UNION–MANAGEMENT

RELATIONS

IN CANADA

FOURTH EDITION

UNION–MANAGEMENT

RELATIONS

IN CANADA

FOURTH EDITION

MORLEY GUNDERSON
UNIVERSITY OF TORONTO

ALLEN PONAK
UNIVERSITY OF CALGARY

DAPHNE GOTTLIEB TARAS
UNIVERSITY OF CALGARY

Addison
Wesley
Longman

Toronto

Canadian Cataloguing in Publication Data

Gunderson, Morley, 1945–
    Union–management relations in Canada

4th ed.
Includes index.
ISBN 0-201-61407-3

1. Industrial Relations – Canada   I. Ponak, Allen M., 1949–   .
II. Taras, Daphne Gottlieb, 1956–   III. Title.

HD8106.5.U54 2001   331'.0971   C00-930677-3

ISBN 0-201-61407-3

Vice President, Editorial Director: Michael Young
Acquisitions Editor: Mike Ryan
Marketing Manager: James Buchanan
Developmental Editor: Suzanne Schaan
Production Editor: Marisa D'Andrea
Copy Editor: Linda Cahill
Production Coordinator: Patricia Ciardullo
Page Layout: Arlene Edgar
Art Director: Julia Hall
Interior Design: Gillian Tsintziras
Cover Design: Gillian Tsintziras
Cover Image: Photonica

Statistics Canada information is used with the permission of the Minister of Industry, as
Minister responsible for Statistics Canada. Information on the availability of the wide range of
data from Statistics Canada can be obtained from Statistic Canada's Regional Offices, its World
Wide Web site at http://www.statcan.ca, and its toll-free access number 1-800-263-1136.

2 3 4 5   05 04 03 02 01

Printed and bound in Canada

Every reasonable effort has been made to obtain permissions for all articles and data used in
this edition. If errors or omissions have occurred, they will be corrected in future editions,
provided written notification has been received by the publisher.

To my family: Melanie Brady and Brendan,
Rory, Jesse and Brady Gunderson

M.G.

To our children: David and Matthew Ponak;
Matthew and Joel Taras; and to each other.

A.P. and D.G.T.

CONTENTS

PREFACE

The New Edition

The publication of the fourth edition of *Union–Management Relations in Canada* coincides with a period of profound social and economic change in this country. Unprecedented global competitive pressures, North American free trade, deregulation, privatization, massive efforts to reduce the public debt, and industrial restructuring towards services and the information economy are just some of the issues that recur in virtually every chapter of this book.

Significant content changes in this edition reflect these issues. The introduction is completely rewritten to emphasize the key features of the field of industrial relations and clearly distinguish it from its nearest rival field, human resource management. Many of the distinctive features of Canadian industrial relations are highlighted, and this chapter anchors the efforts of subsequent chapters to explain noteworthy features of Canadian theory and practice. Chapter 2 is entirely new, and discusses the impetus for unions and collective action. The vocabulary that animates the field is introduced in Chapter 2: "taking wages out of competition," "voice," "equity," "wage-effort bargain," and so on. A number of chapters that bear the same title or topic as in the last edition have been completely rewritten, especially where a new contributing author is involved. Chapter 3 not only examines labour history, but also the development of capitalism and its impact on workers and society. Chapter 7 is a comprehensive treatment of labour law that includes numerous illustrations of the role of law in union–management relations. Chapter 9 provides new discussions on mutual gains bargaining. Chapters 12 and 15, on grievance arbitration and employee involvement respectively, provide new material on arbitration in nonunion settings and on the legal status of nonunion employee representation. Chapter 17, on comparative industrial relations, is entirely recrafted. Every chapter of this edition has been thoroughly updated and revised to reflect recent developments.

The chapters have been reordered to better reflect how previous editions have fared in classroom settings. The book spends more time at the front-end establishing the impetus for collective action and the basis for union–management relations. Chapters are clustered into a logical flow; for example, the chapter on collective bargaining is followed immediately by one on the collective agreement. If agreement is not reached, the next chapter reviews strikes and lockouts. The previous editions situated these three chapters in different sections of the book.

Features that contributed to the popularity of the first three editions remain intact. The book continues to benefit from the participation of many of the country's leading scholars and teachers of industrial relations. In a country as diverse as Canada, this ensures that the experiences in all regions are reflected in analyses, examples, and conclusions. This approach exposes readers to the lively mix of views and perspectives found within a very vibrant industrial relations community. Many chapters present material that is on the leading edge of research in industrial relations and, in some cases, contain analyses that are appearing in teaching materials for the first time. Chapters provide extensive reference lists to direct the interested reader to more specific information and applications of the theory, research, and statistical evidence. Since industrial relations events appear daily on the evening news and in the press, this book pays special attention to how the academic analysis relates to real-world problems and issues.

We are excited by three overarching changes in this edition, which we believe make it more accessible, relevant, and valuable as a reference:

- **The pedagogy has changed substantially.** Each chapter begins with an opening vignette to ground the subsequent discussions. More examples are used than was the case in previous editions, and relevant Websites are given. This fourth edition reflects the realities of individual workers and worksites, and helps future industrial relations practitioners acquire concrete knowledge and applications.

- **The differences between union and nonunion workers are highlighted.** Readers are able to move from chapter to chapter, acquiring specific insights from a variety of perspectives. Students will grasp more clearly the point that union and nonunion workers are covered under different legal frameworks and dispute resolution mechanisms, and form part of distinctive sets of practices designed to suit the union or nonunion setting.

- **Canadian industrial relations contain features that are distinctive, and in some cases, unique.** As competitive and global pressures bring greater awareness of international issues, it is imperative that Canadian students understand the features that make Canada different. We must know ourselves in order to appreciate our place on the world stage. As declining union density in the United States draws considerable attention, it is vitally important that we monitor developments in our own country carefully. Most chapters now explicitly discuss Canada in comparative perspective.

These three new themes—greater applications, union–nonunion differences, and sensitivity to international comparisons—are incorporated throughout the book, and add value without sacrificing any of the rigour of the previous editions.

Features

- *Opening vignette:* Each chapter begins with a vignette, taken from a news article or other text, that draws the reader into the material anecdotally and provides a firm practical context for the following material.

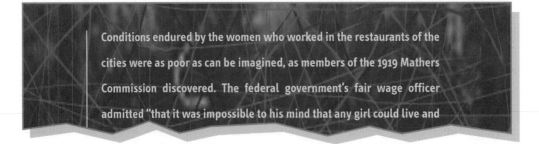

Conditions endured by the women who worked in the restaurants of the cities were as poor as can be imagined, as members of the 1919 Mathers Commission discovered. The federal government's fair wage officer admitted "that it was impossible to his mind that any girl could live and

- *Exhibits:* Each chapter contains several exhibits that provide examples, expand on topics, and provide additional information related to the text.

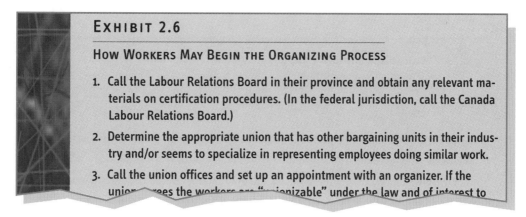

EXHIBIT 2.6

HOW WORKERS MAY BEGIN THE ORGANIZING PROCESS

1. Call the Labour Relations Board in their province and obtain any relevant materials on certification procedures. (In the federal jurisdiction, call the Canada Labour Relations Board.)

2. Determine the appropriate union that has other bargaining units in their industry and/or seems to specialize in representing employees doing similar work.

3. Call the union offices and set up an appointment with an organizer. If the union ~~~es the workers ~~~ "~~ionizable" under the law and of interest to

- *Tables and figures:* Throughout the text, tables and figures are used to present current data, to draw comparisons, and to clarify information by offering it in a clear graphical form.

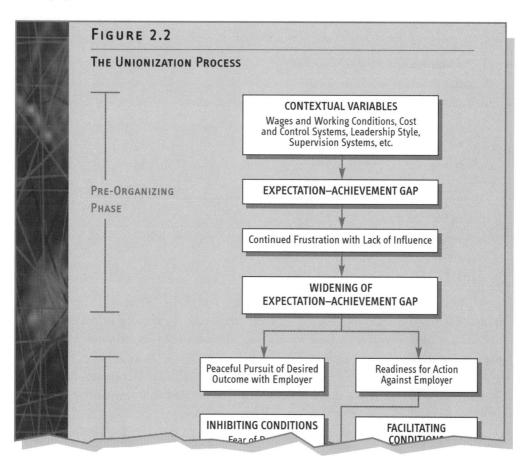

FIGURE 2.2

THE UNIONIZATION PROCESS

PRE-ORGANIZING PHASE

CONTEXTUAL VARIABLES
Wages and Working Conditions, Cost and Control Systems, Leadership Style, Supervision Systems, etc.

EXPECTATION–ACHIEVEMENT GAP

Continued Frustration with Lack of Influence

WIDENING OF EXPECTATION–ACHIEVEMENT GAP

Peaceful Pursuit of Desired Outcome with Employer

Readiness for Action Against Employer

INHIBITING CONDITIONS
Fear of R~~~

FACILITATING CONDITIONS

- *Weblinks:* References to Websites are included throughout the text. Some of these sites provide further information on specific topics discussed in the text, while other links point to industrial relations journals, sources of labour data, union sites, and labour legislation.

 Canadian Labour Congress: www.clc-ctc.ca

AFL-CIO: www.aflcio.org

- *Questions:* Each chapter ends with a series of questions that review the material covered in the chapter and point to possibilities for further discussion or research.
- *References:* The references list not only provides sources for the information within the chapter but also acts as a suggested list for further reading and research.
- *Instructor's Manual:* New to this edition is an *Instructor's Manual* that includes two collective bargaining simulations, several arbitration cases, and other supplementary material.

Acknowledgments

We would like to express our appreciation to numerous colleagues who provided excellent suggestions for material to include in this edition. We are indebted to the reviewers:

P. Andiappan, *University of Windsor*
Charles Beach, *Queen's University*
Travor C. Brown, *Memorial University of Newfoundland*
Diane Castonguay, *McGill University*
Claude Dupuis, *University of Calgary*
Lawrence Fric, *University of Western Ontario*
Mark Julien, *University of Regina*
Andrew Luchak, *Memorial University of Newfoundland*
David McPherson, *Humber College*
Ian Sakinofsky, *Ryerson Polytechnic University*
Robert Swidinsky, *University of Guelph*
Mark Thompson, *University of British Columbia.*

Thanks to A. Tarik Timur, Frederick Jacques, and Kelly Williams, currently PhD students at the University of Calgary, for their comments on portions of the book, with particular acknowledgment to Tarik for his help with obtaining permissions to reproduce copyright materials.

We began this edition under the excellent guidance of Brian Henderson of Addison Wesley Longman, but it was the able stewardship of the post Addison Wesley Longman and Prentice Hall merger team that saw this project through to completion as a Pearson product. We gratefully thank Linda Cahill and Marisa D'Andrea for editing. Finally, Suzanne Schaan and Mike Ryan deserve credit for their determination, persuasiveness, and patience—three attributes we have come to admire greatly.

GENERAL EDITORS

Morley Gunderson (B.A., Queen's University; Ph.D., University of Wisconsin–Madison) holds the Canadian Imperial Bank of Commerce Chair in Youth Employment at the University of Toronto, where he is a professor at the Centre for Industrial Relations (Director from 1985 to 1997) and the Department of Economics. He is also a research associate of the Institute of Policy Analysis, the Centre for International Studies, and the Institute for Human Development, Life Course and Aging, all at the University of Toronto, as well as an Adjunct Scientist at the Institute for Work and Health. He has been a visiting scholar at various institutions: the International Institute for Labour Research in Geneva, Switzerland (1977/78); the National Bureau of Economic Research at Stanford University (1984/85 and 1991–93); the North America Forum at the Institute for International Studies at Stanford (Summer 1994–96); and the Hoover Institution at Stanford (1998/99).

His publications include the books *Women in the Canadian Labour Market* (1998); *Forging Business–Labour Partnerships: The Emergence of Sector Councils in Canada* (1998); *Labour Market Economics: Theory, Evidence and Policy in Canada,* 4th ed. (1998); *Comparable Worth and Gender Discrimination: An International Perspective* (1995); *Pay Equity* (1990); *Women and Labour Market Poverty* (1990); and *Economics of Poverty and Income Distribution* (1983). He has published numerous journal articles on various topics: gender discrimination and comparable worth; the aging workforce, pensions and mandatory retirement; youth employment; public sector wage determination; the determinants and impact of immigration; the causes and consequences of strikes; child-care arrangements and labour market behaviour; workers' compensation and reasonable accommodation; labour market adjustment and training; and the impact of trade liberalization and globalization on labour markets, labour policy, labour standards, industrial relations, human resource management, and workplace practices.

Currently, Professor Gunderson is on the editorial board of the *Journal of Labor Research* and the *International Journal of Manpower,* and he is co-editor of the *Labor Arbitration Yearbook.* He has been a member of the executive board of the Industrial Relations Research Association and an advisor/consultant to various organizations: Labour Canada; Ontario Ministry of Labour; Statistics Canada; Macdonald Commission; Abella Commission on Employment Equity; Canadian Human Rights Commission; Ontario Task Force on Hours of Work and Overtime; Ontario Task Force on Mandatory Retirement; Centre for Policy Studies on Youth and Family; Ontario Pay Equity Commission; B.C. Task Force on Employment and Training; Ontario Workers' Compensation Board; Canadian Policy Research Network; Federal Task Force on Working Time and the Distribution of Work; Ontario Royal Commission on Workers' Compensation; Human Resources Development Canada; British Columbia Royal Commission on Workers' Compensation; the North America Forum at Stanford; the International Labour Organization; and the Harvard Institute for International Development.

Allen Ponak (B.A., McGill University; M.L.I.R., Michigan State University; Ph.D., University of Wisconsin–Madison) is professor of Industrial Relations in the Faculty of Management, University of Calgary, and director of the university's Industrial Relations Research Group. Previously, he held faculty positions at the University of British Columbia and McGill. He has been a visiting scholar at the National Institute of Labour Studies at Flinders University in Adelaide, Australia, and recipient of a Lady Davis visiting scientist position at the Technion in Haifa, Israel.

Professor Ponak has a forthcoming book on essential services dispute resolution and has published numerous articles in such scholarly journals as *Industrial and Labor Relations Review, Industrial Relations,* and *Relations industrielles/Industrial Relations*. He has presented his research at many academic and professional conferences. His work has covered a number of topics including unionized professionals; employee attitudes to collective bargaining; impact of interest arbitration on settlement propensities; discharge and reinstatement in grievance arbitration; delay in grievance arbitration; essential service dispute resolution; and public sector industrial relations. Professor Ponak is a member of the editorial boards of *Relations industrielles/Industrial Relations, Canadian Public Policy,* and the *Employee Responsibilities and Rights Journal*. In 1991–92 he was the national president of the Canadian Industrial Relations Association.

Professor Ponak is experienced in labour dispute resolution, serving as an arbitrator and mediator. Many of his decisions have been reported in *Labour Arbitration Cases*. In 1992 he was admitted to the National Academy of Arbitrators and in 1999 he was named to the Board of Governors of the Academy. He chairs an annual labour arbitration and policy conference in Calgary that has become one of the largest in Canada.

Daphne Gottlieb Taras (B.A., York University; M.A., Duke University; M.B.A. and Ph.D., University of Calgary) is associate professor of Industrial Relations in the Faculty of Management, University of Calgary. Her teaching interests focus on the employment relationship, employee representation, and worksite issues. She has taught organizational behaviour and industrial relations at the undergraduate level and worksite issues at the University of Amsterdam, and she was part of the core teaching team for the Calgary M.B.A. program.

She co-edited the book *Nonunion Employee Representation* (2000). Within industrial relations, her principal research interest is formal nonunion forms of employee representation. She has examined industrial relations and human resources issues in a number of major petroleum firms, including Petro-Canada and Imperial Oil. Dr. Taras has published articles in *Industrial and Labor Relations Review, Industrial Relations, Relations industrielles/Industrial Relations*, and numerous other scholarly journals. She co-edited a symposium for *Journal of Labor Research*. In 1997, she organized a major international conference on nonunion employee representation held in Banff.

Professor Taras has mediated labour relations disputes and has facilitated union–management committees. For the University of Calgary, she acted as mediator in sexual harassment cases. She was co-author of a submission on nonunion representation to the

U.S. Task Force on Reconstructing America's Labor Market Institutions at MIT (1999) and co-author of a submission on right-to-work to the Alberta Economic Development Authority (1995). She was the Faculty of Management's Outstanding New Scholar in 1997 and the recipient of the Dean's Award for Outstanding Research Achievement in 2000. She was elected to the executive board of the Industrial Relations Research Association, and is a member of the editorial board of the *British Journal of Industrial Relations.*

CHAPTER CONTRIBUTORS

Jean Boivin (Ph.D., Cornell University) is co-author, with Jacques Guilbault, of *Les relations patronales-syndicales au Québec* (1989). He is professor of Industrial Relations at the Département des relations industrielles, Université Laval, Quebec. He has published articles and contributed chapters to several books on industrial relations in both French and English. He is a former president of the Canadian Industrial Relations Association and a former member of the Industrial Relations Research Association's executive board. He was visiting scholar at the University of Toronto's Centre for Industrial Relations in 1987–88. His current research interest is in the area of interest-based bargaining.

Richard P. Chaykowski (Ph.D., Cornell University) is a faculty member in the School of Industrial Relations at Queen's University. He has been a visitor at the University of Toronto and McGill University and a visiting scholar at MIT. He is also a co-founder and is currently co-chair of the *Canadian Workplace Research Network*, which supports a national network of human resources and industrial relations researchers in Canada. Dr. Chaykowski's teaching and research interests include public policy in North American labour markets, industrial relations, cooperative approaches to labour relations, the transformation of labour markets and industrial relations systems, and innovation and technological change in the workplace. He is frequently requested to speak on these issues in a wide range of forums in both the private and public sectors, including union and senior management groups, the Conference Board of Canada, as well as branches of the Government of Canada.

His research has appeared widely in such journals as the *Industrial and Labour Relations Review, Industrial Relations,* the *Journal of Labor Research, Relations industrielles, Canadian Public Policy, Canadian Business Economics*, and *Advances in Industrial and Labor Relations.* His books include *Industrial Relations in Canadian Industry* (1992), *Research in Canadian Workers' Compensation* (1995), and *Transition and Structural Change in the North American Labour Market* (1997). His two most recent books, published in 1999, are *Contract and Commitment: Employment Relations in the New Economy* and *Women and Work.*

Esther Déom (Ph.D., Université de Montréal) is a professor of Industrial Relations at the Département des relations industrielles, Université Laval, Quebec. She was Director of the Département des relations industrielles (1994–97) and secretary-treasurer of the

Canadian Industrial Relations Association for many years and was president of CIRA in 1993. She is a member of the editorial board of *Relations industrielles/Industrial Relations*. Her current research is in the area of pay equity and job evaluation, employment equity, and work organization and women. She also acts as a neutral third party in many employment equity committees and was the spokesperson for the Quebec Coalition for Pay Equity. She was also part of the Governmental Consultation Commission for the Pay Equity Legislation.

Ann C. Frost (Ph.D., Massachusetts Institute of Technology) is assistant professor at the Richard Ivey School of Business, University of Western Ontario. She teaches the undergraduate course in organizational behaviour and a graduate course on the management of high performance organizations.

Professor Frost's main research focus has been in the area of workplace restructuring, where she has examined the ability of local unions to deal effectively with changing shop-floor conditions in the steel industry. Articles from this research have appeared in *Advances in Industrial and Labor Relations,* the *Journal of Labor Research*, and *Industrial and Labor Relations Review*. Her current research interests include models of labour–management cooperation, restructuring in the health care sector, and the impact of recent changes in work organization on the careers of low-wage workers. Professor Frost's research has been funded by the Social Sciences and Humanities Research Council, MIT's Industrial Performance Center, and the Russell-Sage and Rockefeller Foundations.

Having voted two years ago for union representation, Professor Frost and her colleagues are still waiting for the negotiation of their first collective agreement.

Anthony Giles (Ph.D., University of Warwick) is associate professor at Université Laval in Quebec City. He teaches undergraduate and graduate courses on industrial relations, collective agreements, industrial relations theory, and comparative and international labour relations. Professor Giles has published articles on a variety of topics and is presently engaged in research on the evolution of the collective agreement, workplace change in multinational corporations, and the impact of globalization on industrial relations.

Doug Hyatt (Ph.D., University of Toronto) is an associate professor of Industrial Relations and Economics at the University of Toronto. His articles have appeared in *Industrial and Labor Relations Review, Industrial Relations, American Economic Review*, and the *Canadian Journal of Economics*. His latest book is entitled *Workers' Compensation: Foundations for Reform* (edited with Morley Gunderson). His current areas of research include public sector collective bargaining, the labour market for child care workers, occupational health and safety, and workers' compensation. During 1998–1999, he was Research Director for the Royal Commission on Workers' Compensation in British Columbia.

Richard Jackson (B.A., M.B.A.) is associate dean and professor of Industrial Relations at Queen's School of Business, Queen's University. He teaches industrial relations, negotiation, dispute resolution, and conflict management. Currently a vice-chair of the Ontario Grievance Settlement Board, he has been active as an arbitrator, mediator, and fact finder in private- and public-sector labour disputes. His publications include books, articles, monographs, and book chapters on the subject of different forms of dispute resolution. He has particular experience with the police and education sectors.

Carla Lipsig-Mummé (M.A., Boston University; Ph.D., Université de Montréal) is professor of Labour Studies and director of the Centre for Research on Work and Society, York University, a research centre working in partnership with the labour movement. Her areas of research and publication have been labour and politics in Quebec, Australia, English Canada, and the United States; trade union strategic repositioning; women, work, and unions; new organizing strategies for labour; the problem of labour internationalism, cultures of militancy, and precarious employment. She has published in *Studies in Political Economy* (Canada), *Journal of Industrial Relations* (Australia), *Relations industrielles/Industrial Relations* (Quebec), *Labour/Le travail* (Canada), *Monthly Review* (United States), *Sociologie du travail* (France), *Sociologie et société* (Quebec), and *Possibles* (Quebec). Formerly a union organizer with the United Farmworkers and International Ladies' Garment Workers Union, she has more recently been a consultant to the executive of the Centrale de l'enseignement du Québec and the Confédération des syndicats nationaux, as well as the Australian Council of Trade Unions, the Canadian Labour Congress, and numerous member unions. She is currently principal investigator for the Training Matters Strategic Project, a five-year SSHRC Network, and project leader of Bridging the Solitudes, a three-year community-university research alliance.

Richard Marsden (Ph.D., University of Warwick) is associate professor of Industrial Relations at Athabasca University, Canada's open university specializing in distance education. He researches social theory to further understanding of the nature, organization, and management of work. He has published in the *Cambridge Journal of Economics, Sociology, Critical Perspectives on Accounting, Organization Studies, Journal of Historical Sociology*, and the *Handbook of Organization Studies*. His book *The Nature of Capital: Marx after Foucault* was published by Routledge in 1999.

David C. McPhillips (M.B.A., LL.B., LL.M.) is an associate professor in the Faculty of Commerce and Business Administration, University of British Columbia. He is also a barrister and solicitor and is an active labour arbitrator and mediator in British Columbia. His teaching and seminar interests include labour law, employment law, industrial relations, and human rights. His articles have appeared in the *Industrial and Labour Relations Review, Relations industrielles/Industrial Relations*, the *Canadian Bar Review, McGill Law Journal*, and *Osgoode Hall Law Journal*.

Noah M. Meltz (B.Com., University of Toronto; Ph.D., Princeton University) is professor of Economics and Industrial Relations in the Department of Economics and the Centre for Industrial Relations, University of Toronto, and professor, School of Business, Netanya Academic College, Israel. He was director of the Centre for Industrial Relations from 1975 to 1985, and principal of Woodsworth College, University of Toronto, 1991–1998. His recent books include *Human Resource Management in Canada* (4th ed., co-author), *Theorizing in Industrial Relations: Approaches and Applications* (co-editor), and *Industrial Relations Theory, Its Nature, Scope and Pedagogy* (co-editor). Recent papers include: "Canadian and American Attitudes Toward Work and Institutions" (co-author) and "Developments in Industrial Relations and Human Resource Practices in Canada" (co-author). He is a past president of the Canadian Industrial Relations Association and was their 1998 recipient of the Gerard Dion Award for contributions to industrial relations. He is the chair of the Advisory Committee on Labour Statistics, to Statistics Canada.

Gregor Murray (Ph.D., Warwick University) is professor in the Département des relations industrielles, Université Laval in Quebec City. He conducts research on trade unionism, work organization, globalization and work regulation, and industrial relations theory. He is the incoming editor of *Relations industrielles/Industrial Relations*.

Frank Reid (M.Sc., London School of Economics; Ph.D., Queen's University) is the director of the Centre for Industrial Relations and a professor in the Department of Economics at the University of Toronto. His publications have appeared in various academic journals in both economics and industrial relations as well as numerous books and chapters in books. His current research continues his established interests in the impact of worksharing, jobsharing, and other alternative work arrangements on employee satisfaction, organizational effectiveness, and job creation. He has also published recently on the labour market and organizational impacts of mandatory retirement, in both Canada and Australia. He has served as a consultant on policy issues to various federal and provincial government agencies in Canada as well as the state and federal governments in Australia and the International Labour Organization.

Akivah Starkman (Ph.D., University of Kent at Canterbury, England) is executive director of the Canada Industrial Relations Board (CIRB). The CIRB is a quasi-judicial tribunal responsible for the administration of industrial relations in enterprises that fall within the authority of the Parliament of Canada. Previously, he was the acting director general and director of operations of the Federal Mediation and Conciliation Service (FMCS). Prior to joining the FMCS, he was the executive director of Labour Canada's Bureau of Labour Information, and the executive coordinator of the Hon. Lloyd Axworthy's Advisory Group on Working Time and the Distribution of Work. In 1995, he was a member of the Governor General's Study Tour, which examined the employee–employer relationship in Canada. Formerly, he was a negotiator and representative for a major Canadian union. He is also a founding board member and past co-chair of the Canadian Workplace Research Network.

Mark Thompson (Ph.D., Cornell University) is William Hamilton Professor of Industrial Relations in the Faculty of Commerce, University of British Columbia. His research has appeared in major journals in Canada, the United States, and Britain, and he has co-edited volumes on comparative industrial relations (published by the Industrial Relations Research Association) and on public sector industrial relations in Canada (published by the IRC Press at Queen's University). He has arbitrated disputes in the public sector for over 20 years. He is a member of the National Academy of Arbitrators and a past president of the Canadian Industrial Relations Association, and he was a governor of the Workers' Compensation Board of British Columbia from 1991 to 1995. He was a member of the Advisory Committee on Labour Management Relations in the Federal Public Service in 1999–2000.

Kenneth Wm. Thornicroft (LL.B., University of British Columbia; Ph.D., Case Western Reserve University) is associate professor of Business Law and Labour Relations with the University of Victoria's Faculty of Business. He was the winner of the Uvic Faculty of Business's graduate teaching award in 1992, and in 1997 he received the faculty's "Professor of the Year" award. Dr. Thornicroft's law practice is restricted to arbitration and alternative dispute resolution. Over the past five years, he has served as a third-party neutral in over 800 disputes. He is an adjudicator with the B.C. Employment Standards Tribunal and is on the roster of the Collective Agreement Arbitration Bureau and the British Columbia Supreme Court's "Trial Overflow Program," and is a listed arbitrator, adjudicator, and wage referee under the Canada Labour Code. Dr. Thornicroft also has acted as a third-party neutral (both as an arbitrator and a mediator) in shareholder and partnership disputes, commercial tenancy disputes, major personal injury claims, and franchise disputes.

Dr. Thornicroft is the author of over 60 journal articles, conference papers, book reviews, and book chapters. His research has been published in the *Labour Arbitration Yearbook*, the *Labor Law Journal*, the *Journal of Labor Research*, the *Canadian Bar Review*, and other journals. His current research focuses on employee and employer rights issues, the grievance arbitration process, and the interpretation and enforcement of employment contracts.

Anil Verma (Ph.D. Massachusetts Institute of Technology) is professor of Industrial Relations and Human Resource Management at the University of Toronto, where he holds a joint appointment at the Faculty of Management and the Centre for Industrial Relations. His primary research interests are in the area of management responses to unionization, participative forms of work organization, and the contribution of human resource management policies—such as employment stabilization practices, profit/gain sharing, and other innovations in industrial relations—to organizational effectiveness and performance.

Professor Verma is the co-author of the following publications, in addition to articles in journals: *Industrial Relations in Canadian Industry* (with Richard P. Chaykowski), *Investing in People* (with Deborah Irvine), and *Contract and Commitment: Employment Relations in the New Economy* (co-edited with Richard P. Chaykowski). He has taught previously at the University of Saskatchewan, the University of California (Los Angeles), and the University of British Columbia, and he worked in the steel industry as an engineer for five years.

CHAPTER 1

Introduction to Canadian Industrial Relations

Daphne Gottlieb Taras, Allen Ponak, and Morley Gunderson

Conditions endured by the women who worked in the restaurants of the cities were as poor as can be imagined, as members of the 1919 Mathers Commission discovered. The federal government's fair wage officer admitted "that it was impossible to his mind that any girl could live and remain decent on $9 a week, which is the minimum allowed by the Alberta Factory Act."

Restaurant workers laboured nine or ten hours a day, often in split shifts, seven days a week, all year, for as small a pay packet as the proprietor could get away with. In some cases, café owners doled out wages a dollar or two at a time. Rent for a cot in the basement could cost as much as $5 a week. Some café owners, afraid of getting caught in one of the far-too-infrequent visits by a Factory Act inspector, would pay their help with a cheque for the minimum wage and then demand that it be cashed at the till so they could take some back.

Restaurant workers were [among] the forgotten underclass of western Canada. The predominantly middle-class suffragists were fighting for things that meant little to women sleeping in café basements. The right to vote, the right to access to the professions, the right to smoke cigarettes in public—what could these things mean to women who were working every day of the year for less than the minimum wage?

Between 1916 and 1922, Edmonton waitresses had succeeded in cutting their work week to 48 hours over six days and bringing wages to about $25 a week but their gains had not come easily. The first significant restaurant strike in Alberta took place in 1916. In 1922, the Edmonton local of the Hotel and Restaurant Employees Union called a strike against four city cafés that were demanding a wage cut of 27.5 percent. The union was offering to accept a cut of 10 percent and the waitresses stayed out 39 days to win their point. Three of the café proprietors then compromised and cut wages only 12.5 percent.

Individually, workers were powerless; when they acted together they could sometimes make things happen.[1]

———————————

They're too young to vote or stay out late, but Tessa Lowinger and Jennifer Wiebe are a force to be reckoned with. Because of the two Grade 12 students, the McDonald's fast food empire has its first unionized outlet in North America in this town [of Squamish] that lies between the formidable rock face of Stawamus Chief Mountain and the Pacific Ocean, 67 km north of Vancouver. It comes as no surprise to many people who live here. "There's a lot of unions in this town," says Lowinger, 16.

Many of the town's 15,000 people are unionized employees at local saw and pulp mills, others at the railway. Both girls' fathers are union members.

So when grumbling about work turned to union talk on July 16 [1998], the teens turned to Lowinger's father, Hans. The mill worker called his local of the Canadian Auto Workers, and then the national office. A union organizer arrived days later. The pair started knocking on the doors of fellow employees, and the union was certified last Wednesday [August, 1998].

> Lowinger and Wiebe aren't hoping for higher wages in the contract the union and McDonald's outlet owner Paul Savage must now negotiate. But they do want changes in the way the mostly teenaged employees are treated.
>
> Lowinger—who has worked at the local McDonald's for more than two years—says some managers berated teenaged employees for making mistakes. Wiebe says she once became sick at work, but wasn't allowed to leave until the next shift arrived. Employees had to find their own replacements if they called in sick, and there were several safety concerns, they say.
>
> "That's not right," says Lowinger's father, who supported his daughter's drive. "If they didn't do those kinds of things to these kids, there wouldn't be a union in there now."
>
> The Squamish certification has bolstered union organizers, who hope other outlets across the country follow suit. "In today's economy we're seeing more and more workers who see these as full-time jobs," says Roger Crowther, the CAW's national representative. And unions want to bring the McJobs under their wing.
>
> The CAW has successfully organized 11 Starbucks and 40 Kentucky Fried Chicken outlets in British Columbia. There are 1050 McDonald's restaurants in Canada.[2]

The vignettes above were chosen to illustrate the type of labour problems that brought the field of industrial relations into being and continue to give the field its relevance and vitality. Anyone who is interested in remaining current by monitoring the status of union organizing should know that only 13 months after the Squamish McDonald's became the chain's only unionized outlet in North America, workers decertified the union. The Canadian Auto Workers blamed the defeat on high turnover.[3] Although the field of industrial relations seems turbulent, this chapter will demonstrate that there is a stable core of assumptions and values that characterize industrial relations for both scholars and practitioners.

SETTING THE BASIC TERMINOLOGY

This is an industrial relations book with a distinctive content and outlook born of its home discipline. There is considerable controversy over the definition of the term "industrial relations." At one time, it was widely accepted that industrial relations focused on union–management relations, and most writing in the field examined unions, collective bargaining, labour laws, strikes, grievance resolution, and other topics derived from the interplay between unions and management. Industrial relations was presumed to regulate the relationship between management and *organized* labour. This definition has become outdated.

The term "industrial relations" was first used in North America in 1912 when American President William Howard Taft and Congress created the Commission of Industrial Relations[4] in response to a 1910 labour dispute that culminated in the bombing deaths of 20 persons in the *L. A. Times* Building by two union leaders. The Commission's mandate was to determine the conditions responsible for conflict and suggest remedies. Prior to the Commission, the term used to describe its field of study was simply "the relations between labour and capital in industry."

Early Canadian terminology embraced such terms as the "Labour Problem" and "Industrial Troubles."[5] One of the first government investigations was a 1903 Royal Commission on Industrial Disputes in British Columbia. One of Canada's earliest labour relations statutes was the *Industrial Disputes Investigation Act* of 1907. Canadians adopted the term "industrial relations" at about the same time the American Commission was publishing its 11-volume report. The Canadian government launched a Royal Commission to Enquire into Industrial Relations in Canada, and its *Report* was issued in 1919. A pamphlet appeared in Canada in 1918 entitled *Industrial Relations*, published by the Canadian Reconstruction Association, which represented 52 members of the Canadian business elite. It vehemently condemned Bolshevism (which in Russia had "consequences of ruin and horror beyond imagination") and espoused "a better understanding between capital and labour." Quite possibly, William Lyon Mackenzie King (the former deputy minister of labour and future prime minister of Canada, and arguably the single most influential individual in Canadian industrial relations) was the ghost author of the pamphlet. Much of the pamphlet contained the same material and style as King's 1918 book *Industry and Humanity* (Ferns and Ostry, 1955: 293), and the term "industrial relations" was adopted throughout his book.

To this day, when we speak of "labour relations" we mean the study of organized labour (unions) and management. This is in contrast to the term "employment relations," which focuses on the relationship between individual employees, including those who are not organized into unions, and their employers. Similarly, labour law deals with collective bargaining matters, while employment law deals with laws covering both union and nonunion employees.

Industrial relations came into being as an academic field because of the magnitude of labour–management warfare and the instability it caused (Abella, 1973) throughout the industrializing world. In Canada, disputes in the coal mines and railways catapulted "the labour problem" to the forefront of social and public policy matters for many generations.[6] The 1919 Winnipeg General Strike terrified politicians and industrialists alike. Workers were discovering that through collective action they could redress the worst abuses of private enterprise and raise their power substantially even in the face of management hostility. Society needed a cadre of experts who could be relied upon to both analyze and solve the increasingly intractable dilemmas in the relations between employers and the workers. Hence, the industrial relations academic field "came to the labor problem to *do* something about labor's inequities in the employment relationship" (Barbash, 1997: 17).

As a result, the industrial relations field has a strong practical orientation. One definition suggested by a leading scholar is that industrial relations is "problem solving [on] behalf of equity in the employment relationship" (Barbash, 1997: 17). During the past century, industrial relations scholars often were social activists and reformers as well as academics, and this tradition of activism provided much the impetus for the field of industrial relations.

The emerging consensus today is that industrial relations is "*a broad, interdisciplinary field of study and practice that encompasses all aspects of the employment relationship.*"[7] Rather than examining only workers organized by unions, industrial relations has begun laying claim to all workers—union and nonunion—in all work settings. Thus, industrial relations consists of both labour and employment relations. By including the elements "study and practice," this definition also captures the idea that the field owes a debt to academics, practitioners, and social activists. This is the definition we accept for this book.

Ordinarily, endless debates about the definition of a key term would be of little interest to most readers. But, as we will describe throughout this chapter, the field is in considerable turmoil, and this grappling over the definition is symptomatic of some of the workplace pressures currently confronting employees, managers, and policy-makers.

TWO DOMINANT CANADIAN APPROACHES: SYSTEMS THEORY VS. POLITICAL ECONOMY

The two most influential approaches in Canadian industrial relations teaching and research have been the systems model and political economy.

Systems Theory

Since the late 1950s, as a result of the widespread fascination of the social sciences in general with systems theory, and the particular application to industrial relations developed by the scholar and practitioner John Dunlop (1958, 1993), much of the field crystallized around a systems model of industrial relations. This model situates the actors (unions, employers, and governments) within their social, political, economic, technological, and legal environment. The actors interact with each other according to a "web of rules" and the results of the system are such matters as wage rates, conditions of employment, strikes and lockouts, productivity rates, and so on. Figure 1.1 shows a simple systems model in industrial relations.

FIGURE 1.1

A FRAMEWORK FOR ANALYZING INDUSTRIAL RELATIONS SYSTEMS (A STRUCTURAL-FUNCTIONAL APPROACH)

ENVIRONMENTAL SUBSYSTEMS	INDUSTRIAL RELATIONS SYSTEM

(EXTERNAL INPUTS)

ECOLOGICAL SUBSYSTEM
- Physical surroundings
- Natural resources
- Climate

ECONOMIC SUBSYSTEM[a]
- Product market
- Labour market
- Money market
- Technology

POLITICAL SUBSYSTEM
- Legislative action
- Executive action

LEGAL SUBSYSTEM
- Statutory law
- Common law
- Administrative law

SOCIAL SUBSYSTEM
- Goals and values as influence on actors in IR system
- Social structures
- Public opinion pressure

ACTORS

LABOUR

GOVERNMENT AND PRIVATE AGENCIES

MANAGEMENT

(INTERNAL INPUTS)

GOALS

VALUES

POWER

MECHANISMS FOR CONVERTING INPUTS INTO OUTPUTS:
- Day-to-day interpersonal relations to satisfy social and psychological needs
- The negotiation process
- Conciliation officer and board
- Mediator
- Fact-finding
- Arbitration of interest and rights dispute
- Creative bargaining, continuous committees
- Special inquiry commissions
- Strikes and lockouts[b]

ORGANIZATIONAL OUTPUTS
- Management rights
- Union recognition
- Union security

WORKER-ORIENTED OUTPUTS
- The wage and effort bargain
- Job rights and due process
- Contingency benefits

FEEDBACK LOOP (FLOW OF EFFECTS INTO INDUSTRIAL RELATIONS SYSTEM AND ENVIRONMENTAL SUBSYSTEMS)

a   This model presupposes but does not explicitly show the interrelationship between the various societal subsystems.
b   A work stoppage may also be considered an outcome or output of the industrial relations system.

Source: A. W. J. Craig and N. A. Solomon, *The System of Industrial Relations* in Canada, 5th Edition. (Scarborough, ON: Prentice Hall).

Alton Craig was one of the earliest Canadian proponents of the systems model, and by the late 1960s, its use in Canada had spread.[8] The term "industrial relations system" was taken by the 1969 Woods Task Force on Labour Relations in Canada to mean "the complex of market and institutional arrangements, private and public, which society permits, encourages, or establishes to handle superior-subordinate relationships growing out of employment and related activities."[9]

The systems approach became popular because of its simplicity and flexibility, and also, it might be argued, because of its ostensible lack of a normative thrust. Scholars became less preoccupied with solving the labour problem, and more involved in simply studying it. This was the heyday of "objective" social science. The pendulum had swung away from social activism towards model building and theory testing. As Craig (1988: 11) put it, the systems approach "has all of the variables which industrial relations practitioners and scholars need for the practice and the study of empirical phenomena." The apparent stability of labour–management interactions during the post–World War II period made the systems approach particularly attractive to North American industrial relations theorists. Many scholars believed that the pattern of industrial relations had been set, that it had, with the entrenchment of collective bargaining and permanent institutions set up to regulate labour–management interactions, reached a "mature" phase. Dunlop and his followers assumed that industrialism is a linear process, moving from turbulence towards a more stable, permanent structure. The glue binding the system is the shared assumptions, or ideologies, of the actors. Progress is made by entrenching and refining the system, and by agreeing to rules and regulations governing conduct and preventing instability. According to its critics, systems theory works fairly well when analyzing measurable variables during periods of calm, but it has difficulty explaining dynamic aspects of industrial relations during turbulent times (Kochan, Katz, and McKersie, 1986).

Political Economy

In Canada there also is a rich tradition of the political economy approach.[10] Political economists tend to focus on macro-level explanations and the identification of forces that shape social and economic relations. They argue that industrial relations are born of the larger organization of relations of production in society. Only by understanding power, the distribution of privilege, and social relations of production can industrial relations be appreciated. Giles and Murray advocate defining industrial relations as the study of "social relations in production." Some argue that conflict is at the very heart of the employment relationship, since employment entails the subordination of employees to the supervision of managers. Conflict is inevitable because in order to increase profits, owners must exploit their workers. The economic aspects of the relationship generate tension.[11]

Because political economists look to the social relations of production rather than institutional mechanisms, there is no imperative to focus on collective bargaining and work settings. They study all workers—be they union or nonunion—and their families. They also study business interests and the corporate elite, and the relationship between the accrual of influence and the development of public policy.

There are enormous differences between the systems approach and political economy. Crudely put, while systems theorists enumerate and scrutinize the *variables* in their models, political economists explore the *arrows and paths* in the model. Critics of systems theory argue that it has a dangerous bias towards consensus and stability, while critics of political economy argue that it exaggerates conflict and exploitation. Both approaches have contributed to our understanding of Canadian industrial relations. Systems work has carefully amassed data and evidence about matters of importance to Canadians such as the terms and conditions of employment, the incidence of industrial unrest, and the relationship between the strength of the economy and changes in the labour market. Political economy has drawn our attention to major public policy concerns such as poverty, fragility of employment for a social underclass, the ability of workers to lobby and have their views heard in government forums, and the relationship between unions and political movements.

One of the characteristics of contemporary Canadian industrial relations scholarship is that systems theory and political economy coexist within the mainstream of the field. The leading academic journal in Canada, *Relations industrielles/Industrial Relations*, frequently publishes contributions from both theoretical orientations. The same rarely can be said of the leading American journals, *Industrial and Labor Relations Review* and *Industrial Relations*, in which labour economists using systems approaches predominate.

EXHIBIT 1.1

SELECTED LEADING JOURNALS IN INDUSTRIAL RELATIONS

CANADIAN

- *Relations industrielles/Industrial Relations* (Laval University).
  Web address: www.fss.ulaval.ca/RevueRI/ReviewRI.html
- *Labour/Le Travail* (Memorial University of Newfoundland).
  Web address: www.mun.ca/cclh/llt/

AMERICAN

- *Industrial and Labor Relations Review* (Cornell University).
  Web address: www.ilr.cornell.edu/depts/ILRrev/
- *Industrial Relations* (University of California at Berkeley).
  Web address: socrates.berkeley.edu/~iir/indrel/indrel.shtml
- *Journal of Labor Research* (George Mason University).
  Web address: www.gmu.edu/departments/economics/jmoiepp/JLR.htm
- *Advances in Industrial and Labor Relations* (JAI Press).
  Web address: www.jaipress.com/

BRITISH

- *British Journal of Industrial Relations* (London School of Economics).
  For backorders: www.swets.nl/backsets/rpt0104.html

INDUSTRIAL RELATIONS AND HUMAN RESOURCE MANAGEMENT: WHAT'S THE DIFFERENCE?

Human Resource Management (HRM) emerged as a subfield of management studies from its initial beginnings as personnel management.[12] The term "human resource" was first used by management guru Peter F. Drucker in his 1954 book *The Practice of Management*. Drucker argues that, unlike other firm resources (equipment, land, money, etc.), the *human* resource has unique qualities: "the ability to coordinate, to integrate, to judge, and to imagine."[13]

HRM has become a dominant focus of management research, often at the expense of industrial relations (Lewin, 1991). The HRM section of the influential (US) Academy of Management has grown exponentially over the past decades. The HRM division of the Administrative Sciences Association of Canada is well established, although it is overshadowed by the Academy of Management. Both the Canadian Industrial Relations Association and the (American) Industrial Relations Research Association have battled membership declines.

Academy of Management: www.aom.pace.edu

Administrative Sciences Association of Canada: www.unb.ca/asac99/ english/mbrshp-frm-engl.html

Canadian Industrial Relations Association: www.business.mcmaster.ca/cira/

Industrial Relations Research Association: www.IRRA.uiuc.edu

The lines between industrial relations (IR) and HRM are blurred. Both fields appreciate that labour is not a commodity, and that people are complex, deserving of dignity, and highly dependent upon their employment. HR managers are familiar with issues raised by unionization, and IR managers are trained to appreciate many personnel planning and compensation issues.[14] In smaller companies, and in nonunion companies, the distinctions between IR and HRM are relatively unimportant. But in some large, partially or fully unionized organizations, HR departments are physically separate from IR departments.

Each field has developed its own expertise and vocabulary and, based on our interviews with managers, it is obvious that certain stereotypes have emerged. IR managers see themselves occupying a tougher, more conflictual world consisting of negotiating and then administering collective agreements and resolving disputes as they arise at the worksite. As a group, they have a fairly cynical outlook. They see HR managers as living in a kinder, gentler world, or, alternatively, as manipulative but naive. By contrast, HR managers feel more connected to firm strategy and believe they have a better understanding of the firm as a whole. They see their counterparts in IR as marginalized, having specific technical expertise that, while vital within the unionized portion of the firm, tends to wax and wane in importance depending on the state of labour relations in the company and industry. They see IR as more reactive, and view themselves as having cutting-edge skills and techniques that can transform the workplace into a more productive and flexible place. Union officers often understand their management counterparts in IR quite well: Although on opposite sides of the bargaining table, union and IR managers share a similar view of the employment setting. But unions sometimes view HRM with deep suspicion. Obviously, there are subtle differences between IR and HRM, but what are they?

Academic treatment of these subjects within universities and colleges does not help clarify the matter. Except for a few free-standing research and degree-granting industrial relations institutes within Canada—at Queen's University, Université Laval, Université de Montréal, and University of Toronto—most industrial relations courses are taught within other faculties, particularly business schools (Chaykowski and Weber, 1993). In the past two decades, there has been enormous growth and development of business and management faculties across the country, and virtually all of them offer courses focusing on the *people* aspects of organizations. Students are offered an array of subjects: organizational behaviour, organizational theory, basic human resource management, and specialty courses in subjects such as compensation and benefits, recruitment and training, and employee development. In addition, students often are offered introductions to industrial relations and some smattering of collective bargaining, labour economics, employment law, and employment dispute resolution methods. Many subtopics within all these courses tend to overlap. Understandably, there is considerable confusion about the place of industrial relations within the larger field of people management and organizational behaviour.

Our experience in the classroom has been that most students believe IR is about unions and do not understand that the field can encompass the full employment relationship in both unionized and nonunion workplaces. As well, there is little appreciation for the important differences that divide IR from HRM. At times, these differences are profound. Although the topics studied within IR and HRM can be identical—for example, the study of wages, the development of employee involvement and participation plans, and so on—each field has its own unique set of assumptions about human behaviour and about the place of collective action within the employment relationship.[15]

The first difference is in the basic paradigm. Human resource management focuses mainly on the individual within the organization: how to enhance the fit among talents, tasks, and behaviours for the purpose of meeting organizational objectives (Horwitz, 1991: 11). According to leading HRM textbooks, the goal is "to influence the effectiveness of an organization's employees" (Heneman et al, 1989: 6).

A widely used American IR text, on the other hand, acknowledges that, despite an ongoing debate over the precise definition of IR, the basic premise shared by most IR scholars is that there exists an inherent conflict of interest between employees and managers. These can be brought into alignment for periods of relative stability, but conflict also is a normal state of affairs. Conflict is not viewed as pathological; however, efforts should be made to reduce the scope and frequency of discord since the parties share the same work setting and have a mutual interest in ensuring its continued viability.[16]

In short, HRM focuses on the shared interests of workers and managers in the success of their enterprise. Conflict is de-emphasized in favour of "win-win" scenarios where problems are solved or put aside to fulfill organizational objectives. By contrast, IR assumes conflict is inherent in the employment relationship, and IR approaches often feature conflictual situations, power struggles, and fixed-sum games involving resource distribution.

Second, HRM tends to be unitarist while IR is pluralist. HRM holds that workers are meant to be absorbed into the corporation fairly seamlessly, minimizing any friction and maximizing the common agenda. Unions generally are treated as external to the organization (and vice versa), akin to uninvited dinner guests. Managers who hold this view often speak of unions as "third parties," and say "we don't believe it is necessary to have any third parties come between us and our employees." HRM textbooks often imply that unions are an "external threat" and the inference is clear that unions cause conflict.

IR recognizes that employee interests and management interests are not necessarily the same and that the two sides may come into conflict. Workers may seek to advance their interests through collective action by, for example, joining a union to increase their power. Unions are the result of, not the cause of, conflict. As Barbash (1984: 49) has put it, "It is the labor problem which creates unions, not unions which create the labor problem." That employees might have dual loyalties—to the firm and to a union—or even a single loyalty to the union against the firm, is an accepted IR concept.

Third, the two fields have different policy implications. HRM guides the development of policies that encourage attachment to the organization, for example, by providing extrinsic or intrinsic rewards to individuals who contribute to corporate performance. The idea is to *align* worker goals with those of the organization, say, by offering profit-sharing schemes. HRM strategies help organizations recruit, select, and motivate employees; compensate them appropriately; and improve the fit between the employee and the organization.

IR focuses on the policies that *regulate* employment relations, particularly the development and administration of collective agreements. The emphasis is on developing rules and procedures through which conflict can be channelled. IR managers are knowledgeable about unionization processes, collective agreement negotiations, prerequisites for lawful work stoppages, and grievance procedures.

Fourth, the unit of analysis—the thing we study—is different. HRM tends to examine the individual, while IR is collectivist. HRM usually is concerned with the harnessing of individual talents. Though HRM often examines the workings of small groups or teams and employee input and participation plans, usually it is from the perspective of either achieving corporate goals or adding value to individual efforts. For example, small, self-managed work teams are applauded when they help increase productivity or solve work scheduling blockages. IR is almost exclusively collectivist in orientation, assuming that individual power in an employment situation is enhanced through coordinated collective mobilization. Since IR accepts that employees often have different interests than their employers, IR then is concerned with how employees band together to advance their interests. And IR is not just about the study of unions: There has been a recent upsurge of interest in using the paradigm of IR to study how nonunion workers represent their interests within their organizations (Kaufman and Taras, 2000). IR studies are concerned with power, employee voice, and the manner in which the terms and conditions of employment are set. What is the bargain—implicit or otherwise—that is struck between workers who provide their services and companies that employ them?

The differences between IR and HRM are set out in Table 1.1.

What can be drawn from this examination of the differences between human resource management and industrial relations? Some policies—wages, benefits, employee participation schemes, to name but a few—can be the result of IR policies, HRM policies,

TABLE 1.1

SIMILARITIES AND DIFFERENCES BETWEEN IR AND HRM

GENERAL STEREOTYPES

	Industrial Relations	Human Resource Management
View of People	Not a commodity	Not a commodity
General Outlook	Tougher, conflictual world	Problem-solving
Place in the Firm	Marginalized to vital, depending on state of labour relations	Connected to firm strategy

DIFFERENCES IN APPROACH (EXAGGERATED FOR CLARITY)

	Industrial Relations	Human Resource Management
Focus	Inherent conflict / Zero-sum	Common interests / Win-win
Assumption	Pluralist / Worker agenda vs. company agenda / Intersection of two organizations	Unitarist / Unions are external
Policy Implications	Regulation, rules, dispute resolution / Voice in the workplace	Attachment, motivation, loyalty / Alignment and harmony
Orientation and Level of Analysis	Collectivist	Individual and small group

or both. At the worksite level, they are virtually indistinguishable, particularly in nonunion settings. Where variability exists in personnel practices within and among firms, the question is whether differences originate from IR strategies, HR strategies, both, or some other organizational imperative. This becomes an important area of investigation when HRM policies are used to forestall unionization. Modern managers are urged to listen to employees, to model expected behaviours, to "walk the talk," and to promote greater employee involvement and participation. These practices could form a cluster demonstrating the use of an excellent progressive HRM philosophy. These same practices could be adopted for the sole purpose of preventing workers from joining unions. We urge students to develop greater sensitivity to the underlying goals of common worksite practices.

Canadian Industrial Relations: The Critical Ingredients

The editors and the majority of our contributors are IR scholars and, in many cases, influential practitioners and policy-makers. At international conferences and meetings, we are frequently asked to compare Canadian industrial relations developments to those of other countries. For example:

- Why is Canadian union density so much higher than that of the US, despite a similar "web of rules," strong economic integration, and overlap in the organized labour movement?

- What is the impact of Canada's labour party, the NDP, on the union movement?

- How have Canadian nonunion workers fared in attaining the protections they need to ensure fair terms and conditions of employment and settlement of worksite disputes?

- As governments have adopted policies of fiscal conservatism (reducing debts and deficits) how have they managed their public-sector workforces in Canada?

- Why is the strike rate in Canada one of the highest in the world?

Answering these complex questions in an introductory chapter is impossible. But in this section, we alert our readers to several important influences on Canadian industrial relations that provide a basis for grappling with these types of questions. Many of our chapter authors provide further insight about unique or noteworthy features of Canadian industrial relations.

Decentralization, Experimentation, and Diffusion

Canada's federal system of government is one of the most decentralized in the world. Broadly speaking, industrial relations belong to the provinces. Only 10 percent of the Canadian workforce is covered by federal labour and employment laws, including employees of the federal government, banks, interprovincial transport, maritime trade, and communications industries. Employees of national companies such as Tim Horton's or

Roots are covered by laws in each of the provinces in which their stores or franchises are located. As a result, from province to province there are differences in minimum wage rates, working conditions, and procedures to follow in the event employees become interested in unionizing.

This decentralization was not by design! In fact, early policy-makers wrote standard laws for all Canadians, assuming that for the efficient development of Canada, and for the "peace, order, and good government" of the nation, employment matters should be centrally regulated. It came as a considerable shock when the British Privy Council declared (in the 1925 *Snider* case)[17] that federal government labour laws were infringing on provincial powers. For over 20 years, the wary federal government withdrew from any activism in labour matters, and wrote only a temporary national labour law in 1944 (known as PC 1003) when World War II gave the federal government extraordinary power for the war's duration. Before and after the war, provinces adopted their own laws.

As a result of this complexity, an unwary practitioner easily can make serious mistakes. Although all provinces and the federal government have adopted similar overall approaches, there are a multitude of small differences. For example, a company such as Petro-Canada can use replacement workers during a strike in Alberta, but cannot do so in Quebec or British Columbia. In some provinces workers who want to be represented by the Steelworkers Union need only sign cards, while in others they must in addition hold a secret ballot vote. On the negative side, there is "too much law and too much inconsequential diversity" in Canada (Sims, 1994: 6). On the positive side, this decentralization has led to a rich tradition of experimentation and the cross-fertilization of ideas.

Canadian Values

Is there a distinctive Canadian culture and approach that affects the practice of industrial relations? Some have made the argument that Canadians are not merely decaffeinated Americans (Taras, 1997). At various points in Canadian evolution, influential groups of citizens and policy-makers within Canada tried to preserve a remnant of their British deference to hierarchy, to authority, together with an overlay of respect for "red Toryism." This important "red Tory" element combines economic conservatism with simultaneously held principles of collective rights and state intervention for the provision of comprehensive social welfare policies. There was no revolutionary overthrow of British influences.

Into this mix was added the unique history and traditions of French Canada, offering alternative social and economic visions embedded in intellectual, linguistic, and cultural influences quite different from those elsewhere in North America. The fierce nationalism of many in Quebec, reflected in successive elections, reinforced the already powerful decentralizing forces within Canada. At the same time, Quebec leaders have dominated federal politics since World War II, with Louis St. Laurent, Pierre Trudeau, Brian Mulroney, and Jean Chrétien enjoying long sojourns as prime minister.

Canadians were encouraged to consider themselves part of a "mosaic" of diverse ethnic groupings, and the notion of a "hyphenated Canadian" was accepted—Italian-Canadian, Jewish-Canadian, French-Canadian, and so on. The settlement of the Canadian hinterland proceeded in a more orderly fashion than was the case in the American West, with major institutions like railways, banks, and the national police (RCMP, formerly NWMP) directing Canadian settlement. It is commonly believed that most Canadians are more deferential to authority than Americans, more accepting of collective rights, and more willing to forgo individual freedoms where they clash with social norms (e.g., Canadian acceptance of gun control, enforced seat belt laws, higher taxation rates than the US, and universal access to medical care). Seymour Martin Lipset (1995) labels Canada as "leftist collectivist" which is likely an overstatement today, but it does capture the historic Canadian tendency towards corporatism.

Corporatism is a system of interest representation in which constituent units are organized into a limited number of non-competitive and functionally differentiated categories, each of which is granted a deliberate monopoly within its respective arena of interest in exchange for observing certain controls on its selection of leaders and behaviour in the articulation of its demands. Thus, business and union associations tend to tame competitive tendencies among firms within a sector in order to stabilize it. There is a strong awareness in this literature of the role of the nation-state (government) as a powerful player that both can apply legitimate coercion on other groups, and also set the public-policy framework within which the other actors must operate.[18]

A contemporary example of how this Canadian impulse to balance individualism with collectivism has had an impact on industrial relations involves the crafting of the 1982 Canadian *Charter of Rights and Freedoms*. The *Charter* guarantees certain fundamental freedoms including freedom of association, freedom of thought, belief, opinion, and expression. But these individual rights are not paramount and absolute (as they are in the US under the *Bill of Rights*). In Canada, Section 1 of the *Charter* holds that fundamental rights are subject to "such reasonable limits as can be demonstrably justified in a free and democratic society." There is a presumption that a fettering of individual rights is necessary for democracy, and there must be an obligation to subordinate some rights for the good of the majority. This balancing act is extremely important in the labour relations arena, where the ability of unions to represent members, collect union dues, and exercise the right to strike depends on a legal regime that allows for collective action even over the protests of individuals who believe their own rights are being diminished.[19]

We believe that it is no coincidence that three of the longest-serving prime ministers in the 20th century—William Lyon Mackenzie King, Pierre Elliott Trudeau, and Brian Mulroney—had substantial training and expertise in industrial relations (though they did not necessarily share the same views on the subject). In the labour relations setting, pragmatism and the ability to find a compromise position for combatants is highly valued, as it is in the political arena. *Seeking a Balance* is the apt title of the 1995 federal task force to investigate reform to Canada's federal labour laws. The title captures the Canadian desire to find that elusive middle ground on which alliances can be fashioned and discord can be minimized.

Multiparty Democracy

The collectivist aspirations of a sizeable segment of Canadians found its expression in a viable political party, the New Democratic Party (called the Cooperative Commonwealth Federation until 1961), and Canadian unions historically formed a close alliance with the NDP. In Quebec, where the NDP did not make inroads, unions aligned themselves with other parties, most recently the Parti Québécois. The movement of unions onto the political stage had enormous ramifications for the regulation of employment relations. Federally, the major labour law (PC 1003) was passed because of the fear that failure to offer basic protections for labour organizing and bargaining to appease unions would drive voters into the arms of the rival CCF. The provincial adoption of strong legislative measures to promote collective rights in employment settings was directly attributable to the influence of the NDP, either as the provincial governing party spearheading labour law reform in a number of provinces (including British Columbia, Saskatchewan, Manitoba, and Ontario) or as a strong and vociferous opposition and a serious electoral threat.

Although many unions aligned their interests with the NDP, it has been increasingly difficult for unions to "deliver" the votes of their members. For example, in the 1990s while union leaders decried the policies of provincial Conservative governments in Alberta and then in Ontario, both Premier Klein and Premier Harris enjoyed tremendous popular support even among unionized workers.

Mackenzie King

Nowhere in the world is there a tighter linkage between a single individual and the development of a long-term statutory regime for labour than in Canada. William Lyon Mackenzie King's imprimatur can be found in virtually all labour policy from the turn of the century to the mid-1940s, and many distinctive features of Canada's approach to this day reflect his thinking.

A brief biography is in order. Mackenzie King was formally educated at the Universities of Toronto, Chicago, and then Harvard for a PhD in labour relations. As a graduate student, he wrote a series of newspaper exposés based on his eyewitness investigations of the appalling conditions in the needle trade sweatshops. These articles, in tandem with his educational qualifications, launched his brilliant parliamentary career.

Mackenzie King entered the newly formed ministry of labour as its resident expert in 1900 and was called upon to investigate and mediate some of Canada's most difficult labour disputes. He was the principal architect of every piece of early labour legislation, and then again, while prime minister during World War II, he oversaw the introduction of comprehensive labour statutes that guaranteed all workers the right to organize and the right of unions to represent the interests of their members.

Mackenzie King's watchword was "conciliation," whether voluntary or by government fiat. Through the magic of the conciliation process, he believed that the veils of self-interest would fall and that the disputant parties would come to appreciate the "public interest." He sought to impose order on chaos and fervently yearned for a humane society in which "Reason" and "Truth" would prevail. To create greater discipline, he drafted laws that emphasized third-party expertise and prohibited work stoppage. The failure of employers to ameliorate abusive treatment of their workers would be a victory for "Evil" just as self-serving and narrow union demands would divert humanity toward disorder. His interventions consistently compelled state involvement to restore industrial peace. He favoured government intervention because he saw it was feasible and felt it to be the morally correct position. He believed, first, that the state realistically could find and employ appropriate third-party expertise (and here he viewed his own early career as the exemplar) and take on the role he described as "impartial umpire," and second, that the state was duty-bound to protect the interests of citizens from the discord created by irrationality between labour and management (Craven, 1980).

Due to his influence, a persistent theme in the development of Canadian labour law has been the preference for reason over passion, and humanism rather than simply macroeconomic planning. There was a strong moral tone in King's energies. In his own words,

> For Industry and Nationality alike, the last word lies in the supremacy of Humanity.
> … The national or industrial economy based on a lesser vision, in the final analysis,
> is anti-social, and lacks the essentials of indefinite expansion and durability. The failure to look beyond the State, and beyond Industry as a revenue-producing process,
> has brought chaos instead of order…[20]

More than 60 years later, the same sentiments were expressed by Paul Weiler (1980: 29) in his important book on Canadian labour policy: "The economic function is the beginning, not the end, of the case for collective bargaining…The true function of economic bargaining consists in its civilizing impact upon the working life and environment of employees."

Among the many elements in Canadian industrial relations that have their origins in Mackenzie King's approach are:

- A ban on strikes and lockouts during the life of the collective agreement. In Canada, a strike is only lawful after the expiry of the collective agreement, when the parties are in a position to bargain. During the collective agreement (which normally is in force for about two years, on average), all disputes must be referred to third-party arbitration for binding resolution.

- Before any strike can occur, there must be a cooling-off period and an attempt at conciliation.

- Various measures are written into labour codes that give ministers of labour power to order investigations into labour disputes that threaten the public interest.
- Government employees were not given the right to unionize until almost two decades after Mackenzie King left office. He felt that unionization of the public service would lead to chaos, as government services to citizens were essential for the welfare of the state and its citizens.

Influence of American Developments

Like many aspects of Canadian life, industrial relations have long been affected by American developments. Given the historic interdependence between the two economies, strengthened by recent free trade agreements and the pervasive influence of American culture, it would be surprising if this were not the case.

More than a century ago, US labour leaders began organizing Canadian workers and integrating them into North American "international" unions. By the early 1900s, international unions dominated the Canadian labour movement, exporting to Canada a union philosophy that came to be known as "business unionism." Business unions were economically and socially conservative, unaffiliated with political parties, and focused on the needs of skilled craft workers. There is no doubt that the US linkages gave Canadian workers access to greater resources and expertise than might otherwise have been the case and likely accelerated union growth in this country. However, American dominance made it difficult for alternative approaches to unionism that might have been more consonant with Canadian needs, such as the earlier formation of a labour political party,[21] to flourish. Even today, one-third of Canadian union members belong to unions such as the Teamsters, Steelworkers, and Food and Commercial Workers, all headquartered in United States. The sole international union located in Canada is the NHL Players' Association, with its Toronto head office.

Canadian and American union linkages have fostered tight linkages in labour law. Mackenzie King's conciliation legislation influenced the US *National Railway Act* of 1928, which in turn was an important stepping stone to the (American) *National Labor Relations Act* of 1935 (also known as the *Wagner Act*). The *Wagner Act* constituted a watershed in the evolution of North American labour law. It outlawed a variety of union-busting tactics, required employers to recognize and bargain with a union chosen by a majority of employees, and established a labour relations board to interpret and apply the new legislation. The result was an enormous surge in union membership. In Canada international unions lobbied hard for similar legislation, and in 1944 the *Wagner Act* principles were adopted into Canadian law alongside the traditional conciliation approach. The 1944 legislation, known as PC 1003, became the basis for Canadian labour law for the remainder of the 20th century.

Today, American influence is felt in another way. American union membership has experienced a precipitous decline in the past 20 years. In an integrated North American economy, where Canada often seems to follow US trends with a time lag, it is an open question whether Canadian unions will undergo the same decline. Management strategies aimed at combatting union growth have been transplanted to Canada, and the workforce structural changes that have contributed to union decline in United States, such as outsourcing and contract work, are prevalent in both countries. The Canadian public sector, the source of most union growth in the last quarter-century, has been declining. Union density in Canada, close to 40 percent in the 1980s, is just over 30 percent at the end of the 1990s.

Nevertheless, it is important to recognize that union density in Canada remains more than double that of the United States, and the fate of US unions should not cause us to believe that unions are less relevant in Canada. At the same time, we need to be cognizant that American industrial relations developments have influenced Canadian trends in the past and will do so in the future.

 American Management Association: www.amanet.org

Why Are Canadian–American Unionization Differences Important?

The similarities and differences between the two countries have had important implications for the treatment of industrial relations in Canadian universities. Historically, Canadian and American rates of union density (the proportion of non-agricultural workers represented by organized labour unions) were virtually identical. The fortunes of the union movements in the two countries began sharply diverging in the 1970s, and today, only 14 percent of American workers belong to unions, compared to more than 30 percent of workers in Canada[22] (see Chapter 4 for details). With the sharp decline of American union density, industrial relations began disappearing from courses and teaching textbooks. American industrial relations scholars were encouraged to examine topics of greater interest in HRM, and many left the field. Employment prospects dwindled for nascent IR managers.

Despite some union decline during the 1990s, the Canadian labour movement remains a significant force in Canadian society. Almost all government services are unionized, including those services, such as policing, air traffic control, education, and health care, which are widely seen as most essential. Most telecommunications, transportation, and hydro employees are unionized. Our automobile industry, resource-extraction industries like logging and mining, and commercial construction all have high rates of union penetration. While some parts of the economy, such as banking, insurance, and retail sales (especially "mall" stores like the Gap or Eddie Bauer) are almost union free, those parts of our economy that are unionized continue to wield a substantial potential impact on our daily lives.

Yet standard Canadian textbooks in such fields as organizational behaviour, organizational theory, strategy, and even accounting and finance, are virtually silent on the strong presence of unions in the Canadian landscape. This is no coincidence. The field of management education has deep roots in the United States, and Canadians tend to adopt American approaches. Until recently, most Canadian business schools hired American-educated professors, and even if they were Canadian citizens, many were strongly influenced by their years of training in the US. Standard textbooks are created for the much larger American market, and are adopted by Canadian classes either directly, or in a "Canadianized" version of the original American text. Even when books are wholly Canadian, the table of contents and rough proportion of topics is drawn from popular American texts.[23]

We believe that Canadian students are being done a disservice by not receiving the exposure to industrial relations that would be warranted by our substantial degree of union density. For example, Canadians should know more about union impact on benefits plans, union pension-based investments, wage setting, and corporate strategic planning. Part of the motivation for this text was to give readers a greater appreciation of the importance of Canadian industrial relations in our more heavily unionized society. It is also necessary to understand that part of the debate over the definition of industrial relations has been sparked by the union decline in the United States. By taking the broadest possible definition of industrial relations—that it is about "all aspects of the employment relationship" and not merely about unions—American scholars and practitioners are fighting to retain their relevance in the face of the disappearance of the very phenomenon on which they had been focused since the origins of the field. Many nonunion workers are not without some systems of representation (Kaufman and Taras, 2000). Most large employers must have health-and-safety committees. About 20 percent of nonunion employees work for an employer who offers some type of council, committee, or forum in order to deal with matters affecting the terms and conditions of employment. Thus, the debate over the definition of industrial relations captures the deep concern of industrial relations scholars that their paradigms (described earlier) must be preserved, reinvigorated, and applied to new areas of study.

Challenges to Canadian Industrial Relations

The preceding discussion reviewed some of the current strains within the academic discipline of industrial relations. To summarize, these are:

1. The challenge to remain a coherent field, with its own intellectual foundation and outlook on the employment relationship, despite the allure of the larger and rapidly growing field of human resource management. The key is to absorb the knowledge and scope of human resource management into industrial relations, without weakening IR's emphasis on collective action, social justice, worksite equity, and the use of power to achieve a different allocation and distribution of resources.

2. Though unions and collective action are a relatively stable and enduring feature of the Canadian workplace, students are given the erroneous impression that unions are irrelevant today, or are incidental players. The challenge is to ensure adequate

coverage of industrial relations topics and concerns in Canadian academic and policy institutions. The fact that over 86 percent of American workers are not unionized has greatly threatened the field of industrial relations in the United States. In Canada, with almost one worker in three covered by unionized work arrangements, and a much higher percentage than that in key industries, there is every reason to incorporate important industrial relations topics into teaching materials. Rarely a week goes by in which industrial relations topics are not front-page news. Canadian citizens should be able to understand developments at the worksite that involve organized labour.

Questions

1. What is the current definition of "industrial relations" and why has it changed over time?

2. What is the difference between systems theory and political economy? Apply each approach to the two opening vignettes in the chapter.

3. Locate an issue of *Relations industrielles/Industrial Relations* and describe the types of topics covered and the approaches used.

4. Why has human resource management posed such a strong challenge to the field of industrial relations?

5. How can you determine whether a manager has adopted an industrial relations or a human resource management paradigm? What questions would you ask a manager to determine his/her underlying assumptions?

6. Locate the front page of one month's newspapers. What types of issues capture media attention?

7. Why is pragmatism and the ability to find a compromise position so highly valued in the development of Canadian public policy towards industrial relations?

8. What ingredients make Canadian industrial relations unique?

9. How have developments in the United States affected industrial relations in Canada?

ENDNOTES

[1] From Warren Caragata, *Alberta Labour: A Heritage Untold.* (Toronto: James Lorimer & Company, 1979), pp. 83–85. Reprinted with the permission of the publisher.

[2] Excerpts from Dene Moor, the Canadian Press. "Fed up with yelling bosses, teens organize McUnion." *The Edmonton Journal* (24 August 1998, Final Edition), p. A6.

[3] "McUnion ousted." News Briefs, *Workplace News* (September 1999), p. 7.

[4] For a comprehensive history of the field, with emphasis on the United States, see Kaufman, 1993.

[5] These terms are taken from titles of William Lyon Mackenzie King's 1899 talks at the Passmore Edwards Settlement House in Bloomsbury, England while he was a PhD student in economics at Harvard. See Ferns and Ostry, 1955, p. 42.

[6] The term "labor problem" was first described as such in North American scholarship by Wisconsin professors Adams and Summer in 1905.

[7] This definition became quite widespread in the late 1980s, and appears on page 1 in a widely used text by Kochan and Katz, 1988.

[8] Alton W. J. Craig, "A Model for the Analysis of Industrial Relations Systems" was presented at the Annual Meeting of the Canadian Political Science Association, June 1967 and reproduced in Jain, 1975. Craig's system model continues to be used in the 1990s in multiple editions of Craig and Norman A. Solomon's textbook *The System of Industrial Relations in Canada.* (Toronto: Prentice-Hall).

[9] *Canadian Industrial Relations.* The Report of the Task Force on Labour Relations. (Ottawa: Queen's Printer, 1969), p. 9.

[10] Giles and Murray, 1988 and 1997. The definition "social relations in production" is attributed to Robert Cox. Major examples of the political economy approach used to analyze the development of the Canadian economy include seminal works by Harold Innis, such as *The Fur Trade in Canada* (Toronto: University of Toronto Press, 1930, reprinted 1956); *Political Economy in the Modern State* (Ryerson, 1946); and *The Cod Fisheries* (Toronto: University of Toronto Press, 1954, reprinted 1978). See also R. T. Naylor, *The History of Canadian Business 1867–1914*, 2 vols. (James Lorimer, 1975); Wallace Clement, *The Canadian Corporate Elite* (Toronto: McClelland and Stewart, 1975); and Wallace Clement and Glen Williams, eds., *The New Canadian Political Economy* (McGill-Queen's University Press, 1989). An excellent example of the political economy approach in Canadian industrial relations is Carla Lipsig-Mummé, "Labour Strategies in the New Social Order: A Political Economy Perspective," in the 3rd Edition of *Union-Management Relations in Canada*, edited by Morley Gunderson and Allen Ponak (Don Mills: Addison-Wesley, 1995), pp. 195–225.

[11] This is in contrast to sociological approaches that find that issues of domination and subordination, powerlessness and alienation, and the conditions of industrialization are the causes of conflict. This is another school of thought in industrial relations. See Barbash, 1984.

[12] Kaufman, 1993 provides an excellent overview of the personnel management (later HRM) and institutional labour economics (later IR) streams of scholarship and practice as they evolved in the United States.

[13] For a comprehensive description of the development of HRM, see Marciano, 1995.

[14] IR and HR practices at eight large Canadian corporations are described in Verma and Chaykowski, 1999.

[15] On similarities, see Lawler, 1990, page 67. On differences, see Horwitz, 1990 and 1991. The most-cited mainstream North American IR journals are listed in Exhibit 1.1. Mainstream HRM research appears in *Human Resource Management* and various Academy of Management publications such as *Academy of Management Journal, Academy of Management Review*, and the *Academy of Management Executive.*

[16] Kochan and Katz, 1988. Paul Weiler, a former British Columbia Labour Relations Board chair, who was instrumental in drafting and applying that province's labour code, and is now a chaired Professor at Harvard University, wrote an important (1980) book on Canadian labour policy which focused on bridging the conflict of interests.

[17] *Toronto Electrical Commissioners* v. *Snider*, in the Privy Council [1925] A.C. 396.

[18] Philippe C. Schmitter. 1974. "Still the Century of Corporatism?" in *The New Corporatism,* edited by F. B. Pike and T. Stritch (Notre Dame: University of Notre Dame Press), pp. 85–131. See also Wolfgang Streeck and Philippe C. Schmitter. 1985. "Community, Market, State—and Associations?: The Prospective Contribution of Interest Governance to Social Order," in *Private Interest Government: Beyond Market and State* (London: Sage Publications), pp. 1–29.

[19] For a good example of the Supreme Court of Canada's approach to the balancing of collective and individual rights see *Lavigne* v. *O.P.S.E.U.* [1991] 2 S.C.R. 211. In that decision the Supreme Court addressed the right of bargaining unit members *not* to pay mandatory union dues, ruling that collective rights superseded the individual rights of an employee named Lavigne who did not want to pay union dues.

[20] King, 1918, p. 28. King was not the only prime minister who wrote on labour. Pierre Elliott Trudeau edited a definitive account of the 1938 Asbestos strike while he was a labour law professor. See *La grève de l'amiante: une étape de la révolution industrielle au Québec* (Montréal: Editions Cité libre, 1956), and the English translation, *The Asbestos Strike* (Toronto: James Lewis & Samuel, 1974).

[21] Under Canada's parliamentary system, so-called "third parties" have the potential to wield far more influence than do US third parties. Thus, while the formation of a labour party may have made little sense in the US, chances for success in furthering union objectives were far greater in Canada. Indeed, European labour parties were formed in the early 1900s.

[22] Union density has also declined in Europe. For explanations of Canadian-US density differences see Gary Chaison and Joseph Rose. 1991. "Continental Divide: The Direction and Fate of North American Unions," in *Advances in Industrial and Labor Relations,* edited by D. Sockell, D. Lewin, and D. B. Lipsky (Greenwich, CT: JAI Press), pp. 169–205; W. Craig Riddell. "Unionization in Canada and the United States: A Tale of Two Countries," in *Small Differences That Matter*, edited by D. Card and R. Freeman (Chicago: University of Chicago Press), pp. 109–147; Noah Meltz. 1985. "Labor Movements in Canada and the United States," in *Challenges and Choices Facing American Labor*, edited by T. A. Kochan (Cambridge, MA: MIT Press), pp. 315–34; and Taras, 1997.

[23] The poor coverage of industrial relations within organizational behaviour texts is detailed in Barling, Fullagar, and Kelloway, 1992, Appendix (pp. 202–205). Twenty-one of the 77 textbooks they list do not mention unions at all. Here is a Canadian example: Over the past few years we have used two editions of the wholly Canadian introductory textbook *Canadian Organizational Behaviour*, written by Steven L. McShane, to teach basic management skills in undergraduate courses at the University of Calgary. Unions were not listed in the first (1992) edition index and merited mention only in five pages of the second (1995) edition. Even Canadian or Canadianized HRM texts often dedicate only one or two chapters to unions. Business strategy texts rarely mention unions, and when they do, the connotation is usually negative, that unions are a threat, limit flexibility, and must be avoided.

REFERENCES

ABELLA, I. M. 1973. *Nationalism, Communism, and Canadian Labour: The CIO, the Communist Party, and the Canadian Congress of Labour 1935–1956*. Toronto: University of Toronto Press.

ADAMS, T. S. and H. L. SUMMER. 1905. *Labor Problems*. New York: Macmillan.

BARBASH, J. 1984. *The Elements of Industrial Relations*. Madison, Wisconsin: University of Wisconsin Press.

———. 1997. "Industrial Relations as Problem-Solving," in *Theorizing in Industrial Relations*, edited by J. Barbash and N. M. Meltz. Australian Centre for Industrial Relations Research and Training (April).

BARLING, J., C. FULLAGAR, and E. K. KELLOWAY. 1992. *The Union and Its Members*. New York: Oxford University Press.

CHAYKOWSKI, R. P. and C. WEBER. 1993. "Alternative Models of Industrial Relations Graduate Programs in Canada and US Universities." Kingston, Ont.: Queen's University Industrial Relations Centre.

CRAIG, A. W. J. 1975. "A Model for the Analysis of Industrial Relations Systems," in *Canadian Labour and Industrial Relations: Private and Public Sectors*, edited by H. C. Jain. Toronto: McGraw-Hill Ryerson Ltd., pp. 2–12.

———. 1988. "Mainstream Industrial Relations in Canada," in *The State of the Art in Industrial Relations*, edited by G. Hebert, H. C. Jain, and N. M. Meltz. Kingston, Ont.: Queen's University Industrial Relations Centre and Toronto: Centre for Industrial Relations, University of Toronto.

CRAVEN, P. 1980. *'An Impartial Umpire': Industrial Relations and the Canadian State 1900–1911*. Toronto: University of Toronto Press.

DRUCKER, P. F. 1954. *The Practice of Management.* New York: Harper and Row.

DUNLOP, J. T. 1958, 1993. *Industrial Relations Systems,* Revised Edition. Harvard Business School Press.

FERNS, H. S. and B. OSTRY. 1955. *The Age of Mackenzie King.* London: William Heinemann, Ltd.

GILES, A. and G. MURRAY. 1988. "Towards an Historical Understanding of Industrial Relations Theory in Canada." *Relations industrielles/Industrial Relations,* 43, no. 4, pp. 780–811.

———. 1997. "Industrial Relations Theory and Critical Political Economy," in *Theorizing in Industrial Relations,* edited by J. Barbash and N. M. Meltz. Australian Centre for Industrial Relations Research and Training (April).

HENEMAN, H. G., D. P. SCHWAB, J. A. FOSSUM, and L. D. DYER. 1989. *Personnel/Human Resource Management,* 4th Edition. Homewood.

HORWITZ, F. 1990. "HRM: An Ideological Perspective." *Personnel Review,* 19, no. 2, pp. 10–15.

———. 1991. *Managing Resourceful People.* South Africa: Juta and Co.

KAUFMAN, B. E. 1993. *The Origins and Evolution of the Field of Industrial Relations in the United States.* Cornell: ILR Press.

KAUFMAN, B. E. and D. G. TARAS, eds. 2000. *Nonunion Employee Representation.* Armonk, NY: ME Sharpe.

KING, W. L. M. 1918, 1973. *Industry and Humanity.* Toronto: University of Toronto Press.

KOCHAN, T. A. and H. KATZ. 1988. *Collective Bargaining and Industrial Relations,* 2nd Edition. Richard D. Irwin, Inc.

KOCHAN, T. A., H. C. KATZ, and R. B. McKERSIE. 1986. *The Transformation of American Industrial Relations.* New York: Basic Books, Inc.

LAWLER, J. J. 1990. *Unionization and Deunionization: Strategy, Tactics, and Outcomes.* Columbia, South Carolina: University of South Carolina Press.

LEWIN, D. 1991. "The Contemporary Human Resource Management Challenge to Industrial Relations," in *The Future of Industrial Relations,* edited by H. Katz. Ithaca: Institute of Collective Bargaining, Cornell University, pp. 82–99.

LIPSET, S. M. 1995. "Trade Union Exceptionalism: The United States and Canada." *Annals of the American Academy,* AAPSS, 538 (March), pp. 115–130.

MARCIANO, V. M. 1995. "The Origins and Development of Human Resource Management," *Academy of Management (Best Papers Proceedings).*

SIMS, A. C. L. 1994. "Wagnerism in Canada: A Fifty-Year Check-Up." H. D. Woods Memorial Lecture. *Proceedings of the 31st Conference.* Calgary, Alberta: Canadian Industrial Relations Association.

———. 1995. *Seeking a Balance: Canada Labour Code, Part 1, Review.* Ottawa, Ontario: Government of Canada.

TARAS, D. G. 1997. "Collective Bargaining Regulation in Canada and the United States: Divergent Cultures, Divergent Outcomes," in *Government Regulation of the Employment Relationship,* edited by B. E. Kaufman. Industrial Relations Research Association 50th Anniversary Research Volume, pp. 295–342.

VERMA, A. and R. P. CHAYKOWSKI, eds., 1999. *Contract and Commitment: Employment Relations in the New Economy.* Kingston: IRC Press, Queen's University.

WEILER, P. 1980. *Reconcilable Differences: New Directions in Canadian Labour Law.* Toronto: Carswell.

CHAPTER 2

Understanding the Unionization Decision

Ann C. Frost and Daphne Gottlieb Taras

There are times when Lori Bonang's wages foil her efforts to be a smiling Starbucks "partner." "How can you be professional, and think about giving someone a latte, when you can't pay the rent?" says Bonang, who earns about $9 an hour.

In a move that's rocked the coffee Goliath, Bonang and 109 other Vancouver-area Starbucks workers have joined the Canadian Auto Workers to negotiate a collective agreement. They have given the union a 92 percent strike vote to bolster its clout.

Talks are under way this week in Vancouver. One of the CAW's priorities is to negotiate a hike in starting wages from about $7 hourly to at least $10.

It's an unusual situation that could have major implications for the Seattle-based chain, which leads the booming market in serving up espressos, cappuccinos, and other caffeine treats.

There are no other unions in any of Starbucks' 1000 gleaming stores across North America. Starbucks officials say they aren't needed because they treat their employees so well. "We believe Starbucks is a great place to work," says Launi Skinner, operations director for western Canada. "Ask partners in our stores. We provide benefits, compensation programs, career opportunities, and a pace where [employees] can enjoy coming to work."

But 23-year-old Bonang and other employees gathered at a downtown coffee shop—not a Starbucks—to help in bargaining aren't buying the company line. Across the table from Bonang, Liz Carr says workers are being reasonable. "We're not asking for six figures a year," says Carr, 29. "I know [my work] is not brain surgery." Carr adds: "Nobody is out to screw Starbucks, but if you want to put a bottom line on it, they're not sharing the pie."

The pie is quite rich. In the year ended October 1, 1996, Starbucks earned $42.1 million on revenue of $696.5 million (US dollars).

The Canadian Auto Workers see a Starbucks agreement in BC as the first step to extracting a larger slice of the company's riches for workers across Canada. First Vancouver, then BC, then every store in the chain.

Some observers have said the CAW's interest in the service sector is linked to its drive to sign up new members for their dues. But CAW spokesman Peggy Nash describes the effort as part of a struggle to bolster working conditions in a service sector made more crucial by high unemployment: "People who need to work are taking jobs whenever they can get them, and when they work in those jobs, they have to live off them."

Carr says that living isn't easy. She works about 30 hours a week, earning a salary of about $9 for each of those hours. She rhymes off her survival strategy: "You have roommates. You eat rice. You only go to movies on Tuesdays and matinees. You don't have a VCR. You go to the library a lot."

The suggestion Carr, Bonang, and Bond try to find higher-paying work prompts shouts of outrage around the table. "Somebody's got to work at Starbucks. Why the hell shouldn't it be me?" says Carr. "And why the hell shouldn't I have a livable wage to do it?"[1]

Workers join unions for a wide variety of reasons and to accomplish a range of objectives. This chapter describes both what unions do and why they attract workers. The functions of unions and their allure are inextricably linked. It is necessary to understand pre-existing conditions in the workplace and what unions offer to best appreciate why people join them.

Canadian Auto Workers: www.caw.ca

The Starbucks vignette that opened this chapter illustrates a number of the motivations workers have for joining a union. Clearly, these Starbucks workers are activated by the economic factors that often come to mind first when considering the decision to unionize. They are seeking to win a living wage through unionization. Their decision to organize will also have broader economic effects should they be successful, by helping to organize the service sector. The unionization of the expanding and largely nonunion sea of low-wage service-sector employment may improve Starbucks' workers' mobility opportunities as well as the well-being of a broader cross-section of service workers. These Starbucks workers also see the union as a way to increase equity in the workplace. They believe that it is only fair that the highly profitable Starbucks share a larger proportion of the pie created in part by its baristas. Unionization may also be a way to participate in an organization of their own. Through their union, workers gain a say over the terms and conditions of employment, have access to a system of due process to ensure protection from unreasonable management actions, and have input into decisions that have an impact on the workplace. Other Starbucks workers may not want to be in a union at all, but if a majority of their co-workers support the union, the law determines that the union will be their bargaining agent.

In this chapter we will review each of these aspects of unions (economic, equity, countervailing power, forced unionism, and voice) and describe the conditions under which each might persuade workers to unionize. We also will provide some insight into an individual's propensity to unionize—not only the determinants of his or her desire to join a union, but also the factors that influence the opportunity to do so. Finally, we will address the changes the new competitive environment is creating in the workplace and assess what these changes mean for unions. What role are unions to play in the future? How can they continue to attract members to ensure their continued relevance and vitality?

THE ECONOMIC RATIONALE

Most people, when they think of what unions are all about, focus on unions' ability to win increased wages and benefits. Such bread-and-butter concerns have traditionally brought many members into unions. Samuel Gompers, the first president of the American Federation of Labor, in 1893, stated labour's singular goal when he responded to the question "What does labour want?" with "more."[2] This traditional function of winning more remains a critical part of what unions do. In the section that follows, we describe two distinct ways in which the economic function of unions appeals to workers: the benefits of collective action for getting a better deal, and the power of unions to take wages out of competition.

Getting a Better Deal

Workers turn to unions because they want to increase their bargaining power in order to negotiate higher wages and benefits than are achieved by their nonunion counterparts. There is an expectation that a union will deliver tangible gains. Figure 2.1 is the 1969 tongue-in-cheek effort of the oil industry's union to use the Imperial Oil mascot (the "Esso Tiger") and advertising slogan "Put a tiger in your tank" against the company in a union organizing campaign promising to deliver improvements in wages and working conditions.

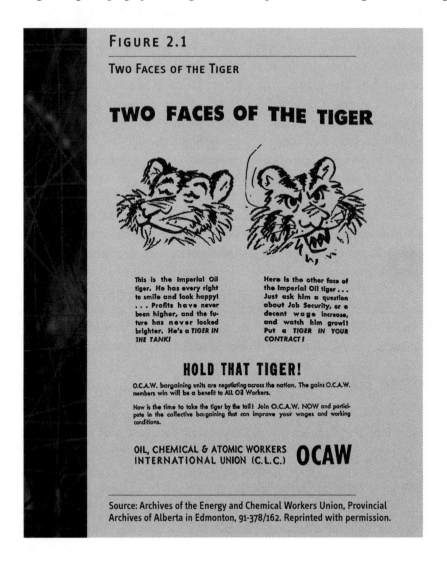

FIGURE 2.1

TWO FACES OF THE TIGER

Source: Archives of the Energy and Chemical Workers Union, Provincial Archives of Alberta in Edmonton, 91-378/162. Reprinted with permission.

The union impact on wages, however, can vary considerably. Richard Freeman and James Medoff (1984), two Harvard economists, show that the union–nonunion wage differential is greatest in industries in which employers enjoy some protection from cut-throat competition. Similarly, where labour is a small portion of total costs, wage differentials can also be significant. In highly competitive industries, such as the apparel industry, or where labour is a large proportion of total costs, union workers earn little or no more than their nonunion counterparts.

Unions' ability to raise compensation (wages and benefits), without creating undue hardship for the firm, usually indicates that profits are above normal. In negotiating successfully with such employers, unions are able to transfer some of these profits from the employer's pocket to the employees'. For example, unions have been highly successful in organizing the automobile, steel, rubber, and telecommunications industries, which are all examples of industries in which employers enjoyed periods of high profitability due to barriers to entry, oligopolistic pricing behaviour, and/or regulated monopoly status. In highly competitive industries, where profit margins are thin, there may be less profit to be transferred to union members through collective bargaining. Unions extract such concessions at the risk of driving such firms out of business. In these settings, unions must appeal to workers on a basis other than higher wages, such as providing a means to check managerial authority or gaining a greater say at work.

The Canadian union–nonunion wage differential is estimated to be in the 10–25 percent range. The differential is largest for unskilled occupations, is larger across small enterprises, is higher for blue-collar than white-collar workers, and is larger during recessions than in boom times (Gunderson and Riddell, 1993). Unions also deliver improved benefits packages. Unionized employees in Canada are 22 to 25 percent more likely to have employer-provided pension plans than nonunion workers (Swidinsky and Kupferschmidt, 1991). The economic effects of unions are explored in Chapter 13.

One example of this process of organizing a highly profitable and oligopolistic industry involves the National Hockey League Players Association, formed in June 1967. The CBC-produced film *Net Worth* documents the struggles of the players in the then six NHL teams to organize and become certified by the Canada Labour Relations Board. For years, team owners had earned large profits from the proceeds of games that could not have been played without the talents of players. They accomplished this by holding pay down. Gordie Howe of the Detroit Red Wings—unquestionably one of the finest hockey players of the 1950s, and indeed of all time—was paid (and accepted) compensation considerably below his value, much to the delight and relief of the club owners. The NHL club owners also did nothing to provide for hockey players at the conclusion of their often short-lived careers. Eventually, players banded together to form the NHLPA and greatly increased their bargaining power, winning higher salaries and valuable pension benefits.[3]

Not all employees want, or need, a union for its economic benefits. People who have high individual bargaining power because they are star performers, or because they have valued skills or attributes, often feel that they can achieve a better deal individually than would be the case if they were part of a collective.

For example, high-tech workers have long believed unions to be irrelevant to their daily work experience. However, as their skills increasingly are in supply and as employers find cheaper, offshore sources of talent, even high-tech workers are beginning to pay attention to union overtures. At the same time, unions understand that workers expect "more" from them, and are struggling to identify those elements of the employment setting with which such workers are less than satisfied. In some cases, wages remain an appropriate focus, but in other settings, the provision of benefits and job security are more important to workers. It is on issues like these that new organizing campaigns, such as the one described in Exhibit 2.1, are being launched.

EXHIBIT 2.1

UNION ORGANIZING STRATEGIES IN SILICON VALLEY

With a Prada bag and the air of an entrepreneur, Amy Dean is an unlikely labour trailblazer. But as head of the AFL-CIO's Silicon Valley office, Ms. Dean, at just 37 years of age, has become the labour movement's chief navigator in the roiling and uncharted seas of the new economy.

To help the valley's horde of temporary workers who have no health insurance, she has taken the unorthodox step of creating a non-profit temp agency that, unlike most for-profit agencies, offers health coverage that temporary workers can afford.

And she has proposed using a hiring-hall concept to provide uninterrupted health and pension benefits to high-tech workers, who often jump from job to job. So far, all her strategizing has failed to strike a chord with the valley's "haves," like software designers, who, happy with their stock options, often think unions are as useful as manual typewriters. Her biggest challenge is figuring out a way for unions to connect to these high-tech workers.

Ms. Dean acknowledges that labour's traditional contracts-are-everything model is largely irrelevant to high-tech workers because it is based on a 1930s notion of people working at industrial behemoths, not agile start-ups, and of workers spending decades at one corporation, not jumping like grasshoppers between companies.

Recognizing this, Ms. Dean has become the foremost exponent of a provocative theory: Labour should return to its craft guild and hiring-hall roots as a way to keep up with the fast-changing high-tech world.

For high-tech workers, who often hold 10 jobs over a career, constantly losing and regaining health and pension coverage, Ms. Dean says unions should be a source of stability and protection. No other institution, she says, is as well-equipped to provide such workers with the two things they say they need most: portable benefits and continual upgrading of their skills.

Her most innovative work has come in seeking to help the thousands of temporary workers who flood in and out of high-tech companies—secretaries, clerks, bookkeepers, software testers. Aided by foundation grants, she has set up a non-profit agency that is placing temporary workers, for the most part

secretaries, who start at $10 an hour, compared with the $8.50 paid by many agencies. Unlike most for-profit agencies, her agency offers low-cost health coverage, paid sick leave, and paid holidays and works with a community college to furnish subsidized courses to upgrade the workers' skills.

Ms. Dean has also set up an association, in essence a fledgling union, where temporary workers can compare notes, air grievances, and map strategies to win better working conditions. The latest idea is to pressure agencies to adhere to a code of conduct requiring health insurance and a respectable wage.

"Is the current model that unions are offering relevant to the knowledge workers of today? No," Ms. Dean said. "Are the principles and benefits that unions offer relevant? Yes."

Source: Steven Greenhouse, "The Most Innovative Figure in Silicon Valley?" *New York Times* (Sunday November 14, 1999), p. 26.

Take Wages Out of Competition

Workers also turn to unions to protect themselves from competitive impulses among firms, that cause top management to try to lower overall firm costs by reducing the rate paid to labour.[4] By bargaining a rate of pay and fixing it for the life of the contract, unions take away management's ability to unilaterally reduce pay. At the same time, unions seek to "organize to the extent of the market" to ensure that all employers in an industry are similarly constrained. Thus, employers are forced to find some other dimension rather than the livelihood of their workers on which to compete.

This interaction between employer strategies and union organizing is illustrated by one of the classic studies in North American industrial relations. John R. Commons documented the process of workers banding together into unions in reaction to the product market expansion.[5] Commons used a case history of American shoemakers from 1648 to 1895. Shoemakers originally organized into city-based guild-like organizations to protect the wages and working conditions of members working in a delimited geographic area (the city of Philadelphia in this case). Employers, confronted with organized shoemakers in one city, simply moved production to a location lacking such organization. In response, the shoemakers' trade union began to organize shoemakers in all centres and got them to agree upon the terms and conditions under which they would work. This process of organizing workers wherever employers moved the work took wages out of competition and forced employers to compete on a basis other than cheap labour: for example, on quality of the goods, diversity of styles, or speed of delivery.

Another example of this process is the strategy followed by the International Brotherhood of Teamsters under the presidency of Jimmy Hoffa in organizing the American trucking industry. Although trucking is a highly competitive industry, by organizing a great proportion of the industry under a Master Freight Agreement, Teamsters effectively took wages out of competition and delivered significant wage and benefit increases to union members.

A similar process occurred during the organization of the mass-production industries in the 1930s and 1940s in North America. With the advent of mass-production technologies, skilled workers (who traditionally had been organized into craft unions) could be replaced by semi-skilled and unskilled workers, many of whom were new immigrants. Such employment practices posed serious threats to the craft unions and their members. The labour movement's response was, once again, to organize to the extent of the market (this time the labour market) and bring the semi-skilled and unskilled into the labour movement.

Indeed, this process of taking wages out of competition largely explains the initial organizing impetus behind the unionization of Canadian workers by American-based international unions.[6] American unions became active in Canada, particularly between World War I and World War II, to prevent Canadian subsidiaries of American-owned firms from using cheaper Canadian labour to undercut American workers. This process was repeated within Canada as unions sought to develop national wage programs to prevent firms from using wage disparities among the provinces as a basis upon which to compete. For example, the Energy and Chemical Workers Union[7] engaged in a formal program of pattern bargaining to keep wages uniform within the petroleum industry. Likewise, highly centralized bargaining structures in British Columbia in which employer associations bargained with a union (or council of trade unions) kept wages and working conditions in the forest products industry and the pulp and paper industry virtually identical across the vast majority of employers.

 Canadian Labour Net: www.geocities.com/CapitolHill/5202/canada/html

This process of organizing to the extent of the market in order to take wages out of competition remains a fundamental goal of the labour movement. The Canadian Auto Workers Union (CAW), which represents workers in the Big Three automotive manufacturers, has watched the industry's employers outsource to smaller, often nonunion, parts suppliers. As a result, the CAW has redoubled efforts to organize these suppliers. Similarly, in Canada's burgeoning film industry, unions are working to organize nonunion film extras. Exhibit 2.2 describes how such extras are substantially less expensive to hire than their unionized counterparts. No doubt the ACTRA union would like to take wages out of competition in order to prevent film industry employers from hiring nonunion workers to the detriment of union members.

Defending workers against market instability remains a relevant union goal, as Canadian and American unions react with alarm to the relocation of firms hoping to capitalize on low wage costs in Mexico and the Far East. The International Labour Organization (ILO) has been attempting to publicize the evils of child labour, sweatshop conditions, and the abuse of workers in countries with weak unions and little protection from exploitation. While the amelioration of the worst conditions for workers is a moral stance, it also is consistent with the goal of organizing to the extent of the market to standardize employment conditions and take wages out of competition on a worldwide basis.

EXHIBIT 2.2

NONUNION EXTRAS PLAN UNION RALLY

Background performers in Toronto's film and TV industry are so angry that they're taking to the streets in protest.

A mass rally and union-organizing campaign planned for this weekend is expected to attract between 500 and 1000 people.

The background performers, also known as extras, are upset that they only earn $7 an hour, compared to the $19.50 earned by extras who are unionized members of ACTRA.

"We would like to be paid $10 or $12 an hour," said Ray Miller, the president of the newly formed Professional Alliance of Canadian Talent. "At $7 an hour, we're grossly underpaid." ACTRA has agreed to support the group's efforts.

Source: "Non-union extras plan union rally." *Calgary Herald* (September 1, 1999), p. D2.

Labour Start (International): www.labourstart.org/

FAIRNESS, EQUITY, AND THE WAGE-EFFORT BARGAIN

In addition to the economic rationales, many people are drawn to unions for reasons of "fairness" or "equity." When firms are highly profitable, workers perceive it is only fair that some of the prosperity born of their efforts be shared with them. Similarly, workers doing a job in one firm believe it is only fair that they be paid the same as other workers doing identical work in similar firms in their industry, regardless of differences in firm profitability. Logically, unions believe that workers in the higher-cost firm should not be forced to bear the brunt of management's inefficiencies.

Unions also serve to increase workers' perceptions of equity within the firm itself. Equity theory, a psychologically based theory of work motivation, posits that people will engage in activities to the extent that they perceive the situation to be fair and equitable. Workers compare what they receive in return for their efforts with what others in similar situations receive for theirs. If this comparison of input to output ratios is equal, then equity is perceived and people will continue with the activity. In assessing inputs, people consider factors such as effort, performance level, education, and time. In assessing outputs they consider factors such as pay, recognition, and other rewards.[8]

Inequity results from people's feelings that they are being over- or under-rewarded. Perceptions of over-reward are rare, but when they occur, people tend to feel guilty and are motivated to work harder or produce higher quality work. When people perceive that they are under-rewarded, however, they try to bring the situation into balance either by working less or lowering the quality of their work. In more extreme instances, they simply quit.

It is natural that workers will look to comparison groups to determine whether their employer is fair. It is quite rankling to discover that another person is paid more, or treated better, for exactly the same type of work.

In periods of relative stability, workers also have a tendency to feel comfort in having achieved some sort of equilibrium between their input of effort and their receipt of compensation for that amount of effort. This is known as the "wage-effort bargain."[9] If management tries to lower the compensation or quality of working conditions, workers attempt to maintain equilibrium by reducing their amount of effort or trying to find other means to restore lost wages. For example, if wages are cut by 5 percent, to achieve a balance workers might decrease their work pace, declare more sick days, develop cynicism about the employer, or even pilfer office supplies. If management desires a higher level of effort, according to this model of behaviour, workers will expect some enhanced compensation. When jobs are enlarged or enriched, it is natural for workers to expect some gain in the form of higher wages, more job security, or better treatment.

If workers feel their equilibrium state is threatened—either by a demand for greater effort or by a reduction in compensation or security—they might turn to a union to redress the balance. Unions can negotiate pay systems that employees perceive to be fair. Union contracts often contain job-evaluation systems to rate jobs on the basis of difficulty, unpleasantness, and responsibility and then pay job incumbents accordingly. Union contracts also often specify the criteria by which job incumbents move from one job to another. And collective agreements "lock in" wage-effort positions so that workers can achieve the stability necessary to develop a psychologically satisfying equilibrium state.

Unions also seek to improve wage equity between bargaining unit and management pay scales. In most unionized firms, the management wage premium tends to be smaller than in nonunion companies. Unions are also concerned with wage inequality within the economy as a whole. In the words of Buzz Hargrove, the President of the Canadian Auto Workers union,

> These are certainly good times if you're wealthy. But what if you're not? Since 1989, the average income of the bottom fifth of all Canadians has fallen 32 percent, the number of poor children has grown by 46 percent, and the number of Canadians living on social assistance has grown by 68 percent. Yet federal spending on social programs, as a percentage of Gross Domestic Product, is at its lowest level since 1949. Good times if you've been invited to the party, not so good if your nose is pressed against the glass. [At the same time] Executive salaries, bonuses, pensions, and other perks reached unprecedented heights. The typical chief executive officer's take-home pay went up 112 percent. The average Canadian worker's after-tax income, meanwhile, *dropped* 9 percent between 1990 and 1997. In real terms, most Canadian workers now earn less than they would have in 1975.[10]

COUNTERVAILING POWER RATIONALE

In addition to economic and fairness rationales, unions are attractive because they are also seen as vehicles for employee power. In order to support our democratic system of government, we prize citizenship behaviours, including voting and the open expression of political beliefs. People are expected through a democratic process to have a say in how they are governed. By contrast, such practices typically stop at the factory gates. Workers are expected to follow all reasonable orders, adhere to company rules and policies, and work faithfully at executing their job duties. Unions are attractive to many workers because they provide workers with some say and a means to check the unfettered exercise of managerial authority.

By joining a union, workers hope to gain additional control over their experience at work. Such additional control comes through both society-wide and worksite-level interventions by unions. At the societal level, unions are a lobbying force of which politicians are well aware. At the workplace level, unions enable workers to have some access to due process, to counter unilateral management action, and to have some input into the codification of the rules that govern their daily work lives. In many cases, workers unionize primarily to gain the latter benefits—mismanagement and capriciousness on the part of first-line supervisors often will do more than low wages to drive employees to unionize.

To Lobby Government and Take Political Action

One of the measures of the vitality of any democracy in the world is the freedom workers enjoy to exercise their collective rights, both at the worksite, and in the larger political sphere. As Lynn Williams (1997:47), Canadian former president of the United Steelworkers of America, has put it, "The heart of the matter is that, in a democratic society, one of the most fundamental rights is that workers have open and non-threatening access to unionization and collective bargaining, if they so choose." The participation of organized labour in the larger political scene of a nation is an important measure of a society's level of democracy.

Because of the progressive and democratic role that organized labour can play within a civil society, one of the repressive measures often taken by dictatorships is the weakening or banning of unions. Conversely, one of the first groups to oppose totalitarian regimes and to work toward their demise is organized labour. One of the best examples of the role of unions in political action is the Dutch Dockworkers and their manifesto distributed throughout the Netherlands on the eve of the Nazi invasion. The Dockworkers listed a number of means of resistance and ended their list with a plea to hide a Jewish child. Similarly, the democratization of Poland was spearheaded by the Solidarity trade union, a union that broke away from Communist control and eventually formed the first democratically elected government of Poland. Social transformation in South Africa included giving blacks the right to vote and unionize.

According to Andrew Sims, head of a federal task force on labour law reform, unions are the only national lobby group available for worker interests. Nonunion workers have little entree into the political arena on issues of concern to them at the workplace because they have no well-established organizations to lobby on their behalf. By contrast, unions have an institutional structure that can be activated to mobilize workers from firm to firm, across industries, and throughout the country (Sims, 2000).

Canada historically has had a labour movement that has actively participated in the country's political life. The Cooperative Commonwealth Federation (CCF) (which in 1961 became the New Democratic Party) was born as an alliance between farm and labour interests. Through the CCF, which achieved electoral success in several provinces, unions were able to lobby for greater statutory protections (see Exhibit 2.3). The Canadian government finally gave workers the right to unionize and compelled firms to recognize unions in 1944, only after Prime Minister William Lyon Mackenzie King perceived that the CCF had gained sufficient momentum that it threatened his electoral chances. Many advances in statutory protections for unions can be attributed to the alliance between organized labour and the CCF/NDP (Bruce, 1989).

This tight alliance has frayed in recent years. Unions refused to support NDP Premier Bob Rae of Ontario in his efforts to introduce a "social contract" in 1993. Some unions withdrew formal support from the NDP. However, even without an overt partnership between labour and a particular political party, unions remain committed to making their presence felt on the political stage.

Unions try to shape public policy and legislation in other ways to benefit their members. Labour recognizes that its collective bargaining strength is strongly influenced by the laws, the policies, the general economy, and the social climate in which it is embedded.[11] Moreover, union members' interests extend beyond the workplace so that unions must also concern themselves with issues like housing, taxation, education, medical services, the

EXHIBIT 2.3

WHAT MAKES CANADA UNIQUE?

North American labour movements differ from those of other countries because of the emphasis on "business unionism"—the preoccupation with protecting and advancing the immediate economic interests of union members rather than engaging in direct participation in politics. However, the Canadian union movement has built a strong alliance with the New Democratic Party (formerly the CCF), making it more of a hybrid movement, practising business unionism in its collective bargaining relationships, but social activism and participation in political processes. Although the NDP has never attained power federally, there have been many instances where the NDP formed provincial governments or led official oppositions. Except for employees of federal undertakings, labour relations fall under provincial jurisdictions.

environment, and the international economy.[12] Through mobilizing workers and forming coalitions with other advocacy groups, trade unions seek, among other things, to protect worker safety and health, to promote managed trade, and to ensure an adequate social safety net. Unions help workers see that they have common interests with fellow workers and make possible the collective action that can protect the vulnerable and improve conditions for all (Bernard, 1998). Sometimes Canadian unions have become active in international relations issues, seeking greater protection from open borders. For example, organized labour was a key player in the coalition of community, church, and farmer groups opposed to the Canada–US Free Trade Agreement in 1988, and, again in 1991, labour led the fight against the North American Free Trade Agreement (Ginden, 1995).

One of the problems with this lobbying role is that union members sometimes do not support the same causes as their leaders. For example, although leaders in the Alberta labour movement fought the rapid deficit-reduction policies of Premier Ralph Klein, many members supported the Klein government and voted to ensure the Conservatives' electoral victory. Another example is provided by the CAW, which favours legislated gun control. However, considerable debate rages within the union as rank-and-file members disagree, often vehemently, with the positions taken by their elected leaders.[13] Some union members deeply resent that the dues they pay to belong to a collective bargaining system are used to support social and political causes with which they personally disagree.[14]

Some workers want unions to be organizations that mobilize workers to express themselves as part of a larger social movement. They expect unions to inform them about political issues and involve them in important causes. Although for a small subset of workers, this role is vital; nevertheless, the Canadian evidence (reviewed later in this chapter) is that this is the least relevant union function to most workers.

 Labour notes (radical site): www.labornotes.org/

To Increase Justice in the Workplace

Unions bring a system of workplace-based representation that reduces unilateral management decision making. By law, each collective agreement must contain a grievance procedure to resolve contractual disputes. The collective bargaining agreement is the document that contains the clauses governing the employment relationship for the life of the contract (generally two or three years). It sets out the myriad details of the employment relationship (see Chapter 10). In doing so, it gives the parties, both union and management, a degree of certainty over the nature of their relationship for a fixed period of time.

Often, collective agreements are copied and bound in small sizes, intended to fit into the pockets of workers and their union shop stewards, to be referred to at work in the event of a dispute. In the famous Canadian film *Final Offer*, auto workers are shown in a tense shop-floor standoff with General Motors in the mid-1980s as their union negotiates an agreement at the Royal York Hotel in Toronto. The workers can quote chapter and verse from their collective agreement. Workers both use it as a shield against management decisions they believe violate their contractual rights and wield it as a sword to get at management.

The Steward: www.thesteward.hypenet.com/canada

The grievance procedure provides workers with due process on the job. The union grievance procedure is an alternative system to the courts accessible by employees. Few wronged employees would take their cases to court—the costs and the length of time a hearing would take prohibit such action in all but the most egregious cases. However, many employees in unionized workplaces take advantage of the grievance procedure to seek redress to wrongs they believe have been committed against them: how promotions were handled, pay for a particular job, or discipline.

There are obvious benefits to employees of having access to this process. Those whose grievances are upheld feel vindicated. Those whose grievances are denied by the independent and neutral arbitrator still, for the most part, believe that through the process they were treated fairly. Without such a process, an aggrieved employee might quit or find other ways of getting back at the employer (through loafing or even sabotage).

It is noteworthy that very few nonunion Canadian companies provide their workers with access to an impartial third party to arbitrate work-related disputes. Even among the companies that do pay a great deal of attention to the provision of justice in the workplace, the overwhelming majority settle disagreements by making a senior human resources executive or vice president the final arbiter in a multi-step system of dispute resolution. Disputes are kept "in-house." Although nonunion workers may take employers to court, this is not a strategy that is taken when an employee wants to preserve a working relationship with the employer.

The union serves a watchdog function for employee interests. Exhibit 2.4 shows two examples of unions challenging managerial decisions through the arbitration process. In the first case, the union unsuccessfully challenged management's application of time-and-motion studies. In the second case, an arbitrator found that the union was correct in arguing that management was unreasonable in refusing to allow workers to take a third washroom break per day without losing pay. In nonunion worksites, there is no mechanism to challenge management's decisions in such matters. Many managers deeply resent having to give up the power to make decisions about employment relationships or work processes, and the flip side of the coin is that many workers are grateful for union protection.

By law, management cannot fire or otherwise punish workers for speaking out through their union. Workers channel their grievances through their union representatives. Any unreasonable management interference with the ability of workers to select and be represented by a union is unlawful. Thus, all things being equal, workers should have a higher sense of security and less fear of reprisal for speaking out within a unionized worksite than in a comparable nonunion setting. Although Canadians by and large are satisfied with their work lives, 51 percent of Canadian workers, both union and nonunion, believe that the possibility of management reprisal exists (Lipset and Meltz, 1997).

EXHIBIT 2.4

TWO EXAMPLES OF UNIONS CHALLENGING MANAGERIAL DECISIONS

CASE 1

The Issue: Whether the employer had a basis to conduct new "time-and-motion" studies. The union filed a policy grievance alleging that the company acted in breach of article 17 of the collective agreement in 1996. Specifically, it was alleged that the company did not provide an adequate reason for doing the new studies because there was no triggering event.

The Arbitrator's Decision: The collective agreement does not restrict the Company's right to initiate time-and-motion studies on jobs with established rates to only those circumstances where there have been triggering events, such as a change in the number of elements in the job, a change in the method of production, or a change in technology. The fact that the nine challenged time-and-motion studies were done on jobs that allegedly had established rates does not create a breach of the collective agreement because it is expressly provided for in article 17.02(a). The Board finds that as a reason, "verification" of the "integrity of the piece rate structure" falls within the Company's entitlement under the agreement. Article 17.02(b) speaks to maintaining a balance of fairness between the Company's interests and the employees' interests by means of correcting both rates that are "too tight" (and therefore unfavourable to the operator) and rates that are "too loose" (and therefore unfavourable to the Company).

Source: Ranpro Inc. and UNITE, Local 2426. Pamela Cooper Picher, arbitrator (August 6, 1999).

CASE 2

The Issue: The company would not permit employees to take paid washroom breaks. The workforce employed by a meat-processing plant was in the habit of taking washroom breaks subject to personal necessity. The company then notified the workforce that washroom breaks were adding to operating expenses and the company would no longer "foot the bill" for these breaks. A new schedule was posted, amounting to an extra 30 unpaid minutes a day. The company allotted two 15-minute breaks, unpaid, when the employees could use the washrooms. If an employee's bladder did not co-operate with the new schedule and the employee needed another break to use the washroom, 15 minutes' pay would be deducted from his or her pay. The union grieved the new policy and asked for damages to be paid to the employees for all their unpaid work.

The Arbitrator's Decision: I do not find that the intent of the parties and the agreement that sprang from that intent allowed the company to act as it did upon this occasion. Even if I am wrong in that conclusion, and the company did have the discretion to so act, I would not find the exercise of that discretion in this instance to be reasonable. I am of the belief that some damages should be paid [to the employees for the amount of unpaid time taken for washroom breaks until the time of the arbitrator's award]. I think it is appropriate here to afford time in which [the parties, union and management] may consider this award and to attempt to find a mutually agreeable resolution. [Failing an agreement] I will render my final determination of quantum if it proves necessary.

Source: Burns Meats, A Division of Burns Foods (1985) Limited, and the United Food and Commercial Workers Union. Paul S. Teskey, arbitrator (March 31, 1993).

As a result of union vigilance, managers feel that unions create rigid and adversarial worksites at a time when managers value flexibility and co-operation. For example, managers frequently complain that it is exceedingly difficult to fire problem employees. There is a great deal of truth to this view. According to a variety of studies, arbitrators reinstate dismissed employees about 50 percent of the time (Williams and Taras, 2000). It is much more difficult to discharge an employee in a unionized workplace than in a nonunion workplace (which is one reason why workers join unions). One solution for management in unionized settings is to pay special attention to recruitment and selection of employees, and if problems emerge, to use reasonable discipline and proper documentation. In unionized settings, personnel management becomes much more important; companies with sophisticated approaches stand a better chance of having their decisions upheld in arbitration than organizations with haphazard personnel arrangements.

To Provide Workers an Opportunity for Meaningful Participation in their Own Organization

For some workers, union activity provides an outlet for needs that are not being fulfilled in other facets of their everyday life, a means of expression missing elsewhere. Groundbreaking early research by Leonard Sayles and George Strauss (1967) on the functioning of local unions identified the factors that caused certain workers to be attracted to a union and to become active in it while other seemingly identical workers were not. Their early field study findings based on the in-depth study of more than 20 local unions continue to be valid more than 40 years later.

People can be attracted to unions because of their level of idealism and discontent with the status quo. For many, the union is seen as a way to have influence not only over workplace issues, but also over larger political issues. Others are drawn to unions for more individual reasons. Many of those who are attracted to unions are highly competent in their current jobs and often find themselves at the top of their promotional ladders. The union offers them another outlet for challenge. Handling grievances, building political support, solving workplace problems all provide people a chance to use creativity that may not otherwise be used on the job. Not only does such activity provide relief from the monotony of many industrial or menial jobs, but doing these things well provides people with a sense of achievement or accomplishment.

Union membership also offers people a social outlet. For many people whose jobs keep them physically tied to a specific workstation or area of a plant, the opportunity to interact with more people on a regular basis is a significant benefit. Further, union activity often requires time away from the job—work in the union hall, meetings with management, the opportunity to travel and attend conventions or company-wide negotiations—which provides respite from the dreariness of everyday workplace life. Finally, others enjoy union membership because it provides them with an outlet for aggression— bored and frustrated by work, union membership allows them a means to vent.

STATUTORY AND "FORCED" UNIONISM

Not all unionized workers choose specifically to be represented by a union or choose a particular union to represent them. Rather, they simply begin working at a worksite that already has been certified by a union, and hence become subject to the pre-existing arrangements.[15] These workers come to the union, not by choice, but by circumstance (see Exhibit 2.5). They might have been attracted to a unionized worksite because of higher pay or greater job protection, but they were not part of the original group of employees whose activities launched the unionization process. They may, or may not, be union supporters. Depending upon the "union security arrangements" (described in Chapter 10) they may be forced to become members of the union, or they may opt out of union membership but have to pay union dues regardless, or some other arrangement might exist. But whether or not they officially join the union, they are nonetheless considered part of a unionized worksite.

Other employees were present during union organizing, but chose not to support the union. Nevertheless, once the majority of their co-workers supported unionization, the workplace became unionized, both for the supporters of the union and for those who opposed it. The only options available to these workers under Canadian laws are to accept the union as their legitimate bargaining agent (regardless of their distaste), or to attempt to bring about a union decertification (an election held to vote the union out). Once unionized, however, employees who wish to get rid of their unions are a distinct minority. When asked in surveys, the vast majority of unionized workers would vote for the union again if given the opportunity. In an American survey (which we describe in a later section of this chapter), 90 percent of current private-sector union members would vote to keep their union, and they believe that a large majority of their colleagues would do the same (Freeman and Rogers, 1998).

EXHIBIT 2.5

REFLECTIONS ON A UNION-JOINING EXPERIENCE

I got my first real job when I was 17, working at a Miracle Mart store that had just opened in a mall near my high school in Montreal. I applied to work Friday nights and Saturdays and filled out the usual application forms. An employee from the personnel department interviewed me to find out where I could work (I ended up in the toy department) and to ensure that I spoke both English and French. She then told me that I had the job, but that I had to join the union before I could start. She showed me the union membership application and the form allowing union dues to be deducted. I said I was only working part time, I didn't need a union, and I sure didn't want to pay union dues. I asked what would happen if I didn't sign. She said that the contract with the union required that all employees join the union and that if I didn't sign she couldn't hire me. I said, "Where do I sign . . .?"

Source: An anonymous colleague's first union experience.

Finally, there are anomalous situations in which workers are forced to unionize. Governments have passed statutes proclaiming that it is in the public interest for specified groups to engage in collective bargaining. For example, university professors in the province of Alberta must be represented by their faculty associations for the purpose of collective bargaining. Teachers' associations in some provinces are creatures of statute, as are some construction unions in Quebec. Sometimes, professional associations, which certify the credentials of their members, also act as bargaining agents. This is the case for public school teachers in Alberta, who must belong to their association (union) in order to be qualified to teach in the public school system.

Thus, the fact that 30 percent of Canadians are unionized does not mean that 30 percent of Canadians voted for or otherwise supported a union. Conversely, many Canadians who are not unionized may, at one time or another, have voted for a union. And still others would like to have a union but cannot convince the majority of their co-workers to support unionization. In a 1997 survey, union members and former members comprised just over one-half of all Canadians who expressed approval of unions, and the remaining support came from people who had never been members of unions (Bibby, 1997:3). On the other hand, many Canadians who are part of unionized worksites never actually chose the union. And other workers became unionized through a government statute, or because their professional association provides both credentials and bargaining. As a result, the union density rate is a poor proxy measure of either the desire to unionize or support of unionization. Thus, the interpretation of unionization rates must be conducted with care.

 "Canadians and Unions" (Angus Reid Survey): www.interlog.com/~wrf/report.htm

THE VOICE RATIONALE

A final rationale for unionization is "voice" (Freeman and Medoff, 1984). Societies have two basic mechanisms for dealing with social or economic problems: exit and voice (Hirschman, 1971). The first is the market mechanism of exit in which an individual expresses his or her displeasure with current conditions by simply going elsewhere. If a store's service is found to be lacking, the shopper walks away. If a restaurant's meal is disappointing, the diner leaves, never to return. If a school fails to deliver expected academic results, parents transfer their children to another. In the labour market, exit translates into quitting—if a worker is dissatisfied with his or her employment conditions (the pay is too low, the supervision too demanding, or the conditions too unpleasant), he or she quits and seeks employment elsewhere. This action, in theory, rewards good employers and punishes bad ones.

The second mechanism for dealing with dissatisfaction is voice. Rather than leave the store or restaurant, never to return, the disgruntled shopper or diner informs the clerk, manager, waiter, or chef of his or her displeasure and seeks to correct the problem. Through the subsequent exchange of a faulty product or the replacement of a too-salty meal, the individual is satisfied and the store or restaurant's performance improves. Likewise, rather than removing their children from a problematic school, parents using the voice option would join with other parents to lobby through the Parent Teacher Association for an improvement in teaching staff, facilities, or resources. In the employment context, voice translates into discussing with the employer conditions that need to be remedied, rather than quitting the job. Exercising the voice option creates a social good: One or more employees taking their grievances to management and having the problems corrected improves the conditions for all.

Clearly, the benefit to workers of the voice mechanism is a potential improvement in job conditions without the costs associated with having to quit, search for a new job, and relocate. The voice mechanism can also increase firm productivity via a number of different mechanisms: the "union shock effect," lowering quit rates, and harnessing worker knowledge and insight regarding the production process, all clearly beneficial to employers as well as workers.

The simple act of becoming unionized often leads to significant improvements in firm performance through what has been termed the "union shock effect."[16] The new presence of a union often serves as a prompt to an employer to professionalize its management, getting it to replace vague, paternalistic, authoritarian personnel practices with explicit rules. In addition, the union communicates with management, possibly leading to improved production methods and a safer workplace. At the same time, access to a voice mechanism allows workers to solve irritating workplace problems whose resolution can lead to increased levels of worker morale and co-operation.

The voice mechanism also lowers quit rates by 20 to 30 percent (Freeman, 1980, 1984), thereby increasing worker tenure and encouraging management investment in training. Increased training, in turn, supports worker productivity. Having some influence over the terms and conditions of employment through the collective bargaining process, as well as the presence of a grievance and arbitration system, are the mechanisms by which quits are reduced. Employers are more likely to invest in upgrading employee skills in situations where the employee is more likely to remain with the firm, thus giving the firm that paid for the training the ongoing benefit of the enhanced skill. At the same time, lower quit rates imply that work groups remain intact longer. As production techniques come to rely increasingly on interdependent functions, team stability pays larger dividends by enabling team members to become more familiar with one another, to develop positive work norms, and to work more productively together.

The union voice function also opens channels of communication between front-line workers and management that yield insights regarding more efficient production techniques. To the degree that worker insights can be tapped to improve operations, product quality and productivity can improve, often dramatically. The benefits of such improvements can then be apportioned through collective bargaining to both management and workers.

While enhanced voice is one reason that workers turn to unions, it is important to note that unionized workers are not likely to report greater levels of job satisfaction than their nonunion counterparts. Even though "satisfaction" is clearly a nebulous term, industrial relations studies have consistently found that unionized workers report equal, or lower, satisfaction than comparable nonunion workers.[17] While the exercise of voice results in measurable benefits, reported work satisfaction is not necessarily one of them.

Voice in the New Competitive Environment

The voice rationale has long been noted as an important impetus to unionization. However, with recent changes in the competitive environment, this function of unions has taken on even greater importance. Competition in many industries and sectors is now much more intense than in the past. Rapid and ongoing technological change, the deregulation of formerly regulated markets, the reduction of trade tariffs, and the intensification of foreign competition have all combined to put increased pressure on Canadian firms. To succeed in an environment in which cost and quality concerns have come to dominate, employers value flexibility, responsiveness, and innovation. For many employers, however, such firm requirements are seen to be incompatible with the perceived rigidities of a union contract, and therefore the payoffs to remaining union free are seen to be greater than ever.

As a result, nonunion employers are becoming more sophisticated. In many sectors, they pay union wages and benefits and have put into place in-house grievance procedures (that sometimes include a worker majority on the panel). However, for precisely the same reasons that employers don't want to be burdened with union representation of their workforce, workers are increasingly seeking out union representation. Workers perceive the rapid changes in the competitive environment as increasing uncertainty, disrupting the wage-effort bargain, and leading to worksite changes that have the potential to negatively affect them. These include the adoption of new technology; the reorganization of work, including broadening jobs, decentralizing decision making, and moving to team forms of work organization; and the implementation of quality- and productivity-enhancing programs with ramifications for employment levels. Workers, increasingly, despite their good pay, benefits, and access to a grievance process, want input over decisions such as these that are having dramatic effects on their daily work experience.

A case in point is the experience of workers at Magna International's Integram plant. Despite union-level pay and benefits, Magna's "Charter of Rights" that guarantees regular meetings between management and workers, "fairness committees" to hear worker grievances, and a hot line set up to field anonymous worker complaints, a majority of Integram workers voted in 1999 to be represented by the CAW. In the words of one 10-year Magna employee, "We want a union so that as the environment of the workplace changes we can have solid input, not a 'façade' committee that never accomplishes anything without the OK of management" (Lippert, 1999: C8).

Clearly, what employees increasingly seem to be interested in gaining is a true voice about decisions that are going to have a direct impact on them on the job. Traditionally, unions have acceded control over the workplace to management, hence the dictum, "management acts and the union grieves." However, this is beginning to change. Increasingly, workers want their unions to speak up for them and to have input into these decisions before they are made. In what follows, we look directly at what North American workers are saying they would like their representatives to do.

 Labour Net Canada: www.labournet.ca/

WHAT WORKERS ACTUALLY WANT FROM COLLECTIVE REPRESENTATION

The chapter so far has discussed the reasons unions have come into being and the reasons why workers have joined them. In this section, we investigate what workers today (both union and nonunion) are saying about what they want unions to do for them (and by logical extension, the kind of union to which they would like to belong). We draw here on two recent surveys, one Canadian and one American. Despite being drawn from different populations operating in quite different labour relations climates, the results of the two surveys are startlingly similar. Traditional bread-and-butter economic issues continue to be important; however, increasingly voice on the job and the ability to have access to decisions at the workplace that affect people's working lives are seen to be valuable. These are what workers are demanding of their unions.

The Canadian Survey

The survey, conducted by John Godard in 1995, interviewed 341 employed Canadians from across the country (not including Quebec). Respondents were asked to rate the extent to which they valued each of 24 activities unions were known to undertake (including economic roles, democratic roles, and voice roles) and how effective they perceived unions to be at each of them.

The survey finds that workers desire high levels of activity by unions in what we would see as traditional union areas: protecting wages and benefits, protecting job security, pursuing grievances, pushing for stronger organizing laws, and supporting workers who elect to strike. And, at the same time, respondents report unions having the most success in achieving their objectives in these same areas.

Godard also evaluates what workers believe unions ought to do. The issues perceived by Canadian workers to be most important include: ensuring workers have a say in union affairs, finding positive solutions to workplace-based conflicts that arise, enabling workers to have a say at work, and representing workers' interests to management. These issues are not generally associated with the traditional bread-and-butter concerns of "business unionism." Rather, they are much more focused on the "voice" and workplace-democracy aspects of what unions can provide for their members. This Canadian survey appears to be telling unions that Canadian workers now expect different things from their unions if unions are to receive their support.

Such desires on the part of Canadian workers are consistent with the kinds of changes that are currently underway in the Canadian economy. Increasingly, narrowly defined jobs, rigid demarcations between jobs, and strict lines of seniority are dissolving as firms seek to gain competitive advantage. To compete in the current environment, firms are finding they require greater levels of flexibility and responsiveness from their workforce, more innovation, and more problem solving at lower levels in the organization. In the midst of this shift, workers are feeling vulnerable: What exactly is my job? Is my job secure? How does the shift to teams affect me? If I suggest productivity improvements, do I leave myself (or my co-workers) vulnerable to layoff? For these reasons, workers want their unions to devote more attention to negotiating over these, more intangible, changes with their employers, and to represent workers' interests in bargaining over new forms of work organization and the introduction of new technology. Workers want to have some input into how the workplace is being restructured. Increasingly, it appears, "the role of the union is to help workers find collective solutions to their work-related concerns" (Hurd, 1996).

The American Survey

In early 1993, the Clinton administration appointed the Commission on the Future of Worker–Management Relations to undertake hearings and to issue recommendations regarding appropriate changes in US regulation of labour–management relations. During this period of intense policy analysis and lobbying from dozens, if not hundreds, of labour and management advocates, Richard Freeman and Joel Rogers, of Harvard and the University of Wisconsin respectively, undertook a national survey of employees to hear from them their perceptions of the state of labour representation in American workplaces (Freeman and Rogers, 1999).

The 1994 telephone survey spoke with 2408 employees: non-supervisory employees and low- and mid-level managers in private-sector establishments of 25 or more employees (a group that is representative of about 70 percent of the employed private-sector workforce in the US). Freeman and Rogers' findings echo many of the themes found in Godard's smaller Canadian survey. Indeed, Freeman and Rogers also surveyed 1000 Canadian private-sector workers in November 1995 and found little difference between their American and Canadian results (Freeman and Rogers, 1999: 36–37).

Freeman and Rogers provide some informative background data. First, the data indicate that the vast majority of employees are sufficiently committed and loyal to their companies to have reasons to want to participate in workplace decisions. Second, at the same time, many employees are concerned about the quality of labour–management relations at their company and are not confident they can trust management. Well over half the respondents consider themselves to have "a lot of loyalty" to their firm. However, only 38 percent have "a lot of trust that the company will keep its promises to them and other employees." The third important background finding from the data is that many employees prefer dealing with management collectively. Some 57 percent agreed that they would "feel more comfortable raising workplace problems through an employee association rather than as an individual." Together, these responses tell us that American workers are committed to their firms, but that they do not entirely trust their employers, and prefer to deal with their employers collectively.

The survey then investigated three specific questions: 1) Do employees want greater participation and representation at their workplaces than are currently provided? 2) What do employees see as essential to attaining their desired level of participation and representation? 3) What solutions do employees favour to resolve any gap between their desired participation/representation and what they currently have?

The answer to the first question is a resounding "yes." Some 63 percent of employees, and fully 72 percent of those employed in manufacturing, want more representation and participation than they have now. In particular, these employees want to have input into decisions regarding work organization, scheduling, compensation, training, technology use, safety, and the setting of work goals. More than three-quarters of those surveyed believe that if workers did have input to decisions in these areas, their company would be "stronger against its competitors," "the quality of products or services would improve," and "employees would enjoy their jobs more."

Most workers surveyed welcomed the adoption of "employee involvement" and other worker empowerment schemes by their employers. (These plans are discussed in greater detail in Chapter 15.) However, most did not believe these programs had gone far enough to encourage worker participation, and less than a third of respondents found these programs to be effective in improving productivity or quality. Overwhelmingly (82 percent of nonunion employees and 91 percent of unionized employees), respondents participating in employee involvement programs at their workplace believed such programs would be "more effective if employees, as a group, had more say in how these programs are run."

What solutions do employees see to the problem of getting access to decision making at the workplace and having true empowerment on the job? Freeman and Rogers find that most employees want "co-operative joint committees with some independent standing inside their companies (whose members are elected by other workers, not appointed by management), and many want unions or union-like organizations." Overall, they want a forum in which labour and management can meet in a co-operative spirit to discuss issues of importance to the workplace, and they want the system of representation to provide workers with effective voice.

The clear message is that most American workers want more involvement and greater say on the job. They want some form of workplace organization that provides them with collective (not just individual) voice and gives independent input into workplace decisions. Workers, for the most part, want influence on the issues that increasingly are affecting them on the job: new forms of work organization, the use of new technology, job safety, and training. They want to be able to select their own representatives to such a body and they clearly prefer co-operative relations with management to traditional conflictual or adversarial ones. If unions are able to adopt such roles and offer such workplace-based services to American workers, workers say they would be drawn to such organizations.[18] The challenge for unions is to achieve the gains that workers expect from them, but at the same time to develop methods of delivering gains without heightening conflict. The two goals are not comfortable bedfellows for most unions.

UNIONIZATION: PROPENSITY AND OPPORTUNITY

Given the findings from these in-depth surveys of North American workers, it appears a considerable number of unorganized employees are indeed interested in some form of collective representation. We will now assess the factors that influence whether or not those interests are translated into union membership. In particular, we will examine an individual's propensity to unionize as well as his or her opportunity.

Why do some workers join unions while others do not? There are two issues embedded within this seemingly simple question. As Gregor Murray (1995: 168–70) explained it, "a distinction should be made here between the *propensity of an individual to join* (the demand for union representation) and his or her *opportunity* to do so (the supply of union representation). Propensity refers to the individual preference, whereas opportunity concerns the context in which those preferences are exercised." For example, consistent findings since the 1970s coming from US data sources show that between 30 and 47 percent of nonunion workers would join a union if afforded the opportunity, a figure significantly higher than the current 14 percent level of unionization.[19] Similarly, one-third of Canadians who are not currently unionized would vote for a union if an election were held tomorrow. So clearly not all workers who approve of unions are currently union members. Table 2.1 reports the findings of the Lipset-Meltz 1996 survey that pertain to support for unions in both Canada and the United States.

Both propensity and opportunity are subjects that have received considerable research attention. Propensity to unionize can be explained by three factors (Barling, Fullagar, and Kelloway, 1992).

1. **Job dissatisfaction**: Employees react to employer practices that are perceived to be unfair, substandard, or capricious. They want better treatment on bread-and-butter issues, greater job protection, and more voice.

2. **Perceived union instrumentality**: Employees are alert to opportunities to advance the terms and conditions of their employment. Employees act instrumentally by shopping around for the best deal and determining that a union can bring advantages. They see unions as attractive instruments because unions will provide countervailing power on behalf of worker interests.

3. **Preconceived views about unions**: Most employees have a general attitude towards unions as institutions. One of the important determinants of these views

TABLE 2.1

CANADIAN AND AMERICAN WORKERS' VIEWS OF UNIONS

	Canada (N=1495) (%)	US (N=1750) (%)
Workers who approve of labour unions	67	70
Workers who believe that as a whole unions are good	52	57
Workers who believe that unions have too much power	40	26
Nonunion employees who, if an election were held tomorrow, would vote for unionization at the workplace	33	47
Nonunion employees who would personally prefer to belong to a union	21	29
Nonunion employees who feel that unions are not needed since workers get fair treatment now	42	37
Nonunion employees who, when hearing of a labour dispute and before knowing all the details, would side with the union	40	57

Source: "Canadian and American Attitudes Toward Work and Institutions," *Perspectives on Work*, vol. 1, no. 3, by Seymour Martin Lipset and Noah Meltz. © 1998, IRRA, by permission.

comes from whether or not a parent supports or is a member of a union, or whether the person has had prior experience with unions. Views about unions often are embedded within employees' larger political and ideological beliefs: If people have pre-existing beliefs that support class feelings, solidarity, and collective action, they are more inclined to support and join unions. If people have an attachment to individualism and a distaste for collectivism, they will be quite reluctant to participate in a union.

Such demographic variables as age, education level, and ethnicity have not been proven to be reliable predictors of union propensity. Apparently, there is no "union profile":

> Some implications follow from this conclusion. For example, over and above being ethically questionable, management attempts to ensure a union-free environment by excluding specific demographic groups would most likely be misguided. Also, it is both unnecessary and unwise for union organizers to target unionization campaigns for specific demographic groups (Barling, Fullagar, and Kelloway, 1992: 36).

Even assuming a certain propensity to join unions can be measured and verified, there remains the issue of opportunity. The factors that affect the opportunity to unionize include the following.

1. **Type of industry and location of employment**: Some industries are more heavily unionized than others. Historically, it has been extremely difficult for unions to organize in the banking and finance sector, whereas unionization is relatively high in heavy manufacturing. There are also geographic differences in unionization opportunities. Workers in heavily unionized manufacturing centres are more likely to come into contact with unions than workers in rural locations, far from union offices.

2. **The nature of the union that traditionally organizes the particular industry**: Some unions are aggressive in their organizing strategies and are willing to devote considerable resources to union organizing. These unions employ talented organizers who are willing to try novel strategies. Other unions may not be willing to expend valuable organizing resources on prospects that are poor because of a prior history of management opposition or knowledge that a large group of union opponents will make victory unlikely. We have been told by a senior union leader that his union is quite reluctant to commence any new organizing activities in Alberta, because the success rate for new certifications is quite low compared to that of other provinces.

3. **The public-policy setting**: We illustrate the importance of public policy with three points. First, Canadian public policy requires employers to take a "hands-off" approach to issues involving employees' decisions to unionize. Employees must be free to make a choice about joining a union without management interference. But public policy makes nonunion status the legitimate default mode of workers (Adams, 1994). Only concerted and sustained action by workers makes new union certifications possible. A second and related issue involves majoritarian principles. Almost all worksites must achieve a threshold level of at least majority support in order to be unionized. Thus, hypothetically, if the one-third of nonunion Canadians who would vote for a union were evenly distributed throughout all worksites, then no worksite would be unionized. Third, not all workers are eligible to belong to unions. For example, many labour codes across the country prohibit the unionization of agricultural workers and/or domestic workers.

4. **Degree and expression of employer opposition**: Although there are many Canadian examples of employer interference in union organizing, the Canadian setting is relatively benign compared to that of the United States. There, a sizeable number of workers lose their jobs illegally each year as a result of employer interference in union organizing. American workers are often required to attend meetings in which they are told the negative consequences of organizing, have anti-union literature delivered to their homes, and can be shown propaganda films developed by a multi-million-dollar consulting industry employed by management to dissuade workers from joining unions. In these circumstances, the opportunity for union joining is severely curtailed despite evidence of high union joining propensity.

Process of Unionization

What triggers unionization efforts among nonunion workers? What is the decision-making process used by employees as they make the transition towards unionization? Generally, unionization is initiated by employee dissatisfaction with pay, treatment, or a lack of voice on the job, or sometimes simply by the recognition that being unionized would provide a better arrangement. The model we present in Figure 2.2 begins with a gap between employees' expectations and their achievements. Awareness of this gap motivates activity leading towards unionization. Union supporters expect that the union can close this expectation–achievement gap.

The ultimate success of union organizing is moderated by the existence of inhibiting or facilitating conditions, including the emotional state of individual workers. Feelings of loyalty to the employer might inhibit union organizing and also prompt employees to give management a chance to solve problems without unionization. Fear of management reprisal might hinder some workers from seeking union support (as it surely does in the United States). Some employees are wary of union methods (i.e., strikes) and dislike adversarialism. Facilitating conditions might include co-workers' positive sentiments about unions, a developing positive relationship with a union organizer, and anger at employer provocation.

The frustration that incites a search for a solution also heightens emotional intensity. The period of union organizing is a tense and difficult time for many workers. The worksite might be divided into pro- and anti-union camps, each vying for the support of their undecided co-workers. Management actions, during both the union–organizing period and the many months or years leading up to the expectation–achievement gap, will be carefully scrutinized. Various unfair labour practices (described in Chapter 7) may be committed by management or the union. Making the unionization decision difficult in many worksites is the knowledge that the vast majority of North American managers will see a pro-union vote as an act of betrayal. Workers worry about the consequences of bringing a union into their job site: Will relationships become even more adversarial? How will normal work interactions be restored?

After the union is certified collective bargaining commences, and over time many workers may develop a sense of having dual allegiances. They are attached to both their employing organizations and their unions. Sometimes these two loyalties can coexist quite harmoniously, while at other times employees must make a choice.

A simplified version of the mechanics of initiating a union organizing campaign are suggested in Exhibit 2.6. These steps are not always followed, and the sequence is sometimes different, but Exhibit 2.6 shows that union organizing can be commenced quite readily. After the union is assured that it enjoys majority support, it will apply for certification by a labour board. Some provinces require a secret ballot vote. Even so, the process can be dizzyingly fast for the neophyte manager. In Ontario, the Labour Relations Board tries to hold a vote within five days of the union's application. The complexities of certification and behaviours that are considered lawful, and those that breach the law, are described in detail in Chapter 7.

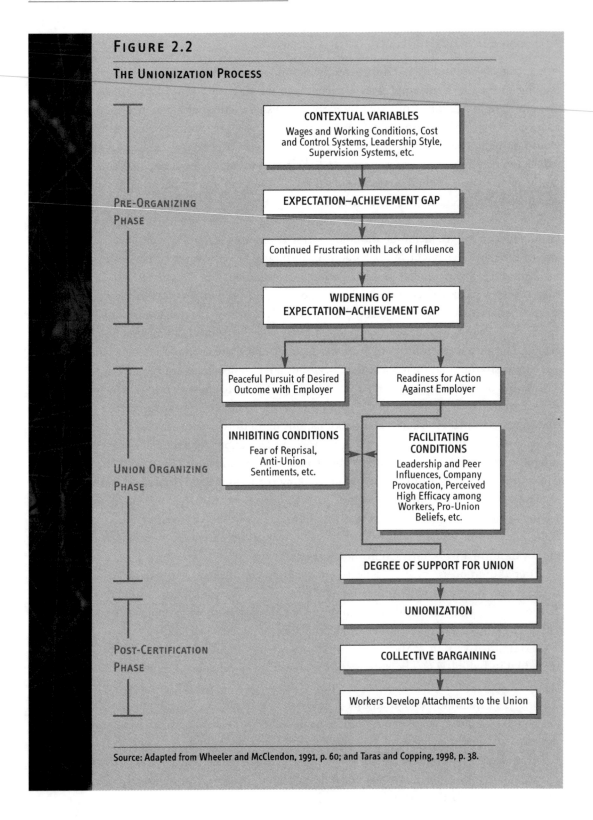

FIGURE 2.2

THE UNIONIZATION PROCESS

PRE-ORGANIZING PHASE

CONTEXTUAL VARIABLES
Wages and Working Conditions, Cost and Control Systems, Leadership Style, Supervision Systems, etc.

EXPECTATION–ACHIEVEMENT GAP

Continued Frustration with Lack of Influence

WIDENING OF EXPECTATION–ACHIEVEMENT GAP

Peaceful Pursuit of Desired Outcome with Employer

Readiness for Action Against Employer

UNION ORGANIZING PHASE

INHIBITING CONDITIONS
Fear of Reprisal, Anti-Union Sentiments, etc.

FACILITATING CONDITIONS
Leadership and Peer Influences, Company Provocation, Perceived High Efficacy among Workers, Pro-Union Beliefs, etc.

DEGREE OF SUPPORT FOR UNION

UNIONIZATION

POST-CERTIFICATION PHASE

COLLECTIVE BARGAINING

Workers Develop Attachments to the Union

Source: Adapted from Wheeler and McClendon, 1991, p. 60; and Taras and Copping, 1998, p. 38.

EXHIBIT 2.6

HOW WORKERS MAY BEGIN THE ORGANIZING PROCESS

1. Call the Labour Relations Board in their province and obtain any relevant materials on certification procedures. (In the federal jurisdiction, call the Canada Labour Relations Board.)

2. Determine the appropriate union that has other bargaining units in their industry and/or seems to specialize in representing employees doing similar work.

3. Call the union offices and set up an appointment with an organizer. If the union agrees the workers are "unionizable" under the law and of interest to the union, they should proceed to the next step.

4. Obtain a list of employees with addresses and phone numbers to help union organizing.

5. In consultation with the union, develop a local union organizing committee to oversee the organizing effort.

6. Articulate the issues that would cause employees to support the union and develop a strategy to get the message out to employees. Follow the union's advice about how to notify the employer and the relevant labour board.

7. Become familiar with the relevant labour statutes and follow the steps (described in Chapter 7) to become certified and then to commence bargaining.

CONCLUSION

As long as the employment relationship is based on an unequal balance of power, employees will likely desire some form of collective representation. This chapter demonstrates that the issues about which employees are most concerned have changed over time and with competitive circumstances. At the same time, unions have had to adapt to this turbulent corporate world with new strategies.[20]

Unions also must hear the message that is being delivered through a variety of surveys, that workers want more say in their work but less adversarialism in achieving it. As union density is declining, even in Canada, unions must struggle to remain relevant and to satisfy the needs of their members. Clearly there is a strong demand for the functions provided by unions, but workers are not entirely convinced that unions are the most desirable vehicle. The next decade will likely test unions' capacities to innovate, to market themselves, and to win support from workers in an increasingly turbulent economy.

The bottom line as to what unions are all about and what attracts people to join them is their representation of collective interests. It is only through collective action that most workers have a chance of matching employers' levels of power. Whether the goal is wage and benefit increases, or increased voice on the job to gain say into the decisions that have fundamental impacts on employees' work lives, or a system of industrial justice to prevent capricious and unilateral managerial action, union representation is often the most established means of achieving it. Perhaps best expressing this sentiment directly is labour's anthem *Solidarity Forever*:

> When the union's inspiration through the workers' blood shall run,
>
> There can be no power greater anywhere beneath the sun;
>
> Yet what force on earth is weaker than the feeble strength of one?
>
> Solidarity forever, for the union makes us strong.

Questions

1. When workers join unions for "more," what are some of the gains—both economic and non-monetary—that they are hoping to achieve?

2. What do the terms "taking wages out of competition" and "organizing to the extent of the market" mean? How are they interrelated? How do they affect business decisions?

3. Give additional illustrations of how the "wage-effort bargain" motivates employee behaviour in situations of wage rollbacks and periods of job insecurity.

4. Roughly 30 percent of Canadian workers are unionized. What does this figure tell us about the demand for unionization? Why is it a poor proxy measure for union demand?

5. What do modern workers want from unions? How can unions design organizing strategies to meet the desires of modern workers?

6. What is the difference between propensity to unionize and opportunity to unionize?

7. What types of issues trigger union organizing?

8. What factors make unions relevant today? What factors make them irrelevant? On balance, what is your view of unions?

ENDNOTES

[1] Ian Bailey, "Drinking a union-made cappuccino: CAW gets Starbucks foothold." *Montreal Gazette* (March 26, 1997, Final Edition), p. F3.

[2] Gompers' response is often misquoted. Gompers actually responded with the much more thoughtful and nuanced statement: "What does labor want? We want more school houses and less jails, more books and less arsenals, more constant work and less greed, more justice and less revenge; in fact, more opportunities to cultivate our better natures." (August 28, 1893. Chicago).

[3] For additional information about collective bargaining in sports, see Paul D. Standohar. *Playing for Dollars: Labor Relations and the Sports Industry* (Ithaca NE: ILR Press, 1996), and his article "Labor Relations in Basketball: The Lockout of 1998–99." *Monthly Labor Review*, 4 (April 1999), pp. 3–9. See also Kenneth A. Kovach, Nancy Greer Hamilton, and Meg Meserole, "Leveling the Playing Field." *Business and Economic Review*, 44, no. 1 (Oct–Dec. 1997), pp. 12–18. To understand similar labour–management pressures in the entertainment industry, see Lois S. Gray and Ronald L. Seeber, eds., *Under the Stars: Essays on Labor Relations in Arts and Entertainment* (Ithaca, NY: ILR Press, 1996).

[4] Frederick Winslow Taylor criticized this tendency to cut labour rates, arguing instead that the focus should be on productivity. See his treatise "The Principles of Scientific Management." *Bulletin of the Taylor Society*, December 1916. Jeffrey Pfeffer begged managers to cease confusing labour costs (a measure that considers productivity per worker) with labour rates (hourly wages) in "Six Dangerous Myths About Pay." *Harvard Business Review* (May–June 1998), pp. 109–119.

[5] John R. Commons' 1909 classic article remains one of the industrial relations field's pre-eminent examples of developing theory from institutional research and case study methods.

[6] Many former international unions in Canada broke away from their American parents in the 1970s and 1980s to become independent national unions. This trend is examined in Gregor Murray's chapter on unions in this volume (Chapter 4).

[7] Today part of the giant Communication, Energy and Paperworkers Union.

[8] Equity theory was developed by J. S. Adams. See his 1965 article.

[9] The concept of the "wage-effort bargain" was developed by W. Baldamus in his 1961 book.

[10] *Labour of Love* Copyright © 1998 by Buzz Hargrove and Wayne Skene. Reprinted by permission of Stoddart Publishing Company Ltd.

[11] Personal interview with Buzz Hargrove, CAW President (March 17, 1999).

[12] CAW Web site: www.caw.ca/policy/cawpol.html

[13] Personal interview with Buzz Hargrove, CAW President (March 17, 1999).

[14] For a fact situation involving a union member's protest against a union's support for a political cause, see *Lavigne* v. *Ontario Public Service Employees Union* (1991), 81 D.L.R. (4th) 545 (Supreme Court of Canada). This issue is described in greater detail in Richard Jackson's chapter on collective bargaining law in this volume (Chapter 7).

[15] In recent years, this issue has been studied by the Work Research Foundation in Mississauga, Ontario, an organization affiliated with the Christian Labour Association of Canada. The WRF has gathered materials in support of the position that "forced" unionism is a challenge to the fundamental freedom of association promised by the Canadian Charter of Rights and Freedoms.

[16] See Slichter, Healy, and Livernash, 1960 for the classic account of this process.

[17] This of course may be due to the fact that union workers feel more able to complain about perceived dissatisfactions at work than do their nonunion counterparts.

[18] Of course, just because workers in the United States want to be unionized does not mean they will become unionized. Most American employers are strongly anti-union and US labour laws make it difficult for employees to unionize in the face of strong employer opposition. See T. A. Kochan, H. Katz, and R. B. McKersie. *The Transformation of American Industrial Relations*. (New York: Basic Books, 1986); and J. J. Lawler. *Unionization and Deunionization*. (Columbia, South Carolina: University of South Carolina Press, 1990).

[19] Task Force on Reconstructing America's Labor Market Institutions. 1999. "Reframing Institutions of Representation." *Blueprint* (Research and Policy Newsletter of the Task Force, Sloan School of Management, M.I.T.), 2, No. 5 (October), p. 9.

[20] For a discussion on supplements to traditional collective bargaining such as ownership campaigns by unions, employee ownership, and "social investing," see various chapters in Estreicher (1998).

REFERENCES

ADAMS, J. S. 1965. "Inequity in Social Exchange," in *Advances in Experimental Social Psychology*, Vol. 2, edited by L. Berkowitz. New York: Academic Press, pp. 267–300.

ADAMS, R. 1994. "The 'Administrative Approach' and Union Growth in Canada and the United States, 1929–1955." *Proceedings of the 31st Conference, Calgary*. Canadian Industrial Relations Association, pp. 29–40.

BALDAMUS, W. 1961. *Efficiency and Effort: An Analysis of Industrial Administration*. London: Tavistock Publications.

BARLING, J., C. FULLAGAR, and E. K. KELLOWAY. 1992. *The Union & Its Members*. Oxford University Press.

BERNARD, E. 1998. "Creating Democratic Communities in the Workplace," in *A New Labor Movement for the New Century*, edited by G. Mantsios. New York: Garland Publishers, pp. 7–19.

BIBBY, R. 1997. "Canadians and Unions: A National Survey of Current Attitudes." Mississauga, Ontario: Work Research Foundation.

BRETT, J. M. 1980. "Why Employees Want Unions." *Organizational Dynamics*, 8, pp. 47–59.

BRUCE, P. G. 1989. "Political Parties and Labor Legislation in Canada and the US." *Industrial Relations*, 28, pp. 115–141.

CARD, D. and R. B. FREEMAN, eds. 1992. *Small Differences That Matter*. Chicago: University of Chicago Press.

COMMONS, J. R. 1909. "American Shoemakers, 1648–1895." *The Quarterly Journal of Economics*, 24 (November).

ESTREICHER, S., ed. 1998. *Employee Representation in the Emerging Workplace: Alternatives/Supplements to Collective Bargaining*. Kluwer Law International.

FREEMAN, R. 1980. "The Exit-Voice Tradeoff in the Labor Market: Unionism, Job Tenure, Quits, and Separations." *Quarterly Journal of Economics*, 94, pp. 643–674.

———. 1984. "Fixed Effects Models of the Exit-Voice Tradeoff." National Bureau of Economic Research Working Paper.

FREEMAN, R. and J. MEDOFF. 1984. *What Do Unions Do?* New York: Basic Books.

FREEMAN, R. and J. ROGERS. 1995. "Worker Representation and Participation Survey: First Report of Findings" in *Proceedings of the Forty-Seventh Annual Meeting of the Industrial Relations Research Association* (January 6–8), Washington, D.C.

———. 1998. "What Do Workers Want? Voice, Representation and Power in the American Workplace," in *Employee Representation in the Emerging Workplace: Alternatives/Supplements to Collective Bargaining*, edited by S. Estreicher. Boston: Kluwer Law International, pp. 3–38.

———. 1999. *What Workers Want*. Ithaca, N.Y.: Cornell University ILR Press.

GINDIN, S. 1995. *The Canadian Auto Workers: The Birth and Transformation of a Union*. Toronto: James Lorimer and Company.

GODARD, J. 1997. "Beliefs About Unions and What They Should Do: A Survey of Employed Canadians." *Journal of Labor Research*, 18, pp. 619–640.

GUNDERSON, M. and C. RIDDELL. 1993. *Labour Market Economics*, 3rd Edition. Toronto: McGraw-Hill Ryerson.

HARGROVE, B. and W. SKENE. 1998. *Labour of Love: The Fight to Create a More Humane Canada*. Toronto: Macfarlane Walter & Ross.

HIRSCHMAN, A. O. 1971. *Exit, Voice, and Loyalty*. Cambridge, MA: Harvard University Press.

HURD, R. 1996. "Contesting the Dinosaur Image—The Labour Movement's Search For a Future," in *A Half Century of Challenge and Change in Employment Relations*, edited by M. Neufeld and J. McElvey. Ithaca, NY: Cornell University ILR Press.

LIPPERT, J. 1999. "Magna hits campaign trail before CAW vote: Could bring in union." *National Post* (October 14).

LIPSET, S. M. and N. M. MELTZ. 1997. "Canadian and American Attitudes Toward Work and Institutions." *Perspectives on Work*, 1, no. 3, Industrial Relations Research Association.

MURRAY, G. 1995. "Unions: Membership, Structures, and Actions," in *Union–Management Relations in Canada*, 3rd Edition, edited by M. Gunderson and A. Ponak. Toronto: Addison-Wesley, pp. 159–194.

SAYLES, L. R. and G. STRAUSS. 1967. *The Local Union*. New York: Harcourt, Brace and World, Inc.

SIMS, A. 2000. "A Canadian Policy-Maker's Perspective on Nonunion Representation," in *Nonunion Employee Representation*, edited by B. Kaufman and D. G. Taras. New York: ME Sharpe.

SLICHTER, S., J. J. HEALY, and E. R. LIVERNASH. 1960. *The Impact of Collective Bargaining on Management*. Washington, D.C.: The Brookings Institution.

SWIDINSKY, R. and M. KUPFERSCMIDT. 1991. "Longitudinal Estimates of the Union Effects on Wage, Wage Dispersion and Pension Fringe Benefits." *Relations industrielles/Industrial Relations* 46, no. 4, pp. 819–838.

TARAS, D. G. and J. COPPING. 1998. "The Transition from Formal Nonunion Representation to Unionization: A Contemporary Case." *Industrial and Labor Relations Review*, 52, no. 1, pp. 22–44.

WHEELER, H. and J. A. McCLENDON. 1991. "The Individual Decision to Unionize," in *The State of the Unions*, edited by G. Strauss, D. G. Gallagher, and J. Fiorito. Industrial Relations Research Association series, pp. 47–84.

WILLIAMS, K. and D. G. TARAS. 2000. "Reinstatement at Arbitration: The Grievors' Perspective." *Relations industrielles/Industrial Relations*, in press.

WILLIAMS, L. 1997. "Facing Tomorrow: A Union Perspective." *Perspectives on Work*, 1, no. 1, Industrial Relations Research Association.

CHAPTER 3

Labour History and the Development of Modern Capitalism

Richard Marsden

In the past, one of the means by which an employee has been able to keep his head above water and prevent being oppressed by the employer has been that the employer didn't know exactly what the employee could do. The only way that the workman has been able to retain time enough in which to do the work with the speed with which he thinks he ought to do it, has been to keep the employer somewhat in ignorance of exactly the time needed.... We don't want to work as fast as we can. We want to work as we think it's comfortable for us to work. We haven't come into existence for the purpose of seeing how great a task we can perform throughout a lifetime. We are trying to regulate our work so as to make it an auxiliary to our lives, and to be benefited thereby.

Most people walk to work in the morning, if it isn't too far. If somebody were to discover that they could run to work in one-third the time, they might have no objection to have that fact ascertained, but if the man who ascertained it had the power to make them run, they might object to having him find out.[1]

The opening vignette is a worker's reaction to 20th century factory management. How society reached that point and what followed is the subject of this chapter.

Any narrative or history of past events is susceptible to the criticism that it is irrelevant to experience of the present; for, by definition, is the past not concerned with events that have "gone by in time," that are "done with," over? By this view, history is a collection of facts about long-since dead kings, queens, famous explorers, politicians, and military leaders. Opening a history book is like entering a musty museum; we find collections of dead facts and artifacts from the past.

Most form a view of the past not by reading histories or visiting museums, but by experiencing the marketing strategies of corporations and by watching television shows and movies. Witness the remarkable popularity of retro-products, testimony to the effectiveness of selling commodities today by marketing nostalgia. As never before, the past is commodified, sold, and consumed, without the necessity of being understood. The most remarkable feature of the most popular television show in America during the 1990s— "Seinfeld"—is that it followed the lives of four people without a past, who were concerned only with the spectacle of the moment. Perhaps history, like a "Seinfeld" episode, consists of only loosely related, fleeting incidents.

Arguably, disregard for history is particularly prevalent among industrial relations practitioners, who are usually a pragmatic, hard-nosed bunch, preoccupied with the immediate problems of the "here and now." An exception is a small minority of union activists, for whom memories of past struggles are as important as "the battle honours of a distinguished regiment ... important reminders to union members of the courage and solidarity that built past gains and that may well be necessary again" (Morton, 1982: 95). Since management's power does not depend on solidarity to the same extent, its exhortatory use of history is less frequent and, with few exceptions, history is not seen as a useful preparation for a career in business.

But let us probe this conventional view of history. It assumes that time is a linear sequence of events, like frames in a movie, moving in a straight line from past to future, like a movie stretches from beginning to end. This linear "arrow of time" approach also assumes that the present whizzes off into the past and disappears. But the past is still with us. We live among the monuments, social and material, of past generations. They constrain and enable how we act. It is for this reason that the object of history, like that of personal memory or recollection, is not the past, but the relationship between the past and the present. Industrial relations have a past, as well as a future. If we understand how they came to be as they are, we are in a better position to act on them.

MERCHANT CAPITAL DISCOVERS AMERICA

In the lagoon of the West Edmonton Mall sits an exact replica of the Santa Maria, one of the ships in which Christopher Columbus discovered America in 1492. It can be rented for functions and it displays the marketing ware of its latest sponsor. An understanding of production relations in Canada is found in its origins, and in the chance discovery of America by merchant-adventurers from northern Italy exploring business opportunities on behalf of Spain and England.

The notable character of northern Italy at the time of Columbus is that it was the centre of the earliest form of capital, "merchant (or trading) capital." Merchant capital can be defined as a form of profit made by traders or merchants by buying cheaply in one place in order to sell at a higher price in another. The strategic location of northern Italy in the Mediterranean allowed its merchants to grow rich on the lucrative trade with India and the Orient, typically, cloth for spices (indeed, Columbus was the eldest son of a poor wool-weaver). Genoa, Florence, and Venice were centres of merchant capital much as today Tokyo, London, and New York are centres of finance capital.

Before merchants could trade cloth they first had to get their hands on it. This led to the creation of the first "modern" employment relation. Cloth was produced by a handicraft system, often by families working in their homes using their own looms and raw materials. The man did the weaving, the woman and children the spinning, cleaning, and other chores, and they sold the cloth they produced at the local market. Producers were organized into trade guilds, associations of master craftsmen, journeymen, and apprentices exercising the same craft, for the purpose of protecting and promoting their common interests. There was no employee/employer division as such. Notable about this guild or handicraft system is the control workers exerted over the creation and sale of the product; they had no intermediary between themselves and the market.

This community of interests was shattered first in Florence during the turn of the 14th century, when guilds based on the various skills involved in producing woollen cloth were disbanded and displaced by a Wool Guild dominated by an elite of merchants. Merchants used the new Guild as an employers' association, proscribing workers from holding assemblies, keeping their wages low, and preventing them from buying and selling raw materials and finished goods. Wool workers were forbidden to trade and prevented from alleviating their powerlessness by organizing.

Merchants now controlled raw materials and finished products and coordinated each step in the production of woollen cloth, as materials passed from one place of work to another from spinner to weaver to dyer. Under this "putting-out" system, merchants often employed thousands of men, women, and children working out of their homes or in workshops using their own tools and machines, paid not for their time, but by the piece. The merchant thus became a producer, a merchant-capitalist, coordinating and controlling the work of previously independent artisans, buying the wool and selling the cloth on the open market. Here the original meaning of 'merchant' developed: "any trader in goods not manufactured or produced by himself."

For decades workers resisted merchants' seizure of power in Florence by riots and strikes and demanded the right to organize themselves into self-governing bodies with a voice in Guild and communal affairs. Half a century of insurrection was crushed by an oligarchy of merchants in the 1380s, resulting in the death or exile of much of its leadership and rank and file. By the mid-18th century the putting-out system was prevalent throughout Europe.

The driving motive of merchant capital—profit through exchange—stimulated the extension of merchants' trading network via speculative adventures. Merchant-adventure was given an added incentive when the commercial supremacy of northern Italy was threatened by the fall of Constantinople (now Istanbul) to the Ottomans (Turks) in 1453, for they imposed high taxes and duties on goods in transit, which added to the already high transport costs of using the overland route to the spice and gem markets of the East. Merchants had a vested interest in cutting out the Ottoman middleman and so interest grew in exploring alternative routes to the East.

In the race for the eastern spice markets, commercial interests vied for access to the latest in information technology to give them a competitive advantage. Today's information technology is computer technology, but then it was navigational technology. Navigators calculated their latitude using the astrolabe, steered by compass; later, the chronometer allowed time to be measured accurately and longitude to be calculated. But the most important technology was the map, for maps revealed information on newly discovered territory and potential trade routes—vital to those looking to invest in new business openings (Jardine, 1996). Cartographers were the computer programmers of the 15th century; Florence was its Silicon Valley. What Columbus had going for him, apart from mercantile seafaring know-how, was that his brother was a cartographer and he had sight of a map, by the Florentine Toscanelli, which strongly suggested that there was a western route to India. Commerce and information technology intertwined from the very beginning.

Columbus, then, was exploring, not so much unexplored territory, as business opportunities. He aimed to forge a new trade route to the spices and gems of India. To his dying day, he thought he had landed on its east coast. This is why native Americans came to be known as "Indians." In this sense, it was the imperative of merchant capital, manifest in the lives of merchant-adventurers, that discovered America.

MERCHANT CAPITALISM IN CANADA

In Italy, merchant capital developed on the backs of sheep. In Canada, it developed on the hides of beaver. It was the growing market for the beaver felt hat in Europe, during the last quarter of the 16th century, that stimulated trade for beaver pelts in Canada, the origin of merchant capital within Canada (Ray and Freeman, 1978). Indian-European trade was facilitated by the Hudson's Bay Co., a new form of business organization: the joint-stock trading company, a privately financed but royally created monopoly, which evolved from the trading partnerships of medieval Italy and is the forerunner of the modern multinational corporation. The HBC's charter was granted by Charles II in 1670, to the "Governor and Co. of Adventurers of England trading into Hudson's Bay." It controlled trade to, from, and within the area defined by its charter, which extended from Labrador to the Rocky Mountains. As a complex exchange system connecting a native trapping network with the fur markets of London, Paris, Leipzig, and Moscow, the HBC was as global as any modern transnational corporation. The nodes in this network were "factors," mercantile agents, and in their "factories," or trading stations, beaver pelts were bartered for European goods.

Fur-trading companies were the only major employers in Canada up until the middle of the 19th century. Settlement was confined to Ontario, Quebec, and the Maritimes and consisted of sparsely populated British colonies with economies based on agriculture, fishing, and the fur trade. The family farm was the main unit of production, and the rural village was the centre of economic activity.

Until the 1850s, those who worked for wages were the exception to the rule, but included men drawn from French-Canadian farm families and Irish immigrants who worked at logging and canal construction, domestic servants, farm labourers, seamen, and skilled craftsmen such as shipwrights and iron workers. Needs that could not be met by the household were satisfied in small, local workshops owned and managed by master craftsmen: saw and grist millers, carpenters, shoemakers, tailors, iron forgers, cabinet makers, distillers, brewers, tanners, and so on. These were generally small scale. The possibility of upward mobility, from apprentice to journeyman to master, fostered a community of interests reinforced by the close, direct, personal, and paternal relations typical of small-scale production. The main societal division was not between master and men, but between a mercantile elite and the farming and fishing families who were indebted to the marketers of their wheat and fish (Heron and Storey, 1986).

Merchants invested the money they made through trade in staples (such as fish, fur and, later, lumber and wheat) in manufacturing commodities for a growing urban market. Artisan workshops, characterized by handicraft techniques, were gradually mechanized to become the factories of the later industrial age. Mechanization increased the scale of production and also the cost of operating a business, and this limited self-employment to the small minority with capital (Palmer, 1992). At the same time, farmers were being forced off the land by mounting debt. These displaced labourers combined with the flood of southern Irish immigrants during the 1840s to form a pool of unskilled labour. They worked in the early factories and on railway, road, and canal construction, thereby establishing the transportation arteries that were to link isolated villages and forge a national market. By the 1850s, there was a workforce of primarily full-time wage earners (Palmer, 1992). The need for a physical infrastructure generated an urban workforce: The demand for houses, factories, and warehouses created the construction worker; the demand for tools and stoves, the foundry worker; and boots and clothes created the shoemaker and tailor. Commerce and urbanization developed hand in hand.

These three causes—the development of workshops into factories, the displacement of labour from the land, and commercial growth of towns—lay behind the metamorphosis of merchant into industrial capital, the making of money by manufacturing commodities. This became possible only with the creation of an interrelationship between employers and employees: by trading the employer's money for workers' capacity to act (their time) and by ensuring that the exercise of that capacity created more value than that paid in wages. Modern industrial relations revolves around bargains over the price of both that capacity to act and its exercise ("time" and "work"—see Exhibit 3.1).

EXHIBIT 3.1

MERCHANTS OF TIME

American labour reformer George McNeill, speaking in the 1890s, summed up the time-work bargain from the workers' perspective:

"Men who are compelled to sell their labour, very naturally desire to sell the smallest portion of their time for the largest possible price. They are merchants of their time. It is their only available capital."

Source: Cited in Palmer, 1992, p. 106.

Industrialization

This movement from merchant to industrial capital entailed the displacement of one type of factory, a merchant company's trading station, by another type of factory, a building or range of buildings with plants for the manufacture of goods. The first factory workers were extremely dependent and subject to close supervision. In England, where manufacturing began, most of the first factory workers were women and children. Within Canada, "three-quarters of the workforce in Toronto's rising clothing industry were female" (Palmer, 1992: 83). In Halifax during the 1870s, "the percentage of children increased from roughly 9 to 22 percent of the labour force in baking." "One in four boys aged 11–15 in Montreal worked for wages, where 42 percent of the industrial workforce in 1871 was composed of women and children" (Palmer, 1992: 99–100). Signalling an end to a way of life in which a measure of self-determination at work was highly valued, the introduction of factories often provoked riots and destruction (Clawson, 1980: 53). All things considered, people preferred the cottage or the homestead to the factory (Thompson, 1968). The first, and indeed subsequent, generations of factory workers did not enjoy the discretion of when and how hard to work. For them the choice was between working on the employer's terms, or not working at all—which isn't much of a choice.

Subcontracting Management

In the first factories, employer-managers provided the premises, raw materials, and operating plant, and subcontracted jobs at a fixed price to skilled craftsmen acting as contractors, or piece-masters, who then employed and paid others to work on the job. Subcontracting was particularly entrenched in shipbuilding, mining, ironworks, and textiles. Managers concentrated on finance, marketing, and purchasing. It was contractors who managed labour, using a mixture of exhortations, threats, rewards, and outright coercion to get work out of workers. There was nothing subtle or hidden about 19th-century management. It was direct and personal rule (Littler, 1982).

Having subcontractors allocate tasks and organize work circumvented the problem of the employer possessing less technical knowledge and skill than his subordinates. It also avoided the need to maintain a large permanent staff in the face of fluctuations in demand. But it had the disadvantage, for employers, of protecting traditional craft skills, and the subcontractors' control over hiring and firing heightened their strategic importance (Nelson, 1975). Subcontracting was eroded by pressure from above and from below during the last quarter of the 19th century. Employers were under competitive pressure to minimize unit labour costs. Since contractors were paid by the piece or for the job, they guarded their profits either by substituting cheaper, semi-skilled labour in place of skilled labour, or by driving their workers harder ("speed-up"). Relations between contractors and workers deteriorated amid charges of "sweated" labour (Exhibit 3.2).

Employers, too, grew skeptical of the value of the intermediate layer of subcontractors, chary of the control they exerted and jealous of the profits they managed to cream in this period of financial stringency. A particular problem was their control over hiring, a practice that proved unable to cope with the increased demand for skilled labour during the 1880s and 1890s. To circumvent this problem, companies centralized hiring by establishing employment departments. This move seriously weakened the power of contractors, for with it they lost the ability to set entry-level wages.

Simply put, employers wanted more control, while increasingly organized workers wanted relief from sweated labour. The limits of the subcontracting system for extracting work had been reached, and it was replaced with a system of salaried foremen.

Salaried Foremen vs. Craft Power

Like contractors, foremen were responsible for how the job was to be done, the tools and often the materials to be used, the timing of operations, the flow of work, the workers' methods and sequence of moves. While foremen (and those remaining contractors) were

EXHIBIT 3.2

"SWEATED LABOUR"

"Workmen protest strongly against the introduction of this intermediary, whom the masters have imposed on them, and whose profits are necessarily obtained from the price of their handiwork. These sub-contractors, from the workman's point of view, are unnecessary, and in any case are only necessary where the master does not understand the details of the working of his business. The masters who have given evidence on this subject have all declared that the only advantage pertaining to this system is that it relieves them from the supervision of their workshops, and that the sub-contractors derive their profits from the extra work which they obtain from the men."

Source: Report of the Royal Commission on the Relations of Labour and Capital of 1889 (cited in Kealey, 1973, p. 29).

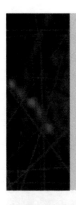

EXHIBIT 3.3

MAINTAINING CONTROL

William Powell, spokesman for the Toronto local of the International Typographical Union, had the following to say about control in the workplace in 1890:

"The work of the composing room is our business. To no one else can we depute it. It is absolutely ours. The talk of running another man's business will not hold. It is ours; we learned it and must control it."

Source: Cited in Kealey, 1973, p. 29.

EXHIBIT 3.4

UNION CONTROL

The *Brockville Daily Times* had the following to say about an 1884 strike at the James Smart Manufacturing Company's foundry:

"The question at issue is simply one of 'control'. It is a fact, however humiliating...that during the past three years of the company's existence, the business has been practically controlled by the Moulder's Union."

Source: Cited in Palmer, 1982, p. 129.

nominally in charge of production decisions, real control was more often than not in the hands of highly skilled craft workers. This was especially true in metal and metal-using industries, the core of the new "industrial revolution." The skill base of their power was supplemented by craft unionism (examined below) which tried to use collective strength to maintain jurisdiction (see Exhibit 3.3).

Skilled workers in the 19th century exercised a great deal of power. Most unions of skilled workers did not deign to negotiate over wages, but unilaterally determined, and told management, the price of their labour. They felt they were the equal of the boss. The "right to manage," asserted as if it were an historical legacy, would have been incomprehensible to 19th-century craftsmen. Their control over the workplace was a natural counterpart of their skill and knowledge of the production process. When technological change threatened to undermine the skill basis of their power, they substituted the collective strength of the union, and the work practices of the artisan age became embodied in the union rule book—a defence against managerial control. Many strikes and lockouts of the 1880s and 1890s centred on the issue of control (see Exhibit 3.4).

Early Craft Unions

Unions emerged spontaneously from informal social groups defending their customary practices and standard of living, both of which were under attack by Canada's developing industrial infrastructure. The first evidence of union organization in Canada is found in New Brunswick and Nova Scotia. "Starting with Halifax building tradesmen and ship-wrights in 1798, and led by printers and carpenters, workingmen formed at least 45 unions in the years before 1850, establishing major centres of skilled labour in Saint John, Quebec, Montreal, and Toronto" (Forsey, 1982: 123). By the 1830s and 1840s skilled workers, particularly in the building, printing, clothing, and shoe trades, were forming trade unions and striking. Saint John, New Brunswick was the trade union capital of British North America from the late 1830s to the late 1850s, with "more, bigger, stronger, and more respected unions than any other place in the North American colonies" (Williams, 1975: 9).

Early unions were confined almost exclusively to male, skilled workers. The obvious need for unions amongst the unskilled, the poorest and weakest workers, had to be set against their vulnerability to employer sanctions and the law. Employers united in fighting unions. Activists often had to work in secret for fear of blacklisting. The power base of the craft union was the skill of its members (see Exhibit 3.5). The unions' control over entry through apprenticeship put them in a position to unilaterally enforce work rules and rates. "When they could, unions in early nineteenth-century Canada set their rates and notified their employers, often in politely worded newspaper advertisements" (Morton, 1982: 96). Enforcement was simple: They would shun employers who flouted the rules. In their defence of the status quo, craft unions gradually developed an industrial relations function based on their unilateral control of the rules of the trade and rates of pay.

A second source of power was the solidarity derived from a collective sense of craft pride. Craft unionists associated with other "respectables," not with their fellow unskilled workers. Thus, from the outset, unions were exclusive and possessed a chauvinism that encouraged attachment to restricted and local priorities. The motivation to take collective action was a defence of privilege. Thus it was that hatters, printers, shoemakers, carpenters "took steps to preserve their respectability by fighting against specialization, unlimited apprentices and hours, and wages that they judged to be inadequate compensation for their skills as well as insufficient for their needs" (Palmer, 1983: 34).

Exhibit 3.5

The Journeyman Printers of York

An extract from the forming statement of the York printers, circa 1830:

"Owing to the many innovations which have been made upon the long established wage of the professors of the art of printing, and those of a kind highly detrimental to their interests, it was deemed expedient by the Journeymen Printers of York that they should form themselves into a body, similar to societies in other parts of the world, in order to maintain that honourable station and respectability that belongs to the profession."

Source: A statement of the York printers, circa 1830, as cited in Williams, 1975, 9.

Finally, unions were small and usually restricted to one locale. Up to 1859, "except for four Amalgamated Society of Engineers [ASE] branches, all seem to have been purely local, and very few seem to have any relations with other unions" (Forsey, 1982: 31). Distance and lack of mobility made communication between them difficult, fostering insularity and hindering solidarity.

The International Unions

The spread of the railway network from 1850 linked discrete labour markets into a national and international labour market, so to control labour supply—a source of their power—unions had to follow suit. Although local unions continued to be formed until the end of the century, they were gradually supplanted by "international" unions, which made their first appearance in the 1850s and spread during the 1860–80 period.

The first international unions were not American, but British; skilled British immigrants brought with them their union consciousness and organizing skill. The British Amalgamated Society of Engineers established branches at Hamilton, Toronto, and Brantford during the 1850s, and others followed. Another British union, the Amalgamated Society of Carpenters and Joiners, established itself in Canada in 1871 with branches in Hamilton, Toronto, Kingston, and St. Catharines. American unions recruited in Canada later. The first to do so was the Iron Molders, in 1861, with members in Montreal, Hamilton, Toronto, London, and Brantford (Williams, 1975: 10). For American unionists, the close physical proximity between the two countries and their similar cultural, linguistic, and social roots created the potential for a single continental jurisdiction for each craft organization. By the 1860s and 1870s, central Canadian workers were part of a continental labour market, marked by large-scale movement back and forth across the Canadian-American border (Palmer, 1983).

The development of international unions illustrates the contradictory forces of unity and sectionalism at the heart of trade unionism. The extension of unionism from its local origins to an international basis was an expression of solidarity with workers in other regions; but it was also a consolidation of sectionalism, for these predominantly craft organizations did not ease the vertical boundaries of union organization. The unskilled were rivals for jobs and a threat to the craft unions' monopoly over labour supply.

The Legalization of Trade Unions

Until the last quarter of the 19th century, workers' ability to combine and take collective action was severely constrained by law. Under the *Master and Servant Act*, for example, it was a criminal offence, punishable by imprisonment, for a worker to quit a job; yet a similar breach of contract by the employer—for example, a failure to pay wages—was only a civil offence. The British *Combinations Acts* (imported into colonial Canada) proscribed collective organizations, and judges declared union activists liable for prosecution for criminal conspiracy in restraint of trade. While the law was used selectively rather than uniformly, its potent threat was one reason trade unionism was restricted largely to skilled workers, whose sense of common identity and craft pride sustained them through legal sanction.

Revision of the legal status of unions was stimulated by the Toronto printers' strike. The Typographical Union struck the Toronto *Globe* newspaper, March 25, 1872, in support of its demand for "A week's work to consist of 54 hours, $10 per week; 25 cents per hour overtime for job printers." The master printers used the common law to argue that unions were conspiracies in restraint of trade and obtained the arrest of the union's Vigilance (strike) Committee. At the subsequent pretrial hearing, the magistrate announced that since unions were illegal combinations, their actions must be unlawful. Before the strikers could stand trial, Prime Minister Macdonald, spurred by political expediency and public pressure, introduced into Parliament two bills: the Trade Unions Bill and the Criminal Law Amendment Bill. The *Trade Unions Act* legalized trade unions by freeing them from the common law liability of restraint of trade, limiting protection to unions registering with the Registrar General of Canada. The *Criminal Law Amendment Act* gave a right to strike, but restricted the exercise of that right to peaceful actions that did not coerce the employer or prevent him from carrying on his business. Coercive acts were illegal, and a combination to carry out a legal act by illegal means was a criminal conspiracy. Trade unionists found these acts restrictive and, through intense political lobbying, succeeded in winning amendments in 1875 and 1876 which "narrowed the definition of criminal conspiracy for the purposes of trade combinations to the performance of acts expressly punishable by law" (Arthurs, Carter, and Glasbeek, 1981). The *Breaches of Contract Act* of 1877 provided that a breach of contract of service should no longer be a crime. These three acts—the *Trade Unions Act*, 1872, the *Criminal Law Amendment Act*, 1872 (as amended in 1875 and 1876), and the *Breaches of Contract Act*, 1877—provided the legal basis of freedom of association in Canada.

The Knights of Labour

Up to 1859, "the only organizations of the unskilled were the two longshoremen's unions" (Forsey, 1982: 31). The unskilled lacked the common identity and organization to withstand employer and legal sanctions and form trade unions. Instead, they—most notably the rafters and canallers—expressed their discontent in less organized forms: desertions, turn-outs, riots (Palmer, 1983: 39). Unskilled workers had to await the militancy and organizing boom of the 1880s to alleviate their disadvantage in bargaining. Its driving force was a very different form of international unionism from the craft unions: the Noble and Holy Order of the Knights of Labour. Originating in Philadelphia, the Knights of Labour aimed to be a worldwide labour body, organizing workers regardless of skill, gender, religion, or nationality: a form of industrial unionism. At its peak, the Order had 700,000 members—12,000 in Canadian "assemblies"—scattered as far afield as Great Britain, Ireland, Belgium, Australia, and Hawaii. The first Canadian assembly was formed in Hamilton in 1867. Although Ontario was the Knights' stronghold, they spread through the industrial and railway towns of the prairie provinces and British Columbia. By unifying workers across regions, industries, occupations, and crafts, the Knights formed the first mass working-class movement in Canadian history (Palmer, 1983: 103–4).

In the United States, the Knights were effectively halted by public reaction to the Haymarket bombing incident in Chicago in 1886. Implicated in the killing of seven policemen, four of their activists were hanged. But in Canada the Knights continued to operate normally, their eventual downfall caused by conflict with the international—American-dominated—craft unions. The cause was a basic philosophical difference, reflected in organizational strategies. The Knights advocated united concerns for all workers, whereas the international craft unions were oriented toward more exclusive interests.

Knights vs. Crafts

The various industry trades and community labour councils, which developed from the 1860s, provided a forum for interaction between Knights and craft unionists. They were also the "local foundations for the creation of the Trades and Labour Congress of Canada (TLC), which first met in Toronto in 1883" (Palmer, 1983: 129). The TLC, Canada's first enduring national labour federation and the forerunner of the Canadian Labour Congress, became a forum for rivalry and conflict between the Knights and the craft unions. As supporters of industrial unionism, the Knights argued that craft unionism weakened class solidarity by contributing to jurisdictional disputes. For this reason, they called for the TLC to devalue its concern with lobbying government in favour of organizing the unorganized. The mounting demands for an extension of industrial unionism, which entailed an organizational campaign that would go beyond craft boundaries, courted opposition from the craft unions (who had a vested interest in maintaining their exclusivity) and their central labour organization in United States, the American Federation of Labor, formed in 1886. The increasingly frequent conflicts between the Knights and the craft unions came to a head in 1902 at the Berlin (now Kitchener) Convention of the TLC, at which narrow craft triumphed over open reformist unionism, and the Knights were expelled. Women and the unskilled—the chief beneficiaries of open unions—"slipped back into a state of unorganized dependence on capital's mercy and the politician's benevolence" (Palmer, 1983: 133).

Taylorism

North America's depression of 1873–79 destroyed excess industrial capacity and provided a starting point for a round of new investment. It also marked the start of a 40-year struggle between employers who wanted to increase their profits by reorganizing work processes and craft workers who wanted to defend their power base.

Just one year before the end of the depression, Frederick Winslow Taylor began work at the Midvale Steel Company, where he worked until 1890. He was to develop a special interest in time and motion. Taylor discovered that the workers under his command were able to use their superior knowledge and skill to restrict output and to control their earnings. Taylor's strategy was to undermine the power of the workgroup, and thereby improve efficiency and profitability, by reducing a reliance on skill and transferring workers' knowledge to managers.

Taylor's objective was to be achieved by the following management practices (often described as the principles of Taylorism). The division of labour is increased by breaking jobs into their component parts—often referred to as the fragmentation of work. Work is simplified, standardized, and deskilled, making labour more substitutable. Less skilled and therefore cheaper workers are substituted for craftsmen, effectively reducing their power. The narrowly defined tasks are evaluated by time study (symbolized by the stopwatch), which analyzes how a specific task can be completed in the shortest time with the fewest motions, providing a quantitative basis for monitoring and comparing worker performance, hence "scientific management."

Having been fragmented, the production process is reintegrated under the coordination and control of management. Managers, not workers, foremen, or subcontractors, now have knowledge of the production process and the ability to plan and direct work. This change marked the separation between the conception and execution of work, or between planning and doing, mental and manual labour. Instead of skilled workers telling management what was possible, management, through time-and-motion study, now determined the best sequence and time of operations and monitored worker performance. Knowledge previously the domain of workers became incorporated into management's own rules and practices.

This reorganization of work along Taylorist lines meshed with a concentration of corporate power. From the turn of the century, a wave of company mergers and takeovers began in the United States and swept over Canada, encouraged by the high tariffs established by the 1880's National Policy. Those American firms establishing branch plants in Canada introduced this new method of managing labour, and Canadian firms often employed managers with American experience or hired American management consultants. By the First World War, scientific management had a firm foothold in Canada. The development of the multinational corporation spread scientific management far afield. Ford and General Motors, for example, established subsidiaries abroad, thus allowing the transfer of techniques and machinery, and also of management techniques. By the mid-1930s, Taylorism had spread across Europe.

 Frederick Winslow Taylor (Stevens Institute of Technology Collection):
www.liv.stevens-tech.edu/collections/taylor/guide/main.html

The Wobblies

Scientific management and technological change diluted skills and increased the need for cheaper, unskilled labour, thereby undermining the craft-dominated mode of production. This demand was met by a massive influx of immigrants early in the 20th century, drawn from the factories and fields of Europe. As foremen grappled with craft workers and their exclusive unions, these new, unskilled immigrant workers were being recruited by a successor to the Knights, the International Workers of the World—popularly known as the Wobblies, supposedly following a Calgary restauranteur's mispronunciation, for whom IWW was "Eye Wobbly Wobbly."

Formed at a Chicago meeting in 1905, the IWW saw its purpose as the emancipation of the working class from capitalism, an objective to be achieved by action at the work-place, the locus of the employer's power. This belief affected the orientation of the Wobblies in two ways: First, economic action, particularly the general strike, had pri-macy over political action; second, the solidarity of the proletariat required that all work-ers in an industry be organized. As a form of industrial unionism, the IWW recruited from those ideologically opposed to the exclusivity of craft unionism: the itinerant, un-skilled workers—loggers, harvesters, longshoremen, and construction workers. For this reason, it was the logging and railway construction camps of the West that provided con-ditions in which the radical industrial unionism of the IWW, and also that of the United Brotherhood of Railway Employees, the American Labor Union, and the Western Federation of Miners, could flourish. The Wobblies went out of their way to overcome the difficulties of organizing this itinerant, ethnically heterogeneous labour force; for ex-ample, they circulated propaganda in at least ten different languages. The IWW's demise was caused mainly by the loss of its membership base with the end of the railway build-ing boom, which dispersed the construction labour force, its main constituency. By the start of the First World War, its membership was falling and its locals disintegrating.

One Big Union and the Winnipeg General Strike

Workers in the West were radicalized by the Russian Revolution and, through their fed-erations of labour, advocated workers' control of industry and general strikes to achieve political change. 1919 was a record year for strikes. The counterpart of the radicalism of western workers against employers was their antagonism to the conservative, eastern-dominated craft unionism. Out of this grew a split in the Trades and Labour Congress, in March 1919, and the birth of "one big union."

The One Big Union (OBU) succeeded the Knights and the Wobblies as an advocate of industrial unionism. Its ultimate goal was workers' control over essential industries; its intended means, the general strike. This philosophy found a receptive audience among the loggers and miners of British Columbia, where the OBU was endorsed by many local trade councils, and especially logging and mining unions. The most prominent incident associated with the One Big Union was the Winnipeg General Strike of 1919, seen by some as about collective bargaining and recognition rights, by others as a challenge to the capitalist system.

The strike is of interest here for what it reveals of the relationship between craft and industrial unionism. Although the immediate issues were modest—union recognition, an eight-hour day—employers cloaked them in revolutionary implications. The immediate stimulus to the general strike was a walkout of building and metal trades workers in support of their demands for wage increases and for employers to recognize the Metal Trades Council. Following a vote among its affiliates, the Winnipeg Trades Council ordered a general strike, and approximately 30,000 workers struck on May 15, 1919, effectively paralyzing the city of Winnipeg. The authorities took it to be a conspiracy to overthrow the government, rather than a simple attempt to obtain basic recognition and bargaining rights, and suppressed the strike. Strike leaders were arrested and charged with "conspiracy to bring into hatred and contempt the governments of the Dominion of Canada and the Province of Manitoba and to introduce a Soviet system of government." Following a year of trials, one of the leaders, R. B. Russell, was convicted and sent to the penitentiary for two years; five others received one-year sentences, one a six-month sentence, and one was freed (Bercuson, 1990).

What was the stance of the craft unions towards this all-too-brief and rare display of labour unity? The Trades and Labour Congress saw the OBU as a competitor for membership and, as a condition of support for the strike, required from the strikers a declaration of allegiance to the TLC, repudiation of the OBU, and assurances of adherence to the constitutions of international unions—terms unacceptable to the Winnipeg strikers (Williams, 1975: 133). Most officers of the international unions were opposed to the strike and shed no tears at its defeat. Attempts to establish industrial unionism were stopped dead in their tracks, union membership fell, and militancy declined. As for the OBU, it experienced a further setback in the Crow's Nest Pass coal strike in 1919, then declined.

"Fordism" and Mass Production

As efficiency-conscious employers restructured work along Taylorist lines, subdividing tasks, accelerating the pace of work, and intensifying operations, workers fought back, defending against the erosion of their skills and hence their power at the workplace. This encouraged the design of machines and plant that would circumvent this resistance to management control: continuous-flow production. Since Henry Ford perfected the flow-line principle of assembly work, it is commonly referred to as Fordism.

The Ford Motor Company was founded in 1903 in Detroit. In its early years, Ford was dependent on skilled labour "because the imperfect and unstandardized parts had to be drilled, milled, ground, planed, and bored before they would fit together satisfactorily" (Gartman, 1979: 195). The assembly procedure was stationary; the team worked together to construct the entire car, which was placed on a wooden horse on the shop floor. Much time was consumed transporting the various components and tools. As production grew, this process multiplied "until the whole shop floor was filled with long lines of stationary positions, a few workers at each" (Ibid.). Ford's innovation, introduced in stages, was to turn this process on its head. Instead of workers moving from job to job, parts were brought to them by conveyors and transporters, obviating the need to move around the workshop, in effect rooting workers to the spot. It was the assembly line, not the worker, that now determined the sequence of operations and the pace of work.

In effect, Ford pushed Taylor's job fragmentation to its logical conclusion and combined it with technical devices for moving material past successive workstations in a continuous flow. These mass-production techniques integrated the production process in a way that allowed a small group of strategically placed workers to shut down an entire plant. This strategic advantage combined with an increasingly homogenized workforce to create the conditions for establishing industrial unionism within these car plants.

Industrial Unionism Becomes Permanent

As we have seen, industrial unionism has a long history. Most prominent are the Knights of Labour of the 1880s, the IWW, and the OBU, but both the Western Federation of Miners and the United Mine Workers of America, in being both vertically and horizontally open, were effectively industrial unions. Since the conflict between the exclusivity of craft unionism and the breadth of industrial unionism is a recurrent theme of Canadian union history, it is worth reiterating the philosophical differences over the purpose of trade unionism that lay behind jurisdictional disputes. Central were the different sources of power of the two types of unions. The power of craft unions lay in eliminating competition between their members and controlling the supply of labour, primarily by regulating the rules governing apprenticeship, the means of acquiring craft skills. To maintain this power base, it was essential to resist mechanization, which eroded the skill component of their work, and to defend their jurisdiction against the encroachments of other workers, skilled and unskilled. The power of industrial unions, in contrast, lay in strength of numbers. Hence the necessity to recruit widely, and their regular clashes with craft unions. The conflict between these open and closed tendencies continued throughout the 1920s and 1930s, and was resolved only by an institutional split in the labour movement in both the US and Canada.

In the US, workers in the mass-production industries were organized by the Congress of Industrial Organizations. The CIO began as a committee of industrial union representatives within the craft-dominated AFL; it became a separate federation in 1937 when jurisdictional disputes with craft unions led to the expulsion of its unions from the AFL. In Canada, the new industrial unions were at first coordinated by a committee of the CIO. Under pressure from the AFL, the TLC expelled these CIO affiliates in 1939. Together with several industrial unions already outside the TLC, the CIO unions in Canada formed the Canadian Congress of Labour (CCL) in 1940. In this fashion, the union movement in the US and Canada was split in two: craft (AFL/TLC) and industrial (CIO/CCL). In 1955, the AFL and CIO merged to form the AFL-CIO, and a year later the TLC and CCL merged to form the Canadian Labour Congress (CLC). This variation and evolution is set out in Table 3.1.

TABLE 3.1

UNIONS: APPROACHES AND EXAMPLES

UNION APPROACHES	EXAMPLES
Craft Unions: along trade lines, exclusive jurisdictions, exclusionary	AFL in US, TLC in Canada (1880s to today)
Co-operatives: improve system, make capitalism work, promote education and literacy, organized on geographic lines	Knights of Labour (1869 to about 1900)
Communists and Syndicalists: class lines, abolition of wage system, use of general strike	IWW (Wobblies) and One Big Union (OBU). Heyday during Winnipeg General Strike
Industrial Unions: sectoral strikes, skilled and unskilled workers, community of interests along industry lines	CIO in US; CCL in Canada (1937 to today)

1955: (US): AFL + CIO = AFL-CIO

1956: (Canada): TLC + CCL = CLC (Canadian Labour Congress)

The increasingly costly conflicts between industrial unions and employers over recognition encouraged development of procedures for institutionalizing this conflict. In the US, the Wagner Act of 1935 recognized the rights of workers in the private sector to belong to a union of their choice, prohibited certain "unfair labour practices" often used by employers to thwart unionization, and required employers to bargain in "good faith" (see Chapter 7). Since industrial unionism in the United States was stimulated by the Wagner Act, Canadian union leaders lobbied for similar legislation. Eventually, the Wagner principles were introduced in Canada through the temporary wartime Privy Council Order 1003, the National War Labour Order, in 1944.

This temporary order became a federal statute in 1948, which was modified and adopted by all ten provinces. Canada had its legal framework for trade unionism and collective bargaining, setting the stage for a sustained period of union growth that continued into the 1990s. The merger of the Trades and Labour Congress and the Canadian Congress of Labour heralded the end of the bitter feud of craft vs. industrial unionism. Both kinds of labour organization could flourish within a unified house of labour, which also would welcome public-sector employees in record numbers in the 1970s. The industrial relations system enjoyed a period of relative stability as employees, through their unions, were able to share in a rapidly expanding economic pie.

 World Trade Union Index: www.fnv.n/~Marcel/unionsen.html

Fordism-Keynesianism

For most of the post–Second World War period, Fordism dovetailed with the institutional framework of collective bargaining and Keynesian management of the economy: stimulating consumer demand through monetary and fiscal policies, investing in industry and social welfare programs, and expanding the public sector. The mass production of Fordism meshed with a mass-consumer society. The aim of the first to keep costs of production down complemented the aim of the last to keep levels of consumption up. In Canada, "Not a single serious recession was experienced during the first 35 years following the end of World War II. In per-person terms, real GDP grew by 2.8 percent per year, providing a real foundation for the greatest increase in living standards ever experienced in Canada" (Stanford, 1999: 189). The difficulty, however, with deficit financing and other measures to maintain consumption is that employers will only increase productive investment if there is a reasonable expectation that it will increase their profits. In the face of a global crisis of stagflation during the early 1970s, this precondition disappeared. It was a stark reminder: For compromises to be possible in industrial relations, there must be something to bargain over.

Restructuring Workplaces and Marketplaces

By the 1970s, Keynesian-Fordism had reached the limits of its possibilities. This was manifest in a long deterioration in the profitability of private business in Canada and other industrial economies, and the coexistence of stagnation and inflation (stagflation), once thought to be impossible by Keynesians. Management's response was to reorganize labour to raise productivity. In the era of industrial capital it was done via Taylorism and Fordism. Now it would be done by re-engineering business processes and McDonaldizing work (Ritzer, 1996). Re-engineering speeds-up production by using information technology to link the knowledge held by individuals remote in space and time, within and across organizations. McDonaldizing redesigns jobs according to criteria of efficiency, calculability, predictability. While we associate it with the fast-food industry, it is rooted in Fordist assembly-line techniques. It has spread from industry to industry, turning workplaces into factories (McUniversity, McHospital). Within service industries, these techniques have been extended from what workers do to how they look, speak, and feel—emotion itself has become a job duty, the "heart" managed (Hochschild, 1983). McDonaldizing has also spread to other countries, turning them into replicas of America. In the 1930s and 1940s these techniques homogenized workers; now they homogenize societies.

The techniques for speeding-up production complement techniques for speeding-up response to markets. Just-in-time inventory systems minimize carrying costs and enable firms to adjust more quickly to changing market conditions. Flexible labour processes and labour markets create the "just-in-time" workforce: a small core of permanent, full-time employees and a large periphery of part-time, casual, on-call, temporary, and sub-contracted workers. The same information technology that makes all this possible gathers information about employees and deposits it in human resource information systems, where worker performance is measured, described, evaluated, examined, and compared (Menzies, 1996: 109–30). The ultimate in flexibility is the virtual organization, unencumbered with physical infrastructure, perfectly responsive to the changing needs of the market. Like the commodities they produce, virtual organizations are disposable. These, and other techniques, replace homogeneous products for mass markets with adaptable products for niche markets, large-scale with small-batch production.

Alongside these developments, competition has increased due to nations moving towards the elimination of tariffs on trade. This was the point of the Free Trade Agreement (FTA) between Canada and the US and the North American Free Trade Agreement (NAFTA) among Canada, the US, and Mexico (which should bring North American tariffs to zero by 2005). Given the role of the World Trade Organization, it is unlikely that tariffs on trade between nations will last much beyond the first quarter of this century. Markets were extended by privatizing public corporations and other non-profit firms, such as Air Canada, Petro-Canada, Canadian National Railway, Manitoba Telephones, the Saskatchewan Wheat Pool, and the Surrey Metro Savings credit union. Finally, markets—especially those in finance, energy, transportation, and telecommunications—were deregulated.

FUTURE CHALLENGES AND LESSONS OF HISTORY

The question for the future is how organized labour will adapt. If free trade, privatization, and deregulation have combined to create more competitive markets, they have also created profound challenges for the labour movement. Unionized garment workers in Montreal now compete with workers in the Ivory Coast and Romania. The sons and daughters of Cape Breton coal miners find their future in the call centres of New Brunswick. Deregulated airlines, telephone companies, and utilities merge with their counterparts worldwide, undermining long-standing work arrangements and compensation practices. Software companies in Vancouver hire programmers in Bangalore, India, who deliver their work by Internet. Contract employees move from job to job, with little loyalty to a particular job and few, if any, ties to their co-workers. The foundation upon which the post–World War II industrial relations system was based—long-term employment expectations that provided incentive for employee voice and a degree of protection from the full forces of the marketplace—has proved ephemeral.

History teaches that unions have adapted to profound economic transformations in the past, moving from craft-based organizations suited to small-scale production to large, heterogeneous industrial unions attuned to mass production. As industry changed, so did worker responses. Today's economic system will require further adaptations; if unionism is to have any continued relevance, it will have to metamorphose yet again to appeal to workers in the 21st-century economy, not the 20th. Otherwise labour organization as we now know it may be reduced to an interesting footnote of a bygone era.

Questions

1. Describe the origins of merchant capital in Canada.

2. Describe the origins of the early unions in Canada.

3. Outline the events surrounding the Winnipeg General Strike.

4. Distinguish between craft and industrial unions.

5. What was the impact of Taylorism on union development?

6. Explain what is meant by the "McDonaldizing" of work.

7. What strategies might unions adopt to appeal to workers in the economy of the early 21st century?

ENDNOTES

[1] A comment on scientific management in 1914 by Alifas, legal representative of the organized federal employees in America, cited in Reg Whitaker, "Scientific Management Theory as Political Ideology," *Studies in Political Economy*, Autumn 1979, no. 2.

REFERENCES

ARTHURS, H. W., D. D. CARTER, and J. H. GLASBEEK. 1981. *Labour Law and Industrial Relations in Canada*. Toronto: Butterworths.

BERCUSON, D. 1990. *Confrontation at Winnipeg*. Montreal: McGill-Queen's University Press.

CLAWSON, D. 1980. *Bureaucracy and the Labor Process: The Transformation of U.S. Industry, 1800–1920*. New York and London: Monthly Review Press.

FORSEY, E. 1982. *Trade Unions in Canada 1812–1902*. Toronto: University of Toronto Press.

GARTMAN, D. 1979. "Origins of the Assembly Line and Capitalist Control of Work at Ford," in *Case Studies on the Labor Process,* edited by A. Zimbalist. New York and London: Monthly Review Press.

HERON, C. and R. STOREY, eds. 1986. *On the Job: Confronting the Labour Process in Canada*. Montreal: McGill-Queen's University Press.

HOCHSCHILD, A. 1983. *The Managed Heart*. Berkeley, CA: University of California Press.

JARDINE, L. 1996. *Worldly Goods: A New History of the Renaissance*. Macmillan.

KEALEY, G., ed. 1973. *Canada Investigates Industrialism: The Royal Commission on the Relations of Labor and Capital 1889*. Toronto: University of Toronto Press.

LITTLER, C. R. 1982. *The Development of the Labour Process in Capitalist Societies*. London: Heinemann Educational Books.

MARSDEN, R. 1999. *The Nature of Capital: Marx after Foucault*. London and New York: Routledge.

MENZIES, H. 1996. *Whose Brave New World?: The Information Highway and the New Economy*. Toronto: Between the Lines.

MORTON, D. 1982. "The History of Canadian Labour, in *Union–Management Relations in Canada*, 1st Edition, edited by J. Anderson and M. Gunderson. Don Mills, Ont.: Addison-Wesley.

NELSON, D. 1975. *Managers and Workers: Origins of the New Factory System in the United States 1880–1920*. Madison: University of Wisconsin Press.

PALMER, B. D. 1982. "The Culture of Control," in *Canada's Age of Industry, 1849–1896: Readings in Canadian Social History*, Volume 3, edited by M. S. Cross and G. S. Kealey. Toronto: McClelland and Stewart.

———. 1983. *Working Class Experience: The Rise and Reconstitution of Canadian Labour, 1960–1980*. Toronto: Butterworths.

———. 1992. *Working Class Experience*, 2nd Edition. Toronto: McClelland & Stewart.

RAY, A. J. and D. FREEMAN. 1978. *"Give Us Good Measure": An Economic Analysis of Relations between the Indians and the Hudson's Bay Company before 1763*. Toronto: University of Toronto Press.

RITZER, G. 1996. *The McDonaldization of Society*. Thousand Oaks, California: Pine Forge.

STANFORD, J. 1999. *Paper Boom: Why Real Prosperity Requires a New Approach to Canada's Economy*. The Canadian Centre for Policy Alternatives/James Lorimer.

THOMPSON, E. P. 1968. *The Making of the English Working Class*. Harmondsworth: Penguin.

WHITAKER, R. 1979. "Scientific Management Theory as Political Ideology." *Studies in Political Economy*, no. 2 (Autumn).

WILLIAMS, J. 1975. *The Story of Unions in Canada*. J. M. Dent and Sons.

CHAPTER 4

Unions: Membership, Structures, Actions, and Challenges

Gregor Murray

Consider three scenarios:

Union A is approached by a number of young nonunion workers from the local branch of a well-known hamburger chain. They are dissatisfied with working conditions, particularly the arbitrary allocation of shift schedules and the macho attitudes of several supervisors. Union A's leaders see this as an exciting organizing opportunity to break into an industry with a low level of unionization, high usage of temporary and part-time workers, minimum wages, and poor benefits. Yet they are wary of squandering organizing resources in this sector, especially in the light of complaints received from a number of their union locals about the diversion of attention and funds away from existing bargaining units towards recruiting new members. They anticipate a fight to the finish, as the employer has a reputation for vigorous opposition to union organizing and has taken steps at other branches to forestall unionization. Further, the costs to Union A of servicing the needs of this small potential bargaining unit might never be matched by the union dues collected from these workers. The union is caught between the desire to *organize the unorganized* and the poor prospects for meaningful organizing success in this important sector of employment without either significant changes in the public policy framework or in its own approach to organizing.

Union B, a major Canadian public service union, is rocked by profound structural change. More than a decade ago, it negotiated one central agreement for the bulk of its membership. Due to government cutbacks, restructuring, and privatization, Union B's membership declined. However, demands on the union are increasing. There are many more negotiations of multiple agreements in newly privatized agencies such as licensing companies, tax collectors, health insurance providers, and among a host of not-for-profit agencies. There are more calls from members requesting advice and representation. Government restructuring is obliging the union to reorganize its own members in new certification contests, and rivalry among unions is increasing. In a ten-year period, Union B moved from easily administered centralized structures to more resource-intensive decentralized operations. Although the union has weathered the storm, it has been unable to develop effective strategies for organizing new members. In fact, it is having difficulty meeting demands on its existing staff and finances are tight due to a shrinking public-sector membership base.

Union C's members are employed by multinational firms in manufacturing. Their jobs are threatened by possible company relocation, either to nonunion American sites or to low-wage plants in Mexico. This problem is hardly new but free trade made it more acute. Union C advocated a proactive policy to protect jobs and working conditions. In the 1980s, it championed RRSP-type worker investment funds to promote employment in its core industries. It pioneered worker retraining and participated in government-sponsored sector training councils. The union also was highly receptive to worker participation in new forms of work organization and had many successes in this regard. Yet there is a membership backlash, as high-involvement worksites are often *lean*

> and sometimes quite *mean*. Union C has many fewer members than it did a
> decade ago, and its members made wage concessions on several occasions in
> order to gain job security provisions and more involvement in workplace deci-
> sions. The leadership of Union C is retrenching. While still advocating mod-
> ernization policies, it is taking a harder line on wage increases and job
> security. Militancy is likely in the next bargaining rounds.

The three scenarios are snapshots of the many challenges faced by Canadian unions.
Servicing the needs of existing membership is an urgent matter, but the long-term survival of unions depends on their ability to recruit new members. There is considerable
stress on union structures that appear out of sync with the new economy. There are
strategic conundrums in the search for the right blend of short-term defensive goals to
protect working conditions and wages of current members and the advocacy role of promoting policies for better workplaces and communities. Unions have multiple mandates
but limited resources.

There are approximately 4 million union members in Canada, distributed among
more than 16,500 union locals. These union members represent over 30 percent of non-
agricultural paid workers (excluding self-employed and unemployed). They negotiate the
terms and conditions of employment of these workers and undoubtedly exert considerable spillover influence on the employment conditions of many other workers. Union
representatives are present in a wide variety of public and private bodies in Canada concerned with labour market and social questions, ranging from health and safety at work
to pay equity, training, and economic adjustment. Unions are among the more important social actors in the Canadian labour market.

This chapter describes union organizations and their actions, while highlighting both
the great diversity of Canadian unions and the challenges they are currently experiencing. The first part concerns the different dimensions of union membership: growth
trends, international comparisons, distribution of union members, and pressures on
union membership. The second part of the chapter looks at the structure of unions and
their internal governance. The final part reviews union actions, both economic and
political.

UNION MEMBERSHIP AND COLLECTIVE BARGAINING COVERAGE

Faced with significant structural adjustments over the last two decades, unions have represented a diminishing proportion of the labour force in many industrialized Western
economies. The recent history of Canadian unionism both confirms and confounds this
trend. In relative terms, union membership in Canada grew more quickly than the non-
agricultural labour force during the two decades from the mid-1960s to the mid-1980s.

This trend stabilized in the last half of the 1980s and reversed in the last half of the 1990s, resulting in a decline of union membership density, expressed as a percentage of non-agricultural paid workers (see Table 4.1). The Canadian pattern is particularly remarkable when compared with declining fortunes of the neighbouring US labour movement. Despite their relative decline as a proportion of paid workers, Canadian unions have performed well. This must not belie the significant pressures—many of which are featured in the opening vignettes—currently operating on union membership.

There are a variety of ways of measuring union membership and relative union presence. Information is available on two key measures: union *membership* and collective bargaining *coverage*. The former refers to the number of individuals who are members of a union; the latter to all persons whose terms and conditions of employment are determined by a union through collective bargaining and who may or may not be union members. Collective bargaining coverage tends to be several percentage points higher than the membership rate.

There also are several sources of such information that depend on different methods of data collection and reporting periods. This chapter draws on the three principal sources of information. First, Human Resources Development Canada, formerly known as Labour Canada, conducts an annual survey of union membership (HRDC and Workplace Information Directorate). Unions are asked to report their own level of membership, which is compiled to give an overview of union membership as a whole (see Table 4.1). This series provides a good historical overview as well as more detailed information on each of the reporting union organizations. However, it is subject to the problems of self-reporting. Second, until 1995, Statistics Canada conducted a detailed annual survey of union organizations, known as CALURA. This was an invaluable source of detailed membership trends by province and gave a very accurate picture of internal union structures. Since there was a time lag of several years before this information was published, the 1995 data are considered relatively recent (Mainville and Olineck, 1999). Finally, since the beginning of 1997, in part to compensate for cancelling CALURA, Statistics Canada has included questions on union membership and bargaining coverage in its monthly Labour Force Survey (LFS). This will be a principal source of data because it draws on the detailed survey of individual experience in the labour market also used to provide estimates of employment and unemployment (see Akyeampong, 1997, 1999). While this kind of survey can only provide an extrapolation of overall union membership, it is reputed to be accurate and also permits more detailed breakdowns by regional, economic, and socio-demographic characteristics. Some provinces also produce data on provincial union movements based on analysis of collective agreements or surveys of unions.

 Human Resources Development Canada Labour Information:
www://labour-travail.hrdc-drhc.gc.ca

Thus union membership figures vary according to the type of measure and the source of the data. Readers should be aware that this is also the case in this chapter and throughout this book. The key distinction in measuring union membership is between *absolute*

TABLE 4.1

CANADIAN UNION MEMBERSHIP, 1911–1999

YEAR	MEMBERSHIP (THOUSANDS)	MEMBERSHIP AS A PERCENTAGE OF NON-AGRICULTURAL PAID WORKERS
1911	133	—
1916	160	—
1921	313	16.0
1926	275	12.0
1931	311	15.3
1936	323	16.2
1941	462	18.0
1946	832	27.9
1951	1029	28.4
1956	1352	33.3
1961	1447	31.6
1966	1736	30.7
1971	2231	32.4
1976	3042	36.9
1981	3487	36.7
1986	3730	37.7
1991	4068	36.3
1992	4089	37.4
1993	4071	37.6
1994	4078	37.5
1995	4003	34.3
1996	4033	33.9
1997	4074	34.1
1998	3938	32.5
1999	4010	32.3

Note: Data on union membership for the years 1911 to 1946 are as of December 31. Thereafter, they refer to January 1 of each year.

Sources: 1911 to 1966: Dion, 1986; 1971 to 1994: Labour Canada, 1994; 1995 to 1998: HRDC, 1999; 1999: Workplace Information Directorate, 1999.

levels of union membership (how many individuals unions represent), and the *relative levels of union membership* (the proportion of represented workers in relation to all workers).

The absolute measure poses three problems. First, the surveys generally exclude small, independent local organizations, and they sometimes exclude professional groupings, such as police and firefighters' associations, that perform union functions. Second, the absolute number does not include workers who are not members of a union, but yet a union negotiates on their behalf. In 1999, for example, it was estimated that actual union membership accounted for 92.4 percent of those persons covered by collective agreements (calculated from Akyeampong, 1999). Third, union reporting may create problems because not all unions have accurate membership-tracking systems. Union membership can fluctuate during the course of a year. Further, unions may under- or over-report their membership in order to increase their importance or reduce their financial obligations in affiliation fees.

The relative measure of union membership, usually referred to as *union density*, expresses the proportion of the labour force that is unionized. If expressed as a proportion of the total civilian labour force, which includes all of those persons who are either employed, self-employed, or seeking employment, then the rate of unionization is lower than if expressed as the proportion of paid workers (LFS survey) or non-agricultural paid workers (HRDC survey). Union density usually is expressed in terms of the latter two measures to facilitate comparisons between countries with varying degrees of industrialization, and because they provide a more accurate gauge of potential union membership. However, density is still not entirely accurate since most Canadian jurisdictions restrict certain categories of employees from unionizing (e.g., managers and supervisory personnel). At the beginning of 1999, HRDC numbers estimated that 32.3 percent of paid non-agricultural workers were union members, with collective bargaining coverage several points higher. The LFS survey found the rate of collective bargaining coverage in 1999 was 32.1 percent of paid employment with a union membership rate of 30.1 percent (Akyeampong, 1999).

Absolute membership figures reflect the relative health of unions, especially in terms of dues income and levels of organizing. Indicators of relative union membership are especially useful for understanding the penetration of unions in different industries and occupations. These two types of measures should be understood as complements because they express different aspects of union membership activity (Bain and Price, 1983: 4). For instance, as is sometimes the case during downturns in economic activity, union density might actually increase while union membership declines or remains stable.

When we compare Canadian union growth with that of other industrialized economies in the 1985 to 1995 period, only the union movements in Denmark, Malta, Norway, and Spain demonstrated a comparable stability. The aggregate membership performance of Canadian trade unions contrasts markedly with the more significant declines in countries such as France, Japan, the United Kingdom, and the United States (ILO, 1997).

TABLE 4.2

UNION DENSITY BY PROVINCE, 1999

PROVINCE	UNION DENSITY (%)	PROVINCE	UNION DENSITY (%)
Newfoundland	38.0	Ontario	26.5
Prince Edward Island	28.4	Manitoba	35.5
Nova Scotia	30.0	Saskatchewan	33.8
New Brunswick	27.4	Alberta	23.0
Quebec	35.9	British Columbia	33.9

Note: Union density is calculated on the basis of union membership and the number of paid workers.

Source: Akyeampong, 1999.

What about variation within Canada? Absolute union membership in all provinces increased significantly over the last two decades. There are, however, significant differences from one province to another. At one end of the scale, Newfoundland consistently exhibits the highest union density (38 percent), followed by Quebec (35.9 percent). Alberta has the lowest union density (23 percent). See Table 4.2.

Three explanations might account for these differences. First, differing industrial structures exist. Employment in Newfoundland, for example, is concentrated in industries that traditionally are strongly unionized. Second, expansion and contraction of regional labour markets also play a role. The rapid expansion of the Ontario labour market has meant that aggregate membership growth has not kept pace with the expansion of employment. Finally, there are important differences in community attitudes to unionism that, despite initial differences in industrial structure, spill over into other sectors when people consider the acceptability of unionism as a way of regulating employment relations. The rate of unionization in large metropolitan areas varies greatly from one area to another. While industrial structure clearly explains some variation, differences in community attitudes about the benefits of unionism also play a role. (For a study of this phenomenon in Edmonton and Winnipeg, see Krahn and Lowe, 1984.)

Canadian vs. US Union Membership

The contrasting fortunes of trade unions in Canada and the United States over the last two decades has sparked considerable research comparing the circumstances of the two labour movements (Kumar, 1993; Riddell, 1993).

Table 4.3 gives an overview of the post–World War II evolution of union membership in the two countries. Whereas they displayed similar patterns of growth throughout the first half of the 20th century, they began to diverge sharply in the mid-1960s. Union membership in the US has diminished in both absolute and relative terms over the past three decades, falling from over 20 million (29.1 percent density) at the beginning of the 1970s to less than 16.5 million (13.9 percent density) at the end of the 1990s. Union density in Canada is now more than twice that of the United States. Moreover, there is a substantial differential in the rate of unionization in all sectors.

The explanation of this divergence appears related to supply rather than demand factors. On the demand side, there is increasing evidence that a substantial minority of nonunion workers in both the United States and Canada indicate an interest in joining a union. In a 1996 comparative survey, Lipset and Meltz (1997) found that 47 percent of nonunion workers in the US and 33 percent of nonunion workers in Canada would

TABLE 4.3

UNION MEMBERSHIP AND DENSITY IN CANADA AND THE UNITED STATES

Year	CANADA		UNITED STATES	
	Membership (thousands)	Percentage of Non-agricultural Paid Workers	Membership (thousands)	Percentage of Non-agricultural Paid Workers
1946	832	24.2	12,254	30.4
1951	1029	30.2	15,139	31.7
1956	1352	33.6	16,446	31.4
1961	1447	30.6	15,401	28.5
1966	1736	30.7	18,922	29.6
1971	2231	32.4	20,711	29.1
1976	3042	36.9	22,153	27.9
1981	3487	36.7	20,647	22.6
1986	3730	37.7	16,975	17.1
1991	4068	36.3	16,568	15.3
1996	4033	33.9	16,269	14.5
1997	4074	34.1	16,110	14.1
1998	3938	32.5	16,211	13.9
1999	4010	32.3	16,447	13.9

Source: Kumar, 1993, pp. 12–13; HRDC and BLS (annual).

vote for unionization at the workplace. On the supply side, there is considerable evidence that Canadian workers have, for a variety of reasons, easier access to unionization. Many American scholars and union leaders point to contrasting public policies as one of the principal explanations for the union density differences. They argue that the revival of trade union fortunes in the US is contingent on securing substantial changes in public policy (Weiler, 1984; Block, 1993). It also has been suggested that Canadian unions have been more innovative (Murray, 1991; Kumar, 1993), pursued new organizing with more vigour than their American counterparts (Rose and Chaison, 1990), achieved political change and favourable public policy more effectively (Bruce, 1989), and pursued a broader social agenda over a longer period (Piore, 1983; Robinson, 1998). However, it might be noted that aggregate union membership in the US recorded a slight increase in 1999—the first in the past several decades. This change, however modest, might be seen to be the result of a certain renewal of unionism in the US. This renewal was symbolized by a change in leadership of the AFL-CIO in late 1995, but, more fundamentally, it is associated with a new emphasis on the importance of organizing new members as opposed to servicing existing members in a number of the key AFL-CIO affiliates (see Bronfenbrenner et al, 1998; Nissen, 1999).

Some authors suggest that due to continental economic integration, there will be increasing pressures to bring Canada's favourable legislative climate for unions more in line with American treatment (Robinson, 1994). One such example was the unsuccessful attempt to bring American-style right-to-work legislation to the province of Alberta in the mid-1990s (Ponak and Taras, 1997). It has also been argued that the cohesive labour relations associated with high levels of union density in many small nations, for example, in Scandinavian economies, can be a source of competitive advantage (Freeman, 1990).

Minority views in this Canada-US convergence/divergence debate should be noted. Troy (1992), in particular, has argued that the divergence between the US and Canadian union movements has been greatly exaggerated by the failure to take account of the greater size of the public sector in Canada and the fact that union movements in both private sectors are in decline. Although it is difficult to disentangle fully this effect, Riddell (1993: 133) has estimated that only 7 percent of the gap between US and Canadian unionization rates is accounted for by the greater proportion of the Canadian workforce in the public sector.

Distribution of Union Membership

Union membership is not evenly distributed throughout the economy. There are significant variations by socio-demographic characteristics, industry, occupation, firm size, and employment status.

A first source of variation is by sex (see Table 4.4). The rate of unionization of women has historically tended to be less than that of men. However, this trend has been reversed over the last decade (Akyeampong, 1998). Roughly 29.3 percent of women, as opposed to 30.9 percent of men, were union members in 1999. This represents a significant change since the 1960s. In 1962, women constituted only 15.4 percent of all union members. This percentage increased steadily: to 23.5 percent in 1971; 31 percent in 1981; 40.6 percent in 1991; and 42.7 percent in 1995. Moreover, while male union membership has grown very slowly over the last two decades, female union membership has increased substantially. For example, from 1983 to 1995, male union membership increased by only 1.5 percent, while female union membership increased by 41.9 percent. (Figures in this section calculated from Mainville and Olineck, 1999.) Thus, underlying a relative stability in union membership is an increasing feminization of the union movement that has significant implications for the character of unions in Canada (see White, 1993; Briskin and McDermott, 1993).

TABLE 4.4

UNION MEMBERSHIP AND COLLECTIVE BARGAINING COVERAGE BY SEX, AGE, EMPLOYMENT STATUS, AND ESTABLISHMENT SIZE, 1999

	UNION MEMBERSHIP (PERCENTAGE)	COLLECTIVE BARGAINING COVERAGE (PERCENTAGE)
Sex		
Male	30.9	33.5
Female	29.3	31.6
Age		
15–24	12.0	13.8
25–44	30.4	33.0
45–54	41.8	44.6
55 and older	34.8	37.1
Employment Status		
Part-time	21.8	23.2
Full-time	32.0	34.7
Establishment Size		
Less than 20 employees	12.2	13.8
20–99 employees	30.5	33.3
100–499 employees	44.1	47.3
500 or more employees	56.6	59.4
Total	30.1	32.6

Note: Estimates calculated from LFS for the first six months of 1999.

Source: "Union Membership and Collective Bargaining Coverage by Sex, Age, Employment Status, and Establishment Size, 1999," reprinted from *Perspectives on Labour and Income*, Catalogue No. 75-001, Autumn 1999, vol. 9, no. 3.

There also are considerable variations in the degree of unionization by industry (see Table 4.5). According to 1999 Statistics Canada figures (Akyeampong, 1999), workers in the education sector are, by far, the most unionized industry group (69.1 percent). They are followed by other industries characterized by a high degree of public ownership or regulation: utilities, public administration, and health care and social assistance. The private service industries remain little unionized (accommodation and food, for instance, with only 6.4 percent unionization).

TABLE 4.5

UNION DENSITY BY INDUSTRY AND SECTOR, 1999

INDUSTRY	ESTIMATED MEMBERSHIP (THOUSANDS)	UNION DENSITY (%)
Goods-producing	905	31.1
Agriculture	3	2.5
Other primary	56	26.4
Utilities	83	68.3
Construction	146	30.2
Manufacturing	651	31.2
Service-producing	2656	29.8
Trade	238	12.6
Transportation and warehousing	253	42.3
Finance, insurance, real estate, and leasing	62	8.3
Professional, scientific, and technical	23	4.0
Management, administrative, and support	36	9.9
Education	645	69.1
Health care and social assistance	667	53.2
Information, culture, and recreation	148	28.0
Accommodation and food	52	6.4
Other	37	8.1
Public administration	493	64.3
Total	3583	30.1
Sector		
Public	1912	70.9
Private	1676	18.2

Note: Estimates calculated from LFS for the first six months of 1999. The totals are variable because of the estimating procedure.

Source: "Union and Density by Industry and Sector, 1999," reprinted from *Perspectives on Labour and Income*, Catalogue no. 75-001, Autumn 1999, vol. 9, no. 3.

Manufacturing, which traditionally has been highly unionized, has experienced both an absolute decline in union membership and a relative decline in union density over the last two decades, falling from 44.3 percent in 1982 to 38.4 percent in 1995 (CALURA) and 31.2 percent in 1999 (LFS). Indeed, the most significant change in union composition over the past two decades has been the declining proportion of union members in manufacturing and the increasing proportion of public-sector workers in the union movement. In 1995, 15.5 percent of union members came from manufacturing, while 39.5 percent were in public services such as health, education, and public administration (Mainville and Olineck, 1999).

The least unionized industries include those that have been growing most quickly. Thus, only 12.6 percent of those working in wholesale and retail trade are unionized, and union density falls to 4 percent in the finance sector. It should be emphasized that the degree of unionization in these two sectors has increased steadily over the past two decades, but the penetration of unions remains extremely weak. This poses a significant challenge for the labour movement because its areas of relative strength seem to be those that are now either in relative decline (manufacturing, primary industries) or facing cutbacks (the public sector). As the employment structure continues to shift towards private services, the future of the Canadian union movement, in many ways, hinges on its ability to navigate this change.

These sectoral differences in the degree of unionization of industries also are apparent by occupational category. There are much higher percentages of union members in some occupations than others. Traditional jobs involving skills in manufacturing, construction, and transport tend to be highly unionized. Unions also have significant presence among professional and technical job categories in the public sector. For example, 80.1 percent of nurses, 77.2 percent of teachers, and 67.4 percent of technical staff in health services are unionized. By contrast, only 5.4 percent of sales and service employees and 8.8 percent of managerial employees are members of a union (Akyeampong, 1999).

The distribution of union members by firm size also is highly variable (see Table 4.4). The overall level of collective bargaining coverage was 32.6 percent of paid workers in 1999. This figure was only 13.8 percent for firms with less than 20 employees, gradually increasing with firm size to a high of 59.4 percent for establishments with more than 500 employees. Fully 52.3 percent of workers covered by a collective agreement worked in firms of 100 or more employees, even though only 33 percent of paid employees worked in such firms. It is well known that unions have a more difficult time securing their presence in smaller firms, and this is reflected in the data on the distribution of collective bargaining coverage by firm size.

Employment status also exerts an effect on the degree of unionization since full-time workers (those working more than 30 hours per week) tend to be more unionized than are part-time workers. Collective bargaining coverage for full-time workers was 34.7 percent in 1999, as opposed to 23.2 percent for part-time workers (Table 4.4). This differential constitutes a challenge for Canadian unions because there continues to be a more rapid expansion of part-time employment than full-time employment, and of contingent or atypical jobs, such as short-term contracts, as opposed to permanent jobs.

Pressures on Union Membership

If Canadian unions have performed fairly well over the last two decades relative to other labour movements, the pressures operating on them are nonetheless very intense. Employment areas in which unions traditionally have been most representative are shrinking, while the areas in which unions have only a tenuous foothold are growing.

There is considerable evidence that the Canadian union movement has proved to be highly adaptable and fairly inventive over the last decade. Several indicators point in this direction: the overall growth in aggregate union membership, continuing high levels of recruitment activity (see, for example, Lipsig-Mummé, 1998), the entry of women into the unionized labour market, and certain successes in obtaining changes in provincial labour laws that facilitate organizing. However, changes in employment structure continue to have a significant impact on union structures. These structure are explored in the next section.

UNION STRUCTURE

Union structure might be envisaged as being made up of several basic building blocks: the certification unit, the union local, the national or international union, the central labour body or congress, and affiliations to international labour organizations by any one of these other levels of union structure.

Components of Union Structure

The cornerstone of all union structures in Canada is the *certification unit* or *appropriate bargaining unit*. This is the defined group of workers for which a labour board or other similar administrative body grants exclusive bargaining rights to a designated agent (a union), after a majority of those workers have indicated support for union representation. (See the discussion of appropriate bargaining units in Chapter 7.) Bargaining units in Canada generally are quite small and bargaining is highly decentralized. With the notable exception of the public sector, the norm is the negotiation of a single agreement between an employer and a union for a single site. The focus of union activity usually is at the level of the certification unit, and unlike many European unions that engage in national-level bargaining, Canada's decentralized union structure has fairly weak vertical integration between different hierarchical levels of union organization.

This decentralization is further exacerbated by the division of powers over labour matters within the Canadian federation. Roughly 10 percent of Canadian workers fall under federal jurisdiction. The other 90 percent are subject to different provincial jurisdictions whose labour codes may vary considerably (Royal Commission, 1985, vol. 2: 672).

Despite this decentralization, the certification unit is most frequently also part of a larger union structure. A *union local* may be made up of one or more of such certification units. Union locals in industries such as construction typically are made up of multiple certification units. In large manufacturing establishments, on the other hand, a union local generally consists of a single certification unit. Union locals have their own form of governance with by-laws, rules of procedure, and periodic elections. There were nearly 16,613 such union locals in Canada in 1998 (HRDC).

Some locals are highly autonomous. Indeed, there are many independent union locals in Canada that have no form of affiliation. Approximately 3.7 percent of union members belong to such locals. Typical examples would include the McGill Non-Academic Certified Employees Association, the Calgary Police Association, and the Loomis Armoured Car Employees Association in Victoria (HRDC, 1998).

Most union locals are part of a larger structure (see Table 4.6). A union local typically is chartered by a *national* or *international union organization* from which it receives its name and its statutes. For example, Local 444 of the National Automobile, Aerospace and Agricultural Implement Workers Union of Canada, better known as the Canadian Auto Workers Union (CAW), organizes Chrysler employees in Windsor. It is a constituent unit of the national union and is governed in accordance with its constitution.

National and international unions organize and charter locals in the industries or professions defined by their constitutions or policies. This is known as a union's *jurisdiction*.

TABLE 4.6

UNION MEMBERSHIP BY CONGRESS AFFILIATION, 1998

	LOCALS	MEMBERSHIP	PERCENTAGE OF MEMBERSHIP
Canadian Labour Congress (CLC)	9817[a]	2,626,740	66.7
Confédération des syndicats nationaux (CSN-CNTU)	2399	242,830	6.2
Centrale de l'enseignement du Québec (CEQ)	305	113,510	2.9
AFL-CIO only	153	82,510	2.1
Centrale des syndicats démocratiques (CSD)	100	73,070	1.9
Confederation of Canadian Unions (CCU)	38	17,020	0.4
Unaffiliated national unions	3793	637,270	16.2
Unaffiliated international unions	8	230	0.0
Independent local organizations	352	144,610	3.7
Total	16,613[b]	3,937,790	100.0

[a] CLC includes 2571 locals with both CLC and AFL-CIO affiliations.

[b] Total of 16,613 does not include the 352 independent local organizations.

Source: *Workplace Gazette*, vol. 3, no. 1. Reproduced with permission of Minister of Public Works and Government Services.

For example, the United Steelworkers of America organized workers in mining, metal transformation, and some areas of manufacturing across North America. The United Brotherhood of Carpenters and Joiners of America organized carpenters in the building trades. The Canadian Union of Postal Workers organized workers of Canada Post. As we will see below, such jurisdictions are being altered by changes in industrial structure and the consequent strategies pursued by unions to diversify their membership base. There were 279 national and international unions operating in Canada at the beginning of 1998 (HRDC, 1998). In 1999, the 15 largest (those totalling more than 50,000 members) accounted for 56.3 percent of all union members in Canada (see Table 4.7).

Most, but not all, of these unions are, in turn, affiliated with *central labour bodies* or *congresses*. For instance, the Canadian Auto Workers Union, a national union, is affiliated to the Canadian Labour Congress (CLC). The United Brotherhood of Carpenters and Joiners of America, an international union, is affiliated with the AFL-CIO in the United States and with the Canadian Labour Congress in Canada.

Canadian Labour Congress: www.clc-ctc.ca

AFL-CIO: www.aflcio.org

These central labour bodies have both a national presence and, in the case of the Canadian Labour Congress, a significant provincial and territorial presence in the form of 12 provincial and territorial federations of labour. Provincial federations organize congress affiliates in their provinces and represent union interests at the provincial government level (which, it should be recalled, is capable of passing labour legislation covering 90 percent of Canadian employees). In Quebec there also are several autonomous central labour bodies or confederations, notably the Confédération des syndicats nationaux (CSN) and the Centrale de l'enseignement du Québec (CEQ).

Labour congresses or confederations also are present at district or regional levels. In the case of CLC affiliates, 125 *district* or *local labour councils* coordinate the activities of congress locals in a particular district, for example, the Sudbury and District Labour Council or the Halifax-Dartmouth and District Labour Council. In Quebec, the Conseils centraux play a similar role for CSN affiliates.

These central labour bodies, as well as many of the national and international unions associated with them, generally maintain *international affiliations*. The Canadian Labour Congress is affiliated with the International Confederation of Free Trade Unions, a grouping of 215 national trade union centres in 125 countries and territories. National and international unions also are affiliated with various international labour federations. For example, many of the public-sector unions in Canada, such as the National Union of Public and General Employees (NUPGE), are affiliated with the Public Services International. International labour linkages are becoming increasingly important. National union leaders now co-ordinate their own meetings to coincide with the G-7

International Confederation of Free Trade Unions: www.icftu.org

TABLE 4.7

LARGEST UNIONS IN CANADA AND THEIR AFFILIATIONS, 1999

RANKING (SIZE)	UNION ORGANIZATION	WEBSITE	MEMBERSHIP (thousands)	(as % of total union membership)
1	Canadian Union of Public Employees—CUPE (CLC)	www.cupe.ca	461.8	11.3
2	National Union of Public and General Employees—NUPGE (CLC)	www.nupge.ca	309.0	8.0
3	National Automobile, Aerospace and Agricultural Implement Workers Union of Canada—CAW (CLC)	www.caw.ca	215.0	5.4
4	United Steelworkers of America—USWA (AFL-CIO/CLC)	www.uswa.ca	200.0	5.0
5	United Food and Commercial Workers International Union—UFCW (AFL-CIO/CLC)	www.ufcw.ca	200.0	5.0
6	Communications, Energy and Paperworkers Union—CEP (CLC)	www.cep.ca	144.3	3.6
7	Public Service Alliance of Canada—PSAC (CLC)	www.psac.com	142.3	3.6
8	Fédération de la santé et des services sociaux—FSSS (CSN)	www.csn.qc.ca	97.0	2.4
9	International Brotherhood of Teamsters—IBT (AFL-CIO/CLC)		93.0	2.3
10	Fédération des syndicats de l'enseignement—FSE (CEQ)	www.ceq.qc.ca	82.6	2.1
11	Service Employees International Union—SEIU (AFL-CIO/CLC)	www.seiu.ca	81.5	2.0
12	Elementary Teachers' Federation of Ontario—ETFO (IND.)	www.etfo.on.ca	62.2	1.6
13	Canadian Union of Postal Workers—CUPW (CLC)	www.cupw-sttp.org	54.8	1.4
14	International Brotherhood of Electrical Workers—IBEW (AFL-CIO/CLC)		57.0	1.4
15	United Brotherhood of Carpenters and Joiners of America—UBC (AFL-CIO/CLC)		56.0	1.4
Total of the largest unions (50,000 or more members)			2256.5	56.3
Smaller unions (fewer than 50,000 members)			1753.5	43.7
Total of all unions			**4010.0**	**100.0**

Source: *Workplace Gazette*, vol. 3, no. 1. Reproduced with permission of Minister of Public Works and Government Services.

summit meeting of the seven largest industrial nations, and union representatives are active participants in coalition meetings held to coincide with regional and international free trade issues. International labour federations try to play a more active role in international labour solidarity issues affecting particular industries, such as cross-border support for strike action in transnational firms.

The next sections focus in more detail on the three most important levels of union structure: labour congresses, national and international union organizations, and union locals.

Central Labour Congresses

The Canadian Labour Congress is the principal central labour congress in Canada. It represented 2.7 million members at the beginning of 1999, approximately 68.8 percent of Canadian union members. There were 93 national and international unions affiliated with the CLC. They pay affiliation fees to the CLC on a per-member basis. The CLC also has a very small number of directly chartered locals, but the major form of affiliation is still through national and international labour organizations. It is such organizations and not the CLC or its provincial federations that provide the bulk of direct services to members. Although the CLC experimented with recruitment in the financial sector in the 1970s, labour congresses usually do not negotiate for their members or recruit new members. That is the role of their affiliated organizations.

Labour congresses thus focus on representational and policy-making activities in the social, economic, and political spheres. CLC representatives participate in a number of national and international bodies to deal with issues such as training, unemployment insurance, and social policy. Provincial federations do likewise at the provincial level. Only the Quebec Federation of Labour, whose distinct status within the Congress was first recognized in 1974 and further clarified at the 1994 CLC convention, tends to assume other roles normally reserved for affiliates, such as the coordination of sectoral bargaining in the Quebec public sector and construction industry.

Affiliated unions zealously maintain their autonomy, and the CLC has very weak formal authority over the activities of its affiliates. Given this weak vertical integration and the Congress's relative lack of financial resources, coordination between the Congress and its principal affiliates depends on consensus building on policy issues and on persuading the affiliates to commit resources to particular campaigns. However, because of increasing conflicts among affiliates involving jurisdictional issues, the CLC has bolstered its disciplinary powers over individual affiliates, thereby limiting the possibility for a union local to switch its allegiance from one national or international union to another. This change was driven particularly by a bitter dispute in the Maritimes' fishing industry between the United Food and Commercial Workers Union (UFCW) and the CAW over the decision of how many UFCW certification units to transfer to the CAW. There have been many other inter-union conflicts over jurisdiction.

The CLC is governed by an executive council that is elected at the triennial convention by union local delegates. The president, two vice presidents, and the secretary-treasurer hold full-time positions. Ken Georgetti, who previously had been president of the British

Columbia Federation of Labour, was elected president in 1999. Other members of the CLC executive usually are senior officers of major affiliated unions. A number of positions are reserved for women union leaders and representatives of visible minorities. The executive and its subcommittees meet at regular intervals between triennial congresses to formulate and implement CLC policy.

The Confédération des syndicats nationaux (CSN) is the second-largest congress. Formerly a confessional or Catholic union movement, but fully secular since the early 1960s, its membership is drawn almost exclusively from Quebec. As a rule, and unlike many CLC affiliates in other provinces, certification is vested solely within the union local (Verge and Murray, 1991: 62). Union locals then affiliate directly to the CSN as well as to one of its eight industrial or sectoral federations and to one of its regional councils (Conseils centraux). That means that union locals are free to re-affiliate with other labour centrals should they be dissatisfied with their representation or services. In the public sector, in particular, there is considerable movement back and forth between different affiliations at the beginning of each bargaining round.

Confédération des syndicats nationaux (CSN): www.csn.qc.ca

Like the CLC, the CSN is administered by a number of full-time executive officers elected at a triennial congress. Its industrial federations do likewise. Unlike the CLC, but like some of the continental European labour congresses, the degree of vertical and horizontal integration of locals within the CSN is highly developed, with meetings bringing together different affiliates at regular intervals.

The Canadian union movement has become increasingly fragmented over the last several decades. In contrast to the 1960s and 1970s, when the CLC could claim to represent nearly three-quarters of Canadian union members, it now represents two-thirds of them (see Table 4.6). This change is not the result of a decline in the overall affiliated membership of the CLC; but rather, it reflects three factors: (1) continued increases in membership of non-affiliated unions, particularly those representing professionals in the health and education sector; (2) a modification in the reporting requirements of Statistics Canada (see CALURA) which, on paper at least, *increased* the number of unaffiliated union members; and (3) the 1982 breakaway from the CLC of a number of US-based affiliated unions, especially in the construction trades, to form the Canadian Federation of Labour (CFL). The CFL took a more conservative approach to union political involvement and social change than that developed by the CLC. At its peak, the CFL represented roughly 200,000 members. Faced with continued membership and financial pressures, it ceased its activities in 1997.

Centrale de l'enseignement du Québec: www.ceq.qc.ca

Other labour congresses in Canada include the Centrale de l'enseignement du Québec, a confederation of Quebec public-sector unions located primarily in the field of education; the Centrale des syndicats démocratiques, a small grouping of Quebec unions that broke away from the CSN in the early 1970s; and the Confederation of Canadian Unions, a loose grouping of independent local Canadian unions with a specific nationalist perspective.

National and International Unions

In terms of the organization of resources and the development of strategies, national and international unions undoubtedly are the most significant organizational level. Major decisions about bargaining, recruitment, and political activity are made here. As befits the decentralization of the Canadian labour movement, national and international unions in Canada are highly diverse in their structures and policies.

Table 4.7 lists unions with more than 50,000 members at the beginning of 1999 as well as their affiliations and Websites. By far the largest is the Canadian Union of Public Employees (CUPE) with roughly 461,800 members in a wide variety of public-sector occupations in municipal employment, public and private transport, and health and education. This is a complex organization with a national office, provincial and often district offices, a national executive board and several full-time executive officers, hundreds of union employees including support staff, a wide range of specialists at its Ottawa headquarters, and a large number of field staff.

The National Union of Public and General Employees (NUPGE) is the second-largest union. Unlike other large national and international unions that provide the bulk of services to their members, NUPGE is, in fact, a federation of highly autonomous provincial government employees unions. The Public Service Alliance of Canada (PSAC) is the seventh-largest union and represents federal government employees. The United Food and Commercial Workers and United Steelworkers of America are the largest international unions in Canada. Both organize primarily in the private sector. The Auto Workers (CAW) and Communication, Energy and Paperworkers Union (CEP) are the largest private-sector national unions.

By international standards, one of the peculiar features of Canadian unionism has been the interpenetration of Canadian and American union structures. Indeed, among industrialized economies, only Ireland and Britain contain this same tight linkage of union structures. The high Canada-US economic integration created spillovers of both craft (AFL) and industrial (CIO) unionism from the US to Canada. A large proportion of Canadian union members have belonged to such "international" unions. An important trend has been the relative decline in the proportion of international or American unionism. At the beginning of 1998, 29.9 percent of Canadian union members belonged to US-headquartered unions (HRDC, 1998). By contrast, 30 years earlier, in 1969, 65 percent of Canadian union members belonged to American-based unions. Thus, there has been almost a complete reversal in the importance of international unionism in Canada.

National unions have been growing much faster than international unions, particularly because of the spread of unionization in the public sector, where almost all union members belong to national unions. There also have been significant breakaways from parent US unions, for example, the CAW's dramatic 1985 split from the United Auto Workers. The move towards greater Canadian autonomy also occurred in other industries, notably in communications and paper in the 1970s and in breweries, woodworking, and energy in the 1980s.

Statistics Canada, Labour, Employment, and Unemployment: www.statcan.ca/english/Pgdb/People/labour.htm

Bureau of Labor Statistics (US): stats.bls.gov/blshome.htm

The Canadianization wave has not always resulted in secession by Canadian affiliates of American unions. There has been a growing movement towards more self-governance by Canadian members of international unions (Thompson and Blum, 1983). From the early 1970s, the CLC adopted a set of minimum standards for the governance of Canadian union members by Canadians. These included provisions on the election of Canadian officers by Canadians, the right to determine policies that deal with national affairs and to speak for their unions in Canada, separate affiliations with international union bodies, and freedom from constitutional or policy constraints to full participation in the Canadian community.

International unions remain a significant feature of Canadian union structure. Of the 15 largest unions listed in Table 4.7, six are international and nine are national. As workers strive to construct cross-border alliances to deal with common problems in the context of the internationalization of production, not only are many forms of international unionism likely to endure, but new forms probably will emerge.

Unions have a wide variety of internal structures that reflect the evolution of particular visions of territorial, occupational, and industrial solidarities as well as administrative arrangements for providing services to members. The great historical conflict was, of course, between craft unionism, which favoured occupational solidarities, and industrial unionism, which sought to organize workers on the basis of industries. Most unions continue to be based on either an occupational or industrial principle. For most unions, however, these organizing jurisdictions have become increasingly blurred over time. Changes in the sectoral distribution of employment have had profound effects on these organizing principles. A significant modification in union structure is thus under way.

First, many previously single-industry unions are involved in mergers. In 1992, for example, three major industrial unions, the Canadian Paperworkers Union, the Communications and Electrical Workers of Canada, and the Energy and Chemical Workers Union merged to create a single new union, the Communications, Energy and Paperworkers Union of Canada (CEP). The Canadian Auto Workers have been extremely active, merging successively in the 1990s with the Canadian Association of Industrial, Mechanical and Allied Workers; the United Electrical, Radio and Machine Workers of Canada; the Marconi Employees' Union; the Canadian Division Brotherhood of Railway Carmen; the Canadian Textile and Chemical Union; the Canadian Brotherhood of Railway, Transport and General Workers; and the Canadian members of the Retail,

Wholesale and Department Store Union. Thus, the merger-mania in the corporate world throughout the previous two decades was matched within the union movement.

Second, many of the international unions in manufacturing have faced declining membership and diminished opportunities for new recruitment activity in their traditional jurisdictions. This has prompted some unions to diversify their areas of recruitment. A striking example of this phenomenon is the Steelworkers, which increasingly recruits in the service sector. Seeking to compensate for significant membership losses in mining and manufacturing, the Steelworkers began organizing security guards, hotel and restaurant workers, and even Wal-Mart (see opening vignette in Chapter 7). Public-sector unions have been recruiting in the private sector. The former National Union of Provincial Government Employees is now the National Union of Public and General Employees (NUPGE, and even further abbreviated to the National Union) in order to better reflect the change in focus. The British Columbia Government Employees Union (a NUPGE component union), which was greatly affected by successive waves of public-sector privatization implemented by the Social Credit government, became particularly active in recruiting members outside the public sector. Many unions in previously well-defined sectors have made selective incursions into other areas, either to compensate for membership losses elsewhere or to respond to changes in the organization of production likely to affect their core membership.

Thus, industrial unionism is giving way to new varieties of general unionism. In the past, there were a few unions that organized in a wide variety of sectors. Such *general unions* were based on neither craft nor industrial jurisdictions. The International Brotherhood of Teamsters, though concentrated in trucking and warehousing, organized in almost any sector and grew to be one of the largest unions in North America. The search for appropriate union structures that can take root in the new service sector is likely to accelerate this transformation of industrial and craft unions into modified forms of general unionism (see Murray, 1998; Yates, 1998).

At the same time, there is a reaction to this trend. In particular, it should be noted that there are a large number of unaffiliated national unions that typically represent professional groups in the public sector, such as nurses and teachers. They have opted not to affiliate with a central labour body such as the CLC because they have been wary of political associations, and they prefer not to lose their sharp sense of occupational attachment. In an era in which jurisdictional lines are becoming muddled, the clearer professional focus of some of these unions has proved to be an impetus for growth. Examples include the nurses' union in Quebec and an increasing number of professional associations, particularly in health care.

Union Locals

The decentralization of Canadian union structure means that many union locals have a high degree of autonomy. Union locals tend to reflect either their craft or industrial union servicing traditions. The craft tradition tends towards a very autonomous union local that organizes a large number of certification units on a regional basis. All dues are paid to that local. It generally has a full-time president who employs business agents to carry out basic servicing activities. The union local is affiliated with a national or international union to which it pays dues on a pro rata basis. The degree of centralization is fairly weak and financial control is vested at the local level. With the growing demands on union services centrally, unions organized along this model have added centralized services, but their ability to perform in an effective manner is limited by union local autonomy and a weak financial capacity at the central level.

The industrial tradition is more centralized. The union local usually consists of one certification unit. Union locals usually have part-time presidents who do not draw their salary from the union, but the locals are serviced by a cadre of full-time officials employed by the national or international union. Some portion of these dues, in conformity with the prevailing constitutional provisions of the organization, are then allocated to the union local. The proportion of dues accruing to the local level varies considerably. The central union body or head office generally develops specialized services delivered by field staff. Steelworkers and CAW are examples of this industrial tradition.

Many of the newer public-sector unions tend to adopt some variation of the industrial union model. Most evolved from government-employee staff associations whose high centralization reflected their employer's structure. While public-sector unions might organize a broad range of employees for a particular government employer, their internal organization, unlike that of industrial unions, is sometimes based on professional category rather than location or administrative unit. They have tended to develop expert services at the head office and have fairly weak local structures. As could be seen in the vignette describing Union B at the beginning of this chapter, decentralization and privatization are exerting increasing pressures on this distribution of responsibilities.

There is considerable pressure on all of these models because of changes in industrial structure. Some models appear better suited to the exigencies of the new service economy than do others. The changing organization of the firm and larger trends in the labour market have had a marked, if highly differential, impact on the structures and strategies of union locals. Most notably, the declining size of existing bargaining units and the small size of many new certifications have prompted some unions to amalgamate different certifications into larger, composite locals.

This is evident in many of the older unions that are characterized by a craft structure and that have traditionally organized a multiplicity of units within a single local and built their servicing structure around this arrangement. In the case of the United Food and Commercial Workers Union, there are new hybrid models where union locals maintain a high degree of autonomy, but there is a tendency to increase the presence of full-time officials paid by the national union to carry out basic services and be involved in policy coordination.

The local structures of industrial-model unions, such as the Steelworkers, also are undergoing significant change (Murray, 1998). With the infusion of smaller certification units, particularly in private services, the Steelworkers gradually altered its local structures, with the average number of certifications per local increasing. This represents a conscious organizing and servicing strategy designed to better meet the needs of new membership groups both in the service sector and in small manufacturing units. Indeed, it aims to create union locals that can adjust to the small size of new units being organized. This strategy also allows the union to achieve a financially viable servicing strategy. The union has done this at times by training full-time lay representatives rather than professional business agents or servicing staff. The increased importance of amalgamated locals naturally pushes unions organized on the industrial model towards greater decentralization in the distribution of services. In the United States labour movement, such an approach is labelled the "organizing model" and this term is increasingly popular in Canada. The objective is to revitalize union recruitment through the reallocation of resources and energies to the recruitment and defence of new groups of workers, most typically on a community basis, whereby union locals try to build bridges with the communities of the workers they seek to represent.

Services and Dues

Canadian unions face increasing demands from their members to provide a wide range of sophisticated services. Basic services include the negotiation and application of collective agreements. While these services might be provided by a lay official such as a union local president or shop steward, or by a full-time official working either for the national or local union, larger certification units generally require complex backup services, such as research and legal assistance. The wider the range of issues dealt with in the collective agreement, the more complex is the range of services required. Thus, in recent years, most unions have added health and safety, pension, and pay equity specialists. There also is an increasing demand for information and advice on company finances, work reorganization, new technologies, and environmental regulations. Many unions provide supplementary services. Unions began as mutual insurance societies to provide benefits to craft workers in times of hardship. Strike pay and supplementary health and insurance schemes are examples of such benefits. Some unions have expanded into other types of individual services such as legal, financial, counselling, and employment advice to members. Other unions have developed collective instruments, such as investment funds, to safeguard and promote employment in particular workplaces.

Whereas most unions used to charge dues on a flat-rate basis, they switched to a percentage basis during the inflationary period of the 1970s. Union dues typically are 1 to 2 percent of salary. For example, monthly dues of Steelworkers are established by the international constitution at 1.3 percent of total salary with provisos for minimum and maximum contributions. The constitution also indicates the percentage distribution of this revenue among different levels of the union. Both the union local and international union receive 44 percent of dues; 7 percent goes to the international strike fund, and smaller amounts are allocated to education (1 percent), political action (1 percent), and organizing (3 percent). Unions with more decentralized traditions, such as the UFCW, have more variable arrangements, since the union local is free to fix its own level of dues from which it then must pay per capita affiliation fees, often on a flat-rate basis, to other levels of the union. Flat-rate dues are a particularly contentious issue for many part-time workers who feel that they are unduly penalized in having to pay a higher percentage of their income in union dues than do full-time workers. This is why a number of unions seeking to attract part-time members have moved away from this kind of dues structure.

Yet, as the demand and the need for services increase, there is a decreased capacity to pay for them. In particular, structural changes in the labour market have resulted in reduced real dues income per member as overall income has remained static with new members often either working part-time or earning less in the general service occupations (Murray, 1998). This has increased the pressure on union services and led to a certain re-thinking of the role of full-time staff in some unions, and especially of the relative division of labour between staff and activists and the role of education and self-empowerment in the provision of services by activists.

Union Governance and Democracy

The union as an organization is characterized by a certain ambiguity, for it is both collective and democratic. It is necessarily collective because its power is derived from its capacity to coordinate the actions of its members in order to achieve common objectives. But if a union is to exercise a degree of power for its members, it invariably exercises a degree of power over them (Hyman, 1975: 65). Craft unions were traditionally illustrative of this point because their power vis-à-vis the employer depended on their control of entry into the trade and their disciplinary powers over those exercising the trade (Clegg, 1976: 30).

Unions also are democratic organizations with constitutions that ensure the protection of individual members and guarantee the right of members to participate in the selection and application of policies and to choose their leaders. The power of the collective over the individual is thus limited by the democratic character of the union as well as by certain legislative and Charter of Rights provisions regarding union elections and strike votes, the ratification of collective agreements, the union's duty to fairly represent members, and the observance of principles of natural justice.

Even if the possibility of participating in the economic life of their workplace and their country is sometimes an important motive for workers becoming union members, it probably is safe to say that the primary objective of most union members is not to enjoy the experience of democracy. Rather, the democratic character of the union is a way of controlling the pursuit of collective goals. Moreover, the attainment of such goals invariably depends on the willingness of individual members to forgo individual prerogatives in favour of democratically agreed-upon collective objectives. The dilemma for union democracy, therefore, is the choice between a stable leadership and efficient organization, on the one hand, and the right of opposition, with all the attendant risks of fragmentation and disorder, on the other (Hemmingway, 1978: 2).

This tension between collectivism and democracy is central to the union organization and affects much of its internal life. Drawing on what a famous observer of life in voluntary organizations labelled the *iron law of oligarchy* (Michels, 1962), a pessimistic vision of union democracy suggests that, sooner or later, leadership ends up being concentrated in the hands of a small elite that is not easily removed from power. The concentration of power can lead to abuse. The image of certain union bosses connected to underworld racketeering in the United States readily springs to mind, and there are cases of such abuse in Canada (see, for example, Kaplan, 1987, on the International Seafarers Union in the 1950s and 1960s). More typically, full-time officials in many unions exercise a tremendous influence on policy outcomes and application.

A more optimistic vision suggests that unions are constantly subject to democratic renewal (Hyman, 1971). Union leaders cannot ignore the real and democratic limits of their power. While such limits are formally part of the governance of the union, they also are highly practical. The constant possibility of election defeat, the potential emergence of organized opposition within the union, the obligation for union officials to account for their actions, and, ultimately, the need to mobilize union members in the pursuit of collective goals while maintaining their satisfaction with union representation—these are all factors that limit the power of union leadership. Most union leaders are preoccupied by the problem of ensuring membership participation. Many have altered their internal union structures to facilitate membership participation, especially that of women and visible minorities, and to better respond to members' needs. Drawing on the traditions of its former parent union in the United States, the CAW constitution provides for a type of ombudsperson procedure, where an independent panel made up of impartial individuals from outside the union will hear any membership complaint about improper internal procedures not resolved through the internal appeal procedure of the union.

There are several possibilities available for membership participation within the union. The most typical form of participation, and the one that generally stimulates high member involvement, is membership input on collective bargaining. Members are asked for input on the objectives of particular bargaining rounds, and they can participate in meetings that frame issues. In addition, the law generally obliges them to formally ratify a decision to accept a collective agreement or strike.

Members also can take on tasks related to the life of the collective agreement or the representation of union members within the establishment. Stewards or workplace representatives are concerned with the application of the collective agreement and the expression of grievances. Workplace health-and-safety representatives are concerned with this aspect of union work. Increasingly, there are other new channels for membership participation and activism on issues such as pay equity and training.

Members also play a role in the administration of the union. The most typical form of participation involves attendance at union local meetings; although, aside from during the most intense periods of collective bargaining, the rate of membership attendance at routine meetings remains very low. Union members also elect their local leaders. The union local must also be represented at other decision-making bodies within union structures. While the number and level of such bodies varies from one union to another, the final decision-making authority in almost all unions is some form of convention or congress to which union locals send voting delegates on the basis of their membership. The frequency of such conventions varies from one to five years or more. Most unions elect their leadership at such conventions, a form of indirect membership elections. Some unions, notably the Steelworkers, elect their leaders by direct membership postal ballot.

Between conventions, most unions provide for other decision-making bodies to deliberate on the implementation of policy. Sometimes, this involves a small number of full-time elected executive members. Sometimes, it involves some form of representative council at which most major locals or territorial or professional groupings would be present. Some unions, for example the Auto Workers, have both an executive and a council meeting every four months to which all locals are requested to send delegates. Many unions also have regional or industry structures that might duplicate these arrangements. In particular, this is the case with the Quebec sections of many national and international unions. Over the past three decades, they have developed forms of self-governance that recognize the *distinct* character of their Quebec membership within the larger union structure. Union locals also send delegates, in principle at least, to the conventions of their national and provincial central labour bodies.

The degree of membership participation in the administration of the union tends to be less than that in the bargaining activities of the union. Most unions nonetheless depend almost entirely on the activism of their members to ensure their daily operations. The dynamism and the influence of a union ultimately depend on the participation of the membership. Most unions invest heavily in membership education in order to train members to administer their organizations. They also seek to ensure that members do participate and to solve the perpetual participation problems that seem to characterize most voluntary organizations. As for individual union members, the scope available to them to participate in the democratic life of their unions can be a training ground for the experience of democracy in the larger society as well as an occasion for developing their own abilities. Many union activists speak glowingly of the tremendous influence that union participation has had on their personal development and of how it has enriched their understanding of society (see, for example, Martin, 1995).

Challenges for Union Structure and Governance

There are a number of common structural adjustments taking place in Canadian unions to reflect the changes in membership composition, the movements in corporate structure, the rise of new identities at work, and the real problems of organizing new groups of workers into unions, especially in private services.

With women participating in the labour force in growing numbers, unions have had to focus on ensuring that women enjoy a more active role in organized labour. The unionization of the public sector brought large numbers of women members into the ranks of unions. Moreover, the growth of private service-sector employment suggests there is an even greater potential for union membership growth among women in the future. However, many women members have charged that unions do not reflect their concerns or accommodate their needs by allowing them to participate in official roles within their unions. Thus, through the 1980s and 1990s, there has been a continuing debate as women have sought to introduce issues such as sexual harassment, child care, maternity leave, employment equity, and pay equity to union agendas. Debate also has surrounded attempts to ensure that women were adequately represented in elected positions and in the different parts of their unions, as well as attempts to eliminate barriers to women's active participation in the life of the union (Briskin and McDermott, 1993: 5). Indeed, women's groups and the feminist movement more generally have been major sources of renewal for many unions. Some union leaderships, for example that of CUPE, now reflect their formative experience in union women's committees and in coalition activity with other feminist groups.

The relative success of women in this endeavour has served as an example to other groups, such as visible minorities, to claim equivalent recognition within the political channels of their unions. Thus, many unions have adopted a variety of employment equity measures to ensure the greater participation of different membership groups. Special internal structures based on specific identities, such as gender, ethnicity, or sexual orientation, also have provided a focus for new activism. Union leaders are sometimes confronted with the potential clash between new activists and traditional membership groups nostalgic for an older, more homogeneous industrial structure.

At the local level, the rise of the composite or amalgamated local has been a response to the importance of smaller unit size in both manufacturing and services. At other levels, as could be seen in the opening vignettes, there is the question of how to create effective coordinating mechanisms in an effort to organize the new groups into viable structures and make links between core and peripheral workers. This is an enduring problem in a large number of unions. Thus, the challenge of fostering participation and giving a sense of ownership to the various diverse groups in the organization will continue to be a major preoccupation of unions.

UNION ACTION

The choice traditionally available to a union is either economic or political action. If its objectives were defined largely in terms of improvement in terms and conditions of employment of its members, a union might rely exclusively on collective bargaining and, ultimately, on recourse to sanctions such as a strike. Alternatively, it might employ various forms of political action, be it through lobbying, the creation of a political party, or even a mass movement, to pursue the same objectives. Moreover, a union might define its objectives more widely, seeking to represent its members not only as wage earners, but also as citizens (Murray and Verge, 1999). Indeed, central union bodies often aspire to be the voice for all workers.

Nature of Union Action

Why do particular union movements emphasize one type of action rather than the other? Many explanations point to the lasting imprint of the formative period of the union movement in a particular country. Did workers already enjoy universal suffrage and was the labour market characterized by shortages or an excess supply of unskilled labour? If a particular country's labour movement played a key role in obtaining the vote, for men at least, it was likely to continue this political role. If there was a shortage of unskilled labour, then the union movement would rely on economic action or collective bargaining. However, if an excess supply of unskilled labour existed, then political action was more likely to improve the lot of the vast majority of unionized workers. In North America, where the market was expanding rapidly and labour shortages were common, and the right to vote came independently of the formation of the labour movement, early unions were typically characterized by the label *bread-and-butter unionism* since they concentrated their efforts in the collective bargaining realm.

The creation of industrial unions was characterized by a period of political ferment leading to the formal obligation on the part of employers to recognize unions where a majority of workers favoured such representation. The consolidation of our current industrial relations regime in the immediate aftermath of World War II, however, tended to emphasize the narrow, economic or industrial character of union representation to the detriment of a broader civic or socio-political role. Increasingly, the Canadian union movement tends to rely on some combination of both economic and political methods.

Collective Bargaining

The classic method of union action is collective bargaining, a subject treated in detail in Chapter 9. It should be emphasized that Canadian unions have long pursued a strategy of wage militancy. Indeed, even during the recession of the early 1980s, the CLC adopted a "no-concessions" policy.

Current shifts in corporate strategy and organization place traditional collective bargaining under severe pressure. At root here is the social reorganization of production at the workplace, which is particularly evident in the use of new production systems and the reorganization of internal labour markets. This results in a dual, and often contradictory, process of *integration* and *differentiation*.

Integration is the ideological reconstruction of the workplace around new production systems and management techniques that seek to mobilize employee enthusiasm and knowledge to achieve greater productivity and competitiveness (Wells, 1996). At one end of the continuum, this might be yet another fad in a never-ending series of managerial initiatives. Alternatively, it might be a complete reformulation of the social system of the enterprise that can seek to integrate (or exclude) certain forms of participation and workers' representative mechanisms into the very culture of the firm. This can involve a range of new managerial practices, including total quality management, quality circles, variable compensation systems, and new forms of worker participation. (See Chapter 15 on employee involvement.) Whatever its orientation, and it certainly varies greatly from one firm to another, this integrative process opens up a range of strategic questions for union organizations, particularly, as could be seen with Union C in the opening vignettes, the extent to which a workers' representative organization can ally its objectives with those of the firm without compromising its watchdog role in the defence of working conditions.

At the same time, there also is a process of differentiation whereby firms seek new levels of *flexibility* by transforming traditional full-time, secure jobs into other categories of employment. These can include part-time, contractual, temporary, or subcontracted work. Also, the firm can identify different profit centres and reorganize production and services into smaller, more highly differentiated units, or it can forgo employment relations altogether in favour of outside contractors. Another aspect of differentiation is the creation of specialist employee categories that function outside traditional promotion and wage systems. Some employers have sought to disconnect or reorganize traditional wage comparisons between firms and units through this same differentiation philosophy. In the retail food sector, for example, there have been numerous franchising activities that result either in de-unionization or increased differentiation among contracts. Similarly, large hotels have recently moved to subdivide their different activities (reception, catering, cleaning, etc.) into distinct businesses, often with different employers. Moreover, as could be seen in the case of Union B at the outset of this chapter, this is far from being strictly a private-sector phenomenon. Public agencies emulate differentiation strategies both in the organization of services and in the wages and working conditions of their direct employees or contracted workers.

Pattern bargaining, the coordination of bargaining objectives and tactics within a particular sector, previously tended to alleviate the effects of this decentralization. The kinds of comparative linkages previously associated with such patterns are difficult to maintain in more competitive product markets, however. There are various new union strategies to deal with these developments. Unions are building broader-based bargaining structures to obtain greater bargaining power in order to create viable servicing structures. While some unions have also espoused new forms of co-operative bargaining techniques, such as interest-based or mutual gains bargaining, others, as was the case of Union C in the opening vignettes, are advocating a return to increased militancy in order to secure a greater share of productivity gains for their members. In terms of bargaining agenda, in addition to traditional and ever-present concerns over job security and remuneration, unions have made some effort to enlarge their bargaining strategies to reflect the changed political economy, the pace of workplace change, and the preoccupations of new groups in the labour market.

In a recent study of national union bargaining priorities and success in Canada, Kumar et al. (1998) identified four areas around which union bargaining agendas are currently structured. In order of importance, they are: 1) the protection of current wages and benefits; 2) the pursuit of an active union and worker role in workplace change, particularly on issues such as consultation and training; 3) limiting the effects of workplace flexibility on workers, in particular on such issues as contracting out and regulating workloads; and 4) the promotion of a progressive agenda on gender, family, and working-time issues through the negotiation of items such as employment equity and time off work for family reasons. In analyzing the degree of success achieved by national unions on these items, Kumar et al. found that unions were achieving a fairly high degree of success on the traditional bargaining agenda (protecting current wages and benefits), but much less success on new items, particularly the effects of workplace flexibility. Unions were, however, able to achieve a high degree of success on gender, family, and working-time issues, but only if these issues were prioritized during negotiations. The strategic challenge for unions is how to strike the appropriate balance between the necessary defensive agenda, driven by employer responses to environmental change, and the more proactive agenda that seeks to connect with both worker concerns to have a voice in their workplaces and the concerns of the new constituencies that unions must organize if they are to maintain and enhance their role in the workplace and in society.

Workplace Reorganization

There is considerable debate within the labour movement over the challenges of workplace reorganization. The new *co-operative* union strategies that focus almost exclusively within the individual firm to the detriment of larger labour market solidarities are particularly contentious. Some unions are tempted by the appeal of enduring, co-operative, strife-free relationships with employers. This kind of new *enterprise unionism* is currently being promoted in a number of countries. Moreover, the threat of unemployment in an era of restructuring and global competition pushes many union leaders towards more collaborative relationships with employers. Most unions have some kind of policy response. Some, such as the CEP and CSN, have actively promoted a co-operative approach to change in the workplace. Others, notably the CAW, have taken a more critical approach.

Hitherto, the effect of workplace reorganization on the union as an institution has not been that dramatic (Betcherman et al., 1994; Kumar, 1995). However, new forms of work design challenge the *Taylorist* form of work organization (Bourque and Rioux, 1994; Rinehart et al, 1997), and might have profound implications for union operations (Bélanger and Murray, 1994). Certainly, collective agreement provisions are reflecting changes in work organization, for example, with more evidence of variable pay, training, and multi-skilling (see Chapter 15 for details).

There is increasing evidence that a union local able to draw on its own internal and external resources is in a better position to play an active role in workplace change (see Frost, 1997; Lévesque and Murray, 1998; Murray et al., 1999). Internal resources include a network of union delegates, time off to take care of union business, and, most importantly, a high degree of membership participation in and support for the union. External resources include the capacity to draw on information, coordination, and solidarity from a wider network, notably from the larger union with which the union local is affiliated. It is therefore especially important for national unions to develop support mechanisms and training for their union locals on workplace change (Kumar et al., 1998b).

Economic Restructuring beyond the Workplace

In the context of current socio-economic transformations both within and beyond the firm, representation beyond the firm is increasingly important. We are witnessing the creation of consultative and representative forums and institutions to deal with such issues as training, sectoral adjustment, productivity, pay equity, and regional economic development. At the national level, the labour movement has played some role in the administration of certain labour market social programs such as employment insurance. For example, one of the four representatives on the Employment Insurance Commission, which is responsible for the system of employment insurance, is only appointed after consultations with the labour movement. However, the CLC's relations with the federal government deteriorated considerably during the 1970s when wage controls were imposed, and never fully recovered. Since that time, consultation between the union movement and the federal government has not been very extensive.

The severity of the recession in the early 1980s prompted many union leaders to diversify union action in the economic sphere. Labour came to define the representation of economic interests more widely, and the government, to a limited degree at least, came to recognize the legitimacy of such representation. A highly visible initiative was the 1984 creation of the Canadian Labour Market and Productivity Centre (CLMPC) to promote more and better-quality jobs. This tripartite body has 11 labour representatives named by the CLC. Moreover, it actively promoted labour participation in a wide range of sectoral initiatives designed to restructure the workplace and modernize industries (CLMPC, 1992). At the instigation of the CLMPC, the Canadian Labour Force Development Board was created in 1991 to establish priorities for labour-force training.

There has been a proliferation of sectoral initiatives to deal with issues of restructuring and training in particular industries (Gunderson and Sharpe, 1998). One of the best known of these is the Canadian Steel Trade and Employment Conference (CSTEC), a bipartite union–employer body that deals with trade and employment-adjustment questions in the steel industry. There are several other sectoral initiatives in auto parts and communications. Moreover, this multiplication of consultative bodies has, to varying degrees, been replicated at the provincial level. Some of these, notably in Quebec (see Charest, 1999; Murray and Verge, 1999), are fairly extensive while others, particularly in Ontario, have been developed only to be struck down following the election of a government of a different ideological stripe keen to jettison the institutions associated with a previous social democratic government.

Another type of economic action concerns new labour vehicles for effecting economic change and protecting jobs. The Quebec Federation of Labour was a pioneer in the creation of its Solidarity Fund in 1984. Operating as a registered retirement savings plan

(RRSP), this fund is designed to channel worker investment into the safeguarding and creation of jobs, primarily through risk capital (Fournier, 1991). This fund benefits from both federal and provincial government tax credits. The Working Ventures and Fondaction (CSN) funds have similar objectives. Several provincial governments have granted special tax recognition to such funds.

Political Action

Political action concerns the defence of the worker both as a wage earner and as a citizen. The importance of political activity as a dimension of union action was confirmed in the Supreme Court of Canada's 1991 landmark decision (*Lavigne* v. *Ontario Public Service Employees Union* (1991) 81 D.L.R. (4th) 545 (S.C.C.)).

Unions exhibit varying attitudes to the role of the market and the need for social changes. On the one hand, there is a commitment by some to *bread-and-butter* or *business unionism*: seeking the best deal possible for their members. On the other hand, many union leaders express a critical view of the workings of the market and argue for the promotion of social and political change as an integral part of union activity. Here we might distinguish between *social* and *social movement unionism* (Robinson, 1994, 1998; Pupo and White, 1994). As opposed to business unionism, both social and social movement unionism embrace a much wider definition of solidarity, i.e., that unions should defend all workers and not just their members. Moreover, both seek to promote the interests of the worker as citizen as well as wage earner and, in so doing, emphasize the importance of unions' political activity. However, the politics of social unionism, deeply rooted in the traditions of industrial unionism in Canada, are more likely to be expressed through a privileged relationship with a social democratic political party, such as the New Democratic Party (NDP), while the politics of social movement unionism are more typically outside of parliament, for example, public protests in coalition with social and community groups. Advocates of social movement unionism are likely to be critical of a narrow emphasis on electoral support for parliamentary social democratic parties and to accentuate the transformative potential of political conflict and public protest. All of these strains of thought coexist within most Canadian unions in one way or another but, at any given time, they will find particular expression so that a union comes to be known as more or less radical in its political activities. Union political involvement varies from no political activity at all to pressure-group tactics to influence the parliamentary or governmental process, direct partisan political action in favour of a particular political party, and coalition activity designed to work with other social groups towards common objectives.

Although most independent unions tend to reject partisan political activity, public-sector cutbacks have sparked many to engage in a much more public political role as increasingly severe restraints have been placed on their ability to bargain collectively (Panitch and Swartz, 1993). Indeed, the affiliation of some formerly independent unions to the CLC, notably the Ontario Secondary School Teachers' Federation in 1998, also highlights this trend. Nowhere is this increased emphasis on political activity more apparent than in the health sector, where nurses' unions have proved to be among the most militant unions in the country over the last decade (see Haiven, 1995). Similarly, the CSN in Quebec is engaged in a wide variety of political activities even though its statutes expressly forbid it to support a particular political party.

In contrast, many CLC affiliates have long maintained a close relationship with the New Democratic Party of Canada and its predecessor, the Cooperative Commonwealth Federation. From the election of 1979, the CLC became increasingly allied with the NDP. Indeed, this process was facilitated when some of the more conservative, business-oriented unions left the CLC to form the Canadian Federation of Labour at the beginning of the 1980s. Many, but not all, CLC affiliates are organically linked to the NDP. The NDP constitution provides for both individual and affiliated membership. Affiliated membership is available to organizations such as unions, farm groups, co-operatives, and women's organizations, and the cost of affiliated membership is generally at a lesser rate than individual membership. Affiliations give organizations direct representation on the different decision-making bodies of the NDP. Leaders of affiliated organizations such as the CAW and the Steelworkers participate actively in policy debates and the selection of leaders.

Both the NDP's distance from government at the federal level and its experience of government at the provincial level have put strains on the relationship between labour and the NDP that are similar to the problems observed between labour parties and union movements in many other countries. The relatively poor showing of the NDP in successive federal elections has led some union leaders to query whether a strong identification with the NDP is really an asset for the representation of their members' interests. Conversely, some in the NDP have wondered whether its alliance with the union movement is really an electoral asset and have promoted an alternative "Third Way," or middle-ground politics. The experience of the NDP government in Ontario in the first half of the 1990s and its implementation of social-contract legislation provides an especially good illustration of the tensions inherent in the relationship between organized labour and the NDP, as well as the gap that separates advocates of social and social movement unionism. The Ontario NDP government suspended free collective bargaining and enacted wage-restraint legislation in the public sector, causing many unions, including the Auto Workers, to withdraw support. Indeed, the tensions over this particular episode have spilled over into the rest of the decade and largely coloured the sometimes acrimonious discussions among Ontario union leaders about appropriate strategies to protest against the policies of subsequent Conservative governments. Nor are such strains unique to the NDP. Similar tensions were observed between Quebec labour unions and the Parti Québécois government of the 1970s and early 1980s, and these have continued through two mandates of the Parti Québécois government in the 1990s.

Unions in Canada have been involved in a variety of other political activities, most notably in coalitions with other groups, as they have sought to influence the outcome of public debates on a range of issues. Faced with the question of how to project the new labour market developments and the preoccupations of their new membership into the larger political and social arena, unions have sought to effect broader coalitions with other social groups.

Most important have been the successive debates on the free trade agreement with the United States and the North American Free Trade Agreement (NAFTA). During these debates, Canadian unions worked with many other social groups (Robinson, 1994). Similarly, some unions have shared platforms with other groups on questions such as the environment, equal rights, and international solidarity. A number of unions have also created special funds to assist their work in this domain. Steelworkers created their Humanity Fund to assist international development projects. The CAW's Social Justice Fund promotes worthy projects both in Canada and abroad. Many unions have, of course, long maintained an active civic and community role in philanthropic work such as the United Way. To cite but one of many examples, the UFCW invests considerable organizational resources in an annual fundraising campaign for research on leukemia.

CONCLUSIONS

This chapter has sought to portray the changing character of unions in Canada. Unions are obliged to come to terms with market changes, but the extent and the direction of adaptation is quite different from one union to another because of the emphasis on different goals.

These changes have been made in a context of relative success. Not only did union membership in Canada increase until the 1990s and then stabilize thereafter, but the labour movement has sought, however imperfectly, to adapt to the major environmental changes of the 1990s. Its strategies have included: increased emphasis on organizing the unorganized, notably through the shift of resources to organizing; the expression of new labour market identities, be they gender, ethnicity, sexual orientation, or otherwise, in policies and bargaining agenda; experimentation with new local structures that take better account of the changing nature of the workplace; attempts to equip union locals to deal with the challenges of workplace change through activist education and new specialist resources; increasing use of new technologies to communicate with members and the general public; an increasing public profile on political and social issues.

These developments presage a change to new union forms that take account of the broader trends in the economy and society. Just as we can now look back on the decline of craft unionism as the passing of an exclusive but effective organizational form, so too can we increasingly discern the limits of the industrial union model, which diffused in a wave of CIO-based organizing throughout Canada in the years of post-war industrial expansion. This model protected its particular membership, primarily male, mass-production workers, through the elaboration of collective agreements. These agreements regulated aspects of the job, while leaving broader questions of work organization in the realm of managerial prerogative. The jurisdiction of the industrial union model was restricted to particular industries, and its organizational form was focused on particular units, generally one agreement per local, with external solidarities being extended only as far as pattern bargaining required some kind of linkage with other units.

The real importance of the new service sector, the significance of workplace reorganization, the changes in union membership and practices, and the continuing mutations of previous organizational forms all point towards the emergence of new union structures. The future of Canadian unions very much depends on the development of these new models, their appeal to an increasingly heterogeneous workforce, and their success in dealing with the problems encountered by workers in their workplaces, their communities, and beyond.

Questions

1. Why did union membership in Canada grow so much until 1990 and then stagnate through the 1990s?

2. Discuss the growing divergence in union density between Canada and the United States. Is it likely to continue?

3. Describe the sectoral differences in the degree of unionization by industry in Canada and the challenges that these pose for unions.

4. How would you explain the basic structural choices that a potential union member has in regard to the type of union he or she might join?

5. How do changes in the larger economy have an impact on the definition of union jurisdictions?

6. What are the different possibilities for a union member to participate in the life of the union? Is the union inevitably an oligarchy?

7. How do you explain the bargaining priorities of national unions and the degree of success achieved?

8. Discuss different ways that Canadian unions have responded to economic restructuring and workplace organization, and the problems that might arise within union locals.

9. Why do unions become involved in political activity? Discuss the relative merits of a partisan as opposed to a non-partisan approach to political activity. Contrast business unionism with social unionism and social movement unionism.

10. What are the challenges for the traditional industrial union model that arise from the growth of employment in private services?

REFERENCES

AKYEAMPONG, E. B. 1997. "A Statistical Portrait of the Trade Union Movement." *Perspectives on Labour and Income*, Statistics Canada, Catalogue no. 75-001-XPE, 9, no. 4, pp. 45–54.

————. 1998. "The Rise of Unionization Among Women." *Perspectives on Labour and Income*, Statistics Canada, Catalogue no. 75-001-XPE, 10, no. 4, pp. 30–43.

————. 1999. "Unionization—An Update." *Perspectives on Labour and Income*, Statistics Canada, Catalogue no. 75-001-XPE, 11, no. 3, pp. 45–65.

BAIN, G. S. and R. PRICE. 1983. "Union Growth: Dimensions, Determinants, and Destiny," in *Industrial Relations in Great Britain*, edited by G. S. Bain. Oxford: Basil Blackwell, pp. 3–34.

BÉLANGER, J. and G. MURRAY. 1994. "Unions and Economic Restructuring." *Relations industrielles/Industrial Relations*, 49, pp. 648–656.

BETCHERMAN, G., K. McMULLEN, N. LECKIE, and C. CARON. 1994. *The Canadian Workplace in Transition*. Kingston: IRC Press.

BLOCK, R. 1993. "Unionization, Collective Bargaining and Legal Institutions in the United States and Canada." *Queen's Papers in Industrial Relations* (1993-4). Kingston: Queen's University Industrial Relations Centre.

BLS (Bureau of Labor Statistics). Annual. "Union Members in 1999." *Labor Force Statistics from the Current Population Survey—BLS*, News Releases, 19 January 2000, http://stats.bls.gov/newsrels.htm.

BOURQUE, R. and C. RIOUX. 1994. "Tendances récentes de la négociation collective dans l'industrie du papier au Québec." *Relations industrielles*, 49, pp. 730–749.

BRISKIN, L. and P. McDERMOTT, eds. 1993. *Women Challenging Unions: Feminism, Democracy and Militancy*. Toronto: University of Toronto Press.

BRONFENBRENNER, K., S. FRIEDMAN, R. W. HURD, R. A. OSWALD, and R. L. SEEBER, eds. 1998. *Organizing to Win: New Research on Union Strategies*. Ithaca: ILR Press.

BRUCE, P. G. 1989. "Political Parties and Labor Legislation in Canada and the US." *Industrial Relations*, 28, pp. 115–141.

CALURA. various years. *Annual Report of the Minister of Industry, Science and Technology under the Corporations and Labour Unions Returns Act, Part II—Labour unions*. Statistics Canada. Cat 71-202. Ottawa: Minister of Industry, Science and Technology. For 1999, see Mainville and Olineck.

CHAREST, J. 1999. "Articulation institutionnelle et orientations du système de formation professionnelle." *Relations industrielles/Industrial Relations*, 54, pp. 439–471.

CLEGG, H. A. 1976. *Trade Unionism Under Collective Bargaining*. Oxford: Basil Blackwell.

CLMPC (Canadian Labour Market and Productivity Centre). 1992. "The Role of Business-Labour Sectoral Initiatives in Economic Restructuring." *Quarterly Labour Market Productivity Review*, no. 1–2, pp. 26–38.

CORNISH, M. and L. SPINKS. 1994. *Organizing Unions*. Toronto: Second Story Press.

DION, G. 1986. *Dictionnaire canadien des relations du travail*, 2nd Edition. Québec: Presses de l'Université Laval.

FOURNIER, L. 1991. *Solidarité Inc.: Un nouveau syndicalisme créateur d'emplois*. Montréal: Éditions Québec/Amérique.

FREEMAN, R. B. 1990. "Canada and the World Labour Market to the Year 2000," in *Perspective 2000*, edited by K. Newton, T. Schweitzer, and J. Voyer. Ottawa: Supply and Services Canada, pp. 187–198.

FROST, A. 1997. "Labour Strategy and Workplace Restructuring: Lessons from Diverse Locals," in *Worker Representation in the Era of Trade Deregulation*, edited by R. Chaykowski, P.-A. Lapointe, G. Vallée, and A. Verma. Selected Papers from the XXXIIIrd Annual CIRA Conference. Quebec: Canadian Industrial Relations Association, pp. 131–142.

GUNDERSON, M. and A. SHARPE, eds. 1998. *Forging Business-Labour Partnerships*. Toronto: University of Toronto Press.

HAIVEN, L. 1995. "Industrial Relations in Health Care: Regulation, Conflict and Transition to the *Wellness Model*," in *Public Sector Collective Bargaining in Canada: Beginning of the End or End of the Beginning?* edited by G. Swimmer and M. Thompson. Kingston: IRC Press, pp. 236–271.

HEMMINGWAY, J. 1978. *Conflict and Democracy*. Oxford: Clarendon Press.

HRDC (Human Resources Development Canada—Workplace Information Directorate). Annual until 1999. *Directory of Labour Organizations in Canada*. Ottawa: Canadian Government Publishing.

———. 1999. *Directory of Labour Organizations in Canada*, http://labour-travail.hrdc-drhc.gc.ca.

HYMAN, R. 1971. *Marxism and the Sociology of Trade Unionism*. London: Pluto Press.

———. 1975. *Industrial Relations*. London: Macmillan.

ILO (International Labour Organization). 1997. *World Labour Report: Industrial Relations, Democracy and Stability*. Geneva, Switzerland: International Labour Office.

KAPLAN, W. 1987. *Everything That Floats*. Toronto: University of Toronto Press.

KRAHN, H. and G. S. LOWE. 1984. "Community Influences on Attitudes Towards Unions." *Relations industrielles/Industrial Relations*, 39, pp. 93–113.

KUMAR, P. 1993. *From Uniformity to Divergence: Industrial Relations in Canada and the United States*. Kingston: Queen's University, IRC Press, Industrial Relations Centre.

———. 1995. *Unions and Workplace Change in Canada*. Kingston: IRC Press.

KUMAR, P., G. MURRAY, and S. SCHETAGNE. 1998a. "Adapting to Change: Union Priorities in the 1990s." *Workplace Gazette*, 1, no. 3, pp. 84–98.

———. 1998b. "Workplace Change in Canada: Union Perception of Impacts, Responses and Support Systems." *Workplace Gazette*, 1, no. 4, pp. 75–87.

LABOUR CANADA, BUREAU OF LABOUR INFORMATION. various years. *Directory of Labour Organizations in Canada*. Ottawa: Minister of Supply and Services Canada.

LÉVESQUE, C. and G. MURRAY. 1998. "La régulation paritaire du changement à l'épreuve de la mondialisation." *Relations industrielles/Industrial Relations*, 53, pp. 90–122.

LFS. Annual. *Labour Force Survey*. Ottawa: Statistics Canada. Catalogue 71-201.

LIPSET, S. M. and N. MELTZ. 1997. "Canadian and American Attitudes Toward Work and Institutions." *Perspectives on Work*, 1, no. 3, pp. 14–19.

LIPSIG-MUMMÉ, C. 1998. "The Language of Organizing: Trade Union Strategy in International Perspective." York University, Centre for Research on Work and Society, Working Paper Series.

MAINVILLE, D. and C. OLINECK. 1999. *Unionization: A Retrospective*. Statistics Canada. Supplement. Catalogue no. 75-001-XPE (Summer).

MARTIN, D. 1995. *Thinking Union: Activism and Education in Canada's Labour Movement*. Toronto: Between the Lines.

MICHELS, R. 1962. *Political Parties*. New York: Collier Books, first published 1911.

MURRAY, G. 1991. "Exceptionalisme canadien? L'évolution récente du syndicalisme au Canada." *La Revue de l'IRES*, 7, pp. 81–105.

———. 1998. "Steeling for Change: Organization and Organizing in Two USWA Districts in Canada," in *Organizing to Win: New Research on Union Strategies*, edited by K. Bronfenbrenner, S. Friedman, R. W. Hurd, R. A. Oswald, and R. L. Seeber. Ithaca: ILR Press, pp. 320–338.

MURRAY, G., C. LÉVESQUE, N. ROBY, and S. LEQUEUX. 1999. "Isolation or Integration? The Relationship between Local and National Union in the Context of Globalization," in *Globalization and Patterns of Labour Resistance*, edited by J. Waddington. London: Mansell, pp. 160–191.

MURRAY, G. et P. VERGE. 1999. *La représentation syndicale: Visage juridique actuel et futur*. Quebec: Les Presses de l'Université Laval.

NISSEN, B., ed. 1999. *Which Direction for Organized Labor? Essays on Organizing, Outreach and Internal Transformations*. Detroit: Wayne State University Press.

PANITCH, L. and D. SWARTZ. 1993. *The Assault on Trade Union Freedoms.* Toronto: Garamond Press.

PIORE, M. 1983. "Can the American Labor Movement Survive Re-Gomperization?" in *Proceedings of the Thirty-Fifth Annual Meeting*, edited by B. D. Dennis. Madison: Industrial Relations Research Association, pp. 30–39.

PONAK, A. and D. G. TARAS. 1997. "Right to Work Study: Submission to the Alberta Economic Development Authority Joint Review Committee," mimeo. Alberta Economic Development Authority.

PUPO, N. and J. WHITE. 1994. "Union Leaders and the Economic Crisis: Responses to Restructuring." *Relations industrielles/Industrial Relations*, 49, pp. 821–845.

RIDDELL, W. C. 1993. "Unionization in Canada and the United States: A Tale of Two Countries," in *Small Differences That Matter: Labor Markets and Income Maintenance in Canada and the United States*, edited by D. Card and R. B. Freeman. Chicago: The University of Chicago Press, pp. 109–148.

RINEHART, J., C. HUXLEY, and D. ROBERTSON. 1997. *Just Another Car Factory: Lean Production and its Discontents.* Ithaca: ILR Press.

ROBINSON, I. 1994. "NAFTA, Social Unionism, and Labour Movement Power in Canada and the United States." *Relations industrielles/Industrial Relations*, 49, pp. 657–695.

———. 1998. "Réactions des centrales syndicales nord-américaines à la restructuration néolibérale," in *L'intégration économique en Amérique du Nord et les relations industrielles*, edited by R. Blouin and A. Giles. Sainte-Foy: Les Presses de l'Université Laval, pp. 119–148.

ROSE, J. B. and G. N. CHAISON. 1990. "New Measures of Union Organizing in the United States and Canada." *Industrial Relations*, 29, pp. 457–468.

ROYAL COMMISSION ON THE ECONOMIC UNION AND DEVELOPMENT PROSPECTS FOR CANADA. 1985. *Report.* 3 vols. Ottawa: Minister of Supply and Services Canada.

THOMPSON, M. and A. A. BLUM. 1983. "International Unionism in Canada: The Move to Local Control." *Industrial Relations,* 22, pp. 71–86.

TROY, L. 1992. "Convergence in International Unionism, etc.: The Case of Canada and the USA." *British Journal of Industrial Relations*, 30, pp. 1–43.

VERGE, P. and G. MURRAY. 1991. *Le droit et les syndicats.* Sainte-Foy: Presses de l'Université Laval.

WEILER, P. 1984. "Striking a new balance: Freedom of contract and the prospects for union representation." *Harvard Law Review*, 98, pp. 351–420.

WELLS, D. 1996. "New Dimensions for Labor in a Post-Fordist World," in *North American Auto Unions in Crisis*, edited by W. C. Green and E. J. Yanarella. Albany: State University of New York Press, pp. 191–208.

WHITE, J. 1993. *Sisters and Solidarity: Women and Unions in Canada.* Toronto: Thompson Educational Publishing, Inc.

WORKPLACE INFORMATION DIRECTORATE (Human Resources Development Canada). 1999. "Union Membership in Canada—1999." *Workplace Gazette*, 2, no. 3, pp. 61–62.

YATES, C. 1998. "Unity and Diversity: Challenges to an Expanding Canadian Autoworkers Union." *Canadian Review of Sociology and Anthropology*, 35, pp. 93–118.

CHAPTER 5

The Management of Industrial Relations

Mark Thompson[1]

Jennifer Tremblay is the industrial relations director of a large Toronto-based manufacturing firm that employs about 4000 production workers and support staff. Early in 1993, Tremblay was assigned to a corporate task force to plan the restructuring of production facilities. The company was preparing to build a new plant in a rural area, a so-called "green-field" site. At the same time, a number of older facilities were being closed or modernized. Reductions in the number of employees at these locations were inevitable. Virtually all blue-collar employees in the firm were represented by unions, most of them by a large international union. Relations between labour and management had been uneven—several large strikes, but also periods of co-operation when productivity was quite high.

The first dilemma Tremblay faced was what to do about union representation at the new site, code-named "Plant '96" in the company. Basically, Tremblay saw three options for management. One possibility would be to do nothing and let the employees decide on unionization.

Perhaps Plant '96 could operate for several years before the union was able to organize the new labour force, most of whom would come from nearby small towns and have little experience with unionization. Probably the end result would be union certification. A second option was to try to change the outcome and prevent the union from winning over the workers. This would be a subtle campaign. The company would avoid hiring people with obvious union backgrounds, pay union wage levels from the first day, and engender a sense of community among the workers. The company would lose no opportunity to inform employees of the benefits of staying nonunion. Tremblay felt that the dominant union in the company would see through the scheme. To attain operational efficiencies quickly, some skilled workers would have to be offered transfers from one of the existing plants. These employees often were active in their local unions and would expect union representation. Finally, many of these tactics bordered on violation of the provincial labour relations act, and the company risked litigation at a time when it was concentrating on getting initial returns for its investment.

Tremblay chose a third option. She approached the international union and offered voluntary recognition at the new plant. As soon as a core group of employees were at work, the company would recognize the union to represent them and future employees and begin negotiating a first collective agreement. However, the collective agreement would be a new document, not borrowed from the existing plants, where many traditional practices and work rules were embedded. This strategy would save the union the expense of an organizing campaign and avoid the divisiveness of pitting the company against the union when co-operation was most necessary. It would also mean that bargaining could deal with the issues of the new plant as they arose. Tremblay was also thinking about the other plants. The planned reductions would be painful for all concerned. The union had the right to resist these changes. If the company were seen as hostile to the union at Plant '96, it could hardly expect co-operation from its unions elsewhere.

Five years later, the collective agreement at Plant '96 was superior to any other in the company from the employer's perspective. Some employees facing layoffs at the older plants transferred to Plant '96 and were enthusiastic about making the operations successful. Some local union leaders resented the cutbacks in their members' jobs, but the international used its influence to avoid confrontations. Overall, the company cut its labour force by 30 percent without major conflict or litigation. Tremblay was convinced her choice had initiated a new era in labour relations for the entire firm.[2]

The array of information and materials on the labour movement and the role of government in Canadian industrial relations is extensive and studied widely. Yet little attention has been paid to the third actor in industrial relations—the employer. This omission is being remedied, spurred in part by developments in the 1980s and 1990s, which focused attention on management's role as a proactive force in industrial relations.[3] As the opening vignette illustrates, management has many strategic options for carrying out industrial relations functions. This chapter provides an overview of the industrial relations policies and practices of unionized Canadian companies, relying on published and unpublished data collected since interest in the role of management became more prominent in Canadian industrial relations. The focus of this chapter will be the management of employment issues in an environment that is at least partially unionized. Human resource management texts treat the employment relationship in nonunion settings.

HR Today Online: www.hrtoday.com/

Managers in any organization must deal with many issues, ranging from the basic strategy of the organization to the implementation of decisions by directors or senior executives. When employees are unionized, or unionization is probable for the organization, labour relations problems must be addressed. Despite their importance to the organization, these issues are seldom mentioned either in the literature of management or in public discussions. Company industrial relations statements tend to be vague and positive, dominated by sentiments such as, "People are our most important asset," or "We need to build more positive relations with our unions," without providing any specifics on management's intentions. These statements cover a wide variety of management policies, ranging from open and vigorous hostility to unionism to acceptance and co-operation with labour organizations.

During the decades following World War II, steady economic growth and relatively low unemployment strengthened labour's bargaining power. Most employers initially concentrated on resisting unions. When labour was successful in winning bargaining rights, management's role was to oppose unions' demands in negotiations. Above all, management of the industrial relations function concentrated on maintaining labour peace. For many companies, labour peace came by granting concessions to unions, often after a strike or difficult bargaining. Ironically, many unionized employers came to rely on advanced human resources policies that resulted from collective agreement provisions, such as fringe benefits or training programs, as tools for recruiting and retaining employees. Other firms concentrated on building positive relations with their unions, usually based on stable employment at competitive rates of pay. Consultation and frequent training opportunities also contributed to a positive industrial relations climate. Finally, some employers never achieved peace, resisting union demands, enduring frequent stoppages, and seeking legislative changes to weaken unions.

With some exceptions, few breakthroughs in employee relations originated from management innovation.[4] Instead, labour maintained the initiative. Unions negotiated the first pensions for non-managerial employees; they raised wages substantially in many industries, promoted occupational health and safety, shortened hours of work, secured medical insurance before government plans appeared, and brought concepts of justice into many workplaces.

After the recession of the early 1980s and a decline in the rate of economic growth, the balance of power between labour and management shifted. In an increasingly market-driven economic climate, many Canadian firms found themselves to be high-cost producers compared with their foreign (or nonunion Canadian) competitors. In addition to reducing overhead costs, eliminating less profitable operations, and refocusing their business strategies, many companies looked for a competitive advantage in their management of human resources. Senior managers wanted to integrate human resource strategies with the firm's general business strategy; management was less likely to merely react to labour's initiatives. Conservative commentators also pointed to the United States, where labour's influence declined dramatically, as a model that Canada should emulate.

These developments focused attention on labour relations as a source of competitive advantage (or disadvantage). During the 1990s, for instance, General Motors in both the United States and Canada had several strikes, while Ford, its largest competitor, enjoyed harmonious labour relations. Ford proved that it could produce successful products on a profitable basis partly because of its success with labour relations, which gave it a competitive advantage over General Motors. By contrast, Eastern Airlines, once an important carrier on the east coast of the United States and in central Canada, collapsed, largely because management and the employees' unions could not agree on how to adapt to the deregulation of the industry.

The major source of data for this chapter is the unpublished results of a sample of 106 major Canadian firms in the private sector that engage in collective bargaining in a substantial way (see Thompson, 1995). Through interviews conducted throughout the 1990s, senior industrial relations executives provided information on many aspects of industrial relations in their firms. The firms ranged in size from 950 to 57,000 employees.

INDUSTRIAL RELATIONS AND MANAGEMENT DECISIONS

Industrial relations considerations affect management decisions in a variety of ways. Overall, industrial relations linkages to specific corporate decisions are strongest in investment in new plants. Research has shown that about half of unionized companies consider industrial relations an important or dominant factor in the decision as to whether to invest or not and in the choice of location. For another quarter of companies, labour matters have no impact, and for the remainder, industrial relations, though considered, is not significant.

There is variation by economic sector, however. The two dominant factors for locating new plants in resource industries, for instance, are the location and quality of a resource (e.g., mineral deposits) and the financial structure (interest rates and taxes). Firms in the service sector, such as large retailers or publishers, locate their operations near their markets, but industrial relations clearly can play a role. When Wal-Mart—a militantly anti-union company in the United States—expanded into Canada through the acquisition of Woolco Stores, it purchased almost all of the nonunion stores but did not buy any of the unionized sites. (Wal-Mart denied that union status was a factor in its decision, stating that it acquired the most profitable locations). Manufacturing companies, which often have the ability to choose among locations for new plants or the expansion of current operations, were often quite careful in their analyses of industrial relations issues. In deciding whether to invest in a new plant, rather than upgrade an existing plant, factors include the current industrial relations climate in the plant, the provisions of the collective agreement there, and the attitude of the union representing workers. Plants where industrial relations are perceived to be poor are clearly at a disadvantage in attracting new investment from their corporate owners. The tactic of building new facilities in rural areas is partly driven by the belief that people in rural areas are less likely to be attracted to unions than their urban counterparts.

For decisions involving adoption of new technology or the reorganization of the company, industrial relations issues are either not significant in major corporate decisions, or management is confident of its ability to deal with these matters successfully. Only one-third of companies indicate that labour relations are significant in these types of decisions, and even fewer consider labour relations when purchasing new components and supplies. It should be noted that, while research has found that the presence of unions was not a significant factor in determining the rate of technological change, they can affect the way in which these changes took place (Betcherman, 1991; Betcherman et al, 1994a).

 Construction Labour Relations Association (Alberta): www.clra.org

MANAGEMENT INDUSTRIAL RELATIONS STRATEGIES

Few Canadian companies that engage in collective bargaining have formal "industrial relations strategies," in the sense of well-articulated policies governing organizational decisions. Instead, employers operate with distinctive sets of principles that guide management policies and behaviours (Purcell, 1987). Although a company's principles may not be stated in writing, industrial relations managers know them quite well and are able to relate specific decisions to the firm's general position. For convenience, in this chapter the combination of principles that guide an employer's industrial relations functions will be called a "strategy."

Firms vary enormously in the extent to which they incorporate industrial relations strategies within their broader human resources policies and larger general corporate strategy. Corporate industrial relations strategies typically evolve over time. Historically, most employers have reacted to the possible unionization of their employees negatively. They still hire lawyers to help them resist certification within the law. The degree of opposition to unionization can be related to the basic human resources position of the firm or industry, experience with unionization, or the ideology of controlling shareholders.

Thus, some employers in the fast-food industry hire young workers with limited skills, set starting pay at or near the minimum wage, offer few opportunities for advancement, and expect high employee turnover. The introduction of a union would upset this system, as organized workers would be expected to press for higher wages, job security, and other possibilities to improve their situation. It is not surprising that McDonald's and Tim Horton's, for instance, vigorously resist unions whenever they appear in one of their franchises (Skogan, 1999).

Public utilities have a much different environment. They employ highly skilled workers who must provide service under all conditions. High skill levels and stable employment fit well with a well-paid unionized workforce. For other firms, the philosophy of management is a factor. The "Big Three" automakers accept unions in their assembly plants, after resisting unionism in the 1930s. In fact, their production strategies may include consultation with unions as a normal management process. By contrast, Magna, the largest auto-parts manufacturer, resists unionism strongly because of the ideology of its principal shareholder.

Constraints on Management Strategies

According to management theories, senior managers are presumed to have considerable latitude in establishing or changing their strategies in most fields, constrained principally by markets or legal regulation. The same flexibility does not always exist for industrial relations issues. Management's freedom of action is always limited by the desire and ability of its unions to resist employer initiatives. Managers may be unsuccessful in persuading their employees' representatives that changes to corporate policies are desirable. Unions are relatively independent organizations, often with the resources to affect management policies when they choose. Even nonunion firms must carefully assess the "union threat" posed by any strategy that works to the disadvantage of the employees. Employees may join a union in order to protect themselves against what they see as unreasonable change in their wages and conditions of work, especially in industries or regions where unionism is well entrenched.

Management Archive (free database): ursus.jun.alaska.edu/
A managerial database to find archived research on various issues.

Unionized firms have to work within the limits their collective agreements impose because these contracts cannot be altered without the consent of the union. The most obvious example would be the problems a firm might face trying to reduce wage levels or to displace workers with a new technology that would enable it to adopt a low-price strategy. This firm might expect its workers to resist these moves vigorously. Depending on the relative bargaining power of the parties, the unionized labour force might thwart management's plans completely.

On the other hand, unions differ in their willingness to co-operate with management plans. The Canadian Auto Workers successfully resisted General Motors's efforts to introduce teamwork concepts into its auto-assembly plants (Kumar, 1999). Other unions have accepted job losses or a reduction in their contractual rights in order to gain rights to participate in joint committees to plan changes in the employer's organization. Thus, Canadian Airlines International would not have survived through the 1990s without the co-operation of its unionized employees, who exchanged wage cuts for equity in the company, a process not available to most nonunion companies. In personal interviews, many Canadian industrial relations executives referred to major strikes as turning points for industrial relations in their firms. Some of these disputes caused management to re-examine its position and promoted improvements in labour relations. In other words, labour resistance caused employers to change their strategies or to formulate new strategies that would not incite labour discord.

Legal considerations also influence industrial relations strategies. Labour relations statutes constrain employer tactics designed to resist unionization or to eliminate unions where they exist. By law, employers must recognize and bargain with unions selected by the majority of employees to represent them. Employers have almost no voice in their employees' choice of a union. Once a worksite is unionized, both union and management are obligated to negotiate in good faith and make every reasonable effort to reach agreement. Such agreements are legally binding, and the law in most jurisdictions requires that they provide for arbitration as the final step of a grievance procedure. Thus, management initiatives in areas covered by collective agreements are subject to challenge through these grievance procedures, further limiting an employer's options (see Chapter 12).

Legislation imposes other constraints on management. Unionized firms are not free to negotiate directly with their employees to implement a strategy. The union is the employees' bargaining agent, and management cannot sidestep the union. Some firms try to evade the law by favouring one union over another, but that process generally carries high risks. Nor can management close an operation and move the work elsewhere without incurring liabilities, which may include retention of the union and collective agreement.

The degree to which unions are established in a firm is a significant factor in management's attitude toward industrial relations. For example, Petro-Canada, formerly a federally owned company, purchased a number of unionized facilities in its early years. Although many other firms in the petroleum industry operate without unions or have employee committees that fulfill some of the roles of unions, Petro-Canada built its policies around the acceptance of unions in the unionized locations it purchased (Taras and Ponak, 1999). When Stelco reduced the scale of its operations, it sought to work co-operatively with the United Steelworkers (who represented almost all of its hourly employees) and succeeded in most cases (Frost and Verma, 1999). By contrast, a number of manufacturing firms, Honda, for example, have built new plants in rural areas, where union influence traditionally is weak. They operated on a nonunion basis (with many of the features of a unionized environment), relying on progressive human resource practices and adroit managers to remain nonunion. Employees at a number of these plants eventually were unionized. Firms with a history of dealings with unions accepted this change, while Japanese firms, unaccustomed to dealing with independent unions, have resisted unionization strongly virtually everywhere in North America.

A major factor in determining the ability of an employer to act strategically is the relative bargaining power of the parties. In the early 1990s, the balance of power at the bargaining table clearly shifted toward management. High rates of unemployment, a decline in labour militancy, plant closures, deregulation, and free trade agreements with the United States and Mexico, all combined to increase the ability of employers to resist union pressures and to obtain their own objectives in collective bargaining. In such an environment, managers were able to negotiate wage freezes or even reductions. Governments in most regions of the country implemented deficit- and debt-reduction practices that led to concessionary bargaining and layoffs in the public sector, further adding to this management advantage. However, an upswing in the economy in the late 1990s lowered unemployment rates and improved the bargaining power of unions, and as a result, higher wage settlements and a strengthening of union bargaining power should appear early in the new decade.

Many Canadian firms have changed their fundamental approach to industrial relations depending upon their circumstances—from confrontation to co-operation or from acceptance of unionism to resistance. For example, Alcan experienced bitter strikes at two major operations (located in British Columbia and Quebec) in the same year. These stoppages, which included sabotage and minor violence, cost the company heavily. The firm maintained operations at a reduced level by using supervisors, an action that antagonized strikers and led to violence. After the stoppages ended, senior management concluded that it had provoked the strikes by making excessive demands on its two unions, and that a more patient and co-operative approach was necessary. The unions involved accepted this new approach. Within a few years, labour relations at both sites had become quite co-operative, even in the face of massive reductions in employment and volatile product markets (Bélanger, 1999).

In summary, the constraints on industrial relations strategy include:

- union power
- union co-operativeness
- union militancy, especially strike propensity
- degree of unionization within the firm
- labour laws
- provisions of the collective agreement

ELEMENTS OF AN INDUSTRIAL RELATIONS STRATEGY

The analysis of industrial relations strategies in Canada is still relatively new. An examination of our survey data and secondary sources shows the common elements of most strategies are: management attitude towards unions, compensation, and workplace practices (Kochan, McKersie, and Capelli, 1984).

The first element is the employer's attitude towards the unionization of its employees, both in terms of existing relationships with labour and the organization of new units. Is there a strong hostility towards unions? If so, the firm is unlikely to share information with unions, to develop consultative mechanisms, or to conduct joint union–management initiatives. The firm might even resist unionization of unorganized plants or try to remove unions where they exist. If the attitude is more accepting of unions, then greater potential exists for more harmonious relationships.

A second element relates to compensation and how wages and employee benefits compare with those of other firms. Some firms are leaders in the labour market and, presumably, find that this position enables them to hire more selectively, avoid labour strife, and retain their workforce. A stable labour force in turn makes investment in training workers feasible. Others prefer a low wage rate and choose to accept high turnover. Training is minimal in these firms, although management may cultivate an image of caring for employee welfare in order to legitimize management authority (Purcell, 1987).

Third, a strategy can be discerned by the manner in which a firm conducts its affairs in the workplace. Has management sought a constructive relationship with its union, has it ignored the union at this level, or has it tried to limit or undermine unions' influence? While most managers have a preference to run union-free workplaces, the issue is whether the firm is translating this preference into managerial practices.

Workplace Today (IR and HRM magazine):
www.workplace.ca/ipm_today.html

Four Strategies towards Unions

Four general strategies for dealing with unions apply to most companies.

1. The *union acceptance* strategy means that the company accepts the inevitability of unionism and collective bargaining for some or all of its operations. These companies may prefer not to have unions, but remain neutral when a union attempts to organize one of their nonunion operations, partly for philosophical reasons, but also because of their broader strategy of working with their unions to the extent possible. Within the framework of collective bargaining, the company seeks to negotiate the most favourable settlements possible.

2. The *union resistance* strategy exists in partially unionized firms that seek to limit the spread of unions to the unorganized parts of their workforce, although they accept the legitimacy of their existing unions. They normally oppose union organizing campaigns within their organizations vigorously. They normally extend terms and conditions of employment negotiated by unions to nonunion employees. This tactic is designed to discourage the spread of unionism by informing employees that improvements in employment are due to management initiative, not union pressure.

3. A third strategy can be called *union removal*. The basic goal of companies using this strategy is to eliminate unions where they exist in their operations. These employers resist negotiating any collective agreements that give unionized employees better conditions than are already provided for nonunion workers. They do this to emphasize the minimal role a union can play. They engage in extensive and continuing campaigns to discourage union activity among their nonunion workers and resist any attempt by unions to organize their employees.

4. Companies that are not unionized but fear that a union may gain a foothold in their organizations may follow a *union substitution/avoidance* strategy. They establish their own forms of representation, designed to make their employees regard unions as unnecessary or inferior to management-sponsored bodies.

Union Acceptance

The best evidence available indicates that the majority of Canadian companies where unions already exist practise the union acceptance strategy. Our survey of 106 private-sector companies with some unionized employees found that 71 percent regarded negotiating the best possible collective agreement as the primary objective of their industrial relations policy. Only 9 percent reported that they concentrated on limiting the influence or spread of unions where they existed. The remaining companies had multiple goals, the most common combination being to negotiate the best possible agreements and to limit the influence or spread of unions. No company reported that its primary goal was removing unions where they existed, and only 3 percent of the companies included the removal of unions with another goal (Thompson, 1995). Another survey of 161 unionized private-sector firms conducted between 1992 and 1994 found similar results. A majority of employers reported that they had taken a tough stance in bargaining in the past decade. About 20 percent reported that they had obtained reductions in wages, benefits, or negotiated restrictions on their authority. Only 9 percent stated that their objective was the reduction or elimination of union influence, and 17 percent had the policy of active avoidance of further unionization (Godard, 1997). At the same time, union acceptance rarely goes as far as enthusiastic co-operation or co-determination, as it does in some European countries.

Inco is one example of the union acceptance strategy. In some respects, the company had little choice. All of its major production facilities are unionized. Labour has a history of militancy in the company. Nonetheless, Inco was able to reduce its employment sharply, by 55 percent between 1980 and 1985, while making substantial improvements in the conduct of labour relations. The parties became more co-operative. Joint consultation grew in scope and importance. New job classifications increased flexibility and productivity. Consultation over job security was incorporated in the collective agreement (Chaykowski, 1999). Stelco is another heavily unionized company that practises union acceptance. Stelco built a new plant in the 1980s and recognized the United Steelworkers, the union at its other operations, before construction was completed. The company did insist, however, on negotiating a new collective agreement for the plant (Frost and Verma, 1999).

Union Resistance

Nevertheless, few Canadian companies are enthusiastic about unions. In the survey of 106 companies, 71 percent preferred not to have a union or opposed unionization actively during an organizing campaign. The obvious question is: "How do Canadian companies react to the prospect of unionization?" The most common answer to this question was: "We try to manage well enough to make a union unnecessary, but we respect our employees' choice if they select one." Companies often attempt to keep unions at bay and attribute any union organizing victories to managerial errors, or local conditions. Exhibit 5.1 illustrates an extreme version of this tendency.

It is noteworthy that most companies already unionized to a substantial degree *do not* oppose unionization actively. By contrast, in the United States, most employers vigorously resist union organizing campaigns, although resistance is less when 40 percent or more of their employees are already unionized. The attitude of many nonunion companies is quite different. Eaton's and the Canadian Imperial Bank of Commerce are two examples of companies that have resorted to various tactics to prevent unionization.

EXHIBIT 5.1

KODAK: KEEPING UNIONS AT BAY

Kodak managers attributed the absence of unions to the company's high pay and good supervision... "We have a reputation of very high standards and very good industrial relations." The implication of this remark was clear. At Kodak, *management* saw to it that the employees got a fair deal, and if a union came in, it was management's fault. For that reason, Kodak executives were embarrassed and their pride badly hurt when a small chemical union organized a Kodak plant outside Toronto shortly after World War II. This was the only Kodak facility in North America ever to be unionized. Since the plant had the same personnel policies as other Kodak units, [the head of IR for Kodak] had to rationalize the Canadian experience by blaming a local plant manager for his "stubbornness and arbitrariness."

Source: Jacoby, 1997, p. 86.

Canadian corporate policies differ from those of American companies. Most American firms probably fall into the union resistance or removal categories. Which path do American companies operating in Canada follow? It is frequently assumed that American companies retain their industrial relations policies when they operate in Canada. In fact, our data showed that the aggressive anti-union practices so popular in the United States are rarely imported into Canada by unionized companies.

Most industrial relations executives of foreign-owned firms report that their head offices have little or no influence on their activities. Management at the foreign headquarters wants to be informed of major events, such as strikes, but seldom dictates policies or practices in its Canadian affiliate. Industrial relations managers normally report to senior management in Canada. General Motors of Canada, for instance, has a Canadian board of directors, including outsiders and senior managers. The vice president of personnel reports to the board of directors in Canada (Kumar, 1999). The manager of another American-owned firm that is almost entirely nonunion in the United States but about 35 percent unionized in Canada declared, "We play by the rules where we operate. In the United States, there are no rules. Here rules exist, and we follow them." No significant differences in industrial relations related to the nationality of the parent company appeared either. In other words, for unionized companies, US, British, and European owners tend to follow much the same policies as their Canadian counterparts (Thompson, 1995). In the United States, a similar pattern has been observed, that is, foreign-owned companies follow local patterns of industrial relations. Ironically, Canadian firms are more likely to intervene in the industrial relations function of their American subsidiaries than owners from other nations (Jedel and Kujawa, 1976).

A case study of ABB, a Swiss-Swedish multinational enterprise that produces electrical equipment in 17 countries reinforces these findings. The company respects national differences in its employment relations. Increased competition in the product market has caused ABB to adopt central policies on common computer software, improved design, and common production methods. Employment relations, however, including the role of employee committees, expanded training, and the role of national collective agreements, all varied among plants in different nations (Bray and Lansbury, 1998).

Union Removal

While none of the large unionized companies surveyed for this chapter had a union removal strategy, there was evidence of this strategy in other firms. The most common employer tactic is to drag out negotiations for its unionized operations. While bargaining is going on, nonunion workers receive wage increases. The employer then informs the unionized bargaining units of the corporate "pattern" and, in negotiations, refuses to offer any terms superior to those already in place. When the number of unionized employees is small, a large employer can hold out in bargaining and through a strike to achieve its ultimate objective, the removal of its union.

Aided by the small size of individual branches and high turnover of union support-ers, chartered banks had such a strategy from 1979 to 1983 (Brody et al, 1993). The Canadian Imperial Bank of Commerce had set the tone of industrial relations for its em-ployees when it engaged in a massive propaganda campaign against unionism. The Canada Labour Relations Board found the employer had committed so many unfair labour practices that the president of the bank was required to write a letter to each em-ployee apologizing and expressing the bank's willingness to abide by the law. Despite such measures, unionism basically disappeared in the banking industry.

In the early 1980s, unions certified six branches of Eaton's Department Store in Ontario, after a 26-month wage freeze and substantial layoffs. Management engaged in an advertis-ing campaign, urging its employees to reject union representation. It asked its employees if they wanted the same reputation as the Auto Workers or Canada Post. When the company refused to negotiate a first collective agreement, a six-month strike followed. One of the four Eaton brothers who owned the chain crossed the picket line to encourage workers to follow his lead. After six months, the union capitulated. It accepted a first agreement with the same wage increase the company had unilaterally granted to its other employees (McQueen, 1998). Amazingly, the Ontario Labour Relations Board concluded that the unilateral wage increases were not motivated by a desire to stimulate decertification petitions.[5] Eaton's ob-tained the result it wanted. Employees in all six stores abandoned their union. In Manitoba, the labour relations board imposed a first contract for a Brandon branch. The company then dismissed half of the employees and demanded concessions from the union. By the end of the decade, these bargaining units, too, had decertified (Palmer, 1992). When Eaton's declared bankruptcy in 1999, employees had no representation during the restruc-turing of the company's assets, and received only legally-required severance pay.

The first McDonald's franchise to unionize in North America was in Squamish, British Columbia in 1998 (see the opening vignette in Chapter 1). The labour move-ment hailed this victory, but it was short lived. The employer launched three separate legal challenges after the union arrived, two of them asserting that workers 19 years of age or less (a majority of McDonald's employees) were "infants" under the law and could not apply for union membership or authorize collection of union dues.[6] In the third challenge, anti-union employees, most of whom made slightly more than the minimum wage, also appeared before the board, represented by a lawyer, to contest the union's ap-plication for certification. The union was successful before the labour relations board, but ultimately lost the support of its members. After 10 months, the Canadian Auto Workers were unsuccessful in negotiating a collective agreement. Some supporters had resigned their jobs. A majority of the remaining workers voted to decertify the union.

Firms without unions, or that follow strategies of union removal or union substitu-tion, often use written surveys to measure employees' views on a variety of subjects. For instance, a large employer in the service sector has unions at a majority of its locations, but strongly resists any union organizing campaigns at new sites and existing nonunion sites. It commissions attitude surveys from time to time in its nonunion establishments to guide its human resource policies.

Union Substitution/Avoidance

While data on the extent of union substitution policies are not readily available, a hand-ful of published accounts describe this strategy. The petroleum industry has several ex-amples of these policies. Imperial Oil has relied upon "joint industrial councils (JICs)" as part of a general strategy to discourage unionization since 1919. Other elements in-clude slightly higher wage scales and generous employee benefits—which are not nego-tiated with unions at any locations (Taras, 1997). JICs were introduced into the Canadian oil industry through the influence of William Lyon Mackenzie King, Canada's first minister of labour and later prime minister. The councils consist of equal numbers of managers (selected) and employees (elected by their peers) who meet regularly to dis-cuss health and safety, recreation, production issues, and occasional grievances (Taras, 1994, 2000; Boone, 2000).

Petro-Canada has "Employee Management Advisory Committees" (EMACs) at several of its nonunion operations. These joint committees meet semi-annually to discuss griev-ances and production issues. Employees receive an information booklet outlining the structure and the powers of the EMAC and containing several other provisions com-monly found in collective agreements, with the notable exceptions of seniority rights, pro-motion criteria, job security, and a formal grievance procedure (Taras and Ponak, 1999).

About 30 percent of employees in the petroleum industry are covered by formal nonunion representation schemes. Despite this substantial presence, the policy has draw-backs. Systems such as JICs consume a great deal of management time and make the em-ployer vulnerable to minor employee pressure tactics and the union threat. Imperial Oil unilaterally cancelled one JIC, and its workers cancelled another at a second location. At Petro-Canada, EMACs have been the basis of successful union certifications (Taras, 1994), and at Imperial Oil an important site rejected the JIC in favour of a large national union (Taras and Copping, 1998).

Since the 1930s, Dofasco, a steel producer located in Hamilton, Ontario, has had a human resources strategy designed to prevent unionization by the United Steelworkers, which had organized the other major steel producers in Hamilton and elsewhere. Dofasco does not have a formal collective representation mechanism for soliciting em-ployees' views. However, it matches the wage rates negotiated by the United Steelworkers at nearby Stelco and adds a profit-sharing plan. It also sponsors social events and recre-ational activities for its employees. There is a concerted effort to foster a sense of com-munity among employees and heavy use of employee involvement plans (Storey, 1983; Harshaw, 2000).

These examples of union substitution strategies, combined with survey results of unionized firms, demonstrate that most Canadian companies would prefer to operate without a union. An equally significant conclusion is that most large companies that already engage in collective bargaining do not oppose union organization vigorously, allowing employees to decide whether they want union representation or not. Once a union is certified, most employers experienced in labour relations seek to negotiate the best collective agreement possible and have found that they can operate successfully in a unionized setting. Data discussed in Chapter 13 show that unionized firms are often more productive than nonunion firms. For large Canadian employers in this situation, the dominant strategy for dealing with unions is union acceptance.

Relative Compensation

All employers must be aware of labour market realities when selecting compensation levels for their employees. Firms whose wages fall below normal levels for the region in which they operate can expect to experience high turnover, employee dissatisfaction, and difficulties in recruiting. For some companies, the savings realized by holding wage costs down offset the disadvantages, especially when the labour force is unskilled. High-wage strategies offer the opposite benefits and costs. High-wage firms are preferred employers in many localities, so they have no difficulty in recruiting staff with strong qualifications. Turnover usually is low, although employee dissatisfaction can still be a problem if other elements of the employment relationship are deficient.

Unionized employers have difficulty pursuing a low-wage strategy, and even nonunion employers in an industry where unions operate also face problems with this policy. Nonetheless, low-wage firms do exist with and without unions. Where unions are present, workers can easily compare wages, and union members expect their unions to negotiate better compensation. Overall in Canada, union members tend to receive wages that are 10 to 25 percent higher than nonunion members in similar circumstances, although there can be considerable variation in the experience of specific work groups (see Chapter 13 on union effects). Apart from their bargaining power, unions bring information on wage levels in other firms to their members' attention, thereby introducing additional market pressures on management in wage determination. In the nonunion environment, employers share compensation data with each other, but typically conceal this information from their employees.

Unsurprisingly, compensation issues are important to managers. In a 1980 survey, Canadian industrial relations managers were asked to rank the importance of bargaining issues on a scale of one to four, with one being the least important. Ninety-five percent of the respondents ranked wage levels as either three or four in importance, and 73 percent also ranked wage administration (skill differentials, incentive pay, etc.) at the same level of importance (Godard and Kochan, 1982).

In my own survey of unionized companies in the 1990s, senior industrial relations executives were asked with which other firms they compared their wages and fringe benefits. Overwhelmingly, these companies compare their compensation to other firms in the same industry or sector. For example, manufacturing firms in Ontario look to other companies in the region facing similar labour market conditions when deciding the appropriate compensation levels for their employees. Naturally, their unions make similar comparisons, reinforcing industry wage patterns. A small proportion of firms compare their wages to other industries, in part because appropriate firms in the same industry may not be available or a single large firm dominates the industry in a region. No firms reported comparing their wages to those in the US or any other foreign country. Except in rare cases, when wage levels may determine the ability of a company to operate successfully, management decisions on appropriate wage rates are based on a combination of the firm's cost structure and the wages other firms pay in the same industry, especially their product market competitors.

Large unionized firms generally pay wages above the average for all firms in their region (Gunderson and Riddell, 1993). Two effects are at work: size and unionization. Overall, large firms pay higher wages than smaller ones, and unionized firms generally pay higher wages than nonunion firms. Interestingly, my survey found that only 40 percent of the firms believed that their compensation was higher than the average for their relevant comparison group in the same industry or region. Almost 55 percent believed their wages and fringes were average compared to other relevant employers. Previous surveys have found a high degree of satisfaction among unionized employers with collectively bargained wage rates (Godard and Kochan, 1982), suggesting that large unionized employers are content to be at or above the average for their industry. Except in rare circumstances, bargaining objectives do not include reducing wages below the levels of domestic competition. Indeed, private-sector wage rollbacks have never been a major feature of Canadian industrial relations, although governments have extracted wage reductions from public-sector employees. Private-sector employers rely on layoffs and changes in the organization of work to reduce labour costs.

Workplace Practices

Canadian employers initiated substantial changes in their operations during the 1990s. Large surveys have shown that almost half of unionized firms engage in some form of employee participation or consultation. Quality and performance-related programs also are popular (Betcherman et al, 1994b; Smith, 1993). Profit sharing is used less often by unionized companies for employees represented by unions (Betcherman et al, 1994b). New initiatives took place alongside traditional and long-standing union–management consultation in such matters as health and safety and technological change.

Definitions of workplace change vary, so direct comparison across firms is difficult. A common employer practice to improve productivity was to reduce the number of job classifications, giving management the right to assign work more flexibly. Job classifications, i.e., rates of pay connected to specified responsibilities, originated as a management technique to control workers. In the changing workplaces of the 1990s, however, detailed descriptions of employees' duties became a barrier to efficiency, at least from the employers' perspective. Inco was a typical case of such change. The company reduced the number of job classifications, and employees were trained to assume additional duties in the enlarged classifications and received higher pay to reflect their new status (Chaykowski, 1999). General Motors agreed to create new job classifications to introduce "multi-tasking," i.e., the amalgamation of job responsibilities, through local bargaining.

New job classifications typically involved a wage increase to reflect added responsibilities (Kumar, 1999). Canadian Pacific Railway won the right to assign workers outside of their classifications for temporary assignments of increasing duration (Coates and Downie, 1999).

When asked what initiatives they had taken to improve labour relations and productivity, managers' most common response (35 percent) was improved communications with their unions and their employees, most often with respect to the operations and financial status of the firm. The focus on production and financial issues was deliberate because the purpose of improved communications with unions and employees was clearly to encourage an appreciation by union leaders and their members of the financial, competitive, and production issues that the employer was facing. Employers believed that they would enjoy a smoother acceptance of changes in their operations if unions understood the reasons for their decisions and the pressures the firm faced. Deliberate efforts were made to steer discussions away from industrial relations issues (e.g., grievances, potential collective bargaining demands).

At Stelco, local management began to share financial and business information with its local unions, going beyond traditional concerns for health and safety. One topic was a joint effort to reduce the reliance on outside contractors. The parties also administered training programs to prepare workers for changes in the firm's product line (Frost and Verma, 1999). Bell Canada initiated regular "forums" with senior union leaders to share information on a wide range of subjects (Verma, 1999).

In Canadian industry generally, line management rather than industrial relations staff typically represented the employer. A common format was regular meetings with union officials to discuss production matters, such as the volume or quality of production. Union representatives had the opportunity to comment or ask questions, but management typically saw these meetings as forums for providing information, not as a form of consultation. Meetings with union representatives enabled management to exchange views with its unions and to discuss issues of mutual concern without at the same time yielding any of its authority to make decisions on matters not covered by the collective agreement. Unions have not become involved in management strategic decisions through these meetings (Wagar, 1994).

In addition to improving communications, another common employer initiative encourages employees to take more responsibility for improving productivity and product quality. About 20 percent of employers instituted formal programs to improve quality. These programs have several names, "quality circles," "total quality management," or "quality improvement" systems. While these programs differ in many important details, they normally include teams of employees, supervisors, facilitators, and technical advisers charged with making specific improvements in the quality of the product or service for which they are responsible (see Exhibit 5.2).

Employee involvement programs were another way for management to change the workplace. These programs, found in about 20 percent of unionized Canadian companies, are designed to solicit employee suggestions on production issues, work schedules,

EXHIBIT 5.2

QUALITY IMPROVEMENT

One of Canada's largest container companies produces thousands of units each day. The containers are shipped to customers who process food, beverages, home-cleaning products, and other goods. The filling of the containers by the company's customers is a high-volume operation. If a container breaks on the customer's production line, the cost to the customer of the interruption in production, cleanup, and damage to equipment can be considerable, as much as $20,000 per incident. The company already had a high-quality product: There were only two to three breaks per 10,000 containers, but the quality improvement program reduced the figure to one break per 100,000 units, better than the American competition. As part of the program, the company also reduced the number of quality inspectors. The company's objective was to lower the rate to a single break for each 200,000 units. The quality improvement program involved bargaining unit members, supervisors, and engineers, who were all invited to suggest changes to the production process to achieve quality targets (Thompson, 1995).

and other workplace problems (see Chapter 15). These usually involve "mixed" teams of employees (union members) and supervisors. Unions usually are wary of employee involvement programs, which are initiated and fundamentally controlled by management and are seen as a threat to unions' role as the exclusive representative of employees in the workplace. In private conversations, some employers have tacitly admitted that they expect employee involvement programs to weaken the militancy of their workers, so labour's concerns may be justified.

In summary, the most common labour relations response of unionized Canadian employers to increased competitive pressures was to co-operate with unions and seek assistance from their workers. It is noteworthy that in adopting these strategies, most employers rejected other, more confrontational approaches. Only two companies stated that they chose to confront their union or to regain management rights that were constrained by the collective agreement. Examples of "concession bargaining," i.e., demanding reductions in the terms and conditions of employment contained in collective agreements, also were rare. Many firms relied on changes to their collective agreements to improve productivity, and companies in some cases had traded new clauses in collective agreements for job security or other benefits to workers. However, most large unionized Canadian companies clearly chose co-operation over confrontation (see Exhibit 5.3).

MANAGEMENT PROCESSES

The responsibility for ensuring that industrial relations strategies are translated into practice is divided among industrial relations staff, human resource departments, and line

> ## Exhibit 5.3
>
> ### Changes in Workplace Practices
>
> - reduced job classifications combined with employee retraining to increase skills
> - enhanced communications with employees and unions with focus on financial and operational issues
> - quality improvement programs
> - employee involvement
> - union–management consultation

managers. Managers of large unionized firms emphasize the importance of the collective bargaining process in meeting corporate objectives. The three major managerial functions in a system of collective bargaining are:

1. preparation for bargaining,
2. the conduct of bargaining, and
3. contract administration.

The resources and talents necessary for each of these functions can vary considerably.

Preparation for Bargaining

Ideally, preparation for bargaining should be an ongoing, year-round process. In practice, however, many organizations seem to wait until several months before the expiry of a collective agreement before beginning active preparation. Most firms compare their wages and fringe benefits to other companies in the same industry, and secondarily to firms in the same region. There are a variety of sources for such information—industry associations, private publications, government surveys, and private surveys. Given this array of information, which normally is not expensive to obtain, most firms can base their bargaining strategies on an extensive knowledge of settlements their competitors in product and labour markets have reached.

The mandate is a major tool for management control of labour costs and is generally approved at the senior management level. Background research for bargaining occurs in the months before negotiations begin. When it is complete, the industrial relations staff must obtain approval from senior management for a bargaining position, commonly known as a "mandate." Negotiators have considerable latitude to settle within their mandate, but must obtain permission from corporate officers if they believe that they must exceed the mandate to obtain a settlement.

 Canadian Labour and Business Centre: www.clbc.ca

Conduct of Bargaining and Contract Administration

Bargaining is conducted according to the principles explained in Chapter 9 of this volume. A member of the industrial relations staff normally is the principal spokesperson for the employer, supported by one or more other industrial relations staff, representatives of line management, and perhaps a financial analyst. Generally, ratification of settlements takes place at the same level of the organization where the mandate was approved. On the other hand, higher levels of authority are often involved when a threat to go on strike is made. The consequences of a stoppage are sufficiently important that the highest levels of management authority are at least informed before a decision is made to reject a union proposal that is backed by a credible strike threat. Often, companies have detailed strike preparedness plans and have taken steps to stockpile finished products and alter inventory systems many months in advance of an anticipated strike.

Chapter 10 of this volume describes the process of contract administration. This function is managed locally in most firms. Local managers may be advised by industrial relations staff reporting to them or by managers at higher levels of the organization. Firms also rely upon outside lawyers to advise them in arbitration matters and to present their cases.

INDUSTRIAL RELATIONS STAFF

Corporate headquarters is directly responsible for major industrial relations policy decisions in a majority of Canadian companies. Some divide the responsibility between headquarters and other levels of authority. Routine approval of decisions by headquarters is rare, except for decisions on the settlement of grievances where authority is widely dispersed. Even in areas where corporate managers do not have operational responsibility, for instance in the monitoring of labour relations, they have significant influence in the formulation of the policies under which lower-level managers will operate.

The location of industrial relations staff confirms the degree of the centralization of decisions. In large firms, approximately one-third of the staff are located at the corporate level. Less than half the staff are located at the plant level, where collective bargaining, grievance meetings, and supervisor training actually take place, while the remainder are located at intermediate levels of the organization.

The high degree of centralization of authority for key industrial relations decisions and policies, especially decisions connected with collective bargaining, indicates that the importance of these decisions, their complexity and political character, and the uncertainty of the business environment outweigh the decentralizing tendencies of the Canadian industrial relations system.[7]

Industrial relations are not purely a staff function. Line managers in most firms have some responsibility for industrial relations activities, supported by industrial relations staff. Because many industrial relations processes can be highly technical and complex, organizations must assign technically competent staff to assist line management and to conduct many specialized functions.

The workload of industrial relations staff can be highly variable. By law, collective agreements must be at least one year in duration, and many agreements are renegotiated once every two or three years. In the periods leading up to the renewal of collective agreements, the demands on industrial relations staff are great, but the workload diminishes considerably after negotiations end. Thus, it is impractical to employ large numbers of staff for collective bargaining when the workload during slack periods may not justify their presence. Although contract administration is an ongoing process, the concentration of this activity at the level of the plant or worksite under the direction of line management limits the contribution of staff specialists (Godard and Kochan, 1982).

The size of industrial relations staff within Canadian companies varies greatly. For example, one firm reported that it had 96 persons employed in industrial relations functions, while two others with the same number of employees had 12 and 22 industrial relations staff respectively. Apart from the extremes, one would expect the number of staff to be related to the number of employees. Overall, the ratio of industrial relations staff to employees is approximately 1:500. Factors such as the number of bargaining units, their dispersion, and industry characteristics are all important determinants of the number of industrial relations staff. In addition, firms with headquarters in the English-speaking provinces and large operations in Quebec often maintain parallel industrial relations staffs for the two language groups. Quebec law requires that most industrial relations functions be carried out in French, so unilingual anglophones are not able to operate there, especially in such functions as measuring the attitude of the workforce or advising managers on the disposition of grievances. Companies with headquarters in Montreal rely on the corporate staff to manage industrial relations in both languages (Thompson, 1995).

What are the traits of successful industrial relations managers? They must be comfortable with conflict. They have to oversee negotiations with unions representing the organization's employees, as well as soothe line managers who are not always happy with the instructions they get from the industrial relations department. IR managers must have a thorough knowledge of labour law and collective agreement language. They must be good listeners, as many problems can be resolved only after hearing other parties tell stories that are important to them. A keen understanding of organizational politics is crucial. Unions are political groups; government policies often affect industrial relations; and employers have their own brand of political behaviours. Stamina and patience are important. Bargaining can be prolonged, and negotiators may have to go over the same issues repeatedly. Finally, IR managers often have to explain the intricacies of workplace labour relations to senior managers. But the authority to make collective bargaining decisions—to determine wages and fringe benefits and to take a strike—is highly centralized and seldom left to line management.

CONCLUSIONS

After more than a decade of employer initiative in industrial relations, several features of management actions have emerged. Firms that have adopted industrial relations strategies tied to their business strategies are satisfied with the results. At present, industrial relations considerations influence a small number of business decisions heavily. It is not clear whether this situation is due to the importance of other factors (such as access to the market or raw materials costs) or the confidence of senior management that they can operate successfully within the general context of Canadian industrial relations.

The hard-line approach of American employers toward their unions and employees has little acceptance in Canada. Although most Canadian employers would prefer not to have a union, in large, unionized firms, the employees' choice of a union is respected. Companies work to maximize their position within the framework of collective bargaining. Large firms are resigned to paying above-average wages and employee benefits, and they accept that collective bargaining raises their visibility in the labour market. Unionized firms did not believe that collective bargaining was a serious barrier to their commercial success. Nonetheless, traditionally nonunion firms continue to vigorously resist unions.

In the face of stronger competitive pressures in the 1980s and 1990s, unionized firms have emphasized communication with their unions and a reliance on existing arrangements for union–management consultation to prove to their unions and employees the economic realities of product markets and to solve operational problems jointly. Labour–management consultation is especially common on the subjects of occupational health and safety, production problems, employee assistance, and technological change. Authority for bargaining decisions is highly centralized, despite decentralized bargaining structures and the shift of responsibility toward line management for some industrial relations processes.

In many respects, the unionized segments of the Canadian economy have performed well without having to remove or severely weaken either the unions or the collective bargaining process. Unionized companies compete successfully in international markets. Productivity and product quality are high. Public policy has played a minor role in the recent initiatives of Canadian employers. But market pressures, fed by international competition, free trade agreements, changing technology, and deregulation will continue to challenge existing strategies and practices.

 Work Index.com (Cornell University): www.workindex.com/
Probably the best IR/HRM site on the Internet.

Questions

1. What are the constraints on management's industrial relations strategies?

2. What are some of the industrial relations issues facing a firm wishing to pursue a low-wage compensation strategy?

3. Distinguish among the broad strategies of union acceptance, union resistance, union removal, and union substitution/avoidance.

4. What are some employer initiatives to improve productivity and industrial relations in the workplace?

5. Discuss the main elements in an employer's preparation for bargaining.

6. What factors would lead to the decentralization of authority for management industrial relations decisions? What factors lead to centralization of authority?

ENDNOTES

[1] Research cited in this chapter was funded by a grant from the Social Sciences and Humanities Research Council. Michael Piczak and Louise Verschelden provided valuable assistance in completing interviews. The author is solely responsible for the views expressed.

[2] Adapted from confidential discussions with a senior industrial relations manager.

[3] For a thorough review of the literature on contemporary management of industrial relations in the United States, the United Kingdom, and Australia, see Fox, et al., 1995.

[4] Some highly paternalistic firms practising "welfare capitalism" were leaders in the implementation of pension plans, profit sharing, and other employee benefits. See Jacoby's 1997 book.

[5] Ontario Labour Relations Board, *Re McKean, et al.* v. *Retail, Wholesale and Department Store Union* v. *T. Eaton Company Limited*, [1987] OLRB Rep. Jan. 3127.

[6] British Columbia Labour Relations Board, *Re P. T. Savage Enterprises Ltd. and National Automobile Aerospace, Transportation and General Workers Union of Canada (CAW-Canada)*, BCLRB No. B508/98.

[7] Kochan and Katz (1988) found similar centralization in the US, where the industrial relations system also is highly decentralized.

REFERENCES

BÉLANGER, J. 1999. "Alcan: Market Pressure and Decentralization of Labour Regulation," in *Contract & Commitment: Employment Relations in the New Economy*, edited by A. Verma and R. P. Chaykowski. Kingston, Ont.: Queen's University IRC Press, pp. 113–136.

BETCHERMAN, G. 1991. "The effect of unions on the innovative behaviour of firms in Canada." *Industrial Relations Journal*, 22, no. 2, pp. 142–151.

BETCHERMAN, G., K. McMULLEN, N. LECKIE, and C. CARON. 1994a. *The Canadian Workplace in Transition*. Kingston, Ont.: IRC Press.

BETCHERMAN, G., N. LECKIE, and A. VERMA. 1994b. "AHRM Innovations in Canada: Evidence from Establishment Surveys." School of Industrial Relations/Industrial Relations Centre, Queen's University at Kingston.

BOONE, D. J. 2000. "Operation of the Production District Joint Industrial Council, Imperial Oil," in *Nonunion Employee Representation: History, Contemporary Practice and Policy*, edited by B. E. Kaufman and D. G. Taras. New York: ME Sharpe.

BRAY, M. and R. LANSBURY. 1998. "Local versus Global: Employment Relations in a Global Corporation," delivered to the 11th World Congress of the International Industrial Relations Research Association, Bologna, Italy (22–26 September).

BRODY, B., K. SEAVER, and T. TREMBLAY. 1993. "The Deunionization of Canadian Banks," in *The Industrial Relations System: Future Trends and Developments. Proceedings of the XXIXth Conference of the Canadian Industrial Relations Association*, edited by T. S. Kuttner. Fredericton, NB: CIRA, 1, pp. 381–396.

CHAYKOWSKI, R. P. 1999. "Adaptation within the Traditional Industrial Relations System: The Development of Labour Relations at Inco Limited," in *Contract & Commitment: Employment Relations in the New Economy*, edited by A. Verma and R. P. Chaykowski. Kingston, Ont.: Queen's University IRC Press, pp. 41–81.

COATES, M. L. and B. DOWNIE. 1999. "The Changing World of Industrial Relations at CPR," in *Contract & Commitment: Employment Relations in the New Economy*, edited by A. Verma and R. P. Chaykowski. Kingston, Ont.: Queen's University IRC Press, pp. 241–292.

CONNORS, P. 1992. "Decision Making Participation Patterns: The Role of Organizational Context." *Academy of Management Journal*, 35, no. 1, pp. 218–231.

FOX, C., W. HOWARD, and M. PITTARD. 1995. *Industrial Relations in Australia: Development, Law and Operation.* Sydney: Longman.

FROST, A. C. and A. VERMA. 1999. "Restructuring in Canadian Steel: The Case of Stelco Inc.," in *Contract & Commitment: Employment Relations in the New Economy,* edited by A. Verma and R. P. Chaykowski. Kingston, Ont.: Queen's University IRC Press, pp. 82–112.

GODARD, J. 1997. "Managerial Strategies, Labour and Employment Relations and the State: the Canadian Case and Beyond." *British Journal of Industrial Relations,* 35, no. 3, pp. 399–426.

GODARD, J. H. and T. A. KOCHAN. 1982. "Canadian Management Under Collective Bargaining: Policies, Processes, Structure, and Effectiveness," in *Union–Management Relations in Canada,* edited by J. C. Anderson and M. Gunderson. Toronto: Addison-Wesley.

GUNDERSON, M. and W. C. RIDDELL. 1993. *Labour Market Economics: Theory, Evidence and Policy in Canada,* 3rd Edition. Toronto: McGraw-Hill Ryerson.

HARSHAW, M. 2000. "Nonunion Employee Representation at Dofasco," in *Nonunion Employee Representation: History, Contemporary Practice and Policy,* edited by B. E. Kaufman and D. G. Taras. New York: ME Sharpe.

JACOBY, S. M. 1997. *Modern Manors: Welfare Capitalism Since the New Deal.* Princeton, New Jersey: Princeton University Press.

JEDEL, M. and D. KUJAWA. 1976. *Management and Employment Practices of Foreign Direct Investors in the United States.* Atlanta: Georgia State University.

KOCHAN, T. A. and H. C. KATZ. 1988. *Collective Bargaining and Industrial Relations: From Theory to Policy and Practice.* Homewood, IL: Irwin.

KOCHAN, T. A., H. C. KATZ, and R. B. McKERSIE. 1986. *The Transformation of American Industrial Relations.* New York: Basic Books.

KOCHAN, T. A., R. McKERSIE, and P. CAPELLI. 1984. "Strategic Choice and Industrial Relations Theory." *Industrial Relations,* 23, pp. 16–39.

KUMAR, P. 1999. "In Search of Competitive Efficiency: The General Motors of Canada Experience with Restructuring," in *Contract & Commitment: Employment Relations in the New Economy,* edited by A. Verma and R. P. Chaykowski. Kingston, Ont.: Queen's University IRC Press, pp. 137–181.

McQUEEN, R. 1998. *The Eatons: The Rise and Fall of Canada's Royal Family.* Toronto: Stoddart.

PALMER, B. D. 1992. *Working Class Experience: Rethinking the History of Canadian Labour, 1800–1991.* Toronto: McClelland & Stewart.

PURCELL, J. 1987. "Mapping Management Styles in Employee Relations." *Journal of Management Studies,* 24, pp. 533–548.

SKOGAN, J. 1999. "Once Upon a Tim." *Saturday Night,* September, pp. 69–73.

SMITH, A. E. 1993. "Canadian Industrial Relations in Transition." *Relations industrielles,* 48, no. 4, pp. 641–660.

STOREY, R. 1983. "Unionization Versus Corporate Welfare: The Dofasco Way." *Labour/Le Travailleur* (Fall), pp. 7–42.

TARAS, D. G. 1994. "Impact of Industrial Relations Strategies on Selected Human Resource Practices in a Partially Unionized Industry: The Canadian Petroleum Sector." Unpublished PhD dissertation, University of Calgary.

———. 1997. "Managerial Intentions and Wage Determination in the Canadian Petroleum Industry." *Industrial Relations,* 36, no. 2, pp. 178–205.

———. 2000. "Contemporary Experience with the Rockefeller Plan: Imperial Oil's Joint Industrial Council," in *Nonunion Employee Representation: History, Contemporary Practice and Policy,* edited by B. E. Kaufman and D. G. Taras. New York: ME Sharpe.

TARAS, D. G. and J. COPPING. 1998. "The Transition from Formal Nonunion Representation to Unionization: A Contemporary Case." *Industrial and Labor Relations Review*, 52, no. 1, pp. 22–44.

TARAS, D. G. and A. PONAK. 1999. "Petro-Canada: A Model of a Union Acceptance Strategy within the Canadian Petroleum Industry," in *Contract & Commitment: Employment Relations in the New Economy*, edited by A. Verma and R. P. Chaykowski. Kingston, Ont.: Queen's University IRC Press, pp. 211–240.

THOMPSON, M. 1995. "The Management of Industrial Relations," in *Union–Management Relations in Canada*, 3rd Edition, edited by M. Gunderson and A. Ponak. Toronto: Addison-Wesley, pp. 105–130.

VERMA, A. 1999. "From POTS to PANS: The Evolution of Employment Relations in Bell Canada under Deregulation," in *Contract & Commitment: Employment Relations in the New Economy*, edited by A. Verma and R. P. Chaykowski. Kingston, Ont.: Queen's University IRC Press, pp. 182–210.

WAGAR, T. H. 1994. *Human Resource Management Practices and Organizational Performance: Evidence from Atlantic Canada*. Kingston, Ont.: IRC Press, Industrial Relations Centre, Queen's University.

CHAPTER 6

Social, Political, and Economic Environments

Frank Reid and Noah M. Meltz

The normal pattern at the General Motors truck plant in Oshawa, Ontario was a rotating shift schedule of two weeks on day shift alternating with two weeks on afternoon shift, but in 1993 when the plant added a night shift, becoming the first automotive assembly operation in North America to run 24 hours a day, it gave employees the opportunity to *volunteer* to work steady nights at a premium wage and reduced hours. The Canadian Auto Workers union supported the idea and agreed to a change of work rules to accommodate the new option.

The 700 employees at the GM truck plant who volunteer to work a steady night shift earn a 10 percent wage premium and work only 7.5 hours while getting paid for 8 hours, effectively adding another 6.7 percent premium to the hourly wage.

Employees find the steady night shift much better than the rotating shifts, which can be even more disruptive to sleeping and eating patterns. Few have elected to go back to the normal rotating shifts pattern, and for those who do, there is a waiting list of employees ready to take their place.

General Motors is also pleased with the volunteer night-shift option as the company has saved the enormous cost of building a new plant. The quality on the night shift equals that of the other two shifts and the night shift has met its production targets.[1]

This innovation by GM and the CAW is an example of what economists would call a compensating wage differential to allocate labour. Compared to the alternative of simply assigning shifts on a rotational basis, using wages to induce voluntary changes in behaviour can be a win-win alternative (i.e., it can make some people better off and make others no worse off—what economists call an increase in efficiency). It can also be more equitable.

The social, political, and economic environments are fundamental determinants of decisions by the three actors in the industrial relations system—unions, management, and government. The purpose of this chapter is to discuss the impact of each of these environments on the actors, and through them on the outcomes of the industrial relations system. While we focus primarily on the impact that the environment has on the actors, we also observe that the actions of the actors can affect the environment. Both unions and management consciously attempt to change the political, social, and legal environments they face in order to influence the laws that are put in place to regulate and enforce standards in the labour market and in the industrial relations system. Our discussion begins with the social environment because that represents the attitudes and values of the population, which in turn affects the political environment and the role people believe the government should play in the workplace.

The political environment represents the vehicle to translate social attitudes into legislation and the mechanisms for its enforcement. The political environment in any country reflects the diverse social views in the population. However, the political environment is not simply a passive response by political parties representing the various views in society. The process is much more complicated. Each political party tries to attain a mandate from a much wider constituency than the formal membership in the party. The parties try to broaden their representation by appealing to as wide a following as possible, and several political parties in Canada have formal ties with the union movement.

The economic environment sets out the limits within which the actors can press for economic improvements in compensation and benefits for employees, and for employers, reduction in labour costs and improvements in productivity and profits. The forces that underlie the operation of the labour market are supply and demand. How these interact, together with the impact of government, are essential components to understanding the industrial relations system.

In discussing each of these environments, we will compare and contrast the situations in the United States and Canada. For unions, on the surface, we should see similar behaviour since many of the same unions bargain in both countries, sometimes with the same companies. We include inter-country comparisons in our discussion of each of the environments since they help illuminate the role of social, political, and economic forces on the outcomes of the industrial relations system.

THE SOCIAL ENVIRONMENT

The social environment represents the combination of attitudes and values of the population toward institutions in society and toward the collective goals of the society. Seymour Martin Lipset and Noah M. Meltz undertook a study (1997) comparing the views of Americans and Canadians on their confidence in the government, unions, and corporations. The study compares the percentage of employees in the two countries who have a lot or a great deal of confidence in the three institutions, with the percentage who have very little confidence. In each country there are more people who have very little confidence in the government, unions, and corporations, than there are who have a lot of confidence. Those in the in-between group, who have some confidence, represent about half of the workforce. People in both Canada and the US seem to have similar feelings towards these institutions.

Major differences emerge between the two countries in attitudes toward the role of government. As indicated in Table 6.1, there was overwhelming agreement in both countries that the gap between rich and poor is too wide, 87 percent in Canada, and 84 percent in the US. However, when asked what role the government should play in narrowing the gap, almost one out of every two Canadians (45 percent), compared with 31 percent in the US, feel that it is the responsibility of government to reduce the difference between people earning high and low incomes. Canadians also are much more strongly committed (73 percent) to the government taking responsibility to preserve society's morality than are Americans (53 percent).

TABLE 6.1

VIEW OF GOVERNMENT

SURVEY RESPONSE	PERCENTAGE OF TOTAL EMPLOYED	
	Canada	United States
Workers who say that the gap between the rich and the poor is too wide	87	84
Workers who feel that it is the responsibility of government to reduce the difference between incomes	45	31
Workers who agree that it is a responsibility of government to ensure the well-being of all citizens	83	72
Workers who feel that it is a responsibility of government to preserve society's morality	73	53

Source: "Canadian and American Attitudes Toward Work and Institutions," *Perspectives on Work*, vol. 1, no. 3, by Seymour Martin Lipset and Noah Meltz. © 1998, IRRA, by permission.

TABLE 6.2

EMPLOYEE VIEWS OF WORK

SURVEY RESPONSE	PERCENTAGE OF TOTAL EMPLOYED	
	Canada	United States
Workers who are somewhat or very satisfied with their job	86	85
Workers who think they were paid fairly in the past year for their main employment	73	74
Workers taking some or a great deal of pride in their work	97	99
Workers who agree that they would do their best regardless of the pay	77	75

Source: "Canadian and American Attitudes Toward Work and Institutions," *Perspectives on Work*, vol. 1, no. 3, by Seymour Martin Lipset and Noah Meltz. © 1998, IRRA, by permission.

In terms of attitudes toward work, Table 6.2 shows that Canadians and Americans have remarkably similar attitudes. The vast majority take pride in their work, are satisfied with their job, would do their best regardless of pay, and think they are paid fairly.

Differences appear when employees in the two countries are asked specifically about how people should be treated in the workplace. In answer to virtually every question that deals with the balance between equity (fairness) and efficiency, Canadians are more supportive of fairness than are Americans, even though both countries support equity in the workplace. For example, as shown in Table 6.3, fewer than half of the workers in Canada (45 percent) think that it is very fair to pay more efficient workers higher salaries, while a majority (57 percent) of Americans think that it is fair.

TABLE 6.3

WORK-RELATED VALUES

SURVEY RESPONSE	PERCENTAGE OF TOTAL EMPLOYED	
	Canada	United States
Workers who believe that it is very fair to pay more efficient workers higher salaries	45	57
Workers who feel that freedom is more important than equality	55	63
Workers who agree with the statement that job security is more important than career advancement	67	61

Source: "Canadian and American Attitudes Toward Work and Institutions," *Perspectives on Work*, vol. 1, no. 3, by Seymour Martin Lipset and Noah Meltz. © 1998, IRRA, by permission.

These tables demonstrate that while there seem to be similar limited levels of confidence in most institutions in the two countries, where the Americans and Canadians part company is on the attitudes toward equality (and fairness) versus freedom and efficiency. Canadians are more supportive of equality and equity than are Americans. As well, Canadians expect government to play a more activist role in the workplace and in society than Americans. This has implications for the political environment.

THE POLITICAL ENVIRONMENT

The political environment has a major impact on the legislative environment, which in turn affects the actors in the industrial relations system. As well, the actors attempt to influence the political and legal environments. How those impacts occur is a complex process, very dependent on the political institutions themselves and the political parties that interact and react within these institutions. The very different recent patterns of trade union growth between Canada and the United States provide a good example of the influence of political institutions. Recently, democratic institutions have had very different effects on the actors in the industrial relations system in the two countries. In the United States, labour policy reform has stalled despite intensive efforts on the part of unions. Canada continues to make adjustments to labour laws in both the federal and provincial spheres.

The political environment in Canada is based on a parliamentary system, in which the party (or parties if there is a coalition) with a majority or plurality of the elected representatives forms the government. In the United States, the congressional system is one of checks and balances with a separately elected president (executive branch), congress (the Senate and House of Representatives), and judiciary. A Democratic president can be rendered ineffective by a Republican congress, and vice versa. In a parliamentary system, a governing party has a greater chance of attaining its objectives. This makes it relatively easier for governments in Canada to pass pro- (as well as anti-) union legislation. In the United States, with the exception of the New Deal period during the Great Depression of the 1930s, it has been much harder for the president to pass labour legislation that is supportive of unions.

The Historical Context: 1900–1949

The political environment for union–management relations has experienced swings during the past century, moving from laissez-faire and even pro-management/anti-union to pro-union and then to lesser support for unions. Prior to the 1940s, with the exception of the First World War, the political environment was not supportive of organized labour. At the beginning of the 1900s, the federal Liberal government passed the *Industrial Disputes Investigation Act* (1907), which gave a form of recognition to unions by requiring a suspension of a strike and the appointment of a conciliation officer—and later, if necessary, a conciliation board—to inquire into the causes of strikes and to recommend terms for an agreement. The recommendations were not binding, and the parties were permitted to resume a strike or lockout after the board's report was made public. There was no protection for employees to form unions.

It was again a federal Liberal government that in 1944 enacted sweeping legislation (PC 1003) that provided for the rights of employees to join unions and introduced a mechanism to enforce the legislation, the Canada Labour Relations Board. This legislation, by virtue of the wartime situation, was deemed to apply not only to workers under the federal jurisdiction, but also to employees under the provincial jurisdiction (approximately 90 percent of all Canadian employees). In 1948 responsibility for labour legislation was returned to the provinces, and PC 1003 for the federal jurisdiction was formally titled the *Industrial Relations and Disputes Investigation Act*.

The political environment in 1944 was crucial for the passage of union-supportive legislation. The Americans had passed similar legislation in 1935, the Wagner Act. What gave a push to the passage of such legislation in Canada was the victory of the socialist CCF Party in Saskatchewan in 1944, and polls showing that in Ontario the CCF was almost even with the Liberals in popular support going into the elections that were expected to take place in 1944. In the same year, the CCF government in Saskatchewan passed legislation that gave both private-sector and public-sector workers the right to organize, bargain, and strike. The federal government not only passed the collective bargaining legislation, but also legislation providing for unemployment insurance and "baby bonuses." Partly as a result of these initiatives, the Liberals were able to co-opt the votes that might otherwise have gone to the CCF and they were again able to form a majority government.

The Post-War Years: 1950–1979

Changes in the political environment in the 1960s and 1970s were responsible for the next major changes in labour legislation in Canada. The Quiet Revolution in Quebec, which began in 1960 with the election of a Liberal government replacing the Union Nationale, led to the passage in 1964 of legislation similar to Saskatchewan's permitting collective bargaining and the right to strike by public-sector employees (government employees, teachers, health care workers).

At the federal level, in 1967, the Liberal government passed the Public Service Staff Relations Act (PSSRA) giving public-sector workers under federal jurisdiction the right to bargain and, under certain circumstances, the right to strike. In the next few years, most of the provinces passed legislation supporting some degree of public-sector collective bargaining. These governments were made up of Progressive Conservative (Ontario), Liberal, and later, NDP (successor to the CCF) governments. The changes in legislation, and the different political parties that introduced them, occurred in a political environment that was moving towards supporting the right of employees in all sectors to form unions and to bargain.

This right was somewhat abridged for three years (1975–78) when the Liberal government of Pierre Trudeau introduced wage and price controls, even though it was elected in 1974 on a platform opposing the proposal for price controls by the Progressive Conservative party. The Anti-Inflation Board (AIB) imposed steadily lower guidelines for wage settlements over the three years of the program and, in conjunction with a restrictive monetary policy, helped to bring down the inflation rate. The AIB was perhaps the most dramatic government intervention in the Canadian collective bargaining process in the post-war period.

The Last Two Decades: 1980–1999

The 1980s and 1990s witnessed another change in the political environment, although in this case the direction was not as clear as in earlier periods. Some of the changes were away from union support, some were toward more union support, and in some cases, particularly in British Columbia and Ontario, the political environment moved back and forth.

In the period 1982–1984, the federal government introduced limitations on the increases in public-sector wages (the so-called 6 and 5 program, indicating the percentage increases in wages that were permitted to federal public servants). Ontario followed suit with a program of 9 and 5, and some other provinces such as British Columbia introduced similar programs, all aimed at containing wage increases in the public sector that might spread to the private sector, or so it was feared.

In the early 1990s there was first a swing toward the NDP and more liberal labour legislation, then a partial swing back, especially in Ontario. NDP governments were elected in Ontario (1990), British Columbia (1991), and Saskatchewan (1991). The first two introduced major changes in labour legislation, with Ontario totally banning the use of strike replacement workers, and BC partially banning their use. Earlier, the province of Quebec had also introduced limitations—though not as encompassing as Ontario's— on the use of replacement workers (see Chapter 16 on Quebec's industrial relations).

The Ontario NDP then reversed direction because of the continuing recession, and in 1993 introduced what was called the Social Contract, which for three years forced a 5 percent reduction in public-sector wage costs by imposing unpaid reductions in work time. The labour movement in Ontario split over the Social Contract. The public-sector unions and the Canadian Auto Workers (CAW) opposed the NDP policy and refused to support the NDP in the next election. The private-sector unions, with the exception of the CAW, supported the government's action, on the grounds that a 5 percent temporary cut in work time was better than the layoff of 13,000 public-sector employees. The split in labour's ranks along with a general dissatisfaction with the NDP and a strong Progressive Conservative platform (The Common Sense Revolution) combined to produce a massive NDP defeat in Ontario in 1995. The political environment had changed again in central Canada. The Progressive Conservatives immediately reversed the union-supportive changes that had been put in place by the NDP.

These swings in the political environment, and in the legislation that often followed the change in the governing parties, must be seen as a factor affecting the bargaining strengths of the actors in the industrial relations system and, ultimately, the outcomes at the bargaining table. Of course, bargaining between unions and management takes place within an economic context. That context, in itself, exerts a major force at the bargaining table. To understand the impact of economic forces, we have to explore what makes up the economic environment and how it affects the industrial relations system.

Canadian Labour Force Development Board: www.clfdb.ca

THE ECONOMIC ENVIRONMENT

The economic environment sets the limits within which employees can press for economic improvements in compensation and benefits, and employers can press for a reduction in labour costs and an increase in profits. Although supply and demand constrain what occurs in the labour market, constraints also result from government legislation and the accompanying rules and regulations, such as employment insurance, minimum wage, and other employment-standards legislation.

The Ideology of a Competitive Labour Market

In this section, we explore what we call the ideology of a competitive labour market; i.e., what makes a labour market tick?

How Competitive Markets Work

Competitive labour markets are assumed to be characterized by a large number of employers and employees of each type of labour so that no single employer or employee has a significant influence on the market wage rate. It is also assumed that there are no artificial barriers to entering any occupation. In a competitive market, each employer is a *wage-taker*, that is, the employer takes the wage as given by the market and decides how many employees to hire in order to maximize profits, given product market conditions and the state of technology.

The supply of labour to any particular occupation (that is, the number of persons who want to work in that occupation) depends on numerous factors, including the wage rate for that occupation; the required levels of skill, training, and experience; working conditions; the status of the occupation; and preferences of labour force members. For any fixed level of the other factors that affect labour supply, an increase in the wage rate for one occupation will make that occupation more attractive, resulting in an increased number of persons who want to work in that occupation.

The demand for labour, that is the number of persons in each occupational group that employers want to hire, depends on factors such as the wage rate for the occupation. The demand for labour is a derived demand; i.e., it is derived from the amount of output the employer wants to produce and technological considerations. For any fixed level of the other factors, a wage increase will tend to reduce the amount of labour employers wish to hire (the number of persons or the number of hours). This reduction occurs for two reasons: the *substitution effect* and the *output effect*. First, for any given level of output, in the long run, employers will tend to substitute capital or other less expensive types of labour for the type of labour that has become relatively more expensive (the substitution effect). Second, an increase in wage costs will increase unit costs and the price of the product being produced, resulting in a drop in sales and a reduction in the derived demand for all inputs including labour (output effect). Both effects work in the same direction, leading to a reduction in the demand for labour as wages increase (i.e., labour demand curves slope downwards).

In the classic, competitive labour market model, there is a particular wage rate, known as the *equilibrium wage*, at which the supply of labour and the demand for labour are equal. At the equilibrium wage, no one would be unemployed; that is, everyone who wanted to work at that wage rate would be able to find work. In other words, the labour market would clear. This simple model can be easily modified to allow for frictional unemployment due to employee turnover in a dynamic labour market. Although unfilled jobs and unemployed workers could coexist in this model, there would be no overall shortage of jobs at the equilibrium wage.

At any wage rate above the equilibrium wage, the supply of labour exceeds the demand for labour, resulting in downward pressure on the wage rate. Conversely, at any wage rate below the equilibrium level, the demand for labour exceeds the supply of labour, resulting in unfilled job vacancies and upward pressure on the wage rate. Consequently, in a competitive labour market, compensation tends toward the equilibrium wage where quantity of labour supplied equals the quantity demanded.

How Wages Allocate Labour: Compensating Wage Differentials

An implication of competitive labour markets, which can be traced back to the work of Adam Smith more than 200 years ago, is that, in the long run, the equalization of the net advantage in each occupation results in compensating wage differentials that offset undesirable non-wage aspects of the job. For example, jobs that are dirty or dangerous or require a long period of training or unduly long hours of work would receive a higher wage that would be just sufficient to offset these disadvantages for the marginal employee. Such differentials serve two economic functions in allocating labour: On the supply side, they attract workers to undesirable occupations and compensate them for tolerating unpleasant working conditions. On the demand side, compensating wage differentials also provide an economic incentive for employers to eliminate undesirable working conditions, provided the cost of eliminating them is less than the cost of paying the compensating wage differential.

The principle of compensating wage differentials can be applied to the use of shift premiums (see opening vignette). For simplicity, suppose that initially there were an equal number of employees working a day shift and a night shift, all employees were required to alternate shifts every two weeks, and there was no shift premium. It can be shown that some employees can be made better off, and no one worse off, if the shift pre-mium is widened sufficiently to induce the required number of employees to volunteer for regular night shift. To ensure that the employer is also not made worse off, assume that the shift differential is created by raising the night-shift wage and lowering the day-shift wage by equal amounts so that labour costs are not increased. Also assume that em-ployees are given the option of continuing to alternate shifts every two weeks, in which case they would earn the same amount over a four-week cycle as they would under the old system. This option guarantees that no employee would be worse off.

For some employees, their personal situation may be such that the extra money from working straight nights is more important to them than the inconvenience of night shift. A few employees may even have reasons to prefer night shift to day shift. The point is that any employees who voluntarily choose to work continuous night shift at the higher wage must be better off, otherwise they would not choose that option over the option of continuing to rotate shifts. Similarly, other employees in different personal situations may find the opportunity to work continuous day shift so appealing that they are pre-pared to accept the lower day-shift wage. Again, these employees must be better off, oth-erwise they would not choose day shift over the option of continuing to rotate shifts. Thus, some employees are made better off and no employee is made worse off by using a compensating wage differential to allocate employees between shifts, rather than rely-ing on the more traditional approach of requiring all employees to alternate shifts. This example illustrates the win-win possibilities of applying economic rationale to solve workplace problems.

What Happens When Competition Is Not Perfect?

Most labour markets differ from the perfectly competitive ideal in several important re-spects. First, although wage rates are influenced by economic forces, these rates generally do not adjust rapidly enough to equate supply and demand as predicted by the competi-tive model. Actual labour markets are often characterized by substantial periods of labour surpluses (unemployment) or, occasionally, periods of labour shortages (job vacancies) even in the absence of institutional factors that impede adjustment such as minimum wage laws, equal pay legislation, or unions. In particular, a reduction in demand for labour often leads to involuntary terminations (layoffs) rather than a lowering of the wage to the equilibrium level. Attempts to explain why wage adjustments do not clear the labour market in a satisfactory period of time have been the source of considerable con-troversy and will be discussed below in the context of barriers to labour market flexibility.

The second reason why actual labour markets differ from the competitive ideal is that many employers are "wage-setters" rather than "wage-takers" as assumed in the competi-tive model. Being a wage-taker implies that the employer can hire any desired amount of labour at the given market wage, but that at a slightly lower wage, the employer would not be able to attract any employees because they would move to a competing firm offer-ing the market wage. Typically, however, employers recognize that if they reduce the wage rate, there may be some reduction in the supply of labour to the firm (or an increase in turnover rates), but they will not lose their entire workforce as assumed in the perfectly competitive model. In fact, survey evidence indicates that teenage workers would require a wage that is 26 percent higher than their current wage to induce them to move to a similar job with a different employer in the same area (Card, 1992: 53). The size of this differential presumably reflects the substantial psychological and economic costs of changing employers, thus giving employers a substantial role as wage-setters.

Employers who are wage-setters rather than wage-takers are said to possess some degree of *monopsony power*, and it can be shown that, in exercising that power to maximize profits, they will pay a lower wage and employ fewer workers than an employer in a perfectly competitive labour market. The extreme case of monopsonistic power is a situation in which there is only one employer of a particular type of labour in the market, such as a school board that is the only employer of teachers in a community, or a hospital that is the only employer of nurses. Such cases of pure monopsony are the polar opposite of a perfectly competitive labour market.

Employers with some degree of monopsony power can also affect the amount of labour supplied to their establishments through their recruiting, promotion, and training procedures as well as through changes in their wage structure or the redesigning of the job.

The Demand for Labour

In this section, we first consider the magnitude of the employment reduction in response to a wage increase, then examine the case of a minimum-wage increase, and finish with a discussion of the issue of deindustrialization.

How Much Does Employment Fall When the Wage Rate Increases: Elasticity of Demand

Many of the changes implemented or proposed in the industrial relations field increase labour costs. Examples include an increase in minimum wages, an increase in wages of female employees through pay equity legislation, an increase in payroll taxes such as Canada Pension Plan premiums, and an increase in pension benefits directly or by indexing benefits to inflation. In the context of a competitive labour market, an increase in labour costs will result in a reduction in employment since the demand curve for labour is downward sloping as discussed previously. In order to make an informed assessment of the potential employment impact of changes in labour costs, it is, however, often necessary to know by *how much* employment will be reduced in response to a given cost increase.

The concept used to measure the responsiveness of employment to labour costs is the *elasticity of demand for labour*, defined as the percentage reduction in employment in response to a 1 percent increase in wages in a particular job (for a given level of wages and prices for the economy as a whole). The percentage reduction in employment associated with a wage increase will be larger under the following circumstances:

- if the firm can easily substitute capital or other types of labour for the type of labour that has increased in cost;
- if a price increase induced by a wage increase would cause a substantial drop in the firm's sales; or
- if labour costs are a substantial portion of total costs so that a wage increase would have a substantial impact on unit costs.

The employment effect will also be greater the longer the time allowed for adjustments to take place.

A review of the empirical evidence suggests that, on average, over a one-year time horizon, employment is reduced by about 3 percent for each 10 percent increase in labour costs (Hamermesh, 1993). In situations where employment is particularly sensitive to labour costs, the employment impact could be twice as large, and in situations where employment is less sensitive to labour costs, the impact may be virtually zero. The evidence also indicates that, on average, the cause of the employment reduction is divided roughly equally between the replacement of the more expensive labour by capital or other types of labour (the substitution effect) and a drop in sales due to the higher price of the output (the output effect).

The Canadian Labour Congress has advocated, as a means of creating jobs, increasing the premium rate for overtime work or completely banning overtime in order to force employers to cut back on it and to hire more employees. A study for the Ontario Task Force on Hours of Work and Overtime calculated that, ignoring the impact on the demand for labour, an increase in the overtime premium from time-and-one-half to double time would increase hourly paid employment in Ontario by 0.5 percent. When taking into account the negative impact on the demand for labour resulting from the increase in labour costs, however, the employment increase would only be 0.2 percent (Robb and Robb, 1987, Table 10).

The Impact on Employment of Raising the Minimum Wage

One goal of a minimum-wage policy is to improve the equity of the distribution of income. A fear in tampering with minimum-wage rates is that if legislation sets the wage above the equilibrium rate, employers may react by reducing minimum-wage jobs. For an employer with monopsony power, however, it can be shown (see Benjamin, Gunderson, and Riddell, 1998: 249–253) that it is theoretically possible for a moderate increase in the minimum wage to actually increase employment. The reason is that the minimum wage causes the employer with monopsony power to become a wage-taker instead of a wage-setter (although in this case the wage is determined by legislation rather than by the market). As the minimum wage increases toward the wage that would have been determined in a competitive market (without monopsony), then employment also increases toward the competitive level. In effect, the legislative intervention offsets the tendency of employers with monopsony power to pay wages below the competitive wage and to hire fewer employees than in a competitive market.

The conventional wisdom that an increase in the minimum wage causes a reduction in employment has been challenged in some important work in the early 1990s by David Card and his associates using American data.[2] An alternative, quasi-experimental methodology was utilized in which minimum-wage increases in one US state were assessed by comparing employment levels to those in another state where the minimum wage did not rise. The second state served as a "control group." This quasi-experimental method used by Card appears to be more reliable on scientific grounds than the time-series analysis that was used in most previous research on the topic. Card found no evidence of negative employment impacts, which led him to conclude that more attention should be given to non-competitive models of the labour market such as the monopsony model. This conclusion has, however, been challenged by other economists (e.g., Baker, Benjamin, and Stanger, 1999) and the topic remains highly controversial.

Deindustrialization

Deindustrialization refers to a shift of employment away from manufacturing and other goods production towards employment in the service sector. This trend is an issue of concern to trade union members and others since many of the jobs in the goods sector are higher-paying, unionized blue-collar jobs and many of the service-sector jobs are lower paying and often nonunion.

There are three fundamental economic forces related to the demand for labour that account for the long-term decline in Canadian manufacturing employment as a percent of total employment. First, as living standards have risen over time, there has been an increase in the consumption of both goods and services, but consumers' preferences for services have increased faster than their preferences for goods. Second, productivity growth has generally been higher in goods industries than service industries. Service industries require greater numbers of workers who are less easily replaced by technology. Third, the demand for labour in Canadian manufacturing has declined as production has shifted to Third World countries with lower compensation costs.

Foreign competition affects manufacturing more than services since services cannot be transported and traded as easily as manufactured goods. Growth in the service sector occurred primarily in the form of a shift in the production of some services and commodities from within manufacturing towards the service sector itself. This has occurred, for example, in many business services (financial, accounting, marketing), security and cleaning services, and cafeteria services. In addition to this shift towards purchasing from within the service sector itself, the demand for services has grown in general.

Within the service sector, which contains almost 70 percent of the workforce, there are enormous differences in employment trends, wage rates, and the extent of unionization. Government employment growth slowed markedly in the 1980s and 1990s after increasing in the 1960s and 1970s. Employment in transportation, storage, communications, and utilities also did not keep up with the overall growth. In contrast, absolute and relative increases occurred in business services, retail trade, consumer services, and education and health. Earnings and the degree of unionization are high in utilities, transportation, storage, communications, government, education, and health, and low in wholesale and retail trade and consumer services. Earnings are high and unionization is low in business services.

The issue of deindustrialization, therefore, is more complex than simply moving from situations of extensive unionization and high wages to situations of low unionization and low wages. Even if the degree of unionization remains unchanged, the long-term trend toward the service sector will produce mixed results in terms of its implications for both unionization and wage rates.

Supply of Labour

The supply of labour to individual occupations depends on the net advantages in each occupation, as discussed above, but the supply of labour to the labour market as a whole requires a somewhat different analysis. Labour supply has both quality and quantity dimensions. The quality dimensions refer to education and training (subjects that have been analyzed within the context of human capital theory) as well as such factors as motivation and alienation (subjects within the purview of human resource management and organizational behaviour).

The quantity dimensions of labour supply are numerous, basically involving the size of our population (births less deaths plus net immigration), the extent to which the population participates in labour market activities, and the hours worked by those who participate in the labour market. The economic determinants of these various components—births, net immigration, labour force participation, and hours of work—have been the subject matter of considerable research on the supply side of labour markets.

Labour Force Participation and Hours of Work

The theoretical framework used for the analysis of employee preferences for hours of work and labour force participation decisions is the "income-leisure choice model," which treats the purchase of "leisure" (a catch-all word for all non-work activities) the same as the purchase of any other commodity. The individual has a fixed amount of time that can be allocated to leisure or to earning income through work. The wage rate indicates the amount of goods and services that can be purchased by giving up one hour of leisure.

In the income-leisure choice model, an increase in the wage rate influences the number of hours the employee desires to work through two effects operating in opposite directions: a *substitution effect* and an *income effect*. On the one hand, the substitution effect of a higher wage means the employee can earn more income and purchase more goods and services for each hour of leisure given up, inducing a substitution of goods for the relatively more expensive leisure. Leisure is more "expensive" because of the higher wage one forgoes by consuming it. The substitution effect means that at a higher wage, the employee will prefer to work longer hours. On the other hand, the income effect of a higher wage means the employee is wealthier and can afford to consume more of both goods and leisure (i.e., work fewer hours).

The empirical evidence suggests that, overall, the income and substitution effects are of roughly equal magnitude—that is, they tend to offset each other. This implies that a wage increase will normally affect desired hours of work only slightly or have no impact. For men, however, the income effect slightly dominates, so that wage increases tend to result in a slight reduction in their desired hours of work (i.e., the male labour-supply schedule is slightly "backward bending"). For women, however, the substitution effect appears to dominate the income effect so that a wage increase tends to increase their desired hours of work (i.e., the female labour-supply schedule is forward sloping) (Benjamin, Gunderson, and Riddell, 1998: 55).

The income-leisure choice model sheds light on several issues that are significant in union–management relations. The standard workweek in Canada has declined dramatically over the last century, influenced by both collective bargaining and employment standards legislation. In Canadian manufacturing, the standard workweek has declined from 64 hours per week in 1870 to under 40 hours per week in the 1990s. In the postwar period, the reduction has been in the form of longer vacations and more holidays, that is, a shorter work year, rather than reduced hours-per-week, in part because the fixed costs of commuting make the reductions in hours-per-week less economical than a longer vacation. The income-leisure choice model suggests that, as productivity and real wage rates have increased over time, the income effect of the wage increase outweighed the substitution effect, resulting in a desire for more leisure and shorter work hours as the wage rate increased (for men but not for women, as discussed above).

The income-leisure choice framework also illustrates how various income maintenance programs (e.g., welfare, employment insurance) can reduce work incentives. This occurs because they provide income and hence reduce the need to work (the income effect), and also because they often tax labour market earnings, usually implicitly by requiring the recipient to forgo all or some of the transfer payment if they work (the substitution effect).

The Aging of the Population

The last decade has seen a continuation of fundamental changes in the demographic composition of the labour force that have important implications for union–management relations. One of these changes is that by the year 2000, the large baby-boom generation (those born between 1947 and 1966) had moved solidly into the middle-aged group (34 to 53 years of age) (Foot and Stoffman, 1996).

Foot and Venne (1990) argue that the movement of the baby-boom generation into middle age has created a mismatch between the typical organizational structure and the demographic structure of the labour force. In the past, the rapidly growing labour force resulted in a "population pyramid" (with a younger population base and fewer persons at the apex in the older age groups), which roughly mirrored the typical pyramidal structure of most organizations (with fewer positions at the higher levels). The population pyramid was transformed, however, as the baby-boom generation was followed by the relatively small baby-bust generation. The result was a mismatching in which the traditional upward career movement was blocked by a lack of senior positions for the baby boomers. Foot and Venne indicate that the degree of mismatch declined during the 1960s and early 1970s, but increased during the 1980s and will continue to worsen during the 1990s and the first decade of the 21st century.

In terms of implications for human resource management, Foot and Venne suggest a change from a traditional linear career path up the traditional hierarchical organization, to a spiral path that combines both lateral and vertical movements. In certain circumstances, there could even be acceptance of a lower position in the hierarchy as a result of downsizing of the organization or increased stress associated with greater competition (Meltz and Meltz, 1992). Such changes would provide new challenges for employees, as well as greater emphasis on planning and retraining. Such changes may also call for complementary policies, such as increased study leaves or sabbaticals and modified compensation structures in which success is related not just to the level of the positions held in the organization, but also to their variety.

The aging of the labour force has other implications for industrial relations and human resource practices. Middle-aged workers tend to be more stable in their attachment to their employer than are younger workers. The aging of the labour force can be expected to reduce voluntary turnover, and this in turn can make unionization a more attractive option. The longer a worker intends to remain with an employer, the more appealing is the investment of effort and money in forming and nurturing a union. In other words, for the greying labour force, the use of "voice" (unionization) becomes more attractive relative to the use of "exit" (quitting) as a way of improving the work environment.

As individuals approach retirement, their preferences in collective bargaining shift towards pension and related benefits and away from an emphasis on wages. There clearly can be sharp differences within a bargaining unit between younger workers with families to support, who are interested in the amount of take-home pay, and older workers who are prepared to accept reduced take-home pay in favour of putting more money into a pension plan. Workers of different ages with differing family responsibilities may also place different emphasis on such factors as health and safety, medical benefits, and seniority and work-time practices including flexible work-time arrangements. Although workers of all ages are interested in job security, this is especially true of middle-aged workers.

The aging of the labour force has also been accompanied by an increasing emphasis on the issue of age discrimination in employment. In almost all Canadian jurisdictions, it is illegal to use age as a criterion in employment decisions such as hiring, promotion,

EXHIBIT 6.1

AGE DISCRIMINATION AND MANDATORY RETIREMENT

- Mandatory retirement refers to a policy of an employer requiring employees to retire at a fixed age (typically 65 years).

- Mandatory retirement constitutes a form of age discrimination, and as a result has been prohibited by legislation in some provinces (such as Quebec and Manitoba) and in the United States.

- Ontario and some other provinces continue to permit mandatory retirement. In Ontario, there is a "cap" of 64 years on the age discrimination provision in the *Ontario Human Rights Code* that allows mandatory retirement by removing protection from age discrimination for employees over age 64.

- The Supreme Court of Canada, in a 1990 Charter of Rights and Freedoms case, ruled that, although the cap was a form of age discrimination, and age discrimination is prohibited under the Charter, it was reasonable for the Ontario government to impose a cap because the abolition of mandatory retirement might have wide-ranging impacts on the industrial relations system.

- Basically, the Supreme Court decision means that any decision to prohibit mandatory retirement will be a political decision made by the provincial legislature rather than by the Court.

or layoffs. Of course, there are typically exceptions related to issues of public safety or where the employer can demonstrate that an age restriction is a bona fide requirement of the job (see Exhibit 6.1).

Increasing Importance of Women in the Labour Force

Another important demographic change is that during the last two decades, the Canadian labour force has been transformed from one that was predominantly male to one approaching an equal balance between men and women. In 1970, men constituted 66 percent of the labour force, double the proportion of women, who constituted only 34 percent. By 1997, however, 53 percent of employees were male and 47 percent female, not far from a 50/50 ratio.[3]

The change in the gender composition was primarily due to a sharp rise in the labour force participation rate of women, mainly reflecting a rise in the participation rate of married women, especially those with children. As well, the male labour force participation rate has declined slightly, largely reflecting a trend toward earlier retirement.

The growing importance of women in the labour force has been accompanied by increased concern regarding the ratio of women's earnings to men's earnings and important changes in legislation governing their pay and working conditions. The pay gap has narrowed over time as women's earnings (for full-time, full-year work) have risen slowly from about 60 percent of men's earnings in the mid-1970s to just over 70 percent in the mid-1990s (Benjamin, Gunderson, and Riddell, 1998: 427). In terms of legislation, *equal pay for equal work* legislation (which requires women to be paid the same as men if they are doing substantially the same job) was generally replaced with *pay equity legislation*. The latter requires that female-dominated jobs be paid the same as male-dominated jobs if the jobs are of equal value based on a composite of skill, effort, responsibility, and working conditions. Gender-neutral job evaluation techniques are used to compare the value of jobs that might be in quite different occupations, such as a secretary and a truck driver.

Because the traditional complaints-based human rights approach was slow and relatively ineffective and tended to be applied mainly to the public sector, the Ontario government, in its 1987 Pay Equity Act, broke new ground by implementing a proactive approach that requires employers (above a minimum size) in both the public and private sectors to evaluate their jobs and to make appropriate adjustments if female-dominated jobs are found to be underpaid relative to male-dominated jobs for the same employer. Changes were phased in between 1990 and 1993, depending upon the size of the employer's workforce. Preliminary evidence suggests that such legislation would only eliminate about 10 to 20 percent of the pay gap, partly because it is restricted to comparisons within establishments (Benjamin, Gunderson, and Riddell, 1998: 450).

Increasing Importance of Part-time and Contingent Work

By the late 1990s, almost one in five employees was working part-time, defined by Statistics Canada as someone usually working less than 30 hours per week at their main job.[4] The part-time employment rate (i.e., part-time employment as a percentage of total employment) has increased steadily from about 4 percent in the mid-1950s to 19 percent in 1998.[5]

Statistics Canada: www.statcan.ca/

The rise in part-time work reflects several of the labour market trends already outlined. On the supply side, the rise in the labour force participation rate of women, particularly married women, resulted in an increase in the proportion of employees desiring to work part-time. Over two-thirds of part-time employees are female. Statistics Canada data indicate that normally about three-quarters of part-timers work part-time voluntarily, although in recessions there is typically an increase in the amount of involuntary part-time work. On the demand side, since services cannot be stored as easily as can goods, the increasing importance of the service sector in the economy resulted in an increase in the demand for part-time employees to meet peak periods of demand.

The federal government's Commission of Inquiry into Part-time Work (1983) found that the productivity of part-timers is generally equal to or higher than that of full-timers, although the compensation of part-timers is often substantially less than that of full-timers doing the same work. To address this inequity, the Commission recommended employment standards legislation to provide equal pay for work of equal value for part-timers and full-timers, with benefits for part-timers pro-rated according to the number of hours worked. However, employer opposition to such recommendations is substantial. In Saskatchewan, the government introduced then withdrew legislation designed to pro-rate part-time benefits. Similarly, the British Columbia government chose not to follow the advice of an independent employment review commission, which had recommended pro-rated benefits for part-time employees.

Unions have often strongly opposed the use of part-time workers, and there have been many strikes in which a major issue was the union's opposition to management proposals to increase the use of part-time employees. The reason for union opposition is that the poor compensation of part-timers is seen as a threat to the employment and compensation of full-time employees. As well, part-time workers are often more difficult to organize. Many employees do prefer part-time work, however, and if the compensation of part-timers is made comparable to that of full-timers, union opposition may diminish. Even in the absence of such legislation, unions have increased their efforts to organize part-time workers, partly as a result of the increase in their numbers.

One of the other reasons for the disadvantage faced by part-time employees is that the Ontario Labour Relations Board, for example, tended to place part-time and full-time employees in separate bargaining units, on the assumption that they do not share a "community of interest." The effect of this was to exclude many part-timers from collective bargaining. Modifications to the Ontario Labour Relations Act (see Exhibit 6.2), introduced by the NDP government in 1992, remedied this situation by directing the Ontario Labour Relations Board to place part-timers and full-timers in the same bargaining unit, unless doing so would cause the certification application to fail. This provision was, however, repealed by the Ontario Conservative government in 1995.

Exhibit 6.2

Provisions for Part-time and Full-time Bargaining Units

Ontario Labour Relations Act (Bill 40 Amendments)

7. (1) Section 6 of the Act is amended by adding the following subsections:

(2.1) A bargaining unit consisting of full-time employees and part-time employees shall be deemed by the Board to be a unit of employees appropriate for collective bargaining.

(2.2) Despite subsection (2.1), the Board shall determine that separate bargaining units for full-time and for part-time employees are appropriate if it is satisfied that less than 55 percent of the employees in a single unit of full-time and part-time employees are members of the trade union on the date the union applies for certification or have applied to become members on or before that date.

Source: © Queen's Printer for Ontario, 1992. This is an unofficial version of Government of Ontario's legal materials.

In addition to the growth of part-time work, there has also been an increase in the utilization of contingent work, i.e., casual, term, contract, temporary, and seasonal jobs. According to Statistics Canada's 1995 Survey of Work Arrangements, non-standard work (part-time and contingent work) now comprises about one-third of employment in Canada (Payette, 1999: 116). Managers report that the main reason for using contingent workers is to provide flexibility to respond to fluctuations in demand. Union representatives suggest that, in addition to providing flexibility, contingent work helps employers to reduce benefit costs and avoid unionization. Union response to contingent work has included resistance strategies (such as prohibiting contingent work and contracting out), accommodation strategies (negotiating work rules and due process for contingent workers), and proactive strategies (such as using union hiring halls for hiring contingent workers and managing pension and benefit plans) (Payette, 1999).

The Brain Drain and Immigration

In the late 1990s, a controversy arose concerning the issue of the "brain drain," i.e., the emigration to the United States of highly skilled Canadians, particularly engineers, computer scientists, doctors, nurses, professors, and managers. Higher earnings and lower taxes in the United States have been suggested as important causes of the brain drain, prompting the minister of finance in 1999 to cite concern about the brain drain as one of the factors motivating his proposal to reduce taxes for the middle class in his next budget.[6]

A Statistics Canada study in 1998 concluded, however, that "there is little evidence in support of a large-scale exodus of knowledge workers from Canada to the United States.... The brain drain was found to be small in a historical sense, small relative to the stock of workers in these disciplines, and small relative to the supply of new workers in these disciplines" (Statistics Canada, 1998: 1). In March 1999, HRDC, in co-operation with Statistics Canada, undertook a special survey of 1995 Canadian university graduates who had moved to the United States. The results of the survey substantiated the conclusion that the brain drain to the United States is small—only 1.5 percent of the 1995 graduating class. Emigrants did, however, tend to be above average—almost half ranked themselves in the top 10 percent of their graduating class (HRDC, 1999: ix–x). Helliwell (1999) also found the brain drain to be of small magnitude in his analysis of US census and current population survey data on the number of Canadians living in the US. Furthermore, these studies showed that Canada gains about four times as many highly skilled workers through immigration from the rest of the world as it loses through emigration to the US.

In spite of this evidence, some writers (Devoretz and Laryea, 1998; Iqbal, 1999) argue the brain drain is important for three reasons: First, the quality issue—those Canada is losing may be the "best and brightest." Second, the "churning argument"—Devortz and Laryea, in their study for the C. D. Howe Institute, argue that replacing emigrants with immigrants is still costly because of administrative and settlement costs and because, at least in the first few years, immigrants earn less than their Canadian counterparts, possibly reflecting a lower productivity level. Third, the data showing a relatively small brain drain focus on Canadians who are permanent residents of the US, but there has recently been an upsurge in Canadians temporarily residing in the US who may become permanent residents in the future.

A further issue is that in many cases there seem to be artificial barriers to the recognition of the qualifications of highly skilled immigrants to Canada. If such barriers reflect an artificial restriction on supply of labour in these occupations, rather than an appropriate evaluation of skills, then Canada may be failing to take advantage of the high levels of skills that many immigrants are bringing to the country.

Interaction of Supply and Demand for Labour

Market forces of supply and demand set the general boundaries for the employment and wage-rate decisions but earnings are also affected by collective bargaining and by government regulations such as minimum wages, training, and education requirements.

Earning Differentials and Efficiency Wages

Empirical studies indicate that the ranking of *occupational* earnings has been fairly stable over long periods of time (e.g., Benjamin, Gunderson, and Riddell, 1998: 345–65). Some changes have occurred, however, which are usually associated either with the decline of an industry (for example, the deterioration in the relative position of the railroads) or a major change in technology (such as the huge increase in air traffic and in the earnings of airline pilots). The dispersion of earnings among occupations seems to have followed cycles of narrowing and widening. Although there was a long-run trend to narrowing until 1971, there has been widening since then.

Evidence also indicates the existence of substantial wage differentials by *industry*, beyond what appear to be required as compensating differentials to reflect variations in qualifications and working conditions. For example, "high-wage" industries, such as tobacco products and petroleum manufacturing, appear to pay 20 to 30 percent above the competitive norm, whereas "low-wage" industries, such as accommodation and food services, tend to pay 20 percent below the competitive norm (Gera and Grenier, 1994). These inter-industry differentials appear to be relatively stable over time and across countries.

A possible explanation for such inter-industry wage differentials is the notion of "efficiency wages," i.e., employers in some industries may find it profitable to pay above the market clearing wage if the higher wage results in higher productivity through mechanisms such as greater work effort, improved morale, and lower turnover. Empirically, however, it is difficult to determine if the observed inter-industry differentials reflect efficiency wages or other economic factors such as employees benefiting from the employer's monopoly power in the product market. As discussed later in the section on barriers to labour market flexibility, efficiency wages can also result in unemployment by preventing the labour market from clearing.

Regional differentials in earnings are affected by the mix of industries and occupations as well as by purely geographical factors. Over time, the regional dispersion of wage rates has narrowed, although there have been cycles similar to those for occupations.

 Bureau of Labour Statistics: stats.bls.gov/blshome.html

Increased Earnings Inequality

During the 1980s and 1990s, there was an increase in the inequality of annual earnings in Canada, in contrast to the fairly constant degree of inequality during most of the post-war period (Statistics Canada, 1999b). The rising inequality of earnings, however, has been ameliorated by the impact of taxes and transfer payments from government—there has been little increase in inequality of income after taxes and transfers (Statistics Canada, 1999a).

If earnings in the service sector are lower and more unequal than in the goods sector, then deindustrialization and the trend toward an increasing proportion of employment in services would increase inequality. Other contributing factors could be the baby boom and an increased premium for education, although evidence suggests they do not account for much of the increase in inequality.

The factor that is most important in explaining the rise in the inequality of Canadian annual earnings is that fewer Canadians were working a "normal" workweek (of 35 to 40 hours). In particular, there was an increase in the number of hours worked by those with high annual earnings. "Unlike the United States, where changes in earnings inequality have been largely a result of changes in the distribution of hourly wages, shifts in Canadian earnings inequality are, at the aggregate level, mainly driven by changes in the distribution of annual hours worked" (Morissette et al, 1993: 3).

Empirical evidence also indicates that there has been some increase in wage inequity or wage polarization in Canada over the 1980s and 1990s. This polarization has been less pronounced in Canada than in the United States, however, because unionization has not declined in Canada as it has in the United States, and unions tend to reduce wage inequality (Lemieux, 1993). Furthermore, there has been a greater influx of more highly educated persons into the Canadian labour market, and this has served to restrain wages at the top of the wage distribution (Freeman and Needles, 1993).

The Proliferation of Computers and the Productivity Paradox

The proliferation of computers and information technology during the 1990s would generally be expected to boost the rate of growth of labour productivity (output per person hour). Instead, annual productivity growth in the 1989–96 period averaged only 0.7 percent in the Canadian business sector, the lowest rate in any decade going back to the 1960s (Sharpe, 1997: 35). Furthermore, a cross-sectional analysis indicates that those sectors that invested more in information technology have, on average, shown lower rates of productivity growth. This productivity paradox is not unique to Canada—it has occurred in a wide range of OECD countries (Sharpe, 1997: 43–44).

Andrew Sharpe has offered three explanations for the paradox that investment in computers has not produced the expected benefits in terms of increased productivity growth. The first explanation is the mis-measurement hypothesis (which he labels "the benefits are here"). This suggests that the methods used to measure productivity at the national level do not adequately capture the impacts of computers. For example, measurement of output in the service sector is problematic. In addition, much of the benefit of computers may be in terms of qualitative change, such as more convenient access to services, rather than an increased quantity of services.

Sharpe's second explanation is the lag hypothesis ("the benefits are coming"). The suggestion is that computers have the potential to increase productivity, but this potential will only be realized with improved organizational structure, more training, and improved computer design. Sharpe's third hypothesis is that "the benefits are never coming." There are several arguments in support of this hypothesis. One is that, in spite of the prevalence of computers in the workplace, the actual magnitude of investment in information technology is a relatively small fraction of total investment, so it should not be expected to have a substantial impact on overall productivity growth. Another explanation is that the benefits of computers are largely offset by their costs in terms of never-ending upgrading, crashes, incompatibility problems, and viruses—problems that are unlikely to ever be eliminated. Sharpe suggests that all three hypotheses probably have some validity, but he feels the third hypothesis (the benefits are never coming) is closest to the mark.

The Macroeconomic Environment

The overall state of the economy, known as the macroeconomic environment, significantly influences many aspects of union–management relations. An expanding economy, for example, leads to higher wage settlements and more strike activity; the latter also tends to increase in periods when there is uncertainty about high levels of inflation. An expanding economy may also facilitate the attaining of broader social goals such as occupational health and safety and pay equity and equal employment opportunities for women. It is also associated with a higher rate of growth of unionization and greater success for unions in certification and decertification applications at the labour relations boards.

In periods when the economy is in recession and temporary layoffs are more prevalent, provisions concerning seniority in layoff and recall assume a greater importance in both the negotiation and the administration of the collective agreement. In cases of permanent layoffs or complete plant shutdown, negotiations concerning severance packages become more prominent. The overall state of the Canadian economy also affects the courts' interpretation of the length of "reasonable notice" required in wrongful dismissal cases under the common law—about one-and-one-half months more notice is required when the economy is in recession than when it is booming (McShane, 1983).

Uncertainty about high rates of inflation tends to result in higher wage settlements and a greater prevalence of cost-of-living adjustment (COLA) clauses in collective agreements. On the other hand, a reduction in uncertainty about the macroeconomic environment can partly explain the significant increase in average contract duration during the 1990s (from under two years in 1990 to almost three years in 1999[7]).

Strategis-Industry Canada (business-related information):
strategis.ic.gc.ca

Swings in the Unemployment Rate

Since the unemployment rate is by far the most prominent measure of the state of the macroeconomic environment, there was a great deal of concern among the actors in the industrial relations system when the Canadian unemployment rate rose to double-digit levels during the recessions of the early 1980s and early 1990s.

Unemployment is measured in Canada by a monthly labour force survey covering about 52,000 households (see Exhibit 6.3). Since Statistics Canada recognizes that there is some ambiguity about the appropriate definition of unemployment rates, it publishes a range of eight unemployment rates with alternative definitions, designated R1 to R8 (Statistics Canada, 1999c). For example, in 1998 when the "official" unemployment rate (R4) was 8.3 percent, its most restrictive definition, the rate for those unemployed for one year or more (R1) was only 1.1 percent. The most comprehensive measure (R8) was 11.5 percent, which included discouraged searchers (0.5 percent), persons waiting for long-term recall and long-term future starts (0.7 percent), and those underemployed, i.e., involuntary part-timers (2.3 percent).

EXHIBIT 6.3

DEFINITION OF UNEMPLOYED IN THE LABOUR FORCE SURVEY

Unemployed persons are those who, during the reference week:

- were without work, had actively looked for work in the past four weeks (ending with reference week), and were available for work;

- had not actively looked for work in the past four weeks but were on temporary layoff and were available for work;

- had not actively looked for work in the past four weeks but had a new job to start in four weeks or less from the reference week, and were available for work.

Source: "Definition of Unemployed in the Labour Force Survey," adapted from *The Labour Force*, Catalogue No. 72-002.

EXHIBIT 6.4

THE CANADA–US UNEMPLOYMENT RATE GAP

A four-percentage-point gap between the unemployment rates in Canada and the United States has emerged over the last two decades.

The Canadian unemployment rate was only slightly (0.5 percentage points) higher than the US unemployment rate during the 1970s, but it was almost two percentage points higher during the 1980s and almost four percentage points higher in the 1990s. Riddell and Sharpe (1998) outline the reasons for the emergence of the gap, summarizing the results of several papers presented at a conference devoted to the issue.

First, about 0.7 percentage points of the gap is due to different definitions of unemployment used in Canada and the United States. Individuals whose job search consists only of looking at job ads are defined as unemployed in Canada but out of the labour force in the United States.

Second, during the 1980s, employment grew by a similar amount in Canada and the United States. The two-percentage-point unemployment rate gap that appeared in the 1980s was due to a relative rise in the labour force attachment of the non-employed, i.e., more people remained unemployed in Canada whereas in the US they were not in the labour force (Card and Riddell, 1993).

Third, the further two-percentage-point increase in the unemployment gap in the 1990s was simply due to a rise in deficient-demand unemployment—the recession of the early 1990s was more severe in Canada and the recovery weaker (Fortin, 1996).

Analytically, it is useful to distinguish deficient-demand unemployment, which refers to an overall lack of jobs in the labour market, from frictional and structural unemployment. Structural unemployment occurs when there is a mismatching of the characteristics of unemployed persons and vacant jobs in terms of geographical location, occupation, or experience. Frictional unemployment occurs when, due to turnover and the fact that it takes time to locate a job, unemployed workers and suitable vacant jobs coexist in the same labour market. New entrants to the labour market can also experience frictional unemployment. The distinction is important because policies to deal with deficient-demand unemployment (e.g., stimulation of the economy through monetary policy or government spending and taxation) differ from policies to deal with frictional or structural unemployment (e.g., education, training, relocation). The distinction is also important for union–management relations because it is the level of deficient-demand unemployment that provides an indication of the overall state of the labour market and affects strike activity, wage settlements, and the other aspects of labour–management relations discussed above (see Exhibit 6.4).

Barriers to Labour Market Flexibility

The pressure of international competition has resulted in increased calls for flexibility in the labour market. A difficult question is why the labour market, and wages in particular, respond so sluggishly to changes in economic conditions. The answer is the subject of considerable controversy.

Keynes (1936) argued that during periods of unemployment, employees are reluctant to accept wage cuts to preserve jobs because inequities would result from the reductions not being spread equally over the whole labour force. Another explanation, given in the context of *efficiency wage models*, is that wage reductions may reduce employee morale and productivity. This argument suggests that it may not be sensible for employers to force wage reductions during periods of unemployment, even if they have the power to do so. Another explanation for the failure of the labour market to clear is that employers in both union and nonunion establishments have an understanding or an *implicit contract* with their employees in which they agree not to reduce wages during economic downturns. The purpose of implicit contracts is to insure risk-averse workers against wage fluctuations in exchange for a slightly lower average wage over the business cycle or to prevent quits by experienced workers in whom the employer has an investment in terms of training.

Some economists have suggested that the wage system could be made more flexible and macroeconomic performance enhanced by the use of bonuses paid through profit-sharing or gain-sharing plans. Gain-sharing plans (e.g., the Scanlon Plan) are based on cost savings or increased production relative to a base period. Profit-sharing is based on increased profits. Gain-sharing plans are more closely related to employee effort than profit-sharing plans because profits can be affected by a wide variety of external developments that are not subject to employee control. Profit-sharing and gain-sharing plans have long been advocated as means of improving productivity but, more recently, potential benefits for macroeconomic performance also have been suggested. Since bonuses paid are not built into base salary, they increase flexibility in the total compensation package. Profit-sharing is more effective than gain-sharing in enhancing macroeconomic flexibility because profits tend to increase in booms and decrease in recessions, but, for the same reason, gain-sharing is more effective than profit-sharing in enhancing employee effort and productivity.

The Impact of the Macroeconomic Environment on Wage Settlements

The wage settlement in any particular set of negotiations will be greatly affected by the magnitude of the average wage settlement in the economy at the time of negotiations. For example, wage settlements in major collective agreements averaged over 5 percent in 1990, then dropped to almost zero (0.3 percent) in 1994, and slowly increased to over 3 percent by the end of 1999.[8] More dramatically, wage settlements that averaged approximately 15 to 18 percent in the mid-1970s (just prior to the introduction of the AIB wage controls) fell to under 4 percent by the early 1980s. What accounts for such changes? (See Exhibit 6.5.)

When the labour market is in balance, the overall supply of labour equals the overall demand for labour, and the economy will experience frictional and structural unemployment but not deficient-demand unemployment. The amount of frictional and structural unemployment at this position is also known as either the "natural unemployment rate"

EXHIBIT 6.5

THE OVERALL RATE OF WAGE CHANGE

Empirical work on the determinants of the overall aggregate rate of wage change, known as the *Phillips Curve*, has established two basic propositions (Wilton and Prescott, 1992):

1. for any given level of expected inflation, wage settlements are high when the rate of deficient-demand unemployment rate is low (i.e., when the labour market is in a boom); and

2. for any given state of labour market conditions, wage settlements fully reflect changes in the expected inflation rate.

The fluctuations in overall wage settlements in Canada reflect these factors—the decline and subsequent rise in wage settlements in the 1990s reflected a sharp rise in the unemployment rate in the recession of the early 1990s and the boom of the late 1990s.

The reduction in wage settlements between the mid-1970s and the early 1980s reflects both a rise in unemployment during the recession of the early 1980s and a decline in expected inflation.

or by the more neutral term, the "non-accelerating inflation rate of unemployment" (NAIRU). The latter name reflects the idea that at such an overall equilibrium position, there would be no labour market pressure for the rate of wage or price change to either increase or decrease.

If the economy is at the NAIRU and is stimulated, for example, by an increased rate of growth of the money supply, the effect in the short run is to reduce the unemployment rate and increase wage settlements. Higher wage settlements are reflected in a higher inflation rate, however, and it can be demonstrated using economic analysis that, in the long run, when expectations about inflation have adjusted to the new higher rate, the economy will return to its original level of unemployment (the NAIRU) and the rate of wage change and inflation will be consistent with the new higher rate of growth of the money supply. Thus, in the short run, reduced unemployment can be "traded off" against higher inflation, but in the long run, such a trade-off is not possible.

If, conversely, the government attempts to reduce inflation by reducing the rate of growth of the money supply, the short-run impact will be an increase in unemployment above the NAIRU, a reduction in wage settlements, and eventually a reduction in inflation. When the lower actual inflation rate is fully reflected in a lower expected inflation rate, the economy can return to its original level of unemployment.

The way in which expectations about inflation are formed plays a crucial role in the adjustment process and has been the subject of considerable debate in the macroeconomics literature. To the extent that labour market participants can accurately foresee the impact of changes in government monetary policy, as suggested by the "rational expectations hypothesis," the short-run adjustment period will be reduced. Unfortunately, evidence suggests that the recession experienced during the "short-run" transition to a lower inflation rate can result in several years of severe unemployment, as revealed in the recessions of the early 1980s and 1990s.

Labour Market Impacts of Free Trade

One of the most significant changes in the economic environment in the 1990s has been the increasing international competition resulting from a series of trade agreements. The bilateral Free Trade Agreement (FTA) with the United States, which took effect in 1989, was followed by the trilateral North American Free Trade Agreement (NAFTA) with the United States and Mexico, which took effect in January 1994. In 1994, in a new round of negotiations under the General Agreement on Tariffs and Trade (GATT), Canada also agreed to a reduction of tariffs in its trade with the global economy, including countries such as India, Brazil, Turkey, Indonesia, and Malaysia.

A question of great concern to many Canadians is how Canada can be expected to compete against countries with much lower wage costs and employment standards? For example, countries such as Mexico and Hong Kong have average hourly compensation costs that are less than one-third the cost in Canada.[9] The answer is that unit labour costs (dollars/unit) are determined by compensation (dollars/hour) divided by productivity (units/hour). If low wages generally reflect low productivity, then unit costs of production are not necessarily lower in low-wage countries. Indeed, some of Canada's toughest competition internationally comes from high-wage, high-productivity countries such as Japan (which has compensation costs about one-half *higher* than Canada) and Germany, with compensation costs almost *double* Canada's (Benjamin, Gunderson, and Riddell, 1998: 185). The concern is, however, that many of the low-wage countries are moving up the productivity spectrum and will become low-wage, *high*-productivity countries, at least until their wages adjust to reflect their increased productivity.

Why has Canada (and most other countries) moved toward free trade in the last few years? The basic argument in favour of free trade is that by allowing production to be located where it is most efficient, costs can be reduced and, in the long run, citizens of all countries can potentially benefit from an increase in their real income. Increased efficiency arises from comparative advantage (which takes advantage of geographical differences in relative ability to produce goods) and economies of scale (which take advantage of longer production runs to utilize mass-production techniques).

The estimated size of the increase in real income resulting from trade liberalization was, however, quite modest. For example, following a review of empirical studies, the Royal Commission on the Economic Union (1985: 331) indicated that real incomes of Canadians could be increased from 3 to 5 percent on average by free trade with the United States. The benefits could be larger if free trade prevented a reduction in Canadian incomes resulting from protectionist trade restrictions that otherwise may have been imposed by the United States. By removing tariff and other trade barriers, free trade may also lead to a dissipation of inefficient market structures, regulatory regimes, and work practices that require protection from the forces of competition in order to survive. These *dynamic* gains from trade can enhance the conventional static gains arising from cheaper imports and increased exports.

Critics of free trade point out that the reallocation of labour and capital to achieve a more efficient outcome in the long run involves a substantial economic dislocation in the short run. If increased efficiency is to be attained, some industries and firms will be put out of business and others will expand. In the short run, layoffs, plant shutdowns, and a rise in structural unemployment are likely to result. Although these adjustment costs can be mitigated by adjustment policies to facilitate relocation and training (and the benefits of free trade should provide the means for such compensation), it is unlikely that there will be complete compensation to the firms and workers bearing the costs of the adjustment.

Equally important, critics have suggested that free trade may lead to a "harmonization" of tax policies, employment standards, and labour relations legislation down to the lowest common denominator as a result of inter-jurisdictional competition for investment and jobs. Gunderson (1998) has argued, however, that there also may be pressure toward upward harmonization by governments (through agreements on minimum standards, such as the Social Charter in Europe) and union and consumer boycotts against practices such as child labour. Pressure for upward harmonization can also occur when social policies are more cost effective, such as Canada's public health-care system compared to the American private-sector model. Individual employers in Canada may have lower costs of production vis-à-vis the United States since major employers in the United States usually pay more toward health care and pensions than in Canada. As a result, these components of labour costs are lower in Canada than the United States. This factor has often been cited as giving an advantage to Canadian automobile plants. On the other hand, these benefits are financed out of taxes, which are higher in Canada.

The same concern is expressed when Canada trades with low-wage countries like Mexico, which also have lower labour standards. The concern here is that plants will relocate and capital will flow into such countries given their lower labour costs. To stem this loss of business and the associated jobs, Canadian governments may be pressured to lower their labour standards until they are more in line with those that prevail in the low-cost countries. Whether free trade will lead to lower standards and regulations, or simply put pressure on excessive regulations for which the benefits do not exceed the cost is an interesting question that merits additional analysis.

Although Canada has now had several years' experience under the FTA and NAFTA, measuring the actual impact of the agreements is difficult because the changes were phased in over a number of years, and because the impacts have been confounded with the effects of other developments such as the implementation of the GST, the recession of the early 1990s, and exchange-rate fluctuations (see Exhibit 6.6).

On the legislative side, there does not yet appear to be a widespread dismantling of Canadian employment law to harmonize with that in the United States. Ongoing assessment of the impacts of Canada's various trade arrangements will no doubt be an important topic of future research.

EXHIBIT 6.6

IMPACT OF FREE TRADE ON EMPLOYMENT IN CANADA

A study of the short-run employment impacts of the Free Trade Agreement by Gaston and Trefler (1997) showed that between 1988 and 1993, employment losses in high-tariff industries averaged 24 percent compared to employment losses of 15 percent in low-tariff industries.

The nine-percentage-point differential between these two figures provides an estimate of the impact of job losses due to the FTA because both the high-tariff and low-tariff industries were affected by the recession and other factors affecting employment.

While the employment loss in those industries most affected by the FTA is substantially higher than the industries in the control group, Gaston and Trefler point out that the loss is still small relative to the job losses attributable to the recession in the early 1990s.

CONCLUSION

This chapter has documented ways in which the social, political, and economic environments constrain the various actors—labour, management, and government—and influence the outputs of the industrial relations system. Although we have discussed a wide range of factors, including demographic trends, legislative changes, deindustrialization, and the macroeconomic environment, our review has only touched on the rich and diverse array of research in this field.

Centre for Industrial Relations, University of Toronto:
www.chass.utoronto.ca/cir

Questions

1. Explain each of the following terms: compensating wage differential; equilibrium wage; wage-taker.

2. Discuss why actual labour markets differ from the competitive ideal.

3. Explain why the economic theory of competitive labour markets predicts that the imposition of minimum wage rates will reduce employment. In light of this expectation, what are the possible explanations for Card's finding that the raising of the minimum had no negative effect on employment?

4. Describe the different types of unemployment that researchers have identified, and discuss why the distinctions are important for purposes of public policy.

5. Describe the income-leisure choice model, and explain how it can be used to shed light on significant issues in labour–management relations.

6. Discuss how the projected aging of the labour force will affect both industrial relations and human resource management practices.

7. What is the magnitude of Canada's "brain drain" and what policies, if any, would be appropriate to alleviate this problem?

8. Outline the magnitude of the gap between the unemployment rates in Canada and the US, and explain the reasons for the gap.

9. Explain the "productivity paradox" and the alternative hypotheses to resolve the paradox.

10. Outline the expected impacts on the industrial relations system of free trade policies.

ENDNOTES

[1] Adapted from information provided in the article by T. Van Alpen, "No sex, please, it's GM night shift." *Toronto Star* (February 24, 1994), pp. A1 and A7.

[2] Card, 1992; Card and Krueger, 1995. See also the Review Symposium on the topic in the July 1995 issue of the *Industrial and Labor Relations Review.*

[3] Statistics Canada. *Canadian Economic Observer*, Historical Supplement, 1997/98, catalogue 11-210, p. 32.

[4] The part-time employment rate was 18.7 percent in 1998. (Statistics Canada. *Historical Labour Force Statistics, 1998,* catalogue 71-201, p. 5).

[5] In the 1950s part-time work was defined by Statistics Canada as normally working less than 35 hours per week—the increase in part-time work would have been even greater if the definition had remained consistent.

[6] "Tax cuts for middle class Martin's priority." *National Post* (September 27, 1999).

[7] HRDC, *Workplace Gazette* (Fall 1999).

[8] Ibid., p. 7.

[9] Data for the year 1995 cited in Benjamin, Gunderson, and Riddell, 1998, p. 185.

REFERENCES

BAKER, M., D. BENJAMIN, and S. STANGER. 1999. "The Highs and Lows of the Minimum Wage Effect: A Time-Series Cross-Section Study of the Canadian Law." *Journal of Labor Economics*, 17, no. 2, pp. 318–50.

BENJAMIN, D., M. GUNDERSON, and W. C. RIDDELL. 1998. *Labour Market Economics: Theory, Evidence and Policy in Canada*, 4th Edition. Toronto: McGraw-Hill Ryerson.

CARD, D. 1992. "Do Minimum Wages Reduce Employment? A Case Study of California, 1987–89." *Industrial and Labor Relations Review,* 46, no. 1, pp. 38–54.

CARD, D. and A. KRUEGER. 1995. *Myth and Measurement: The New Economics of the Minimum Wage.* Princeton, New Jersey: Princeton University Press.

CARD, D. and W. C. RIDDELL. 1993. "A Comparative Analysis of Unemployment in Canada and the United States," in *Small Differences that Matter: Labor Markets and Income Maintenance in Canada and the United States*, edited by D. Card and R. B. Freeman. Chicago: University of Chicago Press, pp. 149–89.

COMMISSION OF INQUIRY INTO PART-TIME WORK. 1983. *Part-Time Work in Canada*. Ottawa: Labour Canada.

DEVORETZ, D. and S. A. LARYEA. 1998. *Canadian Human Capital Transfers: The United States and Beyond*. Commentary no. 115 (October). Toronto: CD Howe.

FOOT, D. K. and D. STOFFMAN. 1996. *Boom, Bust and Echo: How to Profit from the Coming Demographic Shift*. Macfarlane, Walter & Ross.

FOOT, D. K. and R. A. VENNE. 1990. "Population, Pyramids and Promotional Prospects." *Canadian Public Policy*, 16, no. 4, pp. 387–98.

FORTIN, P. 1996. "The Great Canadian Slump." *Canadian Journal of Economics*, 29, no. 4, pp. 761–87.

FREEMAN, R. and K. NEEDLES. 1993. "Skill Differentials in Canada in an Era of Rising Labour Market Inequality," in *Small Differences that Matter: Labour Markets and Income Maintenance in Canada and the United States*, edited by D. Card and R. Freeman. Chicago: University of Chicago Press, pp. 45–68.

GASTON, N. and D. TREFLER. 1997. "Labour Market Consequences of the Canada-US Free Trade Agreement." *Canadian Journal of Economics*, 30, no. 1, pp. 18–41.

GERA, S. and G. GRENIER. 1994. "Interindustry Wage Differentials and Efficiency Wages: Some Canadian Evidence." *Canadian Journal of Economics*, 27, pp. 81–100.

GUNDERSON, M. 1998. "Harmonization of Labour Policies Under Trade Liberalization." *Industrial Relations/Relations Industrielles*, 53, no. 1, pp. 11–40.

HAMERMESH, D. 1993. *Labor Demand*. Princeton, NJ: Princeton University Press.

HELLIWELL, J. 1999. "Checking the Brain Drain: Evidence and Implications." Study 99-3. Toronto: University of Toronto Institute for Policy Analysis.

HUMAN RESOURCES DEVELOPMENT CANADA, in co-operation with STATISTICS CANADA. 1999. *South of the Border: Graduates from the Class of '95 Who Moved to the United States*. Statistics Canada, Catalogue 81-587-XIE.

IQBAL, MAMOOD. 1999. *Are We Losing Our Minds? Trends, Determinants, and the Role of Taxes in Brain Drain to the United States*. Conference Board of Canada, pp. 265–99.

KEYNES, J. M. [1936] 1967. *The General Theory of Employment, Interest and Money*. London: Macmillan.

LEMIEUX, T. 1993. "Unions and Wage Inequality in Canada and the United States," in *Small Differences that Matter: Labor Markets and Income Maintenance in Canada and the United States*, edited by D. Card and R. Freeman. Chicago: University of Chicago Press, pp. 69–108.

LIPSET, S. M. and N. M. MELTZ. 1997. "Canadian and American Attitudes Toward Work and Institutions." *Perspectives on Work: The IRRAS's 50th Anniversary Magazine*, 1, no. 3, pp. 14–19.

McSHANE, S. L. 1983. "Reasonable Notice Criteria in Common Law Wrongful Dismissal Cases." *Industrial Relations/Relations Industrielles*, 38, no. 3, pp. 618–33.

MELTZ, R. L. and N. M. MELTZ. 1992. *Taking Charge: Career Planning for Canadian Workers*. Toronto: Captus Press and Iguana & Associates.

MORISSETTE, R., J. MYLES, and G. PICOT. 1993. *What is Happening to Earnings Inequality in Canada?* Ottawa: Statistics Canada.

PAYETTE, S. 1999. "Contingent Work: Trends, Issues and Challenges for Labour." *Workplace Gazette*, 2, no. 3, pp. 116–19.

RIDDELL, W. C. and A. SHARPE. 1998. "The Canada-US Unemployment Rate Gap: An Introduction and Overview." *Canadian Public Policy*, 24, Special supplement (February), pp. S1–S37.

ROBB, A. L. and R. E. ROBB. 1987. *The Prospects for Creating Jobs by Reducing Hours of Work in Ontario. Background Report to the Ontario Task Force on Hours of Work and Overtime*. Toronto: Queen's Printer.

ROYAL COMMISSION ON THE ECONOMIC UNION. 1985. *Report*. Ottawa: Queen's Printer.

SHARPE, A. 1997. "The Productivity Paradox: An Evaluation of Competing Explanations." *Canadian Business Economics*, pp. 32–47.

STATISTICS CANADA. 1998. "Brain Drain or Brain Gain? What Do the Data Say?" Presentation, October 1, 1998.

———. 1999a. *Income After Tax, Distributions by Size in Canada, 1997*. Catalogue 13-210-XPB, p. 21.

———. 1999b. *Income Distributions by Size in Canada, 1997*. Catalogue 13-207-XPB, p. 22.

———. 1999c. *Labour Force Update: Supplementary Measures of Unemployment*. Catalogue 71-005-XPB, p. 32.

WILTON, D. A. and D. M. PRESCOTT. 1992. *Macroeconomics: Theory and Policy in Canada*, 3rd Edition. Don Mills, Ontario: Addison-Wesley.

CHAPTER 7

Collective Bargaining Legislation in Canada

Richard Jackson

In 1997, the Windsor Wal-Mart store in Ontario was the first of 2600 Wal-Mart stores worldwide to become unionized. The United Steelworkers of America was certified under Section 11 of the Ontario Labour Relations Act even though it won only 28 percent of the representation vote.

Here's how it happened.

From its original Wal-Mart Discount City in Atlanta in 1962, Wal-Mart expanded throughout the world to become the world's largest retail organization. Wal-Mart revolutionized the retailing industry with its unique approach and corporate culture based upon selecting employees who are likely to be good team players and instilling in them a philosophy of superior customer service. Employees at all levels are referred to as "associates" and are taught that their views are valued. The company's team culture includes a general meeting each morning before the store opens and another just after the day's closing. At these meetings, employees are informed about the store's performance and other matters of concern to them and to the company as a whole. Any employee is free to ask questions on any matter of a colleague at any level in the organization and, according to the "sundown rule," is entitled to a full answer by the end of the business day.

Wal-Mart moved into Canada in 1995 by purchasing 122 stores of the Woolco chain. All the purchased stores were nonunion. Seven of the 22 stores Wal-Mart chose not to acquire were unionized.

The United Steelworkers of America began an organizing drive in the Windsor store on April 14, 1996, and filed an application for certification by the Ontario Labour Relations Board (the "Board") on May 2, accompanied by 91 signed cards. At a representation vote on May 9, 151 of the 205 employees present voted against the union and only 43 voted in favour. The union filed a second application, asking that the Board assert its power under Section 11 of the *Labour Relations Act* to certify the union on the basis that the vote did not "reflect the true wishes of the employees in the bargaining unit about being represented by the trade union."

At a lengthy hearing, the Board was told that 84 cards were signed in the first 13 days of the organizing drive. On April 26, an associate told the store manager about the unionization attempt, and he advised the director of associate relations at the Canadian head office, who instructed the district manager to visit the store. The district manager spoke at the morning meeting the next day—an unprecedented occurrence for a Saturday, as was the store manager's ensuring that all employees scheduled for that day would be on time for the meeting. A union organizer also addressed the morning meeting, telling employees that it is illegal for an employer to interfere with an organization attempt or to intimidate prospective members, and that employees did not have to speak to management. The district manager then circulated through the store for several hours, talking to employees. The union noted that from that point on in the campaign, only seven more cards were signed.

The following morning, an employee was given permission to address the meeting. She expressed concern over the prospect of discontent in a unionized workplace and the possibility of losing benefits they now enjoyed. The union was not given the chance to respond because it was already past time for the store to open. Later that day, the store manager told an associate that every aspect of operations would now have to be negotiated, including the profit-sharing program, and that some associates had signed cards under the false impression that they were simply requesting further information.

Once the application was filed, the director of associate relations consulted in-house counsel for advice on what could be said, particularly in view of the corporate culture of openness. Along with several other managers, he spent several days in the Windsor store, answering questions and engaging associates in conversation. Management response to the frequent questions as to what might happen if the union succeeded—including whether the store would close—was that it would be inappropriate to comment on those issues.

The Board decided to ignore the vote and certify the union because the corporate culture made a response of that nature tantamount to confirming employees' fears, and therefore was intimidating or coercive. There was an apparent disparity between this refusal to give substantive answers and the company policies of "openness" and treatment of employees as "partners" in the business. The Board found fault with the company's closure of the morning meeting without allowing the union to reply to the employee's speech and its failure to "distance itself from her comments." A majority of the Board (that is, the Chair and one of two members) decided that these actions intimidated employees, that the results of the vote could not be relied upon as reflecting the true wishes of employees, and that another vote would suffer from the same weakness. It used its power under the *Labour Relations Act* to certify the union.

The other Board member took issue with the majority decision's characterization of the company's actions, noting that union organizers had been able to speak at other meetings and that employees should be given credit for the ability to interpret their colleague's comments. While he, too, wished that the managers had answered the question about the possibility that the store might close, he did note that they had consistently pointed out that issues would be negotiated with a new union.[1]

The Wal-Mart unionization offers insight into how labour boards view managerial actions during a certification campaign and, thus, into the application of labour law. The Board's perspective reflects industrial relations values and the intent of labour law, which is concerned with *actual* (as opposed to theoretical) rights under the labour relations statutes. This point of view is necessarily narrow, in that it may not take into account factors that are extrinsic to the specific situation, such as the company's position in the marketplace or the broader economic circumstances in which it is operating.

The Wal-Mart decision incensed the newly elected Ontario provincial government, which had run on a platform of making the province friendlier to business, partly by rolling back trade union power. It enacted a new statute, the *Economic Development and Workplace Democracy Act*, rescinding the labour board's power to certify without a vote or despite a vote against unionization. It also made an unsuccessful attempt to replace a number of labour board vice-chairs. In the end, the Wal-Mart affair reflected the same clash of values and perspectives that has often made it difficult for those oriented towards business (such as managers and business students) to be certain of exactly what is and is not acceptable under a labour relations act.

 University of Toronto (general information on labour relations and employment law): www.law-lib.utoronto.ca/

Canadian collective bargaining legislation at the end of the 20th century is a microcosm of Canada; our legislation reflects American ideas that are substantially modified by home-grown Canadian values. It is generally more favourable to unions than comparable US labour law, and it is fragmented into 11 jurisdictions—ten provincial and one federal.

From its beginnings around the turn of the century, the collective bargaining system evolved gradually into what became a relatively stable and effective set of mechanisms for the regulation of management–union conflict. It was a regime based in significant part on the trade union principle of collective action and equal treatment of everyone under a collective agreement, differentiated only by seniority and classification.

Since the early 1980s, however, this regime of collective bargaining law has been faced with the emergence of an entirely new set of laws—one of them constitutional—based on a very different principle: the protection and enhancement of *individual* rights. Given that unions exist to give individuals more power, it might appear that laws strengthening *individual* rights would reinforce collective bargaining laws and benefit unions. The reality, however, is very different, and we are witness to a collision of two sets of legal principles that are not entirely compatible. To a very large degree, the key issues in labour law today are the story of the adaptation of one regime to the other.

THE COLLECTIVE BARGAINING SYSTEM TO THE 1980S

To understand the collective bargaining system, it is necessary to know how those who run the system—labour boards, arbitrators, and policy-makers—look at the system and the assumptions that inform their views. Their fundamental premise is simply this: that unionism and collective bargaining provide a way of managing the conflict that inevitably exists between workers and their employers. History makes clear that where potential for conflict exists, it cannot be very long suppressed or successfully avoided. It must be allowed to work itself out, but in a manner that minimizes damage to society. In other words, it must be regulated and, as far as possible, controlled. In addition, despite some modern management and dispute resolution theory, it is naive to believe that there is not a fundamental conflict between the interests of capital (management) on one hand and labour on the other.

The *real* question, then, is: How are those conflicts going to be fought out and resolved? In democracies, the answer—at least with respect to the trade-off between the level of current compensation of employees, the rate of reinvestment in the firm, and payout to the shareholders—is through some form of employee representation and collective bargaining. The collective bargaining system can be thought of as a system for resolving the conflict between employees and employers with respect to compensation and working conditions. This means that the real conflict is about control of the workplace and the distribution of the profits, *with labour law providing the rules of engagement.* Labour boards and arbitrators (and, on very rare occasions, the courts and police) are the referees for this conflict.

Generally speaking, those individuals who sit on labour boards and who act as arbitrators have a deep belief in the importance of the system and in the sanctity of "the process"; they are highly sensitive to their duty to nurture and protect it. They view labour and management as equally legitimate actors playing roles on an important social and economic stage. A large proportion of these referees are lawyers, who naturally view the world through the prism of a legal perspective: Process and equity are much more important than cost and profits, and the words of the collective agreement are law. They tend, often, to be skeptical of management—with very good reason, they would say—and highly sensitive to management's power over individual employees. All too often, management does not understand these realities or ignores them, and the consequences can be expensive, embarrassing, and disruptive, both to the firm and to individual managers.

Principles of Collective Bargaining in Canada

Until the first decade of the 20th century, there was little in the way of actual labour law, although both the criminal and common law had been successfully used by employers to defeat both union attempts at organization and strikes for better wages and working conditions. Existing law was used by business as a weapon against unions; in this, it was aided and abetted by the judiciary. By 1900, however, the law had been rendered more or less neutral on the subject of trade union activity.

Strictly speaking, there is no single "Canadian collective bargaining system." A decision made by the British Parliament in 1925 under the *British North America Act* of 1867 (the statute that, in effect, served as the basis of Canada's constitution until 1982) assigned collective bargaining to the provinces. In the "Snider Case," *Toronto Electric Power Commissioners* v. *Snider, et al.*, the Commission, locked in a labour dispute with its employees, refused to recognize the jurisdiction of a conciliation board appointed under the *Industrial Disputes Investigations Act*, a Canadian federal statute. The Commission maintained that a labour dispute in a Toronto public utility was properly a provincial matter, not federal, because it dealt with a municipality and with civil rights, both of which were provincial responsibilities enumerated under the *BNA Act*. The issue was, in short, whether a labour dispute should be a provincial or federal matter.

The top Canadian court concluded that the federal *Industrial Disputes Investigations Act* did apply to this situation because labour disputes were important enough to the national interest that they should be regulated by the federal government. The British Privy Council, however, disagreed. Their Lordships decided that the dominion (federal) government had exceeded its jurisdiction under the *BNA Act* and that, in the absence of a national emergency, the division of powers under that *Act* must be respected (see Table 7.1). From that point on, labour relations in Canada became principally a provincial matter.

In matters of labour relations, then, the federal government has jurisdiction over the areas listed in Table 7.1, while the provincial governments have jurisdiction over all other businesses and industries. Approximately 90 percent of the labour force falls under a provincial jurisdiction for labour and employment law purposes, while approximately 10 percent falls under the federal jurisdiction. In contrast, US labour law presents the reverse situation; the *National Labour Relations Act* governs most of the labour force. Individual states have limited authority over labour relations.

 The Canadian International Labour Network Site:
labour.ciln.mcmaster.ca/laws.html

Thus, as in so many other aspects of Canadian life, there are *11* different jurisdictions—the ten provinces and the federal, which includes the territories and federally chartered industries. This balkanization of labour relations law has had both positive and negative consequences. Perhaps it would be simpler to have a single set of labour laws for the whole country. But on the other hand, having ten provincial legal domains allows labour legislation to be better tailored to local needs. Some industries are national in nature, however, which suggests that their collective bargaining should also be national in terms not only of structure, but of process and law. Whatever the resolution of this line of argument, having 11 different jurisdictions for labour law has allowed for some interesting experimentation.

TABLE 7.1

DIVISION OF POWERS UNDER S. 91 AND 92 OF THE BNA ACT

AREAS OF FEDERAL JURISDICTION	AREAS OF PROVINCIAL JURISDICTION
Aeronautics	All other areas of commerce
Shipping and Navigation	
Railways	
Banks	
Interprovincial Bus and Transport Companies	
Communications (telephone, television, radio)	
Atomic Energy	

Despite the potential for fragmentation implied by so many different jurisdictions, federal and provincial labour laws in the ten provinces and the federal government have been shaped by many of the same forces and share a number of defining characteristics. The most fundamental of these common influences originated in the United States, by way of the single most important piece of labour legislation in North American history, the *National Labour Relations Act* (1935), known popularly as the Wagner Act.[2]

Northwest Territories government:
pingo.gov.nt.ca/Publications/HR_Manual/toc.htm

The *National Labour Relations Act*

A principal component of the so-called "New Deal,"[3] the *National Labour Relations Act* had both a social and a fiscal goal. At the social level, the New Dealers considered it important to provide workers with a *real,* not just *theoretical,* right to belong to a union; they viewed it as a fundamental democratic right. Just as important, though, was the *fiscal* purpose; the overwhelming challenge faced by the Roosevelt administration was the Great Depression, which was partially a result of insufficient demand. Roosevelt's logic was simple: To increase aggregate demand, it was necessary to increase spending power by raising workers' compensation; to raise compensation, bargaining power had to be increased; to increase bargaining power, more workers had to unionize. Thus, the NLRA was unabashedly one-sided and was explicitly drafted to make it much easier for trade unions to organize workers.

In this, it was hugely successful and, over the next ten years, 9 million workers in the great industries were unionized. One of the main reasons for organized labour's new-found ability to organize workers was that, after many decades of employers defeating unions *before* they got established, typically by such tactics as firing the leaders or defeating the union in a recognition strike, the *National Labour Relations Act* greatly reduced management's ability to impede the formation of a new union. Three elements interacted to achieve this outcome: (1) the creation of a *National Labour Relations Board* to oversee the collective bargaining system and, especially, the process of establishing unions; (2) the development of *certification procedures*, which based union creation and representation rights on the wishes of the affected workers as expressed freely via secret ballot to the Board, without interference by the employer; and (3) the definition of "*unfair labour practices*," a set of rules that made unlawful any management tactics aimed at preventing or defeating unionization attempts and that required the employer to bargain "in good faith" with any union certified by the Board (see Exhibit 7.1).

Thus, the passage of the *National Labour Relations Act* deprived employers of a formidable battery of anti-union weapons used to great effect over many years: firing or discriminating against union organizers, "yellow-dog contracts" (employment contracts that required the employee to pledge never to join a union), blacklisting union sympathizers, threats of plant closure or layoffs in the event of unionization, and the simple refusal to deal with a union.

Exhibit 7.1

Unfair Labour Practices under the Wagner Act

1. Interference with workers' right to organize.
2. Domination of a labour organization.
3. Discrimination against employees for union activity.
4. Retribution against employees for filing charges under the Act.
5. Failure or refusal to bargain in good faith.

Some tactics were more subtle than simply firing and blacklisting union organizers. Designating "domination of a labour organization" as an unfair labour practice under the *National Labour Relations Act* was intended to foreclose a particularly effective anti-union strategy favoured by employers, the so-called company union. This was simply another version of the old "fill the vacuum before the opposition does" trick. Given that perhaps the most potent argument for employees to join a union is to have a collective voice with which to address the company, the existence of an employee association would weaken that argument considerably. A good strategy for an employer, then, would be to set up, and to some extent control, an employee association. Although it would probably have little real power, employees could always argue, "Why do we need a union? We already have representation!" In Exhibit 7.2, a recent Canadian case, Ganeca Transport Inc., provides an instructive example of such an attempt by an employer.

Exhibit 7.2

The Case of Ganeca Transport Inc.

In April 1989, dissatisfied with the results of discussions with their employer over compensation and working conditions, Ganeca's drivers designated three representatives to work out an agreement on the immediate issues and some means of dealing with problems that arise from time to time. While these representatives were able to make considerable progress, the drivers decided in late August to file an application with the Canada Labour Relations Board for certification of the Transport Drivers, Warehousemen and General Workers' Union.

A few days later, the employer invited them to an information meeting and stated that he had been advised by the firm's lawyer not to speak because of the certification application. Nevertheless, he asked what the problem was and participated in the ensuing discussion, which involved primarily the matters still unresolved in the negotiations, as well as the issue of representation. He stated that the unresolved matters would have to be negotiated, which might result in loss of contracts, leading in turn to layoffs and terminations, but that, in any event, he would not negotiate with the Transport Drivers' union. After the drivers withdrew for private discussions, one of the representatives proposed that, instead of joining the Transport Drivers, they should form their own union, which would include drivers and mechanics. This was agreed, and over

the following week, membership cards were signed and collected and a second application filed, this time for the company-supported union. The firm's office manager, who acted as the employer's assistant, called some members and helped collect cards.

Two weeks after the Canada Labour Relations Board ordered a vote to choose between the two unions, the Transport Drivers filed a complaint. The hearing brought out the details of the meeting at which the decision was made to form a new union, the drivers' concerns over the employer's comments with respect to job losses, and the active role played by the office manager in getting the membership cards signed. The Board found that the company union was not sufficiently independent to adequately represent the employees and that the employer had committed an unfair labour practice under ss. 94 and 96 of the *Canada Labour Code*. It dismissed the application for the company union and issued a certificate for the Transport Drivers, Warehousemen and General Workers' Union.[4]

In short, before the Wagner Act, unions could be established only when an employer agreed to recognize and bargain with them (usually having been forced to do so through a "recognition strike"). The American legislative approach made it much more difficult for an employer to defeat a union. Henceforth, unionization would be a decision made by free choice of the affected employees and the process overseen by the National Labour Relations Board. In 1947, to redress an obvious omission in the law, *union* unfair labour practices, such as coercing employees to join the union or interfering with the bargaining rights of another union, were added to the legislation through the Taft-Hartley Act.

The Wagner Act had placed the power of the state solidly behind the American union movement. Given the proximity and influence of the United States, as well as the fact that the vast majority of unionized employees in Canada at that time were represented by international unions based in the US, the Wagner Act was a precedent that immediately placed great political pressure on governments in Canada to emulate it. In 1944, the federal government, acting under its special wartime power, introduced a national labour law known as Privy Council Order 1003 that adopted many of the features of the Wagner Act. After the war, PC 1003 served as a model for provincial legislation, introducing the Wagner principles across Canada.

Mandatory Intervention in the Bargaining Process—The IDIA of 1907

When imported into Canada, the Wagner and Taft-Hartley Act principles of certification procedures, unfair labour practices, the obligation to bargain in good faith, and administration by a specially appointed board were blended with existing federal and provincial legislation. While American labour law had focused on enabling the formation of unionized workforces, Canadian legislation focused in its early years on an entirely different aspect of union–management relations: the regulation of collective bargaining disputes and the prevention of strikes.

Between 1900 and 1907, alarmed by major strikes in vital industries such as railroads and mining, as well as public utilities, the federal government[5] enacted a series of statutes culminating in the *Industrial Disputes Investigations Act* (1907). The most important principle entrenched by this statute was that of compulsory intervention in the collective bargaining process in the form of a tripartite conciliation board (see Exhibit 7.3). The conciliation board process itself was not compulsory but, as a precondition to a legal strike or lockout, such a board had to meet with the parties, conduct an investigation ("fact finding"), and issue a report to the public. It was only upon the completion of these steps that a strike or lockout became legal.

University of Montreal (information on labour relations and employment law): www.droit.umontreal.ca/en/index/html

The Simsgroup (links to all federal and provincial administrative tribunals): www.simsgroup.com/adminsearch.htm

A mechanism championed by Mackenzie King, then minister of labour and later Canada's longest-serving prime minister, the conciliation stage was based on the premise that, if the board itself could not help the parties to achieve a settlement, then publication of its report, with its analysis of the dispute and recommendations for settlement, could mobilize public opinion against one of the parties and so pressure that party to compromise. After the Snider Case and the resulting devolution of most labour relations jurisdiction to the provincial governments, most of the provinces inserted similar provisions into their labour relations statutes.

This is one of a number of paradoxes built into Canadian labour law. On one hand, dispute resolution theory would regard the strike and lockout as positive in that they create the pressure that drives the bargaining process, the threat that forces the parties to make the difficult decisions that are required in bargaining. On the other hand, from a public

Exhibit 7.3

Composition of Boards and Tribunals

The Industrial Disputes Investigations Act started what became a long-standing Canadian tradition of "tripartite" boards for the resolution of labour relations disputes, in the form of conciliation boards, arbitration boards and, indeed, labour boards themselves. Whatever the function and venue, the makeup of the board was similar: one member sympathetic to the point of view of each of the disputing parties, and a neutral chair. The members, while not representatives of the disputing parties in the sense that the union nominee actually belongs to the particular union or the management nominee works for the employer, are experienced labour relations practitioners drawn from the ranks of labour and management generally, and usually are people who are familiar with the sector in question. With the presence of two somewhat partisan but knowledgeable members, the negotiation process continues right in the board's chambers.

policy perspective, overt conflict is considered to be a bad thing, particularly if it inflicts damage or even serious inconvenience on innocent third parties or the public. Hence, while the entire collective bargaining process is built around the ultimate right to strike and lock out—because, in a sense, that threat drives the bargaining process—Canadian labour legislation goes a considerable distance in trying to prevent these from actually occurring.

The Modern Collective Bargaining System

By the 1950s, then, the essential elements of the Canadian collective bargaining system were in place, with relatively minor variations from province to province. The basic system had adopted several features from the US and combined them with home-grown Canadian elements, notably mandatory intervention in the negotiation process as a precondition to strike or lockout (see Exhibit 7.4).

While heavily influenced at the outset by the Wagner Act principles, the character of Canadian collective bargaining legislation gradually evolved to reflect a distinctive Canadian flavour: a considerably stronger role for the state, a greater acceptance of union rights, and a lesser emphasis on individual freedom. These differences in character are manifested in a number of ways, which are set out in the following pages.

EXHIBIT 7.4

THE UNIQUE CANADIAN BLEND

FROM THE AMERICANS:
- Administration by an administrative tribunal (the labour relations board)
- Union formation through the certification process
- The prohibition of "unfair labour practices" to keep the process clean and, in particular, to prevent employers from negatively influencing employees' choice to have a union
- The requirement on both parties to bargain "in good faith" once a union was certified

FROM CANADA:
- Mandatory intervention in the negotiation process as a precondition to strike or lockout
- Mandatory grievance arbitration and prohibition of strikes or lockouts during the life of a collective agreement

The Mechanics of Implementing Free Choice: Certification Procedures

The principle of free choice by those employees who will be affected by unionization is accomplished in practical terms through evidence of majority support for unionization submitted to the labour relations board. This evidence consists of either signed membership cards or ballots in a secret vote conducted by the labour board. There are two basic models for certification among the 11 jurisdictions: the "card" model and the "mandatory vote" model. Under the more common card model, if a union can sign up a sufficiently large number of employees (say, 55–60 percent), the union will be certified without the necessity of a vote; a vote will be held only in the event that the union falls short of the necessary majority for automatic certification. Manitoba's approach is typical. That province's *Labour Relations Act* stipulates that, to apply for certification, a union must show minimum evidence (in the form of signed membership cards) of the support of 45 percent of the bargaining unit employees; with evidence of the support of 55 percent, the board will certify the union without a vote; and, if the union has applied for certification with support between 45 percent and 55 percent, a vote will be conducted, with a majority in favour of unionization among all bargaining unit members necessary for certification.[6] In practice, almost all certifications occur without a vote: The union signs up sufficient employees to be certified outright.

A second basic model for obtaining certification can be found in Newfoundland, Nova Scotia, Ontario, and Alberta. Under the mandatory vote model, borrowed from American labour law, regardless of the initial support a union can demonstrate, a secret ballot must be conducted before the union will be certified. The premise underlying this system is that the true wishes of employees, those advocating and those opposed to union representation, can best be obtained through a secret ballot. To reduce the opportunity for undue employer interference, the vote is typically held within a few weeks of the union's application for certification (and often sooner). If the union obtains a majority of the vote, the union is certified. One advantage of this system is that an employer is more likely to accept the verdict of a secret ballot vote than a simple display of union membership cards. See Exhibit 7.5 for a discussion of appropriate bargaining units.

Nova Scotia Department of Justice:
www.gov.ns.ca/just/regulations/regs/index.htm

Newfoundland Environment and Labour:
www.gov.nf.ca/env/Labour/default.asp

Exhibit 7.5

What Is an Appropriate Bargaining Unit?

Definition: The group of employees represented by a union in a particular organization. The terms and conditions of employment of that group of employees are set out in the collective agreement negotiated by the union and the employer once the union has been certified. To become their certified representative, the union must obtain majority support of the bargaining unit.

The labour board has exclusive authority to determine the appropriate bargaining unit, on the basis of such criteria as **community of interest**—whether

the employees in the proposed unit share some fundamental similarities in terms of the type of work they perform, the way they are compensated, the training/education/background they require.

Some practical considerations: The smaller and more concentrated the unit, the easier it is for the union to obtain a "50 percent plus one" level of support for certification purposes. On the other hand, a small unit may not be the most efficient for bargaining and representation purposes once the union is established. Consider a multi-branch chartered bank, for example; labour boards have determined that an individual branch is the most appropriate bargaining unit, and this is certainly the easiest way for a union to organize the employees. However, the small number of employees in a single branch makes negotiation of contracts and representation of members' rights (e.g., in grievance arbitration) extremely inefficient and expensive for the union. In other words, a unit that covers more people produces economies of scale.

Protection of the Right to Organize

Labour boards take very seriously the right of employees to organize and their own responsibility to protect that right in a meaningful way. Labour relations statutes forbid activities that might interfere with the right of employees to make a free choice about whether or not to join a union. It is important to understand that many labour boards put themselves, not in management's shoes in terms of *intent*, but in the employees' shoes in terms of *inferences drawn*. The fact that management may not necessarily have intended to intimidate or frighten employees (into voting against the union) does not mean that employees were not, in fact, intimidated or frightened. Most labour boards are highly sensitive to management's presumed power to influence employees. After all, management has tremendous latent power—in fact, the ultimate latent power: It can take away someone's job by shutting down the plant, by changing the technology, or by firing.

While management (and many students) often tend to see a battle of equals between management and the union in a certification drive, a labour board typically does not see the protagonists as equal at all—at least in terms of their latent ability to influence employees. Without question, management is perceived to have the upper hand in terms of the power to affect employees' decisions on unionization; management is on the inside; it controls the plant, the equipment, the operation, and the employees' very livelihood. The union is on the outside trying to get in, its only weapon persuasion; it controls nothing. Viewed from the perspective of a labour board, it is a completely unequal struggle and therefore calls for an asymmetrical set of constraints on employer and union actions during such a campaign. Management is severely constrained, particularly in terms of what it may say, while the union is given relative freedom.

In this context, many of the actions taken by Radio Shack in trying to prevent certification of its Barrie warehouse by the United Steelworkers in 1978 were found by the

Ontario Labour Relations Board to have violated the provisions of the *Labour Relations Act*. Indeed, taken in aggregate, Radio Shack's behaviour sank to something of a new low point in employer anti-union behaviour (and, indeed, prompted a record for toughness by a labour board). Among other things, Radio Shack terminated several of its employees for union-organizing activities, circulated an anti-union petition among its employees, threatened to shut down the plant and "move out west" if the union got in, and distributed T-shirts with "I'm a company fink" on the front and "and proud of it" on the back to any employees who wanted one. The board had little difficulty concluding that these actions on the part of Radio Shack were intended to sway the workforce against unionization through fear and intimidation.[7]

While it is not difficult to see that such egregious attempts to intimidate employees would be unacceptable, more subtle management actions can also be problematic. Examples include management personnel following pro-union employees around the workplace, promising wage increases if union organizing fails, and transferring, demoting, or disciplining pro-union employees. Assembling employees for a special meeting, to be addressed by managers on the question of unionization, has something of a "captive audience" aspect of concern to a labour board, at least if not balanced by "equal time" for the union. A management observation that unionization might lower profits, which might, in turn, affect employment levels and job security, could be interpreted by some employees as an implied threat, even though it might, in some objective sense, be true.

In this light, it should certainly be no surprise that a majority of the Ontario Labour Relations Board would have seen in the refusal by Wal-Mart managers to answer the big question—"Will the store close if we unionize?"—an inferred threat (inferred by employees, that is), particularly in the context of both Wal-Mart's record of non-unionization and its self-proclaimed philosophy of dealing candidly and quickly with associates' questions. Management can sometimes find itself in a no-win situation when it comes to certification campaigns in terms of what it can really do and say; it may feel it is "damned if you do and damned if you don't." That may explain a common perception by management that, faced with a certification campaign, the safest, most realistic policy is to say nothing at all.

On the other hand, saying nothing can also be a dangerous strategy, as it was in the Wal-Mart case. Given Wal-Mart's record of 2600 union-free stores, it is easy to understand why employees would want to know Wal-Mart's response to unionization, and what inference they might draw in the face of a refusal to answer. It takes little imagination to understand that local and regional managers would have been in a difficult position when the answer to that question really lay in the hands of a top management and board of directors located in a different country, with a different set of laws, embedded in a different culture.

In discussing the issue of freedom to organize, it must be remembered that "freedom" also implies freedom *not* to organize. Thus, as in the United States, Canadian labour relations statutes prohibit certain union actions that would interfere with employees' wishes not to be represented by a union. For example, intimidation and coercion to sign union cards and threats of job loss should the union get in are typically deemed to be union unfair labour practices.

Choosing to Be Represented by a Union

There is an intriguing paradox associated with the decision by a group of employees to form a union. This is a choice made on an individual basis, but one that will significantly limit subsequent individual freedom of choice in the interests of collective power and action. This has both legal and strategic implications. First, the legal.

In certifying a union, the labour board gives it representation rights for all of the employees in what the board determines to be the "appropriate bargaining unit." The union is afforded "exclusive representation" rights; it becomes the "bargaining agent" for *all* of the employees in the appropriate bargaining unit, whether or not they voted for the union or joined the union, and regardless of whether or not a particular individual even wants to be represented by the union. The union now deals with the employer on any and all aspects of the employee–employer relationship covered by the collective agreement. The wishes of the minority (those who voted against unionization) are thus subordinated to the principle of collectivism, and employees may no longer deal as individuals with the employer.

Just as in a military unit, then, the freedom and wishes of individuals are traded for the power of disciplined and coordinated action by the group. Because it entails a significant trade-off of individual rights and privileges for collective power, the system is open to abuses, either by the union using its power inappropriately or by individuals taking advantage of the union's obligation to work in their interests. Consequently, a number of labour relations statutes include provisions to prevent such abuses and to fine-tune the trade-off.

The Duty of Fair Representation

Balancing the right bestowed upon a union to be the sole representative for *all* employees in the bargaining unit is its obligation to fairly and diligently represent all bargaining unit members, whether or not they are members of, or pay dues to, the union. The union may not discriminate as to how it represents individual members on certain other grounds as well[8]—for example, whether or not the individual in question might be a political rival of the local president.

The duty of fair representation does not mean that the union has no discretion in making its decisions (for example, whether or not to take a particular grievance to arbitration), but typically it must represent the interests of *everyone in the bargaining unit* in a manner that is not "arbitrary, discriminatory, or in bad faith." While some of the provisions regarding duty of fair representation are fairly narrowly drawn and cover only contract administration, the Supreme Court of Canada has made clear that this duty

EXHIBIT 7.6

SHACHTAY VS. CREAMERY WORKERS' UNION (MANITOBA)

Victor Shachtay was a mechanic at the garage of People's Co-operative Limited who was fired for alleged theft of gasoline. After an initial meeting between the union and the company, the union concluded it would be almost impossible to determine who was telling the truth. As a small union run on a volunteer basis, it lacked the expertise to deal with a situation of any complexity. It advised the grievor that, as he had no evidence to support his version of events, there was nothing more it could do. The grievor charged that the union had violated its duty of fair representation, and his case was heard by the Manitoba Labour Board. In allowing his complaint, the board found that the union had failed to take reasonable steps to determine if the grievor had a case. Indeed, information the union turned up in its investigation (which was described by the board report as "perfunctory") was not provided to the grievor. The union was ordered to submit the grievance to arbitration, to pay for independent counsel, and to compensate the grievor in the event he was successful at arbitration.[9]

"arises out of the exclusive power given to a union to act as spokesman for the employees in the bargaining unit."[10] Thus, whether or not duty of fair representation is explicitly set out in a jurisdiction's labour relations statute, it can—at least at a basic level—be inferred from the fundamental reality that, as of the date a union becomes certified, it enjoys the right to represent all employees in the bargaining unit. That right, in other words, brings with it a responsibility (see Exhibit 7.6).

Employment Standards in Manitoba:
www.gov.mb.ca/labour/standards.html?/esg.html

Statutory Recognition and Protection of Union Security

The legal principle of having the union represent all employees in the bargaining unit, whether or not they are members of or support the union, can lead to abuses not only by the union, but by an employee as well. In this regard, an employee who does not support the union and who refuses to join or pay dues, but who nevertheless receives the same benefits from the union's efforts as everyone else, is often characterized, with justification, as someone who is getting a "free ride" at the expense of those who have joined and who pay dues. (Thus, the term "free rider" is part of the union lexicon and refers to someone whom the union has a statutory duty to represent, but who refuses to join or contribute dues.)

For this reason, Canadian labour law generally makes provisions for relatively strong forms of union security arrangements in collective agreements, and goes much further than does its American counterpart in this respect. For example, it expressly recognizes the acceptability of negotiated contract provisions that require union membership and the payment of dues (the various forms such provisions can take are discussed in Chapter 10). In addition to strengthening the union's financial and political power, these provisions eliminate the "free rider" syndrome. A number of Canadian jurisdictions have gone further than *allowing for* these arrangements in their labour acts; five of the provinces[11] and the federal jurisdiction now *require* the employer to deduct membership dues on behalf of all employees in the bargaining unit and remit them to the union (that is, the Rand Formula), and several public-sector statutes require or impose compulsory membership.[12]

The philosophical justification for such provisions is that Canadians long ago accepted collective bargaining as a fundamental element of public policy; therefore, the parties in a collective bargaining relationship should spend their limited time and energy bargaining over matters of wages and working conditions and not over the political or financial status of the union—that is, not over the existence (or otherwise) of the collective bargaining relationship. With the issuance of the certificate, which reflects the wishes of a majority of employees, the question of the bargaining relationship has been settled, and they should move on to the substantive issues of wages and working conditions.

The manner in which this whole area of union security is treated in Canada contrasts with the United States, where the legislation does not go nearly as far in protecting the higher-level forms of union security. Indeed, in a number of states, particularly in the South and in western regions, statutes expressly prohibit compulsory union membership. These are known as "right-to-work" laws, in the sense that no union can legally prevent a person from working on the basis that he or she refuses to join the union; individuals who do not wish to join the union have the "right to work," in other words.

Exhibit 7.7, the BC Hydro case, illustrates the degree to which individual freedom can be constrained within a collective bargaining regime. This may offend some as unacceptable in a democratic society. Others would simply point out that such a trade-off is necessary to afford a union the power to effectively do its job of representing the interests of its constituents. They would no doubt argue, too, that since the law requires the union to negotiate on behalf of, and to represent fairly, *all* those individuals in the bargaining unit and not just those who support the union, then basic fairness and practicality dictate that all those people contribute equally to the cost of the union operations.

Exhibit 7.7

BC Hydro Case

In *British Columbia Hydro and Power Authority and Office and Technical Employees Union, Local 378, and Tottle*, the collective agreement contained a union shop provision. The employer refused to discharge an employee who had been expelled from the union for refusal to pay a disciplinary fine, arguing that the only proper basis for discharge for non-membership would be if the employee had refused to pay proper union dues. The Labour Relations Board did not agree and ordered the employer to discharge the employee.[13]

State Regulation of Dispute Resolution Processes

Collective bargaining disputes can be divided into two main categories: (1) bargaining (or "interest") disputes over the terms of a new collective agreement and (2) "rights" disputes, grievances over the interpretation or application of an existing agreement. We have already noted that state intervention in interest disputes was an early and defining principle of Canadian legislation, by making conciliation or mediation a precondition to a legal strike or lockout. Given that interest disputes take place, by definition, at negotiation time, the logical corollary to this proposition was, of course, that no strike or lockout was legal during the life of a collective agreement. Indeed, Canadian labour statutes typically ban "untimely" sanctions—that is, strikes or lockouts that take place before (1) the collective agreement has expired, (2) the parties have made good-faith efforts to negotiate a collective agreement, (3) some form of third-party intervention has taken place, and failed, and (4) a certain number of days have elapsed. Some go further than this; Alberta, for example, also requires that a strike vote be taken and that the results be filed with the labour relations board, that formal notice of strike or lockout be given, and that the strike or lockout begin on the day specified in the notice.

By contrast, under American legislation, the question of strikes and lockouts during the life of the agreement is a bargainable issue. Under Canadian labour law, the parties—and particularly unions because they use strikes much more frequently than management resorts to lockouts—are significantly restricted in terms of when they may invoke the sanctions of strike or lockout.

Canadian treatment of "rights" disputes (that is, grievances arising over the interpretation or application of the agreement) also contrasts with that in the United States. In almost all Canadian jurisdictions, failing resolution by the parties themselves, disputes that arise out of the collective agreement and during its life must be referred to arbitration by a neutral third party if one of the parties to the agreement insists. In most jurisdictions, the labour relations acts require the parties to include a binding arbitration clause for rights disputes in their collective agreements, deeming one to be present in the event that they do not. For example, the *Industrial Relations Act* of New Brunswick specifies that:

> 55. (1) Every collective agreement shall provide for the final and binding settlement by arbitration or otherwise, without stoppage of work, of all differences between the parties to … the agreement … concerning its interpretation, application, administration or an alleged violation of the agreement, including any question as to whether a matter is arbitrable.

> (2) Where a collective agreement does not contain such a provision as is mentioned in subsection (1), it shall be deemed to contain the following provision:

> Where a difference arises between the parties relating to the interpretation, application or administration of this agreement…[a procedure is described in the statute].

New Brunswick Employment Standards:
www.gov.nb.ca/dol-mdt/empstand/index.htm

The Duty to Bargain in Good Faith

While Canadian law sets out in some detail *procedural* requirements for bargaining (for example, the conditions that must be satisfied prior to a legal strike or lockout), the statutes tend to say very little about the *process* of negotiations; that is, what the parties actually do. Any provision that is legal is also bargainable, and a party may not arbitrarily refuse to even discuss it. The main requirement is that the parties engage in "good faith" bargaining. The *Canada Labour Code*, for example, sets out the following:

> Where notice to bargain collectively has been given under this Part,
>
> (a) the bargaining agent and the employer, without delay, but in any case within twenty days after the notice was given unless the parties otherwise agree, shall
>
>   (i) meet and commence to bargain collectively in good faith, and
>
>   (ii) make every reasonable effort to enter into a collective agreement.

This provision is typical of most of the 11 jurisdictions in that it explicitly mentions two requirements: to negotiate "in good faith" and to make "every reasonable effort."

Collective bargaining is a complex process, with economic, social, political, legal, and strategic and tactical dimensions. It is not a legal process. For this reason, and also because the collective bargaining system is predicated, in a sense, on what amounts to a contest of economic strength and a test of commitment or will—that is, in the form of the strike and lockout—labour boards have been reluctant to venture very far beyond the procedural dimension in their policing of the obligation to bargain in good faith. Without question, such obvious ploys as refusing to meet, attempting to undermine the union or bargain directly with employees, unilateral altering of wages and other terms of employment during the statutory freeze period, the firing of union leaders, insistence on illegal demands, and a refusal to discuss or to provide a rationale for a bargaining position would be seen by labour boards as evidence of bad-faith bargaining. But what about an employer—or, indeed, a union—that simply takes a tough bargaining position?

On one hand, labour boards have made clear that they recognize that collective bargaining is a tough and messy process, that it is not one governed by Marquess of Queensberry Rules, and that labour boards should guard against too close a review of the bargaining process and of allowing itself to be inserted into the process to be used tactically by the negotiators.[14] Nor is it a board's function to compensate for imbalances in bargaining power. Indeed, as noted by the Ontario Labour Relations Board in *The Daily Times*[15] case,

> The parties to collective bargaining are expected to act in their individual self interest and in so doing are entitled to take firm positions which may be unacceptable to the other side. The Act allows for the use of economic sanctions to resolve these bargaining impasses.

And, finally, labour boards should not compensate for one party's lack of bargaining expertise. In this regard, the Ontario Labour Relations Board noted, the existence of the duty to bargain in good faith should not result in a party abandoning the bargaining table for the Board simply because the bargaining process is not working in its favour. A party will not succeed in gaining concessions from the Board that it could not gain during negotiations. Nor will it succeed in recovering opportunities it lost through miscalculation or delay.[16]

On the other hand, labour boards come down hard on parties that they determine have been engaging in "surface bargaining"—that is, going through the procedural motions to make it appear that they are bargaining in good faith but, in reality, conducting themselves in a way intended to frustrate or subvert the process. Given the complexity and messy nature of bargaining, it is often difficult to make such a distinction. However, a board will look at whatever evidence is available and draw its own conclusions. Thus, in the Radio Shack case, as noted earlier, a series of blatant "unfair labour practices" by the employer during the certification campaign gave context for the employer's actions during negotiations, when the union filed a charge of failure to bargain in good faith. The labour relations board already viewed Radio Shack as highly anti-union and, therefore, scrutinized its actions even more closely. Thus, in this context, a series of letters from Radio Shack to every individual employee (see Exhibit 7.8), several demands characterized by the board as predictably unacceptable and shamelessly unreasonable, and the local manager's "thank you" notes to employees who crossed the picket line during the strike were all seen by the board as "surface bargaining" to frustrate the negotiation process and as transparent attempts to undermine the bargaining agent, the union.

Exhibit 7.8

Radio Shack's Letters to Employees

Company memo dated January 9, 1979

Memo to: All Head Office Employees

Ref: Letters from Trade Union

Attached are copies of correspondence the Company has received from the union.

(a) Letter of November 30, 1978, demand to bargain.
(b) Letter of December 05, 1978, request of personal information of full-time employees.

The Company must supply the information or again be attacked by the union. Up until present your *income*, your *job*, and your *personal employment information* has been confidential. This information now has to be sent to the union so Gaye Lambe can go back on radio, television, and the newspaper and *tell all*. The Company is sorry to have to release this previously confidential information, but it has no choice in the matter.

As has been Company policy, we will continue to keep you informed.

The Management

COMPANY MEMO DATED JANUARY 11, 1979, TO WHICH WAS ATTACHED A COPY OF THE UNION'S INITIAL PROPOSALS

TO: ALL HEAD OFFICE EMPLOYEES

Well, *here* it is! From the attached letter you will note the Company has received the *demands* of the union.

We are enclosing both the letter received and the *demands*. Note page *3*, article *6*—"6:01 It shall be a condition of employment that all *members must become and remain* members of the respective union in good standing."

Management *bets* they mean EMPLOYEES instead of members.

We have told you before and we tell you again—*no one* ever has to be a *union* member *TO WORK AT RADIO SHACK*—*NOW* or *EVER*.

This is *Canada*. You are *free* to work without paying Gaye Lambe or the United Steelworkers of America any money.

Again—if you want to join a union—you are free to. If you do not want to— you do not have to.

You will note we have suggested one of three days to commence collective bargaining with the union at the Holiday Inn at Barrie: Tuesday, 16th of January, 1979, or Wednesday, 17th of January, 1979, or Friday, 19th of January, 1979.

The Management[17]

Protection of Workers on Strike and Protection of the Strike Itself

While the degree to which the various Canadian jurisdictions protect the strike and the jobs of workers on strike varies from province to province, all of them do so at a higher level than does American labour law. At the lowest level, most provinces and the federal jurisdiction require reinstatement of legally striking workers.

Several, however, go considerably beyond this and protect the strike itself; they prevent employers from even temporarily replacing workers on legal strikes, using so-called "anti-scab" laws—"scab" being a union slur to refer to anyone who crosses the picket line to work during a strike. British Columbia, for example, forbids the use of outside replacement workers. The Province of Quebec goes so far as to also prevent other employees—either members of the bargaining unit who do not support the strike or supervisors or managers—from performing the work of strikers during a legal strike.

British Columbia Ministry of Labour—Publications: www.labour.gov.bc.ca/labr_pub.htm

Ministère du travail Québec: www.travail.gouv.qc.ca/

For a brief time during the tenure of the NDP government of Bob Rae in Ontario, the Ontario *Labour Relations Act* moved a considerable way towards the Quebec model in that it prevented bargaining unit work being carried out by members of the bargaining unit who did not support the strike or by replacement workers; further, non–bargaining unit personnel (managers and supervisors, for example) could legally refuse to perform bargaining unit work. (This provision was one of many labour-inspired NDP amendments rescinded under the Conservative government's "Common Sense Revolution." This was the first reversal in a long time of a gradual drift towards more pro-union laws. Whether or not this reversal is the start of a new trend remains to be seen.)

The policy rationale for "anti-scab" laws is to eliminate a serious flashpoint for picket line violence when legally striking workers see replacement workers passing through the line. Not only are they violating the putative sanctity of the picket line to take over the strikers' jobs—thus offending the striking workers' understandable proprietary feelings for their jobs—but their actions weaken and possibly neutralize the strike, thus rendering the sacrifices of the strikers useless. To avoid such feelings, therefore, some provinces have simply banned the use of strikebreakers.

First Contract Arbitration

Another manifestation of the heavier degree of state involvement in Canadian labour relations has been the amendment of labour relations statutes in approximately half of the jurisdictions to include provision for the arbitration—by either the labour boards themselves or arbitrators—of first collective agreements in newly unionized situations. The rationale is that, having found itself unionized, the employer should not then be able to frustrate the intent of the statute by subverting the bargaining process so as to effectively foreclose the achievement of a first collective agreement, thereby exposing the union to the possibility of decertification.

Perhaps the best reflection of the philosophical intent behind first contract arbitration is the requirement for triggering it. In this regard, Ontario again provides an interesting and illustrative example. When first contract arbitration was first introduced into the Ontario *Labour Relations Act* under a Conservative government, it could be invoked only when the Labour Relations Board was convinced that the employer had purposely obstructed and undermined the bargaining process in an attempt to rid itself of the union. With the amendments to the *Labour Relations Act* brought in by the New Democratic Party in 1992, however, the trigger for first contract arbitration became, simply, a request from one of the parties—almost always, of course, the union. The further amendments brought in by the subsequent Conservative government returned the trigger to its original form—convincing evidence that the employer had intentionally subverted the bargaining process.

 Ontario Ministry of Labour: www.gov.on.ca/LAB/es/tablee.htm

Labour Boards and Board Remedies

The notion of an administrative tribunal, rather than the court, overseeing and enforcing a statute originated with the American *National Labour Relations Act* in 1935, and was slowly but ultimately widely adopted in Canada. Labour boards are generally seen as more expert than courts (in labour relations), less formal and intimidating, and less conservative. The federal and provincial labour relations boards are independent, quasi-judicial bodies established under various labour relations statutes.

Boards normally have a number of responsibilities relating to union–management relations. In most jurisdictions, their principal responsibilities are to police the union formation function and certify new unions; and to adjudicate charges of bad-faith bargaining, failure to fairly represent, and unfair labour practices. They tend to have extensive investigatory powers and powers to impose remedies. For unionized employees, labour relations boards adjudicate disputes relating to the creation and administration of collective agreements and have the power to decide if a strike or lockout is lawful and, if not, can order an end to it. They are expected to deal with such matters in an impartial manner and in accordance with the relevant legislation; hence, those who work for the boards typically have education and/or experience in such fields as law and industrial relations. Members are often full-time employees of various public- and private-sector unions or human resources managers for corporations.

A typical board comprises a Chair, a number of vice-chairs (full-time or part-time or some of each), and a number of full- and part-time members representing unions or management. Appointments are for specified terms and are usually made on the joint recommendation of labour and management groups. The Chair's responsibilities include the administration of the board and the design and implementation of policies and procedures relating to its activities (see Exhibit 7.9).

While labour boards are governed by the notion that it is their role to provide remedies to those individuals and groups denied their rights under the labour relations statute and not to punish those who have committed those wrongs, their power is still very significant. Radio Shack remedies (in Exhibit 7-10) are tough to counter what the board considered to be blatant violations of the *Labour Relations Act.*

Labour Relations Code in Alberta: www.gov.ab.ca/alrb/resources.html

Alberta Employment Standards Information: www.gov.ab.ca/LAB/facts/empstand/publist.html

Exhibit 7.9

Alberta Labour Relations Board Mission Statement

The mission of the Alberta Labour Relations Board is to support and advance the principles of Alberta's labour relations laws by:

- educating the labour relations community and the public of their statutory rights and obligations;
- developing policies and processes that will assist parties to prevent or resolve disputes over these rights and obligations without resort to litigation; and
- providing timely, appropriate, impartial resolution of disputes.

Exhibit 7-10

The Labour Relations Act

NOTICE TO EMPLOYEES

Posted by Order of the Ontario Labour Relations Board

We have issued this notice in compliance with an Order of the Ontario Labour Relations Board issued after a hearing in which both the Company and the Union had the opportunity to present evidence. The Ontario Labour Relations Board found that we violated the Ontario Labour Relations Act and has ordered us to inform our employees of their rights.

The Act gives all employees these rights:

- To organize themselves;
- To form, join or help unions to bargain as a group, through a representative of their own choosing;
- To act together for collective bargaining;
- To refuse to do any and all of these things.

We assure all of our employees that:

WE WILL NOT do anything that interferes with these rights.

WE WILL NOT threaten our employees with plant closure or discharge or with any other type of reprisals because they have selected the United Steelworkers of America as their exclusive bargaining representative.

WE WILL NOT attempt to get employees to inform on union activities and the desires of their fellow employees.

WE WILL NOT engage in surveillance of employee activities with respect to union organization.

WE WILL NOT intimidate or coerce employees in any way into withdrawing from the United Steelworkers of America or from supporting the United Steelworkers of America.

WE WILL NOT refuse to bargain collectively with the United Steelworkers of America as the certified bargaining agent representative of all employees as directed by the Board in the following units....

WE WILL NOT in any other manner interfere with or restrain or coerce our employees in the exercise of their rights under the Act.

WE WILL make whole the United Steelworkers of America for all losses suffered by reason of our refusal to bargain in good faith as directed by the Board.

WE WILL make whole all bargaining employees who suffered losses by reason of our failure to bargain in good faith as directed by the Board.

WE WILL comply with all other directions of the Ontario Labour Relations Board including:

(1) providing the United Steelworkers of America with reasonable access to employee notice boards in our warehouse facility for a period of one year;

(2) providing the United Steelworkers of America with a list of names and addresses of all bargaining unit employees and to keep this list up to date for a period of one year;

(3) providing the United Steelworkers of America with a reasonable opportunity to be present and to reply to any speech made by management representatives to assembled employees;

(4) providing the United Steelworkers of America with an opportunity to address bargaining unit employees on company time and company premises for a period of time not exceeding 30 minutes following the reading of this notice.

WE WILL bargain collectively with the United Steelworkers of America as the duly certified collective bargaining representative of our employees...and if an understanding is reached, we will sign a contract with the Union.

RADIO SHACK
Dated:
Per: (Authorized Representative)

This is an official notice of the Board and must not be removed or defaced. This notice must remain posted for 60 consecutive working days.[18]

The Law of the Picket Line

Interestingly, picketing during a strike is one aspect of collective bargaining not covered by most labour relations statutes, the exceptions being British Columbia and, for a short time during the NDP government, Ontario. Rather, picket line behaviour is most often regulated through the regular courts, either as civil actions or through charges under the *Criminal Code* of Canada.

When dealing with strikes as civil actions, the court is typically drawn in by employers seeking to have a strike or some particular aspect of a strike "enjoined"—in other words, to have the court issue a cease-and-desist order against some action of the union. In such situations, the courts have had to strike a balance between the competing rights involved. This is not difficult in situations where strikers' behaviour is violent or intimidating. In less serious situations, however, the balancing act between the strikers' rights to communicate their point of view and try to persuade others—suppliers, customers, other workers, and so on—to respond sympathetically—that is, to not cross the picket line—and the rights of those very same groups to cross unimpeded is more complex and difficult.

Strikers have a right to picket peacefully for the purpose of "intending to communicate information for the purpose of persuasion by the force of rational appeal."[19] They have the right to try to convince others—customers, suppliers, and the public, for instance—of the justice of their position. What they do not have the right to do is threaten, intimidate, obstruct, harass, or be violent. It is when the picketers' behaviour strays into the wide, grey area between these extremes that the legal situation becomes murky.

It is the police who are charged with the responsibility of maintaining order on picket lines, a duty that calls for perhaps a higher degree of discretion than most areas of police responsibility. In general, the sole concern of the police is the maintenance of order and the prevention of disorder and violence. Knowing that the picket line can be a serious flashpoint in a labour dispute, particularly when people such as replacements or non-striking workers are crossing it, the police often meet with both parties to mediate a picket line protocol. It is probably fair to observe that, as in most mediated solutions to situations that are or may become violent, such an agreement may well not reflect the strict legal rights of any of the parties involved.

During the 1998 legal strike of cleaners at the Corel Centre, just outside Ottawa, the problem posed by this grey area became particularly noticeable (see Exhibit 7.11). This case also illustrated that the views of judges, no less than anyone else, cover a broad range of perspectives.

EXHIBIT 7.11

PICKETING AT THE COREL CENTRE

The Corel Centre is a multi-purpose arena in which space is leased to a number of tenants, including the Ottawa Senators Hockey Club, several restaurants, a physiotherapy clinic, and the YMCA/YWCA of Ottawa-Carleton. Located in Kanata, Ontario, it draws people from such a wide area that few are within walking distance. The primary route between Ottawa and Kanata is Highway 417, a four-lane highway from which drivers exit onto local streets that provide access to extensive parking lots. Special events, such as hockey games or concerts, draw up to 18,500 spectators, with approximately 7500 passenger vehicles entering the grounds within a 90-minute period.

Of the Corel Centre's 550 employees, about 70 are cleaners, mostly part-time, who are represented by the United Steelworkers of America. In February 1998, the cleaners began a legal strike. They and their supporters began picketing, with 40 to 120 individuals at any one time at 11 locations around the Centre, obstructing the movement of passenger and commercial vehicles and municipal buses carrying other employees, spectators, players, and performers.

In an effort to minimize the traffic chaos, the Ontario Provincial Police (OPP) worked with the Union to develop an "informal protocol" whereby passenger vehicles would be delayed no more than two minutes, commercial vehicles ten minutes, and tractor trailers 30 minutes. While this arrangement worked reasonably when there were no major events, during hockey games the obstructions caused miles-long backups on access roads, prompting drivers to actions like leaving their vehicles on the side of the roads, including Highway 417, and walking to the Centre. Buses were refused access, forcing passengers to get out and walk a considerable distance. There was serious potential for acts even more violent than inconvenienced drivers nudging picketers with cars and engaging in heated verbal exchanges with them.

On March 20, 1998, the Centre's owners applied for an injunction to prevent the picketers from interfering with access to the site. Testimony by OPP officers and others and evidence that included a composite videotape persuaded the Court to grant the injunction on April 2, 1998, on the basis that the legal right to

picket did not include the right to obstruct traffic. In fact, the Court found that the picketers were contravening the *Criminal Code* by preventing people from doing something they had a legal right to do, i.e., making use of public highways. Further, it found that the picketers' actions constituted "nuisance" in that they interfered with the owners' right of enjoyment of their lands and premises. Given that the duty of the police is to enforce the law, the "informal protocol" was found to be illegal. Besides finding that the owners' rights to proper access to their premises outweighed the Union's "right" to obstruct traffic, the Court was convinced that the situation was dangerous enough to warrant measures to control activities on the picket line.

The injunction was overturned by another judge two weeks later, on the grounds that she found there was no evidence of dangerous conditions to justify depriving the Union of its picketing rights, particularly in view of the Union's pledge to her that it would not obstruct traffic, but the Ontario Court of Appeal reversed that decision in late April. The Appeal Court's reasoning rested in large part on the conclusion that the right to picket did not include the right to obstruct traffic. The only change it made in the order was to assign responsibility for enforcing it to the sheriff, rather than to the OPP.[20]

Canadian legislation generally prohibits "secondary picketing"—that is, picketing an employer that is not involved in the dispute. In a recent decision involving a dispute in British Columbia between K-Mart Canada and the United Food and Commercial Workers, in which the union was handing out leaflets at nonunion K-Mart stores, the Labour Relations Board of British Columbia ordered the activity to stop because (1) it clearly fell within the definition of picketing contained in the *Labour Relations Code* and (2) the Code forbids secondary picketing. The Supreme Court found that this definition of picketing was too wide and that, in forbidding even leafleting (which it noted "does not have the same coercive component as a picket line, and does not in any significant manner impede access to or egress from premises") at secondary sites, it offended the freedom of expression provision (s. 2(b)) of the *Canadian Charter of Rights and Freedoms*. Looked at in the shadow of the *Charter*, in other words, a couple of people merely handing out leaflets, even at secondary sites, does not constitute "picketing."[21]

THE ERA OF INDIVIDUAL AND GROUP RIGHTS

The 1980s saw the beginning of a dramatic shift in direction for the collective bargaining system: the superimposition on it of laws and public policies based, not on the principle of collective rights and power, but on individual and group rights—namely, human rights codes, employment equity and pay equity acts, and the *Canadian Charter of Rights and Freedoms*. The principles on which these laws are all based differ from—and, to a considerable extent, conflict with—those underlying the collective bargaining system, and it is the latter that has had to adapt.

The *Canadian Charter of Rights and Freedoms*

The *Charter* was adopted in 1982 as Part I of the *Constitution Act* and, as the name suggests, is now part of the Canadian Constitution. A constitution is a document that sets out and constrains how the various components of government will work and defines limitations on their powers.

As part of the Canadian Constitution, the *Charter* takes precedence over all other laws. Every other statute must be consistent with the *Charter*, which means, in simple terms, that any federal or provincial law can be challenged by an individual or group on the basis of an allegation that its *Charter* rights have been violated by that statute. The ultimate arbiter of such questions becomes the Supreme Court of Canada. This has resulted in a growing controversy over what some see as an "activist" Supreme Court, all too ready to create "judge-made law."

Sections 1 and 2 set out the intent of the *Charter*:

1. The *Canadian Charter of Rights and Freedoms* guarantees the rights and freedoms set out in it subject only to such reasonable limits prescribed by law as can be demonstrably justified in a free and democratic society.

2. Everyone has the following fundamental freedoms:
   a) freedom of conscience and religion;
   b) freedom of thought, belief, opinion and expression, including freedom of the press and other media of communication;
   c) freedom of peaceful assembly;
   d) freedom of association.

Section 32 sets out the domain or coverage of the *Charter*. It applies to laws passed by the Parliament of Canada and the legislatures of each of the provinces.

One of the fundamental freedoms protected by the *Charter* is freedom of association. It was natural that trade unions would see in it the possibility of a constitutional guarantee of the freedom to bargain collectively and to strike—elevating those activities, in effect, to the level of fundamental constitutional rights "beyond the reach of legislators."[22] However, that was not to be. In a series of early *Charter* cases, trade unions attempted to invoke *Charter* protection against, first, Alberta's restriction of provincial public servants' right to strike; second, the federal government wage controls of 1982; and, third, Saskatchewan legislation to prevent a strike in the dairy industry. In each of these cases, collectively known as the "Labour Trilogy," the Supreme Court refused to extend the protection of freedom of association for individuals guaranteed by the *Charter* to these collective activities.[23]

Labour Standards in Saskatchewan:
www.labour.gov.sk.ca/standards.index.htm

While the Supreme Court declined to use the *Charter* to make collective bargaining and striking constitutionally guaranteed rights, so too did it refuse to use the *Charter* to substantially weaken the principle of collectivism that underlies the collective bargaining system, even when that principle is achieved at the cost of individual rights. This was illustrated in what may well have been the most definitive—and clearly was the most instructive—labour relations test of the *Charter* so far. An unwilling member of a bargaining unit challenged his union's right to use any part of his union dues, collected through a Rand Formula provision that compelled payment of dues, to support political causes with which he did not agree. A faculty member at the Haileybury School of Mines, Merv Lavigne, argued that the Ontario Public Service Employees Union's use of dues collected against his will to support generally left-wing political causes—for example, the New Democratic Party, disarmament campaigns, the British Mineworkers' union, and opposition to Toronto's SkyDome—violated his freedom to express himself and to *not* associate. The Court rejected the argument that Mr. Lavigne's freedom of expression under Section 2 (b) had been improperly infringed and, by a majority of four to three, also rejected the argument that his right of non-association implied by Section 2 (d) had been infringed.

The majority having decided that no freedom *from* compelled association was implied by s. 2 (d), all seven justices went on to find that, notwithstanding, *had* they found Mr. Lavigne to have had a right of non-association, and *had* they then found that right to have been infringed by the Rand Formula and the union's policy of supporting certain social and political causes, the heart of the matter would still lie in yet another question: Were those infringements "demonstrably justified in a free and democratic society"? All seven justices decided this hypothetical question in the affirmative[24] (see Exhibit 7.12).

As in the Labour Trilogy, then, the Supreme Court again refused to use the *Charter* to significantly upset the collective bargaining system. In the Trilogy, the Court had refused to extend individual rights into collective rights, while, in Lavigne, it applied the ancient reality that there are no absolute rights in society and that a balance must be struck between competing rights. That balance had been struck with respect to labour relations and collective bargaining in Canada many years before by a combination of legislatures, labour boards, judges, arbitrators, and the parties themselves; the Supreme Court left it intact with its Lavigne decision. Thus, in a direct sense at least, the *Charter* has not had a dramatic impact on the Canadian collective bargaining system. Clearly, however, the potential to upset the system is there, and the *Charter* has had at least an indirect impact on collective bargaining.

Exhibit 7.12

Is Any Right Absolute?

"In this era of human rights, we often hear people claim their rights as if there were no other competing right. Section 1 of the *Charter* recognized that, in any society, no right is absolute. Just as no one has the right to yell 'fire' in a crowded theatre, in any integrated society, there must be limits on virtually any right by any person. The governing principle, again, is striking the appropriate balance *between competing rights of two or more people or groups.*"[25]

The Human Rights Codes

The early 1980s saw the beginning of another major shift in the bedrock of Canadian employment law with the expansion of the provincial and federal human rights codes, first by the provincial legislatures and then by the Supreme Court. At the most basic level, the prohibited grounds for discrimination were extended in many of the provinces, so that, by the end of the 1990s, most human rights laws prohited discrimination on the basis of race, national/ethnic origin, colour, religion, age, sex, marital status, disability, sexual orientation, and creed, while a smaller number of jurisdictions also included such grounds as dependence on alcohol/drugs, nationality/citizenship, pregnancy/childbirth, criminal conviction, ancestry, political beliefs, civil status, language, source of income, social condition, and place of residence. In addition, and more controversially, courts have been willing to "read in" certain grounds for discrimination, even where the legislature has chosen not to. Both the Canadian *Human Rights Act*[26] and the Alberta *Human Rights Code*[27] had sexual orientation read into them on the basis that sexual orientation should fall, by analogy, within s. 15 of the *Charter's* guarantee of equal treatment under the law. Any rule, arrangement, or provision that is directly discriminatory on the basis of a prohibited ground of discrimination in the relevant jurisdiction is, of course, null and of no force.

Human Resources Development Canada—Federal Labour Legislation Site: infor.load-otea.hrdc.drhc.gc.ca

Even more significant for industrial relations is the concept of "adverse impact discrimination." This is the notion that, notwithstanding that a rule or practice may be objective and non-discriminatory on its face (that is, it may *appear* to be neutral and objective), it can nevertheless be discriminatory due to its *impact* on certain groups of employees. The Supreme Court of Canada forcefully articulated this principle in the case of an Ontario sales clerk who, as a Seventh Day Adventist, asked that she not be required to work on Saturday, her religion's Sabbath.[28] The employer insisted that she work a Saturday shift; Ms. O'Malley refused, and was discharged. The Court found that, in order to conclude that Ms. O'Malley had been discriminated against, it was not necessary for Simpson Sears to have *intended* to discriminate against her. Rather, the mandatory Saturday shifts violated her religious principles and disadvantaged her on religious grounds relative to other employees. Thus, the principle of "adverse impact" discrimination was introduced to Canadian law and extended in a series of subsequent Supreme Court decisions. Employers, and unions, became legally obligated to accommodate employees who were the victims, even if unintentionally, of adverse impact discrimination.

Adverse impact discrimination squarely reveals potential conflict between the values underlying the collective bargaining world on one hand and the human rights world on the other. One illustrative case is *Central Okanagan School District No. 32* v. *Renaud.*[29] As in the O'Malley case, the complainant was a member of the Seventh Day Adventist church. Mr. Renaud requested that he not have to work on Saturdays, offering to work on Sundays instead. The employer agreed, but said that he would have to work a Sunday-to-Thursday shift. Unfortunately, under the collective agreement, Mr. Renaud did not have sufficient seniority to be entitled to such a shift; the union objected, threatening to file a policy grievance if the employer went ahead. As a result, no further consideration was given to Mr. Renaud's request. When he refused to work a posted Saturday shift, he was terminated.

The Supreme Court of Canada determined that both the union and employer had discriminated against Mr. Renaud and both had a duty to accommodate him. In a parallel case,[30] a human rights tribunal came to a similar finding and directed that the compensatory damages awarded to the complainant be split equally between the employer and the union.

These cases are harbingers of a new set of values—individual rights—that are being superimposed on the collective values of the collective bargaining world. The clear message is that *both* parties to a collective agreement have a duty to accommodate individuals in order to avoid the discrimination that might result from a normal application to that individual of all of the provisions of the collective agreement. While an employer has a duty to accommodate up to the point of "undue hardship," a union has a similar duty, to a point short of "substituting discrimination against other employees for the discrimination suffered by the complainant."[31] If provisions of a collective agreement, while objective and neutral on their face, are found to be discriminatory, the parties must be prepared to make changes. Mr. Renaud's religious beliefs had to be reasonably accommodated: It would not have been undue hardship had he been allowed to work the Sunday-to-Thursday shift, despite lacking sufficient seniority to qualify under the provisions of the collective agreement.

A 1999 Supreme Court decision, *British Columbia (Public Service Employee Relations Commission) v. BCGSEU,*[32] suggests a more significant potential impact on collective agreements in the future. A female forest firefighter with three years' seniority was terminated when she failed to run 2.5 kilometres in 11 minutes. Evidence was presented at her arbitration hearing that women and men have different aerobic capacities and that women cannot increase their aerobic capacity through training and exercise. The arbitrator found this requirement to be discriminatory and, not satisfied on the evidence that the employer had accommodated the grievor to the point of undue hardship, reinstated her. The case ultimately made its way to the Supreme Court. Most significant about the Court's decision was its strong suggestion that direct (wilful) and adverse impact discrimination should be treated similarly and that the appropriate outcome for a discriminatory rule, requirement, or provision was not simply that the complainant should be accommodated (to the point of undue hardship), but that the rule, requirement, or provision itself should be struck down. This may have interesting implications for collective agreements. For example, had this notion been applied in the Central Okanagan School District case, the result would appear to have been not the accommodation of Mr. Renaud, but the striking down or at least modifying of the seniority provision for shifts.

The concept of seniority is particularly vulnerable to charges of adverse impact discrimination. Seniority lies at the heart of union philosophy and features prominently in collective agreements. It allows unions to gain some measure of control over promotions, the disposition of new positions, the allocation of benefits, and so on, without running the risk of being accused of arbitrariness or favouritism by union members—in addition to its obvious, if imperfect, value as a measure of intrinsic fairness. But the very objectivity of such a criterion as length of service can, in some circumstances, have a disparate impact on certain groups protected under the Human Rights Codes. This is perhaps particularly so for women who, taken as a group, have not been in the labour force as long as men and who therefore tend to have less seniority. The logic is simple: If women as a group have less seniority than men, then collective agreement provisions that distribute benefits on the basis of seniority will tend to disadvantage them. Exacerbating this, women tend to be grouped into lower-paying jobs, or "ghettoized," and seniority provisions can reinforce the barriers to leaving the ghetto.

Shift systems may also have to be re-examined. For example, a general-assignment reporter for the *Toronto Star* repeatedly and unsuccessfully requested that she be allowed to work straight days rather than shifts because of the need to properly care for her small child. She resigned and then grieved that the employer's refusal to accommodate her needs as a mother by putting her on straight days constituted discrimination. The arbitrator dismissed that particular aspect of the grievance, but on the basis that there was insufficient evidence of disparate impact, not on the basis of any conceptual flaw in the logic.[33] The case demonstrated the potential of adverse effect discrimination to affect shift systems, whether seniority-based or not, and the role arbitration can play in applying human rights principles to collective agreements (see Chapter 12).

There may be many potential forms of adverse impact discrimination issues within common collective agreement provisions:

- seniority provisions relating to postings, holidays, schedules
- competitive vs. threshold seniority/job-posting clauses
- deemed termination provisions
- seniority barriers around narrowly defined job "ghettoes"

Pay and Employment Equity

The advent of both pay equity and employment equity also reflects the same superimposition of different values upon Canadian collective bargaining regimes. Pay equity policies are founded upon the premise that salary schedules have systemically discriminated against female employees. Women have tended to be highly concentrated in certain types of jobs—secretarial, clerical, and so on—the so-called "pink-collar ghetto." Such jobs tended to constitute their own bargaining unit within a company—the "administrative-support" group. Pay equity advocates argued that employers undervalued this work ("women's work"), not as part of an orchestrated intention to discriminate against women, but as a reflection of *society's* undervaluation of women's work. They argued that if typical "female" jobs and typical "male" jobs (within the same organization) were analyzed using a single job evaluation scheme based on the same measures of job value—skill, effort, responsibility, and working conditions—then the female jobs would be shown to be systemically underpaid.

In the context of gender issues and pay equity, "systemic discrimination"

> is a form of discrimination that is no one's fault: No one intended it. Work organizations were designed by white males *for* white males on the assumption, then quite valid, that it would be white males who would be working in them. The problem is, however, that white males are different from, and have different needs than, women and various minorities; therefore, a system designed for and by white males poses barriers to the entry and retention of employees other than white males.[34]

For students of industrial relations, the most interesting aspect of this is the role of unions. Bear in mind that, in many cases (that is, where clusters of "female jobs" were unionized), those unions had negotiated the very pay scales that pay equity advocates now argued were systemically discriminatory. Unions have been quick to adjust, however. Though the concept of pay equity was imposed upon collective bargaining regimes from the outside, typically as part of pay equity statutes, unions have used this opportunity strategically, to benefit their female members. Pay equity practices have been harmonized with collective bargaining regimes relatively easily, simply by raising the pay scales of those groups and bargaining units in which there are heavy concentrations of women.

More challenging is the harmonization of another exogenously imposed policy—employment equity. "Affirmative action," as it is known in the United States, is based on a principle which, it can be argued, is in fundamental conflict with the collective values of collective bargaining. Employment equity is a policy under which an employer takes measures to increase the representation in its workforce of certain designated groups—women, visible minorities, the disabled, and aboriginal peoples, in the case of typical Canadian employment equity statutes—who are under-represented in terms of their availability in the general labour force (or working-age population). Thus, for example, an employer trying to increase the proportion of women at various levels of its workforce would try to hire larger numbers of women, but also retain, develop, and promote women wherever possible. The underlying premise of employment equity policies is that women (and the other designated groups) have been victims of "systemic discrimination"—that is, discrimination that is endemic in an employment system designed for and by white men.

Employment equity is founded on a principle—that certain groups have been systemically discriminated against in the past and thus need special treatment now in order to achieve genuine equality—which is, at a certain level, fundamentally at odds with the collective "everyone is equal" principle that informs the traditional collective bargaining regime. The two principles must be reconciled, thus posing yet another challenge for both unions and employers in adapting their collective agreements. The most difficult challenge may lie in adapting the principle of seniority (which unions have traditionally attempted to establish as the dominant criterion for job postings, vacations, shifts, and other benefits under the collective agreement) to the reality that, if the employer has an employment equity plan in place, then women are likely to have less seniority, on average, than men. The challenge, of course, is to adapt the provisions of their collective agreement so as not to render the employment equity plan null. This becomes particularly evident, and important, in the event of a layoff.

CONCLUSION

Canadian labour law, which once simply consisted of the 11 labour relations acts and was based on a relatively small number of simple and well understood principles, has now become a much larger and infinitely more complex collection of laws and policies. The collective values of the traditional labour relations regime have had to adapt to the individual and group values on which human rights codes, employment and pay equity policies, and the *Charter* are built. It is a complex and dynamic mosaic in which the dominant characteristic is, perhaps, change. Labour relations practitioners on both sides of the table are now confronted by a fundamentally new and infinitely more complex set of challenges. We are witness to a fascinating evolution in this body of the law.

Questions

1. Make arguments for and against:
   (a) labour statutes that provide for certification on the basis of a majority of the employees in the appropriate bargaining unit having signed membership cards;
   (b) labour statutes that provide for certification on the basis of a majority of the ballots cast in the certification vote.

2. Prepare arguments both for and against the union shop.

3. Why might it be argued that common collective agreement provisions constitute adverse impact discrimination?

4. Can you think of ways in which such provisions could accommodate the needs of bargaining unit members protected under the Human Rights Codes?

5. How might the seniority provisions of a collective agreement be harmonized with an employment equity plan?

ENDNOTES

[1] *United Steelworkers of America* v. *Wal-Mart Canada, Inc.* [1997] OLRB Rep. 141, 97 CLLC 220–046 (Ont. LRB).

[2] So named because one of the two sponsors of the bill in Congress was Senator Robert Wagner.

[3] The "New Deal" was the name given to President Franklin D. Roosevelt's policies designed principally to pull the United States out of the Great Depression. Taken as a whole, the New Deal injected the state into economic and business matters in a way and to a degree never before seen. In effect, FDR was trying to use the fiscal and law-making power of the state to put people to work, to put money in people's pockets, to reform the banking system, and to buoy confidence in the economic system.

[4] *Ganeca Transport Inc. and Transport Drivers, Warehousemen and General Workers' Union, Local 106*, [1990] CLRB Decision No. 780, Board Files 745-3384, 555-2291, 555-3002.

[5] Remember that this was pre-Snider case (1925), when collective bargaining was still considered to be a federal jurisdiction.

[6] In some provinces and in the federal sector, a simple majority of those voting is required for certification. In several provinces, Manitoba included, the union must obtain a majority of all members of the bargaining unit. In practice, this means that non-voters count against the union.

[7] *United Steelworkers of America and Radio Shack* [1979] 2 CLRBR 281 (OLRB); *United Steelworkers of America and Radio Shack* [1980] 1 CLRBR 281 (OLRB).

[8] The philosophical foundation for the duty of fair representation was laid by the American Supreme Court in a 1944 decision. A number of black railroad firemen complained that the union for their craft, which did not allow black employees to be members, had negotiated a provision with their employer which, if fully implemented, would have ultimately resulted in the layoff of all non-members of the union (that is, black employees). The union had an obligation, in the words of the Chief Justice, "to represent non-union or minority union members of the craft without hostile discrimination, fairly, impartially, and in good faith." *Steeles* v. *Louisville and Nashville Railroad Co.* [323 US 210 (1944)].

[9] *Shachtay and Creamery Workers Union, Local 1* [1986] 86 CLLC 16,033 (Man. L.B.).

[10] *Canadian Merchant Service Guild* v. *Gagnon*, [1984] 1 SCR 509, 9 DLR (4th) 641, 53 NR 100.

[11] Saskatchewan, Manitoba, Ontario, Quebec, and Newfoundland.

[12] For example, the Alberta *School Act* requires that all teachers in the public and Roman Catholic Separate School systems belong to the Alberta Teachers' Association, which also serves as their collective bargaining agent.

[13] *British Columbia Hydro and Power Authority*, 78 CLLC 16,155 (BCLRB).

[14] *Noranda Metal Industries Ltd.* (1975) 1 Can. LRBR 145 (BC) 160–161.

[15] *The Daily Times* [1978] 2 Can. LRBR 446 (Ont.).

[16] *Ottawa Newspaper Guild, Local 205 of the Newspaper Guild, and the Citizen* [1979] 2 Can LRBR.

[17] Supra, note 7.

[18] Supra, note 7.

[19] *Williams* v. *Aristocratic Restaurants (1947) Ltd.* [1951] 3 DLR 769 (SCC).

[20] *Ogden Entertainment Services* v. *Retail, Wholesale/Canada, Canadian Service Sector Division of the United Steelworkers of America, Local 440* [1998] OJ 1769 [Ontario Court of Justice (General Division) McKinnon J.]; *Ogden Entertainment Services* v. *Kay in his representative capacity as Area Representative of Retail, Wholesale/Canada, Canadian Service Sector Division of United Steelworkers of America, Local 440* [1998] 38 OR (3d) 448 (Court of Appeal for Ontario, Robins, McKinlay and Weiler JJ.A.).

[21] *United Food and Commercial Workers, Local 1518* v. *K-Mart Canada Ltd. and the Labour Relations Board of British Columbia* [1999] 2 SCR 1083.

[22] Donald. D Carter. *The Canadian Charter of Rights and Freedoms: Implications for Industrial Relations and Human Resource Practitioners* (Kingston: Industrial Relations Centre, Queen's University, 1991).

[23] The three "Labour Trilogy" cases are as follows: 1) *Public Service Employee Relations Act, Labour Relations Act, and Police Officers Collective Bargaining Act* (1987) 38 DLR (4th) 161 (SCC); 2) *Public Service Alliance of Canada* v. *The Queen in Right of Canada* (1987) 38 DLR (4th) 249 (SCC); and 3) *Government of Saskatchewan* v. *Retail, Wholesale, and Department Store Union* (1987) 38 DLR (4th) 277 (SCC).

[24] *Lavigne* v. *Ontario Public Service Employees Union* (1991) 81 DLR (4th) 545 (SCC).

[25] Supra, note 24.

[26] *Haig* v. *The Queen* (1992), 92 CLLC para. 17,034 (Ont. CA).

[27] *Vriend* v. *Alberta* [1998] 1 SCR 493.

[28] *O'Malley* v. *Simpson Sears*, (1986) 9 CCEL, 185. The case started out as a complaint under the Ontario *Human Rights Code.*

[29] *Central Okanagan School District No. 32* v. *Renaud* (1992), 92 CLLC para. 17,032 (SCC) and Central Alberta Dairy Pool.

[30] *Irene Gohm* v. *Domtar and the Office and Professional Employees International Union, Local 267*, CHRR, Vol. 12, D/161.

[31] Supra, note 29.

[32] *BCGSEU* v. *British Columbia Public Service Employee Relations Commission* [1999] 99 CLLC 145,215.

[33] *Re Toronto Star Newspaper and Southern Ontario Newspaper Guild* 12 LAC (4th) 273 (1990).

[34] R. L. Jackson. *Employment Equity and Ontario Police: Problems and Perspectives* (Kingston: IRC Press, Industrial Relations Centre, Queen's University, 1992), p. 1.

CHAPTER 8

Employment Legislation in Canada

David McPhillips

In 1997, the Supreme Court of Canada pronounced one of the most significant decisions in the history of Canadian employment law. It involved the wrongful dismissal of Jack Wallace from the United Grain Growers. Wallace worked with them for 14 years until his termination in 1986 at age 59. Prior to joining the company at age 45, he did not wish to lose the job security of his previous position without guarantees in his new employment. He sought assurances regarding fair treatment and remuneration. He received such assurances and was promised that, if he performed as expected, he could continue to work until retirement. He enjoyed great success and was the top salesperson in each of the 14 years he was employed. Only a few days after being complimented for his performance, he was discharged without explanation. When he then sued for wrongful dismissal, having never been previously criticized, his employer alleged that he was dismissed for cause. The employer maintained that allegation for two years, withdrawing it only when the legal trial commenced. Mr. Wallace was awarded 24 months' severance pay in lieu of adequate notice of dismissal and due to the bad-faith discharge in spite of earlier promises of security.

> The Supreme Court noted that "A person's employment is an essential component of his or her sense of identity, self-worth, and emotional well-being." Thus, "any change in a person's employment status is bound to have far-reaching repercussions. When the change is involuntary, the extent of disruption is even greater. The point at which the employment relationship ruptures is the time when the employee is most vulnerable and hence, in most need of protection." The Court concluded that, in recognition of this need, the law ought to encourage conduct to minimize the dislocation resulting from the dismissal and "when termination is accompanied by acts of bad faith in the manner of discharge, the results can be especially devastating. [To] ensure that employees receive adequate protection, employers ought to be held to an obligation of good faith and fair dealing in the manner of dismissal, the breach of which will be compensated for by adding to the length of notice."
>
> The Court commented that "I fail to see how it can be onerous to be required to treat employees fairly, reasonably, and decently at a time of trauma and despair. In my view the reasonable person would expect such treatment. So should the law."[1]

This chapter deals with basic laws governing the employment of all workers in Canada. These laws, which exist aside from those offered under collective bargaining regimes, have been created by specific statute and at common law. It is a body of law that affords protection to employees in such fundamental areas as minimum work standards, safety in the workplace, employment contracts at common law, and human rights. The key aspects of this protection are reviewed here, and comparisons are drawn, where appropriate, with the protection provided under collective agreements. The first part outlines the work standards legislation contained in the various jurisdictions. The next part reviews the statutes and common law rules related to individual employment contracts. Human rights legislation pertaining to employment is then covered in the third part.

When most people think of laws relating to employment, they think of the labour relations codes that exist in each jurisdiction. However, those codes govern only the relationships between companies and their unionized employees. Even the collective agreements that are in place, covering about 30 percent of Canadians who are unionized, do not address all aspects of the employment relationship. Employment legislation is designed to provide basic standards covering all workers, nonunion as well as unionized. This legislation is particularly critical in situations where employees may lack effective bargaining power as is frequently the case in the absence of trade union representation. The importance of employment legislation for employees in general and for industrial relations is now widely recognized:

Growing awareness of limitations on the scope and effectiveness of collective bar-gaining has brought a growing realization that direct, substantive legislative inter-vention is often the only answer. Such intervention ... is becoming more pervasive and more fully elaborated. Even for employment relations covered by collective bar-gaining, the legal rights and obligations of the parties can no longer be adequately understood without a grasp of the impact of employment standards legislation, anti-discrimination legislation, health and safety legislation, and the like.[2]

Although Canadian jurisdictions vary in the specific rights conferred on employees, the overall approach is reasonably uniform. As with collective bargaining legislation, sections 91 and 92 of the *Constitution Act, 1981*, which adopted the *British North America Act* of 1867, divide responsibility for employment law between the federal and provincial gov-ernments. Federal employment laws such as Part III of the *Canada Labour Code* (relating to the employment standards), the *Canadian Human Rights Act*, and Part I of the *Canada Labour Code* (labour–management relations) apply to employees of airlines and railroads, banks, the postal service, the federal public sector, and communications firms, which together account for about 10 percent of the workforce. Provincial laws of a similar charac-ter apply to the 90 percent of employees not covered by federal legislation (Figure 8.1).

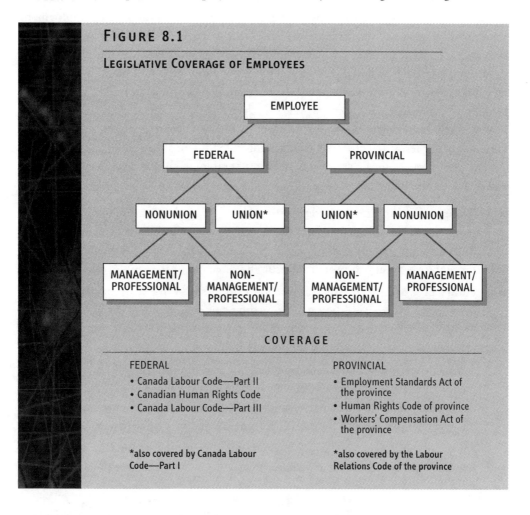

FIGURE 8.1

LEGISLATIVE COVERAGE OF EMPLOYEES

COVERAGE

FEDERAL
- Canada Labour Code—Part II
- Canadian Human Rights Code
- Canada Labour Code—Part III

*also covered by Canada Labour Code—Part I

PROVINCIAL
- Employment Standards Act of the province
- Human Rights Code of province
- Workers' Compensation Act of the province

*also covered by the Labour Relations Code of the province

WHO IS AN EMPLOYEE?

Before most employment laws can be applied, a court, labour board, employment standards board, or human rights tribunal must determine that an individual is an employee as opposed to an independent contractor, apprentice, agent, or partner.[3] (In the latter cases, the parties are governed by the relevant laws of contract, agency, or partnership, respectively.) A number of tests have been developed to determine who is an employee. For example, the control test examines the power of selection, the payment of wages, the right to control the method of doing the work, and the right of suspension or dismissal. The courts will also look at issues such as whether there is limited exclusivity to the services of the "employee" or whether there is any risk or expectation on the part of the "employee."[4] Because more protection is afforded an employee than ordinary contracting parties, the courts, boards, and other tribunals tend to interpret "employee" as broadly as possible.[5]

WORK STANDARDS LEGISLATION

Each jurisdiction sets out minimum standards of work that apply to all employees. These "floors of rights" are contained either in one statute (for example, an employment standards act) or in a series of separate statutes (for example, holidays act, hours of work act) and are intended to set the threshold of rights for all workers, both union and nonunion. It should be noted that in many jurisdictions, these acts or parts of them do not apply to certain groups of employees. For example, overtime-pay requirements may not apply to managers, and some workers, such as farm labourers, fishers, or domestics, may be excluded entirely. However, section 15 of the *Charter of Rights and Freedoms* may eventually result in these exclusions being ruled unconstitutional.

The areas covered in the various jurisdictions' employment standards legislation generally include the following:

1. **Wage protection** provisions deal with such issues as when wages are to be paid, the requirement for a statement of wages, the employer's right to make deductions from earnings, assignments of wages and, in the event of nonpayment, the right of the employee to attach property or sue the directors of the employer.

2. **Hours of work**. Such issues as maximum hours of work daily or weekly before overtime must be paid, the rate of overtime pay, requirements for lunch or coffee breaks, rules regarding split shifts, minimum call-in periods, and minimum consecutive hours free from work are generally covered.

3. **Annual vacation**. Each jurisdiction sets out a minimum annual vacation entitlement (for example, two weeks during each year worked and then three weeks after five years) and states when the vacation leave becomes due. The provisions also set out vacation-pay rates (2 percent, 3 percent) in lieu of paid vacation.

4. **Statutory holidays**. The legislation sets out the minimum number of statutory holidays (Christmas Day, Labour Day, and so on) to which the employee is entitled.

The number varies between five and ten among jurisdictions. The acts also set out technical requirements for entitlement (for example, having worked ten consecutive workdays before the holiday as well as the day following the holiday).

5. **Minimum wages**. The acts or accompanying regulations set out a minimum wage that must be paid to all employees. Some jurisdictions specify separate rates for adults and for younger workers (those under 17 or 18 years of age).

6. **Family leave**. The protections include the right to a paid or unpaid leave for a specific period of time—usually 17 or 18 weeks—during pregnancy and following the birth of a child and, in many cases, a specified period of time for paternity, family leave, or adoption leaves. The provisions also deal with the timing of the leaves and the security rights of the employee on her or his return to work.

7. **Termination**. Each jurisdiction (except the Northwest Territories) sets out a minimum notice period to which most employees are entitled before termination. These notice requirements may not apply if the employee was recently hired or if the employer can prove just cause (such as theft) for termination. In most jurisdictions, the requirement is one of *notice*, so the employer can insist that the employee work during the notice period. In practice, however, the employer often terminates the employee immediately, paying him or her the wages that would be owed for the notice period. Each jurisdiction has its own formula for establishing minimum standards of notice. For example, an employee may be entitled to one week's notice after six months, then two weeks after one year, and then a graduated number up to a certain maximum (generally eight to ten weeks). The federal statute, for example, requires a combination of a short notice period (two weeks) and then severance pay for employees who have worked for at least 12 months.

   Most jurisdictions also have special notice requirements for "mass" (sizeable group) layoffs.

8. **Miscellaneous**. Because the area of work standards is constantly evolving, provisions differ among the various jurisdictions in Canada. Other areas of coverage include clothing or special apparel payments, child employment laws, minimum age levels for employment, bereavement leave, sick leave, and maximum board and lodging charges.

In summary, the minimum standards in each of these areas tend to be just that. They include the basic level of benefits that the governments require employers to make available to their employees. Many employers routinely exceed the minimum standards.

There is also legislation in Canada dealing with the prevention of workplace accidents and diseases. In Canada, the goal of prevention is pursued by a combination of the "external system," wherein defined standards for health and safety are established by legislation, and the "internal system," wherein joint management–labour committees assume certain responsibilities for promoting health and safety at the workplace level. Sometimes the legislation is contained in a specific health-and-safety statute applicable to all employers, but this may be supplemented by a myriad of statutes applicable only to certain industries and administered by different government departments. In all jurisdictions, employees have the right to refuse unsafe work.

The legislation also deals with compensation for workplace accidents and diseases. The principal method for compensating victims who have been disabled by an accident or a disease "arising out of and in the course of employment" is worker's compensation legislation. The key feature of the Canadian schemes is that entitlement does not depend on proof of negligence on the employer's part. In return for this guarantee of no-fault compensation, the worker is precluded from pursuing common law remedies in court against the employer.

 Lancaster House: www.lancasterhouse.com/

It is noteworthy that most of these benefits were originally gained by trade unions but have now been applied to all working people in Canadian society. Presently, most unions negotiate terms in their collective agreements that both greatly improve upon these minimum standards and expand into new areas (paid educational leave, for example).

INDIVIDUAL CONTRACTS OF EMPLOYMENT

Besides the statutory provisions, other protections and obligations are imposed through the existence of individual employment contracts that every employee has with his or her employer. The terms of the employment agreement can arise in any of three ways: by implication through operation of the law, by implication by the past practice of the parties, or by express agreement of the parties. Invariably, the parties do not explicitly agree to or even discuss most of the terms of the employment contract. Nevertheless, because express terms prevail over implied terms, it is wise for the parties to reduce as much as possible to express agreement, particularly in written form.

Implied Terms by Operation of Law
Employee

Important implied terms of any employment contract establish that the employee is under an obligation to work, to not be absent unreasonably, to obey lawful and safe orders, to avoid serious misconduct (which may include dishonesty,[6] impropriety, drunkenness, insolence, and insubordination), to perform in a competent and careful manner (that is, to exercise skill and care), and to account for all property and money he or she receives on the employer's behalf.[7] It has also been held that the employer has the implied right to run the business and to expect the employee to follow instructions.[8]

Each employment contract contains an implied term that the employee will serve honestly and faithfully. The employment relationship is a fiduciary one, which requires good faith, fidelity, and the avoidance of a conflict of interest.[9] This may include the duty to disclose improper conduct by fellow employees[10] and to not disseminate confidential information.[11] Similarly, the solicitation of customers by employees while employed is a breach of the duty; solicitation after leaving employment is normally permitted unless the individual was in a senior position, in which case the fiduciary duty may well continue.[12]

In some jurisdictions, the employment standards legislation includes an obligation on the employee to provide notice of an intention to quit. Moreover, the common law requires an employee to give notice of intent to quit employment.[13] In practice, however, this issue of "wrongful resignation" is rarely litigated as the length of the required notice period is relatively insignificant for most employees. In addition, it may be difficult for an employer to prove damages,[14] particularly in view of the requirement to mitigate, and the cost of litigation acts as a further disincentive.

Employer

The obligations of the employer include paying the employee (at or above the minimum wage) and paying over gratuities.[15]

The most significant implied term in an employment contract, however, is the obligation on the employer to give reasonable notice to the employee in the case of dismissal without just cause.[16] If such notice (or pay in lieu thereof) is provided, there is no breach of the employment contract, and the contract lawfully terminates at the expiration of the notice period or on payment of severance money in lieu thereof. This implied term is a relatively recent addition to the common law, having replaced the 19th-century presumption of yearly hiring. Even today, if the employment contract is for a specific term, as is the case with, say, most professional sport coaches, no such implication of reasonable notice of termination arises, and the contract must be paid in full.[17] Further, the implied term of giving reasonable notice does not arise in cases of an employee's voluntary resignation,[18] frustration of the contract (which occurs when a contract cannot be performed because of some event beyond the parties' control—for example, a fire),[19] retirement,[20] or temporary layoff.[21]

In alleged cases of dismissal, the court has to decide three questions:

1. **Was there an express or constructive dismissal?** An "express dismissal" is an oral or written communication to the effect that the employee is being terminated. A "constructive dismissal" exists where actions by the employer can be construed as the equivalent of a dismissal. Whenever the employer unilaterally changes a fundamental term of the employment contract, such as salary level, job responsibilities, level of status or prestige, fringe benefits, or hours of work,[22] the employee may treat the contract as having been repudiated by the employer and seek the available legal remedies.

   However, *minor* changes to the terms of the employment agreement do not constitute a fundamental change; in these cases, the alteration has to be accepted by the employee. These cases hold that an employer must be allowed a certain degree of latitude with respect to minor changes to the employee's job functions.[23]

This may be especially true where an employee was not hired to fill a particular senior function.[24] Accordingly, there appears to be some leeway in making changes to an employee's job function.[25] In *Canadian Bechtel Ltd.* v. *Mollenkopf,* the Ontario Court of Appeal viewed the power of the employer as being very broad when it stated that "if the employer, although mistaken, acted in good faith and in the protection of its own business interests, the plaintiff would have no right to refuse the [new position].[26]

2. **If there was a dismissal, did the employer have just cause?** Once the fact of dismissal has been established, the employer must show, on the balance of probability, that just cause to terminate without reasonable notice existed. The question is not whether there was a reasonable business explanation for the changes but rather whether there was a proper legal basis to terminate the individual's employment without a reasonable warning. Economic reasons or reorganization of the operations do not constitute just cause,[27] but misconduct, including off-duty behaviour, dishonesty, and disobedience, may constitute cause depending on the particular circumstances.[28] Excessive absenteeism (either culpable or non-culpable)[29] and incompetence[30] may similarly be held to amount to cause. Further, a breach of any implied terms, such as violations of conflict-of-interest requirements[31] or a refusal to accept geographical transfers,[32] may permit the employer to terminate the employee without notice. It is also important that the employer not have condoned or forgiven certain behaviour (a situation that would likely be judged the case if the employer asserted incompetence shortly after giving the employee a merit increase).

3. **If there was no just cause, what is the appropriate remedy for the employee?** In cases where just cause has not been proven, the employee is entitled to reasonable notice of dismissal. It must be emphasized that the employee has no right to retain a job; the common law does not bestow job security. Reinstatement is not available at common law, and the courts have thus far refused to order this remedy on the ground that it is impractical to reinstate employees, particularly those in senior positions.

Additionally, the common law requirement is for notice—that is, a warning period—rather than severance pay. In practice, for reasons of employee morale, confidentiality, and productivity, employers often terminate the employee instantly and remit wages and benefits to cover the notice period, but there is no legal requirement to do so. Although the required notice period is subject to the minimum legislative guidelines already outlined, the courts have held that common law principles require notice periods exceeding the minimum statutory limits in cases of middle and upper management and professional positions and even, in some cases,[33] for blue- or white-collar workers with long seniority. The length of the notice period likely to be required is a function of both the length of time required to obtain similar employment and a reward for past service. These are determined by reference to such factors as the employee's age, total length of service, level of responsibility, length of service in the particular position, level of education, and the availability of similar employment.[34] It is clear from the jurisprudence that there is no fixed formula to determine the appropriate notice period in each case, which makes predictions as to legal outcomes very difficult for both the employer and the discharged employee. It does appear, however, that two years' notice appears to be the upper limit.[35]

The payment covering the notice period includes not only wages but also the fringe benefits (including regular bonuses, stock options, etc.) that would have been bestowed on the employee. Since such benefits normally exceed 25 percent of salary, the dollar amount involved is often significant.

Also potentially affecting any monetary payment awarded by the courts is whether the employee attempted to find another job following his or her termination. An employee entitled to notice has a duty to mitigate or lessen the damages by seeking other substantially similar employment.[36] It should be noted, however, that the legal burden of proof is on the employer to prove that the employee has not done so.[37]

Another issue is whether the discharged employee can obtain punitive damages, or damages for intangible loss such as mental distress, or, in cases of people in the public arena,[38] loss of reputation. Traditionally, most courts, particularly the Supreme Court of Canada, have indicated that such damages are inappropriate in breach of contract cases,[39] but there has been some deviation from this position.[40] Punitive damages can be awarded, however, in cases where a separate cause of action exists, for example, defamation.[41] In any event, very recently the Supreme Court of Canada held in *Wallace* v. *United Grain Growers*[42] that where a company engages in bad faith or unfair dealing in the manner of the dismissal, a court may award compensation for such behaviour by increasing the notice period. See the opening vignette in this chapter for a description of the Wallace decision.

Employers must be extremely careful, therefore, how and under what circumstances they discharge employees. A risk of increased damages exists if the discharge is done in a manner that can be characterized as malicious, vindictive, or harsh (other descriptions used by the courts include abrupt, humiliating, irresponsible, callous, wanton, and reckless) or if totally false and serious allegations of cause (for example, theft) are asserted. In those instances, the court may either award damages for intangible loss or may significantly increase the required notice period without even separately identifying the amount as punitive damages.[43]

The issue of "near cause" has occasionally arisen. This phrase refers to a situation in which the employer's evidence falls short of establishing just cause but there is some evidence that the employee may be partially at fault (for example, some level of incompetence can be demonstrated). Although some decisions have held that the existence of near cause reduces the notice period, higher courts have rejected that notion.[44]

A significant recent development in the area of employment law has been the evolution of a form of job security for non-managerial employees who do not belong to a bargaining unit. Common in other countries, some legislation is included in the federal

EXHIBIT 8.1

THE CONSEQUENCES OF A TEMPER: WHAT IS THE LEGAL SITUATION?

An employee gets angry with his boss and tells her she is the worst manager he has ever had. He then goes home in the middle of the day and does not appear for work the following day. The day after that the employee returns, and the boss informs him he has resigned and in any event he would be fired for insubordination. What is the legal situation for these parties?

jurisdiction, Quebec, and Nova Scotia (England, 1978: 472). Under part III, section 240 of the *Canada Labour Code*, for example, a terminated non-management employee who is not a member of a bargaining unit and has at least 12 months' service may have access to a process of adjudication similar to arbitration under a collective agreement. The adjudicator's remedies include the power to reinstate the employee into his or her previous position. The reinstatement power is discretionary, rather than mandatory, so an adjudicator is free to award damages in lieu of reinstatement where it is felt the latter would be inappropriate.[45] In Nova Scotia, the qualifying period for arbitration is ten years' service, and in Quebec, five years', severely restricting the application of this protection.

Implied Terms by Past Practice

The conduct or past practice of the parties may also be used to decide what terms govern the employment relationship:

> The court does not apply the principles of contract law as though in a vacuum, but reviews the history of the relations between the parties in its entirety so as to arrive at a rational solution in each particular case. The relationship of master and servant in the modern corporate world cannot be determined as though that relationship consisted of a single contract with fixed terms and conditions.[46]

In *Durrant* v. *Westeel-Rosco Ltd.*,[47] the practice of previous executive transfers was held to be indicative of the continuing intent of the parties. It has been said, however, that any imposition of such implied terms for the benefit of the employer must be based on an interpretation that comes within the "bounds of reason."[48]

Employers and employees must be cognizant of the potential changing nature of the implied employment agreement. The courts view their responsibility as interpreting the terms of the employment according to the manner in which the parties would have constructed the relationship at the time in question, which certainly provides a broad opportunity for the exercise of judicial policy-making.

Express Terms
General Rules

Employer and employee are free to agree to express terms that will govern their employment relationship. These agreements, which will prevail over any implied terms, can be either written or oral, although the content of an oral agreement is often difficult to prove.

Both parties must be aware of all terms of the relationship; therefore, express terms that are buried in lengthy contracts or employment manuals may not be enforceable.[49] Although the courts can refuse to enforce terms that have not been voluntarily agreed to, they will, in all likelihood, uphold the application of employment clauses provided that the parties are at arm's length and there has been no coercion or improper influence of any kind on the employee to accept.[50] The courts have very occasionally rejected contracts where there was no real chance to negotiate the contents of the agreement.[51]

Litigation has also arisen in situations in which a term included in an employment agreement has "expired" either because of the passage of time or through fundamental changes in the employee's job responsibilities. For example, notice-of-termination terms have been held to apply no longer if significant time has passed since the employee entered into the employment contract.[52] The employment contract also faces a considerably increased risk of invalidation if the duties of the employee have changed significantly since the time that contract was executed.[53]

Provisions in employment contracts may also be struck down on the grounds that the terms of the agreement were harsh and unconscionable at the time of the making of the contract. The issue appears to have arisen primarily in cases relating to the imposition of oppressive notice periods.[54]

Finally, the terms of the contract must not violate the provisions of statutes or be contrary to public policy. For example, an employment contract may not call for less notice than that required under the applicable minimum employment standards legislation.

Specific Provisions

Express terms may deal with such basic provisions as the date of commencement of employment, salary, the period of probation, and fringe benefits. Employers may also include special terms dealing with cause for termination.

A frequent inclusion by the employer is a term expressly limiting the notice period. As already noted, such a clause must be a reasonable pre-estimate of damages, not a penalty clause.[55] Further, the clause must have been brought to the attention of the employee and continue to remain in effect.[56] For example, in *Wallace* v. *Toronto Dominion Bank*,[57] the Ontario Court of Appeal held that a contract between an employer and employee might, in a given situation, contain terms so onerous or blatantly unfair as to warrant judicial intervention. The majority held on the facts of that case, however, that four weeks' notice of termination could not, in 1971, be said to be either unreasonable or unfair.

Employers frequently attempt to protect their competitive position by inserting specific conflict-of-interest clauses restricting an employee's ability to deal with, for example, confidential information, use of company facilities, or assignment of inventions. As well, a "restrictive covenant" is a clause by which an employer attempts to limit an employee's ability to compete with the employer or work for a competitor even after the employment relationship has ended. The basic rule is that such a clause is presumptively void as being against public policy; the burden is on the employer to demonstrate that it should be enforced. To do so, the employer must demonstrate that there is a proprietary interest to be protected[58] (for example, trade secrets or confidential information); that the clause to protect that interest is reasonable in terms of length of time, geography, and nature of the restriction;[59] and that the provision does not offend the public interest.[60]

Collective Agreements vs. Individual Contracts of Employment

Employees who are covered by a collective agreement must make use of the resources available under that contract. Thus, they are not able to sue for wrongful dismissal in the courts but must pursue their claims through the grievance procedure (ultimately leading to arbitration).[61] They have the benefit of a provision in collective agreements, imposed by labour codes, that prohibits discharge or discipline without just cause. Through the grievance procedure, a wrongfully dismissed employee is able to seek reinstatement (and lost wages) and thereby retain his or her job. Slightly more than half of terminated employees covered by a union contract are, in fact, reinstated, frequently with some back pay (Ponak, 1987: 41).

On the other hand, employers traditionally have been able to terminate nonunion employees, either by establishing just cause or by arbitrarily discharging the employee and giving proper notice. Two new trends have evolved, however. First, courts have significantly increased the common law notice periods so that long-term employees have been awarded 12 to 24 months' pay. This has undoubtedly served to curb the frequency of arbitrary dismissals. Second, three jurisdictions' introduction of statutory rights of

EXHIBIT 8.2

UNION VS. NONUNION: COMPARISON OF THE SAME FACT SITUATION

Darlene Thompson is 50 years old and has worked for Johnson Limited for 26 years. She has been fired for allegedly stealing $3000 in cash from the Company's cash room. In fact Ms. Thompson has been wrongly accused. Her rights in this case are very dependent on her situation.

For example, if Ms. Johnson is a member of a bargaining unit represented by a union, she will approach her shop steward and file a grievance. The union will attempt to settle the matter with the Company and, if they cannot, the matter would go before an arbitrator after about six months. Assuming the truth comes out that she is not responsible, she will be reinstated in her job and awarded her lost wages from the time of her dismissal to the date she is reinstated.

However, if Ms. Thompson is a manager, she must sue for wrongful dismissal in court. Once again, assuming it is concluded that she did not steal the money, she would not be reinstated but would receive a cash award as damages in lieu of notice of approximately one-and-a-half years' wages.

Finally, if Ms. Johnson is a clerk but is not unionized, in most jurisdictions she must file a claim under the basic employment standards legislation, and she would receive approximately two to five months' pay if the company cannot prove she stole the money.

reinstatement for nonunion employees has broadened the concept of job security beyond the unionized sector, although the qualification periods are still lengthy. Nevertheless, it is clear that the vast majority of employees have far more job protection under a collective agreement than under individual contracts of employment (see Exhibit 8.2).

Human Rights Legislation

Each Canadian jurisdiction has passed specific legislation to deal with discrimination. Human rights legislation is designed to prevent discrimination against individuals on the basis of membership in specific groups such as those based on age, sex, race, colour, creed, religion, ancestry, place of origin, marital status, family status, spousal occupation, sexual orientation, mental or physical disability, physical stature, and criminal convictions unrelated to the employment. Organizations of a fraternal, philanthropic, or educational nature are generally exempted from the statutes. Although legislation deals with the prevention of discrimination in many areas (including, for example, housing and public services), this chapter focuses only on those restrictions relating to employment practices.

Enforcement of such an act generally begins with a complaint to a human rights commission or council. (For a list of the Websites of federal and provincial human rights commissions, see Table 8.1.) Most jurisdictions provide for ultimate determination of unsettled cases through a board of inquiry appointed by the minister of the department responsible for the human rights legislation. Appeals from decisions of this board can generally be made to the courts.

TABLE 8.1

Canadian Human Rights Commissions Websites

Human Rights Commission	Website
Canadian (federal)	www.chrc.ccdp.ca
Newfoundland	www.gov.nf.ca/hrc/
Prince Edward Island	www.isn.net/peihrc
Nova Scotia	www.gov.ns.ca/humanrights/default.htm
New Brunswick	www.gov.nb.ca/hrc-cdp/e/index.htm
Quebec (Commission des droits de la personne et des droits de la jeunesse)	www.cdpdj.qc.ca/htmen/htm/1_0.htm
Ontario	www.ohrc.on.ca
Manitoba	www.gov.mb.ca/hrc/
Saskatchewan	www.gov.sk.ca/shrc/
Alberta (Human Rights and Citizenship Commission)	www.albertahumanrights.ab.ca/
British Columbia	www.bchrc.gov.bc.ca/
Yukon	www.yhrc.yk.ca/

Two Supreme Court of Canada decisions—*Bhinder* v. *CNR* and *O'Malley* v. *Simpson Sears*[62]—have made it clear that liability does not depend on an employer's wilful intent to discriminate. Therefore, besides prohibiting intentional, direct discrimination, the acts cover systemic or indirect discrimination that has prohibited consequences (for example, height restrictions that indirectly discriminate against women).

The remedial sections of the human rights legislation are of particular significance. Human rights boards have the power of rectification. They can, for example, order reinstatement of individuals who have been fired or the hiring of individuals who have been refused employment. A board may also award monetary damages (for example, back wages) and order costs to be paid by the losing party.

A critical issue is the power to award punitive damages. On the grounds that human rights legislation is supposed to be educational rather than punitive, upper limits are established under some of the acts that in some cases are extremely low (from $2000 to $5000). Unfortunately, only serious penalties will deter the most irresponsible individuals, so these limits should probably be raised considerably; higher amounts would be awarded only in cases where discrimination is most malevolent and intentional and where deterrence is a major goal (for example, in cases of repeated sexual harassment).

The extent of a board's power to order affirmative action remedies was at issue in the case of *Action Travail* v. *CNR*. In that case, the human rights tribunal ordered that of every four new blue-collar workers hired by Canadian National Railways, one must be a woman until women represented 13 percent of the employees in blue-collar jobs. The decision was overturned by the Federal Court of Appeal but was reinstated by the Supreme Court of Canada.[63]

Hiring Process

Each jurisdiction prohibits discrimination in the area of job advertising. Employers are prohibited from using non-neutral terms that would discourage people of certain groups (for example, people of a certain age, religion, sex, or marital status) from even applying for certain jobs.

In some jurisdictions, application forms and interviews are also covered by the statute. Where there are prohibitions concerning application forms and interviews, the mere asking of a question concerning a prohibited factor is a breach of the legislation. In those jurisdictions without such express protection (Manitoba, Ontario, and British Columbia), a complainant must demonstrate that the answer to the offending question was actually the reason for the refusal to hire.

The object of the prohibition of certain questions is to dissuade employers from acquiring information concerning factors that should not form the basis for a hiring decision. Much of this information may be relevant once the person is hired (for example, age may affect the premiums an employee pays under a group insurance plan), but it should be obtained only after employment begins.

Equal Pay

Besides generally prohibiting discriminatory conditions of work, human rights legislation targets pay discrimination between the sexes. The average female employee in Canada receives an estimated 75 percent of the pay of the average male. The source of the difference has been widely debated, but some of it results from outright pay discrimination (different pay for the same or substantially similar jobs) and some from occupational segregation (the clustering of women in so-called women's jobs, such as secretarial work, child care, nursing, and waitressing). Early legislation required that equal pay be given for identical jobs. To prevent slightly different job descriptions from being given to men and women, most jurisdictions have now adopted the requirement of equal pay for "substantially similar work." The basis for that comparison is the skill, effort, and responsibility required in the similar positions.[64]

Even with legislation of this nature, the gap in earnings has remained. One solution would be to avoid occupational segregation, but there is little likelihood that will occur in the near future. As a result, a movement has arisen to attempt to ensure that traditionally female jobs are paid the same as traditionally male jobs of the same value. This approach is known as "equal pay for work of equal value" in Canada or "comparable worth" in the United States. The federal government was the first to legislate such a provision (in 1978); the Ontario and Manitoba governments have followed suit. This legislation is the subject of much debate, and some legislation has been removed. Opponents claim it does not address the problem of occupational segregation, that it is unworkable on any large scale, that it does not permit the free market to operate, and that it may prove too costly to the economy. Advocates often reply that it may at least narrow the gap (by paying groups such as nurses more money); that the supposedly free market was designed and is operated by men; and that although implementing the principle of equal value will be difficult, it is not impossible, and a failure to do so is a denial of social justice.

Conditions of Employment

Human rights acts contain provisions that prevent employers from refusing to hire because of—or having different terms of employment based on—the prohibited factors. An employer can justify a discriminatory action with the defence of business necessity and the employer must also show that he or she "took reasonable steps to accommodate the complaint, short of undue hardship."[65]

The number of cases dealing with various types of discrimination is now very large. The following provide good illustrations of the issues that arise and how human rights tribunals attempt to resolve them. *Bhinder* v. *CNR*[66] concerned a requirement of the railway that its maintenance electricians wear hard hats. One of the employees, Bhinder, was a Sikh, who was required by his religion to wear a turban. The Supreme Court of

Canada held that, although the railway's policy amounted to discrimination on the basis of religion, the rule had been adopted for genuine business reasons and was a reasonable measure in reducing the risk of injury to employees.

Another case involved an allegation of discrimination on the basis of marital status. Rosann Cashin, a Canadian Broadcasting Corporation reporter in Newfoundland, did not have her contract renewed because her husband (who was head of the fishermen's union) had been named a director of Petro-Canada. Both the original tribunal and the appeal tribunal found that this behaviour constituted discrimination on the basis of marital status but disagreed on the merits of the bona fide occupational qualification (BFOQ) defence put forward by the CBC. The original panel found that a BFOQ was not established:

> A perception that a reporter lacks objectivity, if it exists, may be based on factors which have no bearing on the reporter's actual objectivity. ... For example, if it could be proved that audiences in Newfoundland perceive female reporters to be dishonest or lacking in objectivity, I am not convinced that there would be sufficient jurisdiction for failing to hire female reporters, in the absence of evidence that female reporters were in fact dishonest or lacking in objectivity.

> If it can be said that a perception of lack of objectivity exists without basis, and that the reporter's work has not fallen from his usual high standard, how can it be said that the perception is reasonably necessary to the performance of the job if the job performance remains of high standard? Quite simply, the requirement does not relate to the work if the work is objective, fair, accurate, and balanced. This leads me to the conclusion that the perceived objectivity requirement has not met the objective requirement of the BFOQ test.[67]

The appeal tribunal disagreed, observing:

> When one considers the very high profile and public image of Richard Cashin in Newfoundland, particularly in relation to two of the most important resources of that province and the fact that his wife is a CBC broadcaster reporting on that very subject matter ... we are therefore of the view that perception of objectivity is a valid BFOQ both in the general sense and when applied to the particular circumstances of the complaint.[68]

The Federal Court of Appeal, however, reversed the review tribunal in May 1988 and reinstated the findings of the original board.

In another case, the Federal Court of Appeal struck down a Toronto Dominion Bank drug policy on the basis that the Bank failed to prove the policy was reasonably necessary to assure job performance or that drug testing was the least intrusive of the reasonable methods of assessing job performance.[69]

Discrimination based on sex is subject to similar review. In order to justify differential treatment, the rationale must be truly bona fide and not based on subjective perception of what constitutes a "female" or "male" job.[70] Similarly, size requirements have been held to discriminate systematically against women[71] and thus must be supported by evidence that they are legitimate criteria.

Human rights legislation also regulates harassment. Discussions of harassment generally focus on sexual harassment, but other elements, such as social or religious harassment, may be involved. Sexual harassment is often treated as part of sexual discrimination,[72] but that may not be technically correct. The Manitoba Court of Appeal in *Janzen and Govereau* v. *Platy Enterprises and Tommy Grammas*[73] held, in November 1986, that, although harassment is reprehensible, it cannot be labelled discriminatory. To avoid this problem, many jurisdictions include a separate provision dealing with harassment. For example, the *Canada Human Rights Code* provides that "it is discriminatory practice ... to harass an individual on a prohibited ground of discrimination" (section 13.1). Because employers have been held liable for acts of their employees,[74] many employers have implemented policies dealing with sexual harassment in the workplace.

Supreme Court of Canada (information on labour relations and employment law): www.droit.umontreal.ca/doc/csc-scc/en/index/html

The adoption of affirmative action and employment equity programs is expressly permitted by human rights codes and the *Charter of Rights and Freedoms*. These programs are intended to foster employment equity for groups previously discriminated against by ensuring such actions as pay adjustments, hiring quotas, and promotion standards for the disadvantaged group. In 1987, the federal government introduced the *Employment Equity Act*, which requires federally regulated employers with more than 100 employees to implement employment equity and to collect and annually file data, by designated group, on particular rates, occupational distribution, and income levels for women, visible minorities, aboriginal people, and the physically disabled. Rather than imposing an explicit quota system, the legislation requires each program to contain "an effective enforcement mechanism," the design of which has been left to the employer. Further, as a matter of policy, the federal government, through the Federal Contractors' Program, will require compliance from all companies with 100 or more employees that gain federal government contracts worth more than $200,000. This program extends significantly the employment equity net.

The *Charter of Rights and Freedoms*

It is becoming increasingly clear that the *Charter of Rights and Freedoms* has a direct impact on human rights legislation, primarily through the equality provision:

> Section 15(1) Every individual is equal before and under the law and has the right to the equal protection and equal benefit of the law without discrimination and, in particular, without discrimination based on race, national or ethnic origin, colour, religion, sex, or mental or physical disability.

> (2) Subsection (1) does not preclude any law, program, or activity that has as its object the amelioration of conditions of disadvantaged individuals or groups including those that are disadvantaged because of race, national or ethnic origin, colour, religion, sex, age, or mental or physical disability.

In the case of *Vriend et al.* v. *Province of Alberta*,[75] the Supreme Court of Canada concluded that even though the Alberta legislation did not expressly list sexual orientation as a protected ground, sexual orientation must be read into that Act because otherwise it would be inconsistent with the *Charter*.

The equality rights conferred by Section 15 are, however, subject to Section 1 of the *Charter*:

> The *Canadian Charter of Rights and Freedoms* guarantees the rights and freedoms set out in it subject only to such reasonable limits prescribed by law as can be demonstrably justified in a free and democratic society.

The extent of the courts' willingness to interpret the prescribed rights broadly and their inclination to use the Section 1 limitation will be a major factor in the long-run impact of the *Charter*.

Interestingly, Section 28 sets out an additional right not subject to the limitations expressed in Section 1. Section 28 guarantees sexual equality, stating:

> Notwithstanding anything in this *Charter*, the rights and freedoms referred to in it are guaranteed equally to male and female persons.

Bargaining Unit Employees

Human rights legislation directly applies to all employees, both union and nonunion. Members of bargaining units, however, have added protection from discrimination. First, most of the human rights codes apply explicitly to organizations, such as trade unions and employer organizations. Trade unions are thus prohibited from discriminating and could themselves be the subjects of human rights complaints. Second, most of the labour codes contain provisions imposing on a trade union a duty of fair representation. As a result, a union cannot behave in a manner that can be characterized as bad faith, arbitrary, or discriminatory. If it does, a complaint can be filed successfully with the labour board. Third, collective agreements often contain clauses explicitly or implicitly adopting human rights principles. Discrimination on the part of an employer can then be addressed directly through the grievance process, rather than through the human rights councils.

Questions

1. Are minimum employment standards needed in an advanced society such as Canada?

2. Why does the law not allow the courts to reinstate employees who have been dismissed without just cause at common law? Why do arbitrators have that power?

3. Should an economic recession be grounds for just cause for dismissal? How should it affect the length of notice?

4. What are the principal factors the courts will consider when assessing a notice period at common law?

5. To what extent should discrimination on the basis of the occupation of one's spouse be permitted?

6. What are the problems in the implementation of the principle of equal pay for work of equal value?

7. What effect does employment legislation have on the development of trade unions and collective bargaining?

8. If you had a mental disability and your provincial human rights code did not cover this area, would you still be protected?

ENDNOTES

[1] *Wallace* v. *United Grain Growers Ltd.* [1997] 3 SCR. (http:www.droit.umontreal.ca/doc/csc-scc/en/pub/1997/vol3-html/1997scr3_0701.html). Summarized in H. Levitt, 1997. "Supreme Court of Canada Wrongful Dismissal Decision: Implications for Employers," in *Transitions*, volume 10, no. 1, Murray Axmith.

[2] *Labour Law: Cases, Materials and Commentary*, 4th edition (Kingston, ON: Industrial Relations Centre, Queen's University, 1986).

[3] *de Naray* v. *Gainers Inc.* (1999) 39 CCEL (2d) 303; *Hoskins* v. *Saskatchewan* (1998) 36 CCEL (2d) 155; *Carter* v. *Bell* (1936) 1 DLR 438.

[4] *Doyle* v. *London Life Ins. Co.*, 68 BCLR 285; *MacDonald* v. *Richardson Greenshields of Canada Ltd.* (1985) 12 CCEL 22.

[5] *Montreal* v. *Montreal Locomotive Works Ltd*, (1947) 1 DLR 161; *Mayer* v. *J. Conrad Lavigne Ltd*, (1980) 27 OR 129; *Cooperation Insurance Association* v. *Kearney*, (1964) 48 DLR (2d) 1; *Stevenson, Jordon & Harrison Ltd* v. *MacDonald*, (1952) 1 TLR 101.

[6] *Pliniussen* v. *University of Western Ontario*, (1983) 2 CCEL 1 (Ont. Co Ct).

[7] For a detailed discussion, see Christie, 2nd Edition, 1993, pp. 447–504.

[8] *Tall and Tall Air Ltd* v. *Deconinck and Corporation 5 Ltd*, (1983) 51 NBR (2d) 55 (CA).

[9] *Altschul* v. *Tom Davis Management* Ltd., (1985) 6 CCEL 180; *Mid-Western News Agency Ltd* v *Vanpinxteren et al*, (1975) 62 DLR (3d) 555 (Sask. QB); *Sheather* v. *Associates Financial Services Ltd et al*, (1979) 15 BCLR 265 (SCBC); *Empey* v. *Coastal Towing Company Ltd*, [1977] 1 WWR 673 (SCBC).

[10] *Cartright* v. *Canadian Pacific* Ltd., (1983) 4 CCEL 152; *Swain* v. *West (Butchers), Ltd*, [1936] 3 ALL ER 261 (CA).

[11] *Corporate Classic Caterers* v. *Dynapro Systems Inc.*, (1998) 33 CCEL (2d) 58.

[12] *Alberts* v. *Mountjoy*, (1977) 79 DLR (3d) 108 (Ont. HC); *Canadian Aero Service Ltd* v. *O'Malley et al*, [1974] 1 SCR 592; *Rajput* v. *Menu Foods Ltd*, (1984) 5 CCEL 22 (Ont. HC).

[13] *Forest Automation Ltd.* v. *RMS Industrial Control*, SCBC, unreported, May 24, 1978; *Payzu Ltd* v. *Hannaford*, (1918) 2 KB 248. See, generally, Levitt, 1985, pp. 267–69.

[14] In *H. L. Weiss Forwarding Ltd* v *Omnus et al*, (1972) 5 CPR (2d) 142 (Ont. HC), aff'd (no recorded reasons, Ont. CA), (1976) 1 SCR 776. Moorehouse, J. awarded damages against an employee who quit without notice on the basis of the salary to which the employee would have been entitled during the period of notice. It is our opinion that this view is incorrect since it has no relevance to the actual loss suffered by the employer.

[15] *Barnes* v. *Krisbair Tavern Ltd.* (1982) 82 CLLC 14190; *Shabinsky* v. *Horwitz et al*, (1971) 32 DLR (3d) 318 (Ont. HC).

[16] *Rhodes* v. *Koksilah Nursery*, (1999) 42 CCEL (2d) 179.

[17] *Philip* v. *Expo 86 Corp*, (1986) 13 CCEL 147; *Riddell* v. *City of Vancouver*, (1985) 5 CCEL 55, upheld on appeal; *Hawkins* v. *The Queen in Right of Ontario*, (1985) 8 CCEL 183 (Ont. HC).

[18] *Re Gillingham and Metropolitan Board of Commissioners of Police*, 26 OR (2d) 77; *Sui* v. *Westcoast Transmission* (1985) 7 CCEL 281 (SCBC); *Head* v. *Ontario Provincial Police Force*, unreported, Oct. 14, 1981 (Ont. CA).

[19] *Zalesko* v. *99 Truck Parts*, (1986) 8 CCEL 201; *Yeager* v. *Hastings*, (1985) 5 CCEL 226; *Lockhart* v. *Chrysler*, (1985) 7 CCEL 247.

[20] *Bell Canada* v. *Office and Professional Employees International Union*, [1974] SCR 335, 37 DLR (3d) 561.

[21] *Greene* v. *Chrysler Canada Ltd*, (1985) 7 CCEL 166 (SCBC), upheld, (1985) 7 CCEL 175 (BCCA).

[22] *Clendenning* v *Lowndes Lambert (B.C.) Ltd.* (1999) 41 CCEL (2nd) 58; *Stolze* v. *Ontario* (1998) 35 CCEL (2d) 109; *Lesiuk* v. *BC Forest Products Ltd*, (1984) 56 BCLR 216; *Pearl* v. *Pacific Enercon Inc.*, (1985) 7 CCEL 252.

[23] *Lynch* v. *Richmond Plymouth Chrysler Ltd*, unreported, May 13, 1985, Vancouver Registry No C825918, (SCBC); *Reber* v *Lloyds Bank International Canada*, (1985) 61 BCLR 361 (CA); *Patterson* v. *The Queen in the Right of British Columbia et al*, (1985) 8 CCEL 213 (SCBC); *Longman* v. *Federal Business Development Bank*, (1982) 36 BCLR 115 (SCBC); *Pullen* v. *John C. Preston Ltd*, (1985) 7 CCEL 91 (Ont. HC) at 96; *Canadian Bechtel Ltd.* v. *Mollenkopf*, (1983) 1 CCEL 95 (Ont. CA) at 98.

[24] *Longman* v. *Federal Development Bank*, (1982) 36 BCLR 115 (SCBC) at 124; see also *Reber* v. *Lloyds Bank International Canada*, supra, note 23.

[25] *Pullen* v. *John C. Preston Ltd*, (1985) 7 CCEL 91 (Ont. HC) at 96.

[26] Supra, note 23, p. 98.

[27] *O'Grady* v. *ICBC*, (1975) 63 DLR (3d) 370; *Baker* v. *Burns Foods*, 74 DLR (3d) 762.

[28] *Pliniussen* v. *University of Western Ontario*, (1984) 2 CCEL 1; *Tyrrell* v. *Alltrans Express Ltd* 66 DLR (3d) 81; *Ennis* v. *ICBC*, (1986) 13 CCEL 25; *Himmelman* v. *King's Edgehill School*, (1985) 7 CCEL 16; *Bechard* v. *Chrysler Canada Ltd*, (1979) 1098 DLR (3d) 577.

[29] *Cardinas* v. *Canada Dry Ltd*, (1986) 10 CCEL 1 (Ont. DC); *Zelisko* v. *99 Truck Parts* and *Yeager* v. *Hastings*, supra, note 19.

[30] *Roscoe* v. *McGavin*, (1984) 2 CCEL 287; *Anderson* v. *Pirelli Cables Inc.*, (1985) 5 CCEL 287; *Matheson* v. *Matheson International Trucks Ltd*, (1985) 4 CCEL 271; *Manning* v. *Surrey Memorial Hospital Society*, (1975) 54 DLR (3d) 312.

[31] *Alberts* v. *Mountjoy*, supra, note 12; *Wells* v. *Newfoundland and Labrador Nurses' Union*, SC Nfld., Dec. 13, 1985, unreported.

[32] *Durrant* v. *Westeel-Rosco Ltd*, (1978) 7 BCLR 14; *Lloyd* v. *Canadian Bechtel Ltd*, BCCA, Nov. 15, 1976, unreported; *Page* v. *Jim Pattison*, [1982] 5 WWR 107.

[33] *Cronk* v. *Canadian General Insurance Co.*, 14 CCEL (2d) 1; *Byers* v. *Prince George Downtown Parking Commission*, (1998) 38 CCEL (2nd) 83.

[34] *Bardal* v. *Globe and Mail Ltd*, [1960] 24 DLR 140; *MacAlpine* v. *Stratford General Hospital*, 38 CCEL (2nd) 1.

[35] *Blackburn* v. *Victory Credit Union Ltd.*, (1998) 36 CCEL (2d) 94.

[36] *Ally* v. *Institute of Chartered Accountants*, (1998) 37 CCEL (2d) 212.

[37] *Red Deer College* v. *Michaels*, (1975) 57 DLR (3d) 386, [1976] 2 SCR 324.

[38] *Racine* v. *CJRC Radio Capitale Ltd*, [1977] 2 ACWS 366; *Burmeister* v. *Regina Multicultural Council*, (1986) 8 CCEL 144.

[39] *Addis* v. *Gramaphone*, [1909] AC 488; *Vorvis* v. *ICBC*, (1984) 4 CCEL 237; *Ansari* v. *BC Hydro*, (1986) 13 CCEL 238 (SCBC).

[40] *Williams* v. *Motorola*, (1998) 38 CCEL (2d) 76; *Lockhart* v. *Chrysler Canada Ltd*, (1984) CCEL 43; *Misovic* v. *Acres Dairy McKee Ltd*, (1985) 7 CCEL 163 (Ont. CA).

[41] *Dixon* v. *B.C. Transit*, (1995) 9 BCLR (3d) 108.

[42] [1997] 3 SCR 701; 36 CCEL (2d) 1.

[43] *Wallace* v. *United Grain Growers*, 152 DLR (4th) 1; *Martin* v. *International Maple Leaf Springs Water Corp.*, 38 CCEL (2d) 128.

[44] *Dowling* v. *City of Halifax*, (1998) 33 CCEL (2d) 239; *Steinicke* v. *Manning Ltd*, (1984) 4 WWR 491, 55 BCLR 320, (1984) 4 CCEL 294; *Page* v. *Jim Pattison Industries Ltd*, [1984] 4 WWR 481, (1984) 4 CCEL 283.

[45] *Gulf Canada Products* v. *Griffiths*, (1984) 3 CCEL 140.

[46] *Campbell* v. *MacMillan Bloedel Ltd*, [1978] 2 WWR 686 at 691 (SCBC).

[47] Supra, note 32.

[48] *Rose* v. *Shell Canada*, (1985) 7 CCEL 234 (SCBC).

[49] *Mathe* v. *Klohn Leonoff Ltd*, (1983) 20 ACWS (2d) 517; *Re Maritime Medical Care Inc. and McLaughlin et al*, (1979) 103 DLR (3d) 159; *Chisholm* v. *W. H. Bosley & Company Ltd*, (1980) 5 ACWS (2d) 358.

[50] *Jobber* v. *Addressograph Multigraph of Canada Ltd*, (1983) 1 CCEL 87 (Ont. CA); *Matthewson* v. *Aiton Power Ltd*, (1984) 3 CCEL 69 (Ont. Co Ct), reversed on appeal, (1985) 8 CCEL 312 (Ont. CA); *Lloyds Bank Ltd.* v. *Bundy* [1975] QB 326 (CA).

[51] *Allison* v. *Amoco Production Company*, [1975] 5 WWR 501 (Alta. SC); *Nardocchio* v. *Canadian Imperial Bank of Commerce*, (1979) 41 NSR (2d) (NSSC).

[52] *Ceccol* v. *Ontario Symastic Federation*, (1999) 41 CCEL (2nd) 312; *Wallace* v. *Toronto Dominion Bank*, (1983) 41 OR (2d) 161, leave to appeal denied, (1983) 52 NR 157.

[53] *Lyonde* v. *Canadian Acceptance Corporation Ltd*, (1984) 3 CCEL 220.

[54] *Allison* v. *Amoco Production Company*, supra, note 51; *Matthewson* v. *Aiton Power Ltd*, supra, note 50; *Elsley* v. *J. G. Collins Insurance Agencies Ltd*, [1978] 2 SCR 916.

[55] *Matthewson* v. *Aiton Power Ltd*, supra, note 50; *Maxwell* v. *Gibson Drugs Ltd. et al*, [1979] 103 DLR (3d) 433 (SCBC).

[56] *Lyonde* v. *Canadian Acceptance Corp.* (1984) 3 CCEL 220; *Wallace* v. *Toronto Dominion Bank*, supra, note 52.

[57] Supra, note 52.

[58] *Barton Insurance Brothers* v. *Irwin*, (1999) 40 CCEL (2nd) 159; *Dynamex Canada Inc.*, 37 CCEL (2nd) 41.

[59] *Nelson Burns & Company* v. *Grantham Industries Ltd*, [1983] 42 OR (2d) 705, 150 DLR (3d) 692; *Bassman* v. *Deloitte Haskins and Sells of Canada*, (1984) 4 DLR (3d) 558 (Ont. HC); *Creditel of Canada* v. *Faultless et al*, 81 DLR (2d) 567.

[60] *Green* v. *Stanton*, (1969) 1 WWR 415; *Baker* v. *Lintott*, (1980) 141 DLR 571.

[61] *St. Anne-Nackawic Pulp & Paper Company Ltd* v. *Canadian Paper Workers Union, Local 219*, (1986) 28 DLR (4th) 1 (SCC).

[62] *Bhinder* v. *CNR*, (1986) 9 CCEL 135; *O'Malley* v. *Simpson Sears*, (1986) 9 CCEL 185.

[63] (1984) 5 CHRR at D/2327 [Aug. 22, 1984]; (1985) 6 CHRR at D/2908 [July 16, 1985]; Supreme Court of Canada, June 1987, unreported.

[64] *Re Attorney General for Alberta and Gares, et al*, 67 DLR (3d) 635; *University of Regina*, Sask. Court of Queen's Bench, Oct. 28, 1975, unreported; *Davies, Hickford and Toews and District of Abbotsford*, BC Board of Inquiry, Feb. 1977, unreported; *Jane Bublish* v. *Sask. Union of Nurses*, (1983) 4 CHRR at D/1269.

[65] *O'Malley* v. *Simpson Sears*, supra, note 62, p. 202; *BCGSEU* v. *British Columbia Public Service Employee Relations Commission* (1999) 99 CLLC 145, 215.

[66] Supra, note 62.

[67] *Cashin* v. *CBC*, (1986) 7 CHRR D/3203 [Nov. 25, 1985], at para. 25676–7.

[68] Ibid., (1987) 8 CHRR D/3699 [Jan 23, 1987], at para. 29281.

[69] *Canadian Civil Liberties Association* v. *Toronto Dominion Bank* (1998) 38 CCEL (2nd) 8 38.

[70] *Hartling* v. *Board of Police Commissioners, City of Timmins and Chief Floyd Schwantz*, (1981) 2 CHRR D/487; *Kickham* v. *City of Charlottetown*, (1986) 7 CHRR D/3339 and D/3481; *Dubniczky and Proulx* v. *J. L. K. Kiriakopoulos Company Ltd and Tiffany's Restaurant*, (1981) 2 CHRR D/485; *McDevitt* v. *McMordie's Copper and Brass* (1986) 7 CHRR D/3306.

[71] *Foster* v. *BC Forest Products Ltd*, BC Human Rights Board of Inquiry, April 17, 1979, unreported; *Colfer* v. *Ottawa Board of Commissioners of Police*, Ontario Human Rights Board of Inquiry, Jan 12, 1979, unreported.

[72] *Bell and Korczak* v. *Lades and the Flaming Steer Steakhouse*, (1980) 1 CHRR D/155.

[73] [1987] 1 WWR 355.

[74] *B.(P.A.)* v. *Curry*, (1999) 43 CCEL (2d) 1; *Leblanc* v. *Canada*, (1999) 43 CCEL (2d) 140.

[75] *Vriend et al.* v. *Province of Alberta et al.* [1998] 1 SCR 493.

REFERENCES

BRODY, B., P. ROHANN, and L. ROMPRÉ, 1985. "Les Accidents industriels au Canada: le portrait d'une décennie." *Relations industrielles/Industrial Relations,* 40, pp. 545–66.

BROWN, R. M. 1982. "Canadian Occupational Health and Safety Legislation." *Osgoode Hall Law Journal,* 20.

_____. 1983. "The Right To Refuse Unsafe Work." *University of British Columbia Law Review,* 17, pp. 1–34.

BRYCE, G. and P. MANGA. 1985. "The Effectiveness of Health and Safety Committees." *Relations industrielles/Industrial Relations,* 40, pp. 257–83.

CCH CANADIAN. 1987. *Master Labour Guide.* Don Mills, Ont.: CCH.

CHRISTIE, I. M. 1993. *Employment Law in Canada*, 2nd Edition. Toronto: Butterworths.

DIGBY, C. and W. C. RIDDELL. 1986. "Occupational Health and Safety in Canada," in *Canadian Labour Relations*, edited by W. C. Riddell. Toronto: University of Toronto Press.

ENGLAND, G. 1978. "Recent Developments in Wrongful Dismissal Laws and Some Policies for Defence." *Alberta Law Review,* 16, pp. 470–520.

FISHER, E. G. and I. F. IVANKOVITCH. 1985. "Alberta's Occupational Health and Safety Amendment Act, 1983." *Relations industrielles/Industrial Relations,* 40, pp. 115–39.

FRIDMAN, G. H. L. 1963. *The Modern Law of Employment.* London: Stevens and Sons.

GEORGE, K. 1985. "Les comités de santé et de sécurité du travail: table de concentration ou de négociation?" *Relations industrielles/Industrial Relations,* 40, pp. 512–28.

GLASBEEK, H. and S. ROWLAND. 1979. "Are Injuring and Killing at Work Crimes?" *Osgoode Hall Law Journal,* 17, pp. 506–94.

ISON, T. G. 1983. *Workmen's Compensation in Canada.* Toronto: Butterworths.

LABOUR CANADA. 1981. *Sexual Equality in the Workplace.* Conference proceedings. Ottawa: Labour Canada.

LABOUR LAW CASEBOOK GROUP. 1986. *Labour Law: Cases, Materials and Commentary*, 4th Edition. Kingston, Ont.: Industrial Relations Centre, Queen's University.

LESLIE, G. 1981–82. "The Statutory Right To Refuse Unsafe Work: A Comparison of Saskatchewan, Ontario and the Federal Jurisdictions." *Saskatchewan Law Review,* 46, pp. 235–70.

LEVITT, H. 1985. *The Law of Dismissal in Canada*. Aurora, Ont.: Canada Law Book.

PALMER, E. E. 1982. *Collective Agreement Arbitration in Canada*, 2nd Edition. Toronto: Butterworths.

PONAK, A. 1987. "Discharge Arbitration and Reinstatement in the Province of Alberta." *The Arbitration Journal*, 42, no. 2, pp. 39–46.

SASS, R. 1985. "The Labour Process and Health: An Alternative Conception to Occupational Health and Safety." *Windsor Yearbook of Access to Justice*, 5, pp. 352–67.

SWAN, K. P. and K. E. SWINTON, eds. 1983. *Studies in Labour Law*. Toronto: Butterworths.

SWINTON, K. 1983. "Enforcement of Occupational Health and Safety: The Role of the Internal Responsibility System," in *Studies in Labour Law*, edited by K. Swan and K. Swinton. Toronto: Butterworths.

TUCKER, E. 1986. "The Persistence of Market Regulation of Occupational Health and Safety: The Stillbirth of Voluntarism," in *Essays in Labour Relations Law*, edited by G. England. Don Mills, Ont.: CCH.

UNITED STATES. 1979. *Basic Patterns in Union Contracts*, 9th Edition. Washington, DC: Bureau of National Affairs.

WEILER, P. C. 1980. *Reshaping Worker's Compensation For Ontario*. Ad hoc report to the Ontario Ministry of Labour. Toronto.

CHAPTER 9

Collective Bargaining:
Structure, Process, and Innovation

Richard P. Chaykowski[1]

This vignette is designed to follow the bargaining process over a three-month period in late 1999.[2]

SEPTEMBER 1: About 1100 unionized workers at Inco Ltd.'s Manitoba operations are livid over the company's concessionary package to settle two months of labour negotiations, a United Steelworkers of America spokesman said yesterday. With just more than two week before the current contract expires, the union, which represents the lion's share of the 1400 employees at Inco's operations in Thompson, Man., said no progress over pension and wage issues has been made. But both sides are still talking. Inco's three-year deal with the union expires on September 15.

"We haven't got a whole lot of time here," said Bob Desjarlais, president of Steelworkers Local 6166. "Things are going to happen very quickly here, one way or the other."

SEPTEMBER 16: Hopes to avert a strike at Inco Ltd.'s Manitoba operations seemed futile yesterday as unionized workers began voting on the nickel giant's final contract offer. Results of the vote by 1065 members of the United Steelworkers of America, Local 6166, were expected late last night, only hours before the union moved into a legal strike position at midnight. The bargaining committee has unanimously recommended members reject the Inco offer that would freeze wages for the next three years. "We're expecting the membership to turn down the final offer," said Robert Desjarlais. On September 8, union members voted 98 percent in favour of a strike mandate.

"We're still hoping membership will give [the offer] careful consideration," said Dan McSweeney, Inco spokesman. Nevertheless, the Toronto-based nickel company is prepared for the worst. "We have always required a contract to work. If the outcome of the vote is they've turned down the offer, then we will begin an orderly shutdown of operations," said Mr. McSweeney. Wages are at the centre of the dispute. Inco contends that belt-tightening is essential if the company is to remain competitive.

SEPTEMBER 21: Canadian nickel miner Inco Ltd. said yesterday it had completed a shutdown of its operations in Thompson, Manitoba, just days after locking out more than 1000 unionized workers in a dispute over wages.

SEPTEMBER 28: Inco Ltd. said yesterday that accepting the wage demands of more than 1000 locked-out workers would harm the future of its mining operations in Thompson, Man. "We have to make ourselves look attractive to raise this huge amount of money for capital investment. If we don't, the long-term future is not very bright for Thompson and its mining operation," said Dan McSweeney.

OCTOBER 3: As their longest labour-related shutdown since 1981 stretches to three weeks, both sides in the lockout at Inco Ltd.'s nickel operation in Thompson, Man., are digging in for what could be a long fight. "We've got cabins built at all the picket lines, and they're insulated," said Bob Desjarlais. "We're ready to take them on and our members are in for the long haul," he said. The steelworkers want Inco to give them a 6 percent pay hike over the next three years.

The Toronto-based nickel mining giant locked the doors at its northern Manitoba mines and metal smelting facilities after 86 percent of the 1050 unionized employees rejected the company's "final" offer.

Inco originally sought wage and benefit reductions, but the company's last offer was a wage freeze with a profit-sharing plan if earnings soar. "The reality is that the union wants more money and they want it now," says Dan McSweeney. "But we're seeking a long-term future in Thompson. We want to seize the future, not the moment." Earlier in September, the workers voted 98 percent in favour of giving their negotiators a strike mandate. Desjarlais says massive cost-cutting has already been done in the past three years—and most of it on the backs of the workers. Nearly 400 jobs have been cut through attrition and layoffs since 1996.

Currently neither side is ready to budge and no further meetings have been scheduled. The workers were locked out for two weeks in 1996 and the last strike, in 1981, lasted three months.

OCTOBER 9: Steelworkers launched an attack on Inco Ltd. yesterday as a labour dispute entered a fourth week. The union accused the Toronto-based company of trying to take advantage of its workforce on the key issue of wages and pensions. The steelworkers were particularly upset by Inco's insistence workers accept a three-year wage freeze. The demand, formally rejected by the union on September 15, set the stage for a lockout of the workers at the $1-billion Thompson operation.

OCTOBER 15: Inco Ltd. and the union representing more than 1000 locked-out workers agreed yesterday to seek mediation to break a one-month labour dispute. Representatives of Toronto-based Inco and the Steelworkers called for a Manitoba government mediator to enter the dispute after the two sides held another round of "exploratory talks" yesterday in Thompson.

DECEMBER 10: On Thursday, members of the United Steelworkers' Local 6166 ratified the agreement reached Monday with Inco Ltd., ending the company's 12-week lockout. The vote was 66 percent in favour of the settlement. The three-year agreement, which will run till September 15, 2002 [according to the union's press release], is a victory for the union in that it addresses the wage and pension issues that Inco had refused to negotiate when negotiations broke down in September. The agreement maintains the pattern of increases established among steelworkers in the Manitoba division and those at Inco's Ontario operations.

Collective bargaining is a decision-making process through which union and management negotiators determine the terms and conditions of employment for a specific group of unionized workers. The results of the negotiations are set down in a contract (or collective agreement) that details what the parties have decided with respect to wages, benefits, hours of work, management rights, seniority, and the myriad other matters that may be discussed during bargaining (see Chapter 10 for more on the collective agreement). When major unions and employers are involved, collective bargaining can be a high-profile process that attracts a great deal of media attention. The public may be treated to the spectre of haggard negotiators putting together late-night final offers, followed by early-morning "final final" offers, all amidst public posturing that may be intended to influence popular opinion and possibly garner broader support.

Negotiation processes are critical to the orderly resolution of important issues affecting peoples' working lives. Labour negotiations are often high-stakes situations because they pit workers' pay and working conditions against the labour cost structure of the firm and the degree of managerial authority. In a world that is increasingly globalized, the efforts of the parties to adapt the terms and conditions of employment to rapidly changing and often adverse environmental conditions place extraordinary pressures on union and management negotiators around the bargaining table. But regardless of the initial demands of the parties, at the end of the day they must achieve an agreement if the enterprise is to continue. The dynamics and development of negotiations are well illustrated in the opening vignette. Both Inco and the Steelworkers have had a long history of bargaining together, but this particular set of negotiations proved, nonetheless, to be quite challenging. The difficult economic conditions Inco faced led management to table a tough set of demands that were resisted by the Steelworkers from the outset. The positions were clearly far apart, and negotiations failed to reduce the gap sufficiently to avert a strike. In the end, the parties even tried mediation, but it was probably the costs imposed on the parties by the lengthy strike that most served to force the parties back into negotiations in order to close the deal.

This chapter analyzes the collective bargaining process to demonstrate why the parties behave as they do and to reveal the less visible, but nonetheless important, processes that lie beneath the surface of negotiations. The first section considers the different structures of collective bargaining. The second deals with how the parties actually engage in collective bargaining and the various approaches adopted by management and union negotiating teams. An unsuccessful round of negotiations may be the consequence of poor union–management relations, culminating in a work stoppage. This can, and very often does, impose costs on the workers and firms involved, and sometimes on the broader public. Recognizing these *costs of disagreement*, both unions and management, as well as various governments, have sought ways in which to improve the likelihood that negotiations will be successfully concluded without a work stoppage. The use of alternative approaches to dispute resolution is increasingly prevalent, and these approaches are also considered in this chapter.

THE STRUCTURE OF COLLECTIVE BARGAINING

Bargaining structure is concerned with the number and diversity of employees and employers covered by the negotiation process. Some firms may bargain with only one union to obtain a collective agreement, whereas other firms may engage in collective bargaining with several different unions to obtain a separate collective agreement with each. In both cases, the process of collective bargaining involves negotiations between a management team and one or more union teams. But the question of who management and the union represent and to whom the collective agreement applies may well differ in the two cases. Thus, an appreciation of collective bargaining involves not only an understanding of the process, but an awareness as well of the important elements of bargaining structure.

Collective bargaining is highly decentralized in Canada with negotiations most often occurring between a single employer and a single union. Unlike the situation in Europe, it is relatively rare to have a set of negotiations cover employees in many companies across an entire industry or to involve more than one union at a time. Drawing from on-going practice, six basic bargaining structures can be identified. These structures are differentiated on the basis of: 1) the number of *employers* involved (single vs. multi); 2) for single employers, the number of *establishments* involved (single vs. multi) where establishment is defined as a specific place of business; and 3) the number of unions involved (single vs. multi). Each of these six structures is set out in Table 9.1.

TABLE 9.1

BARGAINING STRUCTURES

STRUCTURE	DESCRIPTION	EXAMPLES	FREQUENCY
1. Single Employer— Single Establishment— Single Union	Localized negotiations at a single place of business or workplace.	Robin Hood Multi-Food and the United Food and Commercial Workers (UFCW) at its plant in Saskatoon; Carleton University and its faculty association; Dominion Textile and most Quebec plants represented by the Fédération canadienne des travailleurs du textile.	Most prevalent
2. Single Employer— Multi-Establishment— Single Union	Negotiation of a common collective agreement across several workplaces by the same employer and union. Makes a great deal of sense where the employer runs an integrated operation across many similar establishments. Efficient for both union and management negotiators.	Characteristic of public-service bargaining, e.g., between the Public Service Alliance of Canada and the federal government; telecommunications where, for example, New Brunswick Telephone negotiates a province-wide agreement with technicians represented by the Communications Energy and Paperworkers Union; retail food industry, where the norm is a regional contract for each of the major supermarket chains and the dominant union, usually the UFCW.	Widespread

STRUCTURE	DESCRIPTION	EXAMPLES	FREQUENCY
3. Single Employer—Single Establishment—Multi-Union	Negotiating partnership between two or more different unions within the same establishment. This situation might arise, for example, if production workers, represented by an industrial union, negotiated together with maintenance workers, represented by a craft union, or where a number of small craft unions join forces.	Pacific Press of Vancouver and the Joint Council of Newspaper Unions.	Rare
4. Single Employer—Multi-Establishment—Multi-Union	Most likely in industries characterized by a few very large employers and a number of small craft unions, such as railways. Coalitions of different operating unions typically negotiate as a group with each major rail company. Negotiations take place across the entire company's operations.	Many different unions that represent workers across Canada at Canadian Pacific may bargain together.	Rare except for railways
5. Multi-Employer—Multi-Establishment—Single Union	Coalition of employers bargaining as a group with a dominant industrial or occupational union.	Found in a number of major industries, e.g., health care, construction, forestry, and garment manufacturing. In trucking, the Teamsters negotiate a series of regional contracts with associations of transportation companies. British Columbia forestry companies have had a tradition of jointly negotiating regional contracts with the Woodworkers Union through an employer bargaining organization, Forest Industrial Relations (FIR).	Less frequent
6. Multi-Employer—Multi-Establishment—Multi-Union	Most centralized form of bargaining. Involves coalitions of unions and employers at a single negotiating table. Restricted almost exclusively to construction industry negotiations where it has usually been introduced only through government pressure following difficult labour disputes.	This extremely centralized structure has been used at various times in Quebec, Alberta, and British Columbia (Rose, 1992).	Rare

Structure is associated with bargaining power, the level of conflict, the type of issues that are negotiated, and the internal politics on each side of the negotiating table (Anderson, 1989). It is difficult to evaluate the bargaining process without knowing to whom the collective agreement that is being negotiated will apply eventually. The 1994–95 professional hockey lockout, an example of a multi-employer bargaining structure, is a case in point. An appreciation of this set of negotiations required an understanding that 26 separate employers operating in two countries were involved, each with different operating costs, financial resources, and philosophies. Thus, little progress across the bargaining table could be made until the management side resolved its internal debate about the necessity of a salary cap. In contrast, bargaining with a single employer usually has less complicated dynamics.

The labour laws of each province contain enough differences to make bargaining across provincial borders very difficult. Union organizing and bargaining unit determination occur worksite by worksite, and often competing unions represent workers in the same industry or occupation, creating a fragmented patchwork of certification arrangements. On an historical basis, the composition and scope of original bargaining units has reflected union attempts to separately organize craft (skilled trades) workers, production workers, and office staff at a given workplace. Labour relations boards have been reluctant to tamper with long-standing industry practices or to require that new bargaining units span more than one establishment or employer for fear of discouraging unionization. Taken together, these factors have produced one of the most decentralized bargaining systems in the world.

There are a few variations to the six basic bargaining structures in Table 9.1. The most important variation is found in situations where multi-establishment negotiations (either single or multi-employer) are combined with single-establishment negotiations. This has been a popular form of bargaining in automobile manufacturing, forestry, hospitals, and some provincial civil services. Under this arrangement, a master collective agreement is usually negotiated first at a central bargaining table. Following completion of the centralized bargaining, further negotiations then take place over local issues on an individual-establishment basis. In the automobile industry, however, local and master negotiations may occur simultaneously (Kumar and Meltz, 1992).

Another interesting variation occurred in the western Canada beer industry during the 1970s and 1980s. While bargaining was formally between single employers and a single union on a multi-establishment basis, the three major brewers (Molson, Labatts, and Carling) agreed among themselves to resist certain concessions being proposed by the union. It was feared that if one of the employers conceded to the union demands, the other two employers would have little choice but to grant the same concessions. The three companies were able to time their individual negotiations such that all three collective agreements expired at the same time and had agreed that a strike against one company would produce an industry shutdown. This prevented the union from playing one company off against the others by threatening a strike that would jeopardize only the struck company's market share, a tactic that had proved very successful in the past. The employers' approach converted the bargaining structure, for practical purposes, from a single into a multi-employer one, greatly enhancing employer bargaining power. This example illustrates why structure can be such an important ingredient in the bargaining process.[3]

Pattern Bargaining

The outcome of negotiated settlements often exercises an indirect influence on others. Thus, any discussion of bargaining structure needs to assess not only those to whom the negotiations formally apply, but also the spillover effect. Pattern bargaining can be defined as a situation in which a key bargaining settlement sets the standard for other settlements. It became an important feature of Canadian industrial relations in the 1950 to 1980 period.

Arthur Ross (1948) explained why wage gains in one set of negotiations can influence the outcomes in another. Ross referred to the range of influence of major settlements on other negotiations as an "orbit of coercive comparison":

> It is when the several locals of a single international union centralize their wage policies and consolidate their strategies, when separate industrial establishments are brought under common ownership, when the state plays an increasingly active role in setting rates of pay, when rival unions compete with one another for jurisdiction, when related unions negotiate together for mutual protection, and when employers organize into associations to preserve a common front that comparisons become coercive in the determination of wages.[4]

For the unions, the benefit of patterning has been to enhance their ability to "take wages out of competition." To varying degrees, the patterning of settlements has occurred in major industries such as steel, mining, and autos. In meat-packing, the major firms and the union actually engaged in centralized or national bargaining that led to standardized wages and contract clauses for a number of years (Forrest, 1989).[5]

But by the 1980s, firms were confronted by a variety of internal and external pressures, including increased competition, the rapid diffusion of advanced technologies, and deregulation and privatization initiatives, which generated increasing diversity in business and employment conditions across establishments (Chaykowski and Verma, 1992; Verma and Chaykowski, 1999). As firms pressured unions to negotiate wages and working conditions, including various pay-for-performance systems, that better reflect the unique circumstances emerging at the establishment level, pattern and centralized bargaining in many industries broke down. Moreover, as economic globalization accelerates into the 21st century, and some firms may (re)locate internationally, the relevant comparison for a settlement in one country may, increasingly, be another settlement around the globe, making union enforcement of pattern bargaining more difficult.

The negotiation of collective agreements in the Canadian auto industry remains an important exception to the decline of pattern bargaining. Each of the Big Three automakers negotiates separately with the Canadian Auto Workers (CAW). But each firm negotiates a national Master agreement covering major items such as wages, shift premiums, the grievance and arbitration mechanism, and hours of work, and which covers all bargaining units at that firm. Then, for each bargaining unit, the firm also negotiates a local agreement that includes establishment-specific items related to issues such as seniority, layoff and recall rules, and wage scales for various job classifications. The CAW typically targets one firm with which to bargain first; the settlement achieved is then intended to serve as a pattern for negotiations with the remaining firms (Kumar and Meltz, 1992). In 1999, the CAW took this a step further by attempting to extend its influence into the largely nonunion auto parts manufacturing sector, which it had been trying, unsuccessfully, to organize. The CAW tried to negotiate an understanding with General Motors that would in essence have required GM to pressure its major (nonunion) parts manufacturer (Magna) to accept unionization. While unsuccessful, this would have allowed the CAW to extend patterning into the parts sector and hence to further "take wages out of competition."

Further Decentralization

The pressures that led to the decline of pattern bargaining had a similar impact on bargaining structure. Though Canadian collective bargaining already is concentrated at the single-employer, single-union level, the few centralized arrangements in place came under substantial pressure beginning in the 1980s. As a result, long-standing centralized bargaining structures in meat-packing, forestry, and textiles were either abandoned or weakened, almost always at the employers' initiative. Pressures for decentralization also emerged in the public sector.

Changes in corporate and regulatory structures partially explain this trend. For example, deregulation and divestiture of rail lines, privatization of government services, and restructuring in both the private and public sectors have created a number of new, smaller, firms.

These trends are not unique to Canada. Many other countries have experienced pressures towards more decentralized collective bargaining, though few started with the degree of decentralization found in this country. Katz (1993: 13) puts forward three explanations for emerging international trends towards the decentralization of bargaining:

> ... decentralization results from shifts in bargaining power, the spread of new work organization that puts a premium on flexibility and employee participation, and a decentralization of corporate structure and diversification of worker preferences.

International evidence supports the conclusion that the first two factors have played a role in decentralization, but that the role of the third factor is probably not substantial (Katz, 1993: 16–17). This tendency toward the decentralization of bargaining is occurring in countries such as the United States, the United Kingdom, and Australia, as well as some European countries.

MODEL OF THE COLLECTIVE BARGAINING PROCESS

Once a bargaining unit has been established and a union has been certified as the exclusive representative of the employees in the unit, collective bargaining becomes the means by which the terms and conditions of the employment contract are established (Bacharach and Lawler, 1981). Although many issues and objectives are initially brought to the negotiating table by both union and management negotiators, the negotiation process typically results in a set of agreed-upon outcomes that may differ quite substantially from the original objectives of either party. Figure 9.1 presents a conceptual framework of the determinants of the outcomes of collective bargaining that identifies the linkages between the goals and power of the union and management, the process of negotiating a contract, and the outcomes of collective bargaining.

The actual *outcomes* of the process of collective bargaining are specified in the clauses of the collective bargaining agreement (refer to Chapter 10). The specific outcomes of collective bargaining that are determined through the negotiation process in turn depend upon the *goals* of the union and management, the *power* that the parties have to achieve their desired objectives, and the statutory requirements that may constrain the bargaining process. The bargaining goals of the union and management are determined by their respective preferences for alternative bargaining outcomes (path A2 of Figure 9.1); the preferences of the parties are in turn determined by a variety of environmental, socio-demographic, and organizational characteristics (path A1 of Figure 9.1). While the relative power of the parties is also determined by various environmental, socio-demographic, and organizational characteristics (path B of Figure 9.1), it is affected by the dynamics of the negotiation process as well. The *negotiation process* (relationship C of Figure 9.1) links the goals and power of both the union and management on the one hand, and the outcomes of collective bargaining on the other hand, and accounts for why the initial objectives of the union and management tend to differ from the results achieved.

Figure 9.1 depicts a rather linear, static framework in order to emphasize the basic relationships at work and to guide the following discussion of the bargaining model. However, the following examination of each of the components of the model will also reveal the complex manner in which they are interrelated and how their effects may change over time.

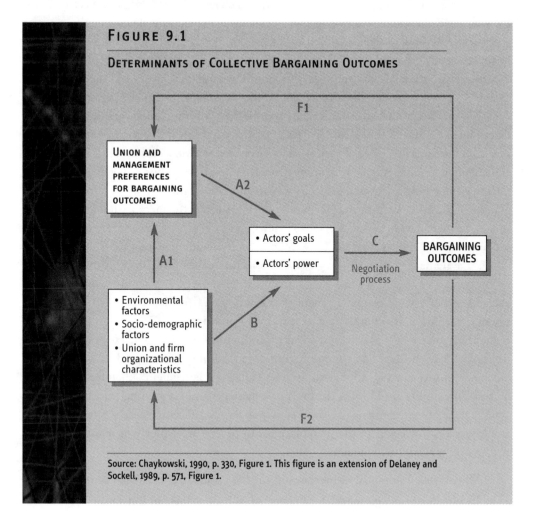

FIGURE 9.1

DETERMINANTS OF COLLECTIVE BARGAINING OUTCOMES

Source: Chaykowski, 1990, p. 330, Figure 1. This figure is an extension of Delaney and Sockell, 1989, p. 571, Figure 1.

Union and Management Bargaining Goals

The priority that management and the union attach to each issue is typically reflective of the goals and objectives of the firm and the membership, respectively. In practice, both the union and management negotiating teams will determine *target* and *resistance* points for each issue they will bargain over in advance of any negotiations. For example, in negotiating over wages, the target point is essentially the most preferred outcome (typically, for the union, a larger wage increase than what management is willing to give), whereas the resistance point is generally taken to be an outcome that constitutes the lowest acceptable (wage) offer to the union and the highest acceptable (wage) offer to management. Wage offers not within the range could create an impasse in negotiations and possibly lead to a work stoppage. In the opening vignette involving the 1999 negotiations between Inco and the USWA, Inco's initial demand for wage and benefit reductions seems to have been far below the USWA's resistance point.

The process of establishing bargaining objectives typically initially involves determining the major issues over which each side (union and management) has unique concerns. Then, for each issue, the union and management negotiating teams must determine the range of acceptable outcomes to their membership and senior management, respectively, in order to formulate specific positions at the bargaining table. Consultation with each party's various constituent groups helps garner approval of both the bargaining issues and the range of acceptable outcomes associated with each issue. Since unions are essentially political organizations in the sense that the leadership and policies of the union are democratically determined, the membership can be expected to have a direct influence on bargaining priorities, but the precise degree of membership involvement varies across unions. Most unions will accumulate a list of future bargaining issues that arise during the term of an existing contract (e.g., emerging health-and-safety issues). In addition, as the end of the contract and beginning of negotiations approaches, unions typically canvass the membership (e.g., through surveys or meetings) in order to elicit the views and priorities of the membership. Exhibit 9.1 illustrates the process that the CAW follows in determining its bargaining agenda.

On the management side, the goals and priorities of the bargaining team usually are an outgrowth of the short- and long-term business strategy and would conform to the goals identified by senior management. For example, a firm that embarks upon a strategy of becoming more competitive by improving product quality as well as productivity may decide that it wants to invest in new production technologies. However, the new technology may be expected to require increased flexibility with regard to work rules or job descriptions already stipulated in the collective agreement; therefore obtaining increased flexibility could form the basis of a management bargaining priority.

The *goals* of management and unions may cover the full range of issues of concern to employees and managers in the workplace. Both parties are typically interested in negotiating over goals in such areas as:

- Wages (i.e., union goal of increases in the base wage over each year of the contract)
- Union security (e.g., mandatory payment of union dues; union shop)

EXHIBIT 9.1

THE DEVELOPMENT OF THE CANADIAN AUTO WORKERS' BARGAINING AGENDA

The CAW does not use a "master contract"; instead, it generally negotiates separate contracts with each company. It may, however, examine contracts in somewhat similar workplaces to see what it can learn from them.

Before collective bargaining actually begins, the union develops proposals during meetings that are open to all members of the local bargaining unit. Then a meeting is called during which each member has an opportunity to vote on the proposals that have been developed for each issue (e.g., wage demands). In addition, the membership would typically elect a bargaining committee from among the members, which would represent them during negotiations. This process allows the CAW to work with the members of the local bargaining unit to develop the set of issues and proposals that will be brought forward to the company at the bargaining table.

During negotiations with the company, other meetings are held (on an "as needed" basis) to vote on offers made by the company. The CAW stresses to each member: "*You* have the final say on whether or not the proposed contract is acceptable."

Source: Adapted from *CAW/TCA Canada.* "Organize Canada—CAW Fact Sheet 1: Questions and Answers about CAW." http://www.caw.ca/join/can/orgcan1/html (December 1999).

- Employee security (e.g., contracting-out; seniority rules on layoffs and for promotions; severance pay benefits)
- Grievance and arbitration procedures (e.g., grievance process)
- Hours and days of work (e.g., daily and weekly hours of work; normal workweek; rules pertaining to shift work)
- Overtime and premium pay (e.g., distribution of overtime among employees; rates of overtime pay)
- Level and structure of compensation (e.g., wage levels and the type of pay system, such as hourly wages versus piece rates versus incentive systems)
- Vacations and leaves (e.g., weeks of vacation; number of paid holidays; provision for education, parental, or bereavement leave)
- Allowances (e.g., pay for clothing, tools, or moving expenses)
- Technological change (e.g., advance notice of the introduction of new technology; retraining)
- Health and safety (e.g., sick leave; disability benefits; rules to ensure safe work practices)
- Fringe benefits (e.g., pension benefits; life insurance; extended health benefits)
- Worker–management relationship (e.g., establishment, membership, and purview of joint committees)

For a particular issue, both the union and the firm will attempt to achieve their most preferred outcomes. In some cases, the interests of management and union are likely to be directly opposed (e.g., on wages). If gains to one party in turn imply that less is available for the other, then the issue is referred to as being *distributive* in nature. For example, wage increases are a good example of a distributive issue: All else being equal, providing more of a firm's earnings to employees as wages implies that the firm then has fewer resources to distribute to the stockholders as dividends or to use for other purposes such as expansion of facilities, modernization, or managerial compensation.

In other areas, the interests of the union and management may have significant elements in common, so that providing more of the outcome will increase the well-being of both the union and management. These types of issues are referred to as *integrative*. For example, establishing joint union–management committees to examine work reorganization that is aimed at increasing productivity could benefit both parties if they agree to share any gains in productivity between them. Alternatively, expenditures that improve workplace health and safety could benefit both workers (directly) and the firm (by lowering accident rates and thereby lowering assessments under the workers' compensation insurance program).[6]

The goals of the union and management are shaped by a variety of influences, including environmental factors, socio-demographic factors, and organizational characteristics. Environmental factors may include the state of the economy, changes in the technology of production, or recent contract settlements in comparable workplaces. Economic factors include macroeconomic influences such as inflation or changes in economic growth. Inflation is an example of a macroeconomic influence that affects union goals. In periods of rapid and prolonged inflation, the union may seek a cost-of-living-adjustment (COLA) clause that provides wage adjustments based upon increases in the Consumer Price Index. The progressive liberalization or expansion of trade is an economic factor that would typically serve to increase competition, which may induce management to try to restrain wage increases in order to limit increases in production costs, especially in firms that have labour intensive production methods.

The introduction of new production technology may affect productivity, unit production costs, product quality, workplace safety or ergonomics, the pace of work, job skills and training requirements, or the number of workers required. For example, introducing a new technology that permits the same level of output, but with higher product quality, using fewer, but more highly skilled, workers may be viewed by management as necessary if the firm is to successfully compete in international markets; but it may also induce the union to bargain for severance packages for employees who are laid off as a result of the introduction of the new technology. Alternatively, the union could seek rules governing transfer rights for displaced workers, or bargain for union involvement in worker training programs.

Socio-demographic factors may include the age or gender composition of the collective bargaining unit. These workforce socio-demographic characteristics may be systematically associated with preferences for certain types of employment outcomes. Consequently, the union leadership may attempt to formulate bargaining goals that incorporate these specific preferences. For example, if the average age of a particular workforce is high, then workers may (on average) exhibit preferences for enhanced pensions or for strong seniority rules governing promotions and transfers—relative to another workforce with a much lower average age. Alternatively, all else being equal, a workforce with a high proportion of females may (on average) express greater preferences for family-related benefits, such as maternity and paternity leaves, child-care facilities, and workplace anti-discrimination programs.

Many private-sector unions were, at first, slow to organize women, in part because they were situated primarily in industries that tended to employ males (such as forestry, mining, rail, and many manufacturing industries such as autos). Unions began to more actively change in the 1970s and 1980s, in part because they recognized that, if they are to expand (or in some cases maintain) their membership levels, they must organize women workers; another reason for the change has been the increasing focus of major unions on organizing workers in the service industries in which many women tend to be employed. While the number of female union members has grown considerably, unions have had to work hard to transform the traditional operation of the union organization and the bargaining goals of the union to meet the needs and goals of women workers. One union that has risen to this challenge is the Canadian Auto Workers. As Exhibit 9.2 illustrates, the CAW leadership recognizes that women workers may have some priorities that go beyond traditional CAW objectives.

Exhibit 9.2

The Extension of Union Priorities to Account for the Changing Female Composition of Membership

Peggy Nash, Assistant to the President of the CAW, has emphasized the importance of giving priority to women's issues in collective bargaining:

> It says that women's issues are union issues and that women's contributions are important though often undervalued. It recognizes that there are often misconceptions about women's roles in the workplace and that our laws are usually inadequate. Most importantly it means that women's issues are important to the union and that the union is committed to women.

According to Nash, the four main areas of special interest to women in collective bargaining are the following:

1. Working conditions (including wages, benefits, and health and safety). Particularly relevant to women workers are pay and employment equity, flexible hours of work, and health issues relevant to pregnant women (such as toxic substances in the workplace).

2. **Maternity and family responsibilities.** Women are concerned with issues such as funding for child care and ensuring that there is no discrimination against pregnant women or women who have child-care responsibilities.

3. **Anti-discrimination and human rights.** Developing policies against harassment and violence against women are priorities.

4. **Giving women a voice** by ensuring women's representation in the workplace and in the union. There is a need to increase the representation of women on workplace committees as well as within the union, on committees, in training programs, and in bargaining activities.

Source: Adapted from *CAW/TCA Canada.* "CAW Women's Bargaining Agenda. Presentation by Peggy Nash, Assistant to the President, at TCA-Quebec Women's Conference." October 16, 1998. http://www.caw.ca/communications/speeches/womenbargaining.html (December, 1999).

Finally, the characteristics of the firm or union can affect their respective bargaining objectives. Changes in business strategy and management goals are also crucially important to bargaining objectives. For example, throughout the 1980s and 1990s, management often sought to enhance productivity (and competitiveness) by pursuing increased flexibility in the deployment of workers or by altering production methods (and hence work organization and job content), all of which typically involved negotiating changes to workplace rules and practices that were well established in collective agreements (Verma and Chaykowski, 1999). As another example, a management strategy of decentralizing authority and decision making within the organization or devolving more authority down to the workplace level may require new workplace organizational structures or some form of employee involvement programs. Bargaining with the union may therefore involve the manner and conditions under which the union will participate in and, indeed, support the establishment of new workplace structures.[7]

Importantly, as Figure 9.1 illustrates, these factors and characteristics *indirectly* influence the goals of the union leadership and management: Each factor acts as a determinant of the preferences of the parties for various types of bargaining outcomes (relationship A1). But the preferences of the parties in turn shape the specific goals or objectives that are sought in the collective bargaining process (relationship A2).

The Concept and Role of Power in Collective Bargaining

The typical observation that two parties engaged in negotiations have unequal leverage or advantage in obtaining their preferred outcome is rooted in the intuitive notion that one party has greater *power*. While power is itself not quantifiable, the concept of power can be defined, and the types of factors that give rise to power with respect to collective bargaining outcomes can be examined.

The Concept of Bargaining Power

The ability of the parties to achieve their desired outcome, or objective, on a given issue will depend on their relative *bargaining power*. The classic conceptual definition of bargaining power is provided by Chamberlain and Kuhn (1986) and includes both the costs associated with a disagreement as well as the costs of agreement. Examples of the *costs of disagreement* may include: the lost production (firm's loss) and wages (employees' loss) associated with a strike or lockout; the withdrawal of labour's active co-operation with management in the workplace (firm's loss); bad publicity associated with a strike (firm's loss); and threatened plant closures (employees' loss). Examples of the *costs of agreement* could include: the direct costs of agreeing to increases in wages and benefits (firm's cost) or possible non-monetary costs associated with agreeing to a joint-participation program (a cost to the union leadership if the membership views union participation with management as "selling out") (Chamberlain and Kuhn, 1986: 180–196). Using the notions of costs of agreement and disagreement, power means:

> ... the ability to secure another's agreement on one's own terms. A union's bargaining power at any point of time *is*, for example, management's willingness to agree to the union's terms. Management's willingness, in turn, depends upon the costs of disagreeing with the union terms relative to the costs of agreeing to them (Chamberlain and Kuhn, 1986: 176).

The power of a particular union (or management) in collective bargaining is clearly expected to vary over time with the specific issue being negotiated, and with the particular negotiating tactics used by the parties (Chamberlain and Kuhn, 1986: 177–178). In the following section, we examine the underlying factors that give rise to bargaining power.

The Determinants of Bargaining Power

The power of the union and management in collective bargaining depends upon a variety of environmental, socio-demographic, and organizational factors. These factors directly determine the power that the union and firm can exert in the negotiation process (refer to relationship B in Figure 9.1).

Environmental factors could include shifts in public support for workers who are on strike, modifications of the legislative framework governing labour relations, or changes in economic circumstances. Environmental influences can therefore affect not just the balance of power but also the goals of the parties.

The effect of public opinion on the relative power of the parties is probably more subtle than other environmental factors. For example, changes in public opinion may involve increased community support for striking workers that could induce the firm to improve its bargaining offers in order to garner public favour. Consequently, union strike strategies may include publicity efforts to encourage the public to boycott the products of the firm. In the broader public sector, popular opinion may be an especially important factor, as we observed in a number of strikes involving nurses and teachers in the late 1990s.

The legal environment is generally believed to be a significant determinant of union power, since legislation can require that certain items be included in the contract or it can place limits on the behaviour or actions of the parties. Amendments to the labour relations legislation of British Columbia and Ontario in the early 1990s were generally viewed as providing increased support for unions (Carter, 1993). The Ontario reforms that prohibited the use of replacement workers during a strike strengthened the effectiveness of the union strike weapon, since the ability of management to operate its facilities during a work stoppage was now limited. In contrast, the set of reforms subsequently undertaken by the Ontario government in the mid-1990s are generally viewed as having reversed the impact of the earlier reforms.

Economic conditions have a primary influence on the relative bargaining power of unions and management. In times of economic growth (an upswing in the business cycle), when the demand for products is increasing, employers will be reluctant to bear the losses associated with a strike, all else being equal. Alternatively, in periods of high unemployment, employment opportunities for workers tend to be fewer, so that, all else being equal, the union membership may be less willing to engage in a prolonged strike. These specific examples illustrate how economic conditions can affect the willingness of the parties to bear the costs of disagreement (in the form of a work stoppage). Another related consideration is the ease with which consumers may substitute other products for the goods that cannot be supplied during a strike. For example, if Canadian steel manufacturers are struck, automakers may seek out other steel suppliers or attempt to substitute away from steel toward other materials (e.g., plastics) in the manufacturing process. In fact, strikes at the outset of the 1990s in the Canadian steel industry appear to have induced both of these effects (Verma and Weiler, 1992).

During the 1980s and 1990s, broader shifts in the Canadian economic context have had a longer-term impact on the relative bargaining power of unions and firms. An intensely competitive business environment has been fostered by numerous factors: changes in foreign and domestic public policies, such as deregulation, and the further strengthening of North-South trade links through the North American Free Trade Agreement (NAFTA); increased capital mobility and (more generally) the globalization of product markets; and the rapid diffusion of advanced production technologies (Verma and Chaykowski, 1999). These influences have created pressures on firms to reduce prices, lower the costs of production, and increase productivity.

Although Canada-US trade has been growing steadily over most of the post–World War II period, the Canada-US Free Trade Agreement and, subsequently, the NAFTA have created trade frameworks that have essentially accelerated the process of economic integration and increased competition. The prospect of creating a trading zone of the Americas in the first decade of the new century would serve to even further extend economic integration and increase competition. Meanwhile, increased capital mobility and new production methods have facilitated the movement of facilities "offshore" to lower-cost regions. This means that, in many cases, firms' production is no longer tied to specific regions or product markets as it may have been traditionally. New production technologies continue to evolve more quickly, are much more rapidly diffused, and are often associated with fewer workers, new skill requirements, and new methods of organizing work. The acceleration of technological advances in production has pressured many firms to maintain competitiveness by acquiring and investing in the latest technologies.

Confronted with these pressures, firms have sought wage concessions or wage freezes or engaged in downsizing their workforces in an attempt to lower costs, attempted to reorganize workplaces and create more flexible work rules, and threatened to close facilities if unions do not co-operate with management demands. In turn, the power of many unions to enforce their own demands has been reduced, largely because the global expansion of markets and increased competition have reduced the ability of unions to "take wages out of competition." Recognizing the implications of bargaining in this new environment, many unions have moderated their wage demands and sought to focus their objectives on membership concerns over employment security. Unions have also carefully considered co-operating with management in its efforts to reorganize work in order to increase productivity, although most unions have developed position papers that state the conditions necessary for their involvement.[8]

The privatization of Crown corporations (e.g., Air Canada) and the deregulation of industries (e.g., transportation and telecommunications) provide good examples of how shifts in public policies can also affect the bargaining relationship through their impact on the economic environment. The deregulation of the airline industry in 1988, and the privatization of Pacific Western Airlines (which later purchased Canadian Pacific to form Canadian Airlines International) in 1983 and of Air Canada in 1989, created significant competitive pressures in the industry (Fisher and Kondra, 1992). By the end of the 1990s, Canadian Airlines International had essentially become unviable, Air Canada had bid to buy the company, and the unions representing workers at Canadian Airlines International faced the long-run prospect of a substantial loss of membership if the takeover proceeded. Recent policy initiatives aimed at deregulating the telecommunications industry are creating similar pressures, which are most noticeable in the market for long-distance telephone services. Unions realize that long-term growth in employee compensation can no longer be readily absorbed by rate increases once common in regulated industries and that, in the long run, increased competition may mean fewer firms and fewer jobs (members).

Diverse **socio-demographic characteristics** may be associated with disparate personal preferences and, therefore, bargaining preferences, amongst the membership. In addition, the membership may be divided in its views on whether or not a particular issue is sufficiently important to warrant a strike if the bargaining objective is not achieved during negotiations. Consequently, union leadership must often account for diverse preferences amongst its membership when formulating bargaining objectives and when assessing the extent of membership support for engaging in a strike to achieve certain bargaining outcomes.

Organizational characteristics that affect power may be broadly defined to include the type of product produced, the technology of production, or the characteristics of the union or firm (e.g., cohesiveness of the union membership, resources available to the union during a strike). If the product is one that can be stockpiled, then management can continue to sell its product during a strike, thereby generating revenues and maintaining its contractual relationships with customers. This capability would minimize the economic impact of a work stoppage on the firm. Alternatively, if the firm produces a good that cannot be stockpiled or a service (which obviously cannot be stockpiled), then a strike would clearly have an immediate impact on the firm's revenues and customer base. For example, the Steelworkers engaged in a 13-week strike against Stelco in 1990 when negotiations broke down. This strike involved lost wages for the workers but also resulted in a significant permanent loss of customers. Verma and Warrian (1992: 114) report that the strike had a lasting effect on the steel industry:

> The company estimated that, during the strike, roughly 5 percent of its customer base had vanished. Some steel-consuming industrial plants had closed, and others had turned to imports. Together, the loss of these customers meant a reduction in demand of 400,000 tons for the Canadian steel industry.

The nature of the technology of production has a direct impact on the ability of management to continue operations during a strike. If the production process enables management employees to operate the facilities themselves, then the impact of a work stoppage could be minimal. For example, in a refinery that requires few workers and is operated by means of control panels, supervisors and managers could maintain operations. During work stoppages in the telephone industry, supervisors have maintained a basic level of service by performing the tasks of operators. Alternatively, the technology of production may require highly specialized skills in the regular workforce; the specialized skill requirements would prevent management from performing the work of skilled workers themselves or hiring replacement workers (where allowed by labour legislation).

One of the most important organizational characteristics of the union is its status as a political organization. For example, the membership may be politically divided in its support for the elected leadership, which could in turn undermine the solidarity of the union or the support provided to the leadership during the negotiating process. In practice, once a tentative agreement has been reached between the union and management negotiating teams, the membership will vote on the "package" offered by the firm. In some cases, the final offer, although endorsed by the leadership, may be rejected in a vote; this would likely serve to affect both the bargaining posture and authority of the leadership. Note that, while a vote that rejects a tentative package may serve to undermine confidence in the leadership and detract from its bargaining position, it may also serve to provide the leadership with a strong mandate to bargain hard for improvements—secure in the knowledge that the membership is fully supportive and possibly prepared to endure a long strike to enforce its demands—thereby increasing the power underlying the union's position. Other characteristics of the union, such as the resources available, can affect its ability to maintain a work stoppage. The magnitude of the union strike fund could directly affect the length of time the membership is willing (or able) to maintain a strike action. Strike funds are accumulated through union dues and are used to provide small payments to workers while they are on strike. Payments are usually made weekly and are aimed at maintaining subsistence requirements.

Intra-organizational dynamics are also important within the firm. The management bargaining team typically serves a variety of interests among managers with different responsibilities. Also, while the union bargaining team must reconcile any settlement with the desires of the rank-and-file membership, so too must the management bargaining team reconcile the negotiated settlement with the goals and objectives of senior management. Centralized bargaining structures in particular may be prone to internal politics, as the objectives of several employers and unions (as the case may be) have to be melded into unified positions that inevitably reflect some compromise.

The various environmental, socio-demographic, and organizational characteristics that affect power operate simultaneously. The particular factors that determine the relative power of the union and management vary considerably over time, across industries, and across jurisdictions—which is why we expect the power of the parties to vary as well. Because the interrelationships among the factors that give rise to power are so complex, we cannot determine, in advance, their net effect on collective bargaining. In practice, this creates a degree of uncertainty in most negotiations; thus an important element in bargaining is the gathering of information about the other side's bargaining power through the give and take of the negotiations.

NEGOTIATING THE COLLECTIVE AGREEMENT: PROCESS AND INNOVATIONS

In the traditional system, once the term of a contract draws near, the union and management engage in negotiations with a view to agreeing upon a new collective agreement, with a specified duration, that provides the specific terms and conditions of employment and methods of administering industrial justice. While the union–management negotiations may lead directly to a settlement, the negotiations may also be punctuated by a work stoppage before a new contract is, ultimately, agreed upon. Figure 9.2 illustrates the linear process that is followed over time as successive contracts are negotiated, abided by for the term of the collective agreement, and subsequently renegotiated. The focus of the following discussion is on the negotiations process itself.

The negotiation process (refer back to relationship C of Figure 9.1) links the goals and power of the parties, on the one hand, with the outcomes of collective bargaining, on the other hand. While the union and management assert their power in order to achieve their goals, the actual process of negotiating the collective agreement can assume its own dynamic, which can itself constitute an important factor in determining the eventual contract outcomes. This section begins with a discussion of the concept of a "zone of agreement," which provides insight into the basis for defining a potential agreement. This discussion is followed by a brief characterization of the manner in which collective bargaining proceeds when a contract requires renegotiation, including a characterization

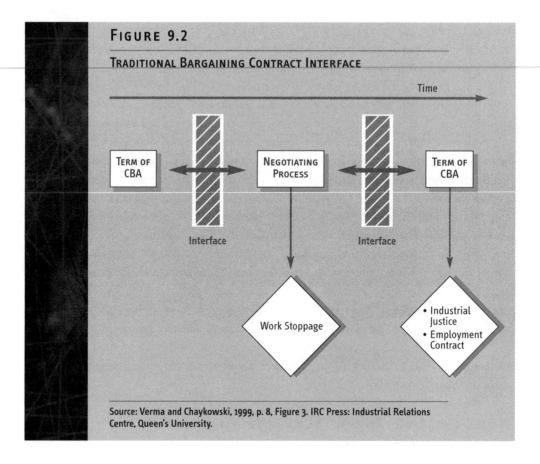

FIGURE 9.2

TRADITIONAL BARGAINING CONTRACT INTERFACE

Source: Verma and Chaykowski, 1999, p. 8, Figure 3. IRC Press: Industrial Relations Centre, Queen's University.

of the process and dynamics of the negotiation process, and a discussion of why (dis)agreement, or impasses, may occur. The final section describes some of the innovations occurring in collective bargaining, largely in an attempt to avoid conflict that leads to impasse.

The Potential for Agreement in Negotiations

Most negotiations involve attempts to resolve numerous complex issues, many of which are typically interrelated. One of the most fundamental concerns is, therefore, whether there even exists a potential basis for agreement. That is, do the *positions* of the parties create a common ground, or are the minimum positions of each party too far apart to permit any common ground? Further, can the parties change their positions on one issue (e.g., wages) during the negotiating process in reaction to changes in positions that occur regarding another issue (e.g., pension benefits)? In practice, it is this type of flexibility and process of trade-offs across outcomes that makes an agreement possible. Defining a "potential zone of agreement" provides a theoretical basis for understanding why an agreement may, or may not, occur.

For a single issue, the notion of a potential "zone of agreement" between union and management negotiators is depicted in Figure 9.3. Consider negotiations over a single issue for which the union seeks an increased value and which management seeks to resist (e.g., wages). In Figure 9.3, the following reference points create a potential zone of agreement between the parties:

- The left-most point (A) represents the lowest value of wages that will induce workers to offer their services, while the right-most point (B) represents the highest level of wages possible that would still permit the firm to operate;

- **UM** represents the minimum wage level that the union will accept (often referred to as the union "resistance point");

- **MM** represents the maximum wage level that management will offer the union (which is often referred to as the management "resistance point").

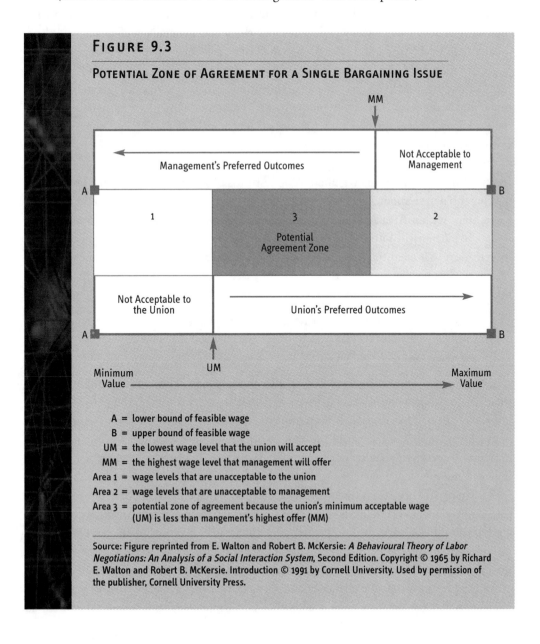

FIGURE 9.3

POTENTIAL ZONE OF AGREEMENT FOR A SINGLE BARGAINING ISSUE

A = lower bound of feasible wage
B = upper bound of feasible wage
UM = the lowest wage level that the union will accept
MM = the highest wage level that management will offer
Area 1 = wage levels that are unacceptable to the union
Area 2 = wage levels that are unacceptable to management
Area 3 = potential zone of agreement because the union's minimum acceptable wage (UM) is less than mangement's highest offer (MM)

Source: Figure reprinted from E. Walton and Robert B. McKersie: *A Behavioural Theory of Labor Negotiations: An Analysis of a Social Interaction System*, Second Edition. Copyright © 1965 by Richard E. Walton and Robert B. McKersie. Introduction © 1991 by Cornell University. Used by permission of the publisher, Cornell University Press.

In the example of bargaining over wages, management may attempt to focus its bargaining strategy on achieving a specific wage level that it believes represents the best that it can do (that is, the lowest wage that it can offer the union). Realistically, management prefers to offer any wage level that is less than MM in Figure 9.3. Since management prefers any wage level less than MM (Area 1 and Area 3), management will certainly prefer wage levels less than UM. However, the union will never agree to any wage offers in Area 1 (i.e., wages below UM), since this area corresponds to wages that are less than the level that is minimally acceptable to the union (UM). But management may not know that wage offers below UM (Area 1) are not acceptable to the union.

From its perspective, the union may focus on a particular wage level that it believes represents the best that can be obtained from management in negotiations (that is, the highest wage it can successfully negotiate). But the union generally prefers any wage level greater than UM (Area 2 and Area 3)—so the union will certainly prefer a wage level that is greater than MM. But management will never agree to any wage demand in Area 2 (i.e., wages above MM), since this area corresponds to wages that are greater than the maximum wage level that is acceptable to management (MM). On its part, the union may not know that wage demands that are greater than MM (Area 2) are not acceptable to the management.

Area 3 is a *potential* zone of agreement because the union's lowest acceptable demand (point UM) is less than management's highest possible offer (point MM). The *existence* of a potential agreement zone will yield a settlement as long as the parties can bargain to some point within Area 3. However, one cannot determine in advance *where within this range* the parties will settle. The process of bargaining allows an exchange of offers and information that encourages management and the union to learn more about their true "resistance" points; in general, it permits both parties to learn more about the *range* of outcomes that is acceptable to each:

> Negotiation ... is back-and-forth communication designed to reach an agreement when you and the other side have some interests that are shared and others that are opposed (Fisher and Ury, 1983: xi).

Obtaining a solution in Area 3 would be made easier if both sides simply revealed their true resistance points; but, in order to gain strategic advantage, the parties will typically not do so. That is, each will attempt to "bluff," to exaggerate their true resistance point, or to employ other tactics in order to obtain a solution closest to their own most preferred wage level; that is, where in Area 3 the parties ultimately settle matters very much to them.

This type of bargaining dynamic assumes that management and the union are bargaining over a single issue or, if more than one issue is being negotiated, that the parties are bargaining over each issue separately. In most cases, however, management and the union negotiate several issues at the same time and negotiations over one issue can affect the bargaining over another. This means that the process of negotiating over one issue can affect the positions that the parties take regarding the other issue. As a consequence, the union and management may seek trade-offs across these two issues because the potential gains in one issue may offset what they must offer for the other issue. For example, this trade-off may be especially appealing because one party (e.g., the union) may place a greater weight on obtaining more of Issue X (e.g., health and safety) than Issue Y (e.g., vacation)—perhaps because the membership places more value on greater health and safety than on more vacation. This type of scenario, which is typical of most negotiations, helps explain why collective bargaining is such a challenging and dynamic process.

Negotiating the Collective Agreement

If a collective agreement is in effect, then near the expiration of the contract the union must give notice to the employer of its intention to bargain for a new collective agreement, after which the parties must meet within a specified period of time; the specific requirements vary across jurisdictions (refer to Table 9.2). The union and management negotiating teams prepare their positions on each issue over which they wish to negotiate.

TABLE 9.2

STATUTORY REQUIREMENTS FOR NOTICE TO COMMENCE AND OBLIGATION TO BEGIN COLLECTIVE BARGAINING FOR RENEGOTIATION OF A COLLECTIVE AGREEMENT IN THE PRIVATE SECTOR

JURISDICTION	PERIOD OF NOTICE TO BARGAIN (BEFORE EXPIRY DATE OF CONTRACT)[d]	OBLIGATION TO BARGAIN (AFTER PROVIDING NOTICE)
Federal	Within 4 months[a]	Within 20 days[b]
Alberta	120 to 60 days[a]	Within 30 days
British Columbia	Within 4 months[c]	Within 10 days
Manitoba	90 to 30 days[b]	Within 10 days[a]
New Brunswick	90 to 30 days[a]	Within 20 days[a]
Newfoundland	60 to 30 days[b]	Within 20 days[a]
Nova Scotia	Within 2 months	Within 20 days[a]
Ontario	Within 90 days[b]	Within 15 days[a]
PEI	Within 2 months[b]	Within 20 days[a]
Quebec	Within 90 days[b]	"Forthwith"
Saskatchewan	60 to 30 days	"Forthwith"

Notes:

a. Union and management may agree to a longer period.

b. Union and management may agree otherwise.

c. Notice is "deemed" given at 90 days before the contract expires.

d. Changes in the notice to bargain are typically stipulated in the collective agreement.

Source: Industrial Relations Legislation In Canada. 1999 Edition. Accessed at http://labour.hrdc-drhc.gc.ca/policy/cb-p/tc-irl.html. Ottawa: Minister of Supply and Services Canada (December, 1999). Reproduced with permission of the Minister of Labour.

In traditional bargaining, each team has a spokesperson. The tone of the meetings has commonly been adversarial, with each team facing the other as "opposites." The union may present its "demands," with the management team withdrawing to examine the requests and subsequently returning to respond with an "offer" (a *position* on each issue of concern). The union will usually then withdraw from the negotiating table to examine the proposal in "caucus." Each side will caucus regularly throughout the negotiating process as each team discusses and debates the merits of the latest offer. Offers are analyzed and evaluated: The economic value of offers related to wages, pensions, holidays, severance packages for laid-off workers, or other issues with a monetary value are "costed"; the merits of offers related to issues with no readily quantifiable value (e.g., changes to promotion rules) are evaluated. This process of preparing and evaluating offers and counter-offers typically continues over many days or weeks until either all issues have been resolved or until an impasse is reached.

If the parties cannot reach an agreement, then either party may request that the government appoint a conciliation officer. (In some jurisdictions, if the conciliator cannot facilitate an agreement, then the government may—but in practice rarely does—recommend that a conciliation board be appointed.) If the impasse continues and the collective agreement has expired, the union has a legal right to engage in a work stoppage and management has a legal right to lock out. Before a strike or lockout becomes legal, certain prerequisites have to be satisfied; typically these include a strike vote and strike notice. While high-profile strikes often catch the attention of the media, and a single strike in a key sector (e.g., in rail or health care) can have a serious impact on the economy, most negotiations lead to a successful settlement without a serious impasse in the negotiations and, of those negotiations that reach an impasse at some point, not all result in an actual work stoppage. This track record of successful negotiations is illustrated by the situation in Alberta. Exhibit 9.3 reveals that over the ten-year period from 1989–98, typically less than 2 percent of the collective agreements that expired in a given year were associated with an actual work stoppage. So, in the larger scheme, collective negotiations prove to be a very successful way of dealing with the need of workers and management to re-contract.

Exhibit 9.3

Expiring Collective Agreements Resulting in Work Stoppages in Alberta, 1989–98

While many of the major strikes that occur catch the public attention, and strikes are generally in the news, the vast majority of collective agreements are settled before they expire. Of those contracts that are not renegotiated before they expire, very few result in a strike or lockout.

A good example of this may be drawn from the Alberta experience with strikes. Overall, 23 percent of employees are union members and roughly 27 percent are covered by a collective agreement (in 1998); this is lower than the national average, but a considerable percentage nonetheless.

In 1998, there were approximately 1373 collective agreements in effect in Alberta, covering around 267,000 employees; by year-end of 1998, roughly 66 percent were in effect, while around 34 percent (or 400) contracts required settlement. Of these, only 1.7 percent resulted in a work stoppage.

FIGURE 9.4

NUMBER OF EXPIRED CONTRACTS VS. PERCENTAGE AT IMPASSE IN ALBERTA, 1989–98

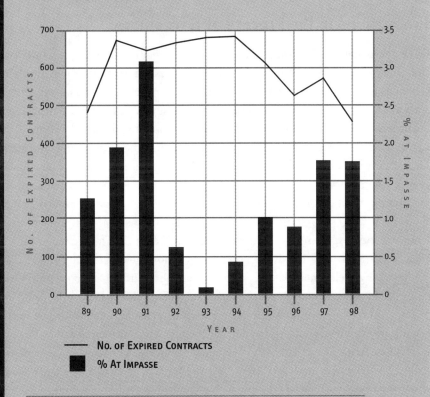

Source: Alberta Labour, www.gov.ab.ca/lab/

As Figure 9.4 illustrates, 1998 was not an unusual year for strikes. The line graph indicates the number of contracts that expired in each year over the 1989–98 period, while the bar graph indicates the proportion of these that ended in a work stoppage. Notice that the proportion of expired contracts that end in a work stoppage varies somewhat in relation to the business cycle, that the proportion of expired contracts is typically less than 2 percent, and that the total number of contracts involving a work stoppage is typically around a dozen or fewer.

Since the number of strikes alone does not convey the impact of strike activity, we usually also consider the number of person-days lost in a work stoppage as well as the effect that a strike may have on other industries.

Even after a work stoppage occurs, the parties will continue their negotiations, often with the help of a government-appointed mediator. While a mediator may assist in achieving an agreement, the process of collective bargaining is affected by a diverse set of factors including: the power of the parties (including the costs associated with a strike or lockout), the skill and personalities of the negotiators, and union and management access to information regarding the true positions of the other side.

 Alberta Labour: www.gov.ab.ca/lab/

Innovations in the Process of Bargaining

Since the issues that are subject to collective bargaining are of consequence to the parties, the process of bargaining is typically pursued strenuously and often results in strained relationships—whether or not a strike or lockout occurs. Achieving a new contract is important in itself, but the union and management also attempt to achieve a resolution to their differences that each considers workable during the term of the collective agreement. The traditional approach to improving the negotiating process, thereby increasing the likelihood of obtaining a collective agreement without an impasse, is to engage in some form of conciliation or mediation. Recognizing that the process of negotiating itself can help the parties to exchange information and to better appreciate their true target and resistance points, many unions and firms have also tended to lengthen the bargaining process, essentially by beginning to exchange information and even to negotiate well in advance of the expiration date of the contract.

Another development has been to increase the number of joint union–management committees as well as to extend the areas of concern that these committees deal with. For example, there are joint committees on such diverse areas as health and safety, work reorganization, job content, technological change, environmental issues, and contracting-out. These committees are often established either by letter of agreement or in the collective agreement and operate during the term of the collective agreement. The benefit from a negotiations standpoint is that the union and management can address problems on an ongoing basis, instead of simply identifying an issue during the term of a contract and "saving" it until the next round of negotiations. This can reduce the number of issues at the bargaining table, allow the parties to address issues before they "become big problems," and allow the parties to discuss issues in a less adversarial setting.

However, these types of developments, including third-party interventions or variations in the length of bargaining, occur in the context of traditional bargaining, and therefore tend not to alter the actual *negotiation process*. The effectiveness of these approaches and developments are therefore constrained by the limitations associated with traditional adversarial bargaining itself.

In recent years, several approaches to improving the process of collective bargaining have been developed in order to avoid costly strikes and lockouts and to improve the quality of the relationship after the negotiations are concluded. The core of these approaches is an attempt to alter the focus of the bargaining and the behavioural approach to negotiating. One of the more successful and widely attempted of these approaches is "interest-based" or "mutual gains" bargaining (MGB).

These techniques are rooted in the generic approach to bargaining referred to as *principled bargaining* (Fisher and Ury, 1983).[9] This approach was developed as an alternative to traditional, confrontational bargaining characterized by situations involving low levels of trust, high conflict, the use of tactics for advantage, a focus on the positions that the parties bring to the negotiations, and an emphasis on win-lose outcomes. Instead of focusing on the *positions* that the parties may assume in a negotiating situation, this approach centres on the underlying *interests* of the parties. Recognizing that the interests of the parties may conflict, Fisher and Ury suggested moving away from traditional adversarial bargaining through four procedures:

• Separating the personalities of the people from the problem under discussion;
• Focusing on the underlying interests of the parties, and not on their bargaining positions;
• Inventing options that give rise to mutual gain, instead of win-lose, solutions;
• In negotiating outcomes, developing objective criteria that involve fairness in both standards and procedures.

The bargaining concepts advanced by Fisher and Ury (1983) are general in nature, so that aspects of principled bargaining have been successfully adopted by negotiators in the process of collective bargaining. Recent analyses of mutual gains bargaining have raised concerns about the inherent limitations to its effectiveness: Since the process is based primarily on behaviourial principles, it may give insufficient weight to either the importance of the relative power of the parties or the institutional context in which the parties function and conduct negotiations (Friedman, 1994; Heckscher and Hall, 1994). However, Friedman has provided suggestions to increase the effectiveness of current practices. These suggestions focus on minimizing barriers to increased trust, altering the roles of the parties in negotiations, and modifying power imbalances between the union and management (Friedman, 1994).

What happens when one party is more powerful than the other? Fisher, Ury, and Patton (1991) acknowledge that MGB cannot guarantee success when the leverage is all on one side. The question of power remains a permanent threat to establishing and sustaining MGB. MGB will be successful if the parties are willing to focus on their common interests and on their will to use tactics based on principles and objective arguments, and not on the manipulation of other party's constraints through coercion.

While there appears to be continued interest in these "principled" types of bargaining innovations, traditional "hard bargaining" probably remains the predominant approach. Even so, anecdotal evidence indicates that some major unions and employers are utilizing principled bargaining, including:

• Petro-Canada and the Communications, Energy and Paperworkers Union (CEP)
• Bell Canada and the CEP

- Cardinal River Coal and the United Mine Workers
- Cominco Fertilizers (Potash Operations) and the United Steelworkers of America (USWA)
- TransAlta Utilities and the International Brotherhood of Electrical Workers
- Algoma Steel and the USWA

There is little systematic evidence currently available regarding the extent of usage of these "principled" approaches, their success, or whether their use tends to be sustained over time. However, Exhibit 9.4 presents a summary of the experiences of a number of prominent firms and unions with mutual gains bargaining in the 1990s that provides insight into some of these issues. The experiences of the parties reveal many of the factors that led the parties to attempt mutual gains approaches; the factors that, in their view, had an impact on the likelihood of the approach succeeding; and a range of considerations that they thought others considering a principled approach, as an alternative to traditional bargaining, might consider.

EXHIBIT 9.4

FROM TRADITIONAL TO MUTUAL GAINS BARGAINING IN CANADA

In October of 1994, the Federal Mediation and Conciliation Service (Human Resources Development Canada) invited representatives of 13 major companies and unions from all sectors of the federal jurisdiction to Ottawa to share their experiences with mutual gains bargaining.

THREE BEHAVIOURS THAT INCREASE THE LIKELIHOOD OF SUCCESS WITH MGB

1. **Openness and honesty:** Full disclosure of information throughout collective bargaining and, in some cases, during the normal business operations of the company.
2. **Trust:** Viewed as perhaps the most critical dimension, but also one of the most difficult to attain, since deeper trust typically evolves slowly over time and often must survive setbacks.
3. **Respect:** At all times.

PROCESS CONDITIONS TO INCREASE THE LIKELIHOOD OF SUCCESS WITH MGB

Joint Organizational Conditions

Training
- Establish joint union and management training in the interest-based approach to bargaining.
- Train at all levels of the organization.
- Recognize that there is a role for a facilitator (i.e., consultant) in training.

Consultancy
- Use an outside facilitator.
- Allow the choice of facilitator to be made jointly between the union and management.

Devote Resources
- Training may require sizeable amounts of financial resources that should be committed on an ongoing basis.
- Time required to develop the process can be substantial.
- Communications regarding the process should be established throughout the management and union.

Management Intra-organizational Factors

Commitment
- Obtain commitment to change from the highest levels.
- Develop commitment that outlasts changes in particular players or champions.

Authority
- Support the authority of the negotiating team to create solutions that the firm will stand by (e.g., ensure no mismatch with top management).

Line Supervision
- Address the needs of first-line supervisors—especially in cases where mutual gains bargaining leads to significant change in the broader, ongoing relationship.

Union Intra-organizational Factors

Education
- Explain the nature of the mutual gains bargaining process and the benefits to the membership.
- Continually educate and inform the membership of any broader change process.

Membership Support
- Cultivate ongoing membership support for the process; some results take time to develop.

Joint Process Conditions

Interests
- Focus on interests and not on positions.
- Stay away from agendas.
- Coordinate communications; explore the use of joint releases to avoid unwanted positioning.

Comprehensive Change
- Approach mutual gains bargaining as part of a broader change in the relationship; it often cannot survive in isolation.
- Use face-to-face, ongoing problem-solving approaches in bargaining.
- Emphasize ongoing problem solving during the term of the contract as well as during negotiations.

Innovate
- Craft your own approach to change.
- In changing your approach to bargaining, create your own procedural rules for engagement.
- Tailor the collective agreement to your particular needs and circumstances.

Source: Excerpted from Chaykowski and Grant, 1995. Reproduced with the permission of the Minister of Public Works and Government Services, 2000.

One serious issue that confounded many attempts to move away from adversarial bargaining was the ability of the firm to meet union concerns over job security, an issue that often arose in connection with the negotiation over issues related to increasing productivity or reducing costs (e.g., increasing workplace flexibility, downsizing). The parties felt that some issues (notably wages) ought to be handled through traditional collective bargaining, whereas others would more readily lend themselves to being channelled through mutual gains bargaining. In deciding which areas are best handled through mutual gains principles, many participants felt that starting with less contentious areas would build confidence and success.

The outcomes of MGB were mixed. Many of the participants suggested that the adversarial approach to collective bargaining may continue to be the best strategy. In some cases, the attempt to adopt MGB had actually harmed the relationship. But other participants experienced improved industrial relations outcomes and measurably better outcomes in organizational performance, including productivity, flexibility, and co-operative relations (Chaykowski and Grant, 1995).

Governments have also recognized that two of the primary "costs" associated with ineffective and conflictual negotiations include the potential damage to the union–management relationship itself and the possibility of a work stoppage due to a strike or lockout. In the case of soured labour–management relations, the effects may show up during the term of the collective agreement through lower trust and morale, an unwillingness to work together, or a reluctance to facilitate workplace change and innovation—each of which could have negative consequences for productivity. In the case of a work stoppage, there is a loss of output to an individual firm that is undesirable; moreover, losses to the economy as a whole can be substantial if strike activity becomes widespread. Even a single strike in a crucial sector—such as auto manufacturing, health care, rail transport, or ports—can have a major and often immediate impact on many other firms connected to these activities; indeed whole sectors can be affected by a single strike, as we saw with the work stoppage associated with the Vancouver dockworkers in 1999.

Some forms of government services are well established (e.g., conciliation) and continue to be mandated in some jurisdictions (i.e., before a strike is allowed); other forms of intervention are more recent and are purely voluntary.[10] In some jurisdictions, the role of government has gradually shifted over time, so that the variety and scope of the voluntary services available to labour and management to support more effective negotiations and improve the overall labour–management relationship have gradually increased. These services tend to be focused on the prevention of a breakdown in negotiations or the escalation of problems, typically by focusing on improving communication and, importantly, on substantively improving the tenor of the labour–management relationship. Figure 9.5 presents the range of services offered by the government of Newfoundland and by the federal government to unions and employers in their jurisdictions. These two examples illustrate how governments in several Canadian jurisdictions have recognized that they can play a more supportive role in the provision of "preventive services" and in the diffusion of constructive new approaches to negotiating.

FIGURE 9.5

BARGAINING-RELATED SERVICES OFFERED BY THE GOVERNMENT OF CANADA AND NEWFOUNDLAND AND LABRADOR

NEWFOUNDLAND CONCILIATION SERVICES
Conciliators provided by the province "assist the parties to reach a collective agreement and avoid a work stoppage."

NEWFOUNDLAND INTEREST-BASED NEGOTIATIONS PROGRAM
"IBN represents a shift from the traditional collective bargaining process, which is usually adversarial...the parties discuss interests rather than state positions... discussion leads to a rational problem-solving approach, which benefits both parties."

Seminars in IBN for management and union staff and members of the collective bargaining team facilitated by mediators provided by the Department of Environment and Labour.

NEWFOUNDLAND PREVENTIVE MEDIATION PROGRAM
"Encourages a shift to a more positive labour relations environment and promotes more responsible collective bargaining in the province."

Neutral consultation with a mediator

First-agreement orientation to the parties about first agreements

Mediator assistance with joint committees

Seminars in communications and joint decision making for supervisors and shop stewards

Mediation of grievances (to avoid arbitration)

Seminars on "relationship by objectives" (better conflict resolution)

GOVERNMENT OF CANADA MEDIATION SERVICES
Mediators are appointed at any time by the minister, but usually following the conciliation process, and the service "is aimed at preventing conflicts and disputes."

GOVERNMENT OF CANADA CONCILIATION SERVICES
Conciliators are appointed before a strike or lockout can legally occur and are appointed "in order to assist them [the parties] in reaching a mutually acceptable solution."

GOVERNMENT OF CANADA PREVENTIVE MEDIATION PROGRAM
Offered during the term of the collective agreement and "designed to help parties build and maintain a constructive working relationship, while providing them with a forum for improving their joint problem-solving skills."

NEGOTIATION SKILLS WORKSHOP
Workshops focusing on "interest-based negotiation" techniques

COMMITTEE EFFECTIVENESS WORKSHOP
Designed to assist the parties in creating and operating joint labour–management committees more effectively

JOINT PROBLEM-SOLVING WORKSHOP
Designed to apply interest-based approaches to ongoing workplace issues

GENERAL FACILITATION
Provided at the request of the parties

"Relationship by Objectives" Workshops
Designed to improve the working relationship of the parties

With the prospect of productivity losses or broader economic impacts beyond the players in a given strike itself, there is a substantial public interest associated with ensuring effective and successful negotiations. With this in mind, the federal as well as provincial governments typically offer a number of proactive services to the labour and management parties to assist them in developing new skills and/or approaches to the entire bargaining process with a view to facilitating better negotiations. One major advantage of the government provision of these kinds of programs is that government can act as a neutral party and can house a set of programs and offer expertise to the parties throughout the economy, thus providing a resource efficiently that is available to all interested parties.

As two examples, the federal government (through the federal mediation and conciliation service in Human Resources Development Canada) and the province of Newfoundland and Labrador (through the labour relations division of the Ministry of Environment and Labour) offer a series of voluntary programs to the parties with the goal of facilitating better labour relations. The range of these kinds of services is depicted in the chart above.

Details about bargaining-related services are available at the following sites: www.gov.nf.ca/env/labour/

labour-travail.hrdc-drhc.gc.ca/doc/fmcs-sfmc

The Outcomes of Collective Bargaining

The final component of the conceptual framework presented in Figure 9.1 is the bargaining outcomes. Generally, the outcomes of collective bargaining include both the contractual agreement as well as impacts at the organizational (i.e., micro) level. At the organizational level, the outcomes of collective bargaining include several basic elements:

1. The immediate contractual results of the collective bargaining process, including the terms and conditions of employment specified in the collective bargaining agreement (see Chapter 10 on the collective agreement).

2. Many aspects of the contract can have effects on the operating efficiency and functioning of the firm. In particular, changes in the collective agreement can have important consequences for compensation systems, productivity levels, and management practices (refer to chapter 13 on union impacts).

3. The tone and dynamics of the negotiations process itself can have a substantial "spillover" impact on the ongoing relationship between employees and managers during the term of the collective agreement. Specifically, whether the negotiations can be characterized as adversarial, bitter, and highly conflictual on the one hand, or more co-operative and positive on the other hand, can affect the conduct of management and employees during the day-to-day operations of the company, and foreshadow the degree of adversarialism at the bargaining table when the contract is due for renegotiation.

Considered across firms and unions, the results of collective bargaining can also have a range of impacts on broader socio-economic (i.e., macro level) outcomes including aggregate economic output (through strike activity and productivity) or inflation (through wage increases).

Taken together, the interrelationships presented in the framework in Figure 9.1 describe the set of factors and processes that determine collective bargaining outcomes. But the model depicted in Figure 9.1 only conveys a *static* sense of the processes. The feedback loops in Figure 9.1 (loops F1 and F2) indicate that there is a *dynamic* element to the process over time because, as noted above, the outcomes achieved in one round of collective bargaining can in turn affect the objectives of the management and union in a subsequent round. This concept of feedback loops highlights the fact that the union–management relationship is a long-term one. The way in which collective bargaining has functioned in previous stages of the relationship affects the way collective bargaining will function in the future.

CONCLUSIONS

The bargaining goals and priorities of unions and firms are being continuously shaped by a variety of environmental factors. In particular, increasingly competitive economic conditions brought on by the internationalization of markets, social pressures for workplace change, and shifts in composition of the workforce over the past 25 years have translated into new concerns and priorities. Both employers and unions have reacted to these pressures at the bargaining table, while governments have engaged in changes to the public-policy environment.

Employers have undergone significant changes in attempting to increase productivity and reduce costs. In many cases, firms have changed organizational structures, reorganized the workplace and introduced new technologies, and altered the nature of their workforces. Organizational changes have included reductions in the number of levels in hierarchies and in the size of the workforce in order to lower the costs of production. Efforts to reorganize work and introduce new technologies have often been accompanied by changes in the number of tasks performed by employees and in employee skill levels. In addition, many firms have attempted to introduce new types of employee compensation systems (e.g., profit sharing or lump-sum payments). Over the past decade, these changes have transformed the bargaining agenda of many employers across industries; for unions, they have highlighted the importance of issues related to job security, the scope of work, job descriptions and work rules, and the basis of pay. The ongoing changes have also affected bargaining structure, weakening traditional pattern bargaining arrangements and placing even more emphasis on decentralized negotiations.

Several emerging trends in the labour movement may be expected to have an important, yet somewhat complex, impact on both the structure and the process of collective bargaining in Canada. First, partly as a result of the changes in employment patterns—including shifts away from traditional areas of union strength in heavy industry toward relatively less-unionized service industries—and somewhat as a result of the ongoing downsizing of workforces across organizations, there has been an erosion of union membership which has served to weaken union strength. Many major unions have therefore begun to organize workers outside of their traditional industries (Kumar, 1993). As examples, the United Steelworkers union has organized taxi drivers and fishery workers, the United Food and Commercial Workers has organized workers in nursing homes, the Canadian Auto Workers has organized rail workers, and the Canadian Union of Public Employees has organized workers in both the airline and longshoring industries (Chaykowski and Verma, 1992: 22). In an especially contentious case, the Canadian Auto Workers recently succeeded over the United Steelworkers for the right to represent miners at the former Mine Mill local at Falconbridge Limited in Falconbridge, Ontario.

Second, there has been considerable merger activity among unions in both the private and public sectors—often among unions that might otherwise, based on their traditional composition and coverage, appear unlikely to join (Kumar, 1993). Although most mergers involve a small and a large union, a recent example of a significant merger among major unions occurred with the integration of the Communications and Electrical Workers of Canada (which is primarily in telecommunications), the Energy and Chemical Workers (organized in the energy sector), and the Paperworkers Union (traditionally in the forest products manufacturing industry) into the Communications, Energy and Paperworkers Union. Many of these types of changes have altered the membership composition of unions and are expected to have significant long-term implications for their priorities and bargaining objectives, their power, and the breadth of their activity (Kumar, 1993: 57). Therefore, by revitalizing their organizing efforts and seeking out advantageous merger possibilities, many unions have developed new bargaining priorities and strategies and have renewed their strength at the bargaining table.

Third, during the formative years of the growth of contemporary unionism, the bargaining priorities of many private-sector unions were traditionally determined by a membership base that was fairly uniform in terms of demographic characteristics (i.e., primarily white and male). While it is the case that the demographic makeup of the labour force generally, and of the labour movement specifically, has become progressively more diverse over the past several decades, the single most important change in the labour force has been the significant and ongoing increase in the labour market participation of women (see Chapter 4). Not surprisingly, a number of women's top bargaining priorities arise from the fact that women now have a strong presence in the labour market and that they want to make women's issues a priority in collective bargaining.

For many firms and unions, the difficult socio-economic challenges of the past decade have translated into increasingly adversarial negotiations as firms have often sought wage concessions, engaged in layoffs, or changed work organization in order to reduce costs and increase productivity, while unions have struggled to protect pay levels and preserve job security. For other organizations, a major challenge has been to achieve better solutions through collective bargaining. This has in turn encouraged the parties to experiment with innovative approaches such as mutual gains bargaining. However, at the close of the 1990s, the traditional approach to collective bargaining remains the centrepiece of Canadian industrial relations.

Questions

1. Identify the major factors that can have an influence on:
   a) the process of collective bargaining;
   b) the outcomes of collective bargaining.

2. Define each of the different types of collective bargaining structures.

3. What types of bargaining structures tend to be most prevalent in Canada? Explain why these types of structures predominate.

4. Indicate why pattern bargaining may be breaking down in Canada. How would you document such a trend? Would you expect it to occur in both the public and private sectors?

5. Using the concepts of bargaining target and resistance points, explain how a management and union bargaining session could lead to:
   a) a zone of potential agreement;
   b) a range of potential disagreement.

6. Explain the difference between *positions* and *interests* in collective bargaining.

7. Analyze a recently completed labour–management contract negotiation using the model in Figure 9.1.

8. Identify an alternative method or approach to collective bargaining that management and unions may use—often in an attempt to avoid strikes and to achieve a settlement. Why might management and the union prefer one method over another?

9. Consider the pros and cons of expanding the role of government in providing voluntary services to unions and employers that help to improve the conduct of negotiations and reduce conflict.

ENDNOTES

[1] The author appreciates the assistance of Bill Murnighan of the Ontario Labour Management Services at the Ministry of Labour in providing bargaining structure data, and thanks Morley Gunderson, Allen Ponak, and Caroline Weber for helpful comments on an earlier version of the paper as well as Daphne Taras for helpful suggestions on this version of the paper.

[2] Excerpts from the *National Post*, September 1, 1999 (C6); September 16, 1999 (C6); September 21, 1999 (C2); September 28, 1999 (C2); October 9, 1999 (D8); October 15, 1999 (C2). Excerpt from Canadian Press Newswire, October 3, 1999. Excerpt from *CAW/TCA Canada*. "Steelworkers Ratify Agreement With Inco Ltd." December 10, 1999. www.uswa.ca/engrel/incoratf.htm.

[3] Since the late 1980s, this bargaining structure has changed, in part because of the rise of small brewers and the merger activity in the industry.

[4] Arthur Ross, *Trade Union Policy* Copyright © 1948 Regents of the University of California © renewed 1976 Arthur Ross.

[5] The three major firms included Canada Packers, Burns, and Swift. The dominant union in meat-packing was originally the United Packinghouse Workers of America, which was succeeded by the Canadian Food and Allied Workers (CFAW); the CFAW merged with the Retail Clerks International Union in 1979 to form the United Food and Commercial Workers (Forrest, 1989: 394).

[6] This simple example assumes that the gains from lower assessments are greater than the cost of the expenditures undertaken to improve health and safety.

[7] The importance of these issues is illustrated by developments in the relationship between the Communications Workers of Canada (CWC) (which recently merged with other unions to form the Communications, Energy and Paperworkers' Union) and Bell Canada. The negotiations leading to the 1991 collective agreement led to the establishment of a high-level joint union–management task force aimed at producing a framework for broad-based workplace reorganization (Chaykowski, 1994).

[8] Each of the United Steelworkers of America, the Canadian Auto Workers, and the Communications, Energy and Paperworkers have developed a rigorous "Statement on Work Reorganization" that either specifies the conditions for union participation in employee involvement programs or guides the approach of the union to workplace change (Kumar, 1993: 93).

[9] This approach is thoroughly discussed in the book *Getting to Yes* by Roger Fisher and William Ury, which arose out of work done through the Harvard Negotiation Project at Harvard University. (See the References section.)

[10] The other characteristic that tends to distinguish the type of service provided is the level or degree of intervention.

REFERENCES

ANDERSON, J. 1989. "The Structure of Collective Bargaining in Canada," in *Union–Management Relations In Canada*, 2nd Edition, edited by J. Anderson, M. Gunderson, and A. Ponak. Don Mills: Addison-Wesley.

BACHARACH, S. and E. LAWLER. 1981. *Bargaining: Power, Tactics, and Outcomes*. San Francisco: Jossey-Bass.

CARTER, Donald. 1993. "The Changing Face of Labour Law." Address to the Annual Spring Industrial Relations Seminar, Queen's University (May 10), mimeo.

CHAMBERLAIN, N. W. and J. W. KUHN. 1986. *Collective Bargaining*, 3rd Edition. New York, NY: McGraw-Hill Book Company.

CHAYKOWSKI, R. P. 1990. "Union and Firm Preferences for Bargaining Outcomes in the Private Sector." *Relations industrielles/Industrial Relations*, 45, no. 2, pp. 326–355.

———. 1994. "Innovation and Cooperation in Canadian Industrial Relations." Paper Prepared for the Canada–United States–Mexico Conference on Labor Law and Industrial Relations. Washington, DC (September 19–20).

CHAYKOWSKI, R. P. and M. GRANT. 1995. "From Traditional to Mutual Gains Bargaining." *Collective Bargaining Review*. Ottawa ON: Human Resources Development Canada (May), pp. 79–88.

CHAYKOWSKI, R. P. and A. VERMA. 1992. "Adjustment and Restructuring in Canadian Industrial Relations," in *Industrial Relations in Canadian Industry*, edited by R. Chaykowski and A. Verma. Toronto, ON: Holt, Rinehart and Winston.

DELANEY, J. and D. SOCKELL. 1989. "The Mandatory-Permissive Distinction and Collective Bargaining Outcomes." *Industrial and Labor Relations Review*, 42, no. 4, pp. 566–583.

FISHER, E. G. and A. KONDRA. 1992. "Canada's Airlines: Recent Turbulence and Changing Flight Plans," in *Industrial Relations in Canadian Industry*, edited by R. Chaykowski and A. Verma. Toronto, ON: Holt, Rinehart and Winston.

FISHER, R. 1994. "Deter, Compel, or Negotiate?" *Negotiation Journal*, 10, no. 1, pp. 17–32.

FISHER, R. and W. URY. 1983. *Getting to Yes: Negotiating Agreement Without Giving In*. New York, NY: Penguin Books.

FISHER, R., W. URY, and B. PATTON. 1991. *Getting to Yes: Negotiating an Agreement Without Giving In*, 2nd Edition. New York: Houghton Mifflin Company.

FORREST, A. 1989. "The Rise and Fall of National Bargaining in the Canadian Meat-Packing Industry." *Relations industrielles/Industrial Relations*, 44, no. 2, pp. 393–406.

FRIEDMAN, R. 1994. "Missing Ingredients in Mutual Gains Bargaining Theory." *Negotiation Journal* (July), pp. 265–280.

HECKSCHER, C. and L. HALL. 1994. "Mutual Gains and Beyond: Two Levels of Intervention." *Negotiation Journal* (July), pp. 235–248.

HUNTER, L. W. and R. K. McKERSIE. 1992. "Can *Mutual Gains* Training Change Labour-Management Relationships?" *Negotiation Journal*, 8, no. 4, pp. 319–330.

KATZ, H. 1993. "The Decentralization of Collective Bargaining: A Literature Review and Comparative Analysis." *Industrial and Labor Relations Review*, 47, no. 1 (October), pp. l3–22.

KUMAR, P. 1993. *From Uniformity To Divergence: Industrial Relations in Canada and the United States*. Kingston, ON: Queen's University IRC Press.

KUMAR P. and N. MELTZ. 1992. "Industrial Relations in the Canadian Automobile Industry," in *Industrial Relations in Canadian Industry*, edited by R. Chaykowski and A. Verma. Toronto, ON: Holt, Rinehart and Winston.

LABOUR CANADA. 1993. *Industrial Relations Legislation in Canada*. Ottawa, ON: Labour Canada.

ROSE, J. 1992. "Industrial Relations in the Construction Industry in the 1980s," in *Industrial Relations in Canadian Industry*, edited by R. Chaykowski and A. Verma. Toronto, ON: Holt, Rinehart and Winston.

ROSS, A. M. 1948. *Trade Union Wage Policy*. Berkeley: University of California Press.

SUSSKIND, L. E. and E. M. LANDRY. 1991. "Implementing a Mutual Gains Approach to Collective Bargaining." *Negotiation Journal*, 7, no. 1 (January), pp. 5–10.

VERMA, A. and R. CHAYKOWSKI. 1999. *Contract and Commitment: Employment Relations in the New Economy*. Kingston, ON: IRC Press.

VERMA, A. and P. WARRIAN. 1992. "Industrial Relations in the Canadian Steel Industry," in *Industrial Relations in Canadian Industry*, edited by R. Chaykowski and A. Verma. Toronto, ON: Holt, Rinehart and Winston.

VERMA, A. and J. WEILER. 1992. "Industrial Relations in the Canadian Telephone Industry," in *Industrial Relations in Canadian Industry*, edited by R. Chaykowski and A. Verma. Toronto, ON: Holt, Rinehart and Winston.

WALTON, R. E. and R. B. McKERSIE. 1991. *A Behavioral Theory of Labor Negotiations: An Analysis of a Social Interaction System*, 2nd Edition. Ithaca, NY: ILR Press.

CHAPTER 10

The Collective Agreement

Anthony Giles and Akivah Starkman[1]

In 1994, Asea Brown Boveri announced that, as part of a rationalization drive across its North American operations, it planned to close its industrial boiler plant in Sherbrooke, Quebec. The closure would mean layoffs for some 400 employees. Shortly afterwards, the company revealed that it would open a new, smaller plant in Hull, Quebec, which would manufacture some of the products previously produced in Sherbrooke.

At the same time, the company told its union that it would grant it recognition in the new plant, but that it wanted to select which employees would be offered a job in the Hull plant and that it wished to make a number of significant changes to the existing collective agreement. For example, the 67 different job classifications in the Sherbrooke plant were cut down to just 2 classifications in the Hull operation. Wage rates were also simplified, with all employees receiving the same hourly rate irrespective of their seniority, experience, or work tasks. In addition, existing rules requiring that layoffs and transfers of employees be done according to seniority were abolished, and all of the employees transferred to the

> Hull plant saw their seniority set back to zero for most purposes. Finally, employees were given a range of new responsibilities in the areas of quality control and training of new employees; and in place of the previous system in which each employee worked alone at a single post, they were now expected to work in teams and to rotate jobs.

Although the exact circumstances surrounding this case were unique, the company's desire to revamp the collective agreement to promote a more flexible style of work organization is representative of a wider trend in Canadian industrial relations. In exploring the content of collective agreements, this chapter will help explain how the rules in those agreements have grown over the years, how they play a vital role in protecting the rights of employees, and why many managers consider them to be a significant constraint.

The mass media usually focus attention on the most dramatic activities of unions and employers—midnight negotiations, nationwide strikes, picket line incidents, and other highly visible events. Less well understood is the tangible result of all the sound and fury that accompanies negotiations—the collective agreement. For unionized workers, "the agreement" (or "the contract") is an important factor shaping their work lives: Stewards, elected union officers, and paid union officials spend much of their time ensuring that management lives up to its side of the agreement; supervisors and human resource managers closely monitor the application of the agreement; and labour arbitrators settle grievances over the interpretation of provisions in the agreement. In short, for those involved in industrial relations on a day-to-day basis, the collective agreement is a matter of critical concern.

THE EVOLUTION OF THE COLLECTIVE AGREEMENT

Before the Second World War, most collective agreements in Canada were very brief and simple (see Exhibit 10.1). Although the issues covered by these early agreements still figure prominently in union–management relations, most modern collective agreements are much longer, more complex, and cover a wider range of issues. In fact, collective agreements in this country (and in the United States) are also longer, broader, and more detailed than are contracts in most other advanced capitalist societies. These distinctive characteristics of Canadian collective agreements emerged as one part of a broader restructuring of industrial relations in the 1940s (MacDowell, 1978).

Early craft unions, like the Carpenters, were often able to defend their interests by exercising control over the supply of skilled labour and instituting a variety of work rules. However, unskilled and semi-skilled workers who flocked into industrial unions in the 1930s and 1940s were in a different position. Lacking uniform skills, workers in industrial unions concentrated on obtaining their goals through negotiations with individual employers. In addition, the political weakness of the Canadian labour movement meant that

EXHIBIT 10.1

COLLECTIVE AGREEMENTS 100 YEARS AGO

In 1901, when Local 713 of the Carpenters Union reached an agreement with contractors in Niagara Falls, Ontario, the contract contained only eight brief clauses:

1. The rate of wages for journeymen carpenters and joiners shall be 25 cents per hour.

2. The hours of work shall be nine (9) hours per day.

3. The rate of pay for legal holidays and overtime shall be time and one-half, except for mill hands.

4. No union man shall take any kind of lump work or sub-contract from a carpenter-contractor.

5. If a contractor applies to the union for men and the union cannot supply them, the contractor can hire any men he likes at any rate of wages, but these men must be discharged before any union man is laid off.

6. Planing mill proprietors shall be bound by these promises only as far as they apply to carpenters and bench hands.

7. Pay days shall be on Saturdays, and the contractor shall pay the men their wages on the job where they are working.

8. The agreement shall go into effect on May 1, 1901, and shall continue for one year.

Source: C. H. Curtis. *The Development and Enforcement of the Collective Agreement* (Kingston: Industrial Relations Centre, Queen's University, 1966), p. 3.

they had to look to the negotiating process as the principal means of advancing their members' interests. They could not act like unions in many European countries, where government legislation played a more important role in regulating the employment relationship.

Even more important than the nature of unionism, however, were the strategies and policies pursued by employers and the government, particularly those adopted in response to the industrial and political unrest of the 1940s. Paradoxically, the fierce resistance of Canadian employers to their employees' attempts to unionize was (and, to a degree, still is) a major cause of the growth of detailed collective agreements. Because employers chose to resist unionization, "unions were generally forced to seek recognition on a plant-by-plant basis, and the process of recognition took on the characteristic of a battle for the hearts and minds of the workers involved. Where the union won, it was typically powerful enough to require management to sign a collective agreement that, over time, became increasingly elaborate" (Adams, 1995: 502). Furthermore, once required to negotiate with a union, most employers tend to seek ways to restrict the workplace activities of unions, to reduce the number of issues subject to union influence, and to adhere to collective agreements in a narrowly legalistic manner, all of which adds to the formality of agreements.

This strategy of limiting the impact of industrial conflict has been abetted by state policy and by the way collective agreements have come to be interpreted by arbitrators. Since 1944, most jurisdictions in Canada have required collective agreements to be binding for periods of no less than one year, and have banned work stoppages during the life of the agreement. Thus, unlike countries where agreements can be renegotiated whenever one side or the other feels some change is warranted, Canadian management and union negotiators must strive for collective agreements that are comprehensive and detailed. Moreover, because most arbitrators hold that management retains authority over any matter not explicitly mentioned in the collective agreement, unions are compelled to channel their concerns into the negotiating process, rather than deal with management more informally. Last, because grievance arbitration (the approved method of resolving disputes during the term of the agreement) is so legalistic, contract language has to be drafted with great care.

Collective agreements have also been influenced by legal developments in another way. General labour statutes, human rights legislation, occupational health and safety acts, and employment standards laws all set out a number of requirements to which the collective agreement must conform. For example, it is illegal to discriminate against employees on a number of specific grounds including age, sex, religion, and disability; in most provinces joint safety committees must be established; and employees must be provided a day off with pay on certain statutory holidays.

The parties have often attempted to incorporate such legal requirements explicitly into the collective agreement, even though this is not strictly necessary (i.e., even if a contract has no anti-discrimination clause, it is still illegal to discriminate). There are several reasons for including these kinds of legal requirements in the agreement. First, the contract provisions are a good way of educating those bound by the contract, employees and management alike, about their legal obligations. Second, through negotiation the parties are able to specify the manner in which the legal requirements might be made to best fit their specific needs (e.g., the composition of a safety committee or what happens when some employees must work on a statutory holiday). Third, by including certain legal requirements in the collective agreement, the issue becomes subject to the grievance procedure, which is usually a speedier and less expensive way to settle problems than through a human rights tribunal or the courts. For all these reasons, the collective agreement plays a central role in Canadian labour–management relations. Still, it must not be forgotten that relationships in the workplace are not fully regulated by formal agreements. In nonunion settings, of course, employment relations are governed by the individual contract of employment and employment legislation. Although some nonunion organizations follow employment policies that are closely modelled on collective agreements, often in an attempt to dissuade their employees from unionizing, individual employees in such workplaces are usually powerless to win improvements in their terms and conditions of employment in the face of employer recalcitrance. Indeed, at their heart, collective agreements reflect a transformation of this relationship into one of collective regulation of employment (see Exhibit 10.2).

Exhibit 10.2

What Makes Canada Unique?

North American collective agreements differ from collective agreements in many other countries in a number of ways:

- Most are negotiated at the level of the establishment and not the industry or regional level.
- They are generally longer and more complex.
- They cover a wider range of issues.

Even though Canadian agreements are often very similar to American agreements, there are some differences:

- Canadian collective agreements commonly contain union security clauses, which are illegal in many US states.
- By law, work stoppages are banned during the term of Canadian collective agreements and grievance arbitration must be used instead; in the US, it is up to the parties to determine these issues for themselves.

The Collective Agreement: An Overview

Anyone who leafs through a collective agreement for the first time finds a bewildering array of clauses, subclauses, appendices, schedules, letters of intent, and other sections, many with mysteriously phrased names (see Exhibit 10.3). Collective agreements are sometimes so complex and legalistic that workers and supervisors barely understand their contents and need to rely on experienced shop stewards, union business agents, and specialized managers. (In fact, one test of the effectiveness of a collective agreement in regulating relationships at the workplace is how familiar workers and supervisors are with its contents. If the union has a strong presence, it is not unusual to see workers keeping a copy of the agreement close at hand and referring to it extensively during arguments with management.) For the student of collective agreements, matters are made worse by the fact that the thousands of collective agreements in effect in Canada at any one time differ from each other quite substantially. After all, each agreement is the product of a unique negotiating relationship, and each is amended many times as the two sides renegotiate the terms and conditions of employment.

Nevertheless, most collective agreements have some basic similarities, as well as a common structure that underlies their many complexities and outward variations. Like most legal contracts, collective agreements are divided into articles (also called sections or clauses), which are usually further divided into subclauses. Almost all collective agreements begin with an article (or a "preamble") explaining the purpose of the agreement. If the agreement is complex, a list of definitions may also appear near the beginning of the document. Most agreements then include a number of clauses that define and regulate the relationship between the union and the employer—clauses setting out the definition of the bargaining unit, outlining management rights and union security, establishing a grievance arbitration procedure, and so on.

EXHIBIT 10.3

TABLE OF CONTENTS OF A TYPICAL COLLECTIVE AGREEMENT

Purpose of Agreement

1. Recognition
2. Interpretation
3. Management Rights
4. Union Representatives
5. No Discrimination
6. Union Dues and Membership
7. Absence for Union Business
8. Union Education Fund
9. Automation
10. Safety and Health
11. Seniority
12. Layoff and Recall
13. Discharge and Discipline
14. Grievance Procedure
15. Arbitration
16. Hours of Work
17. Shift Transfers
18. Overtime
19. Reassignments
20. Classification of Employees

21. Remuneration Systems
22. Productivity Improvement Plan
23. Attendance Improvement Formula
24. Paid Statutory Holidays
25. Vacations with Pay
26. Bereavement Leave
27. Court Duty—Witness or Juror
28. Out-of-Town Assignments
29. Special Leaves
30. Group Insurance
31. Retirement Plans
32. Memorandums of Agreement
33. Entire Agreement
34. Duration

Appendix A—Memorandums of Agreement

Appendix B—Letters of Intent

Appendix C—Forms

Numerical list of classifications

Source: Collective Agreement between Bombardier Inc./Canadair and The International Association of Machinists and Aerospace Workers, Montreal Aircraft Lodge 712, May 10, 1997 to November 30, 2001.

The second major group of articles in the agreement are those specifying hours of work and details of compensation. Here one finds articles that define the normal length of the work day, rules about overtime, rights to time off with and without pay, wage schedules covering different classifications of employees, various wage premiums (such as shift bonuses), and other matters that together constitute what is called the wage-effort bargain.

A third group of clauses in collective agreements deal with how the organization's internal labour market and work system will be operated. For example, agreements often include rules governing how promotions are to be made, how technological changes are to be instituted, how layoffs are to be handled, and so on. Although articles dealing with these matters are not necessarily grouped together in the agreement, they have in common the function of controlling individual and group rights with respect to the allocation of tasks and job opportunities.

The fourth group of clauses typically found in agreements (again not necessarily all in one place) are those that set out conditions with respect to the physical work environment (such as safety rules), behaviour in the workplace (for example, rules on discipline), and the broader "human rights" of employees that must be respected by all of the parties to the agreement.

Exhibit 10.4

Tips on Drafting the Collective Agreement

- Use plain language so that workers and supervisors can understand and work with the provisions in the agreement.
- Avoid ambiguous language that may create difficulties of interpretation later.
- Use terms consistently throughout the agreement.
- Use non-sexist language.
- Pay attention to the relationship between the different clauses, especially when renegotiating part of an agreement that may have implications for other provisions.
- Remember that the agreement must respect legislation regarding employment standards and human rights. Collectively negotiated clauses that do not conform to such legislation are unenforceable.
- When an agreement is reached after the previous agreement has expired, be careful to specify which provisions of the new agreement are retroactive.
- Structure the agreement in a logical way by putting all related clauses together, and use headings, subheadings, a table of contents, and an index to allow workers and supervisors to find their way around the document.
- Put lengthy details in appendices, but remember to refer to them in the body of the agreement as being considered part of the agreement.

Source: Sack and Poskanzer, 1996.

The collective agreement usually concludes with a clause that specifies the duration of the agreement, followed by the signatures of the employer and union representatives. Many agreements also include appendices containing details of particular arrangements considered too lengthy or complex to include in the body of the agreement (such as wage schedules). Lastly, attached to some agreements are letters of understanding, memoranda of agreement, or other supplementary documents; depending on the wording, these may be considered part of the agreement, or they may be unenforceable promises made by one side or the other. Exhibit 10.4 contains suggestions on how to draft a collective agreement.

The remainder of this chapter discusses the four main groups of articles just outlined. Because it would be impossible to discuss every conceivable type of clause in each of the four categories, the emphasis is on types of clauses that are common, generally significant, or of special contemporary relevance.

THE UNION–MANAGEMENT RELATIONSHIP AND THE CONTROL OF CONFLICT

Inherent in the very idea of a collective agreement is the existence of a relationship between an employer and a group of employees acting collectively through a union. Thus, an agreement does more than define the terms and conditions of employment; it establishes and regulates a relationship between two organizations, a process that normally entails conflict over the division of authority and the definition of rights and responsibilities. In practice, the contours of the union–management relationship are defined by three central features of collective agreements: the extent to which joint decision making replaces unilateral managerial authority, the status and role accorded to the union, and the manner in which disagreements and disputes that arise during the life of the agreement are handled.

Management Rights

Most collective agreements contain a *management rights* clause, which acknowledges the employer's right to manage the establishment, subject to other provisions in the collective agreement (see Exhibit 10.5). To understand the function and significance of the management rights clause, we first need to consider the wider issue of authority in the unionized workplace.

In a nonunion workplace, employers enjoy wide discretion in managing the organization and in determining the terms and conditions of employment, working conditions, and the organization of work. Legislated employment standards must be observed, of course, and some individual employees or small groups, particularly those who possess a special skill, may have the leverage to win improvements in their employment conditions. But, on the whole, managers are entitled to run their organizations pretty much as they see fit.

However, when employees unionize, unilateral management control is replaced, to some extent at least, by bilateral control. Indeed, the collective agreement as a whole represents a series of compromises and joint decisions over a range of issues affecting the employees. But although it is clear that the issues spelled out in a collective agreement are no longer the sole prerogative of management, what about issues not dealt with explicitly in the agreement? This question has given rise to considerable controversy over the years.

The traditional view—called the *residual* (or *reserved*) *rights theory*—is that employers retain complete control over any issue not dealt with in the collective agreements. This interpretation has been challenged, not only by labour leaders but also by some industrial relations scholars and arbitrators. For instance, it has been argued that the advent of collective bargaining fundamentally alters the relationship between labour and management by making them equal partners. On this view, it is therefore unfair to give one of the parties all of the rights at the outset and to require the other to whittle away at them. Instead, where a collective agreement is silent on a particular disputed issue, consideration should be given to the whole agreement and to the wider relationship between the parties, or there should even be an obligation to negotiate a joint solution.

Critics of the residual rights theory have not prevailed, however, and managerial authority over issues and decisions not specifically governed by the collective agreement remains largely unimpaired. The major exceptions are cases where it can be shown that, in exercising its rights under the collective agreement, management acted in bad faith, in an arbitrary or discriminatory manner, or for the primary purpose of subverting the collective bargaining relationship (Fisher and Sherwood, 1984).

EXHIBIT 10.5

MANAGEMENT RIGHTS CLAUSES

A "general" management rights clause:

MANAGEMENT RIGHTS

The Corporation has the exclusive right to manage its plants and offices and direct its affairs and work forces, except as limited by the terms of this Agreement and any Memorandums, Letter Agreements, or Supplementary Agreements that by their terms modify this Agreement.

Source: Agreement between Chrysler Canada Ltd. and the Canadian Auto Workers' Union, Production and Maintenance (September 15, 1996).

A "detailed" management rights clause:

MANAGEMENT'S RIGHTS AND FUNCTIONS

12.01 The management of the Company and the direction of the working force, including the right to plan, direct and control store operations, to maintain the discipline and efficiency of the employees and to require employees to observe Company rules and regulations; to hire; lay off or assign employees' working hours; transfer; promote; demote; discipline, suspend or discharge employees for proper cause, are to be the sole right and function of the management.

12.02 The Company shall be the sole judge as to the merchandise to be handled in its stores.

12.03 The foregoing enumeration of management's rights shall not be deemed to exclude other functions not specifically set forth. The management, therefore, retains all rights not otherwise specifically covered in this Agreement.

12.04 The exercise of the foregoing rights shall not alter any of the specific provisions of this Agreement.

Source: Section 12, "Management Rights and Functions," taken from Agreement between United Food Commercial Workers Union, Local 832, and Safeway, May 17, 1998 to November 10, 2001. Reprinted with permission.

But this leaves us with something of a puzzle: If the residual rights approach is so deeply entrenched, why bother to include a management rights clause at all? Even if there is no management rights clause, arbitrators still apply the rule that any issue not dealt with in the collective agreement remains within the prerogative of the employer. Furthermore, most experts admit that the exact wording of the management rights clause only rarely has any importance in determining the outcome of grievances or arbitration cases.

One reason why so many agreements include a management rights clause is that the practice was established in the years during which there still was debate and uncertainty over the issue, a tradition that simply continued long after the debate was settled. Second, since arbitral principles are not cast in stone, the continued inclusion of such clauses may simply reflect management's reluctance to leave itself vulnerable should arbitrators' thinking change. In addition, it has been suggested that management rights clauses are included as a sort of psychological concession to employers, who do not otherwise gain very much in a collective agreement, or as a means of reminding employees that the employer continues to possess a wide range of unilateral rights (Hébert, 1992: 145).

Two different types of management rights clauses are typically found in collective agreements. Some employers prefer a "general" clause that simply affirms the principle of residual rights. Other employers prefer a clause that spells out their rights in some detail, though they are usually careful to also include a phrase making clear that the list is not exhaustive. For unions, the following is crucial: 1) that the clause make clear that the provisions of the collective agreement take precedence over any general management rights; 2) that any reference to management's right to discipline employees be limited to cases where there is "just cause"; and 3) that, if possible, the clause should include a more general statement that the exercise of management rights must be consistent with the spirit of the collective agreement and be applied in a reasonable manner.

Thus, although the management rights clause is sometimes considered to be a mere formality, its significance lies in the underlying issues that it expresses. According to two labour lawyers, the clause is "a battleground for the competing interests of the parties: management wants to assure maximum flexibility by including a clause giving it wide powers as well as specific authority; the union wishes to limit management's discretion by resisting a management rights clause altogether or by narrowing it as much as possible" (Sack and Poskanzer, 1996: 8-5).

Union Rights and Security

When a union becomes the certified bargaining agent for a group of employees, it is said to have been "recognized" by the employer. Most collective agreements contain a clause (often simply repeating the certifying agency's definition of the bargaining unit) making this recognition explicit and defining which employees are members of the unit.

Certain categories of employees are commonly excluded from the bargaining unit, for example, supervisors, security personnel, and employees who have access to confidential information regarding labour relations. More significant is the exclusion of part-time, casual, and temporary employees. From the employer's point of view, excluding such employees from the coverage of the collective agreement is often advantageous because it is thereby possible to pay them at lower rates than unionized full-time workers, to avoid providing them with employee benefits, and more generally to treat them as a flexible, reserve labour force with few job rights. In the past, unions often tacitly or overtly approved of this strategy, not least because it provided full-time, male workers with greater employment security and higher wages, leaving the predominantly female and young peripheral labour force as an inexpensive cushion against risk.

The dramatic growth in recent years of part-time and other "atypical" forms of employment, as well as the expansion of the services sector in which such jobs are concentrated, has led unions to pay more attention to improving collective agreement provisions for these workers. As Figure 10.1 shows, the number of collective agreements that contain provisions regarding part-time workers has increased substantially. Of the various part-time issues that might be dealt with in a collective agreement, seniority appears to be a central preoccupation; other important issues include the hours of work of part-time employees and various types of leave provisions.

In any event, the struggle for real recognition and stability does not end with the recognition clause. First, a union is by nature external to the employing organization. Although the union's members are employees of the organization, the union itself has a separate existence and therefore enjoys no automatic status as a part of the organization. Second, many Canadian employers are hostile to unionism, which means that union members and officials must work continuously to ensure that management respects the role of the union. Third, like any other organization, unions need a degree of institutional stability. Fourth, under existing Canadian labour laws, the collective agreement covers all members of the bargaining unit, not just union members, which means that the union works on behalf of nonunion employees as well as its own members.

For these reasons, unionized employees normally attempt to negotiate a variety of provisions that allow their union to make its presence felt in the workplace and give it a degree of security. For example, the right of the union to appoint shop stewards (whose duties include helping workers prepare and present grievances) stems from the collective agreement. Sometimes the agreement specifies how many stewards are to be appointed, and it usually spells out the circumstances under which they and other union officials may leave their workstations to attend to union business.

The most controversial aspect of union attempts to establish a degree of stability centres on the interrelated issues of union security and the payment of union dues. A variety of types of union security clauses are found in collective agreements (see Exhibit 10.6). The *closed shop* is a system under which an employer agrees to hire and retain only those workers who are members of the union. A *union shop* clause requires that all employees join the union within a specified period of time after having been hired. A *modified union shop* means that, at the time the collective agreement is signed (or, in some cases, the initial certification), the current employees are not obliged to join the union, but all employees hired subsequently must join. *Maintenance of membership* clauses require that employees who have joined the union (and those who join in the future) must remain in the union. *Rand formula* clauses do not impose any requirements regarding union membership, but they do require all members of the bargaining unit,

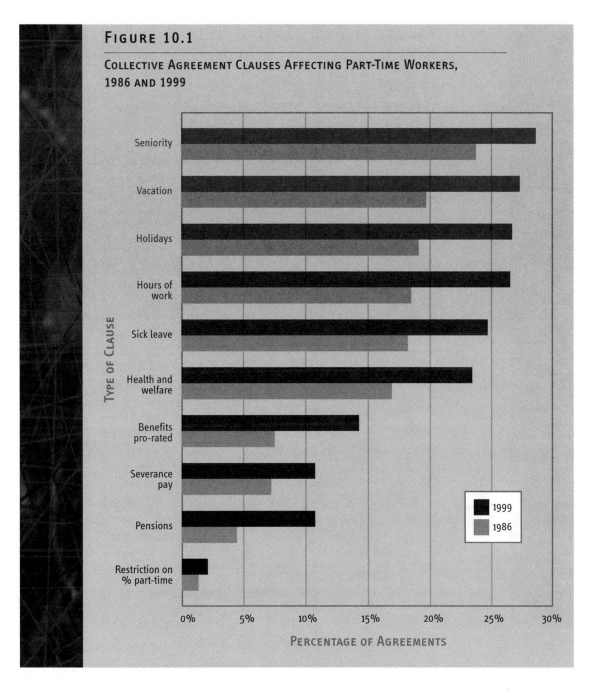

FIGURE 10.1

COLLECTIVE AGREEMENT CLAUSES AFFECTING PART-TIME WORKERS, 1986 AND 1999

whether or not they are union members, to pay union dues. Some Rand formula clauses exempt certain workers from this requirement (for example, if they have religious objections to paying union dues) or permit nonunion members to stipulate that their dues be donated to a charity instead of going to the union. If unions are unable to convince their employer to agree to any form of union security, this is known as the *open shop*.

Exhibit 10.6

Union Security Clauses

A *closed shop* clause:

(4.01) (a)   The Employer agrees to employ only members in good standing of the Union for the performance of all work covered by this Agreement. All employees shall present to the Employer a referral slip, either in person or by facsimile transmission, from the Union prior to commencing employment.

Source: Agreement between the Utility Contractors' Association of Ontario Incorporated and The Labourers' International Union of North America, Ontario Provincial District Council, and its affiliated Local Unions (May, 1998).

A *union shop* clause:

(IV, 2)   All employees in the employment of the Company shall, as a condition of continued employment, maintain membership in good standing in the Union. New employees shall, as a condition of continued employment, become members of the Union thirty (30) days after becoming employed by the Company.

Source: Labour Agreement between MacMillan Bloedel Limited, Powell River Division and Local 76 of the Communications, Energy and Paperworkers Union of Canada (1994–1997).

A *Rand formula* clause:

(10.01)   Subject to the provisions of this Article, the Employer will, as a condition of employment, deduct an amount equal to the monthly membership dues from the monthly pay of all employees in the bargaining unit....

(10.04)   An employee who satisfies the Employer ... that he or she is a member of a religious organization whose doctrine prevents him or her as a matter of conscience from making financial contributions to an employee organization and that he or she will make contributions to a charitable organization...equal to dues, shall not be subject to this Article....

Source: Agreement between the Treasury Board of Canada and the Social Science Employees Association, Social Science Support Group (Expiry June 21, 1999).

The vast majority of major collective agreements in Canada provide for some degree of union security (Figure 10.2). About half of these agreements, because they contain only a Rand formula or no union security provision at all, do not impose any union membership requirements on employees. This proportion has remained virtually unchanged since the mid-1980s. Of the half that do impose some form of requirement, the union shop and the modified union shop continue to predominate. Agreements stipulating a closed shop have grown slightly since the mid-1980s but still represent fewer than 10 percent of all agreements.

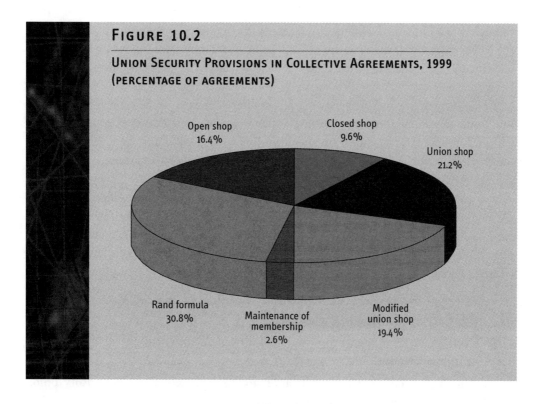

FIGURE 10.2

UNION SECURITY PROVISIONS IN COLLECTIVE AGREEMENTS, 1999 (PERCENTAGE OF AGREEMENTS)

Open shop 16.4%

Closed shop 9.6%

Union shop 21.2%

Rand formula 30.8%

Maintenance of membership 2.6%

Modified union shop 19.4%

Related to the question of union security is the collection of union dues. *Checkoff* refers to the practice whereby employers agree to deduct union dues from the employees' pay on behalf of the union. The checkoff of union dues is partly a form of security and partly a bookkeeping device to provide the union with a regular cash flow and to protect it against loss of dues (and members) through inadvertence or recalcitrance. The vast majority of collective agreements require some form of checkoff, either for all union members or, where there is a Rand formula, for all employees in the bargaining unit.

The predominance of the Rand formula is related to the wider controversies that swirl around the issues of union security and dues checkoff. On one side, many employers claim that union security clauses infringe upon the rights and freedom of individual workers who may not wish to join a union. On the other side, unions argue that the absence of such clauses can easily undermine their effectiveness by allowing nonunion workers to remain on the job while union workers are out on strike. They also contend that such clauses are needed to discourage "free riders"—those workers who, as members of the bargaining unit, are legally entitled to the benefits and protections negotiated by the union, but who might be tempted to avoid their share of the costs and sacrifices by not joining. The Rand formula was devised as a compromise between these two positions; it prevents nonunion workers from taking a "free ride" but does not entail compulsory unionism.

In 21 American states, legislation prohibits unions and employers from negotiating various types of union security provisions, including the closed shop, the union shop, and dues checkoff. These acts are called "right-to-work" legislation and reflect the view that the right of an individual employee to refuse to join a union or pay union dues outweighs the collective rights of the majority of workers in a bargaining unit to ensure institutional security and a fair sharing of the costs entailed in negotiating and administering the collective agreement.

In Canada, right-to-work legislation has not been adopted. In fact, most jurisdictions in Canada require that, at a minimum, the Rand formula be included in collective agreements. Employers and unions are therefore free to negotiate any provision regarding union membership that they wish. Nonetheless, there have been occasional calls to adopt right-to-work legislation in our country.

For example, in the mid-1990s the Alberta government asked the Alberta Economic Development Authority to conduct a study into the possibility of introducing right-to-work legislation in that province. The committee assigned to study the question recommended against the adoption of right-to-work legislation, citing the following reasons (Alberta Economic Development Authority, 1995):

- That right-to-work legislation would not significantly improve Alberta's economic performance or competitive position.
- That right-to-work legislation "may well disrupt Alberta's currently strong and stable labour relations."
- That there is considerable justification to the argument that compulsory union dues are a reasonable means of preventing "free riders."

Workplace Conflict and the Contract

Although collective agreements establish the terms and conditions of employment for a set period, there remain numerous sources of tension that may spark disputes at any time. Unanticipated changes in market conditions may lead to calls for adjustments, such as wage increases if inflation suddenly surges, or wage reductions or other concessions if profitability drops. Similarly, issues not covered by the agreement may suddenly emerge; an example is technological change in the workplace that threatens jobs or disturbs established patterns of pay. More generally, the day-to-day management of work is a permanent source of potential conflict, since employees and their managers do not necessarily see eye to eye on such issues as the pace of work, the style of supervision, and adequate working conditions. Finally, the collective agreement itself may give rise to disputes, since its meaning may not always be clear and its application in particular circumstances may be disputed. For all these reasons, collective agreements usually contain provisions for dealing with conflict.

No-Strike Clause

One of the chief mechanisms for regulating conflict is the *no-strike clause*, in which the parties agree that there shall be no strikes or lockouts during the life of the collective agreement, and instead, that they will use the dispute resolution procedures available under the agreement, e.g., third-party arbitration.

That a majority of collective agreements in Canada contain such a clause is hardly surprising since Canadian labour law generally prohibits the use of strikes or lockouts while the contract is in effect. The legal and contractual prohibitions on the use of work stoppages are not always effective, however, and mid-contract strikes are not uncommon in Canada (see Chapter 11). Because arbitrators tend to look askance at such strikes and have proved willing to assess damages against unions that encourage or condone them, these clauses play an important role in forcing union leaders to restrain their own members, to bring an end to mid-contract strikes, or, at least, to remain uninvolved, thus depriving the strikers of legitimacy and organizational support. In addition, employers can use the threat of applying these clauses as leverage to end the strike on terms that are unfavourable to the strikers (Wells, 1986). Thus, even if no-strike clauses do not actually prevent conflict from breaking out into the open during the life of an agreement, they play an important role in reducing its incidence and effectiveness.

Grievance Arbitration

A second conflict regulation mechanism, found in virtually every collective agreement in Canada, is the *grievance arbitration procedure*. Grievance arbitration procedures provide a means through which any differences between the parties arising from the application, interpretation, administration, or alleged violation of the collective agreement may be settled. Collective agreements usually require that a grievance be taken first to the immediate supervisor. If the grievance is not resolved there, it may be appealed to one or more higher levels of management. If a settlement still does not occur, collective agreements almost always provide for binding settlement by an outside arbitrator or arbitration board (see Chapter 12 for a full treatment of this subject).

For our purposes, it is important to stress that such procedures became required in law at the same time that industrial conflict during the collective agreement was banned; indeed, the requirement that grievance arbitration procedures be included in collective agreements was an attempt to provide workers and unions with a method of dealing with problems while they were legally prevented from exerting pressure through a strike. Grievance arbitration is not a full substitute, since the disputes that are technically arbitrable include only those covered by the collective agreement; moreover, the rule that workers must usually "obey now, grieve later" means that management's decisions must be followed when they are issued, while the aggrieved employee can only complain through the sometimes cumbersome and lengthy grievance procedure. In practice, of course, workers and unions can bring their concerns to the attention of management by using a range of informal tactics, including slowdowns, work-to-rule campaigns, and even sabotage. It is also common for stewards and supervisors to reach informal agreements in response to grievances that are not technically arbitrable.

Labour–Management Committees

Collective agreements sometimes include a special method of raising and discussing non-contractual issues related to labour–management relations—the *labour–management committee.* Plant-level or firm-level labour–management committees, comprised of representatives from both labour and management, can serve as a forum to discuss matters of mutual interest. These can include health and safety, alcohol and drug abuse, working conditions, work schedules, training and retraining, technological changes, quality and efficiency, reduction of waste, and any other issue, depending on the particular situation.

The growth of labour–management committees in recent years has been significant. In the mid-1980s, 38 percent of major collective agreements (covering about 40 percent of workers) provided for such a committee; by 1999, the number had risen to almost 70 percent of agreements (covering more than 75 percent of employees). The effectiveness of labour–management committees varies considerably, often reflecting the nature of the relationship between the parties. Decisions or recommendations normally require mutual agreement. Participation on such committees does allow workers and their unions an opportunity to influence management decisions, but in the absence of mutual agreement, management's decisions prevail.

Joint-Governance Agreements

Another mechanism designed to regulate the relationship between labour and management is the *joint-governance agreement* (Verma and Cutcher-Gershenfeld, 1993). These agreements, which tend to last between four and six years (instead of the more usual two or three), typically involve a trade-off whereby employers secure concessions designed to reduce labour costs and increase productivity, in return for which unions gain greater job security and more involvement in organizational decision making. In some of these agreements, mechanisms are established (like joint committees) that allow what is in effect "continuous bargaining" on issues related to the organization of work. In addition, because of their lengthy duration, joint-governance agreements often contain provisions for mid-term or periodic revisions of wage rates subject to binding arbitration if an agreement is not reached by the parties.

To a certain extent, these agreements can be seen as an attempt to put the union–management relationship on a new, more stable and co-operative footing; however, the fact that they have often been negotiated against the background of threatened layoffs or plant closures raises the question of their long-term durability. Nevertheless, if the duration of collective agreements is taken as a rough indicator of the frequency of joint-governance agreements, it would appear that they are growing in popularity. Across the country, the average duration of major collective agreements has increased from 25.5 months at the beginning of the 1990s to more than 34.1 months by the end of the decade. In Quebec, where such agreements (known there as "social contract agreements") are especially popular, nearly one-quarter of agreements negotiated in the mid-1990s (covering slightly more than 30 percent of employees) had a duration of more than three years (Lacroix et al, 1999).

The Wage-Effort Bargain

The essence of the employment relationship is the exchange of work time for remuneration. Employers agree to pay wages and other benefits, and in return, they become entitled to direct the work activities of employees during the time for which they have paid. Naturally, employers and workers often have different opinions as to what constitutes a "fair wage" or a "fair day's work." Thus, from the exchange of remuneration for work time and effort springs a wide range of issues that are commonly negotiated and set out in collective agreements. Taken together, the provisions in collective agreements that regulate hours of work, compensation, and incentives constitute what is called the wage-effort bargain.

Hours of Work and Scheduling

Most collective agreements specify the number of daily and weekly hours that workers are normally expected to work, the starting and ending times of the workday, the length of meal breaks, rest breaks, wash-up time, and so on (see Exhibit 10.7). However, for a variety of reasons, the "normal" workday or week is not always possible: 40 percent of Canadians do not work a regular, Monday to Friday, daytime schedule (Akyeampong, 1997a). As a result, many collective agreements contain special rules regarding work time. In cases of shift work, for example, there may be a negotiated system of rotating shifts among employees, or shift scheduling may be handled by seniority. Where necessary, the collective agreement will contain provisions regarding workers who are called in to work for short periods, who are asked to be on standby (i.e., remain available during non-working hours), or who must work on weekends.

Because the regular hours of work specified in the collective agreement may sometimes be insufficient due to work volume, collective agreements commonly deal with the issue of overtime. Apart from the question of the premium to be paid, overtime is contentious because of the differing objectives of management and labour. Employers generally want to be able to require that overtime be worked and to choose the employees who will work the overtime. On the other hand, employees and their unions typically prefer that overtime hours be worked on a voluntary basis and that such hours be distributed fairly. Most agreements do not give workers the right to refuse overtime, and, as of the mid-1980s (the last time statistics were gathered on this question), fewer than half provided for equal sharing of overtime hours. Those agreements that do provide for equal sharing use a number of different systems, since overtime can be shared on a plant-wide basis, a department-wide basis, within an occupational bracket, by seniority, or some combination of these.

Collective agreements regulate not only daily and weekly hours, but also the amount of working time over the year. Most agreements include clauses specifying the length of annual vacations. Usually, the length of vacations is tied to length of service, so that the

Exhibit 10.7

Hours of Work Clause

The following clause is typical of an industrial setting where there is shift work.

Article 16: Hours of Work

16.1   Except as otherwise provided in this agreement, the normal working week shall be one of forty (40) hours consisting of five (5) consecutive days from Monday to Friday.

16.1.1 The work week for third (3rd) shift employees is one of thirty-two and one-half (32½) hours consisting of five (5) consecutive days of six and one-half (6½) hours, paid for eight (8) hours.

16.2   Regular Shifts

16.2.1 Working hours shall be as follows:

First shift: 06:45 to 15:25
Second shift: 15:20 to 00:00
Third shift: 23:50 to 06:50

16.2.2 Lunch periods: Employees on the regular first and second shifts and all special shifts will be entitled to a 40-minute unpaid lunch period. Third (3rd) shift employees will be entitled to a 30-minute unpaid lunch period.

16.2.3 Rest periods: Each shift shall include one (1) paid ten (10)-minute rest period.

Source: Collective Agreement between Bombardier Inc./Canadair and The International Association of Machinists and Aerospace Workers, Montreal Aircraft Lodge 712 (May 10, 1997 to November 30, 2001).

longer employees remain with an employer, the longer their vacation periods become. The paid holidays that are provided for in collective agreements (usually between 10 and 13 per year) are less often tied to length of service. Collective agreements may also specify paid or unpaid leaves of absence of various kinds, of which the most common is sick leave.

The growing number of women in the paid labour force and in the labour movement, as well as changes in family structure (Akyeampong, 1999) have given rise to a number of changes in collective agreement provisions regarding working time. For example, unions have sought to improve maternity provisions in collective agreements through expanded monetary benefits, longer leave periods, and the right to accumulate seniority while on maternity leave. Currently, more than half of employees covered by major collective agreements are entitled to a paid maternity leave period longer than that provided through Employment Insurance (compared to fewer than 40 percent in 1986), and nearly 50 percent have full or partial protection of seniority during maternity leave (a level that has remained relatively unchanged over the past decade). In addition to maternity leave, most jurisdictions now provide leave for fathers and for parents who adopt children. However, coverage has been less than complete, and many workers still have no access to extended parental leave or enhanced income support.

These trends have also had implications for approaches to work time and work scheduling, as families struggle to balance the demands of work and home. A number of collective agreements now contain flexible work-time provisions that offer employees some leeway in choosing their start and finish times or compressed workweeks (longer hours over fewer days per week). In addition, provisions that permit leaves for the care of a family member, for bereavement, or for responsibilities such as parent-teacher interviews or professional appointments are intended to build a more "family-responsive" workplace. The extension of coverage has been slow: In 1999, more than 70 percent of collective agreements did not provide for flextime, while nearly two-thirds contained no provision for leave to deal with an illness in the family. Finally, less than 3 percent of agreements contain provisions regarding day-care facilities.

A second labour market trend is the growing importance of education and skills in an economy increasingly based on knowledge, information, and advanced technology. Unions have attempted to expand educational leave provisions, primarily to enable their members to attend job-related or union-sponsored educational programs. Provisions allowing paid or unpaid job-related education leave are now contained in slightly more than 30 percent of major agreements, covering about 45 percent of employees. Collective agreements are more likely to put the emphasis on training rather than education leave.

A third labour market trend is an increased polarization in patterns of working time and income. The proliferation of part-time, temporary, and casual work has increased the number of people who work fewer hours than the traditional 40-hour workweek. At the same time, however, the number of people working longer hours has also increased. These trends can be seen in Table 10.1, where the decline in the number of collective agreements setting the workweek at 40 hours has been accompanied by an increase in the number of agreements specifying a shorter workweek. Interestingly, the proportion of collective agreements in which there is *no* provision covering standard weekly hours took a huge jump in the 1990s. In 1990, 15 percent of agreements (covering 9.6 percent of employees) had no provision for standard weekly hours; by 1999, 26.6 percent of agreements (covering 28.3 percent of employees) had no such provision. This shift may be evidence of the growing frequency of non-standard work-time patterns. What the table does not reveal, however, is the growing number of workers who regularly put in overtime after their "normal" workweek: For the labour force as a whole, in 1998 "just under a million Canadians put in an average of 8.7 paid overtime hours per week, and another one million worked an average 9.5 unpaid overtime hours" (Hall, 1999: 34).

International Labour Organization Main Database: www.ilo.org/

Given the persistently high levels of unemployment over the last two decades, as well as the fact that many employees who work shorter hours would prefer to work full time, these trends have sparked calls to reduce or redistribute working time (Donner, 1994).

Table 10.1

Standard Weekly Working Hours under Major Collective Agreements (various years)

Hours	Percentage of Agreements[a]			
	1986	1990	1994	1999
Less than 35	1.9	2.4	2.9	2.3
35 to 39	38.9	40.2	41.2	43.2
40	54.5	53.4	52.1	50.5
More than 40	4.7	4.0	3.7	4.0
Totals	100.0	100.0	100.0	100.0
Number of agreements	802	946	861	733

[a] These figures are based on those collective agreements in which hours of work are specified on a weekly basis. See Endnote 1.

Within the collective agreement, a reduction or redistribution of working time could be achieved in several ways: shortening the "standard" workweek, restricting the use of overtime, increasing overtime premiums, increasing the availability of leave provisions, or permitting early or phased-in retirement. Some recent collective agreements have begun to experiment with these methods, notably in the automobile and communication sectors. Provisions designed to share work on a voluntary basis have also started to become more common: In 1999, 10 percent of major collective agreements contained clauses permitting two or more employees to share an existing job, up from fewer than 4 percent in 1986.

Compensation

Wages are at the heart of the collective agreement. For most employees, their pay is the chief determinant of their standard of living and one of the main reasons they are in paid employment. For the employer, compensation costs have a significant impact on competitiveness and financial performance. Thus, an important aspect of the collective agreement is the wage level; but just as important is the way the agreement affects the wage structure, wage premiums, and whether wages are linked to performance. In addition, the compensation received by employees includes not only their wages, but a range of other monetary benefits as well.

Wage Structures

Sometimes all of the employees covered by a collective agreement receive the same wage rate or salary, but it is more usual for agreements to set out a number of different wage rates (generally hourly rates for production employees and weekly, monthly, or annual rates for office workers and professionals). The pattern of differentials between these rates is known as the *wage structure*. Two types of such structures are common. First, different jobs may be paid differently. For example, in a pattern common to collective agreements in the steel industry, jobs in the Lake Erie Steel Company plant are grouped into 28 classes with a differential of 20.7 cents per hour between each class. Thus, a general labourer (Job Class 2) is entitled to a $0.207 per hour premium over the base rate of $18.47, giving a total of $18.677 per hour; a millwright in Class 16 receives an hourly premium of $3.105; an industrial mechanic (Class 21) benefits from a premium of $4.14; and so on.

The second common type of wage structure is where wages are linked to length of service. Such systems are common where there are few opportunities to progress upwards through various job classifications. For instance, agreements covering white-collar and professional employees often set out a number of pay steps within each job category, with employees moving up one step at set intervals of time. In some cases, progression through these increment levels is also tied to satisfactory job performance. It is also common for the two types of structures to be combined, resulting in a wage or salary "grid" in which the wage rate of an individual employee is determined both by his or her specific job and length of service (see Exhibit 10.8).

Recently there has been some interest in a third type of wage structure—*pay-for-knowledge*—in which wages are determined by the skills and knowledge that employees possess rather than the particular job that they perform (Celani and Weber, 1998). In some professions this has been a long-standing practice, e.g., where teachers' salaries are tied, in part, to their level of education. Recent attempts to develop pay-for-knowledge systems for other workers reflect the desire of employers to encourage multi-skilling of employees and increase their flexibility and discretion in the deployment of workers. Although growing in popularity, pay-for-knowledge pay structures remain far less common than other, more traditional wage structures, especially in unionized establishments (Betcherman et al, 1994: 40–42).

The setting of rates for particular jobs can give rise to much controversy, since subjective judgments about the relative worth of particular tasks and skills cannot be avoided. Jobs done predominantly by women workers have frequently been placed low down on the wage hierarchy because the classification process has been dominated by male assumptions about the nature of skill and ability (Warskett, 1993; Lamson, 1986). In order to redress this, some collective agreements specify that equal pay be accorded to men and women for performing similar work, or work deemed to be of comparable worth; around 15 percent of major agreements now contain such a provision, compared to fewer than 6 percent in 1986. In addition, many Canadian jurisdictions have some kind of pay equity legislation. Because of such legislation, the federal government agreed to provide several classifications of workers represented by the Public Service Alliance of Canada a total of $3.6 billion in pay equity payments covering the period 1985 to 1998.

EXHIBIT 10.8

A WAGE GRID

The grid below illustrates a wage structure that is linked to both the type of job (classified into Salary Groups) and the length of service (the five "steps"). Note that employees in Salary Group 2 only have two steps instead of five.

For purposes of illustration, the rates are shown for only five of the thirteen groups, and, although the actual agreement sets out the rates for each group on an hourly, biweekly, monthly, and annual basis, only the biweekly rates are included in this extract.

SALARY STRUCTURE—OCTOBER 1, 1998 (BIWEEKLY RATES)

SALARY GROUP	STEP 1	STEP 2	STEP 3	STEP 4	STEP 5
Salary Group 2 (e.g., Clerk II)	—	—	$1008.39	—	$1084.60
Salary Group 5 (e.g., Cheque Control Clerk)	$1169.94	$1210.67	$1256.00	$1303.13	$1352.11
Salary Group 8 (e.g., Autoplan Technical Writer)	$1459.43	$1514.57	$1572.61	$1634.02	$1698.59
Salary Group 11 (e.g., Senior Technical Architect)	$1836.11	$1909.87	$1984.76	$2065.18	$2147.88
Salary Group 13 (e.g., Senior Database Administrator)	$2147.88	$2235.00	$2326.59	$2420.36	$2517.48

Source: Collective Agreement between Insurance Corporation of British Columbia and Office & Professional Employees' International Union, Local 378 (1996–1999).

Performance-Based Wage Systems

In all of the wage structures discussed above, an individual's wage or salary rate is *fixed*, either in relation to his or her specific job, length of service, or level of education or skill (or some combination of these factors). However, some collective agreements provide for *performance-based pay*, usually as a supplement to the basic rates.

One traditional method of linking pay to performance is known as *piecework*, in which workers' pay is determined, at least in part, by their rate of output (the number of "pieces" they produce). These systems can be quite complex, since circumstances like machine breakdown and other necessary interruptions in work have to be taken into account. Because each task must have a piecework rate set for it, the administrative costs can be high, and the setting of rates may give rise to considerable conflict. For these reasons, only about 5 percent of contracts (mostly in the clothing and forestry industries) incorporate a piecework system.

Another method of linking pay to performance is through the use of bonuses, which can be paid to individuals, groups, or all employees based on some measure of performance. When paid to individuals, bonuses are generally based on supervisors' evaluations and are known as merit bonuses. For groups of employees, bonuses are commonly based on some measure of productivity or cost savings achieved in their work area or department. Finally, profit-sharing and stock ownership plans link employees' remuneration to the broader performance of the firm.

Performance-based pay is often favoured by employers, who argue that it stimulates work effort and rewards above-average performance. Unions have been more skeptical, believing that such schemes introduce an element of subjectivity and uncertainty into the compensation package, and that they may create competition between workers that will undercut collective solidarity. Less than 15 percent of collective agreements currently include any form of wage incentive plan.

Wage Levels, Adjustments, and Premiums

The wage *level* is the amount of pay for each classification of employee. For much of the 1980s and 1990s, Canadian employers have attempted to improve their competitiveness by reducing labour costs. During the 1993 recession, a record number of major agreements contained wage freezes or cuts: 44.8 percent of agreements negotiated that year, covering nearly two-thirds of unionized workers, provided for either no increase or a reduction in wages. This marked a substantial rise from the 4.4 percent of such agreements a decade earlier. Since 1993, as the economy improved, the number of major collective agreements containing wage freezes or cuts has declined steadily, but real wages (that is, wages adjusted to account for inflation) actually declined in Canada in the 1990s.

Another innovation proposed by some employers as a means of reducing total compensation costs is the use of *two-tiered* wage structures, in which new employees are paid lower rates than incumbent employees. In some cases these differences disappear as the new employee progresses, but in others the differential is permanent. Unions have fiercely resisted this strategy because it creates two classes of employees, thus threatening the principle of equality of treatment. The prevalence of two-tiered agreements peaked in the latter half of the 1980s and has subsequently declined, although the issue has resurfaced lately in Quebec (see Chapter 16).

Another method of lowering labour costs has been to use lump-sum payments (sometimes called "signing bonuses") in place of all or part of an increase in actual wage rates. Such payments reduce increases in wage-related benefits and premiums and, because they are not included in wage rates, allow subsequent contract renegotiations to begin from a lower base. Lump-sum payments have received only limited acceptance in Canada.

In one-year agreements wage and salary rates are generally fixed, but in multi-year agreements there is often a provision for *wage adjustments*. For example, the agreement might provide for an increase in the wage rates or salary levels at one or more points in time during the life of the agreement. Another method of adjusting the wage level is the inclusion of a "reopener clause," in which the parties agree to renegotiate the wage level at a particular point in time.

Collective agreements can also provide for wage adjustments through cost-of-living-allowance (COLA) clauses. COLAs are a special form of premium that began to grow in popularity in the 1950s and became especially common during the inflationary 1970s. The basic idea is that wages should be adjusted to the rate of inflation so that workers' purchasing power is maintained during the life of the agreement, thereby allowing the parties to agree to multi-year contracts without risking the erosion of negotiated wages by unanticipated inflation. Actually, very few COLA clauses provide full protection against inflation: Some COLAs are triggered only above a certain level of inflation; some are capped (limited to a certain amount of increase); some do not cover the whole contract period; and some do not provide for a full adjustment to the rate of inflation (Wilton, 1980). The decline in the rate of inflation since the early 1980s has meant that many of the remaining COLAs have not been triggered, thus aiding the efforts of employers to remove such protection from collective agreements: Whereas nearly 30 percent of major agreements settled in 1981 contained COLA clauses, less than 14 percent of those reached in 1998 contained such clauses.

Finally, the wages received by employees can be augmented by a variety of *wage premiums*, which are supplements to basic pay that arise from certain circumstances, such as shift work, overtime, or work on holidays and weekends. The most usual rate for overtime hours is time-and-one-half, though a small number of agreements simply prescribe straight time for excess hours, and some agreements require more than time-and-one-half. Some collective agreements also have special overtime rates for days worked in excess of the normal workweek. Besides specifying wage premiums, agreements often include special payments for certain circumstances, such as travel allowances for remote worksites, clothing and tool allowances, meal allowances for employees working overtime, "call-in" pay, standby pay, and so forth.

Employee Benefits

Compensation includes much more than the actual pay received by employees. In fact, more than 30 percent of total compensation costs in Canada are represented by *employee benefits*. The most common types of benefits found in collective agreements are pensions, long-term and short-term disability plans, sick leave plans, extended health care, life insurance, and dental insurance (see Figure 10.3). The collective agreement usually spells out the details of the various plans, the eligibility rules (often linked to length of service), and the respective contributions of employer and employees towards the costs of the plans. In fact, so widespread are such plans that they can no longer accurately be referred to as "fringe" benefits; they are central features of the overall compensation package.

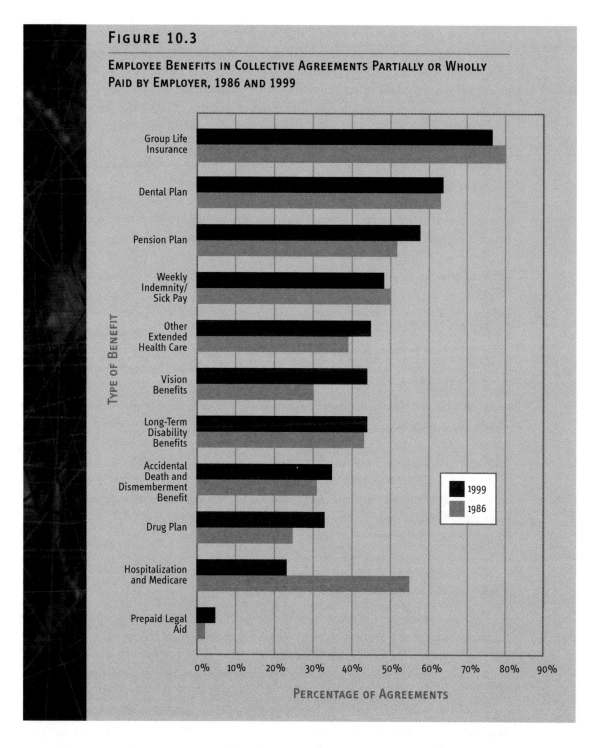

FIGURE 10.3

EMPLOYEE BENEFITS IN COLLECTIVE AGREEMENTS PARTIALLY OR WHOLLY PAID BY EMPLOYER, 1986 AND 1999

Of the various types of benefits that are found in collective agreements, pension plans have probably given rise to the most controversy. Generally speaking, unions regard pension contributions, whether paid by the employer or the employee, as deferred wages. On this basis, they argue that the administration of pension funds should be the joint responsibility of unions and employers. Employers have taken a different view. Since most pension plans in the unionized sector are defined-benefit plans that set out the specific pension benefits, employers argue that, so long as they ensure that these benefits are paid, they should retain control over the funds accumulated and the disposition of any "surplus assets" from pension funds. Currently, only about one-third of pension plans in major collective agreements provide for union participation in the administration of the fund, although this represents a significant increase since the mid-1980s when less than 10 percent contained such a provision. An even smaller number (2.4 percent) give unions unilateral control.

The recent economic and political climate has not been conducive to the introduction of new benefits. Indeed, as with wages, many employers have attempted to reduce benefits or to shift a higher proportion of the costs of benefit packages to employees. Nonetheless, recent years have seen the emergence of one new type of benefit that is likely to grow in popularity in the future—prepaid legal services. The Canadian Auto Workers' union and the large automakers have negotiated collective agreements providing for a legal services plan financed by employer contributions. Under the plan, union members receive a range of free legal services. Recent CAW agreements have also contained such new benefits as employer-sponsored child-care programs and the availability of workplace advocates to provide assistance to women facing harassment on the job or abuse at home.

In conclusion, the wage-effort bargain, encompassing provisions on working time, wages, and employee benefits, is a prominent feature of the collective agreement. Indeed, unionization is often seen solely as an attempt by employees to offset the power of the employer to determine the wage-effort trade-off. However, the employment relationship is much more than a simple exchange of time for money: Even after wages and working hours have been agreed on, the organization and control of the workforce and the workplace naturally give rise to a host of issues, many of which centre on disputes between employers and employees over the control of jobs.

THE CONTROL OF JOBS AND WORK

In the absence of unions, management normally controls decisions that affect the internal labour market and the organization of work: how many workers to employ, whom to hire, the types of jobs to be established, the assignment of individual employees to particular tasks, how tasks are to be performed, the rate of production, whom to promote, how layoffs are to be handled, and so on. For management, decisions about such matters revolve around its concern to minimize labour costs and to maximize productivity. In practice, this means that managers want the rules regulating the internal labour market and the work process to be as flexible as possible.

These issues look very different from the workers' standpoint. In particular, workers and their unions are concerned that too much managerial flexibility can result in a sense of permanent insecurity for employees, a lack of autonomy for workers and work groups, and the abuse of discretion by managers. Unions have therefore traditionally sought some input into the management of the internal labour market, especially on matters that affect job security. The efforts to secure job rights inevitably conflict with management's desire for flexibility and control, so collective agreements often contain negotiated provisions arising from the struggle for the control of jobs.

Entering the Internal Labour Market

The struggle for control over jobs begins with the processes of hiring and job assignment, which collective agreements regulate in a variety of ways. For example, collective agreements may address hiring and job-assignment decisions by: stipulating the minimum qualifications or training for new or reassigned employees, establishing union–management apprenticeship programs, requiring that vacancies be filled from within the organization when possible, or restricting supervisors and other non-bargaining unit personnel from performing tasks normally done by union members.

Newly hired employees are usually put on probationary status. About two-thirds of major agreements specify probationary periods for new employees, usually of less than five months, but occasionally for lengthier periods. The significance of probationary status is that such employees are often not entitled to a number of the protective features of the collective agreement, particularly protection against dismissal if their performance is not judged acceptable. Thus, the use of a probationary period permits management to retain a considerable amount of control over hiring.

Another method by which collective agreements can affect the hiring process is through closed shop arrangements or hiring halls. As discussed earlier, closed shop agreements are a form of union security—the only one that regulates the hiring decisions of the employer. The longshoring industry offers a good example of the way union hiring halls function. On the Vancouver waterfront, the composition of work gangs and the allocation of gangs and individual workers to particular tasks are controlled by the workers themselves through a union hiring hall and a joint union–management dispatch system. In this way, longshore workers have been able to exercise a considerable amount of control over hiring, job assignment, and production (Jamieson and Greyell, 1995).

Work Rules

Once employees have been hired and trained, another issue arises: How is the actual work to be performed? Management has traditionally regarded decisions about the speed and quantity of production, the way tasks are defined, the number of employees assigned to particular operations, and so on, to be within its domain. On the other hand, workers and their unions have sometimes sought to win influence over these matters. The speed of an assembly line, or the number of employees allocated to a particular task, for example, is an issue of efficiency from management's point of view. From the point of view of employees, however, it is an issue of quality of working life and the level of employment. The result of this divergence of interests is a struggle over the "frontier of control"

(Gilson, 1985). Although such disputes often involve informal tactics and result in unwritten arrangements, they are sometimes formalized through the collective agreement.

One type of work rule that is occasionally negotiated is workload. For example, school teachers in a number of provinces have negotiated average and maximum class sizes. Another type of work rule arises in cases where a job classification system is in place. In such circumstances, it is not unusual for collective agreements to restrict the assignment of individual workers to jobs within their classification or to prohibit supervisors and other employees not in the bargaining unit from performing tasks for which there is a classification. The construction trades in particular attempt to maintain strict control over which workers are permitted to do certain tasks.

Systems of collectively negotiated job classifications have been criticized in recent years by employers on the grounds that they prevent the most efficient allocation of labour. As a result, two types of modifications to existing structures of job classifications have become more common. First, recent research indicates that job classification systems are being simplified through the reduction of the number and type of job classes (Beaucage and Lafleur, 1994). Second, some employers and unions have introduced measures in collective agreements designed to promote new ways of organizing work. For example, recent agreements in a number of industries have sought to widen the range of tasks employees carry out by requiring or encouraging multi-skilling. In some cases, multi-skilling is encouraged through bonuses, as in the case of an agreement between Cami Automotive and the CAW that provides maintenance workers with a $500 per year multi-skilling bonus, or at Dow Chemical in Ontario and Fraser Inc. in New Brunswick where hourly flexibility bonuses have been negotiated. In still other cases, like the MIL Davie shipyard in Lévis, Quebec, multi-skilling has been achieved in return for job security provisions. In addition to multi-skilling, employers have also sought to reorganize work through the introduction of techniques like teamwork and quality circles. Because

EXHIBIT 10.9

AUTONOMOUS TEAM CLAUSE

The parties agree to create autonomous work teams, each under the responsibility of a team leader who works with the employees.

The team leader position will replace that of assistant foreman. Team leaders will be selected according to the provisions of article 30.10 of the collective agreement.

Given the need for training and the impact that the creation of autonomous work teams can have on the organization of work, the parties agree to introduce this new concept on an experimental basis in one department, one area, or one workshop. The details of implementation will be determined by agreement between the parties.

Source: A translation from the French into English of an excerpt taken from La Convention collective de travail intervenue entre MIL Davie Inc. et Le Syndicat des travailleurs du chantier naval de Lauzon Inc., 1995–2000. Translated by Daphne Gottlieb Taras. Reprinted with permission.

such innovations may affect salary differentials, job classifications, and patterns of authority in the workplace, they are often introduced through the collective agreement (see Exhibit 10.9, and Chapter 15). Such arrangements have often proved to be fragile, however, especially when they have been introduced in the context of negotiations focused on finding a solution to a short-term financial crisis.

Movements within the Internal Labour Market

After they are hired, employees may change jobs within the bargaining unit for a variety of reasons—the need to replace another employee who is absent or on leave, winning a promotion to a better job, a lateral transfer to a different department that suddenly needs extra help, and so forth. The way these movements within the internal labour market are managed is a central feature of the collective agreement.

Unions generally favour the principle of seniority—that is, the idea that long-serving employees, because they have invested a considerable portion of their working lives in the organization, are entitled to preferential treatment in job opportunities and security against layoffs. In addition, seniority rights "provide an element of due process by limiting nepotism and unfairness in personnel decisions" and serve "to buttress the bargaining power of unions by curbing competitive and aggressive behaviour that pits one worker against another" (Gersuny, 1982: 519). Although some managers favour a limited use of seniority as a means of reducing tensions over promotion and other decisions, most prefer to retain control over such decisions because they believe that they are in the best position to judge which employees are the most (or least) deserving.

In the majority of major collective agreements, promotion decisions must take some account of seniority (Figure 10.4). A small number of these specify that seniority is the only factor to be taken into account, but the great majority provide that seniority will be one criterion (along with skill and qualifications), or that it will be the deciding factor only if all others are equal (see Exhibit 10.10). Even where qualified by other factors, seniority may still be the most important criterion because skill and ability can be difficult to assess, and because management sometimes finds it simpler to use seniority in cases where there is not a great difference in ability (Chaykowski and Slotsve, 1986).

It is important to remember that seniority is used in many other decisions besides the regulation of internal movements. Seniority is often used in determining who is offered overtime, who is given first choice of vacation periods, and who is given preference in the choice of particular shifts, as well as in governing workforce reductions. In addition to these cases of "competitive seniority" (so called because it is used to settle competing claims among employees), seniority also commonly determines the level of benefits of individual employees (e.g., the length of vacations, eligibility for pensions, etc.).

The pervasive use of seniority as a criterion in decisions concerning the allocation of jobs and benefits means that agreements frequently go into considerable detail about how seniority is calculated, and it is not unusual for them to require the posting of seniority lists at regular intervals. In fact, although the basic idea of seniority is easy to grasp, its measurement and application is often extraordinarily complex (Slichter, Healy,

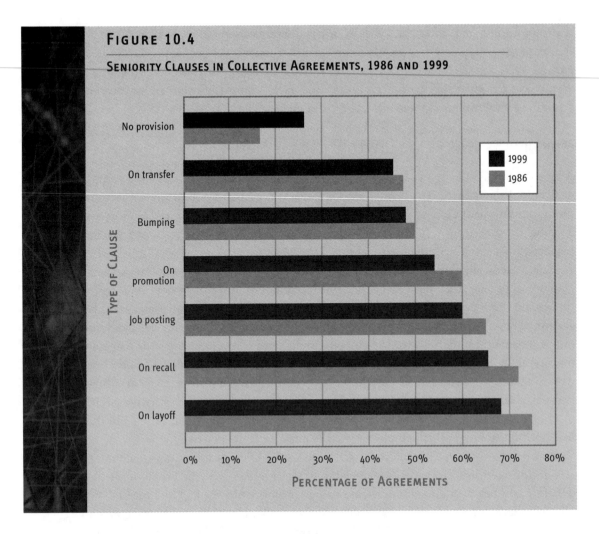

FIGURE 10.4

SENIORITY CLAUSES IN COLLECTIVE AGREEMENTS, 1986 AND 1999

and Livernash, 1960). For example, seniority can be calculated organization-wide, at the level of the establishment or department, or within an occupational group. A single agreement may use each of these methods for a different purpose, which means that each employee might have several different levels of seniority at the same time.

Aside from the complexity of its calculation, the use of seniority has become contentious in recent years for two other reasons. First, because it favours employees with more years of continuous service, seniority has been challenged on the grounds that it serves as a mechanism of systemic discrimination against women and other comparatively recent entrants to the labour force (Forrest, 1993). Second, as part of the wider pattern of detailed job regulation in North American collective agreements, seniority and other provisions that hamper employers' ability to increase flexibility in the organization and management of work have been criticized. Figure 10.4 indicates that there has been a noticeable decline in the prevalence of seniority clauses since the mid-1980s: The proportion of agreements containing no reference to seniority on the decisions listed has increased from around 17 percent to about 26 percent, and the use of seniority has shrunk in each of the areas named, though by varying amounts.

Exhibit 10.10

Sample Seniority Clause

The weight given to seniority vis-à-vis other criteria depends on the exact wording of the clause. The following clause illustrates two common formulas. For some positions (section 12.4.a), the employee with the most seniority will be given the promotion provided that he or she meets the minimum level of "ability, qualifications, and merit." This is known as the "sufficient ability" formula. For other, higher-level positions (12.4.b), seniority only comes into play when these other factors are "relatively equal," a formula known as "relative ability." Another common formula (not illustrated here) is where seniority is given equal weighting with the other criteria.

Article 12—Seniority

12.1. a) Where the Company determines it necessary to fill a vacant position, other than entry level, within the scope of this Agreement, the position shall be posted. Vacancies will be open to applicants for ten (10) days. It will be the policy of the Company that, in filling posted positions, present members of the staff will be given first consideration.

12.4. a) When filling a posted position ranked below that of Manager Customer Service II, seniority shall prevail subject to ability, qualifications, and merit.

b) When filling a posted position at the level of Manager Customer Service II and above, the Company shall select the candidate who, based on ability, qualifications, and merit is determined by the Company to be best suited for the position, and in the event two or more candidates are relatively equal, the Company shall appoint the more senior.

Source: Excerpts from the Collective Bargaining Agreement between Saskatchewan Wheat Pool and Grain Services Union (ILWU—Canadian Area) covering Employees of the Country Services Division (Operations), February 1, 1996 to January 31, 2000. Reprinted with permission.

Exiting the Internal Labour Market

Employers want to be free to reduce the labour force as they see fit, whereas workers and their unions want to avoid job losses, especially during periods of high unemployment. In theory, it is possible to negotiate a clause giving employees guaranteed employment security, but only around 15 percent of major collective agreement contain such clauses, predominantly in the public sector. Furthermore, few employment guarantees are absolute; most are limited to either a particular group of employees (e.g., the most senior) or to certain circumstances. Finally, a collectively negotiated employment guarantee is only effective for the duration of the collective agreement, and only so long as the firm stays in business. In practice, the main role of the collective agreement is to determine *how* workforce reductions are effected.

Seniority plays an important role in determining which employees are to be laid off. In almost 70 percent of agreements, seniority has to be taken into account, and in just fewer than two-thirds of agreements, seniority is also used to establish the order in which employees are recalled from layoffs. Furthermore, collective agreements may also contain "bumping rights." "Bumping" is the practice of allowing senior employees who have been laid off to take the jobs of more junior employees, who may, in turn, take the jobs of even more junior employees. In theory at least, the displacement of a very senior employee can set off a series of bumps down through the seniority list, much like the fall of a row of dominoes. Around half of collective agreements contain bumping provisions, though the great majority restrict a worker's ability to bump, either by limiting it to certain locations, or requiring a certain level of ability.

In addition to the method of effecting layoffs, collective agreements can offer other forms of protection for employees. One basic type of protection is the requirement that employers notify employees and the union of impending layoffs in order to give them time to make adjustment plans. Although one might think that such provisions would be common, only a little more than half of major agreements make any mention of layoff notification, and of these, the vast majority provide for less than 45 days' notice. It is possible that the existence of legislation requiring advanced notice of layoffs in most Canadian provinces, and at the federal level, makes the achievement of parallel collective agreement provisions less pressing.

Some collective agreements have severance pay plans, and a small number (particularly in the primary metal and transportation equipment sectors) provide for supplementary unemployment benefits. Other examples of workforce reduction protection in agreements include: provisions regarding the distribution of work among employees during slack periods, rights to new job openings in other establishments run by the employer, early-retirement provisions, and the continuation of benefits in the case of layoffs. But layoff notices, severance pay, supplementary unemployment benefits, and the like only cushion the impact of job loss. Although such provisions may help prevent hasty or unnecessarily drastic reductions, employers still retain the power to reduce the workforce at their discretion. Indeed, despite the emphasis that unions have put on improving job security during the 1980s and 1990s, and despite substantial gains in a few cases—including agreements between the federal government and the Public Service Alliance of Canada and between Canada Post and the Canadian Union of Postal Workers—there has been no widespread improvement in any of these types of security.

One particularly contentious area related to workforce reductions is the practice of contracting-out, where an employer hires another firm to do work for it rather than using existing employees or hiring new employees. For example, many large institutions, such as universities, subcontract their cleaning operations to independent firms. Because contracting-out threatens the jobs of existing employees or prevents growth of the unionized workforce, it is bitterly opposed by workers and their unions. Management, on the other hand, typically wants to be able to contract out, primarily to reduce labour costs (since smaller, specialized firms are not likely to be unionized and often pay lower wages), but also to exercise leverage over its existing employees by raising the possibility of contracting-out at the negotiating table.

Unions have had some success in introducing collective agreement provisions restricting the use of contracting-out. Between 1986 and 1999, the incidence of such provisions in major collective agreements grew from 36.4 percent to 53.4 percent. In most of the cases where there is a restriction, contracting-out is prohibited only if it leads to layoffs or if the contract is with a nonunion firm. Only a small minority of agreements provide a complete ban on contracting-out.

Technological Change

Differences between workers and employers over the handling of technological change have been occurring since the Industrial Revolution, but in times of economic restructuring, these disputes become particularly sharp. Management seeks ways to cut labour costs and increase productivity through technology, while workers' concerns about job security and the integrity of their skills are heightened. Between the mid-1980s and the mid-1990s, there was a slow but steady increase in the proportion of collective agreements that included provisions regarding technological change, but in the last several years this trend appears to have reversed; currently, slightly more than half of major collective agreements deal specifically with technological change, virtually the same as in the mid-1980s. Fewer than 50 percent of major agreements require the employer to notify and/or consult with the union in advance of technological changes; fewer than 20 percent provide for labour–management technological-change committees; and fewer than 10 percent require that special layoff notices be provided to employees affected by technological change. Some form of training or retraining of employees affected by technological change is mandated in about one-fifth of agreements, and an even smaller number provide workers with any form of income or employment security in the case of technological change. Finally, more than 45 percent of agreements (covering nearly 50 percent of workers) contain no reference at all to technological change. In a few jurisdictions, legislation exists that allows for the reopening of collective agreements (Craig, 1986). In general, employers in Canada have been steadfast in their determination to preserve their control over the process of technological change.

 Unite Canada (union site offering policy papers): www.unite-svti.org/

THE CONTROL OF WORK BEHAVIOUR AND THE WORK ENVIRONMENT

To this point, we have looked at how collective agreements affect the union–management relationship, the contours of the wage-effort bargain, and the regulation of the internal labour market and the organization of work. To complete the discussion, we must examine a fourth set of issues—those arising from the social and physical environment in which work is performed. Collective agreements cannot possibly regulate even a small proportion of the issues, tensions, and relationships that spring from the social and physical setting of work. However, negotiated rules frequently do come into play in three general areas: human rights, workplace behaviour, and occupational health and safety.

Human Rights and the Collective Agreement

We have seen throughout this chapter that the collective agreement codifies a wide range of employee and employer rights. For employees, the agreement establishes their right to be paid a certain wage rate and receive certain benefits, to have their seniority taken into account in numerous decisions, and so on. For management, the management rights clause and prevailing arbitral opinion work together to preserve a considerable degree of authority over the workplace. But the issue of "rights" also crops up in collective agreements in a broader way, through various types of clauses that protect employees from certain types of actions by management, by other employees or, indeed, by their own union (Scott, 1996).

One common way in which the human rights of employees are protected through the collective agreement is the nondiscrimination clause (see Exhibit 10.11). Such clauses typically prohibit discrimination on the basis of sex, race, religion, union activity, and other objectionable grounds; this protection is usually expressed in a general way so that it covers hiring, promotion, job assignment, compensation, and other areas where discrimination may occur. Around half of major collective agreements in Canada currently include such a clause, usually written by the parties themselves, but sometimes merely incorporating the human rights code of the relevant government.

EXHIBIT 10.11

NONDISCRIMINATION CLAUSE

EQUAL APPLICATION OF THE AGREEMENT

The Corporation and the Union, in their respective fields, have been leaders in adopting and effectuating policies against discrimination because of race, colour, religion, age, sex, national origin, sexual orientation, or disability. The terms and conditions of agreements between the Corporation and the Union have always been applied equally to all employees, regardless of such considerations.

In order to assure full knowledge and understanding of the foregoing principles on the part of employees and all agents and representatives of the Corporation and the Union, the parties hereby incorporate the same in this Agreement. Any employee who claims that, in violation of said principles, said employee has been denied rights guaranteed by this Agreement or the Ontario Human Rights Code may complain as provided in the grievance procedure. [...]

Source: Agreement between Chrysler Canada Ltd. and the Canadian Auto Workers' Union, Production and Maintenance (September 15, 1996).

EXHIBIT 10.12

SUBSTANCE ABUSE TESTING

The parties agree that it is in the best interest of all concerned to promote a safe working environment. Accordingly, the Union has no objection to pre-employment and post-incident substance abuse testing. The cost of such testing is to be paid for by the employer. Should an individual test positive, such is cause for immediate dismissal. The employer is responsible to notify the Union on an employee testing positive.

Source: Excerpts from the Bricklayers Provincial Collective Construction and Maintenance Agreement (May 1, 1997 to April 30, 1999), between the Masonry Contractors Association of Alberta and the International Union of Bricklayers and Allied Craftsworkers and it's Affiliates, Local Unions # 1 and 2 of Alberta. Reprinted with permission.

Other rights clauses are aimed at protecting specific groups. For example, around one-third of collective agreements contain special protections for older workers and for disabled workers, especially in terms of opportunities to transfer to suitable jobs. Clauses specifically targeted at the problem of sexual harassment have also become more common and are now found in slightly more than one-third of agreements.

Several recent agreements (e.g., between the federal government and its employees, and between the CAW and the major auto manufacturers) now treat same-sex couples on a par with other common-law couples for the purposes of collective agreement provisions.

Finally, some collective agreements contain clauses with respect to the right to privacy where employers use various means of surveillance. The collective agreement between Canada Post and its employees, for example, limits the use of the "watch and observation system" to the purposes of "protecting the mail and the property of the State against criminal acts" and expressly prohibits its use "as a means to evaluate the performance of employees and to gather evidence in support of disciplinary measures unless such disciplinary measures result from the commission of a criminal act." The growing use of technology as a means of controlling employees has increased union efforts to protect their members' right to privacy through the collective agreement. Although still not widespread, clauses regulating testing for AIDs and drug use (see Exhibit 10.12), electronic surveillance in the workplace, and the monitoring of electronic mail are likely to grow in coming years.

Behaviour and Discipline at Work

The modern workplace is pervaded by rules established by management to regulate the behaviour of employees. The purposes of such rules include safety concerns (e.g., procedures in nuclear plants), hygiene considerations (e.g., cleanliness in a food-processing factory), attempts to maximize work time (e.g., limitations on break periods), customer relations (e.g., the attempt by one airline to ban the wearing of earrings by its male flight attendants), general standards of decorum (e.g., "no fighting"), and efforts to reinforce the structure of authority (e.g., respecting the decisions of supervisors). These examples may be rooted in very different circumstances, but they have an important feature in common: They are rules established by management, the enforcement of which entails an array of disciplinary sanctions.

Collective agreements usually grant management the power to institute rules of behaviour and to mete out punishment, subject to the employees' right to grieve. Unions usually prefer not to incorporate specific rules in the collective agreement, since this preserves their right to dispute disciplinary action. Most collective agreements allow management to suspend or discharge employees provided that there is "just cause"—a criterion that is almost always arguable. Some contracts, however, include specific rules and/or penalties (see Exhibit 10.13).

The imposition of discipline is subject to a number of procedural limitations in some collective agreements, such as the right of an employee to be represented by a union at disciplinary meetings with management, or the requirement that an employee's disciplinary record be "cleared" after a specified period of time (usually one to three years).

EXHIBIT 10.13

SPECIFIC DISCIPLINE CLAUSES—EXAMPLE

ABSENTEEISM CONTROL PROGRAM

Unauthorized absences [including late arrivals and early departures] are recorded within a moving 12-month period. According to the number of absences accumulated by the employee during the 12 months immediately preceding the last unauthorized absence, the following disciplinary measures will be applied:

NUMBER OF ABSENCES DURING THE 12 MONTHS PRECEDING THE LAST UNAUTHORIZED ABSENCE	DISCIPLINARY MEASURES TO BE APPLIED
4th absence	Verbal reprimand
5th absence	Written reprimand
6th absence	1-day suspension
7th absence	5-day suspension
8th absence	2-week suspension
9th absence	Discharge

Source: Convention collective entre Bridgestone/Firestone Canada Inc., usine de Joliette, et Le Syndicat des travailleurs(euses) de Bridgestone/Firestone de Joliette (CSN) (March 4, 1996 to August 31, 1999). Translated by authors.

Health and Safety

Work kills, maims, and sickens at a horrifying rate: In 1997, more than 800 industrial fatalities occurred in Canada; almost 800,000 workers were injured on the job; and more than 17 *million* worker-days were lost to disabling injuries and illnesses (Human Resources Development Canada, 1999).

Occupational health-and-safety issues are not solely technical questions. As one authority in the field points out: "In all technical questions pertaining to workplace health and safety there is the social element. That is, for example, the power relations in production: who tells whom to do what and how fast. After all, the machine does not go faster by itself; someone designed the machinery, organized the work, designed the job" (Sass, 1982: 52). At times the core issue is money. From the point of view of a small number of employers, improved occupational health and safety may involve short-term losses in efficiency, as well as the extra costs of administration and protective equipment. The report of the public inquiry into the 1992 Westray Mine explosion that killed 26 workers observed that, among the factors that contributed to the tragedy, "Management, through its actions and attitudes, sent a ... message [that] Westray was to produce coal at the expense of worker safety" (Richard, 1977: 21). Occasionally, workers themselves resist efforts to increase safety. Shortcuts are enticing when pay and performance are judged on speed of production (as in some coal mines). Sometimes workers take risks out of bravado or a supposedly macho approach to the job. Nonetheless, at many job sites, health and safety is a matter not of dollars and cents but of life and death, and both employers and unions place great emphasis on accident prevention.

Some of the clauses in collective agreements already discussed (such as rules affecting the pace of work) have an indirect effect on health and safety. More directly, collective agreements typically address health and safety by establishing special safety programs or joint committees, and some agreements make specific provisions obliging the employer to furnish and pay for safety equipment, allowing employees the right to refuse to perform unsafe work, or dealing with particular issues like work with video display terminals.

In most Canadian jurisdictions, occupational health-and-safety committees are required by law, even in nonunion workplaces. Such legislation usually gives workers the right to refuse to perform tasks that they believe are hazardous or potentially injurious. Recent legislation also requires that information be provided on hazardous materials used in the workplace. Such requirements are typically referred to as Workplace Hazardous Materials Information System (or WHMIS for short). In addition to these legislative requirements, however, the inclusion of provisions in collective agreements—such as those that allow employees to obtain information about and/or refuse unsafe work—enables unions to deal with specific problems through grievance and arbitration procedures rather than having to rely solely on the enforcement of health-and-safety laws or the policies agreed on by joint committees.

CONCLUSION

Given the largely unfettered power of management to rule over a nonunion workforce, collective agreements represent a step towards industrial democracy (see Exhibit 10.14). Yet judged against the democratic standards that govern political life in our society, collective agreements represent only a partial step in the direction of full economic democracy. Collective agreements *do* make a difference, but employers have been successful in retaining many of their traditional prerogatives. Indeed, the manner in which collective agreements are administered, particularly with respect to management residual rights, serves to legitimize and bolster managerial powers.

The collective agreement reflects these basic authority relationships and also the ebb and flow of economic and political power in society. For example, the 1980s and 1990s were marked by recession, high rates of unemployment, and a resurgent conservatism. The bargaining power of unions deteriorated, and Canadian employers took advantage of this situation to launch an offensive against many of the provisions in collective agreements. Unions and workers have been confronted with employer demands to reduce or freeze wages and benefits, to tie compensation more closely to productivity, and to make work rules and job classifications more flexible. Even management proposals for greater

EXHIBIT 10.14

UNION VS. NONUNION

Although some nonunion organizations provide many of the same benefits and follow many of the same rules as those found in collective agreements, there are several crucial differences between the two settings.

- Collective agreements are negotiated by a democratically elected, independent representative of the employees; in the nonunion setting, employees might be consulted, but they have no collective counterweight to management decisions.

- Collective agreements are bilaterally negotiated contracts that fix the terms and conditions of employment for a set period of time; terms and conditions of employment in the nonunion sector can usually be changed unilaterally by employers with little notice.

- Collective agreements provide employees with a set of rights that can be enforced through the grievance arbitration procedure; in the nonunion sector, individuals who feel aggrieved have a more difficult time pursuing justice.

- Collective agreements generally provide superior terms and conditions of employment than those found in equivalent nonunion organizations.

- Collective agreements tend to promote equal treatment of similar groups of employees in many areas; in the nonunion sector, inequality is more pronounced.

- Collective agreements introduce a measure of democracy to the workplace; nonunion organizations are, at best, benevolent dictatorships.

employee participation in decision making, quality circles, and autonomous work groups have at times been coloured by anti-union motivation, since these techniques often seek to strengthen employees' identification with the firm's goals, which can weaken union solidarity.

Nevertheless, the collective agreement remains at the centre of the Canadian industrial relations system. It provides both a detailed set of rules to govern the workplace and a benchmark of union ability (or inability) to win for its members a voice in the management of the workplace. For the union, the negotiation and administration of the collective agreement is the cornerstone of its activity, and to union members it represents the tangible results of union membership. Whatever changes take place in Canadian industrial relations will undoubtedly be reflected in the content and substance of the collective agreement.

Questions

1. Obtain a collective agreement and categorize its contents according to the four general types of clauses outlined in this chapter.

2. Describe the distinctive characteristics of Canadian collective agreements. Discuss the reasons for these characteristics.

3. Outline the arguments for and against the residual rights theory of managerial prerogatives. In your view, does this doctrine promote or retard organizational effectiveness?

4. Discuss the different types of union security clauses found in collective agreements. In your opinion, does the Rand formula establish a balance between individual and collective rights?

5. Describe the ways in which collective agreements might be used to remove the barriers to equality faced by women workers and by workers with disabilities.

6. What are the various wage incentive systems? Why are they not commonly found in collective agreements?

7. Discuss how the conflict between management's concern with efficiency and workers' concerns with job security and working conditions is manifested in collective agreements.

8. Discuss the recent moves by Canadian employers to alter many of the traditional features of collective agreements in their favour. What are the likely long-run effects?

9. Why do collective agreements sometimes include provisions that are already required by legislation, such as employment standards legislation, human rights codes, or occupational health-and-safety legislation? Give examples.

10. What do you think the typical Canadian collective agreement will look like ten years from now and why?

ENDNOTES

[1] Unless otherwise noted, the statistics cited in this chapter were provided by the Workplace Information Directorate, Human Resources Development Canada. These statistics cover all bargaining units in Canada with 500 or more employees.

REFERENCES

ADAMS, R. J. 1995. "Canadian Industrial Relations in Comparative Perspective," in *Union–Management Relations in Canada*, 3rd Edition, edited by M. Gunderson and A. Ponak. Don Mills: Addison-Wesley, pp. 495–526.

AKYEAMPONG, E. 1997a. "Work Arrangements: 1995 Overview." *Perspectives on Labour and Income*, 9 (Spring).

———. 1997b. *A Statistical Portrait of the Trade Union Movement.* Statistics Canada, Catalogue no. 75-001-XPE.

———. 1999. "Unionization—an Update." *Perspectives on Labour and Income,* 11 (Autumn), pp. 45–65. Statistics Canada, Catalogue no. 75-001-XPE.

ALBERTA ECONOMIC DEVELOPMENT AUTHORITY. 1995. *Final Report.* Joint Review Committee, Right-to-Work Study (November 30).

BEAUCAGE, A. and C. LAFLEUR. 1994. "La négociation concessive dans l'industrie manufacturière canadienne pendant les années 1980," in *Proceedings of the XXXth Annual Conference of the Canadian Industrial Relations Association,* edited by E. Déom and A. Smith. Quebec: CIRA.

BETCHERMAN, G., K. McMULLEN, N. LECKIE, and C. CARON. 1994. *The Canadian Workplace in Transition.* Kingston: IRC Press.

BROWN, D. J. M. and D. M. Beatty. 1999. *Canadian Labour Arbitration*, 3rd Edition. Aurora: Canada Law Book.

CELANI, A. and C. L. WEBER. 1998. "Pay-for-Knowledge Systems: Guidelines for Practice." Industrial Relations Centre, Queen's University, Current Issues Series. Kingston: IRC Press.

CHAYKOWSKI, R. P. and G. A. SLOTSVE. 1986. "Union Seniority Rules as a Determinant of Intra-Firm Job Changes." *Relations industrielles/Industrial Relations*, 41, pp. 720–37.

CRAIG, A. W. J. 1986. "Technological Change, Labour Relations Policy, Administrative Tribunals and the Incidence of Technological Change Provisions in Major Collective Agreements," in *Is There a New Canadian Industrial Relations?* edited by M. Thompson. Proceedings of the 23rd Annual Meeting of the Canadian Industrial Relations Association. Quebec: CIRA.

DONNER, A. (Chair). 1994. *Report of the Task Force on Working Time and the Distribution of Work.* Ottawa: Human Resource Development Canada.

FISHER, E. G. and L. M. SHERWOOD. 1984. "Fairness and Managerial Rights in Canadian Arbitral Jurisprudence." *Relations industrielles/Industrial Relations*, 39, pp. 720–37.

FORREST, A. 1993. "Women and Industrial Relations: No Room in the Discourse." *Relations industrielles/Industrial Relations*, 48, pp. 409–440.

GERSUNY, C. 1982. "Origins of Seniority Provisions in Collective Bargaining." *Labor Law Journal*, 33 (August), pp. 518–524.

GILSON, C. H. H. 1985. "Changes in the Nature of Grievance Issues Over the Last Ten Years: Labour Management Relations and the 'Frontier of Control'." *Relations industrielles/Industrial Relations*, 40, pp. 856–64.

HALL, K. 1999. "Hours Polarization at the End of the 1990s." *Perspectives on Labour and Income*, 11 (Summer), pp. 28–37.

HÉBERT, G. 1992. *Traité de négociation collective.* Boucherville: Gaëtan Morin.

HUMAN RESOURCES DEVELOPMENT CANADA. Various dates. *The Workplace Gazette, Collective Bargaining Bulletin,* and *The Wage Settlement Bulletin,* Government of Canada.

———. 1999. "Statistical Analysis: Occupational Injuries and Fatalities, Canada" (May 10).

JAMIESON, H. R. and B. R. GREYELL (Commissioners). 1995. *Report of the Industrial Inquiry Commission into Industrial Relations at West Coast Ports* (November 30).

LACROIX, M., M. HEBERT, N. AMYOT, A. CHARBONNEAU, and T. PLANTE. 1999. "Long-Term Collective Agreements and Reopener Clauses." *Workplace Gazette,* 2 (Fall), pp. 42–57.

LAMSON, C. 1986. "On the Line: Women and Fish Plant Jobs in Atlantic Canada." *Relations industrielles/Industrial Relations,* 41, pp. 145–156.

MacDOWELL, L. S. 1978. "The Formation of the Canadian Industrial Relations System During World War Two." *Labour/Le Travailleur,* 3, pp. 175–196.

PALMER, E. E. and B. M. PALMER. 1991. *Collective Agreement Arbitration in Canada,* 3rd Edition. Toronto: Butterworths.

RICHARD, Justice K. P. (Commissioner). 1997. *The Westray Story: A Predictable Path to Disaster.* Report of the Westray Mine Public Inquiry. Halifax: Province of Nova Scotia.

SACK GOLDBLATT MITCHELL. 1993. *Words and Phrases: A Dictionary of Collective Agreement Language.* Toronto: Lancaster House.

SACK, J. and E. POSKANZER. 1996. *Contract Clauses: Collective Agreement Language in Canada,* 3rd Edition. Toronto: Lancaster House.

SASS, R. 1982. "Safety and Self-Respect." *Policy Options* (July–August), pp. 50–53.

SAXE, S. D. and B. C. McLEAN. 1995. *Collective Agreement Handbook: A Guide for Employers and Employees.* Aurora: Canada Law Book.

SCOTT, T. 1996. "Human Rights Issues and the Collective Agreement." Industrial Relations Centre, Queen's University, Current Issues Series. Kingston: IRC Press.

SLICHTER, S. H., J. J. HEALY, and E. R. LIVERNASH. 1960. *The Impact of Collective Bargaining on Management.* Washington, D. C.: Brookings.

VERMA, A. and J. CUTCHER-GERSHENFELD. 1993. "Joint Governance in the Workplace: Beyond Union-Management Cooperation and Worker Participation," in *Employee Representation,* edited by B. E. Kaufman and M. M. Kleiner. Madison, WI: Industrial Relations Research Association.

WARSKETT, R. 1993. "Can a Disappearing Pie Be Shared Equally?: Unions, Women, and Wage Fairness," in *Women Challenging Unions: Feminism, Democracy, and Militancy,* edited by L. Briskin and P. McDermott. Toronto: University of Toronto Press.

WELLS, D. 1986. "Autoworkers on the Firing Line," in *On the Job: Confronting the Labour Process in Canada,* edited by C. Heron and R. Storey. Kingston: McGill-Queen's University Press.

WILTON, D. A. 1980. "An Analysis of Canadian Wage Contracts with Cost-of-Living Allowance Clauses." Discussion Paper 165. Ottawa: Economic Council of Canada.

CHAPTER 11

Strikes and
Dispute Resolution

Morley Gunderson, Douglas Hyatt, and Allen Ponak[1]

Strikes by the United Food and Commercial Workers (UFCW) and employers in the hog-slaughter industry illustrate various principles in the strike literature.

In November 1997, the United Food and Commercial Workers Union (UFCW) went on strike against Maple Leaf Foods in Edmonton. The plant, formerly Gainers, owned by Peter Pocklington, had gone through a violent strike in 1986 when replacement workers were brought in. The 1997 strike was to call the company's bluff when it threatened to close the plant if concessions were not made. The strategy backfired, however, and the plant was closed. While this appeared to be a miscalculation on the part of the union, many workers had also "grown tired of the increasing uncertainty about their future" and others "were angry over what they believed was the lack of respect they received."

Subsequently, in March 1998, perhaps believing that the company's threats were credible, striking workers in Burlington, Ontario voted to accept the company's offer under the threat of a plant closure. Wage cuts of around $9 per hour were involved, which the company argued were necessary to bring its costs in line with major US competitors. In return for the wage cuts, the company agreed to give each worker a one-time cash payment of between $10,000 and $33,000, regardless of whether they stayed with the company. Presumably, the unusual settlement was part of a strategy to ensure that the remaining workers would be content with their pay: Those who wouldn't be content would leave; those who stayed at the lower wage would have the lump-sum payment; and new workers would be willing to sign on for the lower pay and, importantly, would be paid the same as incumbent workers (rather than there being a two-tiered wage structure).

The settlement soon led to domino effects and a strike at Quality Meat plants in Toronto and Brampton in December 1998. That company also demanded wage concessions, citing "competition at home, especially from Maple Leaf Foods as well as from US processors... we're dictated by international supply and demand conditions."[2]

This chapter provides an overview of the causes and consequences of strike activity in Canada. First, a description of the frequency, size, and duration of strikes and their distribution by industry and province is presented. The functions and causes of strikes are then discussed, focusing on both economic and non-economic causes. In addition, the role of dispute resolution procedures in reducing strike activity is outlined. Finally, the chapter concludes with a brief discussion of the potential consequences of strikes.

Strikes are one of the most visible outcomes of union–management relations in Canada, and they are often used as a barometer to gauge the health of the industrial relations system. (Hereafter, strikes refer to both strikes and lockouts unless otherwise noted.) As the opening vignette shows, strikes can play a variety of functions both in the union–management relationship and in society: They support bargaining demands, reveal information on the parties' true settlement points, establish reputations, place pressure on both sides to make negotiating concessions, solve intra-organizational bargaining problems, provide a safety valve to release pent-up frustrations, support or protest government policy, enhance political consciousness, and show solidarity with workers' causes elsewhere. Just as strikes have different purposes, it is also clear there is a complex set of conditions that are likely to combine to cause a strike. In any given union–management relationship, the prevailing economic conditions, community characteristics, internal dynamics of the union and management organizations, the nature of the relationship, and the history of collective bargaining may contribute to producing a settlement or a strike. Strikes also have costs. For workers, a strike almost always means

EXHIBIT 11.1

WE'RE NUMBER 1!

On an international basis, Canada has always had a high volume of strike activity, usually second only to Italy. This has occurred in part because strikes in Canada tend to be of long duration. From 1986 to 1995, however, Canada has achieved the dubious distinction of having the highest strike rate (days lost per worker) of *all* G-7 Industrial Nations (the United States, Germany, France, the United Kingdom, Italy, and Japan). Over that period, Canada's strike rate was about 2.5 times the average of the G-7 Industrial Nations, and also about 2.5 times that of the average of the 24 nations of the Organization for Economic Co-operation and Development.

Source: Calculations from data given in Sweeney and Davies, 1997.

substantial loss of income while the strike lasts. The union may provide strike pay, but the amount is usually only sufficient for basic subsistence needs. If the strike shuts down operations, the employer may be faced with loss of profit, loss of customers, and a permanent decline in market share. The same may happen to other employers who rely on the services of an employer who is shut down because of a strike. The public may also be affected if, for example, the major employer in a small town is shut down or a service on which people rely, such as mass transit, is no longer available. These issues are of particular importance given our high strike rate by international standards (see Exhibit 11.1).

MEASURING STRIKE ACTIVITY

As with most seemingly simple statistics, the measures of strike activities are replete with problems—problems that are accentuated when comparisons are made over long periods of time or across diverse countries. These problems[3] include what to count as a strike (in Canada strikes involving a total loss of less than ten working days are excluded), how to treat political strikes or protests, how to classify people who may not officially be on strike but are not working because of the strike, and how to determine when some protracted strikes have ended. Quantitative studies of strike activity are also difficult to compare because of differences in the measures used (Stern, 1978). As well, the format for publishing strike statistics can change. For example, prior to 1982 the United States classified work stoppages involving six or more workers as a strike. After 1982, only stoppages involving 1000 or more workers are included in the series. This has led some researchers to question the appropriateness of generalizations based on large strikes, although others find that small and large strikes both have similar underlying determinants (Garen and Krislov, 1988; Skeels, McGrath, and Arshanapalli, 1988).

Most developed nations, Canada included, publish strike statistics in three series: (1) frequency or number of strikes per year; (2) total number of workers involved in strikes;

and (3) volume or total days lost through strikes, often expressed as a percentage of working time. These raw measures do not, however, directly indicate the average size of each strike (that is, the average number of workers involved) or the average duration (that is, the average length of time each worker remains on strike). Hence, the raw measures by themselves do not indicate if a high volume of strike activity, as measured by days lost, resulted from a large number of strikes (frequency), a large number of workers involved in each strike (size), a series of long strikes (duration), or some combination of these three components.

As illustrated in Table 11.1, however, some basic manipulations of the raw numbers enable the calculation of the three components of the total volume of strike activity—frequency, size, and duration. These three components, when multiplied together, give the overall volume of strike activity, or total days lost (Forchheimer, 1948). Expressed as a percentage of time worked, this is a measure of the relative degree of overall strike activity in the economy.

To put this latter measure in perspective, a figure of 1 percent of working time lost due to strikes would imply that about 1 day out of every 100 working days would be lost due to strikes. A figure of 0.40 percent implies about 1 day per year lost (based on 250 working days in a year). The average time lost in the period since 1976 is slightly under half of that (i.e., 0.18 percent), which implies slightly under a half-day per year per worker lost due to strikes.

CANADIAN STRIKE ACTIVITY

Strike activity in Canada has been historically quite volatile. The percentage of working time lost due to strikes has ranged from a low of 0.01 in the Depression of 1930, to a high of 0.60 in 1919 after the First World War and 0.59 in 1976. Even in these years of peak strike activity, considerably less than 1 percent of total working time was lost due to strikes. Table 11.1 reveals that there have been distinct phases: moderate levels of strike activity in the prosperous years of the early 1920s, low levels in the depression years of the late 1920s and early 1930, low levels in the war years 1939–45, a spurt in 1946 followed by moderate levels until the mid-1960s, extremely high levels from 1970 to 1981, moderate and declining levels throughout the 1980s, and a sharp drop in the 1990s.

Strike activity generally drops in periods of recession and stagnant economic activity. Since the recession of the early 1980s, and especially during the 1990s, strike activity has declined markedly, perhaps heralding an end to the wave of strike activity that began in the mid-1960s. While strike activity in Canada has been declining markedly in recent years, there are notable deviations in that trend. There was a noticeable increase in strike activity in 1996 and 1997, attributable to a number of large and long-lasting strikes in the public sector (i.e., the Canada Post and Ontario Teachers' Federation strikes in 1997 as well as the CAW strike against General Motors in Ontario in 1996). Furthermore, in 1996, there were a large number of short "days-of-protest" strikes in Ontario, especially in the public sector, to protest against policies of the newly elected Conservative government.

TABLE 11.1

VARIOUS MEASURES OF STRIKE ACTIVITY, CANADA, 1901–1998

Year	Frequency[a]	Size[b]	Duration[c]	Person-Days Lost[d]	VOLUME As Percentage of Working Time[e]
	(1)	(2)	(3)	(4)	(5)
1901	99	243	30.6	737,808	—
1902	125	102	16.0	203,301	—
1903	175	219	22.4	858,959	—
1904	103	111	16.9	192,890	—
1905	96	130	19.7	246,138	—
1906	150	156	16.2	378,276	—
1907	188	181	15.3	520,142	—
1908	76	343	27.0	703,571	—
1909	90	201	48.6	880,663	—
1910	101	220	32.9	731,324	—
1911	100	292	62.4	1,821,084	—
1912	181	237	26.5	1,135,787	—
1913	152	267	25.6	1,036,254	—
1914	63	154	50.5	490,850	—
1915	63	181	8.3	95,042	—
1916	120	221	8.9	236,814	—
1917	160	314	22.4	1,123,515	—
1918	230	347	8.1	647,942	—
1919	336	443	22.8	3,400,942	0.60
1920	322	187	13.3	799,524	0.14
1921	168	168	37.1	1,048,914	0.22
1922	104	421	34.9	1,528,661	0.32
1923	86	398	19.6	671,750	0.13
1924	70	490	37.7	1,295,054	0.26
1925	87	333	41.2	1,193,281	0.23
1926	77	310	11.2	266,601	0.05
1927	74	301	6.8	152,570	0.03
1928	98	179	12.8	224,212	0.04
1929	90	144	11.7	152,080	0.02
1930	67	205	6.7	91,797	0.01
1931	88	122	19.0	204,238	0.04
1932	116	202	10.9	255,000	0.05
1933	125	212	12.0	317,547	0.07
1934	191	240	12.5	574,519	0.11
1935	120	277	8.7	288,703	0.05
1936	156	223	8.0	276,997	0.05
1937	278	259	12.3	886,393	0.15
1938	147	139	7.3	148,678	0.02
1939	122	336	5.5	224,588	0.04

TABLE 11.1 (CONT'D.)

VARIOUS MEASURES OF STRIKE ACTIVITY, CANADA, 1901–1998

Year	Frequency[a]	Size[b]	Duration[c]	Person-Days Lost[d]	Volume — As Percentage of Working Time[e]
	(1)	(2)	(3)	(4)	(5)
1940	168	361	4.4	266,318	0.04
1941	231	377	5.0	433,914	0.06
1942	354	322	4.0	450,202	0.05
1943	402	543	4.8	1,041,198	0.12
1944	199	378	6.5	490,139	0.06
1945	197	488	15.2	1,457,420	0.19
1946	226	614	32.4	4,494,833	0.54
1947	234	442	22.9	2,366,339	0.27
1948	154	278	20.7	885,793	0.10
1949	135	347	22.1	1,036,818	0.11
1950	161	1,200	7.2	1,388,110	0.15
1951	258	392	8.9	901,625	0.09
1952	219	513	24.6	2,765,506	0.29
1953	173	315	24.1	1,312,715	0.15
1954	173	327	25.3	1,430,300	0.15
1955	159	378	31.2	1,875,400	0.19
1956	229	387	14.1	1,245,824	0.11
1957	245	329	18.3	1,477,105	0.13
1958	258	425	24.4	2,673,481	0.24
1959	216	440	23.4	2,226,891	0.19
1960	274	180	15.0	738,701	0.06
1961	287	341	13.6	1,335,081	0.11
1962	311	239	19.1	1,417,361	0.11
1963	332	251	11.0	916,991	0.07
1964	343	293	15.7	1,580,421	0.11
1965	502	342	13.4	2,301,088	0.17
1966	617	667	12.6	5,179,993	0.34
1967	522	483	15.8	3,975,792	0.25
1968	581	385	22.7	5,077,609	0.32
1969	597	514	25.2	7,733,287	0.46
1970	544	481	25.0	6,539,500	0.39
1971	569	421	11.9	2,854,480	0.16
1972	598	1,180	10.9	7,716,287	0.43
1973	724	484	16.4	5,761,150	0.30
1974	1,217	487	15.6	9,222,256	0.46
1975	1,170	431	21.6	10,877,291	0.56
1976	1,040	1,524	7.3	11,544,170	0.53
1977	806	270	15.3	3,320,050	0.15
1978	1,057	379	18.4	7,357,180	0.32

TABLE 11.1 (CONT'D.)

VARIOUS MEASURES OF STRIKE ACTIVITY, CANADA, 1901–1998

Year	Frequency[a]	Size[b]	Duration[c]	VOLUME Person-Days Lost[d]	As Percentage of Working Time[e]
	(1)	(2)	(3)	(4)	(5)
1979	1,049	441	16.9	7,819,350	0.33
1980	1,028	427	20.8	9,129,960	0.37
1981	1,049	325	25.9	8,850,040	0.35
1982	679	684	12.3	5,702,370	0.23
1983	645	511	13.5	4,440,900	0.18
1984	716	261	20.8	3,883,400	0.15
1985	829	196	19.3	3,125,560	0.12
1986	748	647	14.8	7,151,470	0.27
1987	668	871	6.5	3,810,170	0.14
1988	548	377	23.7	4,901,260	0.17
1989	627	709	8.3	3,701,360	0.13
1990	579	467	18.8	5,079,190	0.17
1991	463	547	9.9	2,516,090	0.09
1992	404	371	14.1	2,110,180	0.07
1993	381	267	14.9	1,516,640	0.05
1994	374	216	19.9	1,606,580	0.06
1995	328	455	10.6	1,583,061	0.05
1996	330	854	11.9	3,351,820	0.11
1997	284	907	14.0	3,610,196	0.12
1998	378	616	10.6	2,465,530	0.08

[a] Number of strikes in existence during the year, whether they began in that year or earlier.

[b] Average number of workers involved per strike, calculated as the number of workers involved (from the basic data source, not shown on the table) divided by the number of strikes.

[c] Average days lost per worker on strike, calculated as total person-days lost (column 4) divided by the number of workers involved. This is a measure of the average length of time that each worker who is on strike remains on strike. An alternative measure of duration is the average length of each strike, which can be calculated as the days lost divided by the number of strikes (i.e., frequency of column 1).

[d] Product of frequency (strikes) times size (strikers/strikes) and duration (days lost/striker). Numbers are approximate because of rounding.

[e] Beginning in 1975, potential working time is based on employed workers. Prior to 1975, working time is based on paid, non-agricultural workers.

Sources: 1901–1945—Labour Canada, *Strikes and Lockouts in Canada*, various issues.

1946–1975—Calculations by the authors based on the Bureau of Labour Information, *Work Stoppage File*.

1976–1998—Figures for columns 1, 4, and 5 are from Human Resources Development Canada, Workplace Information Directorate, adapted with the permission of the Minister of Public Works and Government Services Canada 2000, http://labour-travail.hrdc-drhc.gc.ca/doc/wid-dimt/eng/ws-at/table.cfm. Figures for columns 2 and 3 are calculated by the authors as discussed, respectively, in notes b and c above. Both calculations required data on the total number of workers involved from the Web address above.

Exhibit 11.2

A 'Withering Away' of the Strike?

The decline of strike activity in the 1980s and 1990s is not confined to Canada and the United States. It has also occurred in western Europe, and especially in otherwise strike-prone countries like Italy and the United Kingdom. Interrelated reasons for the decline include (Aligisakis, 1997):

- The high unemployment of the last 20 years;
- Industrial restructuring and new technology, which are not conducive to worker mobilization;
- A political decision on the part of the Italian trade unions, especially in the public sector, to pursue more peaceful labour relations;
- Restrictive legislation under Thatcher in Britain;
- Increased worker participation in the joint management of the organization.

Undoubtedly, globalization has also played an important part since both labour and management run a greater risk of permanently losing market share to other countries if the organization is shut down due to a strike.

While the recent decline of strike activity may have occurred across many countries, it may be premature to conclude that the strike has "withered away" (see Exhibit 11.3).

A breakdown of the time pattern of strike activity for the public and private sectors respectively (Gunderson and Hyatt, 1996; Gunderson and Reid, 1995) indicates that strike activity has declined since the mid-1970s in both sectors; however, the decline has been more rapid in the private sector compared to the public sector. As such, the public-sector share of total strike days lost has increased since the mid-1970s. In fact, in 1991, a record high of 57 percent of all strike days lost was accounted for by public-sector strikes, although in more typical years they account for around 20 to 30 percent of all strike activity—approximately their same percentage of total employment (see Chapter 14).

The recent decline in strikes is an international phenomenon, also having occurred in the United States and western Europe (Aligisakis, 1997). Whether this reflects a "withering away" of the strike or a temporary phenomenon is an interesting and important question (see Exhibits 11.2 and 11.3).

Cyber Picket Line (British list of strikes around the world):
www.cf.ac.uk/ccin/union/

Components of Strike Activity

The first three columns of Table 11.1 indicate the contribution of each of the components of strike activity—frequency, size, and duration—to the overall volume of strike activity. With the exceptions of both World Wars, Canada has almost always had strikes of fairly long duration compared to most other countries. Over the full period 1901 to 1998, the average strike lasted 18.8 days, though it dropped to 16.6 days in the 1980s,

EXHIBIT 11.3

THE NEWS OF MY DEATH IS PREMATURE

While the strike rate, or proportion of contracts signed after a strike in the private sector, has clearly declined (9.5 percent in the 1990s, compared to 15.1 percent in the 1980s, as shown in Table 11.4) strikes have not "withered away." As indicated in the table below, strike rates declined markedly in the recession of the early 1990s to a low of 2.7 percent in 1993. After 1993 however, strike rates rebounded to double-digit levels after the mid-1990s, indicating that the strike weapon is "alive and well" (although opponents of the adversarial system will argue that the cure may well "kill the patient"). Clearly, strikes have dissipated but they have not disappeared. To paraphrase Mark Twain, "the news of my death is premature."

PROPORTION OF AGREEMENTS IN THE PRIVATE SECTOR SIGNED AFTER A STRIKE, 1990–98

YEAR	STRIKE RATE
1990	12.6
1991	5.6
1992	11.9
1993	2.7
1994	7.8
1995	9.3
1996	12.2
1997	10.2
1998	12.7

and 13.8 days in the 1990s. This recent drop in duration, which has been accompanied by a decline in strike frequency, has resulted in a substantial reduction in the percentage of working time lost due to strikes. The 1970s were a particularly volatile period in Canadian industrial relations, and this is reflected in strike activity. Two very large strikes occurred in 1972 and 1976—the Common Front general strike of public employees in Quebec, and a Day of Protest throughout Canada in opposition to wage controls introduced by the federal government the previous year. The average size of strikes in these two years increased dramatically as a result. The frequency of strikes also increased because the average length of contracts shortened during the inflationary cycle of the 1970s. This meant that more contracts were being negotiated each year and hence the potential for strikes rose.

Contract Status at Time of Strike

It is useful to distinguish strikes by the status of the contract at the time of the strike because different kinds of strikes may well have different underlying causes. First-contract or recognition strikes occur over the establishment of the first collective agreement following the certification of the union; contract-renewal strikes occur over the renegotiation of an existing collective agreement; mid-contract strikes occur during the term of an existing collective agreement.[4]

Table 11.2 provides information on the status of the contract at the time of the strike. From 1986 to 1998, the vast majority of strike activity according to all measures was accounted for by regular end-of-contract disputes that occur during the renegotiation of an existing collective agreement. This result is not unexpected, since the overwhelming majority of contract negotiations occur in this category and since strikes during the term of the collective agreement are illegal. Recognition or first-agreement strikes accounted for 15.5 percent of strikes and lockouts, but because they tended to occur mainly in small establishments, they involved only 1.9 percent of workers on strike. In spite of their illegality in all jurisdictions except Saskatchewan, mid-contract strikes during the term of an existing collective agreement accounted for 6 percent of all work stoppages and 24.0 percent of workers involved in strikes. Because they were illegal, these strikes tended to be of short duration, however, explaining why they only accounted for 3.8 percent of person-days lost because of strikes.

Although the earlier periods are not shown in the table, mid-contract strikes as a proportion of all strikes have declined substantially since the 1970s—from 25.2 percent in the 1970–79 period to 11.8 percent in the 1980–85 period, to 6.0 percent between 1986 and 1998. Research would be needed to establish the reasons for this decline. Some of the change may be due to the emergence of new grievance arbitration procedures (for example, expedited arbitration and grievance mediation) and employment standards innovations (for example, health-and-safety committees and advance layoff notice) to deal with problems that arise during the term of the collective agreement. As well, with the

TABLE 11.2

STRIKES AND LOCKOUTS BY CONTRACT STATUS FOR VARIOUS MEASURES OF STRIKE ACTIVITY, CANADA, 1986–1998

CONTRACT STATUS	STRIKES AND LOCKOUTS (%)	WORKERS INVOLVED (%)	PERSON-DAYS LOST (%)
First agreement	15.5	1.9	4.1
Renegotiation of agreement	76.3	72.0	85.3
During term of agreement	6.0	24.0	3.8
Other[a]	2.2	2.1	6.8
Total	100.0	100.0	100.0

[a] Includes instances where there was no collective agreement before the work stoppage and where the conclusion of a final agreement was not a basic issue.

Source: Calculations by the authors based on data from the Human Resources Development Canada, *Work Stoppage File.*

increased use of just-in-time delivery, mid-contract strikes could be particularly disruptive, leading management to take defensive moves against them (e.g., increasing the use of supervisory personnel who would not go on strike) so as to reduce the likelihood of their being used.

Clearly, the underlying causes of these different types of strikes may differ. First-contract strikes may reflect the inexperience of the parties, an especially important factor because this inexperience is likely to lead to misperceptions and a lack of knowledge about the other's position. They may also arise as a continuation of bitter and difficult union organizing campaigns. Mid-contract strikes, on the other hand, usually occur in response to a particular work situation or working condition and may reflect pent-up frustration and lack of confidence in the grievance procedure. Such strikes may also be a way for union members to show discontent over the contract negotiated by their leadership. All too often, the discussion and analysis of strikes assumes that they are a relatively homogeneous phenomenon, and therefore all strikes are analyzed as regular end-of-contract disputes. Most certainly, the determinants of strikes may differ depending on the type of strike.

Industry and Regional Variation

As indicated in Table 11.3, there is considerable industrial and some regional variation in strikes in Canada and also considerable variation within an industry or province over brief periods of time. Between the 1980s and 1990s, the average strike time lost per worker fell by more than half, from 0.46 days to 0.19 days. In the 1990s, the most strike-prone parts of the economy were the primary industries (e.g., fishing, forestry, and mining), followed by manufacturing, with transportation/utilities, and public administration and construction clustered close behind. The industries that were *not* strike-prone were agriculture, finance, trade, and services. A fairly similar picture prevailed in the 1980s, although construction moved down the strike-prone ranking from the 1980s to 1990s and public administration moved up (to almost twice the average). Days lost due to strikes declined in all industries between the 1980s and 1990s, although the decline was small in public administration. As such, public administration moved from being a slightly below-average strike-prone sector, to one that is almost twice the average, currently similar to such conventionally strike-prone industries as construction and transportation/communication.

The provincial figures do not exhibit the same degree of variation. In the 1980s, Newfoundland, British Columbia, and Quebec had the highest volume of strike activity. To a large degree, this reflects the concentration of strike-prone industries in those provinces. This is borne out in econometric studies that indicate strike probabilities in the private sector in Canada are fairly similar across regions when other factors, including industrial distribution, are held constant.[5] In the 1990s, there was greater convergence in strike activity across the provinces, with the conventionally strike-prone provinces of Newfoundland, Quebec, and British Columbia reducing their strike activity the most, moving very close to the national average. For each of these provinces, strike activity dropped to about one-quarter of its 1980 level, while the average across all provinces dropped to slightly more than one-half.

TABLE 11.3

PERSON-DAYS LOST PER EMPLOYED WORKER BY INDUSTRY AND PROVINCE, CANADA, 1980–1998

	1980–89	1990–98
Industry		
Agriculture	0.01	0.00
Other primary industries	1.81	0.69
Manufacturing	0.99	0.44
Construction	0.98	0.31
Transport/utilities	1.04	0.35
Trade	0.12	0.10
Financial	0.09	0.02
Services	0.19	0.10
Public administration	0.43	0.32
Province		
Newfoundland	1.09	0.25
Prince Edward Island	0.07	0.00
Nova Scotia	0.32	0.07
New Brunswick	0.25	0.29
Quebec	0.60	0.15
Ontario	0.31	0.22
Manitoba	0.11	0.12
Saskatchewan	0.20	0.11
Alberta	0.18	0.08
British Columbia	0.81	0.21
Average	0.46	0.19

Note: Calculated as person-days lost due to strikes and lockouts divided by the number of employed workers in each industry and province.

Source: "Person-Days Lost per Employed Worker by Industry and Province, Canada, 1980–1998," adapted from *Labour Force Information*, Catalogue No. 71-001.

Strike Rates and Settlement Stages

Another measure of strike activity is the strike rate or proportion of collective agreements that are signed after a strike has occurred. This information is provided in Table 11.4, which shows the stage at which each collective agreement was settled (hence the term "settlement stage"). The last column of Table 11.4 indicates that from 1980 to 1998, 12.9 percent of private-sector agreements were signed after a strike. The strike rate in the private sector was lower (9.5 percent) in the more recent 1990–98 period than in the earlier 1980–89 period (15.1 percent).

In the more recent period of 1990–98, 59 percent of the private-sector agreements were settled at the stage of direct bargaining, with an additional 28.4 percent settled with the assistance of conciliation or mediation. The use of third-party arbitration is extremely rare in the private sector (1.6 percent)—the parties being loathe to hand this decision over to a third-party arbitrator.

In the public sector, strike rates initially appear considerably lower, at 3 percent in the 1990–98 period. This apparently low rate may be misleading because the public sector had a substantial proportion of contracts settled through direct legislative intervention (22.4 percent in the 1990–98 period). In some cases, legislation takes place *after* a strike

TABLE 11.4

SETTLEMENT STAGES, MAJOR COLLECTIVE AGREEMENTS—PUBLIC AND PRIVATE SECTORS, 1980–98

PROPORTION OF AGREEMENTS SIGNED AT EACH STAGE[a]

Settlement Stage	Early Period 1980–1989		Later Period 1990–1998		Full Period 1980–1998	
	Public	Private	Public	Private	Public	Private
Direct bargaining	46.3	45.1	50.5	59.1	48.2	50.7
Conciliation	11.9	17.8	6.3	13.5	9.4	16.1
Post-conciliation	3.1	7.1	2.7	5.3	2.9	6.4
Mediation	9.9	12.8	9.5	9.0	9.7	11.3
Post-mediation	2.7	0.7	1.1	0.6	2.0	0.7
Arbitration	8.6	0.9	4.2	1.6	6.6	1.2
Strike	4.2	15.1	3.0	9.5	3.7	12.9
Legislated[b]	12.7	0.2	22.4	0.9	17.0	0.4
Other, Unknown	0.6	0.3	0.3	0.5	0.5	0.3
Total	100.0	100.0	100.0	100.0	100.0	100.0

[a] In order for the data to be defined consistently across time periods, contracts covering 200 or more workers in the federal jurisdiction were excluded after the 1986 settlement year and construction contracts after the 1983 settlement year. Thus, the table includes non-construction contracts covering 500 or more employees.

[b] Includes contracts reopened under the Ontario Social Contract of 1993. These amounted to 12.5 percent of the 22.4 percent in the period 1990–1998 and 5.6 percent of the 17 percent over the full period 1980–1998.

Source: Calculations by the authors based on data from the Bureau of Labour Information's Major Wage Settlements database, for major collective agreements of 500 or more employees. Reproduced with permission of the Minister of Human Resources Development Canada.

has occurred; in others, legislation suspended collective bargaining and imposed collective agreements. Furthermore, arbitrated settlements are much more common in the public sector. Combining arbitrated collective agreements with agreements achieved after a strike or through legislation would show that between 1990 and 1998, public-sector collective agreements were achieved by the parties themselves (or through the assistance of a mediator or conciliator) only about 70 percent of the time. By comparison, private-sector negotiations successfully produced collective agreements 88 percent of the time. The special circumstances of the public sector are discussed in Chapter 14.

Summary of Basic Picture

Historically, there have been wide fluctuations in the various components of strike activity in Canada. From the mid-1960s to the early 1980s, strike activity was particularly high, but it has dropped markedly during the 1980s and especially 1990s. Whether this is simply a short-run phase or the beginning of a long-run trend reflecting greater competitive pressures is an important but unanswered question.

Although most strikes occur during the renegotiation of a collective agreement, a substantial number of illegal strikes occur during the term of the collective agreement. Recognition or first-agreement strikes occur quite often; however, they do not involve many workers and hence do not contribute much to the total person-days lost because of strikes.

There is substantial industry and regional variation. In the 1980s, Newfoundland, British Columbia, and Quebec had the highest volume of strike activity, in part because they have a concentration of strike-prone industries, including fishing, mining, construction, lumber, and pulp and paper. In the 1990s, strike activity dropped markedly across almost all industries and it dropped the most in the otherwise strike-prone provinces so that there has been considerable convergence of strike activity across provinces. It is of particular note that strike activity in public administration did not drop by much. As such, its strike activity was almost twice the national average in the 90s, similar to that of such conventionally strike-prone industries as construction and transportation/communication.

In the 1990s, almost 90 percent of private-sector agreements were settled by direct bargaining or with the aid of conciliation or mediation. Slightly less than 10 percent required a strike, and very few required legislation or arbitration. Conversely, in the public sector, about 70 percent were settled by direct bargaining or with the aid of conciliation. Almost 30 percent were settled by other means: legislation (22 percent), arbitration (4 percent), or a strike (3 percent).

FUNCTIONS AND CAUSES OF STRIKES

Strikes can serve a variety of functions (and disfunctions) with those functions being intricately related to the causes and determinants of strikes.

Functions of Strikes

Since strikes can serve a variety of purposes and can occur for a variety of reasons, it is not really feasible to talk about a unique cause of strike activity. Strikes may occur to win recognition for a particular union or to win concessions from the other side. They may serve an important information-generating function through shedding light on the true settlement points of both parties and on the internal trade-offs being made within both the union and the firm. They may simply be mistakes or accidents made by the parties, like the UFCW's miscalculation at Maple Leaf Foods' Edmonton plant (see opening vignette), given the complexities and uncertainties of the bargaining process. Strikes may reflect pent-up, unresolved grievances over working conditions or be spontaneous acts in response to a particular working condition. (The latter often results in a strike during the term of an existing collective agreement—termed a wildcat strike). Strikes may be a cathartic event providing a safety valve for pent-up frustration, or they may be a political act of worker solidarity or even a way of getting a vacation. They may also be used by union leaders to solidify the rank and file, to find out what they really want and are prepared to give up, or to lower their expectations as the strike runs its course. The parties may also use strikes to establish or enhance reputations for subsequent rounds of bargaining; this factor can complicate the analysis of strike activity, since the ultimate purpose of the strike may appear unrelated to the events at hand.

Strikes can also occur over a range of issues. Conventionally, strikes occur over wages. However, in recent years job security and working time have emerged as prominent strike issues. These issues have become more prominent because downsizing and restructuring have increasingly threatened the jobs of the typical union member, and those who remain employed have often seen the pace of their workload intensify. These issues have been prominent in a number of recent high-profile strikes. The Ontario teachers' strike of 1997 was sparked by a fear of job loss associated with education restructuring and by concern over loss of preparation time. The Canada Post strike in the same year was sparked by concerns over job cuts as well as possible increases in the pace of work associated with mail delivery.

Strikes can be extremely difficult phenomena to analyze, in part because they involve bluffs and posturing, as well as the "calling" of bluffs. The illustration from the 1999 auto industry negotiations in Exhibit 11.4 provides insights into the complexity of bargaining table behaviour and the role of the strike or at least its threat.

Causes or Theoretical Determinants of Strikes

Theories of the causes of strikes endeavour to relate measures of strike activity to various observable characteristics that are believed to affect strike activity. Such characteristics, or strike determinants, can involve variables related to the social, economic, political, and legal environment in which the parties operate and the characteristics of their respective organizations as well as of the negotiators and the bargaining process itself.

EXHIBIT 11.4

THE STRIKE THAT ALMOST WAS

On October 5, 1999 the CAW negotiated a settlement with Daimler-Chrysler that followed the pattern established with Ford earlier in the year. In that earlier Ford negotiation, the CAW had taken the unprecedented step of releasing the first offer by the company to the rank and file in the plants. This had the predictable effect of solidifying the rank and file to take strike action if necessary.

In the subsequent Chrysler negotiations, the CAW took another unusual step—threatening to strike if Daimler-Chrysler did not compel one of its major parts suppliers, Magna, to voluntarily recognize the union at one of its plants in Windsor where an organizing drive was underway. The CAW has been trying to organize the parts suppliers because by around 2003, 80 percent of the jobs in the auto industry are expected to be in the parts industry. As Sam Gindin (assistant to the CAW president) indicated, "you can't be this little island of unionized workers surrounded by deunionization" (*Globe and Mail,* October 23, 1999, p. B14).

While the objective was important for the union, it is unlikely that the rank and file at Daimler-Chrysler could have been mobilized for a sympathy strike to facilitate unionization in parts suppliers where there is little history of unionism and worker solidarity. As CAW president Buzz Hargrove indicated: "Bargaining is about posturing and getting yourself in certain positions...Sometimes you stick your neck out. In this case, I got clipped a bit...I put myself in a box and I know that...It was a gamble I took to make Magna a separate strike issue. But in the end, I could not justify a strike on the Magna issue alone" (*Toronto Star,* October 7, 1999).

While Hargrove describes himself as "getting clipped a bit," the facts are that the Magna demand was dropped in part for company concessions to invest more in the Windsor assembly plant and to avoid job losses in the Ajax trim operation. If he was "clipped a bit," he clearly did not pay for the clipping! He was able to negotiate terms that were of clear benefit to his existing membership.

Any theory that tries to indicate how these observable characteristics affect strike activity must confront a basic dilemma; such variables do not have a direct impact on the level of strike activity so long as the variable's effect on each party's bargaining power is understood by both. For example, it is often stated that strike incidence is high at the peak of a business cycle because labour has more bargaining power at that time (since workers have job opportunities elsewhere, and employers are reluctant to lose business). To the extent that this is also known by employers, however, management has an incentive to increase its offer to avoid the strike. The factor giving labour more bargaining power, therefore, has implications for the magnitude of the settlement but not necessarily for strikes. Differential bargaining power is a theory of wages, not of strikes. In a world of perfect information, strikes would serve no useful function; each party would realize each other's position and settle accordingly, dividing up the savings from the avoidance of a costly strike. Hence, the often-cited statement by Hicks (1963: 146–47): "The majority of actual strikes are doubtless the result of faulty negotiation.... Any means which enables either side to appreciate better the position of the other will always make a settlement easier; adequate knowledge will always make a settlement possible."

At the theoretical level, there have been a number of attempts to identify a causal connection between strikes and a variety of observable variables that appear to be determinants of strikes. One procedure is to assume that the parties base their offers and demands on different factors. Rees (1952), for example, argued that unions base their demands on current or lagging indicators such as employment and the cost of living, while management bases its offers on leading indicators such as business failures, security prices, and new contracts. Mauro (1982) theorizes that firms make their offers on the basis of product prices, while employees base their demands on the consumer price index. Kaufman (1993) argues that both parties base their positions on expected inflation, but they have divergent views about its expected level. In all these circumstances, the parties' offers and demands may not offset each other, and strikes may ensue. Although these theories do provide an explanation for strikes, they do not explain why such divergences in expectations or in the determinants of offers and demands should persist.

An alternative perspective[6] views strikes as serving the purpose of eliciting information from employers, who tend to have more information on the true state of their product market and financial position. Given this situation of asymmetric or private information on the part of employers, unions try to prevent them from bluffing about the true state of their financial position. They do this by compelling the firm to endure a strike if it argues that wage concessions are necessary because of its bad financial position. In such circumstances, the firm can endure the strike only if its particular situation is so adverse that the loss of output from the strike is not as costly as a high wage settlement. In essence, the firm is compelled to accept a package involving lower employment (via a strike that is costly) if it insists that its particular situation is adverse; this, in turn, deters bluffing about its true position. It is the firm's particular situation relative to the general state of the economy that is at issue, not the general state of the economy itself. The former is private information; the latter (that is, the business cycle) is public information.

This asymmetric-information perspective is appealing since it provides a theoretical rationale for the existence of strikes. It is not clear, however, that such private information—held only by the firm—is so important in today's world of sophisticated information processing. In addition, it is not clear why the parties would not agree to contractual arrangements whereby compensation depends upon the true state of the firm, as that information is revealed over time.

A third perspective emphasizes that strikes will depend on the joint or total cost to both parties of using the strike as opposed to other mechanisms for sorting out differences between the parties.[7] As discussed previously, strikes serve a variety of functions—eliciting information, establishing reputations, solving intra-organizational problems, venting frustrations, protesting government policy, supporting workers' causes elsewhere—or they may just be mistakes or accidents. In other words, strikes help the parties sort out their differences over the division of the wealth of the enterprise and over everyday employment practices. These purposes can also be served by other mechanisms, including continuous bargaining, joint committees, grievance arbitration, voluntary arbitration, and absenteeism and turnover. All of these mechanisms are costly in terms of uncertainty and their use of real resources.

Simply put, the argument for the joint-cost perspective is that whatever the function or benefits of strikes—and there are many—they are used less often and less intensely when they are costly relative to the other mechanisms that can serve the same purposes. Similarly, if strikes are mistakes or accidents, they will be made less often when the costs of such mistakes are high. It is the joint cost to *both* parties that is important. If a certain factor or variable increases the cost of a strike to only one of the parties, that party will have to "bribe" the other with more favourable settlement terms to reduce the likelihood or duration of a costly strike. The fact that a variable has a differential effect on the parties means that it has implications for settlement terms as well as strike incidence. However, incidence and duration are reduced even though the cost of strikes is higher for one party, since the cost to that party is a component of the total cost to both parties. For example, if unemployment insurance became available to workers on strike, the joint-cost theory predicts that the use of strikes would increase because, in effect, the state would be subsidizing the cost of this method of dispute resolution. It also predicts that settlement terms would be more favourable to the union because, in effect, the bargaining power of the union would be enhanced.

It is interesting that both of the most recent theoretical developments in the strike literature—the asymmetric-information models and the joint-cost perspective—predict that strike activity will be reduced when strikes are costly. The asymmetric-information models predict this on the basis that the firm will opt for the strike to get wage concessions when the cost of the strike to the firm is low. The joint-cost model predicts that strikes will be used more often when the costs are low because strikes are thereby more appealing than the other procedures for solving basic differences at the workplace.

The recent theoretical developments in the strike literature emphasize the importance of strikes as an information-generating mechanism, compelling the parties to articulate their preferences and trade-offs (including those within the organization) and to reveal what otherwise might be private information. They also emphasize focusing on the costs and benefits of strikes relative to other mechanisms for solving basic differences at the workplace. Although often formidable in their mathematical procedures, these models essentially formalize ideas that have long been recognized in institutional industrial relations. More important, they provide a convenient way of incorporating a wide array of institutional industrial relations variables, including policy variables, as strike determinants. In essence, they suggest the *causal* mechanism whereby the institutional industrial relations variables affect strike activity. That is, strike activity is likely to be higher if the variable increases the need for the strike to elicit information from the parties (if, for example, the variable increases uncertainty, misinformation, divergent expectations, or intra-organizational differences) or if the variable reduces the cost of using the strike as opposed to other mechanisms for solving basic differences at the workplace.

Categorizing Strike Determinants

There are almost as many ways of categorizing the causes of strikes as there are ways of classifying strikes themselves. To a certain degree, the categorization reflects the perspectives of the different disciplines that have contributed to our understanding of strike activity. Economists have focused on the economic environment (notably the business cycle, market characteristics, and inflationary expectations); sociologists have focused at the macro level on class conflict and dramatic changes in the social system and in the relations of production, and at the micro level on the process of bargaining and on interpersonal relations; political scientists and historians have emphasized the political environment and the importance of the strike in achieving political ends; and industrial relations analysts have emphasized dispute resolution procedures and characteristics of the bargaining structure and relationship.

For our purposes here, we have categorized the determinants of strikes as either economic or non-economic factors, the latter including legal and procedural factors, political and historical factors, characteristics of the various actors and of the bargaining structure, and personal and interpersonal relationships. Many of these categories are obviously interdependent and overlapping; they are used simply as a convenient way to summarize the current theoretical and empirical literature and to illustrate its interrelatedness—and at times the isolation of particular disciplinary perspectives.

ECONOMIC DETERMINANTS OF STRIKES

The economic determinants of strikes can be categorized according to the ways in which strikes have been analyzed empirically: the early studies of strikes and the business cycle; the more recent studies of the time pattern of aggregate strike activity; recent cross-section studies that seek to explain variation in strikes across industries, unions, regions, cities, or collective agreements; and recent studies that use hazard function procedures to analyze determinants of strike duration.

Business Cycles and Strike Cycles

The earliest economic studies of the time pattern of aggregate strike activity focused on the relationship of strikes to the business cycle. The expectation was for a positive relationship, with strikes being highest at the peak of a business cycle. The reasoning for this theory (usually derived in an ad hoc fashion) was that at the peak of a business cycle—when unemployment is low and profits are high—workers are willing to incur the cost of a strike, largely because they are then more likely to be able to find jobs elsewhere and because they feel employers can pay more since profits are high and inventories low. This line of reasoning, however, begs the question of why the parties should not settle for large wage increases in such circumstances. More bargaining power in the hands of labour should lead to larger wage settlements, not necessarily more strikes. In spite of their inadequate theoretical explanation, the earliest studies of aggregate strike activity tended, with some notable exceptions, to find a positive relationship between strikes and the business cycle.[8]

Recent Studies of Time Pattern of Aggregate Strike Activity

The more recent studies of the time pattern of aggregate strike activity differ from the earlier studies because they endeavour to establish a more rigorous theoretical relationship between strikes and various measures of business cycle activity, and also because they use more sophisticated statistical techniques to try to disentangle the complex relationship between strikes and various measures of economic activity.

Many of the recent studies take as their departure the model developed by Ashenfelter and Johnson (1969). Theirs was the first attempt to develop a formal model whereby strikes resulted from optimizing behaviour. The essence of their model is that a firm decides on the "optimal" profit-maximizing duration of the strike by trading off strike costs with expected future wage costs in its profit-maximizing decision. Subsequent theoretical work has analyzed the analogous decision with respect to unions, both parties, and when union leaders and management have objectives that differ not only from each other's, but also from their constituents' (Eaton, 1973).

Although the recent studies differ considerably in the precise specification of the variables, most relate various measures of aggregate strike activity to a variety of explanatory variables reflecting measures of aggregate business conditions.[9] Even though particular studies always have some exceptions, the empirical results generally find economic factors to be important determinants of the time pattern of aggregate strike activity. In particular, strike activity diminishes in periods of high unemployment and increases in periods of inflation or when real wages are eroded. In Canada, economic factors have been more successful in explaining the frequency of strikes than their size or duration, and they have been less successful in explaining strikes before the Second World War when union organizing strikes were prominent. The ability of economic factors to explain strikes is highest for contract-renewal strikes, second-highest for first-agreement strikes, and lowest for strikes during the term of the contract.

The relationship between economic factors and strike activity is weaker in Canada than either in the United Kingdom or, especially, in the United States. This weaker relationship between strikes and economic factors in Canada may occur for a variety of reasons.

1. Because Canada has a smaller population than either the United Kingdom or the United States, its strike activity may be more dominated by "unusual" events.

2. To the extent that long-duration strikes are more prominent in Canada and strike duration is not as explicable by economic factors as is strike incidence, Canadian strike activity (at least for measures involving duration) will appear to be less dependent on economic activity.

3. Strikes during the life of the contract are more often illegal in Canada than in the United States, where the right to strike during the contract is often negotiable. Since there is more pressure in Canada to wait until the contract expires before striking, it is less likely that strike activity will reflect economic conditions at the time of the strike. In essence, in Canada there is less flexibility to strike in response to current economic conditions, although illegal mid-contract strikes occur frequently, and they appear to be responsive to economic factors.

4. There may simply be differences in the political and sociological environments of Canada and the United States that make Canadian strike activity less dependent on economic activity (Vanderkamp, 1970).

Cross-Section Studies and Economic Variables

The importance of economic factors in explaining strike activity has also been tested in cross-section studies (sometimes pooling time-series data also), which try to explain differences in strike activity across unions, cities, regions, or industries.[10] Empirical studies at the micro level, using the collective agreement as the unit of observation, are particularly informative since their analysis is at the level of the bargaining unit, where bargaining actually occurs, and they often incorporate numerous explanatory variables describing the negotiation environment.[11]

Unfortunately the cross-section studies of strike activity are exceedingly difficult to compare because of the different units of observation (for example, industry, union, region, collective agreement) and the different variables used to explain strike variation or to control for the other relevant factors. In general, however, it appears that characteristics of the economic environment are not as consistently or quantitatively important in explaining strike activity in the cross-section studies as they are in the aggregate time-series studies. Presumably, the effect is dominated by non-economic factors that do not change much over time (and hence that do not "explain" much of the variation in the time pattern of aggregate strike activity).

Hazard Estimates of Strike Duration

A number of recent econometric studies[12] have focused on analyzing strike duration by examining the strike settlement probabilities as the strike progresses (termed the "hazard rate"). Generally, as the strike progresses, the probability of settling the next day (the conditional strike probability) declines, implying that the remaining life expectancy of the strike actually increases as the strike progresses. Much of this simply reflects the fact that the composition of the remaining strikes increasingly consists of strikes that are hard to settle, the easy ones having been settled earlier and dropped out of the sample. When these factors are controlled for, the conditional settlement probabilities increase substantially as the strike progresses, although there is no consensus on the exact configuration of those settlement rates. The evidence appears to indicate, however, that the expected duration of strikes is counter-cyclical (that is, decreases at the peak of the business cycle) while strike incidence is pro-cyclical.

NON-ECONOMIC DETERMINANTS OF STRIKES

It is somewhat of a misnomer to categorize some determinants of strikes as non-economic since many of these factors (such as a legislative change) may alter the costs and benefits of strikes to the parties. Conversely, many of the economic or market variables may operate through intervening variables categorized as non-economic.

Numerous studies have emphasized the non-economic determinants of strikes, focusing on behavioural, organizational, and political aspects.[13] Many of the studies attempt to relate strike activity to one or more of the following aspects: characteristics of the community, union and management organizations, the negotiation process, the bargaining parties, the legal and historical context in which bargaining occurs, personality factors, and the broader socio-political environment.

Worker and Community Characteristics in Mobilizing Workers

Sociological investigations of the determinants of strike activity have viewed strikes as an example of collective behavior. As a result, sociologists especially have attempted to identify characteristics of the community and the union that may increase the mobilization and threat potential of the bargaining unit.

Resource mobilization theories emphasize that strikes are more likely when unions have the strength and resources to mobilize individual workers into collective action.[14] This ability to mobilize resources can be associated with a wide range of factors such as male dominance of the industry and other personal characteristics, as well as with characteristics of the community,[15] large plant sizes (Enderwick and Buckley, 1982), and the "explosion of class consciousness" that often accompanies major strikes and strike waves (Kelly, 1988; Langford, 1996).

Frustrated Expectations and Collective Action

Wheeler (1985) emphasizes that strikes are not so much the result of rational calculations on the part of parties; rather, they tend to occur when individuals are frustrated over the gap between their expectations and their economic and social circumstances. This individual frustration gets translated into collective action when certain preconditions are present, including group solidarity. Wheeler indicates how this perspective is able to explain considerable strike behaviour.

Godard (1992) also emphasizes the importance of strikes as a behavioural manifestation of worker discontent through a "collective voice." Based on Canadian data, his research provides evidence that strikes are more likely in workplaces where there is a lack of autonomy or progressive managerial practices, where union leaders are under pressure to appear militant, and where large operations create a sense of alienation.

Political Environment

A general political environment that is favourable to labour may facilitate the mobilization of workers into forms of collective action like strikes. It may also, however, facilitate labour unions making gains at the political level through social policies that can benefit labour, and this may move the forum for collective action from strikes at the workplace to action at the political level. Overall, therefore, it is not clear whether a general political environment that is favourable to labour will increase or decrease strikes at the workplace. It is also difficult to separate the independent effect of the general political environment from other factors that are at work simultaneously.

Within Canada, Quebec has tended to have a political and legislative environment that "favours" labour, and yet it has a high level of strike activity (see Chapter 16). In the United States, strikes increased in the 1930s within the pro-labour environment of the New Deal, and they decreased in the anti-labour environment of the Reagan era. Labour was also more likely to "lose" strikes in an anti-labour political environment like the 1980s and to "win" them in a pro-labour environment like the New Deal era.[16] Similarly, in Britain, strikes decreased substantially in the 1980s in a political and legal environment that was not supportive of labour (Ingram, Metcalf, andWadsworth, 1993). These examples illustrate that strike activity is likely to increase within a pro-labour political environment and to decrease within an anti-labour political environment, perhaps reflecting changing expectations. There is, however, also considerable international evidence indicating that strikes appear to be less likely in corporatist, social-democratic political environments where labour has considerable influence over the negotiation of social programs that can benefit labour.[17] Clearly, more research in this area would be welcome to sort out the underlying relationship between the general political environment and strike activity.

A number of studies have emphasized strikes as the manifestation of a political struggle between labour and management for power and control at the shop-floor workplace level.[18] From this perspective, strike activity can be altered by various institutional and organizational factors; nevertheless, it is an inevitable by-product of the struggle between labour and capital for control at the workplace.

Union and Management Organization Characteristics
Intra-organizational Conflict

A major component of the bargaining process is the negotiations that occur within the union and management sides (Ghilarducci, 1988). Often there is a great diversity of interests that result in potentially conflicting goals and priorities for the collective bargaining process. Factions and different degrees of militancy often exist within the union on the basis of age, sex, occupation, seniority, or political affiliation, as well as between union leaders and the rank and file. Unless mechanisms exist within the union to resolve these conflicts, the potential for a strike may increase because of the inability of union members to agree on management's offers. For example, studies (Gramm and Schnell, 1994; LeRoy, 1992) indicate how the decision to cross the picket line and return to work (a decision that signals internal conflict within the union and that can effectively end the strike) is related to the individual characteristics of strikers, characteristics such as seniority, income, and racial identification with union leadership.

Management officials also may have major disagreements over priorities and the stand to be adopted on various issues at the bargaining table. Although this type of conflict is most pronounced in the public sector, where differences between management and elected officials are common, it is not unusual for line and staff managers in the private sector to have disputes during collective bargaining.

Inadequate Decision-Making Authority

Inadequate decision-making authority, particularly on the management side, increases the probability of a strike. For example, in the 1960s and early 1970s, the final decision on management's position often resided in the US headquarters of Canadian subsidiaries, leading union negotiators to believe that the management negotiators were little more than messengers who ran back and forth between the table and top management. In such situations, the likelihood of a strike can increase for two reasons. First, union leaders may feel that the only way to bring the real decision makers to the bargaining table is to apply pressure through a strike. Second, not having the real decision makers involved in the day-to-day negotiating process increases the likelihood that they have either unrealistic expectations about the point of settlement or inaccurate perceptions of the expectations of the union.

Foreign Ownership and Multinationals

Related to the notion of inadequate decision-making authority within foreign-owned firms, a number of studies have examined the extent to which such firms may be more strike-prone than domestically owned firms. The issue is complicated, however, by the fact that foreign-owned firms tend to be large multinationals that have considerable bargaining power because they can diversify their production to other plants (Rose, 1991). The issue is especially important in the Canadian context, given the significant role of foreign ownership and multinationals. Canadian studies that have used statistical techniques to control for the influence of other determinants of strikes have produced mixed results.[19] Studies of multinational management practices, discussed in Chapter 5, show that companies tend to adapt their industrial relations practices to conform to the country in which they are operating.

Size and Number of the Bargaining Units

Knowing the impact of the size of the bargaining unit on strike activity is important because labour relations boards can influence bargaining unit size in their certification decisions. There is also the perception that some of Canada's poor strike record is attributable to the proliferation of small bargaining units, which characterize its decentralized bargaining structure. The limited empirical evidence that is available on this topic, however, suggests that, other things being equal, strikes are less likely in single-plant bargaining units[20] and in smaller bargaining units.[21] This also suggests that strikes may decline even more in the future if the trend to smaller bargaining units continues (see Exhibit 11.5).

EXHIBIT 11.5

FEWER STRIKES, MORE CONFLICT?

Hebdon, Hyatt, and Mazerolle (1999) provide empirical evidence for Ontario indicating that strikes are less likely in smaller bargaining units and with independent local unions that are representative of non-traditional forms of employee representation. Over time, smaller bargaining units are becoming more prominent, reflecting the growth of small firms, decentralized bargaining, and the fact that most large bargaining units are already organized in the public sector. Non-traditional forms of employee representation that tend to be more co-operative and non-adversarial are also growing in importance in such forms as enterprise unions, joint health-and-safety committees, plant-level work councils, and independent local unions that are not affiliated with national or international unions.

The fact that strikes are less likely in smaller bargaining units and under non-traditional forms of employee representation suggests that strikes are likely to decline even more in importance if these forms of employee representation become more prominent. The authors also find, however, that these alternative forms of representation are associated with greater individual expressions of conflict such as grievance arbitrations and health-and-safety complaints. In essence, smaller bargaining units may lead to less *collective* conflict like strikes, but more *individual* conflict like grievances and health-and-safety complaints. As such, future dispute resolution should emphasize internal conflict resolution procedures such as peer review panels, mediation, labour–management committees and joint forums, as well as internal problem solving and process consultation among union and management decision makers.

Negotiator and Bargaining Process Characteristics

Union and Management Trust or Hostility

Interpersonal sources of conflict may make it extremely difficult for union and management representatives to accept the position of the other side, to back down from an extreme position taken early in bargaining, or to compromise. As a result, hostility and a lack of trust may increase the probability of a strike.[22]

Negotiator Skills and Experience

As previously noted, Hicks (1963) stated that most strikes are the result of faulty negotiations. Inexperienced negotiators are more likely to provide incorrect cues to their opponents, generating unrealistic expectations about the terms of settlement. Moreover, inexperience may lead a negotiator to become overcommitted to a position that may be unacceptable. Movement from that position may then be impossible without a loss

EXHIBIT 11.6

FROM SIT-IN TO LOVE-IN

A bitter three-week strike occurred between the Canadian Auto Workers and General Motors in October 1996, including the occupation of a parts plant in Oshawa that the company wanted to sell. GM was also hit by strikes in the US in Dayton, Ohio in 1995 and in Flint, Michigan in 1998. These disputes and the accompanying poor labour relations likely contributed to GM's loss of market share and the associated fall in its stock price.

These events may have served as a catalyst for both sides to improve labour relations to facilitate their joint survival. GM, for example, appointed labour relations managers who were prepared to work with and share information with the union. As GM's chief negotiator, Al Green, indicated, "I spent a lot of time getting to know Buzz [Buzz Hargrove, CAW president]...The union and the company have spent much time exchanging information about the business challenges. There are very real challenges that threaten the existence of both of us" (*Globe and Mail*, October 23, p. B14).

The spirit of co-operation led to a settlement at 5 p.m. on October 19, 1999, well before the usual 11th-hour settlement (or later) that typifies negotiations. More surprisingly, and "absolutely unheard of" in the words of CAW president Buzz Hargrove, the CAW bargaining team gave the GM negotiating team a standing ovation that was returned by the GM team for about eight minutes.

Whether the mutual love-fest will last and survive a possible downturn in the auto industry will likely depend on the extent to which both parties can translate the new-found spirit of co-operation in the collective bargaining arena into everyday actions at the workplace level.

of face, both for the other side and for the negotiator's own constituency. Thus, a lack of skill and experience on the part of either or both negotiators is likely to increase the probability of a strike.[23]

Bargaining History

Whether or not a strike is going to occur in a given round of negotiations may be affected as much by the historical context of the relationship as by current economic and non-economic conditions. Past struggles and hostilities may well exacerbate subsequent conflict; the parties may develop a habit or pattern of conflict. Alternatively, strikes may serve as a safety valve and learning experience, thereby decreasing subsequent conflict. The negative experience of a strike may also discourage subsequent conflict through what is known as a "teetotaller" effect (see Exhibit 11.6). The empirical studies[24] generally yield conflicting results on these effects, although the Canadian evidence tends to suggest that long strikes in previous contracts have a sobering teetotaller effect, reducing subsequent conflict, while short strikes leave unresolved issues that lead to more strikes in subsequent rounds.

CBC Interactive Site (provides a brief history of strike activity in Canada): cbc.ca/news/indepth/strike/index.html

DISPUTE RESOLUTION PROCEDURES

All Canadian jurisdictions have established a number of procedures, usually involving the intervention of a neutral third party, to help the parties resolve their disputes (Ponak and Falkenberg, 1989). Some purposes of third-party intervention are to: provide information and help the parties articulate their preferences and trade-offs; provide a period for emotions to ebb and hostilities to cool off; solve interpersonal and political problems through enabling the parties to save face by yielding to the suggestions of a third party; bring public awareness to, and perhaps put pressure on, the parties; and in the most extreme form of intervention—compulsory interest arbitration—to provide a substitute for the strike. These objectives are facilitated to varying degrees by a variety of forms of third-party intervention, including conciliation, mediation, fact-finding, and arbitration.[25]

Types of Dispute Resolution Procedures
Compulsory Conciliation

Canada was one of the few countries to adopt a system of compulsory conciliation during the early 1900s. In the current context, most jurisdictions require conciliation as a precondition to a work stoppage. Typically, at the request of either party, a government conciliator is appointed by the provincial ministry of labour. The conciliator meets with the parties and reports the possibilities of a settlement to the minister of labour. After the report has been filed and a specified period of time has elapsed (usually seven or fourteen days), the union obtains the right to strike and management the right to lock out. In some jurisdictions, if conciliation is unsuccessful, the dispute is forwarded to a conciliation board (usually tripartite), also charged with investigating the dispute and reporting to the minister.

Mediation

Although the terms "mediation" and "conciliation" are sometimes used interchangeably, mediation is often reserved for the voluntary use of a neutral third party, often a non-government professional, who gets involved after the conciliation process is exhausted and possibly when the strike is in progress. Mediation usually is more interventionist than conciliation, with the mediator not just providing information at the early stages, but also suggesting compromises at subsequent stages, and ultimately even suggesting proposals and possibly settlement terms. The mediator's views can be used or ignored by the parties (hence the importance of trust and confidence in the mediator); they need not involve a recommendation, and they are usually not made public, except possibly in public-sector disputes.

Fact-finding

Fact-finding, a task often performed by conciliation boards, is a more formal process than mediation. The fact-finder (or fact-finding board) is charged with the responsibility of investigating the issues in dispute and making formal recommendations to the labour relations board and possibly to the public. As in mediation, however, the recommendations of the fact-finder do not have to be adopted by the parties.

Typically, the fact-finding process includes formal briefs from both union and management as well as a formal hearing where both parties are allowed to present their views. In some situations, however, the term "fact-finding" is used (as the word implies) to refer to a stage in which a third party simply helps the parties compile the relevant facts before any intervention by a conciliator or mediator.

Arbitration

Arbitration is the strongest form of third-party intervention, since it involves the establishment of terms and conditions of the collective agreement by a third-party arbitrator. Such arbitration is termed "interest arbitration" to distinguish it from "rights or grievance arbitration," the latter involving a neutral third party to interpret the existing collective agreement. Interest arbitration usually serves as a substitute for the strike in situations in which strikes are banned, as is often the case for various elements of the public sector, such as police, firefighters, hospital workers, teachers, and the civil service. Canadian jurisdictions vary considerably in requirements for interest arbitration for the different elements of the public sector (see Chapter 14). Although the arbitration decision itself is binding on both union and management, the decision to engage in arbitration may be voluntary. Such voluntary arbitration is rare, however, compared to compulsory arbitration, which is required by law if the parties cannot come to an agreement.

Arbitration, especially in its compulsory form, has been criticized as an unacceptable strike substitute since it does not provide the same inducements to the parties to settle as would a strike. Specifically, arbitration has often been found to chill genuine collective bargaining. This "chilling effect" is said to occur because the parties may hold back concessions during bargaining, believing that the arbitrator is likely to split the difference between their final positions. Arbitration has also been criticized because it may create a "narcotic effect," making the parties dependent on the arbitrator to determine their terms and conditions of employment. The existing empirical evidence (reviewed in Ponak and Falkenberg, 1989) in general does not yield conclusive results on the existence of chilling and narcotic effects.

Other Forms of Dispute Resolution

In the Canadian public sector, the government has often taken an alternative approach to resolving disputes, especially strikes by public employees. More and more frequently, both the federal and provincial governments have been willing to pass special back-to-work legislation requiring the termination of a strike and forcing the parties back to the bargaining table (see Chapter 14). Thus, strikes may be reduced through mediation and fact-finding, prohibited and replaced by arbitration, or ended through special legislation.

Social Contracts

Especially in the 1990s in the private sector in Quebec, a number of long-term contracts have been signed in traditionally strike-prone industries like pulp and paper and steel (see Chapter 16). The agreements have generally been for longer than the conventional maximum of three years—a maximum that is usually required by law, but that the government has extended in these cases in the hope of fostering labour relations peace. Conventionally, wage arbitration is required after three years. In return for forgoing the right to strike that is implied by such long-term contracts (since strikes during the term of collective agreements are not allowed), labour has generally been guaranteed job security as well as a promise of continued investment in plant and equipment (often facilitated by government). The Quebec government has been involved not only in supporting the investment in plant and equipment, but also in facilitating the negotiation of these social contracts. The term "social contracts" is often used to describe these contracts since they involve all of the social partners (labour, management, and governments) in negotiating private collective agreements with a view towards enhancing private outcomes such as industrial peace, job security, and investment that also serve broader social purposes. The term social contracts is also used to describe the programs imposed by various provincial governments in the early 1990s whereby mandatory unpaid days of leave were imposed on public-sector workers as an alternative to layoffs (Gunderson and Hyatt, 1996: 256).

Effect of Dispute Resolution and Other Policy Variables

There is very little empirical evidence on the effect of various dispute resolution procedures or other labour relations policy variables on the level of strike activity. This is particularly unfortunate since, by definition, such variables could be manipulated to reduce the level of strike activity, if this outcome was considered desirable. In contrast, other possible strike determinants, such as the economic variables and the season, region, and industry are subject to little or no policy manipulation.

Specific Laws

The few empirical studies that have included policy variables have generally simply added a variable to reflect the impact of a particular law such as the Landrum-Griffin Act (Ashenfelter and Johnson, 1969), right-to-work laws (Gramm, 1986), state penalties for public-sector workers who go on strike or prohibitions on school districts to reschedule teacher strike days to qualify for state aid (Montgomery and Benedict, 1989; Olson, 1984, 1986), the availability of unemployment insurance for workers on strike (Hutchens, Lipsky, and Stern, 1992; Ondrich and Schnell, 1993), or an index of labour law changes that affect collective bargaining and union power (Ingram, Metcalf, and Wadsworth, 1993). These studies generally find that laws and policies designed to discourage strikes or make them more costly or difficult do tend to reduce strike activity.

Prohibitions on the Right to Strike in the Public Sector

A number of empirical studies have also examined the extent to which legislative prohibitions on union activity and the right to strike in the public sector have deterred strikes.[26] Most find public-sector strike activity is deterred, but by no means eliminated, by prohibitions and penalties on the right to strike (see Exhibit 11.7).

Labour Relations Policy Variables

A comprehensive analysis of the impact that a wide range of Canadian labour relations policy variables have on strike activity is summarized in Table 11.5, based on the econometric studies cited in the source. The first column gives the effect of each policy variable on strike incidence—that is, the probability that the contract will be settled following the occurrence of a strike. These changes should be interpreted relative to the average strike incidence of 15.9 percent; that is, over the period 1967–1985 almost 16 percent of contracts involved a strike. The second column gives the effect of each policy variable on strike duration—that is, the length of the strikes that occurred

EXHIBIT 11.7

DOES PROHIBITING THE RIGHT TO STRIKE REDUCE DISPUTE COSTS?

Currie and McConnell (1991) find that granting public-sector workers the right to strike does lead to significantly higher strike frequencies, compared to when the right is prohibited and arbitration is required. Furthermore, the cost per dispute is much higher when the dispute takes the form of a strike rather than an arbitration. For these reasons, dispute costs (strikes plus arbitrations) increase because the cost increase due to increased strikes is greater than the cost saving due to reduced arbitrations. They argue that this must be traded off against higher wage costs, which tend to occur under arbitration. These general conclusions tend to hold up when their data is reanalyzed to account for discrepancies in their legislative coding and the content of the relevant statutes, as well as the actual practice (Gunderson, Hebdon, and Hyatt, 1996).

The analysis becomes even more complicated, however, since prohibiting the right to strike among public-sector workers leads to more grievances. In essence, restricting the right to strike simply redirects conflict into other costly forms such as grievances (Hebdon, 1991; Hebdon and Stern, 1998). This suggests that while dispute costs (strikes plus arbitrations) may be lower when strikes are prohibited, this may not be true when other forms of dispute, such as grievances, are also considered.

(which averaged 35 days over that period). The discussion here will focus on those variables that had a statistically significant (as denoted by an asterisk *) and quantitatively large impact on strike activity, since they are of most policy relevance.

The existence of a conciliation officer and board is associated with a substantial 12.8 percent reduction in the likelihood that a strike will occur. A mandatory strike vote (a majority of bargaining unit members must vote in favour of the strike before it can occur) is associated with an 11.1 percent reduction in strike incidence as well as a reduction of seven days in the duration of strikes. Dues checkoff is associated with a substantial 9.1 percent reduction in the likelihood of a strike but a 6.4-day increase in the duration of strikes. The existence of automatic reopener provisions (whereby the collective agreement can be reopened in the event of technological change that was unanticipated at the time the contract was signed) is associated with a 3.4-day reduction in the length of strikes.

The most controversial, and perhaps unexpected, result is that legislation prohibiting the use of replacement workers (so called "anti-scab" legislation) is associated with a 24.4 percent increase in strike incidence and a 6.9-day increase in the length of strikes.

TABLE 11.5

EFFECT OF LABOUR RELATIONS POLICY VARIABLES ON STRIKE ACTIVITY

LABOUR RELATIONS POLICY VARIABLE	EFFECT ON INCIDENCE (PERCENT)	EFFECT ON DURATION (DAYS)
Average Incidence and Duration	15.9	35.0
Conciliation officer	-7.9	1.2
Conciliation officer and board	-12.8*	-1.1
Cooling-off period (days)	0.2	0.5
Mandatory strike vote	-11.1*	-7.4*
Employer-initiated vote option	18.9*	-1.5
Dues checkoff	-9.1*	6.4*
Prohibition on replacement workers	24.4*	6.9*
Negotiated reopeners	-5.4	1.5
Automatic reopeners	6.6	-3.4*

* Statistically significant at p < .05 level.

Source: Strike incidence effects are from Gunderson, Kervin, and Reid (1989) based on Labour Canada's Major Collective Agreements (500 or more employees) database for the years 1971–1985. Strike duration effects are from Gunderson and Melino (1990) based on Labour Canada's Work Stoppage File for strikes of any size for the years 1967–1985. A non-technical summary of these studies, and the qualifications that are appropriate given the nature of the data, are given in Gunderson, Melino, and Reid (1990).

While these magnitudes are large, they should be regarded with caution since they are based exclusively on the anti-strikebreaking provisions that were introduced in Quebec in 1977; other pro-labour legislative changes were also introduced in Quebec at the same time (see Chapter 16). But consistent with these results, Lacroix and Lesperance (1988) also found for the period 1961–81 that bans on replacement workers and laws permitting secondary picketing have led to increased strike incidence in Quebec, Ontario, and British Columbia.

A number of theoretical explanations have been offered for why the restrictions on the use of replacement workers can lead to increased strike activity. In their review of the game theory analysis of strikes, Kennan and Wilson (1989) indicate that banning replacement workers actually increases the union's uncertainty about the firm's willingness to pay to end the strike since that willingness is no longer constrained by the firm's option of using replacement workers. When the firm could use replacement workers, the union knew that this would place an upper limit on the firm's willingness to pay to end the strike—that upper limit is removed if replacement workers are not an option. As well, a ban on replacement workers makes the strike a more attractive weapon to the union compared to other mechanisms such as continuing to work without a contract (Cramton and Tracy, 1992). Whatever the reason, the limited evidence from Canada suggests that legislative bans on replacement workers are associated with an increase in both the incidence and duration of strikes. These results continue to hold based on an updated and more extensive analysis that also includes the effect that the ban on replacement workers has on wages (see Exhibit 11.8).

CONSEQUENCES OF STRIKE ACTIVITY

Strikes are of policy interest in large part because of their perceived effects on the parties themselves, on third parties, and on the economy as a whole. Canada's poor strike record by international standards has been cited as a possible contributor to its poor productivity performance and as a possible concern to foreign investors and importers. Although conjectures abound, there is very little rigorous statistical analysis of the effects of strikes, certainly much less than that of strike determinants. Nevertheless, a few empirical studies estimate the diverse consequences of strikes.

With respect to the effect of strikes on wages, Canadian studies show mixed results.[27] Based on US data, McConnell (1989) finds that strikes lead to lower wage settlements. There is some Canadian evidence indicating that the costs of a strike for workers are outweighed by the wage gains for shorter strikes but not for longer ones (Ng, 1993; Reid and Oman, 1991). This tends to confirm the industrial relations stereotype that unions "win" short strikes, but "lose" long ones.

The empirical evidence also indicates strikes to have the following effects:

- Negative effects on the stock-market value of struck firms.[28]
- Negative feelings towards the government as well as replacement workers, police, and management in the case of public-sector disputes (Langford, 1996).

Exhibit 11.8

What Effects Do Legislative Bans on Replacement Workers Have?

Cramton, Gunderson, and Tracy (1999a, 1999b) analyzed the effect on wages and strike incidence and duration in large bargaining units in Canada over the period of January 1967 to March 1993. Bans on replacement workers existed in British Columbia from January 1993 and Ontario from January 1993 to November 1995, as well as in Quebec since February 1978. Their results suggest that the bans on replacement workers were associated with the following effects:

- An increase in the probability of a strike occurring of 0.12, a substantial magnitude relative to the average probability of 0.16.
- An increase in the length of the strike of 32 days, a substantial magnitude relative to the average of 59 days for strikes that occurred.
- An increase in real wages of 4.4 percent over the life of a contract or almost 2 percent per year.
- A net gain to the union of almost $3 million (wage gain of almost $4 million less strike cost of $1 million) and a net loss of almost $5 million to the firm (wage loss of almost $4 million plus strike cost of $1 million) in a typical contract renegotiation under a ban on replacement workers.

With such large gains and losses to the parties, it is not surprising that the legislative ban on replacement workers generates such intense controversy.

The authors emphasize that their analysis deals only with the effect that a legislative ban on replacement workers has on wages and strike incidence and duration. Other important dimensions beyond the scope of the analysis include: picket line violence; the post-strike relationship between strikers, employers, and replacement workers; the balance of power and the viability of the collective bargaining system itself; and even workplace injuries.

- Increasing workplace injuries (see Exhibit 11.9).
- Negative psychological consequences for the workers involved in the strike (McBride, Lancee, and Freeman, 1981; Stoner and Arora, 1987).
- Galvanizing community support for strikers (Gilson, Spencer, and Granville, 1989; MacDowell, 1993).
- Cathartic and constructive effects on labour–management relations (Beatty and Ganz, 1989).
- Mixed effects on productivity.[29]
- No dramatic effects in general, in part because the parties adjust before, during, and after the strike.[30]

Certainly, the consequences are not as substantial as is often portrayed in the media at the time of a strike. Gunderson and Melino (1987), for example, indicate that in the North American auto industry the typical pattern has been for inventories to be built up

EXHIBIT 11.9

STRIKES, REPLACEMENT WORKERS, AND WORKPLACE INJURIES

The conventional argument for banning the use of replacement workers during a strike is to reduce the picket line violence that often occurs when replacement workers are used. Empirical evidence based on data for New York in the 1970s (Allen, 1994) indicates that strikes can lead to increased workplace injuries as firms hire replacement workers who are unfamiliar with the jobs and the associated dangers. The injuries could also occur if there is a "speed-up" after the strike to replace lost output.

prior to a strike through increased production and increased prices, with the latter having deterred consumption. After a strike, inventories were again restored in the same fashion. The authors indicate that "both consumers and producers rationally respond to the expected and the actual event of the strike through a variety of inter-temporal adjustments; and, while the initial effects are in some instances quite pronounced, the long-run effects are usually minimal" (p. 1). But, as the survey evidence of Tang and Ponak (1986) indicates, the perceived costs of strikes differ dramatically across different organizations.

Strike Page North American Listings: igc.apa.org/strike/

Further, it must be emphasized that the empirical literature on strike effects tends to focus on private-sector strikes, where customers usually have options in terms of other suppliers or of postponing purchases. In the public sector, the situation is quite different because of the essential nature of many of the services and the lack of alternatives. Here, the third-party effects on the general public can be quite substantial; this is, of course, the rationale for binding interest arbitration as an alternative to a strike. In the quasi-public sector and for regulated utilities (for example, telephone, transportation), the situation is likely to fall in between those of the private and public sectors; third parties (that is, customers) usually have some alternatives, although they are not as readily available as in the private sector. This threat of a loss of customers puts some pressure on the parties to settle—more so than in the public sector, but less so than in the purely private sector.

CONCLUDING COMMENTS

Although there is a voluminous literature on strike determinants, most of it simply relates measures of strike activity to a variety of variables for which data are available. Little effort is made to understand the causal mechanisms through which these observable factors affect strike activity. Recent theoretical work has somewhat improved on this lack of analysis by emphasizing that strikes have benefits, especially in terms of the information they generate, and that whatever the function of strikes, they will be used less when the joint costs to both parties are great relative to the costs of other mechanisms for achieving the same end.

On the empirical side, the most important recent advances involve the use of large-scale data sets that have the individual contract (that is, the collective agreement) as the unit of observation. This is important, not only because this is the level at which bargaining actually occurs, but also because it can enable the incorporation into the study of a number of characteristics of the bargaining unit. It can also enable the construction of longitudinal data sets involving bargaining rounds for the same bargaining pair. Such longitudinal data, in turn, are important because they facilitate controlling for the effect of otherwise unobserved factors that may give rise to persistent strike-proneness. In addition, a beginning has been made in analyzing the effect of labour relations policy variables, an important consideration since these are the levers that can be manipulated to alter strike activity. The recent theoretical and empirical advances may help explain a variety of phenomena associated with Canadian strike activity: the high level by international standards, the increase, especially from the mid-1960s to the mid-1970s, and the decline since the mid-1970s.

Since the mid-1960s, the Canadian economy has been subject to considerable growth involving new entrants into the market and new unionization. New bargaining relationships carry with them little mutual information about each party's "resistance points" and involve a desire on the part of each to establish a reputation. In addition, in the 1970s the economy was subject to numerous shocks, including oil price changes, unanticipated inflation, and trade shocks, and these increased uncertainty, especially concerning the firm's ability to pay. They put a premium on the strike as a mechanism to elicit information and re-establish the appropriate division of the firm's rents (or above-normal profits). The greater uncertainly also led to shorter contracts, increasing the number of times the parties were exposed to the risk of an end-of-contract dispute. This, in turn, may have led to an increased use of renegotiation strikes as opposed to mid-contract dispute resolution procedures such as grievances, joint committees, and continuous bargaining (although the extent to which these serve as substitute dispute resolution procedures remains empirically unknown and an interesting subject for research).

Canada's high strike record reflects not only these information problems, but also a concentration of strike-prone, resource-based industries, which tend to be strike-prone in other countries as well. Information problems are exacerbated by the open nature of the Canadian economy and the extent of foreign trade and possibly even foreign control. In addition, Canadian unions negotiate a wide range of items. In contrast, in many European countries, many of these issues (for example, hours of work) are addressed at the political level, where the unions are involved as partners in establishing a broad social contract.

With respect to the decline in strike activity that has occurred since the mid-1970s, the joint-cost and asymmetric-information perspectives also provide some insights. That period has been characterized by intense international competition and dramatic restructuring and downsizing. It is no longer the case that information is asymmetric, with firms knowing more about the true state of demand and ability to pay than do workers; rather, both parties know that economic difficulties prevail, and this has been revealed through the trend towards downsizing and restructuring. There is less uncertainty about the "economic rents" or excess profits to bargain over, since such rents have been dissipated by international competition. In essence, there is less need to fight over the "spoils" when there are no spoils to divide! The joint cost to both parties of engaging in strikes is also higher since competitors from abroad may permanently replace the lost output and the jobs associated with that output. Furthermore, multinationals may locate their new plants and investment in countries where there is less risk of strikes. This is especially the case since just-in-time delivery systems put a premium on being able to deliver products and services with a high degree of certainty and reliability.

In essence, in recent years the cost of using the strike mechanism has increased and the benefits have declined—the latter especially in terms of eliciting information from the parties. This may explain some of the decline in strike activity that has occurred in Canada, at least since the 1970s. Since these economic pressures are stronger in the private sector than in the public sector, this may also explain why strike activity has declined more precipitously in the private sector than in the public sector. The increase in the cost and the decline in the benefits of using the strike mechanism may also explain some of the increased use of alternative dispute resolution procedures and co-operative as opposed to adversarial bargaining that has occurred. These may be necessary for the joint survival of both business and jobs in times of intense international competition, when business investment and plant location decisions are increasingly made on an international basis. Just as "necessity is the mother of invention," it may also be the mother of innovation in alternative dispute resolution procedures.

Although these explanations of our changing pattern of strike activity are plausible, it must be admitted that neither the state of theory nor evidence in the strike literature gives us a very complete—some would say even adequate—explanation of the various dimensions of strike activity over time or across various industries, regions, countries, and bargaining units. For every generalization and empirical regularity there is an exception; often no generalizations are possible. Strikes remain somewhat of a mystery, an area where we should be modest about our ability to predict behaviour and consequences. This uncertainty reflects the variety of institutional, economic, and process factors that impinge on the parties, as well as the fact that if strikes and their outcomes were completely predictable, they would serve little purpose.

Questions

1. What measures of strike activity are typical? What information does each provide about strikes?

2. Describe the main function that strikes serve.

3. Describe four main dispute resolution mechanisms.

4. How does mediation work to reduce the likelihood of a strike?

5. In your opinion, what impact do strikes have on the Canadian economy? Why might this impact differ among sectors (private, regulated, public)?

6. "Unequal bargaining power on the part of one of the parties in the negotiation process has implications for wage determination, not for strikes." Discuss.

7. Why may one expect the relationship of strike cycles to business cycles to differ in Canada and the United States?

8. Discuss how strikes may arise because of an asymmetry of information between employers and employees. What does this imply about the effect of changing economic conditions?

9. Discuss the joint-cost perspective as a theory of strikes. Given this perspective, how would you expect strike activity to be affected by each of the following:
   a) compulsory conciliation?
   b) the availability of unemployment insurance for workers on strike?
   c) an increase in unemployment?

10. What impact would you expect free trade between Canada and the United States to have on strike activity in Canada?

11. Use the joint-cost perspective and the asymmetric-information theories of strike activity to explain the following empirical "facts" about strike activity in Canada:
   a) its high level relative to other countries.
   b) its increase between the mid-1960s and mid-1970s.
   c) its decline since the mid-1970s.
   d) the greater decline in the private sector compared to the public sector.

ENDNOTES

[1] The authors acknowledge material in this chapter that appeared in previous editions of this textbook: Anderson, Gunderson, and Ponak (1989) and Gunderson, Hyatt, and Ponak (1995). Readers should consult those earlier versions, especially for references to the earlier literature, since such references have often been removed from this current version.

[2] Based on articles from *The Globe and Mail* (December 5, 1997), p. A2; (March 7, 1998), p. 83; and (December 8, 1998), p. B3. Reproduced with permission from *The Globe and Mail*.

[3] Discussions of measurement problems are given in Aligisakis (1997), Cameron, (1983), Franzosi (1989), Garen and Krislov (1988), ILO (1990), Lacroix (1986b), Segella (1995), Sweeney and Davies (1997), Shalev (1978), and Stern (1978).

[4] In Canada, mid-contract and other illegal strikes have been described and analyzed in Jones and Walsh (1984) and Ng (1987).

[5] Dussault and Lacroix, 1980; Gunderson, Kervin, and Reid, 1986; Swidinsky and Vanderkamp, 1982.

[6] Abowd and Tracy, 1989; Cramton, Gunderson, and Tracy, 1999b; Cramton and Tracy, 1992, 1994; Hayes, 1984; Kennan and Wilson, 1989; McConnell, 1989; Tracy, 1987.

[7] Cousineau and Lacroix, 1986; Gunderson, Kervin, and Reid, 1986; Gunderson and Melino, 1990; Kennan, 1980; Maki, 1986; Reder and Neuman, 1980; Siebert and Addison, 1981.

[8] Reviewed in Kennan (1986).

[9] References to the large number of specific studies that relate strikes to these different measures of aggregate business conditions are contained in the chapter on strikes in the previous edition of this volume (Gunderson, Hyatt, and Ponak, 1995). Other recent contributions include Beggs and Chapman (1987), McConnell (1989).

[10] References to the particular studies are given in Gunderson, Hyatt, and Ponak (1995).

[11] Abowd and Tracy, 1989; Budd, 1994, 1996; Card, 1990; Cramton, Gunderson, and Tracy, 1999a, 1999b; Cramton and Tracy, 1992, 1994; Cousineau and Lacroix, 1986; Dussault and Lacroix, 1980; Gramm, 1986, 1987; Gramm, Hendricks, and Kahn, 1988; Gunderson, Kervin, and Reid, 1986, 1989; Gunderson and Melino, 1990; McConnell, 1989, 1990; Schnell and Gramm, 1987; Swidinsky and Vanderkamp, 1982; Tracy, 1986, 1987; Vrooman, 1989.

[12] Card, 1990; Gunderson and Melino, 1990; Harrison and Stewart, 1989; McConnell, 1990; Ondrich and Schnell, 1993; Tracy, 1986, 1987; Vrooman, 1989; and earlier references cited in Kennan, 1986.

[13] Excellent recent reviews and discussions of many of these studies are given in Edwards (1992) and Kaufman (1993).

[14] Cohn and Eaton, 1989; Franzosi, 1989; Korpi and Shalev, 1980.

[15] Church, Outram, and Smith, 1990; Martin, 1986; McClendon and Klass, 1993; Ng, 1991, 1993; Schutt, 1982; Tomkiewicz, Tomkiewicz, and Brenner, 1985.

[16] Cohen, 1990; Goldfield, 1991; Kaufman, 1993.

[17] See Chapter 17 in this volume as well as Edwards (1992) and references cited therein.

[18] Many of these studies are discussed in Edwards (1986).

[19] Cousineau, Lacroix, and Vachon (1991) find strike activity to be less in foreign-owned firms. Ng and Maki (1988) find it to be the same, but that members of national unions are more likely to strike than are members of international unions. Budd (1994) finds no difference in strike activity between foreign-owned firms and Canadian-owned firms, nor between members of national or international unions. He argues that the differences disappear when adequate control variables are included to control for the effect of other determinants of strike activity, especially industry and firm size. Budd (1994) also reviewed the results from a number of similar studies in the United Kingdom and Ireland, and found that there is no consensus regarding the effect of foreign ownership.

[20] Cousineau and Lacroix, 1986; Ingram, Metcalf, and Wadsworth, 1993; Schwartz and Koziara, 1992; Swidinsky and Vanderkamp, 1982.

[21] Currie and McConnell, 1991; Cramton, Gunderson, and Tracy, 1999b; Godard, 1992; Gramm, 1986, 1987; Gunderson, Kervin, and Reid, 1986, 1989; Hebdon, Hyatt, and Mazerolle, 1999; Swidinsky and Vanderkamp, 1982.

[22] Horn, McGuire, and Tomkiewicz (1982) find mistrust and lack of communication between union and management to be important predictors of teacher strikes.

[23] For teachers, Montgomery and Benedict (1989) found that bargaining experience led to fewer and shorter strikes.

[24] See the discussion in the previous edition (Gunderson, Hyatt, and Ponak, 1995) for a discussion of the evidence.

[25] The terms "conciliation," "mediation," and "fact-finding" are sometimes used interchangeably and are often used differently in different jurisdictions as well as in different labour relations laws. Hence, the terminology used here should be regarded as a common, but not exclusive, way of defining these concepts.

[26] Currie and McConnell, 1991; Gunderson, Hebdon, and Hyatt, 1996; Ichniowski, 1988; Olson, 1986, 1988; Partridge, 1988; Zimmer and Jacobs, 1981.

[27] Lacroix (1986a) cites numerous studies that find that strikes lead to higher subsequent wage settlements; however, his own results suggest that this is sensitive to the specifications of the estimation equation. Card (1990) finds no relationship between strikes and subsequent wage settlements, except for very long strikes which lead to lower wage settlements.

[28] Becker and Olson, 1986; Davidson, Worrell, and Garrison, 1988; DeFusco and Fuess, 1991; Greer, Martin, and Reusser, 1980; Neumann, 1980.

[29] Strike effects on productivity have been found to be both negative (Flaherty, 1987) and positive (Knight, 1989). Other studies have found negative productivity effects in linked industries that supplied or depended upon the struck industries being stronger than in the struck industries themselves (McHugh, 1991).

[30] Gunderson and Melino, 1987; Hameed and Lomas, 1975; Knight, 1989; Maki, 1983; Neumann and Reder, 1984; Paarsch, 1990.

REFERENCES

ABBOTT, M. G. 1984. "Specification Tests of Quarterly Econometric Models of Aggregate Strike Frequency in Canada," in *Research in Labor Economics,* edited by R. Ehrenberg. London: JAI Press Inc.

ABOWD, J. and J. TRACY. 1989. "Market Structure, Strike Activity, and Union Wage Settlements." *Industrial Relations,* 28, pp. 227–50.

ALIGISAKIS, M. 1997. "Labour Disputes in Western Europe: Typology and Tendencies." *International Labour Review,* 136, pp. 73–94.

ALLEN, D. 1994. "How Strikes Influence Work Injury Duration: Evidence from the State of New York," *Proceedings of the Forty-Sixth Annual Meeting.* Madison, Wisconsin: Industrial Relations Research Association, pp. 306–314.

ANDERSON, J. C., M. GUNDERSON, and A. PONAK. 1989. "Strikes and Dispute Resolution," in *Union–Management Relations in Canada,* 2nd Edition, edited by J. Anderson, M. Gunderson, and A. Ponak. Don Mills, ON: Addison-Wesley.

ASHENFELTER, O. and G. JOHNSON. 1969. "Bargaining Theory, Trade Unions, and Industrial Activity." *American Economic Review,* 59, pp. 35–49.

BEATTY, C. and J. GANZ. 1989. "After the Strike: Changing the Teacher Board Relationship." *Relations industrielles/Industrial Relations,* 44, pp. 569–589.

BECKER, B. E. and C. A. OLSON. 1986. "The Impact of Strikes on Shareholder Equity." *Industrial and Labor Relations Review,* 39, pp. 425–38.

BEGGS, J. and B. CHAPMAN, 1987. "An Empirical Analysis of Australian Strike Activity: Estimating the Industrial Relations Effect of the First Three Years of the Prices and Incomes Accord." *Economic Record,* 63 (March), pp. 46–60.

BUDD, J. 1994. "The Effect of Multinational Institutions on Strike Activity in Canada." *Industrial and Labor Relations Review,* 47, pp. 401–16.

———. 1996. "Canadian Strike Replacement Legislation and Collective Bargaining: Lessons for the United States." *Industrial Relations,* 35, pp. 245–60.

CAMERON, S. 1983. "An International Comparison of the Volatility of Strike Behaviour." *Relations industrielles/Industrial Relations,* 38, pp. 767–84.

CARD, D. 1988. "Longitudinal Analysis of Strike Activity." *Journal of Labor Economics,* 6, pp. 147–76.

———. 1990. "Strikes and Wages: A Test of an Asymmetric Information Model." *Quarterly Journal of Economics,* 105, pp. 625–59.

CHURCH, R., Q. OUTRAM, and D. SMITH. 1990. "British Coal Mining Strikes 1893–1940: Dimensions, Distribution and Persistence." *British Journal of Industrial Relations,* 28, pp. 329–50.

COHEN, I. 1990. "Political Climate and Two Airline Strikes: Century Aviation in 1932 and Continental Airlines in 1983–85." *Industrial and Labor Relations Review,* 43, pp. 308–23.

COHN, S. and A. EATON. 1989. "Historical Limits on Neoclassical Strike Theories: Evidence from French Coal Mining, 1890–1935." *Industrial and Labor Relations Review,* 42, pp. 649–62.

COUSINEAU, J. and R. LACROIX. 1986. "Imperfect Information and Strikes: An Analysis of Canadian Experience, 1967–82." *Industrial and Labor Relations Review,* 39, pp. 377–87.

COUSINEAU, J., R. LACROIX, and D. VACHON. 1991. "Foreign Ownership and Strike Activity in Canada." *Relations industrielles/ Industrial Relations,* 46, pp. 616–29.

CRAMTON, P. and J. TRACY. 1992. "Strikes and Holdouts in Wage Bargaining: Theory and Data." *American Economic Review,* 82, pp. 100–21.

———. 1994. "The Determinants of US Labour Disputes." *Journal of Labour Economics,* 12, pp. 180–209.

———. 1998. "The Use of Replacement Workers in Union Contract Negotiations: The US Experience, 1980–1989." *Journal of Labour Economics,* 16, pp. 667–701.

CRAMTON, P., M. GUNDERSON, and J. TRACY. 1999a. "Impacts of Strike Replacement Bans in Canada." *Labor Law Journal,* 50, pp. 173–79.

———. 1999b. "The Effect of Collective Bargaining Legislation on Strikes and Wages." *Review of Economics and Statistics,* 81, pp. 475–87.

CURRIE, J. and S. McCONNELL. 1991. "Collective Bargaining in the Public Sector: The Effect of Legal Structure on Dispute Costs and Wages." *American Economic Review,* 81, pp. 693–718.

DAVIDSON, W., D. WORRELL, and S. GARRISON. 1988. "Effect of Strike Activity on Firm Value." *Academy of Management Journal,* 31, pp. 387–94.

DeFUSCO, R. and S. FUESS. 1991. "The Effects of Airline Strikes on Struck and Nonstruck Carriers." *Industrial and Labor Relations Review,* 44, pp. 324–33.

DILTS, D. 1986. "Strike Activity in the United States: An Analysis of the Stocks and Flows." *Journal of Labor Research,* 7, pp. 187–99.

DUSSAULT, F. and R. LACROIX. 1980. "Activité de Grève: un test des Hypothèses Explicatives Traditionnelles." *Canadian Journal of Economics,* 13, pp. 632–44.

EATON, B. C. 1973. "The Worker and the Profitability of the Strike." *Industrial and Labor Relations Review,* 26, pp. 670–79.

EDWARDS, P. K. 1986. *Conflict at Work: A Materialist Analysis of Workplace Relations.* Oxford: Basil Blackwell.

———. 1992. "Industrial Conflict: Themes and Issues in the Recent Research." *British Journal of Industrial Relations,* 30, pp. 361–404.

ENDERWICK, P. and P. J. BUCKLEY. 1982. "Strike Activity and Foreign Ownership: An Analysis of British Manufacturing 1971–73." *British Journal of Industrial Relations,* 20, pp. 308–21.

FLAHERTY, S. 1987. "Strike Activity, Worker Militancy, and Productivity Change in Manufacturing, 1961–1981." *Industrial and Labor Relations Review,* 4, pp. 585–600.

FORCHHEIMER, K. 1948. "Some International Aspects of the Strike Movement." *Bulletin of the Oxford University Institute of Statistics,* 10, pp. 9–24.

FRANK, J. A., M. J. KELLY, and B. D. MacNAUGHTON. 1982. "Legislative Change and Strike Activity in Canada, 1926–1974." *Relations industrielles/Industrial Relations,* 37, pp. 267–83.

FRANZOSI, R. 1989. "One Hundred Years of Strike Statistics: Methodological and Theoretical Issues in Quantitative Strike Research." *Industrial and Labor Relations Review,* 42, pp. 348–62.

GAREN, J. and J. KRISLOV. 1988. "An Examination of the New American Strike Statistics in Analyzing Aggregate Strike Incidence." *British Journal of Industrial Relations,* 26, pp. 75–84.

GHILARDUCCI, T. 1988. "The Impact of Internal Politics on the 1981 UMWA Strike." *Industrial Relations,* 27, pp. 371–84.

GILSON, C., I. SPENCER, and S. GRANVILLE. 1989. "The Impact of a Strike on the Attitudes and Behaviour of a Rural Community." *Relations industrielles/Industrial Relations,* 44, pp. 785–802.

GODARD, J. 1992. "Strikes as Collective Voice: A Behavioral Analysis of Strike Activity." *Industrial and Labor Relations Review,* 46, pp. 161–175.

GOLDFIELD, M. 1991. "The Economy, Strikes, Union Growth and Public Policy During the 1930s." *Proceedings of the 1991 Spring Meeting of the Industrial Relations Research Association.* Madison, WI: IRRA. pp. 473–483

GRAMM, C. 1986. "The Determinants of Strike Incidence and Severity: A Micro Level Study." *Industrial and Labor Relations Review,* 39, pp.361–75.

———. 1987. "New Measures of the Propensity to Strike During Contract Negotiations, 1971–1980." *Industrial and Labor Relations Review,* 40, pp. 406–17.

GRAMM, C., W. HENDRICKS, and L. KAHN. 1988. "Inflation Uncertainty and Strike Activity." *Industrial Relations,* 27, pp. 114–29.

GRAMM, C. and J. SCHNELL. 1994. "Difficult Choices: Crossing the Picket Line During the 1987 National Football League Strike." *Journal of Labor Economics,* 12, pp. 41–73.

GREER, C., S. MARTIN, and T. REUSSER. 1980. "The Effect of Strikes on Shareholder Returns." *Journal of Labor Research,* 1, pp. 217–30.

GUNDERSON, M., R. HEBDON, and D. HYATT. 1996. "Collective Bargaining in the Public Sector." *American Economic Review,* 86, pp. 315–26.

GUNDERSON, M. and D. HYATT. 1996. "Canadian Public Sector Employment Relations in Transition," in *Public Sector Employment in a Time of Transition.* Madison, WI: Industrial Relations Research Association.

GUNDERSON, M., D. HYATT, and A. PONAK. 1995. "Strikes and Dispute Resolution," in *Union–Management Relations in Canada,* 3rd Edition, edited by M. Gunderson and A. Ponak. Don Mills: Addison-Wesley.

GUNDERSON, M., J. KERVIN, and F. REID. 1986. "Logit Estimates of Strike Incidence from Canadian Contract Data." *Journal of Labor Economics,* 4, pp. 257–76.

———. 1989. "The Effect of Labour Relations Legislation on Strike Incidence." *Canadian Journal of Economics,* 22, pp. 779–94.

GUNDERSON, M. and A. MELINO. 1987. "Estimating Strike Effects in a General Model of Prices and Quantities." *Journal of Labor Economics,* 5, pp. 1–19.

———. 1990. "The Effects of Public Policy on Strike Duration." *Journal of Labor Economics,* 8, pp. 295–316.

GUNDERSON, M., A. MELINO, and F. REID. 1990. "The Effects of Canadian Labour Relations Legislation on Strike Incidence and Duration." *Labor Law Journal,* 41, pp. 512–18.

GUNDERSON, M. and F. REID. 1995. "Public Sector Strikes in Canada," in *Public Sector Collective Bargaining in Canada,* edited by G. Swimmer and M. Thompson. Kingston: IRC Press.

HAMEED, S. M. and T. LOMAS. 1975. "Measurement of Production Losses Due to Strikes in Canada: An Input-Output Analysis." *British Journal of Industrial Relations,* 13, pp. 86–93.

HARRISON, A. and M. STEWART. 1989. "Cyclical Fluctuations in Strike Durations." *American Economic Review,* 79, pp. 827–41.

HAYES, B. 1984. "Unions and Strikes with Asymmetric Information." *Journal of Labor Economics,* 2, pp. 57–83.

HEBDON, R. 1991. "Ontario's No-Strike Laws: A Test of the Safety Valve Hypothesis." *Proceedings of the 28th Conference of the Canadian Industrial Relations Research Association.* Kingston, Ontario: CIRA.

HEBDON, R., D. HYATT, and M. MAZEROLLE. 1999. "Implications of Small Bargaining Units and Enterprise Unions on Bargaining Disputes." *Relations Industrielles/Industrial Relations*, 54, pp. 503–24.

HEBDON, R and R. STERN. 1998. "Tradeoffs Among Expressions of Industrial Conflict: Public Sector Strike Bans and Grievance Arbitrations." *industrial and Labour Relations Review*, 51, pp. 204–21.

HICKS, J. R. 1963. *The Theory of Wages,* 3rd Edition. New York: St. Martin's Press.

HORN, R. N., W. J. McGUIRE, and J. TOMKIEWICZ. 1982. "Work Stoppages by Teachers: An Empirical Analysis." *Journal of Labor Research,* 3, pp. 487–96.

HUTCHENS, R., D. LIPSKY, and R. STERN. 1992. "Unemployment Insurance and Strikes." *Journal of Labor Research,* 13, pp. 337–54.

ICHNIOWSKI, C. 1988. "Police Recognition Strikes: Illegal and Ill Fated." *Journal of Labor Research,* 9, pp. 183–97.

ILO. 1990. *Meeting of Experts on Statistics of Strikes and Lockouts.* Geneva: International Labour Organization.

INGRAM, R., D. METCALF, and J. WADSWORTH. 1993. "Strike Incidence in British Manufacturing in the 1980s." *Industrial and Labor Relations Review,* 46, pp. 704–17.

JONES, J. C. H. and W. D. WALSH. 1984. "Inter-industry Strike Frequencies: Some Pooled Cross-sectional Evidence from Canadian Secondary Manufacturing." *Journal of Labor Research,* 5, pp. 419–25.

KAUFMAN, B. 1993. "Research on Strike Models and Outcomes in the 1980s: Accomplishments and Shortcomings," in *Research Frontiers in Industrial Relations and Human Resources,* edited by D. Lewin, O. Mitchell, and P. Sherer. Madison, Wisc.: Industrial Relations Research Association.

KELLY, J. 1988. *Trade Unions and Socialist Politics.* London: Verso.

KENNAN, J. 1980. "Pareto Optimality and the Economics of Strike Duration." *Journal of Labor Research,* 1, pp. 77–94.

———. 1986. "The Economics of Strikes," in *The Handbook of Labor Economics,* edited by O. Ashenfelter and R. Layard. Amsterdam: North Holland.

KENNAN, J. and R. WILSON. 1989. "Strategic Bargaining Models and Interpretation of Strike Data." *Journal of Applied Econometrics,* 4, pp. 87–130.

KNIGHT, K. 1989. "Labour Productivity and Strike Activity in British Manufacturing Industries: Some Quantitative Evidence." *British Journal of Industrial Relations,* 27, pp. 365–74.

KORPI, W. and M. SHALEV. 1980. "Strikes, Power and Politics in the Western Nations: 1900–1976," in *Political Power and Social Theory,* edited by M. Zietlin. Greenwich, Conn.: JAI Press.

LACROIX, R. 1986a. "A Microeconometric Analysis of the Effects of Strikes on Wages." *Relations industrielles/Industrial Relations,* 41, pp. 111–26.

———. 1986b. "Strike Activity in Canada," in *Canadian Labour Relations,* edited by W. C. Riddell. Toronto: University of Toronto Press.

LACROIX, R. and A. LESPERANCE. 1988. "New Labor Laws and Strike Activity." *Relations industrielles/Industrial Relations,* 43, pp. 812–27.

LANGFORD, T. 1996. "Effects of Strike Participation on the Political Consequences of Canadian Postal Workers." *Relations industrielles/Industrial Relations,* 51, pp. 563–82.

LeROY, M. 1992. "Multivariate Analysis of Unionized Employees' Propensity to Cross Their Own Union's Picket Line." *Journal of Labor Research,* 13, pp. 285–92.

MacDOWELL, L. 1993. "After the Strike: Labour Relations in Oshawa, 1937–1939." *Relations industrielles/Industrial Relations,* 48, pp. 691–710.

MAKI, D. 1983. "A Note on the Output Effects of Canadian Postal Strikes." *Canadian Journal of Economics,* 16, pp. 149–54.

———. 1986. "The Effect of the Cost of Strikes on the Volume of Strike Activity." *Industrial and Labor Relations Review,* 39, pp. 552–63.

MAKI, D. and K. STRAND. 1984. "The Determinants of Strike Activity: An Interindustry Analysis." *Relations industrielles/Industrial Relations,* 39, pp. 77–91.

MARTIN, J. E. 1986. "Prediction of Individual Propensity to Strike." *Industrial and Labor Relations Review,* 39, pp. 214–27.

MAURO, M. J. 1982. "Strikes as a Result of Imperfect Information." *Industrial and Labor Relations Review,* 35, pp. 522–38.

McBRIDE, A., W. LANCEE, and S. FREEMAN. 1981. "The Psychological Impact of a Labor Dispute." *Journal of Occupational Psychology,* 54, pp. 125–33.

McCLENDON, J. and B. KLAAS. 1993. "Determinants of Strike-Related Militancy: An Analysis of a University Faculty Strike." *Industrial and Labor Relations Review,* 46, pp. 560–73.

McCONNELL, S. 1989. "Strikes, Wages, and Private Information." *American Economic Review,* 79, pp. 810–15.

———. 1990. "Cyclical Fluctuations in Strike Activity." *Industrial and Labor Relations Review,* 44, pp. 130–43.

McHUGH, R. 1991. "Productivity Effects of Strikes in Struck and Nonstruck Industries." *Industrial and Labor Relations Review,* 44, pp. 722–32.

MILNER, S. and D. METCALF. 1993. "A Century of Strike Activity," in *New Perspectives on Industrial Disputes,* edited by D. Metcalf and S. Milner. London: Rutledge.

MONTGOMERY, E. and M. BENEDICT. 1989. "The Impact of Bargainer Experience on Teacher Strikes." *Industrial and Labor Relations Review,* 42, pp. 380–92.

NEUMANN, G. R. 1980. "The Predictability of Strikes: Evidence from the Stock Market." *Industrial and Labor Relations Review,* 33, pp. 525–35.

NEUMANN, G. R. and M. W. REDER. 1984. "Output and Strike Activity in US. Manufacturing: How Large are the Losses?" *Industrial and Labor Relations Review,* 37, pp. 197–211.

NG, I. 1987. "Determinants of Wildcat Strikes in Canadian Manufacturing Industries." *Relations industrielles/Industrial Relations,* 42, pp. 386–96.

———. 1991. "Predictors of Strike Voting Behaviour." *Journal of Labor Research,* 12, pp. 123–34.

———. 1993. "Strike Activity and Post-Strike Perceptions Among University Faculty." *Relations industrielles/Industrial Relations,* 48, pp. 231–47.

NG, I. and D. MAKI. 1988. "Strike Activity of US Institutions in Canada." *British Journal of Industrial Relations,* 26, pp. 63–73.

NOEL, A. and K. GARDNER. 1990. "The Gainers Strike: Capitalist Offensive, Militancy, and the Politics of Industrial Relations in Canada." *Studies in Political Economy,* 31, pp. 31–72.

OLSON, C. A. 1984. "The Role of Rescheduled School Days in Teacher Strikes." *Industrial and Labor Relations Review,* 37, pp. 515–28.

———. 1986. "Strikes, Strike Penalties, and Arbitration in Six States." *Industrial and Labor Relations Review,* 39, pp. 539–51.

———. 1988. "Dispute Resolution in the Public Sector," in *Public Sector Bargaining,* 2nd Edition, edited by B. Aaron et al. Washington: Bureau of National Affairs.

ONDRICH, J. and J. SCHNELL. 1993. "Strike Duration and the Degree of Disagreement." *Industrial Relations,* 32, pp. 412–31.

PAARSCH, H. 1990. "Work Stoppages and the Theory of the Offset Factor: Evidence from the British Columbia Logging Industry." *Journal of Labor Economics,* 8, pp. 387–418.

PARTRIDGE, D. 1988. "A Reexamination of the Effectiveness of No-Strike Laws for Public School Teachers." *Journal of Collective Negotiations in the Public Sector,* 17, pp. 257–66.

PONAK, A. and L. FALKENBERG. 1989. "Resolution of Interest Disputes," in *Collective Bargaining in Canada,* edited by A. Sethi. Toronto: Nelson.

REDER, M. and G. NEUMANN. 1980. "Conflict and Contract: The Case of Strikes." *Journal of Political Economy,* 60, pp. 371–82.

REES, A. 1952. "Industrial Conflict and Business Fluctuations." *Journal of Political Economy,* 60, pp. 371–82.

REID, F. and A. OMAN. 1991. "Do Unions Win Short Strikes and Lose Long Strikes? *Proceedings of the 28th Conference of the Canadian Industrial Relations Association.* Kingston, Ontario: CIRA.

ROSE, D. 1991. "Are Strikes Less Effective in Conglomerate Firms?" *Industrial and Labor Relations Review,* 45, pp. 131–44.

SCHNELL, J. F. and C. L. GRAMM. 1987. "Learning by Striking: Estimates of the Teetotaller Effect." *Journal of Labor Economics,* 5, pp. 221–41.

SCHUTT, R. 1982. "Models of Militancy: Support for Strikes and Work Actions Among Public Employees." *Industrial and Labor Relations Review,* 35, pp. 406–22.

SCHWARZ, J. and K. KOZIARA. 1992. "The Effect of Hospital Bargaining Unit Structure on Industrial Relations Outcomes." *Industrial and Labor Relations Review,* 45, pp. 573–90.

SCREPANTI, E. 1987. "Long Cycles in Strike Activity: An Empirical Investigation." *British Journal of Industrial Relations,* 25, 99–124.

SEGELLA, M. 1995. "Industrial Conflict in Developed and Developing Countries: Extending a Western Strike Model." *Relations industrielles/Industrial Relations,* 50, pp. 393–417.

SHALEV, M. 1978. "Problems of Strike Measurement," in *The Resurgence of Class Conflict in Western Europe Since 1968,* edited by C. Crouch and A. Pizzorno. London: MacMillan.

SIEBERT, W. and J. ADDISON. 1981. "Are Strikes Accidental?" *Economic Journal,* 91, pp. 389–404.

SKEELS, J. 1982. "The Economic and Organizational Basis of Early United States Strikes, 1900–1948." *Industrial and Labor Relations Review,* 35, pp. 491–503.

SKEELS, J., P. McGRATH, and G. ARSHANAPALLI. 1988. "The Importance of Strike Size in Strike Research." *Industrial and Labor Relations Review,* 41, pp. 582–91.

SMITH, D. A. 1972. "The Determinants of Strike Activity in Canada." *Relations industrielles/Industrial Relations,* 27, pp. 663–78.

——. 1976. "The Impact of Inflation on Strike Activity in Canada." *Relations industrielles/Industrial Relations,* 31, pp. 139–45.

STERN, R. N. 1978. "Methodological Issues in Quantitative Strike Analysis." *Industrial Relations,* 12, pp. 32–42.

STONER, C. and R. ARORA. 1987. "An Investigation of the Relationship Between Selected Variables and the Psychological Health of Strike Participants." *Journal of Occupational Psychology,* 60, pp. 61–71.

SWEENEY, K and J. DAVIES. 1997. "International Comparisons of Labour Disputes in 1995." *Labour Market Trends,* 105, pp. 121–56.

SWIDINSKY, R. and J. VANDERKAMP. 1982. "A Micro-Economic Analysis of Strike Activity in Canada." *Journal of Labor Research,* 3, pp. 456–71.

TANG, R. Y. W. and A. PONAK. 1986. "Employer Assessment of Strike Costs." *Relations industrielles/Industrial Relations,* 41, pp. 552–70.

TOMKIEWICZ, J., C. TOMKIEWICZ, and O. BRENNER. 1985. "Why Don't Teachers Strike?" *Journal of Collective Negotiations in the Public Sector,* 14, pp. 183–90.

TRACY, J. S. 1986. "An Investigation into the Determinants of US Strike Activity." *American Economic Review,* 76, pp. 423–36.

———. 1987. "An Empirical Test of an Asymmetric Information Model of Strikes." *Journal of Labor Economics,* 5, pp. 149–73.

VANDERKAMP, J. 1970. "Economic Activity and Strikes in Canada." *Industrial Relations,* 9, pp. 215–320.

VROOMAN, S. 1989. "A Longitudinal Attitude of Strike Activity in US Manufacturing." *American Economic Review,* 79, pp. 816–26.

WALSH, W. 1975. "Economic Conditions and Strike Activity in Canada." *Industrial Relations,* 14, pp. 45–54.

WHEELER, H. 1985. *Industrial Conflict: An Integrative Theory.* Columbia, S.C.: University of South Carolina Press.

ZIMMER, L. and J. JACOBS. 1981. "Challenging the Taylor Law: Prison Guards on Strike." *Industrial and Labor Relations Review,* 34, pp. 531–44.

CHAPTER 12

The Grievance Arbitration Process: Theory and Practice

Kenneth Wm. Thornicroft[1]

A grievance:

Janet Jones, an auto mechanic employed by Big City Automotive Ltd., was very upset—her $500 Christmas bonus had just been paid to her and she was shocked to discover that income tax had been deducted; she was expecting a cheque for the full amount of the bonus. She immediately went to see the bookkeeper to get the matter sorted out. The bookkeeper told Ms. Jones that since the bonus was "income," it was necessary to deduct income tax. The bookkeeper suggested to Ms. Jones that if she was still dissatisfied she should speak with the company's general manager, Brian Brown.

Ms. Jones went to Mr. Brown's office and launched into a tirade about a number of matters, including the fact that other (male) mechanics were earning more per hour than she was and that, in general, the wages paid by Big City were less than those of other comparable automotive shops. She demanded an immediate 10 percent raise and that she be issued a cheque for the "full amount" of her Christmas bonus.

Mr. Brown responded that he was not going to change her bonus cheque and that, further, no employee would be getting a pay raise unless the union was decertified. Ms. Jones immediately called the local business representative of her union; in the grievor's words, "I was just furious; ready to kill." The union representative was not in the office so Ms. Jones simply left a message for him to return her call "as soon as possible." Ms. Jones returned to Mr. Brown's office and stated that since her shift was over she was leaving for the day. Mr. Brown replied that her shift was not over and that she should "get back to work." Mr. Brown then stated to Ms. Jones that she was not "chained down" and could be "replaced on a minute's notice." Finally, Mr. Brown—who was by now at least as agitated as Ms. Jones—stated: "If you're so unhappy, why don't you just do us all a favour and quit?" Ms. Jones then picked up some—but not all—of her tools, approached the bookkeeper and told her to "get my walking papers ready," and then she walked off the job (this was about 10 minutes before the end of her shift) without punching out her time card.

The next morning, a Friday, Ms. Jones returned to the shop to pick up the rest of her tools; she never spoke with Mr. Brown that day. The following Saturday morning, Ms. Jones called Mr. Brown to apologize and asked to meet him for a cup of coffee. During their brief meeting they discussed a number of matters, including Ms. Jones' possible return to work, but ultimately Mr. Brown was unwilling to allow Ms. Jones to return to work unless she agreed to "try and help me get rid of the union," something Ms. Jones was unwilling to do.

Prior to this incident, Ms. Jones was considered to be a diligent and productive worker (perhaps the most productive worker in the shop) and one who had never before engaged in any sort of workplace misconduct. On Monday of the following week, Big City forwarded a Record of Employment to Jones, which indicated code "E" (the code for "quit") in the space provided for "Reason for Issuing This ROE." Ms. Jones immediately contacted her union representative who stated that he would "look into the matter" and then probably file a grievance on her behalf.[2]

In general, federal and provincial labour laws prohibit strikes and lockouts during the term of a collective bargaining agreement. For example, section 58 of the BC *Labour Relations Code* states that collective bargaining agreements must contain the following provision (or the equivalent): "There must be no strikes or lockouts so long as this agreement continues to operate."[3]

It is sometimes assumed that the government, by way of such provisions, has legislated a form of *quid pro quo*—the "no-strike" provision is given up by the union in exchange for the employer's undertaking not to lock out the bargaining unit employees during the term of the agreement. However, it is more accurate to characterize both the no-strike and no-lockout provisions as one side of the coin, with the *grievance arbitration* process as the other. Thus, rather than resorting to the use of economic pressure tactics such as strikes, lockouts, and picketing, disputes about the parties' respective rights and obligations under their collective bargaining agreement can be resolved through the grievance arbitration process without a work stoppage and without having to initiate a court action.

The grievance arbitration process is a very important factor in the overall union–management relationship. In many ways, grievances serve as a barometer of the underlying labour climate. There is evidence that unresolved grievances can have a "spillover effect" leading to lower organizational efficiency and productivity and increased workplace conflict (Lewin, 1999; Brett and Goldberg, 1979).

A *grievance* is "an allegation, usually by an individual [employee], but sometimes by the union or management, of misinterpretation or misapplication of a collective bargaining agreement or of traditional work practices" (Doherty, 1989). A collective bargaining agreement is simply an employment contract between an employer and a particular group of employees, and thus a grievance is, in effect, an allegation of breach of contract. However, rather than pursuing an action for breach of contract in the civil courts (with the attendant delay and expense), labour relations practitioners originally established an alternative form of dispute resolution, namely grievance arbitration, as their preferred mechanism for resolving disputes about the meaning, interpretation, or application of a collective bargaining agreement. What began as a purely voluntary system has evolved into a compulsory statutory scheme whereby the parties are now required, by law, to resolve their contract disputes through grievance arbitration.

The success of alternative dispute resolution methods developed in the labour relations context, and in particular mediation and arbitration, has spurred the adoption of these procedures in many other settings. Today, it is not uncommon to find arbitration clauses in nonunion employment contracts, franchise agreements, and commercial leases. Further, some nonunion firms have instituted grievance systems, but third-party arbitration is rarely a component of such systems, calling into question the perceived procedural fairness of many nonunion grievance processes (Peterson and McCabe, 1994). Even where arbitration is used in nonunion settings, concerns about fairness may arise (Zack, 1999). (We return to this issue later in the chapter.)

Quite apart from the use of arbitration in other settings, the range of disputes now addressed by grievance arbitrators in union settings has dramatically expanded over the past few decades. The courts have ruled that a wide variety of disputes that arise in union settings—disputes that traditionally were adjudicated by the courts or other administrative tribunals—can now *only* be adjudicated through grievance arbitration.[4] For example, if Ms. Jones does, in fact, have a legitimate wage-discrimination claim, rather than filing a human rights complaint, she is best advised to file a grievance.

Grievance arbitration was originally conceived as an equitable, inexpensive, and expeditious solution to the problem of contract disputes between union and management. Grievance arbitration has been lauded as an effective mechanism for improving workplace democracy and for providing employees with a meaningful "voice" in matters affecting their employment (Freeman and Medoff, 1984). Despite such favourable comment, however, others have argued—with some justification—that the contemporary grievance arbitration process is in need of repair: The process is too slow, too expensive, and overly "legalistic." In light of these criticisms, both policy-makers and labour relations practitioners have modified existing grievance arbitration processes and have formulated alternative systems for resolving workplace disputes. In this chapter, we shall describe the modern grievance arbitration process, outline some of the criticisms of the process, and examine some of the more innovative approaches to resolving workplace disputes.

GRIEVANCE PROCEDURES IN CANADA

At the outset it is important to distinguish grievance or *rights arbitration* from *interest arbitration.* In interest arbitration, a neutral third party, after hearing the submissions from both union and management, determines the terms and conditions of the parties' collective bargaining agreement. Parties occasionally voluntarily agree to settle their dispute by interest arbitration; much more often, it is mandated by legislation as a substitute for the right to strike or lock out in the event of a bargaining impasse. Interest arbitration is very infrequently used in the private sector but is commonly used to settle, for example, disputes involving police and firefighters. When striking employees are ordered back to work by ad hoc legislation, the "back to work order" is often accompanied by a direction that the dispute be resolved by interest arbitration (see Chapter 14 for a discussion of interest arbitration).

Rights or grievance arbitration, on the other hand, is exclusively concerned with the enforcement of rights and obligations arising from the parties' collective bargaining agreement. In essence, interest arbitration is concerned with the determination of the terms and conditions of a collective agreement (especially wages and benefits), whereas grievance arbitration concerns the interpretation of an agreement already in force. In this chapter, we shall focus our discussion on grievance arbitration.

The Internal Grievance Process

Collective bargaining agreements invariably include an internal two- or three-step process in which the grievance is reviewed at successively higher levels of the organization. A typical grievance procedure is set out in Figure 12.1. The process typically begins with the local union representative (usually the shop steward) filing a grievance, either orally or (usually) in writing, alleging a violation of the collective agreement. For example, Ms. Jones' shop steward might take the position that, as a matter of law, Ms. Jones did not quit, and since the employer did not discharge her, she ought to be able to return to work. Prior to a grievance being filed, the shop steward and Mr. Brown might discuss the matter between themselves in an attempt to informally resolve the dispute. Many workplace disputes are resolved either prior to, or shortly after, a formal grievance is filed. The local shop steward will usually draft the grievance on behalf of the *grievor* (the party on whose behalf the grievance is filed—in the United States, this party is called the *grievant*). It should be noted that bargaining unit employees rarely have the authority to file

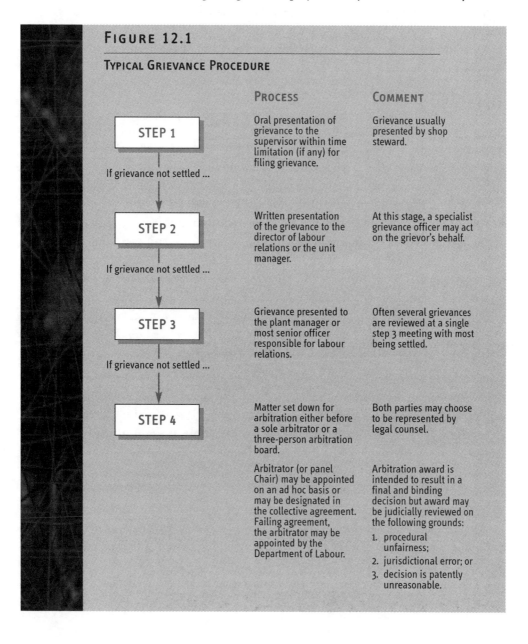

FIGURE 12.1

TYPICAL GRIEVANCE PROCEDURE

	PROCESS	COMMENT
STEP 1 If grievance not settled ...	Oral presentation of grievance to the supervisor within time limitation (if any) for filing grievance.	Grievance usually presented by shop steward.
STEP 2 If grievance not settled ...	Written presentation of the grievance to the director of labour relations or the unit manager.	At this stage, a specialist grievance officer may act on the grievor's behalf.
STEP 3 If grievance not settled ...	Grievance presented to the plant manager or most senior officer responsible for labour relations.	Often several grievances are reviewed at a single step 3 meeting with most being settled.
STEP 4	Matter set down for arbitration either before a sole arbitrator or a three-person arbitration board. Arbitrator (or panel Chair) may be appointed on an ad hoc basis or may be designated in the collective agreement. Failing agreement, the arbitrator may be appointed by the Department of Labour.	Both parties may choose to be represented by legal counsel. Arbitration award is intended to result in a final and binding decision but award may be judicially reviewed on the following grounds: 1. procedural unfairness; 2. jurisdictional error; or 3. decision is patently unreasonable.

a grievance on their own behalf—the decision to file a grievance rests with the union and thus not all "gripes" are formalized into a grievance.[5] Even so, many "gripes" are nevertheless resolved between the union and the employer on an informal basis.

As the grievance proceeds through the internal dispute resolution procedure, the grievance may be settled or withdrawn, but failing resolution or withdrawal, the final step is an arbitration hearing before a neutral arbitrator or three-person arbitration board. Not all grievances that proceed through the final step of the internal grievance process end up in arbitration. For a variety of reasons—the fundamental importance of the dispute, costs, union bargaining strategy, or internal union politics—the union may decide not to refer the dispute to arbitration. In the vast majority of cases, grievances are settled internally, thereby avoiding the expense, delay, and conflict inherent in the arbitration process. For example, a Quebec study found that 97 percent of grievances were settled short of arbitration (Foisy, 1998); similar results have been reported elsewhere (Graham and Heshizer, 1978; Gandz, 1979).

Time Limits

Very often, the collective agreement will provide for a "limitation period"—if the grievance is not filed within the time limited by the agreement, the employer is not obliged to consider the matter at all (i.e., the grievance is not *arbitrable*). The vast majority of collective agreements contain time limits within which grievances must be filed; most often agreements require that grievances be filed within a few weeks after the dispute occurred. In British Columbia, Manitoba, Ontario, and Quebec, arbitrators have been given the statutory authority to override time limits or other procedural irregularities relating to the grievance. Of course, there are always strategic considerations involved in refusing to deal with a grievance that is "out of time." Will the same issue merely arise once again in another grievance? Will the unresolved conflict "spill over" into the workplace? Will the unresolved dispute simply appear as an agenda item in the next round of collective bargaining?

Sole Arbitrator or Three-Person Board?

Once referred to arbitration, the grievance may be decided by a single arbitrator or by a three-person arbitration board. In the latter case, the union and management each name one person (referred to as a "nominee") to the board and a neutral Chair is selected by the parties or appointed by some third party—for example, the minister of labour or the labour relations board. The Chair effectively is the decision maker, however, since the panel need only reach a majority, not a unanimous, decision. In the event neither nominee agrees with the Chair's decision, it nonetheless stands as the final award.

Although there are regional variations, most arbitration awards are issued by sole arbitrators; nevertheless, arbitration boards continue to be used in about one-quarter to one-third of all cases despite the additional costs and lengthier hearings and deliberations boards entail (Thornicroft, 1993). Some parties strongly subscribe to the view that the presence of their nominee on the board ensures that their particular position will be, if not accepted, at least fully aired.

Costs

A frequently voiced complaint about the grievance arbitration process is its cost. Relative to the costs of litigating civil claims in the courts, arbitration appears to be a comparative bargain, but the costs of arbitration can hardly be characterized as modest. Although there are no grievance "filing fees" (unlike the courts) and no direct out-of-pocket expenses for the grievor (unlike the civil claimant who must retain, at his or her own expense, legal counsel), grievance arbitration nonetheless involves significant expense. Some portion of the employees' union dues must be allocated to hire legal counsel (or to pay the salary of an internal union "grievance officer") and to pay the arbitrator's fees and expenses. Both parties, of course, are responsible for paying the fees of their own legal counsel or representative; the arbitrator's fees and expenses are shared between the parties. Unlike in the civil courts, the successful party cannot recover its fees and expenses from the unsuccessful party. In some US states, the practice is for the unsuccessful party to pay the arbitrator's entire fee; however, that is not the situation in Canada.

Arbitrators' fees reflect the time spent on pre-hearing matters (pre-hearing conferences, advance rulings on procedural matters, scheduling the hearing and issuing hearing notices, etc.), presiding at the hearing, reviewing the parties' written submissions, conducting research, and preparing reasons for decision. An arbitrator's fee for sitting and writing an award can range from $500 to over $2500 per day plus related expenses (such as transportation costs, hearing-room rental, etc.)—these costs appear to vary more by region than by individual arbitrator. The costs payable to the arbitrator for a one-day hearing can easily range from $2500 to over $5000. If the parties have opted for an arbitration board, the fees and expenses payable to the nominees will increase the total costs payable. Even if the nominees are not being paid a fee for sitting on the board (say, for example, where the union nominee is a salaried union official rather than an "independent" nominee), there are still additional overhead costs, such as time away from regular duties to prepare for and attend the hearing, that must be taken into account.

The parties (employers more often than unions) may choose to be represented by legal counsel whose fees can range from $100 to over $300 per hour, adding up to somewhere between $2500 and more than $10,000 for a one-day case. Many unions, and increasingly, large employers, do not utilize the services of independent legal counsel, preferring instead to rely on in-house "grievance officers" (union) or "labour relations officers" (employer) whose duties include appearing before arbitrators. In such cases, a fair assessment of the costs of arbitration must include some allocation of the officer's wages and benefits and related overhead expenses.

To put the costs of arbitration into perspective, consider a small employer, say 10 to 20 bargaining unit employees, and its associated union local. With an annual dues base of between $5000 and $10,000, how many arbitrations could the union afford to take on in a given year, taking into account all of the other activities that it wishes to undertake on behalf of its members (such as collective bargaining)? Is it any wonder that most grievances are settled short of arbitration? Increasingly, arbitration has become the preserve of those large unions and employers that have the institutional resources to arbitrate contentious disputes—small employers and unions are constrained to find some other way to resolve their disputes. The high costs associated with collective agreement administration, including grievance arbitration, may well explain, at least in part, the recent trend of smaller unions merging with larger unions (Chaisson, 1996).

The Union's Duty of Fair Representation

Unions are not required to take each and every unresolved grievance to arbitration. However, in deciding to either settle or withdraw a grievance, the union must not be motivated by some improper or discriminatory purpose. Under both Canadian and US labour laws, unions have a statutory duty of fair representation (DFR). If a bargaining unit employee believes that he or she has been treated unfairly by the union, a complaint may be filed with the labour relations board. For example, if Ms. Jones's union determined that she had, in fact and in law, quit her employment, it might decide—if the matter could not be amicably resolved—not to take her grievance to arbitration. Ms. Jones might challenge the union's decision through a DFR complaint, but if the union reached its decision in good faith, after a reasonable examination of all relevant considerations, the union's decision could not be successfully challenged. While DFR complaints are not uncommon, relatively few succeed. For example, in British Columbia the labour relations board has received over 200 DFR complaints each year for the past several years; however, in 1998 for example, only four of the 245 complaints filed that year resulted in a finding that the union had, in fact, breached its DFR obligation. Chapter 7 discusses this topic in more detail.

The Arbitrator's Authority and the Substance of Grievances

Although employers have the right to file grievances against the union, most grievances are filed by the union against the employer. For the most part, the employer can simply apply the collective agreement in a manner consistent with its own view of its rights and obligations (though it may subsequently be found to have acted in error). If the union disagrees with the employer's view, its remedy is to file a grievance. It should also be noted that until such time as an arbitrator rules otherwise, bargaining unit employees are bound to respect the employer's view regarding the interpretation of the collective agreement. In accordance with the so-called "work now; grieve later" principle, employees who dispute the propriety of their employer's directions or orders must nonetheless comply or else risk being disciplined for insubordination; the appropriateness of the direction or order is a matter for the arbitrator to decide (Brown and Beatty, 1997, para. 7: 3610).

Most union-initiated grievances are filed on behalf of individual employees and are often referred to as *individual grievances,* for example, where an employee claims that he or she was wrongfully denied a job promotion or that a certain disciplinary action was inappropriate. Other times, the dispute affects a number of employees or even the bargaining unit as a whole, for example, whether or not the "night shift" employees are entitled to a shift premium under the collective agreement or whether a profit-sharing bonus has been correctly calculated. Such grievances are referred to as *group* or *policy* (or *union*) *grievances.*

Grievances may be filed regarding any term or condition of the collective agreement, including seniority rights, pay and benefits, promotions, and layoffs. Quite frequently, grievances are filed concerning employee discipline or discharge. In discipline and discharge grievances, the onus of proof (and the corresponding obligation to proceed first at the hearing) rests with the employer to show that it had *just cause* to either discipline or terminate the grievor. In all other cases, the party filing the grievance (invariably the union) bears the burden of proof. In discipline and discharge grievances, it is appropriate to place the burden of proving just cause on the employer because it is the employer who is best able to explain why the employee was disciplined or terminated. If the employer is unable to prove that it had just cause for the particular disciplinary action meted out, the arbitrator will cancel the disciplinary action. If some lesser disciplinary action was appropriate given the conduct in question (say, a suspension but not termination), the arbitrator can substitute a lesser penalty, including giving the grievor "one last chance" to salvage his or her job (Bamberger and Donahue, 1999).

A grievor who was discharged without just cause may, if he or she wishes (and that is not always so), be reinstated to his or her former position (a remedy that is generally unavailable in a nonunion "wrongful discharge" lawsuit). Such *reinstatement orders* are generally accompanied by an order for monetary compensation (referred to as a *backpay order*) reflecting the grievor's lost wages during the period between discharge and reinstatement. In all cases where a grievance is upheld, the arbitrator has a great deal of discretion to fashion an appropriate compensatory remedy, which may involve the payment of money, directions regarding the employer's records or policies, or declaratory orders. Arbitrators cannot impose some sort of penalty on the employer for having violated the collective agreement, unlike judges who can award "punitive damages" as a way of punishing a civil defendant (Casey, 1999).

Not only do arbitrators have substantial flexibility in fashioning arbitral remedies, but the range of disputes for which any sort of remedy may be granted has dramatically expanded over the last several decades. As grievance arbitration was originally envisioned, the arbitrator's authority or *jurisdiction* was limited to interpreting and applying the express terms of the collective bargaining agreement. That is no longer the case. In 1974, the Supreme Court of Canada held that arbitrators must take into account relevant legislation when interpreting collective agreements and must override the express language of a collective agreement when it conflicts with external legislation, for example, human rights or employment standards legislation.[6]

In 1986, the Supreme Court of Canada clearly stated that legislatively mandated grievance arbitration procedures effectively ousted the courts' general jurisdiction to deal with disputes that could otherwise be the subject of a court action. Thus, an employer's civil suit against its union for damages suffered as a result of an illegal strike was dismissed on the ground that the employer was obliged to proceed with its claim through the grievance arbitration process.[7]

In 1990 the Supreme Court ruled that arbitrators were empowered to apply the *Canadian Charter of Rights and Freedoms,* for example, to declare a collective bargaining provision null and void because it conflicted with a *Charter* right.[8]

In 1995, this trend was extended still further—the Supreme Court held that an arbitrator is a "court of competent jurisdiction" for purposes of granting constitutional remedies (for example, awarding compensation) for a breach of a *Charter,* as opposed to a collective agreement, right.[9]

The law is evolving so that any dispute that could be said to "arise from the collective agreement" can only be adjudicated through arbitration. Thus, claims for invasion of privacy,[10] defamation,[11] monetary claims for reimbursement for property damage,[12] and perhaps even human rights claims[13]—to list but a few examples—may all fall within the exclusive domain of the arbitrator. This trend is all the more remarkable because once an arbitrator has rendered a decision, it is considerably more difficult to have that decision overturned than if the same decision had been issued by a court.

Enforcement and Review of Arbitration Awards

Arbitrators do not have the formal authority to ensure that the parties comply with their awards, but an arbitration award can be filed in a registry of the provincial superior court and thereafter may be enforced as an ordinary court order. A party who continues to ignore an arbitrator's order after it has been filed with the court risks a fine or even imprisonment for contempt of court. In light of these potential sanctions, few parties flout an arbitrator's order. Rather, the losing (or only partially victorious) party might seek to overturn the arbitrator's decision through a process known as *judicial review* whereby the courts are asked to reconsider the arbitrator's award.

A "review" is not an "appeal" and the courts have generally taken a "hands-off" approach to arbitrators' decisions—the courts refer to this as *judicial deference.* A court will not overturn an arbitrator's decision simply because the court disagrees with the arbitrator's analysis and conclusions. So long as the arbitrator is acting within his or her jurisdiction, the decision cannot be overturned unless it can be said to be "patently unreasonable"—in other words, there was no evidence to support the conclusions reached by the arbitrator or the decision is otherwise rationally indefensible.[14]

The courts have shown a greater willingness to intervene when the arbitrator, in the court's view, obviously misstated a general legal principle, appears to be biased, or failed to ensure that the hearing was conducted in a procedurally fair manner. Nevertheless, even when the court does overturn (or quash) an arbitrator's decision, the usual remedy—unless the arbitrator was acting without any authority whatsoever—is a referral for rehearing before the same or another arbitrator. In light of that position, it behooves the parties to ensure that their arbitrator is a judicious, competent, knowledgeable, and fair-minded individual. Where are such individuals to be found?

ARBITRATORS: CHARACTERISTICS AND TRAINING

The arbitrator profession is largely unregulated. There is no legal impediment to anyone "hanging out a shingle" and announcing their availability to arbitrate unresolved grievances. In reality, a small number of individuals conduct the majority of arbitrations within any given province. The parties are usually unwilling to allow inexperienced arbitrators to adjudicate their disputes. Many collective agreements contain a roster of experienced arbitrators who are called on, in rotation, to arbitrate unresolved grievances. If the minister of labour or labour board is requested to appoint an arbitrator, they will invariably draw a name from their own panel of experienced, acceptable arbitrators.

As a result, in almost every province there are a few arbitrators who are extremely busy, and many others who are quite underutilized. A study found that 13 arbitrators issued 76 percent of the arbitration awards in Ontario (Gandz and Warrian, 1977), and similar levels of arbitrator concentration have been reported elsewhere (Thornicroft, 1993). The growing utilization of expedited arbitration (discussed in more detail later) may lead to a reduction in the reliance on a small corps of arbitrators. For example, in Ontario since the introduction of expedited arbitration in 1979, 20 arbitrators completed a training program and were added to the province's list of approved arbitrators; these newly trained arbitrators issued 20.3 percent of the awards rendered in 1985–86 and over one-quarter of their caseloads involved non-expedited arbitration (Rose, 1991).

Most labour relations practitioners have well-defined views about what makes a good arbitrator, and experience and good judgment are two characteristics that are likely to appear on any list of desired attributes (Westercamp and Miller, 1971). In a survey of nearly 300 members of the American Arbitration Association the following attributes were listed as being the most important (in descending order): personal integrity; experience, both as an arbitrator and within labour relations generally; and perceived neutrality. The respondents did not believe that a legal education was particularly necessary to succeed as an arbitrator although a majority of arbitrators are lawyers (Allen and Jennings, 1988).

The typical arbitrator is a relatively older male, university trained in law or labour relations and experienced in labour relations as a union or management advocate, labour relations board member, or university professor (Lewin, 1999). Most arbitrators do not work full-time although in each province, especially Ontario, Quebec, and British Columbia, there is a small corps of full-time arbitrators. Unlike professions such as law, medicine, and engineering, there is no self-governing regulatory body for arbitrators. However, many arbitrators are members of one or more of the following organizations (all of which hold annual conventions or workshops): the National Academy of Arbitrators (which has an extensive code of ethics), the American Arbitration Association, the Society of Professionals in Dispute Resolution, the Industrial Relations Research Association, and the Canadian Industrial Relations Association. In addition, in some provinces the arbitrator community has established a local organization—for example, the British Columbia Arbitrators' Association.

There is little formal training provided to prospective arbitrators, although in recent years there have been initiatives in Ontario, Newfoundland, Alberta, and British Columbia to offer a structured training program for new arbitrators. Such programs typically involve a rigorous selection process for trainees, seminars on the law of evidence and arbitration procedure, and decision-writing workshops; often the trainees are asked to attend a series of actual arbitration hearings conducted by experienced arbitrators and are then required to draft decisions for review and critique. Although relatively inexperienced labour arbitrators have a difficult time establishing a professional foothold, many are finding that their adjudicative expertise can be applied in a number of other settings such as nonunion employment disputes; disputes regarding franchise, partnership, and shareholder agreements; and insurance claims.

Of course, before an arbitrator can be appointed, there must be an unresolved dispute that has been formalized into a grievance. There is a large body of research concerning grievance-filing behaviour, the topic to which we now turn.

WHO FILES GRIEVANCES AND WHY?

Grievances are one mechanism that bargaining unit employees can utilize to voice their dissatisfaction with the status quo (Lewin, 1999.) Some employees—especially those who are comparatively well paid or whose alternative job prospects are bleak—may view filing a grievance (i.e., a "voice" response) as a preferable alternative to quitting (i.e., an "exit" response) (Cappelli and Chauvin, 1991). Research on individual grievor characteristics has found grievors to be younger, less well-educated, more highly skilled, and more likely to be members of minority groups than employees who have not filed grievances. As well, employee loyalty to the firm is a factor; highly loyal employees are more prepared to "suffer in silence" rather than file a grievance (Lewin, 1999).

The *grievance rate* refers to the number of grievances filed per bargaining unit employee. Although lower grievance rates often indicate a better union–management relationship (Gandz, 1979; Gandz and Whitehead, 1982), a low rate does not necessarily imply an absence of workplace dissatisfaction. A comparatively low grievance rate may be attributed to managerial domination of the bargaining unit employees or to the employees' fear of retaliation if they file grievances. On the other hand, a high grievance rate may reflect union domination of the workplace (Lewin and Peterson, 1988), the fact that the union's internal constitution obliges it to file and even arbitrate certain types of grievances (e.g., terminations), the length of the current agreement (some "collective bargaining issues" may be expressed as grievances if the next round of bargaining is not imminent), or the fact that the employees do not have the right to strike (Hebdon and Stern, 1998). Other factors that affect the grievance rate include supervisors' behaviour, the extent to which shop stewards and supervisors prefer to resolve matters informally rather than through the formal grievance process, the industry, the rate of technological change, the state of the local labour market, and the general organizational climate (summarized in Lewin, 1999). Since early resolution of grievances is usually believed to benefit all parties, some researchers have identified the determinants of early settlements (e.g., at the first or second step): co-operative bargaining relationships (Turner and Robinson, 1972), experienced first-line supervisors (Knight, 1986a), a willingness to learn from past grievances (Knight, 1986b), and the exclusion of lawyers from the settlement process (Deitsch and Dilts, 1986); all these factors appear to make early settlements more likely.

"Legalism" in Grievance Arbitration: Bane or Benefit?

It has become fashionable in recent years to decry the creeping "legalism" of the grievance arbitration process. Lawyers are well entrenched in the grievance arbitration process, in most cases at the initiative of the parties themselves. However, this criticism goes beyond the mere involvement of lawyers in grievance arbitration. More than ever before, the arbitration process has taken on the "look and feel" of a courtroom trial—arbitrators seem to be overly concerned with applying "arbitral principles" as derived from the large body of arbitration case law, dealing with evidence on the basis of court-derived rules, and focusing on the parties' respective legal rights rather than the underlying equities of the actual dispute. Most arbitrators or arbitration board chairs are lawyers, and parties (especially management) often choose to retain legal counsel to appear on their behalf at the arbitration hearing.

Presumably, parties retain lawyers in order to improve their chances of success, although the available evidence suggests that may be somewhat of a false hope (Block and Steiber, 1987; Thornicroft, 1994). Some parties may choose legal representation because they do not have the expertise, time, or organizational skills to prepare and present a case on their own. Regardless of the reason why parties choose to retain legal counsel, it does seem clear that lawyers' involvement in the grievance arbitration process tends to delay the process, an issue to which we now turn.

Justice Delayed, Justice Denied

Grievance arbitration was originally conceived as an expeditious and inexpensive mechanism for resolving disputes arising from collective bargaining agreements. Regrettably, there is mounting evidence that the grievance arbitration process is not particularly expeditious, although it must always be borne in mind that, for the most part, arbitration proceeds comparatively faster than does a civil lawsuit and that the vast majority of grievances are settled before arbitration. Nevertheless, in a survey of 360 union and management advocates, the union representatives identified "delays by the other side" as the most serious fault with the arbitration process (Berkeley, 1989). It is not uncommon for a grievance that ultimately proceeds to arbitration to take nearly a year to be resolved, that is, from the date the grievance was filed to the date the arbitrator's decision is issued (see Table 12.1). More troubling, over the past two decades, the average elapsed time from initial filing to issuance of the arbitrator's award has doubled (Ponak et al, 1996).

There are two main components of delay in the grievance arbitration process—pre-hearing and post-hearing delay—the former, by far, being the larger component.[15]

Pre-hearing delay may be attributed to a variety of factors, including the congested schedules of prominent arbitrators and the parties' legal counsel or other representatives, unavailability of witnesses, and time spent addressing the grievance in the internal (often two- or three-step) grievance process. This latter source of delay might be

TABLE 12.1

STUDIES OF DELAY IN GRIEVANCE ARBITRATION

Study	Jurisdiction	Time Frame	Pre-Hearing Delay	Hearing to Award	Total Delay*
Goldblatt (1994)	Ontario	1971–1973	212	37	256
Fricke (1976)	Alberta	1973–1975	157	46	214
Kochan and Katz (1988)	USA	1975	—	—	223
Labour Arbitration Cases	Canada	1975	—	—	283
Stanton (1983)	BC	1966–1981	—	—	240
Winter (1983)	Ontario	1980	258	36	301
Rose (1986)	Ontario	1983	—	48	342
F.M.C.S (1988)	USA	1985–1987	281	64	345
Olson (1990)	Alberta	1985–1988	268	70	345
Labour Arbitration Cases	Canada	1987–1988	366	101	428
Barnacle (1991)	Ontario	1983–1986	168	—	240
Thornicroft (1993)	Newfoundland	1980–1991	146	35	181
Foisy (1998)	Montreal	1993–1996	467	55	522

*Total Delay (calendar days) may not equal sum of "Pre-Hearing Delay" and "Hearing to Award" due to missing information and multi-day hearings.

Source: Adapted, with additional references, from Ponak and Olson, 1992.

eradicated if the parties agreed to streamline their internal grievance process by eliminating one or more of the internal steps. Exhibit 12.1 comments on this necessity.

Once the parties finally get to an arbitration hearing, matters tend to proceed quickly. Although cases may drag on because an insufficient number of days have been set aside to hear the evidence (thus necessitating an adjournment to another date convenient to all parties and their counsel), arbitrators typically render a decision within six to eight weeks after hearing all the evidence. Generally speaking, decisions in discipline and (particularly) discharge cases are rendered more quickly compared to other cases. One study suggests that grievances arising in the public sector take longer to conclude than similar private-sector cases perhaps because of the bureaucratic nature of many public-sector organizations (Ponak and Olson, 1992; Foisy, 1998). Other sources of delay in the grievance arbitration process include the use of tripartite panels (versus sole arbitrators) and representation by legal counsel (Ponak and Olson, 1992; Thornicroft, 1994).

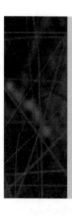

Exhibit 12.1

"Time Marches On"

In many relationships there are four or five grievance steps, in each of which no more takes place than had occurred in a preceding step. The union merely repeats what it has said before, and the employer representative merely uses a previous answer as a rubber stamp. While all this transpires, to no effective purpose, the grievant waits for justice and time marches on.

Source: Seitz, 1981.

While delay may be a lesser concern in certain types of cases, it is a particular problem in discharge grievances because the grievor cannot return to work until the grievance is resolved in his or her favour. Moreover, some studies have found that arbitrators are less likely to order reinstatement where there has been substantial delay in getting to a hearing (Adams, 1978). Even if the grievor is returned to work, say, one year after discharge, the remedy may prove to be rather unsatisfactory because the grievor might have found a new job and might be reluctant to return to his or her former position or, indeed, may have relocated to another city or province in search of new employment. While the grievor will undoubtedly receive some sort of monetary award in any event, many employees—if offered the opportunity of a timely reinstatement—would prefer both backpay and reinstatement. Similarly, employers are not indifferent to delay in discharge cases because, of course, their liability for backpay increases with the passage of time. If a grievor is reinstated, the employer may face the ticklish situation of dealing with not only the grievor but also another employee who may have been hired as the grievor's replacement.

GRIEVANCE OUTCOMES AND ARBITRAL REMEDIES

There is substantial interest in who wins and who loses in arbitration and the factors that affect these results. For this reason, researchers have looked at factors that might be systematically related to arbitration decisions.

Arbitrator Characteristics

Unlike judges, arbitrators are not bound by precedent nor by the technical rules of evidence; each case must be decided on its own merits. Assuming the grievance is upheld, the appropriate remedy will depend on the nature of the grievance. Remedies can range from a simple declaratory order (e.g., management has the right to contract out certain equipment maintenance work), to monetary orders, to employee reinstatement orders (either unconditionally or on terms, and with or without backpay). The courts, when reviewing arbitral remedies, have repeatedly stressed that awards will not be set aside simply because they are unconventional or "creative."

Although arbitrators have considerable flexibility in fashioning their awards, there is some concern that arbitrators tailor their awards so that neither party is unduly offended.

Since arbitrators are selected by mutual agreement of the parties, arbitrators may have an incentive to "keep the scales in balance." Such behaviour may be motivated by the "decision statistics" or "box scores" that are compiled by some unions and employers. Arbitrators, not surprisingly, often declare that they have no idea what their decision ratios might be and contend that they only base their decisions on the merits of the case before them. Although some research suggests that arbitral outcomes are influenced by arbitrators' background characteristics such as age, education, and experience, several other studies have concluded that arbitrators' background characteristics have little, if any, impact on arbitrators' decision making (Bemmels, 1990; Lewin, 1999). Legal training also has little effect on outcome. The overwhelming evidence is that lawyer-arbitrators do not decide cases any differently than arbitrators who are not members of the legal bar (Thornicroft, 1994).

Legal Representation

The efficacy of legal representation is a matter of considerable empirical debate. Various studies have shown that when one party is represented by legal counsel and the other is not, the represented party is more likely to prevail (Wagar, 1994); thus, it is not legal counsel per se that makes the difference but rather the "imbalance" in legal representation (Block and Steiber, 1987). Of course, this observed effect could merely be a statistical artifice reflecting the fact that parties are less willing to incur the expense of legal representation when the merits of their case appear doubtful.

In a contrary finding, an analysis of all Newfoundland arbitration decisions issued between 1980 and 1992 indicated that parties were not more likely to prevail when represented by legal counsel (Thornicroft, 1994). Considered collectively, the available empirical evidence suggests that lawyers have little, if any, impact on grievance arbitration outcomes when each or neither party is represented but may favourably shift the odds (in favour of the represented party) when only one party is legally represented. These findings imply that unions and employers could reduce their arbitration costs if they would mutually agree not to retain legal counsel to appear on their behalf at the arbitration hearing—a policy that has been embodied in some private expedited arbitration schemes. For example, the Canada Post and CUPW contract includes Article 9.63: "The parties agree not to use lawyers to represent them in regular arbitration."

Grievor Characteristics

Labour relations researchers have also examined whether or not grievors' personal characteristics, or the characteristics of the grievance itself, are systematically related to grievance outcomes. For example, one study found that arbitrators treated grievors whose misconduct involved alcohol rather more leniently than grievors whose misconduct could be traced to the use of narcotics (Thornicroft, 1989). Not surprisingly, and consistent with the theory of "progressive discipline" (namely, that repeated acts of misconduct will be met with increasingly more severe penalties), grievors with poor work records are less likely to succeed in arbitration compared to grievors with unblemished work histories (Thornicroft, 1989, 1994).

Perhaps the most commonly examined personal characteristic is gender (Bemmels, 1988, 1991). There are two competing "gender hypotheses": the "chivalry" hypothesis (which operates in favour of women, particularly given that most arbitrators are male) and the "evil woman" hypothesis (which operates to the detriment of female grievors). Despite a great many studies, no clear empirical consensus has emerged. Among some 17 published studies, ten found a pro-female bias, one found an anti-female bias, and six found gender to be wholly irrelevant (Thornicroft, 1995). These results, however, are all based on an analysis of arbitration awards; there may be gender-based differences in grievance-filing behaviour or arbitration-referral behaviour which have yet to be systematically investigated.

ALTERNATIVES TO CONVENTIONAL GRIEVANCE ARBITRATION

Mounting criticisms of traditional grievance arbitration have led many parties to explore alternatives such as *expedited arbitration* and *grievance mediation.*

While there are many variants, expedited arbitration generally involves procedures designed to reduce the delay and expense associated with traditional grievance arbitration. For example, in an expedited arbitration system the parties may agree that:

- the matter will be heard by a sole arbitrator rather than a tripartite panel;
- the arbitrator will issue (either immediately upon the conclusion of the hearing or within one or two days thereafter) an oral decision to be followed by a brief written award;
- all evidence will be submitted in the form of written witness statements with no oral testimony whatsoever, or the number of witnesses may be limited (say, one witness for each party);
- neither party will retain legal counsel; and
- the hearing is subject to some time limit, say one or two hours, which may allow a sole arbitrator to hear several cases in a single hearing day.

An expedited arbitration process may be established by mutual agreement of the parties or may be imposed by statute, as is the case in Ontario and British Columbia. The former are voluntary systems, whereas the latter are established by legislation and may be invoked without joint agreement.

One of the first examples of a statutory expedited arbitration system was implemented in British Columbia in the early 1980s. The labour relations board could mediate and arbitrate grievances at the request of one of the parties. Between 1981 and 1986, approximately 600 applications were received each year of which some 69 percent were settled through mediation (Thompson, 1992). The current British Columbia expedited

arbitration system was established in 1994. Once appointed under the expedited procedure, the arbitrator must render a decision within 21 days of the hearing. Approximately
45 percent of all cases referred for expedited arbitration during the first two years of the
program were concluded less than 100 days from date of grievance to issuance of award,
a considerable improvement over traditional arbitration (Thornicroft, 1996). The British
Columbia system also includes the appointment of a settlement officer who attempts to
achieve a mediated settlement prior to arbitration. Between 1994 and 1998, 80 percent
of all cases submitted to the expedited process were settled this way. Ontario's system is
similar and also includes grievance mediation. Nearly one-half of all matters referred for
expedited arbitration are resolved by settlement officers.

The Ontario system, like that in British Columbia, can be invoked regardless of the
nature of the grievance and, at least in Ontario, it would appear that the types of cases
that proceed to expedited arbitration differ little from those sent to conventional arbitration (Rose, 1991). The British Columbia experience thus far indicates that about one-
quarter of all expedited arbitration applications concern discipline or termination
cases.[16] In addition to being faster, expedited arbitration has resulted in significant cost
savings to the parties (Rose, 1991).

British Columbia Ministry of Labour: www.labour.gov.bc.ca

Private expedited arbitration systems (usually, but not always, set out in the parties'
collective agreement) are relatively rare but are becoming increasingly more common.
One of the older systems in Canada is the Canadian Railway Office of Arbitration, established in 1965, which provides for a single arbitrator who often hears five to seven
cases in a single day and is obliged to render a decision within one week. The evidence
is usually submitted only in written form (witnesses are rarely called) and the use of
lawyers is discouraged; significant time and cost savings have been reported (Picher,
1991). Other private systems have been established by Inco, Canada Post Corporation,
and in the BC health care and longshore sectors (Thompson, 1992; Arbogast, 1991).
Under the longshoring system, a "job arbitrator" is on call 24 hours a day and issues immediate "on-the-spot" decisions when called upon to resolve certain types of disputes.

Grievance mediation is another effective alternative to the grievance arbitration system. It is sometimes incorporated as a voluntary step in either an expedited or conventional grievance arbitration process. The labour relations statutes of several provinces
(British Columbia, Saskatchewan, and Ontario) provide for the appointment of a settlement officer, i.e., a grievance mediator, with mutual consent of the parties.

In grievance mediation, a trained third-party neutral (the mediator) assists the employer
and the union representatives in reaching a voluntary settlement of the grievance. Mediators
usually endeavour to clarify the issues in dispute, seek out the parties' respective "bottom
lines," and may even offer proposals for settlement. Unlike an arbitrator, a mediator has no
independent authority to resolve the dispute. If the grievance cannot be resolved through mediation, the only remaining option—other than withdrawal of the grievance—is arbitration.
During mediation, information may be disclosed to the mediator that would not otherwise

be disclosed to the other party. To protect the integrity and efficacy of the mediation process, all such disclosures remain confidential even after the mediation process had ended; generally, all matters discussed during mediation are protected from subsequent disclosure during an arbitration hearing. Moreover, if a mediated settlement is reached, the settlement is on a "without prejudice" basis so that no precedent is created with respect to any future dispute regarding the same issue.

Some of the benefits of grievance mediation include the following.

1. Faster resolution of cases. There is no waiting for a written decision.

2. Cost savings. Mediation is usually less expensive than arbitration (e.g., settlement officers appointed under the BC *Labour Relations Code* are provided at no cost to the parties).

3. Less adversarialism. The focus of mediation is reaching a mutually acceptable agreement rather than winning a rights dispute. To put the matter another way, in a dispute settled by arbitration, only one party wins; in a mediated dispute, both parties win.

4. Improved labour–management relations. The positive experience of settling disputes through mediation may enhance the probability of future disputes being resolved amicably and without resort to some form of adjudicative process (Feuille, 1999).

Although grievance mediation often involves a formal process whereby a mediator is either appointed or privately retained solely for the purpose of mediating the dispute, many arbitrators endeavour—either at the invitation of the parties or on their own motion—to effect a settlement of the dispute prior to commencing the formal arbitration hearing. Indeed, some arbitrators are specifically appointed because of their skills as a mediator. The arbitrator's mediation function has now been formalized in the BC *Labour Relations Code:* "an arbitrator may...encourage settlement of the dispute and, with the agreement of the parties...may use mediation, conciliation, or other procedures at any time during the arbitral proceedings to encourage settlement" (s. 89(h)).

There is little published research on the effect of grievance mediation in Canada. In the pre-hearing mediation process used by the Ontario Crown Employees' Grievance Settlement Board, approximately 70 to 80 percent of all cases were resolved prior to the hearing stage (Fraser and Shime, 1989). In the Ontario construction industry, a negotiated settlement was reached through grievance mediation in 87 percent of all cases during the period 1980 to 1984 (Whitehead, Aim, and Whitehead, 1988). In the United States, voluntary grievance mediation has resulted in significant time and cost savings in such diverse sectors as coal, telephone, electric power, manufacturing, petroleum refining, retail drug, local government, secondary education, and mass transit (Goldberg, 1989). It has been estimated that of those grievances referred to mediation, some 80 percent have been resolved short of arbitration (Skratek, 1993). This success rate may reflect, at least in part, the fact that parties who agree to mediate a particular grievance are predisposed to settlement.

Overall, the evidence indicates that expedited arbitration and grievance mediation are effective mechanisms for resolving disputes more efficiently than traditional arbitration procedures. The time and cost savings clearly are compelling; in addition, grievance mediation may also improve the parties' problem-solving ability and their overall bargaining relationship. Both grievance mediation and expedited arbitration offer sufficient promise to warrant their expanded use and further empirical evaluation.

 Canadian Centre for Policy Alternatives: www.policyalternatives.ca/

Employer Promulgated Arbitration in Nonunion Settings

Quite apart from nonunion arbitration requirements that may arise under certain statutes like the *Canada Labour Code*, a recent development has been the voluntary adoption of arbitration to settle employment disputes in nonunion organizations. Because employees are not represented by a union, arbitration in nonunion settings is introduced unilaterally by the employer—hence the term, "employer promulgated arbitration." Thus far, experience with nonunion arbitration systems has occurred almost exclusively in the United States, but it has begun to spread into Canada through American firms with nonunion operations in this country. In 1999, it was estimated that almost as many employees were covered by employer promulgated arbitration in the United States as by collective agreement arbitration procedures (Zack, 1999).

Why would a nonunion company voluntarily adopt arbitration processes? Two main reasons have been advanced. First, it makes good sense as part of a strategy of progressive human resource management that gives employees an avenue to resolve perceived injustices, bringing a sense of fairness to the workplace. A useful by-product might be the forestalling of unionization since the employer has provided nonunion employees with one of the main benefits of union certification. A second reason is less benign. In the United States, the costs of court litigation have skyrocketed, with employees occasionally winning huge awards against their employers in highly publicized cases. Arbitration is a substitute for litigation and many employers that have adopted an arbitration process have made the use of arbitration a condition of the employment contract. In other words, employees give up their right to sue their employer in court over, for example, termination of employment for some alleged shortcoming.

 Labor Net (American, union-oriented): www.labornet.org/

Unionized employees also relinquish their right to go to court, but in a unionized situation the arbitration process is carefully negotiated between the union and employer and backed by the union's considerable institutional power and resources. While fairness in the arbitration process is not absolutely guaranteed, it is at least safeguarded. The main criticism of employer promulgated arbitration systems is that they may lack basic fairness, tilting the outcome heavily in favour of the employer. For example, the employee, who typically lacks any expertise in arbitration, may be precluded from having representation

Exhibit 12.2

Due Process in Nonunion Arbitrations

Excerpts from Due Process Protocol for Mediation and Arbitration:
    ...The focus of this Protocol is on standards of exemplary due process.

Right of Representation

Choice of Representative. Employees considering the use of or, in fact, utilizing mediation and/or arbitration procedures should have the right to be represented by a spokesperson of their own choosing.

Fees for Representation. The amount and method of payment for representation should be determined between the claimant and the representative. The arbitrator should have the authority to provide for fee reimbursement, in whole or in part, as part of the remedy in accordance with applicable law or in the interests of justice.

Access to Information. Adequate but limited pre-trial discovery is to be encouraged and employees should have access to all information reasonably relevant....

Mediator and Arbitrator Qualification

Roster Membership. Mediators and arbitrators selected for such cases should have skill in the conduct of hearings, knowledge of the statutory issues at stake in the dispute, and familiarity with the workplace and employment environment. Regardless of their prior experience, mediators and arbitrators on the roster must be independent of bias toward either party. They should reject cases if they believe the procedure lacks requisite due process.

Conflicts of Interest. The mediator and arbitrator has a duty to disclose...conflicts of interest.

Authority of the Arbitrator. The arbitrator should be bound by applicable agreements, statutes, regulations, and rules of procedure...[and] should be empowered to award whatever relief would be available in court under the law.

Compensation of the Mediator and Arbitrator. Impartiality is best assured by the parties sharing the fees and expenses of the mediator and arbitrator. In cases where the economic condition of a party does not permit equal sharing, the parties should make mutually acceptable arrangements to achieve that goal if at all possible. In the absence of such agreement, the arbitrator should determine the allocation of fees.

Source: Excerpted from Zack, 1999, pp. 90–94.

or from participating in the selection of the arbitrator. This is especially egregious in a situation in which the employee has to agree to arbitration in order to be hired.

These concerns, combined with the rapid spread of employer promulgated arbitration and several important court cases on fairness,[17] have led to an unusual experiment. Several organizations with stakes in employer promulgated arbitration, including the

National Academy of Arbitrators, the American Bar Association, the labour movement, and the American Civil Liberties Union, negotiated a set of rules designed to satisfy concerns over fairness. This set of rules, known as the "Due Process Protocol," establishes a voluntary framework for employer promulgated arbitration schemes (Exhibit 12.2). Among other things, the protocol provides representation rights to employees, access to information prior to the hearing, participation in the selection of the arbitrator, and the creation of a roster of experienced, neutral arbitrators. It is predicted that arbitration for nonunion employees will spread, and with the Protocol in place, nonunion arbitration has the potential of meeting the "same goals of employee fairness that spawned the labor–management model of dispute resolution" (Zack, 1999: 89).

CONCLUSION

Grievance arbitration plays a central role in the union–management relationship. It was originally conceived as an equitable, inexpensive, and expeditious mechanism for resolving contract disputes. This still remains true in a comparative sense. For example, arbitration is a much less expensive and more accessible procedure to remedy a wrongful discharge than a lawsuit in the civil courts. The grievor need not incur expenses for pursuing his or her grievance—that cost is absorbed through the payment of union membership dues. Unlike civil litigation, the grievance arbitration process is largely within the exclusive control of the parties themselves; the parties are free to select their own decision maker; the parties can jointly determine the most appropriate procedure. Grievance arbitration has also been lauded as an effective mechanism for improving workplace democracy and for providing employees with a meaningful voice in matters affecting their employment.

Notwithstanding its benefits, however, serious concerns have been raised about the effectiveness of grievance arbitration. It has been suggested that grievance arbitration, as presently constituted, is too slow, too expensive, and overly legalistic. In light of these criticisms—all of which have at least some merit—both policy-makers and labour relations practitioners have attempted to formulate alternative systems for resolving workplace disputes such as expedited arbitration and grievance mediation.

The available evidence indicates that both processes are effective in terms of promoting and effecting settlement of disputes and produce substantial savings in both time and money. In future, we can expect more experimentation with these and similar processes to return arbitration to its original roots: to serve the needs of the participants in the labour relations system.

Questions

1. To what extent can the grievance process be utilized as a mechanism for employees to "voice" their concerns about workplace issues?

2. It has been said that the grievance process is the quid pro quo for a no-strike/no-lockout clause in the collective agreement. Is this a "fair" trade-off?

3. Some parties choose sole arbitrators while others prefer to use three-person panels. What are the pros and cons of each format?

4. What remedy does a bargaining unit employee have when the union does not take his or her unresolved grievance to arbitration?

5. What changes, if any, would you propose to the contemporary grievance arbitration process to ensure that it is a relatively quick, inexpensive, and just process?

6. How does "expedited arbitration" differ from "conventional arbitration"?

7. Do you feel that lawyers should be banned from the grievance arbitration process? Why or why not?

8. Can measures be introduced into nonunion (employer promulgated) arbitrations that will make them as "fair" as those in the unionized setting?

ENDNOTES

[1] This chapter is a revision of a chapter that appeared in the third edition, co-authored by K. W. Thornicroft and G. Eden.

[2] Case adapted from author's files.

[3] BC *Labour Relations Code*, RSBC 1996, c. 244 as amended, s. 58.

[4] See *Weber* v. *Ontario Hydro* (1995), 125 DLR (4th) 583 (SCC); *New Brunswick* v. *O'Leary* (1995), 125 DLR (4th) 609 (SCC).

[5] This is to be contrasted with the US situation where, by virtue of section 9(a) of the *National Labour Relations Act*, bargaining unit employees "shall have the right at any time to present grievances to their employer and have such grievances adjusted...."

[6] *McLeod* v. *Egan* (1974), 46 DLR (3d) 150 (SCC).

[7] *St. Anne Nackawic Pulp & Paper Co.* v. *C.P.U., Local 219* [1986] 1 SCR 704, 28 DLR (4th) 1 (SCC).

[8] *Douglas/Kwantlen Faculty Assn.* v. *Douglas College* (1990), 77 DLR (4th) 94 (SCC).

[9] Supra, note 4.

[10] *Weber* v. *Ontario Hydro*, supra, note 4.

[11] *Re Fording Coal* (1997), 69 LAC (4th) 430.

[12] *New Brunswick* v. *O'Leary*, supra, note 4.

[13] For a discussion as to why arbitration is not an entirely appropriate forum to address human rights complaints, see Carter (1997).

[14] *Dayco* v. *C.A.W.-Canada* (1993), 102 DLR (4th) 609 (SCC).

[15] In turn, pre-hearing and post-hearing delay may be more finely subcategorized. For example, pre-hearing delay includes delay associated with selecting an arbitrator as well as delay in fixing a hearing date once an arbitrator has been selected. It would appear that different factors come into play at each subcategory. Thus, lawyers are associated more with delay in fixing a hearing date than with delay in selecting an arbitrator, see Ponak et al (1996).

[16] *British Columbia Ministry of Labour Annual Report 1997/1998*—available on the Ministry's Website: www.labour.gov.bc.ca.

[17] *Gilmer* v. *Interstate Johnson Lane Corporation* (1991), US Supreme Court, 500 US 29.

REFERENCES

ADAMS, G. A. 1978. *Grievance Arbitration of Discharge Cases.* Kingston, Ontario: Industrial Relations Centre, Queen's University.

ALLEN, A. D. and D. F. JENNINGS. 1988. "Sounding Out the Nation's Arbitrators: An AAA Survey." *Labor Law Journal,* 39, pp. 423–31.

ARBOGAST, M. W. 1991. "Resolving Issues and Improving Relationships Through the Use of Expedited Arbitration," in *Proceedings of the 28th Conference of the Canadian Industrial Relations Association.* Kingston, Ontario: CIRA, pp. 533–42.

BAMBERGER, P. and L. DONAHUE. 1999. "Employee Discharge and Reinstatement: Moral Hazards and the Mixed Consequences of Last Chance Agreements." *Industrial & Labor Relations Review,* 53, no. 1, pp. 3–20.

BARNACLE, P. J. 1991. *Arbitration of Discharge Grievances in Ontario: Outcomes and Reinstatement Experiences.* Kingston, Ontario: Industrial Relations Centre, Queen's University.

BEMMELS, B. 1988. "The Effect of Grievants' Gender on Arbitration Outcomes." *Industrial and Labor Relations Review,* 41, pp. 251–262.

———. 1990. "Arbitrator Characteristics and Arbitrator Decisions." *Journal of Labor Research,* 11, pp. 181–92.

———. 1991. "Gender Effects in Grievance Arbitration." *Industrial Relations,* 30, pp. 150–162.

BERKELEY, A. E. 1989. "The Most Serious Faults in Labor Management Arbitration Today and What Can Be Done to Remedy Them." *Labor Law Journal,* 40, pp. 728–733.

BLOCK, R. N. and J. STEIBER. 1987. "The Impacts of Attorneys and Arbitrators on Arbitration Awards." *Industrial and Labor Relations Review,* 40, pp. 543–555.

BRETT, J. and S. B. GOLDBERG. 1979. "Wildcat Strikes in Bituminous Coal Mining." *Industrial and Labor Relations Review,* 32, 465–83.

BROWN, D. and D. BEATTY. 1997. *Canadian Labour Arbitration,* 3rd Edition. Aurora, Ontario: Canada Law Book.

CAPPELLI, P. and K. CHAUVIN. 1991. "A Test of an Efficiency Model of Grievance Activity." *Industrial and Labor Relations Review,* 45, pp. 3–14.

CASEY, J., editor. 1999. *Remedies in Labour, Employment and Human Rights Law.* Toronto: Carswell.

CHAISSON, G. 1996. *Union Mergers in Hard Times.* Ithaca, New York: Cornell University Press.

DEITSCH, C. R. and D. A. DILTS. 1986. "Factors Affecting Pre-Arbitral Settlement of Rights Disputes: Predicting the Method of Rights Dispute Resolution." *Journal of Labor Research,* 7, pp. 69–78.

DOHERTY, R. E. 1989. *Industrial and Labor Relations Terms: A Glossary,* 5th Edition. Ithaca, New York: ILR Press.

FEUILLE, P. 1999. "Grievance Mediation," in *Employment Dispute Resolution and Worker Rights,* edited by A. E. Eaton and J. H. Keefe. Champaign, Ill.: Industrial Relations Research Association Series.

FOISY, C. 1998. "Is Arbitration Too Slow and Legalistic?" in *Conference Proceedings of the 16th Annual University of Calgary Labour Arbitration Conference,* edited by M. Hughes and A. Ponak. Calgary: Industrial Relations Research Group and University of Calgary.

FRASER, D. and O.B. SHIME. 1989. "The Ontario Grievance Settlement Board," in *Proceedings of the 26th Conference of the Canadian Industrial Relations Association.* Laval, Quebec: CIRA, pp. 567–78.

FREEMAN, R. B. and J. L. MEDOFF. 1984. *What Do Unions Do?* New York, NY: Basic Books.

FRICKE, J. G. 1976. "An Empirical Study of the Grievance Arbitration Process in Alberta." Edmonton, Alberta: Alberta Labour.

GANDZ, J. 1979. "Grievance Initiation and Resolution: A Test of the Behavioural Theory." *Relations industrielles/Industrial Relations,* 34, pp. 778–792.

GANDZ, J. and P. J. WARRIAN. 1977. "Does It Matter Who Arbitrates?—A Statistical Analysis of Arbitration Awards in Ontario." *Labour Gazette,* 77, pp. 65–75.

GANDZ, J. and J. D. WHITEHEAD. 1982. "The Relationship Between Industrial Relations Climate and Grievance Initiation and Resolution." *Proceedings of the 34th Annual Meeting,* Industrial Relations Research Association. Madison, Wisconsin: IRRA, pp. 320–28.

GOLDBERG, S. B. 1989. "Grievance Mediation: A Successful Alternative to Labor Arbitration." *Negotiation Journal,* 5, pp. 9–15.

GOLDBLATT, H. 1974, *Justice Delayed...The Arbitration Process.* Toronto, Ontario: Labour Council of Metropolitan Toronto.

GRAHAM, H. and B. HESHIZER. 1978. "The Effect of Contract Language on Low-Level Settlement of Grievances." *Labor Law Journal,* 30, pp. 427–432.

HEBDON, R. and R. STERN. 1998. "Tradeoffs Among Expressions of Industrial Conflict: Public Sector Strike Bans and Grievance Arbitrations." *Industrial and Labor Relations Review,* 51, pp. 204–221.

KAUFFMAN, N., D. VANSWAARDEN, and C. FLOYD. 1994. "Values and Arbitrator Selections." *Labor Law Journal,* 45, pp. 49–54.

KNIGHT, T. R. 1986a. "Correlates of Informal Grievance Resolution Among First-Line Supervisors." *Relations industrielles/Industrial Relations,* 41, pp. 281–98.

———. 1986b. "Feedback and Grievance Resolution." *Industrial and Labor Relations Review,* 39, pp. 585–98.

KOCHAN, T. and H. KATZ. 1988. *Collective Bargaining and Industrial Relations,* 2nd Edition. Homewood, Illinois: Richard D. Irwin, Inc.

LEWIN, D. 1999. "Theoretical and Empirical Research on the Grievance Procedure and Arbitration: A Critical Review," in *Employment Dispute Resolution and Worker Rights,* edited by A. E. Eaton and J. H. Keefe. Champaign IL: Industrial Relations Research Association.

LEWIN, D. and R. B. PETERSON. 1988. *The Modern Grievance Procedure in the United States.* Westport, Conn.: Quorum Books.

OLSON, C. 1990. "Time Delays in Grievance Arbitration." MBA Thesis, University of Calgary.

PETERSON, R. B. and D. M. McCABE. 1994. "The Nonunion Grievance System in High Performing Firms," *Proceedings of the 1994 IRRA Spring Meeting.* Madison, Wisconsin: IRRA, pp. 529–34.

PICHER, M. D. 1991. "The Canadian Railway Office of Arbitration." *Labour Arbitration Yearbook,* 1, pp. 37–54.

PONAK, A. and C. OLSON. 1992. "Time Delays in Grievance Arbitration." *Relations industrielles/Industrial Relations,* 47, pp. 690–708.

PONAK, A., W. ZERBE, S. ROSE, and C. OLSON. 1996. "Using Event History Analysis to Model Delay in Grievance Arbitration." *Industrial and Labor Relations Review,* 50, pp. 105–121.

ROSE, J. B. 1986. "Statutory Expedited Grievance Arbitration: The Case of Ontario." *The Arbitration Journal,* 41, pp. 30–45.

———. 1991. "The Emergence of Expedited Arbitration." *Labour Arbitration Yearbook,* 1, pp. 13–22.

SEITZ, P. 1981. "Delay: The Asp in the Bosom of Arbitration." *The Arbitration Journal,* 36, pp. 29–35.

SKRATEK, S. 1993. "Grievance Mediation: How to Make the Process Work for You." *Labor Law Journal,* 44, pp. 507–511.

STANTON, J. 1983. *Labour Arbitrations: Boon or Bane for Unions?* Vancouver, B.C.: Butterworth and Company.

THOMPSON, M. 1992. "Expedited Arbitration: Promise and Performance." *Labour Arbitration Yearbook,* 3, pp. 41–53.

THORNICROFT, K. Wm. 1989. "Arbitrators, Social Values and the Burden of Proof in Substance Abuse Discharge Cases." *Labor Law Journal,* 40, pp. 582–93.

———. 1993. "Accounting for Delay in Grievance Arbitration." *Labor Law Journal,* 44, pp. 543–55.

———. 1994. "Do Lawyers Affect Grievance Arbitration Outcomes?" *Relations industrielles/Industrial Relations,* 49, pp. 357–372.

———. 1995. "Gender Effects in Grievance Arbitration... Revisited." *Labor Studies Journal,* 19, pp. 35–44.

———. 1996. "The Timeliness of Expedited Arbitration in B.C.: The First Two Years." *Labour Arbitration 1996.* Vancouver, BC: Continuing Legal Education Society of BC.

TURNER, J. T. and J. W. ROBINSON. 1972. "A Pilot Study on the Validity of Grievance Settlement Rates as a Predictor of the Union-Management Relationship." *Journal of Industrial Relations,* 14, pp. 314–22.

WAGAR, T. H. 1994. "The Effects of Lawyers on Non-Discipline/Discharge Arbitration Decisions." *Journal of Labor Research,* 15, pp. 283–293.

WESTERKAMP, P. R. and A. K. MILLER, 1971. "The Acceptability of Inexperienced Arbitrators: An Experiment." *Labor Law Journal,* 22, pp. 763–70.

WHITEHEAD, J. D., E. M. AIM, and L. A. WHITEHEAD. 1988. "Dispute Resolution in Canada: Selected Examples of Recent Innovations," in *Selected SPIDR Proceedings 1987–1988.* New York, NY: SPIDR, pp. 200–218.

WINTER, C. 1983. *Grievance Arbitration Cost and Time, 1980.* Toronto, Ontario: Research Branch, Ontario Ministry of Labour.

ZACK, A. 1999. "Agreement to Arbitrate and Waiver of Rights Under Employment Law," in *Employment Dispute Resolution and Worker Rights,* edited by A. E. Eaton and J. H. Keefe. Champaign IL: Industrial Relations Research Association.

CHAPTER 13

Union Impact on Compensation, Productivity, and Management of the Organization

Morley Gunderson and Douglas Hyatt

The CAW recently negotiated contracts with the Big Three automakers that included substantial wage increases for all of its members. As well, the union negotiated "fringe" benefits that would appeal to its membership at all different age groups. Generous pensions were negotiated for the older workers, tuition allowances for older family members with children in university, and child-care allowances for younger family members with preschool children.

The union also negotiated substantial retroactive pension increases for its membership that was already retired. At first glance, this may seem odd because these retirees are not voting members. The incumbent older workers, however, are voting members, and they realize that what is now done for retirees will soon be done for them when they retire.

The union even tried to get Daimler-Chrysler to pressure one of its parts suppliers, a Magna corporation plant in Windsor where an organization drive was underway, to voluntarily recognize the union. Although this demand was subsequently dropped, it does illustrate the attempts of the union to influence the way in which the organization is run, since subcontracting to parts suppliers is increasingly important in that industry.

The impact of unions on compensation provides an excellent example of an area in which our understanding can be furthered by a judicious blend of industrial relations with knowledge from another discipline—in this case, economics. This theme is portrayed throughout this chapter as it moves from a discussion of union power, to the methods used by unions for attaining their objectives, to the actual impact of unions[1] on wages, wage structures, fringe benefits, productivity, and the management of the organization itself.

UNION POWER AND METHODS FOR AFFECTING COMPENSATION

Union power as well as various market conditions affect the ability of unions to garner compensation increases for their members.

Internal Power

The power of a union to fulfill its goals depends, in part, on a consensus within the union with respect to those goals. This agreement must come from the various groups within the union, from the leadership and the rank-and-file members, and from other unions and affiliated bodies. Jurisdictional disputes, rank-and-file discontent with union leadership, and rivalry within the membership can all dissipate the energies of the union and prevent it from marshalling its power.

External Power and Elasticity of Demand for Labour

A union's power to realize its wage demands depends not only on its internal strength but also on the particular objective circumstances it faces. Many of these factors can be summarized under the determinants of the elasticity of demand related to substitute products, substitute inputs, and labour costs as a proportion of total costs.

Substitute Products

If there are few good substitutes for the products or services produced by unionized labour, union wage cost increases may be passed on to the consumer in the form of price increases without a substantial reduction in the demand for those products and, therefore, without a fall in the derived demand for union labour. This may occur, for example, if a tariff or import quota protects the product from foreign competition, if the product is advertised through the union label or a "social label" (see Exhibit 13.1), if sufficient time has not passed (i.e., the short run) so that substitute products are not yet available, if the industry is in decline so that new nonunion firms are not entering (see Exhibit 13.2), and if the whole industry is organized so as to prevent the substitution of nonunion-made products for union-made products.

EXHIBIT 13.1

IS THE SOCIAL LABEL REPLACING THE UNION LABEL?

In earlier days of union organizing, the union label indicating that the product was "union made" was an important strategy to inhibit the substitution of nonunion products for union products. Good trade unionists would not purchase products without the union label.

In recent years, the "social label" has been proposed whereby the product would be labelled as being produced under satisfactory working conditions and without the use of child labour. The hope is that good, socially minded citizens would not purchase products without the social label.

Multinationals have also been under pressure to adopt voluntary corporate codes of conduct, especially under the threat of consumer boycotts. Advocacy groups have exposed the working conditions involved in multinational production, and especially in subcontractors that produce for multinationals.

For more information about these practices, see: www.corpwatch.org

EXHIBIT 13.2

MILKING A DEAD COW: AN "END-GAME" STRATEGY

In declining industries, there may be very little threat of new entry from nonunion firms. In such circumstances, unions may engage in an "end-game" strategy whereby they demand high wage increases in spite of the declining demand because they know that the lower-paying nonunion firms are not likely to enter the industry, given that it is in decline. In such circumstances, unions may be able to garner a larger *share* of profits, even though overall profits are declining (Lawrence and Lawrence, 1985).

Difficulty in Using Substitute Inputs

If there are few good and cheap substitute inputs for union labour, or if it is technologically or institutionally difficult to substitute other factors of production for union labour, unions can obtain wage increases with less worry about substitutes being used for unionized labour. Hence, unions are very concerned about technological change and alternative processes that represent a substitution of capital for union labour. Restrictive work practices ("featherbedding" rules) are also designed, in part, to prevent the substitution of other inputs for union labour. Professional associations also try to control the substitution of less highly trained workers for professionals.

Another possible substitute for union labour is nonunion labour. Firms may try to use such labour by contracting out or by assigning work to probationary workers or supervisory

personnel who are not in the bargaining unit. Obviously, unions try to control the use of such nonunion labour, in part through union security provisions whereby unions do the hiring (hiring halls) or whereby all persons in the bargaining unit are required to join the union as a condition of employment (union shop) or to pay union dues (agency shop or use of the Rand formula).

To the extent that a reserve of low-wage labour in the economy is also a threat to union labour, unions may try to reduce that reserve by supporting policies like full employment, income maintenance, and restrictive immigration, and they resist programs such as "workfare," which require recipients of welfare or social assistance to work. If the size of the low-wage labour pool cannot itself be controlled, unions at least want to make that pool of labour more expensive. To do this they may support wage-fixing policies (minimum wages, equal pay, "fair" wages on government contracts, and wage-extension decrees) as well as labour standards programs that make the use of such nonunion labour more expensive (see Exhibit 13.3). This is not the only reason for union support of these policies, but it may be one reason.

Craft unions can protect the jobs of their members through such mechanisms as the hiring hall, apprenticeship ratios, and restrictions on who can practise in the trades. Similarly, professional associations can restrict the use of non-professionals through occupational licensing or certifications.

Labour Cost Portion

In general, if the costs of unionized labour are a small proportion of the total costs of a firm, the firm can more easily absorb union wage increases; the resultant cost increases simply do not matter much relative to the total cost picture of the firm. This may be the case, for example, for certain skilled craft workers and small professional groups, and for capital-intensive industries. It may, in part, explain the reluctance of these groups to merge with larger groups within whose wage demands their own demands would be subsumed.

Non-Competitive Markets

The degree of competition prevailing in the environment affects the power of unions and hence their ability to win gains for their members. Non-competitive situations can prevail in the product market and in the labour market, with both situations affecting the power of unions.

Monopoly in the Product Market

A firm that has a monopoly in the product market has a greater ability to pay out of monopoly profits (see Exhibit 13.4), and unions can garner high wage increases in such circumstances. In addition, if the firm is a regulated monopoly, it may be concerned about its public image and hence willing to "buy" good labour relations by paying high wages; it may also feel that it can obtain permission to pass any wage increase on to the public in the form of rate increases. Working in the other direction, monopolies may have a greater ability to pay, but they may also have a greater ability to resist union wage demands. They may use their monopoly profits to resist unionization or to set up structures (for example, using capital equipment or extensive nonunion supervision) that weaken the power of unions or that enable employers to withstand a lengthy and costly strike. Empirically, however, the dramatic decline in union wages that has occurred under deregulation suggests that unions in the regulated sectors are able to appropriate some monopoly profits and that union wage gains are higher in non-competitive product markets.

Public-Sector Employees

There is a presumption that unions in the public sector can become quite powerful because their employers are not subject to a competitive profit constraint. In essence, says

EXHIBIT 13.4

STRANGE BEDFELLOWS

The recent attempted takeover of Air Canada by Onex would have led to the merger of Air Canada and Canadian Airlines, a merger that subsequently occurred without Onex. Many were concerned that this would create a monopoly, especially because foreign airlines are restricted from competing.

There was also general surprise when the CAW president, Buzz Hargrove, supported the Onex-led merger—union leaders do not generally support business takeovers because the restructuring generally leads to job losses and demands for concessions on wages and work rules. In this particular case, however, guarantees were provided that any job reductions would occur through attrition and retirements. As well, any resulting monopoly situation could benefit both the employer and the union.

the theory, the political constraint in the public sector is not as binding as the profit constraint in the private sector. Union wage increases can be passed on to taxpayers, who must have the essential services and cannot buy them elsewhere, who are often ill-informed about the "tax price" of public services, and who exercise their democratic prerogatives only occasionally by voting on a package of issues of which the wage costs of services may be only a small part. Of real concern is the possibility that public-sector employers may try to save on current wage costs by granting liberal compensation to be paid by future taxpayers, possibly when another political party is in power. Such deferred wages can come in the form of regular seniority-based wage increases, liberal retirement pensions, or job security.

Although these arguments do suggest that public-sector unions should be quite powerful, there are also forces—usually more subtle ones—working in the opposite direction. Taxpayers are scrutinizing government with increasing severity, and they may sympathize more with employers, forgetting that it takes two sides to create a dispute. Politicians may seek to curb inflation and private-sector settlements by moderating public-sector wage settlements, and they may even prolong or foster strikes to gain the media exposure that is crucial to their prominence. Employers in the public sector, unlike those in the private sector, do not usually lose their (tax) revenues during a strike. Some US jurisdictions have also experimented with having citizen observers present in collective bargaining.

Monopsony

Non-competitive conditions also prevail in labour markets that are dominated by a single employer—termed a *monopsonist* to indicate that the firm is a monopolistic buyer of labour. Such a firm is so large relative to the size of the local labour market that it has to raise wages to attract additional workers; conversely, it does not lose all of its workforce if it lowers wages. A monopsonist is extremely sensitive about raising wages to attract additional workers because it knows it will have to pay these higher rates to its existing workforce in order to maintain internal equity of the wage structure. This fact serves to depress wages paid by the monopsonist relative to what it would pay if it were a competitive buyer of labour.

Canadian Association of Labour Media: www.calm.ca/

Monopsonists are ripe for union organizing because union wage increases, at least within a certain range, can actually lead to their hiring more labour. This paradoxical result occurs because when faced with a fixed union wage that they must pay to all their workers, monopsonists are no longer constrained in their hiring decisions by the fact that they have to raise wages to attract additional workers; all workers are paid the union rate for each job. Thus, the wage demands of unions, at least for a range of wage increases, are not constrained by the possibility of reduced employment opportunities. Clearly, these circumstances afford room for considerable bargaining in that there is a range of wage increases that the monopsonist can absorb. With so much to gain and lose, one would expect a high degree of conflict in organizing and in bargaining—an observation that seems borne out in the isolated one-industry towns that characterize monopsony.

MEASURING THE UNION IMPACT

Attempts to quantify the impact of unions have met with numerous estimation problems. The most important are those of separating cause and effect and of controlling for quality differences.

Separating Cause and Effect

Conventional wisdom suggests that causality runs in the direction of unions' causing higher wages in the union sector. Causality, however, may also operate in the other direction. That is, unions are more likely to be formed in situations in which high wages already exist because they are easier to organize and because the higher wages may enable workers in such sectors to afford to buy more of everything, including union services (Ashenfelter and Johnson, 1972). Furthermore, workers in high-wage firms are reluctant to leave or "exit" because of the high wages—hence they turn to "voice" (e.g., through unions) as the mechanism to improve the non-wage aspects of their situation (Freeman, 1976; Freeman and Medoff, 1979, 1984). The causality in such a situation runs from high wages (and hence reduced exit) to unionization (as the form of voice).

An appealing element of this perspective is that it reconciles the views of industrial relations analysts, who emphasize the importance of the union in achieving due process and job security at the workplace, with the views of economists, who emphasize the wage impact of unions. Unions are associated both with higher wages for their members and with job security and due process at the workplace.

Quality Differences

Firms that pay the higher union wage rate are likely to have a queue of applicants and hence they can be more selective than nonunion firms in their hiring and recruiting procedures, thereby obtaining higher-quality workers with more education, training, and experience, as well as more of such typically unobserved characteristics as motivation. Working in the opposite direction, it may be more difficult for employers to dismiss poorer-quality workers in the union sector or if poorer-quality workers try to obtain secure union jobs. For these reasons, it is important to control for the reverse causality and the quality differences in estimating a pure union wage impact.

Measurement Techniques and Data

The impact of various factors that can affect wages is usually controlled through the use of multiple-regression analysis, which indicates the effect on wages of each explanatory variable, including a measure of unionization, while holding the other wage-determining factors constant. The regression equation is estimated on various types of data: cross-sections of aggregate or macro data relating wages in an industry, city, or state to the proportion of the industry, city, or state that is unionized;[2] micro data sets[3] that have the individual worker as the unit of observation;[4] and panel or longitudinal data that follow the same individuals over time.[5]

UNION IMPACT ON COMPENSATION

In varying degrees, the numerous empirical studies of the impact of unions attempt to account for the measurement problems just discussed. Unions can affect various aspects of compensation, including wages and wage structures, nonunion wages, and fringe benefits.[6]

Impact on Wages and Wage Structures

In a recent review of the evidence based on the different methodologies, Kuhn (1998: 1037) concludes "there is abundant and robust evidence that identical workers in North America earn about 15 percent more in unionized than in nonunion jobs." This is in the mid-range of the 10–25 percent noted in other Canadian reviews (Benjamin, Gunderson, and Riddell, 1998: 556; Renaud, 1997: 217).

The union impact on wages tends to be larger in recessions and smaller at the peak of the business cycle, reflecting the fact that union wages are less sensitive to economic fluctuations than are nonunion wages (in part because union workers have long-term wage contracts).

The union impact is higher for blue-collar and less skilled workers than for white-collar and more skilled workers.[7] Generally, union workers tend to get a "flat" union premium, but that amount declines with productivity-related characteristics such as experience, education, and skill. This phenomenon gives rise to union wage profiles that are higher but flatter (i.e., start higher but rise less steeply) than do nonunion wage profiles with respect to such factors as age, experience, and education. This finding is consistent with the view of unions as institutions that blunt the impact of market forces by gaining a constant increase for members, but having their wages increase less than the wages of nonunion workers for increments in productivity-related characteristics.

Thus, with respect to the overall dispersion of wages, unions exert two opposing effects. They narrow wage differentials that reflect such factors as skill, education, and experience; however, they widen the overall dispersion by creating a new source of dispersion—the union–nonunion wage differential. There is some evidence that the equalizing effect dominates, so that unions tend to reduce the overall dispersion of wages.[8]

The union–nonunion wage gap tends to be similar for men and women, based on US data.[9] However, based on Canadian data[10] researchers find the union wage impact tends to be larger for females than for males, but females benefit less from unions because they

EXHIBIT 13.5

THE DECLINING UNION WAGE IMPACT

In his comprehensive review of the Canadian evidence, and based on his own analysis, Renaud (1997) indicates that the union–nonunion wage differential in Canada:

- was approximately 15 percent at the beginning of the 1970s;
- rose throughout the 1970s to a peak of around 25 percent by the end of the 70s;
- fell throughout the 1980s to around 10 percent by the end of the 1980s.

He also concludes (p. 223): "In the coming years, the size of the union–nonunion differential might keep shrinking. Forces like freer-trade and the deindustrialization of the Canadian economy will make it more difficult for unions to do what industrial relations specialists were first noting that they were doing, that is taking wages out of competition."

Some recent evidence suggests that this prediction is correct. Gunderson, Hyatt, and Riddell (1999) found that by 1997, Canadian workers covered by a collective agreement earned 8 percent more than persons not covered.

Whether this decline in the union impact reflects a decline of union power or a strategic reorientation to other objectives such as employment and job security or less costly forms of employee "voice" remains an interesting and important question.

are less likely to be covered by a collective agreement. These opposing effects offset each other, so that, overall, unions neither increase nor decrease the male–female wage gap.

Although the limited empirical evidence that exists is not always in agreement, most studies suggest that the union impact on wages is greater in decentralized than in centralized structures.[11] Somewhat surprisingly, the empirical evidence suggests that the union impact tends to be smaller in the public than the private sector, although there is considerable diversity in this result.[12]

Importantly, the union wage impact appears to have increased in the 1970s and declined in the 1980s, reaching a level of around 10 percent in the early 1990s (see Exhibit 13.5).

Impact on Nonunion Wages

Unions can affect the wages of nonunion workers through a variety of mechanisms. To the extent that unionized wage increases reduce employment opportunities in the unionized sector, the excess supply of labour from that sector should serve to depress wages in the nonunion sector. This effect may, however, be mitigated if unions are able to "featherbed" (require the use of excess amounts of labour in the union sector).

On the demand side, the demand for nonunion labour—and hence the nonunion wage—is affected in an indeterminate manner by an increase in the wages of union workers. The demand for nonunion labour may increase to the extent that nonunion labour is substituted for the now more expensive union labour. Unions will certainly resist such a substitution, but it still occurs in a number of ways—for example, through contracting-out, using nonunion supervisors, or even relocating production to a nonunion sector. In addition, output demand may shift from the products produced by the more expensive union sector to those produced in the cheaper nonunion sector. (This effect may be minimized if the whole sector can be organized.) On the other hand, the demand for some nonunion labour may decrease to the extent that it is complementary to (i.e., works in tandem with) union labour or to such an extent that firms reduce their scale of output (in the extreme, perhaps even closing down) in response to the higher union labour cost; in such circumstances firms may employ less of both union and nonunion labour.

Other forces are at work institutionally whereby nonunion wages are affected by unionization. As discussed previously, unions can affect nonunion wages by supporting wage-fixing legislation, which applies mainly to the nonunion sector. In addition, nonunion firms may raise their wages to avoid the threat of becoming unionized. In the extreme, they may pay wages in excess of the going union wage rate to avoid what they regard as other costs associated with becoming unionized, notably interference with managerial prerogatives (Taras, 1994). Nonunion firms may also be compelled to raise their wages so as to compete with unionized firms for a given workforce or to restore traditional wage relativities that existed before unionization. The last argument, however, ignores the fact that nonunion firms should not have to worry about recruiting problems or restoring traditional wage patterns because they will have a supply influx of workers who cannot get jobs in the high-wage union sector (in essence, market forces suggest that their recruiting problems are lessened and that there is reduced pressure to maintain a traditional wage pattern).

Clearly, unions affect the wages of nonunion workers through a variety of institutional, market, and legislative forces. Since these forces do not all work in the same direction, it is not possible to state theoretically the expected impact of unions on the wages of nonunion workers; one must appeal to the empirical evidence. Earlier studies tended to find that unionism lowered the wages of nonunion workers but by a small amount—less than 3 or 4 percent (Kahn, 1978, 1980; Lewis, 1963). Other studies, however, including more recent ones, have found small positive effects of unions on the wages of nonunion workers.[13]

Impact on Employee Fringe Benefits

Empirical evidence[14] indicates that unions increase the employee benefits of their members even more than they increase their wages. This may occur for a variety of reasons.

To the extent that unionization makes workers better off, they can afford to buy more of everything, including employee benefits; this will be especially important if they enter the higher tax brackets and employee benefits are not taxed. In addition, unions, being a political institution of "voice," can be expected to represent the wishes of the average worker (more specifically, the median voting member) as opposed to the marginal worker whose interest is most likely to be represented by the mechanism of exit or mobility. Since the average worker is more likely than the marginal worker to be older, with seniority, and with a family, the collective preferences are more likely to favour employee benefits, especially pensions and life, accident, and health insurance.

Employee benefits, as a form of deferred compensation, may also be more prevalent in unionized establishments than in nonunion ones.[15] Employers may prefer deferred compensation because it provides a threat that can be used to ensure effort from their employees. The threat is the possibility of dismissal and therefore the loss of deferred wages. Deferred wages can also provide employees with an interest in the financial solvency of the firm. In addition, deferred compensation reduces turnover, since employees who quit would lose some or all of their deferred wages (for example, pension and vacation rights). Employees may willingly accept a deferred wage if they are given a sufficiently high wage to compensate for some of it being deferred (and hence its receipt being uncertain), or if they are provided with sufficient guarantees that the employer will ultimately pay. Such guarantees have more credence when they are provided in a collective agreement, which, for example, prevents arbitrary dismissal and reinforces the legal obligation to provide the promised payments. In essence, unionization makes the payment of fringe benefits in the form of deferred wages a feasible compensation scheme. Hence one can expect such employee benefits to be associated with unionization.

UNION IMPACT ON PRODUCTIVITY, PROFITABILITY, EMPLOYMENT, AND INVESTMENT

While the impact of unions on various dimensions of compensation tends to receive the most attention, increasing attention is being given to the impact of unions on other dimensions, including productivity, profitability, employment, and investment. In the global economy, these other dimensions can have crucial implications for the joint survival of both unions and their organizations.

Impact on Productivity

Although recognized for a long time by industrial relations analysts (Slichter, Healy, and Livernash, 1960), the potential positive impact of unions on various aspects of productivity has only recently been analyzed and quantified by labour economists.[16] As Freeman and Medoff (1984) indicate, there are two dominant views of trade unions. The monopoly view regards unions as creating economic inefficiency by raising wages above the competitive norm, by inducing strikes, and by requiring featherbedding work rules that compel the employer to use inefficient amounts of union labour. An alternative view is that unions have positive effects on productivity by reducing turnover, "shocking" management into more efficient practices, improving morale and co-operation among workers, providing information about the collective preferences of workers, and improving communications between labour and management.

The literature on the impact of unions on various aspects of productivity examines the *direct* effects on productivity after controlling for the fact that the union wage premium results in an *indirect* productivity increase by inducing firms to substitute capital for labour and by enabling them to hire more productive workers. This indirect effect on productivity leads to inefficiencies,[17] since management will use excessive amounts of capital and nonunion labour relative to higher-priced union labour. Management will also utilize excessively high-quality union labour.

With respect to the direct effect on various aspects related to productivity, unions have been found to lower quit rates,[18] to increase tenure with the firm (Addison and Castro, 1987), to enhance quality (see Exhibit 13.6), and to raise productivity or output per worker.[19] There is not universal agreement in the latter area, however, and the results are often sensitive to the type of data used and the specification of the output equation.[20] There is also conflicting evidence on the effects of unions on productivity in the public sector, although most studies show unions there to have had no net effect, either positive or negative.[21]

EXHIBIT 13.6

THE IMPORTANCE OF UNION SUPPORT FOR QUALITY IMPROVEMENTS AND ORGANIZATIONAL PERFORMANCE

Quality improvement is generally regarded as a key ingredient of firm performance in a world of global competition. As such, it is crucial to know if unions enhance or impede quality improvements.

Empirical evidence based on US data indicates that quality circles are more likely to survive in unionized environments (Drago, 1988). Quality circles are a form of employee participation in the management of the organization. They involve a work group that meets voluntarily, typically once per week, to discuss, analyze, and solve problems common to the work group.

Cooke (1992) also finds quality improvements to be higher in workplaces with employee participation than in the more traditional workplaces with no participation. Of particular note, the greatest quality improvements occurred in firms with joint union–management administration of the program. If management unilaterally ran the program, there was no quality improvement, as was also the case when there was traditional adversarial bargaining with no employee involvement. Additional US evidence on the positive effects that co-operative union involvement has on product quality and other dimensions of firm performance is given in Cooke (1989, 1990, 1994).

Based on Canadian data from unionized establishments, Wagar (1997) finds co-operative union–management relations are associated with a wide range of perceived positive organizational outcomes, including decreased resistance to change; reduced conflict, turnover, and absenteeism; improved morale, innovation, productivity, and product quality; and reduced job insecurity. In another study, Wagar (1998) found similar positive effects on perceptions of productivity, product/service quality, and customer/client satisfaction.

Exhibit 13.7

Unions and Gain-Sharing

Various forms of gain-sharing (bonus or profit-sharing) plans have been introduced to encourage work effort and enhance productivity. When they are introduced in unionized establishments, unions may or may not be involved in the design, administration, and monitoring of the program. Based on data from 217 establishments in the US and Canada, Kim and Voos (1997) found that there was no significant difference between managers' perceptions of the success of such programs in union compared to nonunion establishments. However, this was because the positive effect of gain-sharing in union establishments *when unions were involved* with the program was offset by the negative effect in union establishments when unions were *not* involved. In essence, if gain-sharing is to be successful in unionized establishments, it is crucial that unions be involved in its design and implementation. If they are not involved, the program can be counterproductive. Based on Canadian data, Wagar (1997) also found productivity, quality, and organizational performance to be positively related to a positive co-operative labour–management climate.

Kaufman (1992) found profit-sharing plans to be more successful in unionized compared to nonunion establishments. Interestingly, Cooke (1994) found gain-sharing to enhance productivity more in unionized compared to nonunion establishments, but because unions were able to appropriate more of the gains through higher wages, gain-sharing contributed less to profits in unionized firms than in nonunion firms.

Some analysts also offer evidence that unionized environments have more strenuous working conditions than nonunion ones, with, for example, a structured work setting, inflexible hours, and a faster work pace.[22] This may reflect the fact that unionism is more likely to occur in response to such working conditions or that some employers are able to respond to the union wage advantage by changing the conditions of work, partly to take advantage of a higher-quality workforce.

The labour relations climate in the workplace can also influence the productivity of union workers. A good union–management relationship can amplify the productivity-enhancing effects of unions, especially through information sharing and a focus in bargaining on mutual gains rather than on rules that control the behaviours of the parties (see Exhibit 13.7). Conversely, a poor industrial relations climate can exacerbate the negative impacts on productivity. A number of studies have found negative productivity effects where labour relations are generally bad, as evidenced, for example, by a large number of grievances or strikes.[23]

Impact on Profitability

Although these productivity-inducing effects probably offset some of the wage cost increases resulting from unionism, they are unlikely to offset all of them. If they did, one

EXHIBIT 13.8

DOES THE STOCK MARKET ADJUST TO REFLECT THE COST OF UNIONS?

Based on US evidence, Ruback and Zimmerman (1984) find that the stock market value of a firm falls by about 1.4 percent when a petition to hold a union election is put forward, by a further 1 percent if the petition succeeds, and by a further 1.4 percent if the election succeeds and a union is certified. The cumulative drop in the share value turns out to be very close to the cost of a 15 percent wage increase associated with unionization, which is the typical wage impact. This suggests that the stock market perfectly adjusts to reflect the cost increase associated with unions, at least as reflected in expected wage increases. To the extent that the stock market should adjust to reflect the *cost* increase, this suggests that the wage impact of 15 percent may be a good reflection of the net cost increase that would also include other factors such as fringe benefits and productivity.

EXHIBIT 13.9

ARE UNIONS LIKELY TO KILL THE GOOSE THAT LAYS THE GOLDEN EGG?

If unions reduce profitability, it is possible that they could cause firms to go into bankruptcy. Based on US evidence, Freeman and Kleiner (1999) find that this does not occur. Unionized firms are no more likely to declare bankruptcy than nonunion firms. As such, they conclude: "Unions reduce profits but they do not 'destroy the goose that lays the golden egg.' They would be foolish to do so, and while they may make mistakes in collective bargaining (just as management may), they are not so foolish as to force organized firms out of business." As such, they indicate (p. 510) that unions do not contribute to Samuel Gomper's "worst crime" when he stated, "the worst crime against working people is the company which fails to operate at a profit."

would expect to see managers, or at least shareholders, welcoming unions—a phenomenon rarely observed (except in cases of "company unions" that management controls). At least some union wage gains must represent real gains to union workers and real costs to employers, otherwise one would not see workers organizing or employers resisting unionization. The empirical evidence also generally confirms that unionization reduces profitability and the stock market value of firms[24] (see Exhibit 13.8) but not to the point of inducing bankruptcy (see Exhibit 13.9).

Impact on Employment

If unions raise wages and costs, it would appear that this should lead to reduced employment as firms substitute capital for the more expensive labour and as some reduce their output (perhaps even going out of business) because of the higher costs. These are the basic substitution and scale effects (movement along the labour demand curve) of textbook labour economics. Unions, however, do not simply bargain over wages and allow employers to choose the level of employment. Unions also bargain over employment levels, both directly and indirectly, in such forms as no-layoff provisions, restrictions on subcontracting and overtime, featherbedding work rules, restrictions on plant closings, and requirements for additional plant investments. Thus, powerful unions could increase *both* wages and employment.[25] The extent to which a union would opt for one or both of these elements it values depends, in part, on the collective preferences of the membership. If the jobs of the voting members are reasonably secure, they may opt for wage increases knowing that their own jobs are not at risk. However, if their own jobs are at risk (as is increasingly the case with downsizing and plant closings), they may opt for employment guarantees. Casual empiricism suggests that unions bargain over employment as well as wages, and limited empirical evidence also suggests this to be the case. Certainly unions have been able to prevent employers from reducing the employment of union labour by as much as they would like to given the union wage increase. Of course, unionized plants may have had still higher employment had they not also received higher wages.[26]

Impact on Investment

Unions can have an impact on the investment decisions of firms though various mechanisms. They may encourage investment by inducing firms to substitute capital for the more expensive union labour. They may also bargain directly for more investment in specific plants to sustain employment. Unions may discourage investment, however, to the extent that investors are reluctant to invest in unionized sites. In the extreme, if a plant goes out of business because of higher union costs, then there is no investment. Firms may be especially reluctant to invest in situations where unions are likely to appropriate the benefits of successful investments (termed the "hold-up" problem) since it is difficult to move capital once it is in place. The empirical literature generally finds a negative effect of unions on investment.[27]

UNION IMPACT ON MANAGEMENT OF THE ORGANIZATION

Unions can have a substantial impact on the way management runs the organization—restricting the otherwise unfettered rights of management (within the law) to run the firm in what could be an arbitrary or even capricious manner with respect to employees. They may do so by regulating specific provisions (e.g., seniority) in the collective agreement as well as in the grievance procedure for interpreting and breathing life into the agreement. Unions have also been instrumental in encouraging—and at times helping to enforce—legislative employment standards, which regulate such factors as minimum wages, pay and employment equity, hours of work and overtime, paid vacations and holidays, maternity leave, and employee termination. They can also be involved in joint union–management committees (most noticeably on health and safety), and union representatives may even be on the board of directors of the company.

Legislative Assistance

Legislative initiatives have often helped unions achieve due process and circumscribe the otherwise unfettered rights of management in the employment relationship. This aid has taken a variety of forms: the legal obligation to recognize a certified union as the workers' exclusive bargaining agent and to bargain in good faith; the legal recognition of collective agreements and of the grievance procedure with its own jurisprudence; and the establishment of employment standards and health-and-safety legislation that effectively give government backing and enforcement to a number of issues over which unions might otherwise have to negotiate. On many issues, legislative initiatives have used the existing machinery of collective bargaining and the union's communications network to provide effective enforcement. Such is the case, for example, in the health-and-safety area (with the use of joint committees as part of the "internal responsibility" system) and in pay equity (with unions to be involved in job-evaluation procedures and in the allocation of awards pertaining to equal pay for work of equal value).

Examples of Impact on Management of the Organization

Given their emphasis on the rights and well-being of workers, unions' effects on the management of the organization have been mainly on those dimensions of managerial decision making that impinge most directly on the workforce. Many of these are discussed in Kaufman and Kaufman (1987: 342), who conclude, "Union firms in our sample are significantly more likely to have grievance procedures, job-posting systems, and other restrictions that limit management's prerogative in promotion, classification, and job assignment" (see Exhibit 13.10).

At the hiring stage, the union impact is usually negligible; this lack of effect normally extends for a brief probationary period, when managerial discretion is largely unfettered. The exception is the situation in which unions have negotiated union security clauses

EXHIBIT 13.10

THE IMPACT OF UNIONS ON HUMAN RESOURCE PRACTICES

Human resource practices can be used strategically by organizations to enhance productivity and hence firm competitiveness and performance. Ng and Maki (1994) examine the impact of unions on 37 human resource practices in Canadian manufacturing firms. They find that unionization leads to more formal managerial practices such as job posting, formal probationary periods for new hires, and explicit criteria governing promotion, all of which tend to reduce managerial discretion. Unions, however, tend to reduce the use of formal appraisal systems that are often associated with individual incentive pay systems involving merit pay and piece rates.

Similar results are generally found in other studies including Balkin (1989), Bemmels (1987), Freeman and Kleiner (1990), and Kaufman and Kaufman (1987).

involving a "closed shop" (only union members can be hired). This is often coupled with the union's running a "hiring hall" (the union acts as the employment agency, having the exclusive right to refer employees to the firm). These forms of union security provisions are rare, however, existing mainly in some areas of construction and longshoring.

Unions, however, can have a more indirect effect at the hiring stage. They tend to reduce the use of formal selection tests (Cohen and Pfeffer, 1986) as well as the resources firms devote to recruitment sources so as to expand the applicant pool (Koch and Hundley, 1998), the applicant pool already being expanded by the union wage premium.

After the hiring and probationary period, the union impact becomes more prominent. Almost invariably, collective agreements contain clauses requiring "just cause" for discipline and discharge; situations involving these clauses are the most common source of grievance arbitration cases. Seniority provisions regulating managerial discretion in matters such as promotion, transfer, layoff, and recall are also very common in collective agreements as well as a common source of grievance arbitration cases.

Restrictions on contracting-out are also prevalent in collective agreements, in part because employers can undercut the power of a union by contracting out certain jobs to the nonunion sector. This issue is currently highly contentious; management wants the right to contract out as part of its increased drive for flexibility, and unions fear the loss of union jobs, especially in the current climate of downsizing. Policy-makers also have some concern that contracting-out may be used as a way of getting around legislative intervention in such areas as employment standards and equal pay legislation. Often the subcontracting goes to self-employed individuals or to small firms, where the legislation is more difficult to enforce. In part to enhance their own job security, unions have also bargained for investment guarantees in their own plants, and they have even bargained for organizations to put pressure on their parts suppliers to voluntarily recognize the union (opening vignette).

Regulations on job assignment (who can do what work) can also restrict managerial discretion. The extreme form of these rules often involved featherbedding practices such as the requirement that containers be unloaded and reloaded at ports or that a fireman be maintained on diesel engines. Other restrictions on managerial discretion include the right to refuse overtime and requirements for advance notice or transfer rights in the case of plant closings or technological change. In most circumstances, however, these restrictions are not prominent features of collective agreements; they are more often introduced by legislation.

Some empirical evidence suggests that the large increases in shareholder wealth that occurred as a result of the takeover boom of the 1980s, and that were larger in unionized firms subject to takeover, were a result of the increased managerial discretion in running the firms after the takeover (see Exhibit 13.11).

Some Unintended Side Effects

In some instances, union practices that restrict managerial discretion can have unintended side effects. For example, seniority provisions can be an obstacle to attempts to achieve pay and employment opportunities that are equal for men and women since

EXHIBIT 13.11

DO THE SUBSTANTIAL GAINS TO SHAREHOLDERS IN TAKEOVER FIRMS COME FROM UNIONIZED WORKERS?

The 1980s witnessed a remarkable takeover boom involving mergers and acquisitions, often of unionized firms that paid substantial union wage premiums and fringe benefits, and that placed considerable constraints on managerial authority in running the organization. Based on US evidence, Becker (1995) found that the average returns to shareholders from the takeover activity were higher in unionized firms that were taken over (41 percent) compared to nonunion firms (35 percent). He calculates that these effects are *equivalent* to a loss of 8 percent of annual earnings of unionized workers, which is approximately half of the union wage premium. This larger gain to shareholders in unionized establishments that are taken over suggests that these additional gains come from more restrictions placed on the wages and fringe benefits of workers in unionized establishments, and from fewer restrictions placed on managerial authority.

Becker reviews a small number of other studies, most of which find negligible negative effects on wages and benefits from takeover activity. This suggests that the larger gains to shareholders in unionized establishments that are taken over come mainly from reduced restriction on managerial authority after the takeover.

Perhaps this is why, in the proposed Onex takeover of Air Canada and merger with Canadian Airlines, guarantees were made to the union that there would be no wage or involuntary employment reductions. Perhaps the gains were to come from increased managerial discretion in the operation of the companies. Of course, the gains to shareholders could also come from other factors such as economies of scale and monopoly pricing.

women tend to accumulate less seniority (especially if they leave the labour market for child-rearing). Seniority provisions can also be an obstacle in accommodating the needs of disabled persons at the workplace. Requirements for specific ratios of apprentices to journeymen can inhibit firms from expanding their training to meet certain shortages. Prohibitions on the use of part-time labour can inhibit employers from reducing overtime and sharing the available work. Requirements for severance pay and advance notice and concern over unfair or unjust dismissal cases can make employers reluctant to hire new workers who might eventually have to be laid off.

Restrictions in the Public Sector

In many parts of the public sector, unions try to bargain over broader issues that may encroach on managerial authority. Such is especially the case with professional employees who invariably want more say in the management of the organization, and who often possess the expertise to make such decisions.

The limited empirical evidence available in this area tends to suggest that public-sector unions do have a considerable impact on the management of the organization.

Teachers, for example, often bargain over pupil/teacher ratios, curriculum content, class sizes, placement of suspended students, and the selection and transferring of students (Hall and Carroll, 1973; Woodbury, 1985). Goldschmidt and Stuart (1986) conclude that these items usually put severe constraints on the ability of school districts to adapt to changing circumstances. On the other hand, in a study of the US federal civil service, Beyer, Trice, and Hunt (1980) find that when a union is present and articulates its position, supervisors tend to be more aware of and use policies to deal with equal employment opportunities as well as employee problems with alcoholism.

CONCLUSION

Unions tend to increase the compensation of their members (usually by around 15 percent) and slightly reduce the compensation of nonunion workers. The union impact is largest for blue-collar and less-skilled workers. In fact, union workers tend to get a flat wage premium, but then receive relatively low returns for increases in such factors as skill, education, and experience. Overall, unions have probably reduced wage disparities and had a larger impact on employee benefits than on wages. The union premium is similar for men and women, although some Canadian evidence suggests it is larger for females. Women, however, tend to be less unionized and receive fewer benefits of unionism for that reason.

Unionism may be a result of, as well as a cause of, high wages, and union workers may differ from nonunion workers in terms of unobserved, as well as observed, characteristics. Also, unionized establishments may adjust to costly union wage increases by raising their hiring standards and altering their work conditions. Unions may also have a beneficial impact on productivity, which may offset some of the wage cost increase associated with unionization, albeit unionization does reduce profitability.

Unions reduce managerial discretion through provisions in collective agreements, through the grievance procedure, and through support of legislative regulation of the work environment. Although intervention is limited at the hiring and probationary stages, it later becomes substantial through seniority provisions and requirements for "just cause" in cases of discipline and discharge. Other regulations pertain to contracting-out, job assignments, and, to a lesser degree, safety, worktime practices, plant closings, and technological change (the latter issues are more often the subject matter of legislation than of collective bargaining).

Public-sector employees, mainly professionals, have done more direct bargaining than private-sector workers over what might be perceived as managerial issues. This likely reflects a combination of professional concern over these issues and a realization that they can be an important way of affecting working conditions and job security.

This decade will be an interesting one for analyzing the impact of unions on a variety of outcomes—wages, job security, fringe benefits, productivity, and managerial discretion. Unions are clearly on the defensive in the United States, and this situation is likely to affect Canadian unions, especially given the spread of foreign competition, deregulation, and freer trade. In these circumstances, employers are likely to want more managerial discretion and flexibility, and unions are likely to seek more job security and better fringe benefits, such as generous retirement pensions (in part as a work-sharing device). However, this conflict also provides the opportunity for the parties to deal creatively with challenges stemming from the dramatic changes in the Canadian industrial relations system and its environment.

Global competition, trade liberalization, and the greater international flow of capital are likely to have a profound impact on union goals and strategies, and ultimately on wage and other outcomes. Unions may simply not be able to continue to obtain wage premiums of 15 percent because this higher labour cost will lead to more imports of lower-priced foreign-produced goods. As well, employers may locate their plants in countries where labour costs are not as high.

In essence, it is difficult for unions to "take labour out of competition" now that the labour market is international. Labour will be under pressure to adopt more international strategies. It will also have to focus less on wages and other outcomes that impose costs on employers and more on ensuring due process and "voice" mechanisms that may be less costly to employers. There will also be more emphasis on labour–management cooperation and on reducing adversarial bargaining. Unions will also likely have to direct more of their efforts toward the political level to influence governments into increasing the "social wage." It is clear that the next few years pose some interesting and important challenges and opportunities for unions.

Questions

1. "The power of unions depends on the economic environment in which unions operate." Discuss.

2. Discuss the determinants of the elasticity of demand for union labour in both the construction industry and the public sector, indicating what this should imply about the ability of unions to achieve wage gains in those sectors.

3. "Unions can have no long-run impact on wages because if they did then unionized firms would go out of business." Discuss.

4. Discuss the impact of unions on the wages of nonunion workers.

5. Discuss how unionized firms may adjust their hiring standards and working conditions when faced with unions. What does this imply about the measured union–nonunion wage differential?

6. Discuss the mechanisms whereby unionism may be a response to high wages as well as a cause of high wages. What does this imply about the measured union–nonunion wage differential?

7. Why may fringe benefits be a preferred form of compensation for union members even more than for nonunion members?

8. Discuss the mechanisms whereby unions can affect productivity. What does this imply about the costs to the firm that result from unionization?

9. Discuss the various ways in which unions may affect managerial discretion in running the organization. Is such union impact greater in the public or the private sector?

10. What effects would you expect global competition and trade liberalization to have on the impact of unions?

ENDNOTES

[1] The goals of unions are discussed in Chapter 2 in this volume. No attempt is made here to review the empirical literature exhaustively. Lewis (1986a) reviews approximately 200 US studies and Jarrell and Stanley (1990) review 114 US studies of the union impact on wages alone. Benjamin, Gunderson, and Riddell (1998) review 15 Canadian studies and Renaud (1997) reviews 20 Canadian studies of the wage impact.

[2] Comprehensive reviews of these earlier macro studies are contained in Lewis (1963) for US studies prior to 1963 and in Lewis (1983) for studies after 1962.

[3] Reviewed in Lewis (1986a, 1986b), with methodological problems also discussed in Andrews, Stewart, Swaffield, and Upward (1998).

[4] Such studies often control for the selection bias that may occur if union workers are sorted into the union sector on the basis of unobserved characteristics that also affect wages. Canadian studies that deal with the selection bias include Kumar and Stengos (1985), Renaud (1998), Robinson and Tomes (1984), and Simpson (1985).

[5] In the panel studies, the analyst makes the reasonable assumption that the conventional unobserved factors (for example, motivation) remain constant for each individual. The union impact is identified when these individuals change their union status over time. Unfortunately, this methodology gives rise to problems of its own since only a small sample of individuals change their union status, and when they do so, it is often under unusual circumstances and other factors are also often changing, thereby making it difficult to disentangle a pure union impact. It has generally been the case that estimates of the union impact obtained from longitudinal panel data are slightly smaller than those obtained from cross-sectional data. US studies using longitudinal data include Jakubson (1991), Mellow (1981), Mincer (1983), and Moore and Raisian (1983). Canadian studies include Grant, Swidinsky, and Vanderkamp (1987), Robinson (1989), and Swidinsky and Kupferschmidt (1991). Freeman (1984) reviews the methodological problems with such studies.

[6] Reviews of this evidence are contained in Hirsch and Addison (1986), Kuhn (1998), and Lewis (1963, 1986a, 1986b). Reviews of the Canadian evidence are given in Benjamin, Gunderson, and Riddell (1998) and Renaud (1998).

[7] Based on Canadian data; however, White (1994) indicates that professionals benefit from unionization.

[8] Belman and Heywood, 1990; Freeman, 1980a; Hyclack, 1980; Meng, 1990; Quan, 1984. Freeman (1993) finds that about one-fifth of the increase in wage inequality for males over the period 1970 to 1987 in the US can be attributed to the decline of unionization over this period. Based on Canadian data, Lemieux (1993, 1998) finds that unions reduce overall wage inequality for men, but not for women because higher-wage women tend to be unionized.

[9] Almost 50 studies reviewed in Lewis (1986a, 1986b).

[10] Christofides and Swidinsky, 1994; Doiron and Riddell, 1994; Kumar and Stengos, 1985; Lemieux, 1993; Renaud, 1998.

[11] Reviewed in Davies (1986: 242–45).

[12] Reviews are contained in Ehrenberg and Schwartz (1986), Freeman (1986), Lewin, Horton, and Kuhn (1979), and Mitchell (1983) all based on US data, and Renaud (1997, 1998), Riddell (1993), Robinson and Tomes (1984), and Simpson (1985), based on Canadian data.

[13] Corneo and Lucifora, 1997; Ichniowski, Freeman, and Lauer, 1989; Rosen, 1969; and Zwerling and Thomason, 1995. Neumark and Wachter (1995) find positive effects at the city levels and negative effects at the industry level.

[14] Freeman, 1981; Freeman and Medoff, 1984; Ichniowski, 1980; Renaud, 1998.

[15] For Canadian evidence, see Swidinsky and Kupferschmidt (1991).

[16] Brown and Medoff, 1978; Clark, 1980; Freeman and Medoff, 1979, 1984; and others comprehensively reviewed in Belman (1992).

[17] Estimates of the output loss due to these inefficiencies are 0.14 percent of gross national product (GNP) in the United States according to Rees (1963) and 0.10 percent of GNP according to De Fina (1983).

[18] Blau and Kahn (1983), Freeman (1980b), Leigh (1979), and Rees (1994), all using US data; Swidinsky (1992) using Canadian data.

[19] Studies reviewed in Belman (1992), Benjamin, Gunderson, and Riddell (1998), Freeman and Medoff (1984), and Hirsch and Addison (1986).

[20] See, for example, Maki (1983) and Mitchell and Stone (1992), which are based on Canadian data.

[21] Earlier studies are reviewed in Freeman (1986). In a more recent study, Hoxby (1996) finds unions to have had a negative effect on the productivity of US public school teachers.

[22] Duncan and Stafford (1980) estimate that about two-fifths of the union–nonunion wage differential reflects a compensating wage for these more demanding working conditions. Kalachek and Raines (1980) find that employers are able to offset some of the union wage cost increase by more stringent hiring standards, notably with respect to the education qualifications of their workers.

[23] Belman, 1992; Bemmels, 1987; Flaherty, 1987; Ichniowski, 1986; Kochan, Katz, and Mower, 1985; Maki, 1983; Read, 1982.

[24] Laporta and Jenkins (1996) and Maki and Meredeth (1986) based on Canadian data; Abowd (1989), Becker and Olson (1989, 1992), Belman (1992), Bronars and Deere (1990, 1994), Brunello (1993), Hirsch (1991a, 1991b), Machin (1991), Machin and Stewart (1996), Ruback and Zimmerman (1984), and Voos and Mishel (1986) based on US data. Reviews are given in Addison and Hirsch (1989), Becker and Olson (1989), and Hirsch (1999). Based on US data, Allen (1987) found that unions reduced costs in the construction of large office buildings due to the fact that union hiring halls were able to coordinate the casual market in skilled labour. Unions, however, increased costs in other areas of construction. Based on Canadian data, Laporta and Jenkins (1996) also found that unions actually increased profitability in industries with large numbers of competitive firms but they reduced profits in industries that were dominated by a few firms (i.e., unions could appropriate monopoly profits). Interestingly, Pearce, Groff, and Wingender (1995) found that shareholder wealth does not appear to increase when unions are decertified, perhaps because of the costs involved in implementing the new managerial policies designed to deal with the change from a union to a nonunion environment.

[25] Formal models of what are termed "efficient wage and employment contracts" are set out in Benjamin, Gunderson, and Riddell (1998: Chapter 15), Kuhn (1998), and Pencavel (1991). These studies also review the limited empirical literature on the topic.

[26] The empirical evidence, reviewed in Hirsch (1999), indicates employment growth to be lower in union compared to nonunion plants, although much of this simply reflects the predominance of unions in large firms and sectors where growth is slow. Even after accounting for this, however, Long (1993) finds employment growth in Canadian manufacturing to be lower in unionized compared to nonunion plants. Similar evidence for the US is provided in Freeman and Kleiner (1990).

[27] Allen (1988), Becker and Olson (1992), Bronars, Deere, and Tracy (1994), Cooke (1997), Hirsch (1991a, 1991b, 1992) for the US; Denny and Nickell (1991) for the United Kingdom; Odgers and Betts (1997) for Canada; with reviews in Kuhn (1998) and Hirsch (1999). An important exception is Menezes-Filho, Ulph, and Van Reenen (1998) who find that the negative effect of unions on investment disappears

when one controls for the fact that unions are less prominent in the high-tech industries that invest considerably in R & D. They argue that the greater emphasis on jobs compared to wages by British unions could also explain the reluctance of British unions to deter investment. As well, at a more aggregate level, Karier (1995) does not find any evidence indicating that firms in heavily unionized industries in the US are more likely to transfer their investments out of those industries and into foreign countries.

REFERENCES

ABOWD, J. 1989. "The Effect of Wage Bargains on the Stock Market Value of the Firm." *American Economic Review,* 79, pp. 774–809.

ADDISON, J. and A. CASTRO. 1987. "The Importance of Lifetime Jobs: Differences Between Union and Nonunion Workers." *Industrial and Labor Relations Review,* 40, pp. 393–405.

ADDISON, J. and B. HIRSCH. 1989. "Union Effects on Productivity, Profits and Growth." *Journal of Labor Economics,* 7, pp. 72–105.

ALLEN, S. 1987. "Can Union Labor Ever Cost Less?" *Quarterly Journal of Economics* (May), pp. 347–73.

———. 1988. "Productivity Levels and Productivity Change Under Unionism." *Industrial Relations,* 27, pp. 94–113.

ANDREWS, M., M. STEWART, J. SWAFFIELD, and R. UPWARD. 1998. "The Estimation of Union Wage Differentials and the Impact of Methodological Choices." *Labor Economics,* 5, pp. 449–74.

ASHENFELTER, O. and G. JOHNSON. 1972. "Unionism, Relative Wages and Labour Quality in US Manufacturing Industries." *International Economic Review,* 13, pp. 488–507.

BALKIN D. 1989. "Union Influence on Pay Policy: A Survey." *Journal of Labor Research,* 10, pp. 299–309.

BECKER, B. 1995. "Union Rents as a Source of Takeover Gains Among Target Shareholders." *Industrial and Labour Relations Review,* 49, pp. 3–19.

BECKER, B. and C. OLSON. 1989. "Unionism and Shareholder Interests." *Industrial and Labor Relations Review,* 42, pp. 246–62.

———. 1992. "Unions and Firm Profits." *Industrial Relations,* 31, pp. 395–415.

BELMAN, D. 1992. "Unions, the Quality of Labour Relations, and Firm Performance," in *Unions and Economic Competitiveness,* edited by L. Mishel and P. Voos. Armonk, New York: M. E. Sharp, Inc.

BELMAN, D. and J. HEYWOOD. 1990. "Union Membership, Union Organization, and the Dispersion of Wages." *Review of Economics and Statistics,* 72, pp. 148–53.

BEMMELS, B. 1987. "How Unions Affect Productivity in Manufacturing Plants." *Industrial and Labor Relations Review,* 40, pp. 241–53.

BENEDICT, M. and L. WILDER. 1999. "Unionization and Tenure and Rank Outcomes in Ohio Universities." *Journal of Labor Research,* 20, pp. 185–202.

BENJAMIN, D., M. GUNDERSON, and W. C. RIDDELL. 1998. *Labour Market Economics: Theory, Evidence and Policy in Canada,* 3rd Edition. Toronto: McGraw-Hill.

BEYER, J. M., H. M. TRICE, and R. E. HUNT. 1980. "The Impact of Federal Sector Unions on Supervisors' Use of Personnel Policies." *Industrial and Labor Relations Review,* 33, pp. 212–31.

BLANCHFLOWER, D. and R. FREEMAN. 1992. "Unionism in the United States and Other Advanced Countries." *British Journal of Industrial Relations,* 31, pp. 56–79.

BLAU, F. D. and L. M. KAHN. 1983. "Unionism, Seniority, and Turnover." *Industrial Relations,* 22, pp. 362–73.

BOOTH, A. 1995. *The Economics of the Trade Union.* Cambridge: Cambridge University Press.

BRONARS, S. and G. DEERE. 1990. "Union Representation Elections and Firm Profitability." *Industrial Relations,* 29, pp. 15–37.

———. 1994. "Unionization and Profitability: Evidence of Spillover Effects." *Journal of Political Economy,* 102, pp. 1281–88.

BRONARS, S., G. DEERE, and J. TRACY. 1994. "The Effects of Unions on Firm Behaviour." *Industrial Relations,* 33, pp. 426–51.

BROWN, C., and J. MEDOFF. 1978. "Trade Unions in the Production Process." *Journal of Political Economy,* 86, pp. 355–78.

BRUNELLO, G. 1993. "The Effect of Unions on Firm Performance in Japanese Manufacturing." *Industrial and Labor Relations Review,* 45, pp. 471–87.

CHRISTOFIDES, L. and R. SWIDINSKY. 1994. "Wage Determination by Gender and Visible Minority Status: Evidence from the 1989 LMAS." *Canadian Public Policy,* 20, pp. 34–51.

CLARK, K. 1980. "The Impact of Unionization on Productivity: A Case Study." *Industrial and Labor Relations Review,* 33, pp. 451–69.

COHEN, Y. and J. PFEFFER. 1986. "Organizational Hiring Standards." *Administrative Science Quarterly,* 31, pp. 1–24.

COOKE. W. 1989. "Improving Productivity and Quality Through Collaboration." *Industrial Relations,* 28, pp. 299–319.

———. 1990. "Factors Influencing the Effect of Joint Union-Management Programs on Employee-Supervisor Relations." *Industrial and Labor Relations Review,* 43, pp. 587–603.

———. 1992. "Product Quality Improvement Through Employee Participation: The Effect of Unionization and Joint Union-Management Administration." *Industrial and Labor Relations Review,* 46, pp. 119–34.

———. 1994. "Employee Participation Programs, Group-based Incentives, and Company Performance: A Union-Nonunion Comparison." *Industrial and Labor Relations Review,* 47, pp. 594–609.

———. 1997. "The Influence of Industrial Relations Factors on U.S. Foreign Investment." *Industrial and Labour Relations Review,* 51, pp. 3–17.

CORNEO, G. and C. LUCIFORA. 1997. "Wage Formation Under Union Threat Effects." *Labor Economics,* 4, pp. 265–92.

DAVIES, R. J. 1986. "The Structure of Collective Bargaining in Canada," in *Canadian Labour Relations,* edited by W. C. Riddell. Toronto: University of Toronto Press.

DeFINA, R. H. 1983. "Unions, Relative Wages, and Economic Efficiency." *Journal of Labor Economics,* 1, pp. 408–92.

DENNY, K. and S. NICKELL. 1991. "Unions and Investment in British Manufacturing Industry." *British Journal of Industrial Relations,* 29, pp. 113–21.

DOIRON, D. and W. RIDDELL. 1994. "The Impact of Unionization on Male-Female Earnings Differentials in Canada." *Journal of Human Resources,* 29, pp. 504–34.

DRAGO, R. 1988. "Quality Circle Survival." *Industrial Relations,* 27, pp. 336–51.

DUNCAN, G. and D. LEIGH. 1980. "Wage Determination in the Union and Nonunion Sectors: A Sample Selectivity Approach." *Industrial and Labor Relations Review,* 34, pp. 24–34.

DUNCAN, G., and F. STAFFORD. 1980. "Do Union Members Receive Compensating Wage Differentials?" *American Economic Review,* 70, pp. 335–71.

EHRENBERG, R. and J. SCHWARZ. 1986. "Public Sector Labor Markets," in *Handbook of Labor Economics,* edited by O. Ashenfelter and R. Layard. Amsterdam: North-Holland, pp. 1219–68.

FLAHERTY, S. 1987. "Strike Activity, Worker Militancy, and Productivity Change in Manufacturing: 1961–1981." *Industrial and Labor Relations Review,* 40, pp. 585–600.

FREEMAN, R. 1976. "Individual Mobility and Union Voice in the Labor Market." *American Economic Review Proceedings,* 66, pp. 361–68.

———. 1980a. "Unionism and the Dispersion of Wages." *Industrial and Labor Relations Review,* 34, pp. 3–23.

———. 1980b. "The Effect of Unionism on Worker Attachment to Firms." *Journal of Labor Research,* 1, pp. 29–62.

———. 1981. "The Effect of Unionism on Fringe Benefits." *Industrial and Labor Relations Review,* 34, pp. 489–509.

———. 1984. "Longitudinal Analysis of the Effects of Trade Unions." *Journal of Labor Economics,* 2, pp. 1–26.

———. 1986. "Unionism Comes to the Public Sector." *Journal of Economic Literature,* 24, pp. 41–86.

———. 1993. "How Much Has De-unionization Contributed to the Rise of Male Earnings Inequality?" in *Uneven Tides: Rising Inequality in America,* edited by S. Danziger and P. Gottschalk. New York: Russell Sage Foundation.

FREEMAN, R. and M. KLEINER. 1990. "The Impact of New Unionization on Wages and Working Conditions." *Journal of Labor Economics,* 8, pp. 8–25.

———. 1999. "Do Unions Make Enterprises Insolvent?" *Industrial and Labour Relations Review,* 52, pp. 510–27.

FREEMAN, R. and J. MEDOFF. 1979. "The Two Faces of Unionism." *The Public Interest,* 7, pp. 69–93.

———. 1984. *What Do Unions Do?* New York: Basic Books.

GOLDSCHMIDT, S. M. and L. E. STUART. 1986. "The Extent and Impact of Educational Policy Bargaining." *Industrial and Labor Relations Review,* 39, pp. 350–60.

GRANT, E. K., R. SWIDINSKY, and J. VANDERKAMP. 1987. "Canadian Union–Non-Union Wage Differentials." *Industrial and Labor Relations Review,* 41, pp. 93–107.

GUNDERSON, M., D HYATT, and W. C. RIDDELL. 1999. *Pay Differences Between the Government and Private Sectors.* Ottawa: Canadian Policy Research Network.

HALL, W. and N. CARROLL. 1973. "The Effects of Teachers' Organizations on Salaries and Class Size." *Industrial and Labor Relations Review,* 26, pp. 834–41.

HIRSCH, B. 1991a. "Union Coverage and Profitability Among US Firms." *Review of Economics and Statistics,* 73, pp. 69–77.

———. 1991b. *Labor Unions and the Economic Performance of Firms.* Kalamazoo, MI: Upjohn Institute for Employment Research.

———. 1992. "Firm Investment Behavior and Collective Bargaining Strategy." *Industrial Relations,* 31, pp. 95–121.

———. 1999. "Unionization and Economic Performance: Evidence on Productivity, Profits, Investment, and Growth." Vancouver: Fraser Institute.

HIRSCH, B. and J. ADDISON. 1986. *The Economic Analysis of Unions: New Approaches and Evidence.* Boston: Allen and Unwin.

HIRSCHMAN, A. 1970. *Exit, Voice and Loyalty.* Cambridge, Mass.: Harvard University Press.

HOXBY, C. 1996. "How Teachers' Unions Affect Production." *Quarterly Journal of Economics,* 111, pp. 671–718.

HYCLACK, T. 1980. "Unions and Income Inequality." *Industrial Relations,* 19, pp. 212–15.

ICHNIOWSKI, C. 1980. "Economic Effects of the Firefighters' Union." *Industrial and Labor Relations Review*, 33, pp. 198–211.

———. 1986. "The Effects of Grievance Activity on Productivity." *Industrial and Labor Relations Review*, 40, pp. 75–89.

ICHNIOWSKI, C., R. FREEMAN, and H. LAUER. 1989. "Collective Bargaining Laws, Threat Effects, and the Determination of Police Compensation." *Journal of Labor Economics*, 7, pp. 191–209.

JAKUBSON, G. 1991. "Estimation and Testing of the Union Wage Effect Using Panel Data." *Review of Economic Studies*, 58, pp. 971–91.

JARRELL, S. and T. STANLEY. 1990. "A Meta-Analysis of the Union-Nonunion Wage Gap." *Industrial and Labor Relations Review*, 44, pp. 54–67.

KAHN, L. 1978. "The Effect of Unions on the Earnings of Non-Union Workers." *Industrial and Labor Relations Review*, 31, pp. 205–16.

———. 1980. "Union Spillover Effects on Unorganized Labor Markets." *Journal of Human Resources*, 15, pp. 87–98.

KALACHEK, E. and F. RAINES. 1980. "Trade Unions and Hiring Standards." *Journal of Labor Research*, 1, pp. 63–76.

KARIER, T. 1995. "U.S. Foreign Production and Unions." *Industrial Relations*, 34, pp. 107–18.

KAUFMAN, R. S. and R. T. KAUFMAN. 1987. "Union Effects on Productivity, Personnel Practices, and Survival in the Automotive Parts Industry." *Journal of Labor Research*, 8, pp. 333–50.

KAUFMAN, R. T. 1992. "The Effects of IMPROSHARE on Productivity." *Industrial and Labor Relations Review*, 45, pp. 311–22.

KIM, D. and P. VOOS. 1997. "Unionization, Union Involvement, and the Performance of Gainsharing Programs." *Relations industrielles/Industrial Relations*, 52, pp. 304–29.

KOCH, M. and G. HUNDLEY. 1998. "The Effect of Unionism on Recruitment and Selection Methods." *Industrial Relations*, 36, pp. 349–70.

KOCHAN, T., H. KATZ, and N. MOWER. 1985. "Worker Participation and American Unions," in *Challenges and Choices Facing American Unions*, edited by T. Kochan. Cambridge: MIT Press.

KUHN, P. 1998. "Unions and the Economy: What We Know and What We Should Know." *Canadian Journal of Economics*, 31, pp. 1033–56.

KUMAR, P. and T. STENGOS. 1985. "Measuring The Union Relative Wage Impact: A Methodological Note." *Canadian Journal of Economics*, 18, pp. 182–89.

LAPORTA, P. and A. JENKINS. 1996. "Unionization and Profitability in the Canadian Manufacturing Sector." *Relations industrielles/Industrial Relations*, 51, pp. 756–76.

LAWRENCE, C. and R. LAWRENCE. 1985. "Manufacturing Wage Dispersion: An End Game Interpretation." *Brookings Papers on Economic Activity*, 1, pp. 47–106.

LEE, L.-F. 1978. "Unionism and Wage Rates: A Simultaneous Equations Model with Qualitative and Limited Dependent Variables." *International Economic Review*, 19, pp. 415–34.

LEIGH, D. 1979. "Unions and Nonwage Racial Discrimination." *Industrial and Labor Relations Review*, 32, pp. 439–50.

LEMIEUX, T. 1993. "Unions and Wage Inequality in Canada and the United States," in *Small Differences that Matter: Labor Markets and Income Maintenance in Canada and the United States*, edited by D. Card and R. Freeman. Chicago: University of Chicago Press, pp. 69–107.

———. 1998. "Estimating the Effects of Unions on Wage Inequality in a Panel Data Model with Comparative Advantage and Nonrandom Selection." *Journal of Labor Economics,* 16, pp. 261–91.

LEWIN, D., R. HORTON, and J. KUHN. 1979. *Collective Bargaining and Manpower Utilization in Big City Governments.* New York: Universe Books.

LEWIS, H. G. 1963. *Unionism and Relative Wages in the United States.* Chicago: University of Chicago Press.

———. 1983. "Union Relative Wage Effects: A Survey of Macro Estimates." *Journal of Labor Economics,* 1, pp. 1–27.

———. 1986a. *Union Relative Wage Effects: A Survey.* Chicago: University of Chicago Press.

———. 1986b. "Union Relative Wage Effects," in *Handbook of Labor Economics,* Vol. 1, edited by O. Ashenfelter and R. Layard. New York: Elsevier Science Publishers.

LONG, R. 1993. "The Effect of Unionization on Employment Growth of Canadian Companies." *Industrial and Labor Relations Review,* 46, pp. 691–703.

MACHIN, S. 1991. "Unions and the Capture of Economic Rents: An Investigation Using British Firm Level Data." *International Journal of Industrial Organization,* 9, pp. 261–74.

MACHIN, S. and M. STEWART. 1996. "Trade Unions and Financial Performance." *Oxford Economic Papers,* 48, pp. 213–41.

MAKI, D. R. 1983. "Trade Unions and Productivity: Conventional Estimates." *Relations industrielles/Industrial Relations,* 38, pp. 211–25.

MAKI, D. and L. MEREDITH. 1986. "The Effect of Unions on Profitability: Canadian Evidence." *Relations industrielles/Industrial Relations,* 41, pp. 54–68.

MELLOW, W. 1981. "Unionism and Wages: A Longitudinal Analysis." *Review of Economics and Statistics,* 63, pp. 43–52.

MENEZES-FILHO, N., D. ULPH, and J. VAN REENEN. 1998. "R & D and Unionism: Comparative Evidence from British Companies and Establishments." *Industrial and Labor Relations Review,* 52, pp. 45–63.

MENG, R. 1990. "Union Effects on Wage Dispersion in Canadian Industry." *Economic Letters,* 32, pp. 399–403.

MINCER, J. 1983. "Union Effects: Wages, Turnover and Job Training," in *New Approaches to Labor Unions,* edited by J. D. Reid, Jr. Greenwich, CT: JAI Press.

MITCHELL, D. 1983. "Unions and Wages in the Public Sector: A Review of Recent Evidence." *Journal of Collective Negotiations in the Public Sector,* 12, pp. 337–53.

MITCHELL, M. and J. STONE. 1992. "Union Effects on Productivity: Evidence From Western US Sawmills." *Industrial and Labor Relations Review,* 46, pp. 135–45.

MOORE, W. and J. RAISIAN. 1983. "The Level and Growth of Union/Non-Union Relative Wage Effects, 1967–1977." *Journal of Labor Research,* 4, pp. 65–80.

NEUMARK, D. and M. WACHTER. 1995. "Union Effects on Nonunion Wages: Evidence from Panel Data on Industries and Cities." *Industrial and Labour Relations Review,* 49, pp. 20–38.

NG, I. and D. MAKI. 1994. "Trade Union Influence on Human Resource Management Practices." *Industrial Relations,* 33, pp. 121–35.

ODGERS, C. and J. BETTS. 1997. "Do Unions Reduce Investment? Evidence from Canada." *Industrial and Labor Relations Review,* 51, pp. 518–36.

PEARCE, T., J. GROFF, and J. WINGENDER. 1995. "Union Decertification's Impact on Shareholder Wealth." *Industrial Relations,* 34, pp. 58–72.

PENCAVEL, J. 1991. *Labor Markets Under Trade Unionism: Employment, Wages and Hours.* Cambridge, Mass.: Basil Blackwell.

QUAN, N. 1984. "Unionism and the Size Distribution of Earnings." *Industrial Relations,* 24, pp. 270–77.

READ, L. 1982. "Canada Post: A Case Study in the Correlation of Collective Will and Productivity," in *Research on Productivity of Relevance to Canada,* edited by D. J. Daly. Ottawa: Social Science Federation of Canada.

REES, A. 1963. "The Effect of Unions on Resource Allocation." *Journal of Law and Economics,* 6, pp. 69–78.

REES, D. 1994. "Does Unionization Increase Faculty Retention?" *Industrial Relations,* 33, pp. 297–321.

RENAULD, S. 1997. "Unions and Wages in Canada." *Selected Papers from the 33rd Annual CIRA Conference.* Quebec: Canadian Industrial Relations Association, pp. 211–226.

———. 1998. "Unions, Wages and Total Compensation in Canada." *Relations industrielles/Industrial Relations,* 53, pp. 710–27.

RIDDELL, W. 1993. "Unionization in Canada and the United States: A Tale of Two Countries," in *Small Differences that Matter: Labor Markets and Income Maintenance in Canada and the United States,* edited by D. Card and R. Freeman. Chicago: University of Chicago Press.

ROBINSON, C. 1989. "The Joint Determination of Union Status and Union Wage Effects: Some Tests of Alternative Models." *Journal of Political Economy,* 97, pp. 639–67.

ROBINSON, C. and N. TOMES. 1984. "Union Wage Differentials in the Public and Private Sectors: A Simultaneous Equations Specification." *Journal of Labor Economics,* 2, pp. 106–27.

ROSEN, S. 1969. "Trade Union Power, Threat Effects, and the Extent of Organization." *Review of Economic Studies,* 36, pp. 185–96.

RUBACK, R. and M. ZIMMERMAN. 1984. "Unionization and Profitability: Evidence from the Capital Market." *Journal of Political Economy,* 92, pp. 1134–57.

SCHEUR, S. 1999. "The Impact of Collective Agreements on Working Time in Denmark." *British Journal of Industrial Relations,* 37, pp. 465–81.

SIMPSON, W. 1985. "The Impact of Unions on the Structure of Canadian Wages: An Empirical Study with Micro Data." *Canadian Journal of Economics,* 18, pp. 164–81.

SLICHTER, S., J. HEALY, and R. LIVERNASH. 1960. *The Impact of Collective Bargaining on Management.* Washington: Brookings Institution.

SWIDINSKY, R. 1992. "Unionism and the Job Attachment of Canadian Workers." *Relations industrielles/Industrial Relations,* 47, pp. 729–751.

SWIDINSKY, R. and M. KUPFERSCHMIDT. 1991. "Longitudinal Estimates of the Union Effects on Wages, Wage Dispersion and Pension Fringe Benefits." *Relations industrielles/Industrial Relations,* 46, pp. 819–38.

TARAS, D. 1994. "Impact of Industrial Relations Strategies on Selected Human Resources Practices in a Partially Unionized Industry: The Canadian Petroleum Sector." Ph.D. dissertation, Faculty of Management, University of Calgary.

TREJO, S. 1993. "Overtime Pay, Overtime Hours and Labor Unions." *Journal of Labor Economics,* 11, pp. 253–78.

VOOS, P. and L. MISHEL. 1986. "The Union Impact on Profits: Evidence from Industry Price-Cost Margin Data." *Journal of Labor Economics,* 4, pp. 105–33.

WAGAR, T. 1997. "Is Labor-Management Climate Important: Some Canadian Evidence?" *Journal of Labor Research,* 18, pp. 163–74.

————. 1998. "The Labour-Management Relationship and Organizational Outcomes." *Relations industrielles/Industrial Relations,* 52, pp. 430–46.

WHITE, F. 1994. "The Union/Non-Union Earnings Differential for Professionals." *Proceedings of the 30th Annual Conference of CIRA.* Quebec: Canadian Industrial Relations Association, pp. 269–79.

WOODBURY, S. 1985. "The Scope of Bargaining Outcomes in Public Schools." *Industrial and Labor Relations Review,* 38, pp. 195–210.

WUNNAVA, P. and B. EWING. 1999. "Union-Nonunion Differentials and Establishment Size." *Journal of Labor Research,* 20, pp. 177–83.

ZWERLING, H. and T. THOMASON. 1995. "Collective Bargaining and the Determinants of Teachers' Salaries." *Journal of Labor Research,* 26, pp. 468–84.

CHAPTER 14

Public-Sector Collective Bargaining

Allen Ponak and Mark Thompson

In November 1995, 120 hospital laundry workers in Calgary began a wild-cat strike to protest the planned outsourcing of laundry services. Two years earlier they had accepted pay cuts of 28 percent to help their hospital meet its budget and preserve their jobs. With the announcement that the laundry function was to be privatized and sent to a nonunion firm in Edmonton, the workers, members of CUPE, walked out. The next day, laundry workers at another hospital, belonging to a different union, joined the strike and other unionized health-care workers followed. The striking laundry workers received considerable support from doctors, nurses, and most importantly, the general public. The province was galvanized by the courage of the lowest-paid workers in the health-care system. One magazine commented that the "David-and-Goliath nature of their struggle had strong appeal for Albertans. The traditional reticence about organized labour was largely absent from the public response to these particular workers" (McGrath and Neu, 1996: 25). Public opinion surveys showed that three-quarters of Calgarians supported the strike.

Eventually, more than 2500 workers from six hospitals and nine nursing homes walked off the job. Many more who remained at work launched work-to-rule campaigns in support of the strikers.

In the end, the laundry workers won a longer notice period and severance pay, but the strike also represented the first major reversal in the "no-blink" approach of the Conservative government of Ralph Klein. Since its election in 1993, the Klein government had massively cut public expenditures in health and education as part of its goal of reducing provincial budget deficits. The so-called "Klein Revolution" became the model emulated by Ontario and other provinces. The laundry workers' strike, however, drew attention to health care and general public concern that health-care reductions were too fast and too deep. As the strike escalated, the government announced that it was cancelling a scheduled $53 million cut to health-care spending, and Klein conceded that "we're taking a bit of a detour" and that his government had underestimated the "human factor." With this, public support for the government was restored, and Klein maintained his image as a tough but populist leader.[1]

This chapter reviews the evolution, distinguishing features, and special problems of collective bargaining in the Canadian public sector. Collective bargaining functions differently in the public sector than in the private sector, in particular because of some pronounced differences in public- and private-sector employers. These differences, as well as other factors, have given rise to persistent problems in dispute resolution and wage determination. More recently, the very role of government itself has been undergoing change.

The laundry workers' strike illustrates the tensions of public-sector industrial relations—disputes are highly visible; they touch on services that affect the public at large; and politics are central to many decisions. It also illustrates how changes in the role of government, as shown by the decision to contract out laundry services previously provided by public employees, can affect industrial relations. The public sector is the most heavily unionized part of the Canadian economy. In the 1970s employees in health care, education, and government at all levels embraced collective bargaining in numbers not seen since the industrial unionism drives of the 1930s and 1940s. The collective bargaining process in which these new union members engaged affected the way public services were provided, disrupted those services from time to time, contributed to higher levels of taxation, and created a whole new set of pressures on public managers and government budgets.

Governments' response to these developments has been intertwined with attitudes about the role of government itself. Historically, the public sector has been important to Canada. Public agencies and branches of government built much of the country, thanks to a legacy of colonialism, a weak private sector, and the fear of US domination. Public institutions were created to promote public ends in transportation, communications, cultural spheres, and social endeavours, that is, in the complete infrastructure of a modern society (Thompson, 2000). The state provided the overwhelming majority of all educational services, transportation systems, and a public broadcasting system. After the Second World War, Canadian governments generally accepted Keynesian economics, which called for government intervention to reduce major fluctuations in the business cycle and maintain high levels of aggregate demand to achieve full employment (Haiven, McBride, and Shields, 1991). The basis for the modern welfare state was established after World War II, with universal health care, public pensions, and social assistance of various kinds. By 1999, Canada ranked in the middle of developed countries in terms of gross domestic product consumed by government, higher than the United States or Japan, but well below northern Europe. This level is consistent with other mid-sized developed nations with relatively open economies. Canada's low population density also contributes to the cost of public services (Thompson, 2000).

Beginning in the late 1980s the traditional approach of government underwent critical scrutiny in Canada and elsewhere. Governments of all political stripes, from conservative to socialist, embarked on a path leading to the reduction of the role and size of government (Beaumont, 1995). In many countries, Canada included, massive public debt levels lent urgency to the debate.

New policies emphasized free market forces. Keynesian economic policies fell into disfavour. Virtually all levels of government restricted spending, and per capita spending by government declined throughout the 1990s (Thompson, 2000). Major government-owned enterprises, from airlines and telephone companies to liquor stores, were sold to the private sector. Work formerly performed by public employees, including snow removal, highway maintenance, safety inspections, and licensing, were contracted out. Hospitals and recreation centres were closed, university class sizes increased while tuition skyrocketed, and new user fees were imposed on a variety of services. Not surprisingly, these and other changes placed great stress on the public-sector collective bargaining system.

SIZE AND SCOPE OF THE PUBLIC SECTOR

For purposes of this discussion, the public sector is defined to include federal and provincial civil services, municipalities, health care, education, and government enterprises (for example, the Canadian Broadcasting Corporation, Hydro-Québec). Table 14.1 provides data on public-sector employment in mid-1999. Reliable employment information was not available for government enterprises, and they were not included in the table.

Total public employment was estimated at 2.68 million in 1999, comprising more than 22 percent of all employees in Canada. With government enterprises, the public-sector proportion of employment is more than one-quarter of the overall economy. Health care and education are by far the largest components of the public sector, accounting for nearly three-quarters of all public employees. The federal government employs relatively few people, contrary to popular perceptions. On an international comparative basis, Canada ranks slightly above the OECD average in terms of the ratio of public to overall employment (Swimmer, 2000).

Data in Table 14.1 confirm the impact of government policies introduced in the last half of the 1990s aimed at reducing the role of government. Total employment fell in education and in the provincial and federal civil services. Overall, public-sector employment as a proportion of the total economy declined from 25 percent to 22 percent. Put another way, while employment in the rest of the economy expanded, public-sector employment hardly grew at all, thus accounting for a significantly smaller part of the economy as a whole. To put this decline into perspective, it should be noted that public employment increased at an annual rate of 7 percent between 1946 and 1975 (Foot and Thadaney, 1978) and was still increasing by 1 percent a year into the late 1980s and early 1990s.

The reversal in public-sector growth rates was achieved in three principal ways: the sale of government assets and enterprises (privatization), the turning over of work previously performed by public employees to private contractors (contracting-out), and the reduction in the level of public services (Thompson, 1995).

TABLE 14.1

PUBLIC-SECTOR EMPLOYMENT, 1994 AND 1999

AREA OF PUBLIC SECTOR	1994 (THOUSANDS)	1999 (THOUSANDS)	ANNUAL PERCENTAGE CHANGE 1994–1999
Education	772.9	749.4	-0.5
Health & welfare	1150.3	1224.6	1.1
Local government	216.3	260.5	3.4
Provincial government	242.6	213.4	-2.0
Federal government	275.8	228.1	-2.9
Total public sector	2657.9	2676.1	0.1
Total economy	10,600.4	11,940.6	
Public-sector proportion of total economy	25.0%	22.4%	

Source: "Public-Sector Employment, 1994 and 1999," adapted from Statistics Canada, *Employment, Earnings, and Hours*, Catalogue No. 72-002. Figures are for July of the reporting year.

Privatization has taken several forms, but has most often involved the sale of Crown corporations to private-sector firms engaged in the same or related industry. For example, the federal government sold two aircraft manufacturing firms to Boeing and Bombardier, and the British Columbia government sold its gas distribution system to companies already active in the province (Thompson, 1995). In other cases, for example, Alberta Government Telephones (now Telus), Petro-Canada, and Air Canada, the government owners of these companies issued public shares, which were widely distributed.

The contracting out of services previously performed by public employees to the private sector has also been extensive, particularly at the municipal level, in hospitals, and in educational institutions. The most common candidates for contracting-out are solid waste disposal (i.e., garbage collection), building maintenance and security, laundries, food services, snow removal, and road and highway maintenance (Thompson, 1995). Canada Post has contracted out janitorial services for some of its facilities, and private firms run many university food services. Social services, such as group homes for the disabled, have also been shifted to the private sector.

A third strategy to reduce government is simply to decrease or eliminate specific public services, reducing employment at the same time. This approach has been especially noticeable in health care with the closure of acute-care hospitals, the elimination of certain departments (e.g., surgical wards), or the reduction in the number of beds (Swimmer, 2000). In Saskatchewan, for example, a number of rural hospitals have been closed, and in Calgary two large acute-care hospitals were shut down (the largest of the two, the Calgary General Hospital, was physically demolished). Beyond health care, other examples of reduced services include cutting back the number of outdoor ice rinks in Montreal parks, closing university departments, shortening library operating hours, or simply reducing the number of staff in various government departments (see Exhibit 14.1).

Taken together, privatization, contracting-out, and service reductions reversed four decades of public employment growth. In Manitoba, provincial government employment fell by 22 percent between 1991 and 1997, and in Ontario it fell by 20 percent in just two-and-a-half years beginning in 1995. Similar patterns were evident in most of the other provinces (Swimmer, 2000).

Exhibit 14.1

How to Reduce Public Employment

- Privatize: Sell government-owned companies to the private sector (e.g., Air Canada).
- Contract Out: Have services previously performed by government employees done by private-sector contractors (e.g., garbage collection, hospital laundry).
- Reduce Services: Reduce the amount of services, shrinking employment levels (e.g., shorter operating hours, fewer government offices).

DEVELOPMENT OF PUBLIC-SECTOR COLLECTIVE BARGAINING

Public-sector collective bargaining did not become widespread in Canada until the mid-1960s. Previously, few public employees engaged in formal collective bargaining, with the exception of blue-collar municipal workers. Today the situation is totally reversed. It is difficult to find a public employee group not covered by a collective agreement. Canada's two largest unions (Canadian Union of Public Employees and National Union of Provincial and General Workers) operate almost exclusively in the public sector, and the level of collective bargaining in the public sector far exceeds that found in the private sector. Slightly more than half of all union members in Canada work in the public sector (Akyeampong, 1999).

Table 14.2 reports the latest available information on union density for various components of the public sector. The level of unionism ranges from 75 percent unionized in provincial government to 50 percent in health and social services (with the bulk of nonunion employment in health care found in offices of physicians and dentists, which arguably should not be included as public sector at all).[2] The union density rates in the public sector are obviously much higher than the rate of one-third unionized for the economy as a whole and the 22 percent rate for the private sector (Akyeampong, 1999). With the exception of a drop in union density for provincial government employees, public-sector unionization rates have remained stable through the 1990s.[3]

TABLE 14.2

PUBLIC-SECTOR UNION DENSITY

AREA OF THE PUBLIC SECTOR	PERCENT UNIONIZED	
	1991	1998
Local government	67.9	65.3
Provincial government	94.9	74.6
Federal government	72.5	70.5
Educational services	75.3	73.2
Health and social services	50.9	55.9
Overall economy	35.1	32.5

Sources: 1991: Statistics Canada, Corporations and Labour Unions Return Act. Part II, Labour Unions, Appendix 1.5, Catalogue No. 71-202, unpublished information provided by Labour Union Section, 1992, and unpublished data provided by Labour Force Survey Program.

TABLE 14.3

MEMBERSHIP OF PUBLIC-SECTOR UNIONS (THOUSANDS)

Unions	1980	1994	1998
PSAC	155.7	167.8	142.3
NUPGE	195.8	307.6	309.0
CUPE	257.2	409.8	389.3
Teachers' unions	276.8	404.6	404.6
Nurses' unions	78.1	166.5	166.2
Police unions	34.5[a]	43.5	42.2
Firefighters' unions	19.4[a]	27.2	30.8

[a] Membership is for 1986.

Source: Labour Canada, *Directory of Labour Organizations*, 1980, 1994, and 1998; and Rose, 1995, Table 1. Reproduced with permission of the Minister of Human Resources Development Canada.

While local, provincial, and federal employees are represented by their own national unions, teachers and registered nurses thus far have remained in provincially based independent labour organizations. Police officers and firefighters also are heavily organized. Police belong to independent local or provincial associations while firefighters are represented mainly by the International Association of Firefighters. Almost all unionized public employees except firefighters belong to Canadian-based national unions. Table 14.3 sets out membership patterns of the various public-sector labour organizations, and mirrors recent declines in public employment.

Canadian Union of Public Employees: www.cupe.ca

Canadian Union of Postal Workers: www.cupw-sttp.org

Association–Consultation

The current extent of public-sector unionism belies its recent origin. Associations of public employees existed before 1900, and then, as now, these workers shared at least some of the many concerns of their private-sector counterparts in terms of salaries and employment conditions (Logan, 1948). Early in the 20th century, Canadian public employees spurned unionism and collective bargaining. Instead, they formed public employee associations. These organizations avoided union tactics, especially strikes, and were independent of any labour body. Management personnel, to the most senior positions, often were active in these associations and even occupied positions of leadership. A major function of these organizations was consultation with the employer, regarded as the best means of influencing the salaries and working conditions of their members.

EXHIBIT 14.2

ASSOCIATION–CONSULTATION MODEL OF EMPLOYMENT RELATIONS

- non-certified employee organizations
- minimal dues, minimal budget, few, if any, permanent staff
- unaffiliated to labour movement
- membership included senior levels of management
- rejected collective bargaining, grievance arbitration, strikes
- periodic consultation with government over wages and conditions of employment
- employer makes final decision on all employment matters

This approach to employer–employee relations is referred to here as "association–consultation" (see Exhibit 14.2). It was the prevalent form of public-sector labour relations until the mid-1960s, when it yielded to the more familiar unionism and collective bargaining approach. The transition from association–consultation to union–collective bargaining began in the 1950s, accelerated in the mid-1960s, and was virtually complete by the mid-1970s.

Unions and Collective Bargaining

Why did association–consultation decline so rapidly, starting in the 1960s? The answer lies in problems with the "consultation" component of association–consultation, which was based on the belief that consultation was an adequate means for employees to address their employment concerns. In the long run, consultation proved disappointing. Weaknesses not foreseen at the outset ultimately created great dissatisfaction.

In practice, consultation delivered much less than envisioned (see Exhibit 14.3). The range of issues open to consultation proved narrower than employees wanted. Wages were typically the subject of salary briefs only. No mechanisms existed to resolve differences between the parties on contentious issues. The powers of the consulted party were only advisory; if the employer rejected a proposal, the status quo prevailed (Frankel, 1960).

Disenchanted with consultation, staff associations became advocates of collective bargaining. At the same time, they began modelling themselves along traditional union lines, excluding management personnel from their membership, hiring full-time staff experts, eliminating no-strike clauses from their constitutions, merging with competing or complementary organizations, and in some cases affiliating with the Canadian Labour Congress.

The major catalyst in the movement to full collective bargaining was the removal of legal obstacles. Saskatchewan had set a precedent in 1944 by including civil servants under the coverage of the provincial *Trade Union Act*, undermining the proposition that government sovereignty prevented public-sector bargaining. Other governments slowly

Exhibit 14.3

"A Big Blob of Jello"

A disgruntled member of the British Columbia Government Employees' Association summed up his feelings on the eve of the association becoming a bona fide union:

"When I came into the association, it was just a blob of jello. You could push it one place to try to change things and it popped out in another place in the same old way. I had been working as a gold miner at Bralorne and came out of the Mine, Mill and Smelter Workers' Union into the association. What a jolt it was to become part of a company union with a lot of bosses in leadership.

"We never made any 'demands' on the Employer. Only requests, going to Victoria every year with reams and reams of briefs and hoping for the best. It was when we got the LCB employees [Liquor Control Board] into their own group that we started changing the association into a union.

"Before that, it was just a big blob of jello with people with hundreds of different jobs and different problems all going to the same branch meetings."

Source: McLean, 1979, p. 97.

accepted that certain limitations in their own discretion might be necessary if rights—to which public employees now felt strongly entitled—were to be ensured. In many jurisdictions, the substitution of arbitration for the right to strike overcame misgivings about work stoppages. Gradually, the legislative environment began to change from one hostile to the collective bargaining model to one that supported it.

The most important breakthrough for employee associations seeking collective bargaining occurred in 1963. Astute political lobbying by employee organizations persuaded the newly elected federal government of Prime Minister Lester Pearson to promise collective bargaining rights for the federal civil service (Edwards, 1968). The Public Service Staff Relations Act (PSSRA) was enacted several years later and more than 100,000 federal employees were soon covered by collective agreements. In 1965, the *Quebec Labour Code* extended bargaining rights to all public employees in that province, and 40,000 workers started their first round of bargaining. Political pressure mounted for other governments to emulate these examples. One by one, the remaining provinces enacted collective bargaining legislation for various groups of public employees.

By 1975, the rights of virtually all public employees to engage in collective bargaining were established and protected by law. Access to certification procedures, conciliation machinery, and labour boards, together with public employers' acceptance of unionism and collective bargaining, launched one of the most sustained periods of union growth in Canadian history. Once committed to collective bargaining, public-sector organizations wasted little time exercising their newly acquired rights. Existing associations converted themselves into unions, eliminating the need for extensive membership campaigns, and unionization spread rapidly. By the late 1970s, most eligible public employees in the country were covered by collective agreements.

DISTINGUISHING FEATURES OF PUBLIC-SECTOR COLLECTIVE BARGAINING

As public-employee unionism spread rapidly, it became obvious that bargaining did not work quite the same way in the public sector as in the private sector. Certain important differences between public- and private-sector employers, employees, and legislation combined to produce distinctive bargaining dynamics.

Employer Differences

Many of the distinctive features of public-sector labour relations stem from differences between public employers and private employers. Decision-making structure and authority differ between the two sectors, typically being much more diffuse in the public sector. Most public employers (a small number of government enterprises excepted) do not have a profit motive. They are evaluated on the services they provide or on political considerations. Federal and provincial government employers also enjoy the ability to legislate—an advantage unmatched by their private-sector counterparts. Each of these features can have substantial implications for bargaining dynamics in the public sector.

Political considerations dominate management's view of work stoppages. While strikes normally impose financial hardships on private-sector employers, public employers often save money from a strike if revenues continue. For example, a municipality retains property taxes even if services are interrupted. On the other hand, public-sector strikes frequently disrupt services that are not easily substituted for (e.g., schools) and that affect large numbers of people. Ultimately, the decision about a work stoppage will involve a political assessment of the consequences by the public employer.

The political element in public-sector bargaining translates into substantial efforts by the parties to make their case to the public, particularly with respect to work stoppages. Thus, negotiations may take place not only at the bargaining table but in the media, as each side attempts to win public support. Teachers and hospital workers, for example, usually frame their bargaining demands not in terms of better wages and working conditions but in terms of improvement in the quality of education or health care.[4] Public employers take great pains to justify back-to-work legislation in the name of the public interest, not on the grounds that such tactics enable them to achieve a particular bargaining objective.

Canadian public-sector employers are still groping for the right organizational form for labour relations. The Quebec provincial government developed a highly centralized bargaining structure, but a series of major disputes under this format resulted in legislation forcing a degree of decentralization (Grant, 2000). The City of Vancouver and a dozen surrounding suburban communities have at various times given full bargaining authority to an employers' association as have several municipalities in the British Columbia interior. Several provinces created a small number of health-care regions with budget authority, effectively eliminating individual hospitals from bargaining. In education, provincial bargaining has become widespread as governments seek to control costs (Thomason, 1995). In Quebec and New Brunswick, provincial government officials represent management at the bargaining table in health care and social services negotiations, while a government observer is part of the employer bargaining team in Saskatchewan hospital negotiations (Haiven, 1995). The British Columbia government established a "Public Sector Employer's Council" in 1993 to coordinate bargaining for the entire public sector in the province. It issues wage and benefit guidelines, which effectively bind the various public-sector employers (Thompson, 2000).

Provincial Health Authorities of Alberta: www.phaa.com

British Columbia Public School Employers: www.bcpsea.bc.ca

Federal and provincial governments play a dual role in labour relations. They are both large employers and holders of sovereign authority over their territories, with the power to legislate the rules under which they and their employees must function. The power to legislate tempts governments to adjust labour relations rules in their own self-interest as employers. Between 1991 and 1996, the federal government and most provincial governments rolled back or froze wages for public employees through legislation (Swimmer, 2000).

Employee and Union Differences

Public–private sector differences that exist on the employer side are not matched on the employee and union side to the same degree. Pressures on public-sector union leaders to achieve collective bargaining objectives are not very different than the pressures on their private-sector counterparts. While the subject matter of negotiations might vary between the two sectors, bargaining is still focused on the traditional issues of "wages, hours, and conditions of employment" in both sectors. The major cost of strike action—immediate loss of income—also is the same for public- and private-sector employees. Such costs have similar consequences for employees in the two sectors, except that public-sector workers have little reason to fear their employer will close permanently.

There are, however, demographic differences between public- and private-sector employees, and by extension, their unions. Perhaps most significantly, the public sector employs a higher proportion of women than does the private sector; overall, 57 percent of the public-sector workforce is female. Union density among men and women is very similar; thus 58 percent of public-sector union members are female. In comparison, about one-third of private-sector union members are women (Akyeampong, 1999). Furthermore, the public sector contains a higher proportion of white-collar workers and professionals than does the private sector. These differences mean that whereas most private-sector unions are essentially blue collar and male dominated, public-sector unionism is heavily white collar and female. Similarly, virtually all professionals who engage in collective bargaining are employed in the public sector.

One important implication of these differences is the heightened significance it gives to employment and pay equity issues and anti-discrimination regulations. Public-sector unions with a large female membership have been among the strongest advocates of workplace equity. In 1999, the Public Service Alliance of Canada settled a long-standing pay equity case against the federal government, which resulted in a multi-billion-dollar payout to many women employees who had been found to be underpaid because of their gender. Unions composed of professional employees might also be expected to attempt to negotiate over issues relating to professional concerns, possibly creating clashes over managerial prerogatives and policy (Ponak, 1981). Teacher unions, for example, have bargained over student/teacher ratios, curriculum development, and limits on the inclusion of disabled children in the classroom (Thomason, 1995).

Public Service Alliance of Canada: www.psac.com

Policy and Legislative Distinctions

The right of public employees to unionize and engage in collective bargaining is enshrined in law, much as it is in the private sector. Public employers are obliged to recognize and bargain in good faith with labour organizations that enjoy majority support. Public-sector collective bargaining legislation is extremely diverse, however, compared to the private sector. Whereas private-sector legislation in each of the provinces and at the federal level generally follows principles derived from PC 1003 (enacted in 1944) as well as earlier conciliation legislation (see Chapter 7), there is no similarly accepted framework in the public sector. Hence considerable differences exist in legislation between the public and private sectors and in the treatment of different groups of public employees.

Table 14.4 sets out public-sector labour legislation at the federal level, in each province, and in the two territories. Most jurisdictions have several statutes for public employees. Except for municipal employees, most public employees do not fall under general private-sector labour codes. For example, in seven provinces collective bargaining for teachers is governed either by a special statute established for that purpose (e.g., the *Teachers Collective Bargaining Act* in Nova Scotia), the basic legislation governing education (e.g., the *Public Schools Act* in Manitoba), or some combination of these statutes and the general labour code (e.g., in Ontario).

Even where superficially it may appear that labour relations are governed by the general private-sector statute, as in the case of hospital workers in six provinces, there may be special provisions within the general labour code or in other legislation that create distinctive regulatory procedures. In British Columbia and Newfoundland, for example, hospital unions must negotiate coverage of essential services with their employer prior to striking. In Alberta, provisions of the labour relations code prohibit strikes by hospital workers and set out an arbitration system. In Quebec, other statutes replace the labour code for bargaining structure and the maintenance of essential services (Hébert, 1995; Haiven, 1995).

Public Service Staff Relations Board: www.pssrb-crtfb.gfc.ca

Newfoundland Department of Labour: www.gov.nf.ca/env/Labour

The multiplicity of statutes and diversity of approaches governing the public sector reflect both the absence of a generally accepted labour law model for public employees and the dual role of government as employer. As various groups of public employees

TABLE 14.4

PUBLIC-SECTOR LABOUR LEGISLATION BY JURISDICTION

Jurisdiction	General Private Sector	General Municipal	Police	Firefighters	Hospitals	Teachers	Civil Service	Government Enterprise
Federal	Canada Labour Code	Canada Labour Code	Canada Labour Code	Public Service Staff Relations Act	Public Service Staff Relations Act	Public Service Staff Relations Act	Public Service Staff Relations Act	Canada Labour Code
British Columbia	Labour Relations Code	Labour Relations Code	Labour Relations Code/Fire and Police Service Collective Bargaining Act	Labour Relations Code/Fire and Police Service Collective Bargaining Act	Labour Relations Code/Health Authorities Act	Labour Relations Code	Public Service Labour Relations Act/Labour Relations Code	Labour Relations Code
Alberta	Labour Relations Code	Labour Relations Code	Police Officers Collective Bargaining Act/Police Act	Labour Relations Code	Labour Relations Code	Labour Relations Code/School Act	Public Service Employee Relations Act	Labour Relations Code
Saskatchewan	Trade Union Act	Trade Union Act	Police Act	Fire Department Platoon Act	Trade Union Act	Education Act	Trade Union Act	Trade Union Act
Manitoba	Labour Relations Act	Labour Relations Act	Labour Relations Act/Police Act/City of Winnipeg Act	Labour Relations Act/Fire Departments Arbitration Act	Labour Relations Act/Essential Services Act	Public Schools Act	Civil Service Act/Essential Services Act	Labour Relations Act
Ontario	Labour Relations Act	Labour Relations Act	Police Services Act/Public Service Act (Ontario Provincial Police)/Public Sector Dispute Resolution Act	Fire Protection and Prevention Act/Public Sector Dispute Resolution Act	Labour Relations Act/Hospital Labour Disputes Arbitration Act/Public Sector Disputes Resolution Act	Labour Relations Act/Education Quality Improvement Act	Crown Employees Collective Bargaining Act	Crown Employees Collective Bargaining Act
Quebec	Labour Code	Labour Code	Labour Code/Police Act	Labour Code	Labour Code/Public Service Act	Labour Code	Labour Code/Public Service Act	Labour Code/Public Service Act
New Brunswick	Industrial Relations Act	Industrial Relations Act	Industrial Relations Act/Police Act	Industrial Relations Act	Public Service Labour Relations Act	Public Service Labour Relations Act	Public Service Labour Relations Act/Civil Service Act	Public Service Labour Relations Act

TABLE 14.4 (CONTINUED)

PUBLIC-SECTOR LABOUR LEGISLATION BY JURISDICTION

Jurisdiction	General Private Sector	General Municipal	Police	Firefighters	Hospitals	Teachers	Civil Service	Government Enterprise
Nova Scotia	Trade Union Act	Trade Union Act	Trade Union Act	Trade Union Act	Trade Union Act	Teacher's Collective Bargaining Act	Civil Service Collective Bargaining Act/Highway Workers Collective Bargaining Act	Trade Union Act
Prince Edward Island	Labour Act	Labour Act	Labour Act/Police Act	Labour Act	Labour Act	School Act	Civil Service Act	Civil Service Act
Newfoundland	Labour Relations Act	Labour Relations Act	Labour Relations Act/Royal Newfoundland Constabulary Act	Labour Relations Act/City of St. John's Fire Department Act	Public Service Collective Bargaining Act	Teacher's Collective Bargaining Act	Public Service Collective Bargaining Act	Public Service Collective Bargaining Act/Labour Relations Act (Hydro)
Yukon	Canada Labour Code	Canada Labour Code	—	—	Canada Labour Code	Education Act	Public Service Staff Relations Act	—
Northwest Territories	Canada Labour Code	Canada Labour Code	—	—	—	Public Service Act	Public Service Act	—

Source: Applicable statutes as of January, 2000. Reproduced with the permission of the Minister of Labour, 2000.

sought enabling legislation for collective bargaining, legislators experimented freely (Goldenberg, 1988), while protecting their own and the public interest. As well, the early experience with bargaining differed widely across the country, again giving rise to distinct regulatory approaches. For example, Ontario's decision to enact a specific statute to regulate labour relations for teachers, complete with its own tribunal and extensive fact-finding provisions, reflected a particularly volatile initial bargaining experience in that province (Downie, 1992).

While it is difficult to generalize, public-sector statutes differ most from the private-sector model in three areas. First, there tends to be less discretion given to labour relations boards with respect to *certification and recognition*. A number of statutes—for example, the federal *Public Service Staff Relations Act* (Finkleman and Goldenberg, 1983)—have established occupational bargaining units, an approach very different from the discretion given labour boards in the private sector. British Columbia established three bargaining units under its provincial civil service law (PSLRA) as did the Northwest Territories under its Public Service Act. Also in contrast to private-sector practice, a number of organizations were granted statutory representation rights, particularly in the case of teachers' unions, faculty associations, and to a lesser degree, civil service unions.

A second area of difference has been the tendency to restrict the ***scope of bargaining*** in many parts of the public sector. Private-sector negotiators are almost universally free to bargain over whatever issues they choose. General private-sector labour code requirements that bargaining proceed over "wages, hours, and working conditions" have been interpreted very liberally. Less negotiating latitude is permitted under a variety of public-sector statutes. The PSSRA removes classifications; criteria for promotion, transfers, and layoffs; technological change; and pensions from the scope of bargaining. Similar constraints on bargaining scope are found in a majority of provincial civil service statutes. Local government employees, teachers, and hospital employees are frequently covered by non-negotiable pension plans. The negotiating scope for police and firefighters may be limited, particularly with respect to disciplinary arrangements and superior–subordinate relations, owing to the paramilitary nature of these services. Since the early 1980s, many governments have legislated temporary wage controls, effectively removing wages from the negotiations during some rounds of bargaining.

Dispute resolution procedures provide a third, and the most controversial, major area of legislative difference between the public and the private sectors. Almost all private-sector employees enjoy a right to strike over the renegotiation of a collective agreement once certain preconditions (e.g., a strike vote) have been satisfied. Public-sector employees, by comparison, are much more fettered (see Exhibit 14.4). Frequently their right to strike is removed and replaced by arbitration, even in situations, as for New Brunswick firefighters and Alberta nurses, in which a general labour code provides basic statutory coverage. If strikes are permitted, the preconditions are normally more severe than in the private sector. Quebec public employees cannot withdraw their services until agreement is reached on maintaining certain functions deemed essential; federal civil servants must participate in a two-stage conciliation process before their right to strike becomes operative; and fact-finding is a precondition to work stoppages for Ontario teachers.

The proclamation of the *Charter of Rights and Freedoms* in 1982 was initially viewed by unions as a vehicle for challenging some of the restrictions in public-sector legislation. A series of Supreme Court decisions, however, have limited the Charter's impact (Swinton, 1995). In three decisions that together are referred to as the Labour Trilogy,[5] the Supreme Court ruled that freedom of association does not include the right to strike, the right to bargain collectively, or the right to choose a bargaining agent. These decisions enable governments to continue to restrict the right to strike for certain employees; uphold various bargaining restrictions, particularly wage controls; and leave unchanged the statutory naming of bargaining representatives. While the decisions did not give new constitutional protection to labour to strike or bargain collectively, neither did they undermine traditional union strength (Swinton, 1995).

EXHIBIT 14.4

PRIVATE- VS. PUBLIC-SECTOR LEGISLATION

BARGAINING
- Private—almost everything is negotiable
- Public—variety of restrictions on what can be bargained and arbitrated

CERTIFICATION
- Private—any bona fide labour organization can represent employees; labour board determines bargaining unit
- Public—labour organization may be specified in legislation; employee choice restricted; bargaining units established in legislation

STRIKES
- Private—almost all employees have the right to strike
- Public—many employees prohibited from striking or must carry out certain designated services during a strike

WAGES
- Private—unions and employers bargain over wage rates
- Public—wages set unilaterally by legislation during parts of 1970s, 1980s, and 1990s

STRIKES AND DISPUTE PROCEDURES

Of all the issues in the public sector, the treatment of strikes has been the most difficult. Policy-makers are clearly divided, as demonstrated by the diversity of dispute resolution procedures in use. For example, half the provinces allow their civil service to strike, the other half do not. Teachers have the right to strike in most provinces, but not in Manitoba or Prince Edward Island. Both advocates and opponents of a right to strike can offer strong arguments in support of their position (see Exhibit 14.5).

Opponents of strike rights for public employees make their case mainly on the grounds that public-sector work stoppages impose too much inconvenience on the public. Private-sector disputes often do not affect third parties seriously, since there are usually substitutes available for products cut off by strikes. This is in sharp contrast with the public sector. The effects of strikes by teachers, postal workers, air traffic controllers, and transit workers, among others, inevitably go beyond the employees and employers directly involved at the bargaining table, disrupting heavily used and irreplaceable services. In stoppages involving employees such as hospital workers, police, and firefighters, service interruptions may pose immediate danger to the health and safety of those who by necessity rely on the struck services. For these reasons alone, it is argued, public employees should be prohibited from striking.

These arguments have not gone unchallenged. Analysis of public employee strikes suggests that damage to the public is much less than commonly claimed (Adell, Grant, Ponak, 2000; Gunderson, 1995). Many public-sector employees perform services that

EXHIBIT 14.5

ARGUMENTS FOR AND AGAINST PUBLIC-SECTOR STRIKES

RESTRICT PUBLIC-SECTOR STRIKES
- Strikes inconvenience and possibly endanger the public.
- They give unions too much power leading to over-generous wages and working conditions.
- They create destabilizing and tumultuous political confrontations.

PERMIT PUBLIC-EMPLOYEE STRIKES
- Strike impact is exaggerated; most public employees are not essential.
- Techniques are available to ensure truly essential services are maintained, reducing public risk.
- Strike substitutes, like arbitration, are inefficient and produce poor contracts.

are not essential, at least in the short run. In truly essential services, techniques exist to protect the public during work stoppages, such as requirements that certain essential employees remain at work. Recent research has shown that managers and employees can be remarkably innovative at providing essential services even in the face of a complete withdrawal of services (Adell, Grant, and Ponak, 2000).

But the strongest argument in favour of the right to strike in the public sector lies in the lack of acceptable substitutes for strikes. Removing the right to strike from the collective bargaining process necessarily implies replacing it with some other mechanism capable of resolving disputes. Many of those who defend the right to strike contend that they are not so much enamoured of the strike weapon as they are disillusioned with the alternatives, such as arbitration and final-offer selection (Weiler, 1980). Strike substitutes are criticized on the grounds that they weaken the collective bargaining process, lead to excessive third-party intervention, and generally produce inferior collective agreements (Ponak and Falkenberg, 1989).

Public-Sector Strike Record

To help assess the debate about the right to strike, it is important to begin with an examination of the strike record. Table 14.5 presents public-sector strike frequency and volume (person-days lost) from 1975 to 1998, inclusive, and also shows public-sector strike frequency and volume as a proportion of the economy-wide strike frequency and volume (public and private sectors combined). There are wide fluctuations from year to year both in terms of absolute public-sector strike volume and frequency and the public sector's share of overall strike activity. These yearly fluctuations notwithstanding, there has been a discernible decline in annual public-sector strike activity since 1984. From 1975 to 1984, the average annual public-sector strike volume was relatively constant at

TABLE 14.5

PUBLIC-SECTOR WORK STOPPAGES BY YEAR

YEAR	NUMBER OF WORK STOPPAGES	AS A PERCENTAGE OF TOTAL WORK STOPPAGES IN CANADA	PERSON-DAYS LOST (IN THOUSANDS)	AS A PERCENTAGE OF TOTAL PERSON-DAYS LOST IN CANADA
1975	234	20.0	2025	18.6
1976	225	21.6	2219	19.2
1977	191	23.7	801	24.1
1978	212	20.1	1189	16.1
1979	208	19.8	2385	30.5
1975–79 (mean)	*214*	*20.9*	*1724*	*21.1*
1980	244	23.7	3194	35.0
1981	271	25.8	2211	25.0
1982	121	17.8	895	15.7
1983	95	14.7	2129	47.9
1984	108	15.1	572	14.7
1980–84 (mean)	*168*	*20.4*	*1800*	*28.1*
1985	158	19.1	628	20.1
1986	128	17.1	796	11.1
1987	105	15.7	885	23.2
1988	76	13.9	2167	44.2
1989	139	22.2	1658	44.8
1985–89 (mean)	*121*	*17.7*	*1267*	*27.0*
1990	119	20.6	786	15.5
1991	115	24.8	1429	56.5
1992	80	19.8	496	23.4
1993	85	22.3	362	22.6
1994	55	14.7	414	25.8
1990–94 (mean)	*91*	*20.7*	*696*	*27.1*
1995	55	16.8	183	11.6
1996	76	23.0	1393	41.6
1997	59	20.8	1971	54.6
1998	119	31.5	642	26.0
1995–98 (mean)	*77*	*23.3*	*1047*	*38.0*

Source: Calculations based on special data from Workplace Information Directorate, Human Resources Development Canada. Reproduced with the permission of the Minister of Public Works and Government Services (formerly Supply and Services) and the Minister of Labour.

approximately 1.8 million days lost per year. Afterwards, annual public-sector strike volume declined by more than one-third. The number of public-sector strikes has shown a consistent downward trend as well, from an average of more than 200 strikes per year in the late 1970s to less than half of that number in the 1990s.

Part of the explanation for the decline in public-sector frequency and volume lies in the general decline in work stoppages experienced by Canada and most other industrial countries since the late 1980s (see Chapter 11). At the same time as public-sector strike volume has been declining, the public sector's share of strike activity has increased. In the last half of the 1990s, public employees accounted for approximately 38 percent of all person-days lost in Canada, up from approximately 27 percent in the previous 10 years. Thus, while it can be said that public-sector strike activity is declining, it is equally true that public-sector strikes loom much larger within the overall Canadian industrial relations system. Concern about public-sector work stoppages, therefore, is not misplaced.

Compulsory Arbitration

Compulsory arbitration is a substitute for strikes in the Canadian public sector. Because public-sector strikes inconvenience the public and pose political risks to elected officials, they are frequently prohibited by law and replaced by arbitration. Several forms of arbitration exist. The most common format in Canada is *conventional interest arbitration*. Under this system, if the negotiating parties cannot reach a settlement, they submit their differences to an arbitrator (or arbitration panel) who issues a binding award based on the parties' arguments. This award becomes, in effect, the new collective agreement. Under conventional arbitration procedures, arbitrators are free either to accept the position that one of the parties has submitted or to fashion their own solution on any particular issue.

Where compulsory arbitration systems are in place they have eliminated virtually all work stoppages. Misgivings about arbitration are not based on its effectiveness at preventing strikes, but rather on the effect it has on the likelihood of the parties reaching agreement during negotiations. Canadian industrial relations place a high value on the ability of labour and management to resolve differences themselves through the give and take of the bargaining process. Almost all available evidence indicates that conventional arbitration systems lead to a lower rate of negotiated settlements than do systems in which strikes are permitted. After a review of major empirical studies up to 1988, Ponak and Falkenberg (1989) estimated that right-to-strike systems achieved settlement rates of 90 percent, but that under conventional arbitration systems settlement rates fell to between 65 and 70 percent. Similar results have been reported for the Ontario public sector (Rose and Piczak, 1996).

The ability of parties to settle their differences under conventional arbitration is reduced because the possibility of an arbitration award is not a sufficient threat to induce the tough compromises necessary to reach a settlement. The possibility of a strike, by comparison, usually is a sufficient threat. It is important to note, however, that the parties do reach agreement in at least 65 percent of their negotiations, demonstrating their fundamental preference for negotiated settlement.

In an effort to encourage the parties to reach agreement in the absence of a strike threat, *final-offer selection* (FOS) has been suggested (Stevens, 1966). Under FOS, the arbitrator must choose, without alteration, either the position submitted by management or that submitted by the union. Arbitrators cannot, as they can under conventional arbitration, split the difference between the positions submitted by the two parties; rather, they are obliged to accept one party's position or the other's. The idea behind FOS is that the two parties would rather make the concessions needed to achieve settlement during negotiations than face the risk of an arbitration award in which the other side's position, in its entirety, could be incorporated into the new collective agreement.

Final-offer selection is required in several statutes in the United States, especially for police and firefighters, but is rarely used in Canada. Although the US experience generally shows that FOS is capable of producing a higher rate of negotiated settlements than conventional arbitration, it is rejected in Canada by all parties, arbitrators included. FOS can lead to poor collective agreements if neither side submits reasonable proposals and it produces a damaging win–lose mentality in the labour–management relationship. Under conventional arbitration, in contrast, the arbitrator is able to fashion a decision that is likely to reflect some compromise between the final positions submitted by the two sides.

Designation Model

Lack of confidence in arbitration led to development of a dispute resolution model that permits strikes and protects the public. First introduced in the federal sector (PSSRA), the designation model is now used for at least part of the public sectors in six provinces (Adell, Grant, and Ponak, 2000). This approach permits work stoppages but requires that certain employees be "designated" to remain on the job to provide essential services. The number and role of such employees is generally subject to negotiation between the parties and, in the absence of agreement, a labour relations tribunal makes the final determination. Under the PSSRA, the proportion of employees designated within a given bargaining unit has varied from 2 percent or less among librarians and social science support services to 100 percent of air traffic controllers, firefighters, and veterinary scientists (Swimmer, 1995).[6] In Montreal, transit workers may strike but must provide service during rush hour. In British Columbia, up to 65 percent of striking nurses were required to remain at work, depending on the services they were providing.

In theory, the regulated strike model could satisfy the needs of policy-makers, unions, and employers. The union exercises its right to strike. It is under pressure to settle because the majority of its members are forgoing their paycheques and the employer is in partial operation. The employer is under pressure because it is unable to provide normal levels of service and may be forced to mount a strenuous effort to maintain even its limited operations. The public interest is protected because the designated employees maintain essential services.

EXHIBIT 14.6

NEGOTIATING THE LEVEL OF ESSENTIAL SERVICES

In an interview, a British Columbia management negotiator summed up his frustration with the difficulty of negotiating the level of essential services as follows:

"It's...massive, time consuming, incredibly wasteful...the essential services process. I would say without exaggeration in the fifteen years I've been a labour negotiator, of all the things I've done, however cooperative or uncooperative they've been in the union-management process, it is the most single wasteful exercise."

Source: Adell, Grant, and Ponak, 2000.

In practice, it becomes obvious that designating the "correct" proportion of bargaining unit personnel is crucial to the success of this dispute procedure. If too many employees are designated, the pressure on the employer may be inconsequential; if too few employees are at work, even minimum service requirements may not be met and the union may enjoy a bargaining advantage. Thus, negotiations between the union and employer to determine the proportion of employees who will not strike are often difficult and protracted. For example, in the face of an impending strike of 2000 non-professional employees at the Vancouver General Hospital, management took the position that all 2000 employees were essential, while the union claimed that none of its members should have to "scab on their own union's strike" (Weiler, 1980). Eventually the labour board designated 100 employees as essential. In an excellent review of essential service procedures during nurses' strikes in five provinces between 1988 and 1991, Haiven (1995) found that labour tribunals tend to set designation levels too high, preferring to err on the side of caution. In one Quebec hospital, 110 percent of the usual nurse complement was required during a tight labour market for nurses. Even with high levels of coverage, Haiven found that many hospitals failed to prepare adequately for strikes, resulting in chaotic conditions.

Recent research concludes that, despite the practical difficulties of implementation so vividly described in Exhibit 14.6, the designation model has great potential to satisfy the conflicting interests of all participants. Moreover, there is good evidence that the parties gain confidence over several rounds of bargaining and that, after some frustrating early experience, subsequent negotiations over which services to maintain prove easier (Haiven, 1995; Adell, Grant, Ponak, 2000). For these reasons, the designation model is likely to continue to spread within the public sector.

Emergency Legislation

Legislation to end particular strikes has long been a feature of the public sector. Table 14.6 shows that 76 public employee strikes, the great majority of which were legal, were terminated through special legislation between 1965 and 1999. In most cases, arbitration

TABLE 14.6

EMERGENCY LEGISLATION IN THE PUBLIC SECTOR

YEAR	FEDERAL	QUEBEC	ONTARIO	BC	SASK.	OTHERS	TOTAL
1950–64	0	0	0	0	0	0	0
1965–69	0	4	1	0	1	1	7
1970–74	0	2	2	1	0	0	5
1975–79	2	5	6	4	1	0	18
1980–84	0	8	3	1	2	3	17
1985–89	2	3	2	1	3	0	11
1990–94	2	1	3	2	0	0	8
1995–99	2	1	2	2	2	1	10
Total	8	24	19	11	9	5	76

Source: Updated from Thompson and Ponak (1995, Table 15-9), and Human Resources Development Canada, Highlights of Major Developments in Labour Legislation, 1993–94 to 1998–99 (HRDC Website).

was also invoked to resolve the issues in dispute once the strike was terminated, but more recently, as was the case in the postal workers' strike in 1997 and the Saskatchewan nurses' strike in 1999, the legislation also set the actual wages and terms and conditions of employment. Thus, in these disputes the final contours of the collective agreement were not left to the determination of an arbitrator, but were set unilaterally through legislation by the employer.

The use of special legislation has not been evenly distributed across the country. One-third of the back-to-work laws were enacted in Quebec, a province marked by particularly tumultuous public-sector disputes as well as a tradition of legislative intervention in industrial relations (Grant, 2000). Given the relatively small size of its workforce, Saskatchewan has also seen a high utilization of legislation to end strikes. Conversely, the federal government has resorted to legislation infrequently.

The incidence of back-to-work legislation peaked in the 1975 to 1984 period and has been relatively stable at a lower level since. The decline as well as the overall impact of government reliance on emergency legislation have sparked considerable debate. Some observers believe that the use of special legislation to end otherwise legal strikes is part of a fundamental retreat by governments from any kind of free collective bargaining system for public employees (Haiven, McBride, and Shields, 1991; Panitch and Swartz, 1993).

Other observers are less ready to accept that frequent use of back-to-work legislation marks the end of free collective bargaining in the public sector (Thompson and Swimmer, 1995; Swimmer, 2000). Strike activity in the public sector has dropped substantially, a function of general economic circumstances, labour market conditions, and mature bargaining relationships. As well, the need for governments to intervene has been reduced by the introduction of sophisticated labour tribunals like the Essential Services Commission in Quebec and the spread of the designation model. While critical of the overuse of back-to-work laws, these observers argue that the incidence of such legislation is declining for sound industrial relations reasons.

COMPENSATION ISSUES

Questions surrounding public employee compensation, though less visible than those involving dispute resolution, have proven almost as troublesome. From the inception of collective bargaining, a public perception arose that government employees were overpaid and too successful at winning generous wage increases. Private employers complained that government wage settlements established patterns that the private sector, limited by profit-loss considerations, could not match. Union officials countered by claiming that such allegations were untrue and that seemingly high wage increases reflected the need of some groups of low-paid public employees to catch up to the private sector. Furthermore, union officials argued, even if a few government employees were paid more than their private-sector counterparts, there was nothing inherently wrong with government being a wage leader. Public employers should be model employers, setting standards for the rest of the community.

Public–Private Wage Differentials

Philosophies and perceptions aside, the following factors suggest that compensation in the public sector will usually exceed the private sector (Gunderson, 1995):

1. Political pressures are less stringent than the profit constraint.
2. There is pressure on government to be a model employer.
3. The public sector is more highly unionized.
4. Wage surveys on which public-sector wage increases are based tend to focus on large, higher-paying private employers.
5. Public employers have the ability to defer costs to future taxpayers.

There are also reasons for public-sector compensation to lag the private sector. First, the public sector has traditionally provided more job security than the private sector, which should lead to a private-sector wage premium. Second, the public sector is much more likely to be singled out for special wage restraints, depressing wages. Third, government is much more likely to intervene in public-sector strikes, depriving more powerful public-sector unions of the opportunity to win large wage increases (Gunderson, 1995). For a number of occupations, like university professors, the public sector is effectively the only employer (monopsony power), giving the employer a bargaining power few private-sector employers enjoy.

Empirical studies confirm that the upward bias outweighs the downward pressures, although the difference is not large. Data show that public employees enjoy a wage premium of between 5 and 10 percent more than their private-sector counterparts, and that public-sector fringe benefits are slightly more generous than in the private sector. The public-sector advantage is greatest at the provincial and local level, is larger for women than for men, is greater at the lower ranges of the pay scales, is negative at senior levels, and has been diminishing for a number of years. The research also shows that there is no significant spillover effect from the public to the private sector; i.e., public-sector wage levels do not drive up wages in the private sector (Gunderson, 1995). The studies upon which these conclusions are based predate the wage controls introduced in the early 1990s and the reversal in public-sector employment growth. Taking these factors into account may well demonstrate that the public-sector wage premium has disappeared. Indeed, the federal government has had to offer special bonuses to hire and retain staff in certain high-demand occupations.

Further insight into public- and private-sector wage differentials can be gained by examining time series data on wage changes in the two sectors. Table 14.7 reports annual wage increases between 1979 and 1999, based on collective agreements involving 500 or more employees. It shows the wage changes for the private and public sectors as a whole and also disaggregates the public-sector data by major group. From the table it can be observed that since 1979, unionized private-sector employees have received substantially higher cumulative wage increases than unionized public employees. Between 1979 and 1999, private-sector employees won wage increases of 156 percent; public employee wages increased by 140 percent. In only six of twenty years did public employees negotiate higher wage settlements than their private-sector counterparts. Since 1990, the private sector has always been ahead. Looking at the various components of the public sector, we can see in Table 14.7 that local government employees received the largest overall wage increases and that federal government employees received the lowest increases. Taking the data in this table as a whole, there is no support for the contention that unionized public-sector wage settlements have outstripped those in the private sector; indeed the reverse appears true.

Public-Sector Wage Controls

The imposition of wage controls during the 1980s and 1990s targeted exclusively at public employees caused public-sector wage increases to lag those in the private sector. The federal Anti-Inflation Program of 1975 covered both the public and private sectors, but it showed governments that restricting the compensation of public-sector workers was attractive politically.

The first round of wage restraint programs aimed exclusively at the public sector was initiated in the early 1980s when the Canadian economy fell into a severe recession, causing government revenues to fall sharply. With the encouragement of Prime Minister Pierre Elliott Trudeau, every province in the country restricted public-sector compensation in

TABLE 14.7

AVERAGE ANNUAL PERCENTAGE WAGE CHANGES, MAJOR COLLECTIVE AGREEMENTS, 1979–1999

YEAR	OVERALL PRIVATE	OVERALL PUBLIC	FEDERAL	PROVINCIAL	LOCAL	EDUCATION/ HEALTH/ WELFARE	CROWN	UTILITIES
1979	10.8	9.2	8.4	9.1	9.4	8.2	12.4	9.1
1980	11.6	10.9	11.3	11.3	10.8	10.8	11.1	10.2
1981	12.7	13.2	12.7	13.5	12.7	13.5	12.7	13.3
1982	9.7	10.6	8.3	11.8	12.1	11.4	10.6	12.3
1983	5.4	4.6	5.5	5.0	5.7	3.6	5.6	6.6
1984	3.2	3.9	5.0	5.2	3.3	3.1	4.6	2.6
1985	3.4	3.8	3.2	4.4	4.7	3.4	4.0	3.4
1986	3.0	3.8	3.6	3.9	4.9	3.6	3.7	2.8
1987	3.8	4.2	3.4	4.5	4.2	4.2	2.6	2.0
1988	4.9	3.9	3.5	4.3	4.6	3.8	3.1	3.0
1989	5.3	5.3	4.2	5.7	6.1	5.9	4.0	5.0
1990	5.9	5.6	5.3	5.8	4.9	5.4	4.5	5.3
1991	4.3	3.5	1.7	3.9	5.1	3.8	4.4	2.3
1992	2.3	1.5	1.7	1.0	4.6	1.4	3.0	3.1
1993	0.9	0.5	0.0	0.3	0.7	0.7	2.3	1.5
1994	1.2	0.0	0.0	0.1	0.8	0.3	2.0	0.3
1995	1.4	0.6	0.0	0.9	0.6	0.5	0.8	0.4
1996	1.7	0.5	0.0	0.2	1.1	0.5	0.4	0.9
1997	1.8	1.2	3.2	1.2	1.2	1.0	1.4	1.6
1998	1.8	1.6	2.2	1.6	1.5	1.3	2.2	1.4
1999	2.2	1.9	3.1	1.6	2.0	1.7	2.3	2.4
Cumulative (%)	155.9	139.5	130.5	150.2	165.0	132.1	156.4	143.7

Source: Data until 1992 based on Appendix A and Appendix B in Gunderson (1995), both of which were compiled from Labour Canada, Bureau of Labour Information, *Major Wage Settlements;* data from 1992–1999 from Statistics Canada, *Wage Increases in Collective Agreements*, CANSIM matrix 4049.

1982 and 1983, either through a formal system of wage controls or through spending limits. A review of the impact of the restraint programs in British Columbia, Manitoba, Ontario, and New Brunswick, found that: (1) there was no direct relationship between provincial economic growth and the degree of restraint; (2) wage increases varied considerably among different groups within the public sector of each province; and (3) the number of provincial civil servants rose during the restraint period (Thompson, 1988).

The wage restraint programs of the 1980s generally lasted no more than three years (with the exception of British Columbia where controls remained until 1987). However, shortly after collective bargaining over wages resumed in the early 1990s, a new round of wage controls began, again confined to the public sector. The main impetus for the new restraint programs was pressure on government to reduce spending to tackle public debt. Wage control programs also fit well with sentiment in favour of a smaller role for government and were part of broader campaigns that included privatization, contracting-out, layoffs, and reduction in services.

Beginning in 1991, seven provinces plus the federal government passed legislation either reducing or freezing wages. In some cases, the controls were introduced in stages, with subsequent stages harsher than the initial stage. In Newfoundland, Nova Scotia, and Manitoba, wage freezes introduced in 1991 were followed by wage rollbacks in 1994 (Swimmer, 2000; Fryer, 1995). The Quebec Liberal government legislated wage freezes in 1992 and 1993; the subsequent Parti Québécois government achieved similar results by negotiations beginning in 1995. To reduce some of the pain, rollbacks in many provinces were achieved, at least partially, through unpaid days off work. In Manitoba, for example, employees had ten unpaid days off, which accounted for most of their wage reduction.

None of the three westernmost provinces, Saskatchewan, Alberta, and British Columbia, imposed wage controls through legislation. Instead, wage restraints were introduced through bargaining after significant public-sector funding reductions. The Alberta provincial government embarked on a program to reduce funding to health care, education, and its own administration by more than 20 percent over three years. At the same time, public employees were asked to take a 5 percent pay cut. In the collective bargaining that followed, most groups agreed reluctantly to wage reductions, usually in the form of a combination of unpaid days off and outright salary decreases (Ponak, Reshef, Taras, 2000). In Saskatchewan, an NDP government used mutual gains bargaining in 1995 to conclude a three-year agreement with annual increases of 1 percent and job guarantees for the first year of the contract (Swimmer, 2000). The British Columbia government, which enjoyed the benefit of a buoyant economy longer than the rest of the country, followed a four-year contract that had provided modest increases with two years of negotiated wage freezes beginning in 1998 (Swimmer, 2000).

The most tumultuous wage restraint exercise took place in Ontario. In the first part of the 1990s, the NDP government, faced with a ballooning deficit, attempted to negotiate a combination of cost savings and public-sector restructuring with close to 1 million public employees represented by several different unions. In doing so, it asked that existing collective agreements be reopened and scheduled wage increases rescinded. Public-sector unions bitterly opposed the Ontario government's approach. Negotiated agreements, which included a combination of wage reductions and unpaid days, were ultimately achieved with most unions. But bargaining took place under a government deadline, after which the Social Contract Act—which contained the government's contract objectives—was to go into effect. The labour organizations that had helped elect the NDP government felt betrayed (Fryer, 1995), and this disenchantment was a major factor in the government's defeat and replacement by a Conservative government led by Mike Harris in 1995. The new government enacted legislation that removed important job protections (like successor rights in the event of privatization) and then negotiated a four-year contract with no wage increases. This contract was signed after a five-week strike and union-orchestrated "days of protest" amidst calls for a province-wide general strike (Swimmer, 2000).

In a recent review of the wage control experience in the 1990s, Swimmer (2000) concluded that the governments that achieved reductions through negotiations were just as successful at meeting their fiscal goals as governments that relied on legislated solutions. In particular, the jurisdiction that engaged in the most co-operative bargaining approach, the province of Saskatchewan, also managed to achieve the highest relative budgetary surplus (as measured against provincial GDP) in 1997. Ontario and Quebec, which relied on a combination of legislation and adversarial bargaining, remained in the worst relative deficit positions.

CONCLUSIONS

Public-sector collective bargaining has gone through three distinct phases. The first phase, which lasted from the 1960s until the early 1980s, was marked by rapid unionization, the liberalization of labour laws, strong public-sector employment growth, and high wage settlements as unions sought to "catch up" to the private sector. This phase, then, can be thought of as an expansionary one both in terms of public-sector collective bargaining and of the role of government in general.

The second phase, which lasted through most of the 1980s, was one of restraint. It was characterized by wage controls aimed exclusively at public employees and by low wage settlements even in the absence of formal controls. Employment growth began to slow, unions reached a saturation point in terms of public-sector organizing opportunities, and strike volume began to decline, although at a slower rate than in the private sector. Public-sector labour laws remained largely intact, but it was obvious that governments could and would suspend such laws to impose wage controls, issue back-to-work orders, or deem entire groups of employees as essential and hence unable to strike. Federal and provincial governments, though proclaiming the virtues of the emerging philosophies favouring less government, had not as yet abandoned Canada's traditional commitment to an active public sector.

The third phase in public-sector collective bargaining, a period of retrenchment, began in the 1990s. This phase has been characterized by a commitment on the part of governments to reduce the size of the public sector through privatization and contracting-out and through outright decreases in government services. Layoffs have become a common feature of public employment, reversing a long tradition of job security as an important ingredient of government employment. The 1990s also saw the widespread renewal of public-sector wage restraints, with significant wage decreases for many employees. Time lost due to public-sector strikes has continued to decline.

The events in this latest phase of public-sector collective bargaining have been driven by two developments. One has been a change in the way in which governments view their own role, resulting in reductions in the part governments play in many spheres of economic, social, and cultural activities. The rethinking of the philosophical limits of government coincided with a period of recession and high public debt, which placed practical limits on the scope of government undertakings. As a result, severe pressures were placed on the public-sector collective bargaining system as unions, employees, and public-sector managers all attempted to cope with a very different environment than the one that shaped the original contours of the system.

The future of collective bargaining for public employees will depend on several factors. First, it is difficult to envision a genuine collective bargaining system if wages and benefits are excluded from negotiations because of legislated wage controls (or the threat of legislation, which has much the same effect). Since the early 1980s, public employees in the federal jurisdiction and in most provinces have seen their wages controlled through legislation for long periods. The first period of controls lasted approximately three years, after which there was a return to wage bargaining, and then a second round of controls was introduced. These controls lasted for much of the 1990s and were only lifted after governments had largely eliminated their budget deficits. Some semblance of real collective bargaining had resumed at the end of the 1990s, but unions remain very wary of further government intervention.

Wage controls may well become a fixture in the public sector as a way of attacking the overall debt and reducing personal taxes, and because controls on public employee compensation may be seen as consistent with the goal of reducing government. Moreover, politicians have correctly concluded that controlling the wages of public employees is politically popular and that union attempts to fight controls have thus far been largely ineffectual. As a result, wage control programs hold few political risks, making them relatively easy to establish. A meaningful system of collective bargaining is unlikely under permanent wage controls. Erosion of the quality of services under wage restraint is slow, but likely to be inevitable.

The fate of the right to strike is a second factor that will affect the future development of industrial relations in the public sector. Strike volume in the public sector has declined sharply since the mid-1980s, a trend consistent with the drop in private-sector strike activity. However, the decline in public-sector strikes may be attributable to the effect of wage controls (which removes an often contentious issue from negotiations) and the willingness of governments to use back-to-work legislation if necessary. If wage controls are lifted, a dramatic increase in public-sector strike activity might follow, especially if employees attempt to recoup the losses of the wage control period. This in turn could produce more legislation to end strikes. A collective bargaining system in which one of the more important rules (i.e., the right to strike) constantly changes is one that is likely to be marked by a great deal of frustration, mistrust, and turbulence. The designation model may hold promise of establishing a set of rules that both parties can accept, thereby providing more stability.

A third factor that will help determine the future direction of public-sector collective bargaining is the response of unions. Unions representing public employees are the largest in the country and make up half the labour movement. Despite this apparent strength, they have been unsuccessful at reversing policies that are clearly contrary to the interests of their members. Contracting-out frequently results in the transfer of jobs to nonunion and lower-paid workers; the sale of government assets typically results in job losses; and reductions in government services usually mean layoffs. Even where services have been diminished, union leaders have seldom been able to rally a general public that is more likely to see public-sector unions as a narrowly based interest group.

Given this environment, a number of union strategies have been suggested. One set of strategies involves relying on the traditional union tool of negotiations to attempt to obtain contract language that will protect union members. Reliance on negotiations often is buttressed by extensive use of litigation before arbitration tribunals, labour boards, and courts (Thompson, 1995). The Canadian Union of Postal Workers has employed this strategy to achieve, among other things, limits on contracting-out and a high degree of job protection in the event of work rationalization. At least one observer has suggested that the viability of this approach is dependent on the internal efficiency of the union itself and that a number of public-sector unions need to significantly improve the delivery of union services to their membership if they hope to advance their collective bargaining agenda (Rose, 1995).

A second set of strategies involves enhancing overall union power through the building of coalitions and alliances with other unions and with community-based groups (Panitch and Swartz, 1993; Rose, 1995). It has been noted that unions have not even been able to coordinate their activities within a particular sector. For instance, the four or five health-care unions found in each province (e.g., nurses, support staff, technicians) have rarely established strong working relationships. Where inter-union alliances have been formed, they have strengthened union power considerably. Examples include Quebec Common Front actions involving most of the province's public-sector unions, the coalition of private- and public-sector unions formed in British Columbia in 1983 to oppose anti-union legislation, and the co-operation between the National Union of Provincial and General Employees and the Public Service Alliance of Canada during the latter's nationwide strike in 1991. In each one these cases, the coordination contributed to whatever degree of union success was achieved.

Finally, a former public-sector union leader suggests that unions must be much more willing to jettison their traditional adversarial mentality if they are to have any hope of achieving tangible gains for their members (Fryer, 1995). It is argued that the economic realities of the 1990s gave governments very little choice but to reduce the level and scope of the public sector. While recognizing that problem solving is a two-way street, Fryer argues that public-sector unions can be most effective by attempting to work together with governments to bring about necessary changes while protecting the interests of their members. The approach taken in British Columbia through sectoral negotiations is seen as a model for this kind of strategy.

Even if union leaders prove capable of devising new strategies, it is likely that the expansion phase of public-sector collective bargaining has ended. Collective bargaining can still flourish, even in the face of public-sector decline. It has proven resilient in private-sector industries, like textiles and clothing, which have been in a state of decline and restructuring for decades. Indeed, meaningful collective bargaining can assist the process of change to the benefit of all participants. Such a scenario is possible in the public sector if both parties are prepared to abandon old habits. For employers this means refraining from legislative intervention that eliminates wage negotiations, ends legal strikes, and otherwise manipulates the rules in a way guaranteed to sow mistrust and anger. For unions it means accepting that the expansion years of the 1960s and 1970s are over and adjusting to the economic and political realities of the new century.

Questions

1. Explain the role consultation played in the development of public-sector collective bargaining.

2. Describe the key differences between private- and public-sector employers, and discuss the implications of these differences for collective bargaining in the public sector.

3. Some public employees (for example, most municipal employees) fall under general private-sector labour legislation, while others (for example, federal civil servants) are governed by special public-sector statutes. Discuss the merits of the respective approaches.

4. Why is the question of dispute resolution procedures such an important issue in the public sector?

5. "Public employees should have the right to strike." Discuss.

6. "Public-sector wage controls are justified by the necessity of keeping public-sector wage increases behind private-sector wage increases." Discuss.

7. Describe the changes in the role of government during the past ten years, and indicate the implications of these changes for public-sector collective bargaining.

8. If you were a public-sector union leader, how would you respond to the changing role of government in order to best advance the interests of union members?

ENDNOTES

[1] Adapted from Ponak, Reshef, and Taras (2000).

[2] Given the way in which union density statistics are reported by Labour Canada it was not possible to exclude private medical offices from other parts of health and social services in calculating density rates.

[3] We are unable to explain the drop in provincial government union density between 1991 and 1998 and believe that the 1991 union density may have been overestimated in the 3rd edition of the book (from which the 1991 data in Table 15-2 are taken). It is noted that union density rates for provincial government employees provided by Rose (1995) and Thompson (2000) report provincial union density in the 70 percent range, which is much more consistent with current reported levels, and suggests that provincial public service union density has remained relatively stable.

[4] For a good illustration of how parties attempt to publicly frame bargaining issues for strategic advantage, see the discussion of the 1987 Toronto teachers' strike in Thomason (1995).

[5] These cases are as follows: 1) *Re Public Service Employee Relations Act, Labour Relations Act, and Police Officers Collective Bargaining Act* (1987) 38 DLR (4th) 161 (SCC); 2) *Public Service Alliance of Canada* v. *The Queen in Right of Canada* (1987) 38 DLR (4th) 249 (SCC); and 3) *Government of Saskatchewan* v. *Retail, Wholesale, and Department Store Union* (1987) 38 DLR (4th) 277 (SCC).

[6] A 1982 court decision significantly altered the designation process under the PSSRA. The federal government can now declare that full service must be maintained, virtually guaranteeing that almost all employees providing the service will be deemed essential. For example, prior to the ruling, approximately 10 percent of air traffic controllers were deemed essential because most commercial aviation would be suspended during a strike. Following the ruling, 100 percent of air traffic controllers must remain on the job because the government has decreed that commercial aviation must continue normally (Swimmer, 1995). This has removed in practice the ability of a number of groups to engage in even a limited strike.

REFERENCES

ADELL, B., M. GRANT, and A. PONAK. Forthcoming, 2000. *Striking a Balance*. Kingston: Queen's University, IRC Press.

AKYEAMPONG, E. 1999. "Unionization—an Update." Statistics Canada, Catalogue no. 75-001-XPE. *Perspectives* (Autumn 1999), pp. 45–65.

BEAUMONT, P. 1995. "Canadian Public Sector Industrial Relations in a Wider Setting," in *Public Sector Collective Bargaining: The End of the Beginning or the Beginning of the End*, edited by G. Swimmer and M. Thompson. Kingston: Queen's University, IRC Press.

DOWNIE, B. M. 1992. "Industrial Relations in Elementary and Secondary Education: A System Transformed," in *Industrial Relations in Canadian Industry*, edited by R. Chaykowski and A. Verma. Toronto: Dryden.

EDWARDS, C. 1968. "The Public Service Alliance of Canada." *Relations industrielles/Industrial Relations* 23, pp. 634–41.

FINKELMAN, J. and S. GOLDENBERG. 1983. *Collective Bargaining in the Public Service: The Federal Experience in Canada*. 2 vols. Montreal: Institute for Research on Public Policy.

FOOT, D. K. and P. THADANEY 1978. "The Growth of Public Employment in Canada," in *Public Employment and Compensation in Canada: Myths and Realities*, edited by D. K. Foot. Scarborough, Ont.: Butterworths.

FRANKEL, S. 1960. "Staff Relations in the Canadian Federal Public Service: Experience with Joint Consultation," in *Canadian Public Administration*, edited by J. E. Hodgetts and D. C. Corbett. Toronto: Macmillan.

FRYER, J. 1995. "Provincial Public Sector Labour Relations," in *Public Sector Collective Bargaining*, edited by G. Swimmer and M. Thompson. Kingston: Queen's University, IRC Press.

GOLDENBERG, S. 1988. "Public Sector Labour Relations in Canada," in *Public Sector Bargaining*, 2nd Edition, edited by B. Aaron, J. Grodin, and J. Stern. Madison, Wis.: Industrial Relations Research Association.

GRAHAM, K. 1995. "Collective Bargaining in the Municipal Sector," in *Public Sector Collective Bargaining*, edited by G. Swimmer and M. Thompson. Kingston: Queen's University, IRC Press.

GRANT, M. 2000. "Quebec," in *Regional Differences in Industrial Relations*, edited by M. Thompson, J. Rose, and A. Smith. Canadian Industrial Relations Association.

GUNDERSON, M. 1995. "Public Sector Compensation," in *Public Sector Collective Bargaining,* edited by G. Swimmer and M. Thompson. Kingston: Queen's University, IRC Press.

HAIVEN, L. 1995. "Industrial Relations in Health Care: Regulation, Conflict and Transition to the 'Wellness Model'," in *Public Sector Collective Bargaining,* edited by G. Swimmer and M. Thompson. Kingston: Queen's University, IRC Press.

HAIVEN, L., S. McBRIDE, and J. SHIELDS. 1991. "The State, Neo-Conservatism, and Industrial Relations," in *Regulating Labour,* edited by L. Haiven, S. McBride, and J. Shields. Toronto: Garamond Press.

HÉBERT, G. 1995. "Public Sector Bargaining in Quebec: The Rise and Fall of Centralization," in *Public Sector Collective Bargaining in Canada,* edited by G. Swimmer and M. Thompson. Kingston: Queen's University, IRC Press.

LOGAN, H. A. 1948. *Trade Unions in Canada.* Toronto: Macmillan.

McGRATH, A. and D. NEU. 1996. "Washing our Blues Away; The Laundry Workers Strike Alberta." *Our Times,* 15, no. 1 (March/April).

McLEAN, B. 1979. *A Union Amongst Government Employees. A History of the BC Government Employees' Union.* Vancouver: BC Government Employees' Union.

PANITCH, L. and D. SWARTZ. 1993. *The Assault on Trade Union Freedoms.* Toronto: Garamond Press.

PONAK, A. 1981. "Unionized Professionals and the Scope of Bargaining." *Industrial and Labor Relations Review,* 34, pp. 396–407.

PONAK, A. and L. FALKENBERG. 1989. "Resolution of Interest Disputes," in *Collective Bargaining in Canada,* edited by A. Sethi. Toronto: Nelson.

PONAK, A., Y. RESHEF, and D. G. TARAS. 2000. "Alberta," in *Regional Differences in Industrial Relations,* edited by M. Thompson, J. Rose, and A. Smith. Canadian Industrial Relations Association.

ROSE, J. B. 1995. "The Evolution of Public Sector Unionism," in *Public Sector Collective Bargaining,* edited by G. Swimmer and M. Thompson. Kingston: Queen's University, IRC Press.

ROSE, J. B. and M. PICZAK. 1996. "Settlement Rates and Settlement Stages in Compulsory Interest Arbitration." *Relations Industrielles/Industrial Relations,* 51, no. 4, pp. 643–663.

STEVENS, C. 1966. "Is Compulsory Arbitration Compatible with Bargaining?" *Industrial Relations,* 5, pp. 38–52.

SWIMMER, G. 1995. "Collective Bargaining in the Federal Public Service of Canada—The Last Twenty Years," in *Public Sector Collective Bargaining,* edited by G. Swimmer and M. Thompson. Kingston: Queen's University, IRC Press.

———. 2000. *Public Sector Labour Relations in an Era of Restraint and Restructuring.* Canadian Policy Research Networks.

SWIMMER, G. and M. THOMPSON. 1995. *Public Sector Collective Bargaining.* Kingston: Queen's University, IRC Press.

SWINTON, K. 1995. "The Charter of Rights and Public Sector Labour Relations," in *Public Sector Collective Bargaining,* edited by G. Swimmer and M. Thompson. Kingston: Queen's University, IRC Press.

THOMASON, T. 1995. "Labour Relations in Primary and Secondary Education," in *Public Sector Collective Bargaining,* edited by G. Swimmer and M. Thompson. Kingston: Queen's University, IRC Press.

THOMPSON, M. 1988. "Public Sector Industrial Relations in Canada: The Impact of Restraint," in *Proceedings of the Annual Spring Meeting, 1988, of the Industrial Relations Research Association,* edited by B. Dennis. Madison, WI: IRRA.

———. 1995. "The Industrial Relations Effects of Privatization: Evidence from Canada," in *Public Sector Collective Bargaining,* edited by G. Swimmer and M. Thompson. Kingston: Queen's University, IRC Press.

————. 2000. "Public Sector Industrial Relations in Canada: Adaptation to Change," in *Strategic Choices in Reforming Public Service Employment: An International Perspective*, edited by C. Dell-Aringa and B. Keller. New York: St. Martin's Press.

THOMPSON, M. and A. PONAK. 1995. "Public Sector Collective Bargaining," in *Union–Management Relations in Canada*, 3rd Edition, edited by M. Gunderson and A. Ponak. Don Mills, Ontario: Addison-Wesley.

THOMPSON, M. and G. SWIMMER. 1995. "The Future of Public Sector Industrial Relations," in *Public Sector Collective Bargaining,* edited by G. Swimmer and M. Thompson. Kingston: Queen's University, IRC Press.

WEILER, P. C. 1980. Reconcilable Differences: New Directions in Canadian Labour Law Reform. Agincourt, Ont.: Carswell.

CHAPTER 15

Employee Involvement in the Workplace

Anil Verma and Daphne Gottlieb Taras

The following vignette outlines employee involvement at the Chemainus sawmill, Weyerhauser Ltd. (formerly MacMillan Bloedel).

Since January 1985, the union and management at the Chemainus sawmill, Weyerhause, Ltd. (formerly MacMillan Bloedel) have embarked upon a program to change traditional employee relations. This Vancouver Island sawmill is the site of an older sawmill dating back to the 1920s, which shut its doors in 1983. It was restarted in 1986 under an innovative new agreement that committed both management and union to explore new solutions to enhancing productivity. After extensive consultations and consideration of various proposals, in June 1986, the employees voted to accept an addendum to their collective agreement that effectively commits the parties to "team policies."

Production at the plant is carried out in teams. Workers are paid according to a pay-for-knowledge-and-skill (PKS) scheme in which workers rotate through different jobs and spend time learning them. Pay is tied to learning new skills. For example, on the trim team, an operator starts at the edger drop workstation and then goes on to the chipper, the hula trimmer, the mountain trimmer 1 and 2, the resaw drop, the quad drop and, lastly, the vertical resaw workstation. At each stage, the worker must be trained by a co-worker already qualified to operate that machine. After a certain number of hours on a new machine, the worker must be tested and "validated" through tests and demonstrations. It takes about three years to master all the jobs within the trim team.

There is no formal requirement to rotate and learn new skills. But everyone is required to master at least two workstations. In 1998, on average, employees had mastered five workstations.

The team policies and the associated pay-for-knowledge-and-skill system create several opportunities for greater employee involvement compared to the traditional workplace. To begin with, the creation of the PKS involved intensive consultations with the union and workers. At the workplace, workers are involved with their supervisor in setting standards for training. For example, the minimum and maximum hours for qualifying on a machine were set jointly by the workers and their foreman. Workers are also heavily involved in training although they are not required to do so. Lastly, they are jointly involved with their foreman in testing and validating new skills learned by a co-worker. Thus, the creation of teams and the PKS has led to an increase in employee involvement in workplace tasks.[1]

Employee involvement (EI)[2] in decision making is not a new idea. Yet, despite its intuitive appeal and its compatibility with demands for higher quality and innovation, the diffusion and effective implementation of EI remain elusive. Managers routinely underestimate the difficulties of making the transition from traditional to high-involvement workplaces. Despite the failures, EI has continued to grow in popularity as firms break with traditional forms of work design in the hopes of achieving more innovative and productive workplaces.

Throughout the 20th century, work tended to be organized in a top-down, "command-and-control" system. At the top of the pyramid were high-level executives who designed strategy and approved company policy. The middle held gradations of staff and management who executed policy, supervised shop-floor employees, and reported operational results back up the chain of command. At the bottom were the mass of employees who followed orders and produced goods and services. This traditional organization is increasingly regarded as anachronistic in an era of heightened global and domestic competition, shortened product and technology life cycles, and greater employee expectation of involvement and satisfaction at work. The command-and-control system has given way to a new philosophy involving decentralized decision making, team production, and enhanced opportunities for employee involvement (Kaufman and Taras, 1999). The growth of direct participation for employees signifies one of the more important changes occurring within the industrial relations system.

In this chapter we address the EI forms and the extent of their diffusion. We examine their effect on performance and satisfaction. The legal status of employee involvement in both nonunion and unionized workplaces is reviewed, and the role of public policy is described. Finally, we discuss the effect of employee involvement on employer–employee and union–management relations.

EMERGENT FORMS OF EMPLOYEE INVOLVEMENT

Employee involvement initiatives can be classified on a number of dimensions. These include the nature of the employees' participation, the impact of participation upon organizational decisions, and the types of issues addressed. Some types of EI can be installed quite easily into existing organizational structures and processes, while other EI initiatives require substantial organizational redesign.

Participation

Involvement or participation in decision making can take many forms (Dachler and Wilpert, 1978). First and foremost, there is the issue of *direct* versus *indirect* forms of participation. Do workers make their needs and views known to management directly, or do they channel their sentiments through an agent who speaks to management on their behalf? Collective bargaining and the legislative process use elected representatives and hence participation is indirect. Work or quality teams have direct participation because the individual is personally involved. Direct involvement can be at the *individual* or the *group level*. Suggestion schemes are a mild form of involvement at the individual level. A quality circle is an example of group participation.

The second dimension of participation is the extent to which participation is allowed. *Consultation* is a milder form of participation because it does not imply decision-making authority. *Equal say* in decision making for all parties and the power to implement decisions are much stronger forms of participation. Some highly participative forums may also contain a mechanism to resolve any disputes among the parties participating in decision making.

The third dimension of participation is the substantive content of decision making, i.e., the set of issues over which decision making is exercised. This may be limited to a small cluster of issues such as the administration of training programs, health-and-safety concerns, or quality control. It can also be broadened to include any issues arising from the terms and conditions of employment, or the entire production processes. In some cases, participative forums may have an open-ended mandate to consider any relevant workplace issues.

Canadian industrial relations studies have relied almost exclusively on knowledge gained through an examination of indirect participation through unions, collective bargaining, and grievance procedures. How does the introduction of direct forms of participation affect relations among the actors within the industrial relations system? There are troubling questions. Is direct participation compatible with indirect participation or does it, as is often alleged, supplant the need for indirect representation? Is EI capable of meeting employees' needs for economic advances, fairness and equity, countervailing power, and voice (Chapter 2) without unions? To what extent might EI be used in managerial strategies of union avoidance, substitution, or replacement (Chapter 5)?

Industrial Relations Research (UK-based forum on industrial relations): www.mailbase.ac.uk/lists-f-j/industrial-relations-research/

Integration into Organizational Structure

EI programs can be divided into two categories based on the degree to which the EI program affects structures and work processes within the firm (Cutcher-Gershenfeld, Kochan, and Verma, 1991). The first is self-contained, that is, EI is not accompanied by any significant corresponding changes in organizational structure, procedures, or other subsystems. Quality circles generally do not threaten or require a change in the traditional hierarchy of the organization and are add-on features that require relatively little effort to implement. Perhaps for this reason, they became the most popular form of employee involvement in the US in the 1980s.

The second type of employee involvement is characterized by its high degree of integration with, and impact on, the organization. A host of changes in organizational structures and procedures are required. Autonomous work groups, in their very design, are intended to challenge the traditional hierarchical structure of authority. Because their impact on the organization is substantial, such forms require a large investment of funds and effort and are more difficult to implement. This explains, in part, why the diffusion of these forms has remained well below that of the first type.

EMPLOYEE INVOLVEMENT VS. SCIENTIFIC MANAGEMENT

We describe the philosophy of scientific management to provide the traditional context that is under attack. One of the most influential, controversial, and perhaps most misunderstood pioneers of the industrial age was Frederick Winslow Taylor (1865–1915). His scientific management movement continues to have a huge impact on the way industrial society produces work (Taylor, 1911). He and his followers believed that the key to a stable and prosperous society was the determination of the "one best way" to organize the firm for greatest productivity (Kanigel, 1997). Management was to devise the optimal way of doing the job and the worker was to follow scientifically derived instructions. The worker was not meant to be "thinking" about the production process lest she or he should tamper with the most efficient way of doing the job. At one point, Taylor argued that any involvement of the worker with the production process might be "fatal" to success. Unions responded to scientific management by negotiating collective agreements that clearly specified divisions of responsibilities and the types of rigid work rules most appropriate to factory systems. Because EI is essentially a reversal of this aspect of Taylorism, it poses significant challenges to many deeply embedded labour–management practices.

Principles of Scientific Management:
melbecon.unimelb.edu.au/het/taylor/sciman.htm

Today, Taylor is most widely known—and vilified within pro-union circles—for the "time-and-motion" studies that led to specialization and segmentation of labour and assembly-line speed-ups that put tremendous pressure on workers. But at the turn of the last century, Taylor observed widespread chaotic and capricious management practice, tyrannical foremen with the power to fire workers for any—and no—reason, and workers whose only protection from job loss or downward pressure on wages was collective "soldiering" (or slowdowns in production). To move towards a better world, in which soldiering would be unnecessary and both workers and owners could prosper from greater society-wide productivity, Taylor recommended a set of practices that were quite revolutionary for his time. In addition to endorsing the usual separation of managers from workers, he proposed four main practices:

1. Lowering unit production run costs and compensating workers for their greater efficiency by paying them substantially higher wages;

2. Carefully studying and experimenting with methods of production to find the best method to achieve optimal levels;

3. Paying great attention to selection and sympathetic training of employees, with relevant and timely feedback on work performance; and

4. Developing a climate of co-operation between workers and managers. Managers would take a greater role than previously in understanding actual work processes for the purpose of implementing scientific methods.

Within these precepts, and the quotes in Exhibit 15.1, are found many of the underpinnings of contemporary management practices such as gain-sharing, employee involvement in productivity enhancements, and even total quality management. At Bethlehem Steel Company, Taylor's methods were used to increase productivity by 280 percent, while workers' wages rose by 60 percent.

Biography of F. W. Taylor and links to his works:
www.ideafinder.com/facts/inventors/taylor.htm

The modern break from Taylorist principles is the removal of the dichotomy between workers and managers. Today, workers in an EI mode are expected to think, plan, and contribute their brains and energies to the enterprise that employs them.

But Taylor also foresaw that management's temptation to simply lower labour rates whenever possible, while maintaining high productivity, would be the greatest threat to the success of scientific management.[3] After a flurry of activity to implement an employee involvement plan, many companies simply forget over time that workers must be adequately compensated (both in terms of wages and other non-monetary issues such as job security) for the greater efforts they expend. Sometimes the provision of appropriate training is neglected, or competitive pressures in the marketplace cause a climate of fear and defensiveness rather than co-operation. Indeed, we believe that failure to follow Taylor's four precepts is one of the main reasons that employee involvement plans go awry.

EXHIBIT 15.1

THE PRINCIPLES OF SCIENTIFIC MANAGEMENT, AN EXCERPT

FREDERICK WINSLOW TAYLOR ON INCREASED EFFICIENCY

"Nineteen out of twenty workmen throughout the civilized world firmly believe that it is for their best interests to go slow instead of to go fast. They would say "[if you make me go faster at my job] I know that the only result would be that half of us would be out of a job before the year was out." They firmly believe that that would be the result of a great increase in efficiency, and yet directly the opposite is true.

"Nineteen-twentieths of the real wealth of this world is used by the poor people, and not the rich, so that the workingman who sets out as a steady principle to restrict output is merely robbing his own kind. That group of manufacturers which adopts as a permanent principle restriction of output, in order to hold up prices, is robbing the world. From what does the progress the world has made come? Simply from the increase in the output of the individual all over the world."

ON THE DEVELOPMENT OF SCIENTIFIC MANAGEMENT

"There has been, until comparatively recently, no scheme promulgated by which the evils of rate cutting could be properly avoided, so soldiering has been the rule. Scientific management [was] first step that was taken in an earnest endeavor to remedy the evils of soldiering. The increasing of the output per individual results, of course, in cheapening the product; it results, therefore, in larger profit usually to the owners of the business; it results also, in many cases, in a lowering of the selling price. Without any question, the large good which so far has come from scientific management has come to the worker. Under scientific management, they look upon their employers as the best friends they have in the world; the suspicious watchfulness which characterizes the old type management, the semi-antagonism or the complete antagonism between workmen and employers is entirely superseded, and in its place comes genuine friendship between both sides.

"If this surplus can be made so great, providing both sides will stop their pulling apart, will stop their fighting and will push as hard as they can to get as cheap an output as possible, that there is no occasion to quarrel. Each side can get more than ever before."

Source: Taylor, 1916, pp. 66–75.

DEVELOPMENTS IN THE CANADIAN WORKPLACE

The contemporary workplace context within which employee involvement practices are being adopted is turbulent. Increased competition due to growing international trade, deregulation, privatization, and the introduction of flexible technologies (e.g., computer-based information and process technology) has put pressures on firms to meet ever higher standards of quality, cost, innovation, and flexibility. Canadian firms have two broad options to cope with the new challenges. The first option is to lower wages to levels prevailing in the competitor economies. For a variety of reasons, this option is not feasible for most Canadian firms. Even if Canadian wages were cut substantially they would still remain well above wages in several countries.

An alternative strategy would be to maintain higher wages but seek a comparative advantage through product innovation, quality, service, and specialization. Porter (1980, 1990) calls this a differentiation strategy by which firms seek to differentiate their products from those of the low-cost producers. Successful differentiation requires that the firm employ technological and organizational innovation to develop new products quickly. These products must be of a high quality and come with reliable service so that they can fetch the premium price needed to support high wages. The success of this strategy depends on mobilizing a highly skilled, trained, flexible, and motivated workforce. The Tayloristic dichotomy between managers who "think" and workers who "do" must be supplanted by a system that encourages a partnership among the various hierarchies of the firm for the purpose of achieving comparative advantage.

What kind of workforce could cope with these demands? Under conditions of increasing competition and flexible technologies, workforces would have to become highly skilled and trained, involved with the production process, and flexible and adaptable to shifting market conditions. In high-wage countries, firms are competing internationally by differentiating their product rather than by lowering wages (Porter, 1980, 1990). The high value-added manufacturing places greater demands on employees' skills, adaptability, and involvement.

Employee involvement does not occur in isolation of other human resource practices. Innovative policies are required in four key areas: training, employee involvement, work organization, and compensation.

Creation of a highly skilled workforce requires that firms invest more resources in *training*. The emphasis on quality and innovation within the differentiation strategy also means that firms must get their workers more involved in the production process. Hence, a greater emphasis on participation may be expected. *Equity theory* suggests that people are motivated to seek equitable rather than maximum rewards, i.e., the same rewards that other people with comparable skills and experience receive. *Expectancy theory* suggests that people are motivated only when they believe that expended efforts will generate commensurate rewards. Put together, these two theories imply that, unless workers share in the fruits of their labour, it is unlikely that they will expend maximum effort.

High-involvement policies and programs are unlikely to be effective unless they are complemented with a set of policies that promote *sharing*.[4] Sharing need not be confined to financial matters alone. It can also mean information dissemination. To promote EI, many organizations began, in the 1980s, to share information widely with all levels of employees. Sharing can also be extended to privileges; removal of hierarchical privileges such as preferential parking, cafeterias, and washrooms for managers can also promote the perception that workers are equal partners in the enterprise.

As competition forces firms to move to higher value-added products and greater investment in skills there will be greater pressure to move away from Tayloristic to more *flexible forms of work organization* (Gerwin and Kolodny, 1992). Greater employee involvement requires broader multi-skill training. Team-based work organization, in which workers have multiple skills and greater responsibility for decentralized decision making, is much more compatible with a high value-added workplace that is competing on the basis of high quality and innovation.

From the preceding discussion, it becomes obvious that the pressures leading firms to explore the introduction of EI practices have a great deal to do with productivity, flexibility, and competition—management's agenda—and less relationship to workers' desire for a stronger voice in the operations of the worksite and better terms and conditions of employment. Contemporary surveys of workers' attitudes (described extensively in Chapter 2: Godard, 1997; Freeman and Rogers, 1999) show that modern workers expect greater participation at work and want more open communications and less adversarial relations with management. By introducing EI practices and meeting the employer agenda, firms are also in the happy position of being able to deliver greater voice to workers.

The Diffusion of Employee Involvement and Other Innovations

Information on the extent of EI and other innovations in Canadian workplaces has been scant and available only sporadically (Table 15.1). The 1993 Human Resource Practices Survey (HRPS) was limited to four industries (wood products, fabricated metal products, electrical and electronic products, and business services) across 714 establishments (Betcherman et al., 1994). Another survey, the Working with Technology Survey (WWTS) was conducted in 1985 (Long, 1989; Betcherman and McMullen, 1986) and repeated in 1991 (Betcherman, et al., 1994). Although the measures used by these surveys are not all identical and, therefore, not directly comparable, results from the Canadian surveys are presented along with results from US surveys to put them in context.

Workplace Innovations, Workplace Information Directorate, Human Resources Development Canada: labour-travail.hrdc-drhc.gc.ca/wip/

As indicated in Table 15.1, some form of employee involvement was reported by 43 percent of Canadian establishments in the HRPS Survey. Respondents were asked if the establishment had any of the popular forms of employee involvement such as quality circles, quality-of-worklife programs, or total quality management initiatives. This figure likely overestimates the average for all sectors because of its bias towards manufacturing where workplace innovations have generally preceded those in the service and public sectors. The survey results show that EI is spreading quickly.

TABLE 15.1

INCIDENCE OF WORKPLACE HR PRACTICES: CANADA AND US

PERCENT OF ESTABLISHMENTS REPORTING EACH PRACTICE

HR PRACTICES	CANADA		US	
Survey	HRPS Survey 1993[a]	WWTS Survey 1985[b]	M.I.T. Survey 1992[c]	GAO Survey 1987; CEO Survey 1990[d]
Employee Involvement	43.1—includes quality circles, total quality management, quality-of-worklife	14.2—quality circles; 19.4— other problem-solving groups 47.5—WWTS 1991	78.2—of any coverage; 64.0—covering at least 50% of the workforce	61—1987 QCs only; 66—1990 QCs only; 70—1987 Groups other than QCs; 86—1990 Groups other than QCs
Training	31—1987 Human Resource Training & Development Survey; 70—1991 National Training Survey	n/a	32—Off-the-job; 45.1—Cross training	n/a
Flexible work organization				
Job Rotation	22.5	n/a	n/a	n/a
Job Enlargement	21.1	n/a	n/a	n/a
Job Enrichment	21.4	21.9	n/a	60 (1987); 75 (1990)
Self-directed Work Teams	15.7	11.0	n/a	25 (1987); 28 (1990)
Variable Pay				
Profit-Sharing	21.6	25.0	44.7	65 (1987); 63 (1990)
Employee Stock Option Plans	14.1	n/a	n/a	61 (1987); 64 (1990)
Pay-for-Skill	14.5	7.4	30.4	40 (1987); 51 (1990)
Gain-Sharing	6.5	9.7	13.7	26 (1987); 39 (1990)
Other Incentive Pay	6.4	n/a	n/a	Individual incentive: 87 (1987); 90 (1990) Team incentive: 59 (1990)

[a] Betcherman, G., K. McMullen, N. Leckie, and C. Caron. 1994. *The Canadian Workplace in Transition*. Kingston, ON: IRC Press.

[b] Long, R. J. 1989. "Patterns of Workplace Innovations in Canada." *Relations industrielles/Industrial Relations*, 44, no. 4 (Autumn), pp. 805–25.

[c] Osterman, P. 1994 "How Common is Workplace Transformation and Who Adopts it?" *Industrial and Labor Relations Review*, 47, no. 2, pp. 173–188.

[d] Lawler, E. E., S. A. Mohrman, G. E. Ledford. 1992. *Employee Involvement and Total Quality Management: Practices and Results in Fortune 1000 Companies*. Copyright © 1992. Reprinted by permission of Jossey-Bass, Inc., a subsidiary of John Wiley & Sons, Inc.

The prevalence of training in a significant number of firms is well indicated.[5] Statistics Canada's 1987 Human Resource Training & Development Survey found that 31 percent of the establishments reported formal in-house training programs. The National Training Survey taken in 1991, which defined training more broadly to include both internal and external training as well as various forms of on-the-job training, found training practices prevalent in 70 percent of establishments surveyed. Whatever the precise estimate, it is clear from these data that training as a human resource practice has also become widespread.

Flexible forms of work organization such as job rotation, job enlargement and enrichment, and self-directed work teams were reported by 15.7 to 22.5 percent of the establishments. At least one of these practices was used in 37 percent of the firms surveyed (Betcherman et al., 1994: 34). Variable pay practices such as gain-sharing, profit-sharing, employee stock ownership plans, and pay-for-skill were reported by 6.5 to 21.6 percent of the establishments.

Self-Directed Work Teams (provides links to team resources): users.ids.net/~brim/sdwth.html

Within the unionized sector exclusively, the *1995 Overview of Innovative Workplace Practices* reports that of the 298 collective agreement settlements achieved that year, approximately 77 percent included some innovative or adaptive practice at the workplace level. Just over one-fifth of settlements addressed issues relating to the organization of work processes, including provisions for restructuring or flattening hierarchies, reductions in job classes, the establishment of work teams, and other related interventions. An example of a provision introducing greater flexibility among tradesmen is reproduced in Exhibit 15.2. Almost 95 percent of agreements changed non-wage provisions such as hours of work or introduced flexible schedules or wage provisions to give lump-sum payments, signing bonuses, incentive pay (including gain-sharing, profit-sharing, employee ownership plans), pay-for-knowledge or skill premiums, or performance-related bonuses. Nearly half of agreements offered training or retraining. Almost 45 percent of settlements included the use of committees and employee involvement and participation initiatives. Of these committees, about a quarter are used explicitly to facilitate information sharing and general employee participation schemes. But, commented the report, there were very few settlements that reported employee participation and information sharing without the use of committees. However, "this low frequency is due to the strong focus on joint committees and joint labour–management approaches to information sharing, employee involvement, and employee participation because these are bargained outcomes. In a unionized environment, the first level of participation is the legitimate involvement of the union and this is achieved through a labour–management committee structure."

Thus, both theory and empirical evidence in this section suggest that employee involvement does not stand in isolation of other complementary human resource practices in the workplace.

EXHIBIT 15.2

TRADES FLEXIBILITY

Here is an excerpt from an agreement between Stone-Consolidated Inc. La Baie Quebec, and Federation of Paper and Forest Workers (672 office, clerical, and production employees) dealing with greater trades flexibility:

"In the course of carrying on his trade, an employee may perform related duties and tasks. These related tasks are intended to make it easier for the employee to carry on his trade and may be related to tasks that are normally part of another trade. These related tasks do not require highly specialized training or a licence issued pursuant to a statute or regulations.

"Further, where a job requires the assignment of employees from more than one trade to facilitate the work, employees will assist one another in complying with the technical requirements of each trade, for each task involved in the job.

"The parties agree on the creation of a group of on-call tradesmen. Their primary duties are related to emergencies and breakdowns that occur during on-call periods. In addition, they will perform tasks as needed in any department of the plant. Where an emergency job...has to be done or where a breakdown makes an immediate repair necessary...the on-call tradesman, working alone or as part of a crew, performs all the work he is capable of performing, regardless of his trade....

"...Employees on the pay list who held a regular tradesman position on the date the 1990–93 collective agreement was ratified will not be laid off from their department because of the application of the [Tradesmen Flexibility Program]."

Source: Workplace Information Directorate, Human Resources Development Canada. "Workplace Innovations: Dialogue on Changes in the Workplace." *Collective Bargaining Review* (April 1996), pp. 81–90. Reproduced with the permission of the Minister of Human Resources Development Canada.

 Employee Involvement Association: www.eia.com/

A GENERAL THEORY OF EMPLOYEE INVOLVEMENT

The adoption of EI in practice has been driven more by its intuitive appeal than by its efficacy established through scientifically tested theories. Yet, if employee involvement is to become widespread in practice it is important to develop a theoretical framework to guide policy and research. In this section, we provide a brief overview of the principal theoretical ideas found in the EI research. Briefly, we examine the theoretical foundation for the efficacy of EI, the factors that influence its adoption, the consequences of EI, and issues arising from EI implementation in unionized environments.

Theoretical Foundations for Employee Involvement

At the policy level, the introduction of employee involvement has been driven by two distinct underlying philosophies. The first approach is derived from a moral, ethical, and socio-cultural base. Its main precept is that greater say in decision making is crucial for those who are affected by these decisions, an ideal that is as pertinent to the workplace as it is to democratic societies. The European notion of industrial democracy and the systems of co-determination that exist in Germany and several other countries in western Europe are good illustrations of this approach. It should be noted that most instances of industrial democracy in Europe have taken the form of indirect rather direct participation and are mandated by law.

The second approach, championed by Japanese and North American firms, derives from the utilitarian principle that innovative workplace practices (such as employee involvement) are a means to other important ends such as higher quality and productivity. In this view, employee participation leads to better outcomes for all parties because it improves productivity and creates more satisfied and energized workers.

There is no single theory of why employee involvement would produce positive outcomes. Rather, a number of theories such as expectancy theory, attribution theory, and equity theory among others, have been combined to develop models that predict the outcomes of EI (Cotton, 1993). A review of the relationship between discretionary effort and the organization of work is reviewed by Appelbaum and her colleagues (2000). They argue that three components are needed: motivation, skills, and opportunity for participation. A selected number of models are reviewed here, very briefly, to show how and why positive effects of participation on productivity and affective responses such as job satisfaction may be expected.

Sashkin (1976) suggested that the psychological and cognitive effects of employee involvement are likely to produce "ownership" of decisions. In this model, EI is also seen as leading to shared norms and greater information flow. These outcomes, in turn, will lead to increased commitment, higher quality, and a greater capacity for adapting to change. Locke and Schweiger (1979) argue that employee involvement may increase productivity through two different mechanisms: cognitive effects such as better communication and better understanding of the job, and motivational effects such as greater "ownership" from ego involvement and increased trust.

In other models, employee involvement is seen as reducing role conflict and role ambiguity (Schuler, 1980). Employee involvement may also strengthen expectancy links between performance and rewards because the employee will know more about the behaviours that are rewarded (Lee and Schuler, 1982). Conger and Kanungo (1988) modelled participatory effects through increased self-efficacy information such as enactive attainment, vicarious experience, verbal persuasion, and emotional arousal. These effects lead to a strengthened belief in personal efficacy, which in turn leads to behaviours necessary to accomplish task objectives.

Lastly, some scholars have modelled effects of participation within the structural context of groups. Tjosvold (1991) proposed that participation leads to more opportunities to discuss problems, creating constructive interactions in the form of a co-operative context and productive controversies. These interactions, in turn, lead to effective problem solving, which can be expected to result in high productivity and morale.

Factors Leading to EI Adoption

One of the more striking findings in the EI literature is that there is considerable diversity of practices among establishments—even of approximately similar sizes and within the same industries. The pace of diffusion is difficult to assess (Gittleman, Horrigan, and Joyce, 1998: 113). However, we have sufficient case studies that allow the classification of five categories of triggers for EI adoption (Verma, 1990; Jackson and DiGiacomo, 1997).

Crisis

External shocks like loss of profits; loss of markets; and financial crises caused by recessions, deregulation, and so on, are the factors that induce the vast majority of firms to adopt greater employee involvement.

A manager at NB Tel observed that "We used to have slow, infrequent change. Now we have daily wrenching change… Revenues are a monthly adventure!" Given regulatory and technological change, and rising customer expectations, the company "had no chance of surviving with a hierarchical bureaucracy." When asked why NB Tel decided to restructure workplace practices, he declared that "Survival, survival, survival are the three main reasons!" (DiGiacomo, 1997).

Implementation of EI involves its own costs that can be quite high. A crisis, therefore, is a double-edged sword when it comes to introducing EI. On the one hand, the crisis provides an incentive for change but, on the other hand, implementing EI requires resources that may be scarce during a crisis. Experience seems to suggest that a crisis of moderate proportions provides the best combination of conditions for successful implementation. A firm careening into bankruptcy is unlikely to have the resources to invest in EI.

Crisis in the Labour–Management Relationship

In a smaller number of cases, EI adoptions take place in the aftermath of a crisis in the labour–management relationship. Some adversarial relationships in a downward spiral keep getting more conflictual until they assume crisis proportions. At this point, the parties introduce a number of initiatives to improve relations, and EI can be a part of that effort. For example, the turmoil caused by a nationwide strike in 1969 in the Canadian petroleum industry led the parties to develop their own mutual gains approach to bargaining, long before this approach was adopted by professional negotiators.

Workplace Problems

In a small number of cases, certain crises specific to the workplace account for the need to adopt greater employee involvement. EI was adopted at Manitoba Telephone Systems and the CEP Union largely in response to the need to reduce stress on the job (Verma and Cutcher-Gershenfeld, 1993). At Abitibi-Price's paper plant in Alma, Quebec, in the 1980s, there were between 150 and 200 grievances yearly among 900 workers, and Alma had the poorest quality products and largest accumulated number of days lost to strikes of any Abitibi-Price plants. Labour relations were so acrimonious that the company considered plant closure. Against this backdrop, the union and management came together in the early 1990s, and after consulting with numerous small groups in the plant, developed a "Vision 2000" statement (reproduced in Exhibit 15.3). Between 1991 and 1996, only one grievance was recorded, client satisfaction increased by three to six times the previous levels, and production costs were reduced.

Emulation

EI professionals communicate with each other through extensive networks. Word is thus passed on about cutting-edge practice from one organization to another. Some companies, especially those that benchmark themselves against the best methods, adopt EI simply because they find that EI has won acceptance among leading-edge firms. The introduction of EI programs in the Canadian oil industry follows this pattern (Taras and Ponak, 1999). The Internet makes available a number of Websites through which managers submit and receive information.

EXHIBIT 15.3

ABITIBI-PRICE ALMA PAPER PLANT "VISION 2000" STATEMENT

- Each employee acts and thinks as if the plant was his.
- Each employee decides and goes ahead, with no need for approval from his boss.
- Each employee has enough information to allow him to participate efficiently in the success of his team and his enterprise.
- Each employee is responsible for the work of his team, and knows the impact of his actions on the other members of the team.
- All know and act in function of the concept "supplier/client." This concept is omnipresent in everything we are undertaking up to the user of our products and/or our services.
- Criteria for success are clear, known, and requested by all and everyone: unionized employee, manager, supplier, client.
- Total quality is a predominant concern and a way of life.
- Recognition of one's worth is based on performance and excellence.

Source: Quoted in Chamberland (1997). Reproduced with the permission of the Minister of Public Works and Government Services, 2000.

Proactive Adoption

Another small group of firms adopt EI because they anticipate problems they are likely to face in the future and they want to be prepared. These organizations truly believe that EI is a better way to manage and to compete. These are typically large companies or members of large conglomerates such as Boeing, Bell Canada, and Motorola. Often, innovative workplace practices are initiated by senior management in a top-down fashion, but there is a preparedness at the most senior levels of the company to provide training, incentives, and an organizational environment that encourages innovation (Jackson and DiGiacomo, 1997).

The Organizational Consequences of EI

There are many areas of change following the introduction of greater EI in an organization. For the sake of brevity and focus, three areas where the impact of EI is felt most are considered below. These are also the areas that need the most attention in the formative period when the foundation for EI effectiveness is laid.

Training

As discussed earlier, one of the most important requirements when introducing EI is training. The traditional organization invests only a modest sum in training and most of that is directed at management or at training in technical and functional skills. Effective implementation of EI requires that training be increased in both magnitude and scope. Training in problem-solving skills and team-based skills are a must. Notably successful companies in Canada appear to be investing roughly five to seven days of training per employee per annum on an ongoing basis (Verma and Irvine, 1992).

Successful companies use training in the context of EI for three distinct purposes. First, training is used to inform and socialize employees into appreciating the value of employee input and the organizational need to improve quality and productivity. Firms have been generally quite successful in raising awareness of EI and in getting employees to identify with strategic goals of the business. The second task for training is to provide employees with a set of basic skills in problem solving so that they can begin to get involved. Finally, training is used to upgrade skills, to disseminate information about the firm's strategic direction, and to renew interest on an ongoing basis.

First-line Supervision

First-line supervisors are among the first managers directly affected by the introduction of EI (Klein, 1988; Klein and Posey, 1986). Experience shows that if EI is to be meaningful, certain changes must occur in the quality and quantity of first-line supervision.

In many organizations, the introduction of EI has been followed by a decrease in the amount of direct supervision and by the redefining of the role of a supervisor from monitor to coordinator and facilitator (Klein, 1988). If EI is effective, workers do not need as much supervision. Organizations have terminated the employment of cadres of supervisors, making employee involvement an immediate and measurable contributor to the corporate bottom line.

Employee Involvement in the New Game:
www.fdmmag.com/articles/03aco.htm

Whatever supervisors remain on payroll must have their expectations and job duties dramatically altered by EI. If workers are learning problem-solving skills, they need a different kind of support. Supervisors are becoming "coaches" and "facilitators," whose skills are used for employee training, promoting communication flows with other parts of the organization, developing benchmarks, and assisting with the acquisition of information. Often, supervisors who were selected for traditional organizations and who are accustomed to "command and control" styles are unable to make the difficult transition to high-performance work settings. They become casualties of EI.

Information Flow

The medium- to long-term consequences of EI for the organization are in the areas of information flow and access. A hierarchical organization is characterized by a protocol for information flow both horizontally and vertically. The introduction of EI creates a demand for information that severely tests the old protocol in which employees at progressively lower levels of the organization had access to less and less information.

Organizations have developed a wide variety of ways to deal with increasing demands for access to information. In some companies, employee teams include staff representatives from support departments like accounting, engineering, and maintenance. The support staff become a link between the team and other departments for access to information. But usually there are not enough such personnel to allow them to be assigned to every employee team. In many situations, it becomes problematic for non-managerial employees to request and receive technical or cost data from other departments. Yet, the need to increase flow of information is urgent if EI is to be effective and successful.

The Effect of EI on Productivity and Satisfaction

Numerous studies have been conducted to measure the effects of participation on individual and organizational outcomes since the 1950s.[6] Here the results are summarized to provide an overview.

Employee Involvement: A Strong Link to Productivity: epfnet.org/polei.htm

More than 50 research studies (see Table 15.2) demonstrate that it has not always been possible to show a direct, significant, and positive impact of EI on bottom-line measures of cost and productivity (Locke and Schweiger, 1979; Miller and Monge,

1986). While a majority of studies do show a positive impact, the effects frequently vary and a number of studies have found no effect. The positive effects of participation are more clearly observed in the case of job satisfaction where the evidence supports the finding of a small but positive impact. Case studies of the effects of lean production in the automobile industry on worker outcomes such as empowerment, work pace and workload, and health have found negative results (Graham, 1995; Lewchuk and Robertson, 1996). In the American steel industry, practices that link pay to performance, share information with workers, provide employment security, or involve workers in decisions

TABLE 15.2

EFFECT OF EMPLOYEE PARTICIPATION ON PERFORMANCE AND SATISFACTION (SUMMARY OF RESEARCH STUDIES)

Form of Participation	RESULTS ON PERFORMANCE			RESULTS ON SATISFACTION		
	Positive Finding	Negative Finding	No Effect	Positive Finding	Negative Finding	No Effect
Participation in Work Decisions	11 studies (73%)	1 study	3 studies	4 studies (50%)	1 study	3 studies
Overall summary	Positive	—	—	Mixed	—	—
Consultative Participation	4 studies (80%)	—	1 study	3 studies (75%)	—	1 study
Overall summary	Positive	—	—	Positive	—	—
Short-Term Participation	1 study (9%)	—	10 studies	2 studies	—	5 studies
Overall Summary	—	—	No Effect	—	—	No effect
Informal Participation	5 studies (80%)		1 study	17 studies (85%)	—	3 studies
Overall Summary	Positive	—	—	Positive	—	—
Employee Ownership	3 studies (100%)	—	—	4 studies (80%)	—	—
Overall Summary	Positive	—	—	Positive	—	—
Representative Participation	1 study (25%)	1 study	2 studies	4 studies (50%)	2 studies	2 studies
Overall Summary	—	—	No effect	—	—	No effect

Note: The entries in the cells show the number of studies in that category with the percentage of all studies in that category shown in parentheses. The overall conclusion is considered positive if more than two-thirds of the studies indicate a positive finding.

Source: This table is derived from J. L. Cotton, D. A. Vollrath, K. L. Froggatt, M. L. Lengnick-Hall, and K. R. Jennings. 1988. "Employee Participation: Diverse Forms and Different Outcomes." *Academy of Management Review*, 13, no. 1, pp. 8–22. The table has been simplified to make it more reader friendly. A complete list of the studies included in the table appears in the original publication.

do not affect job satisfaction. Rather, job satisfaction in this mature, male-dominated industry was influenced by good employee–management relations and flexible practices that help balance work and family (Berg, 1999). The most recent comprehensive study of 44 manufacturing facilities across the United States from 1995 to 1997 reports positive effects on performance measures "that are large enough to be important to the companies in our study but not so large as to strain credulity" (Appelbaum et al, 2000: 19).

A number of case studies also have provided evidence of positive effects, and some are glowing testimonials for EI programs. It is hard to interpret this evidence. For example, the vast majority of reported cases involve success stories. Rarely does the case-study literature touch on cases that may have failed. There are no reliable estimates of the failure rate among EI programs. However, anecdotal evidence places the attrition rate as high as 40 percent in the first two or three years following introduction (Rankin, 1986), possibly indicating that organizations are still at an early stage in the learning curve for EI implementation. Many case studies are written by those who are directly involved with the initiative such as the managers or consultants responsible for design and implementation. Thus, many case studies suffer from lack of objectivity or the rigour of scientific investigation.

There are also methodological problems in isolating the precise contribution of EI programs as distinct from the effects of technology or markets or other changes that happened simultaneously with EI. As a rule, positive EI impacts were reported when there also were changes in technology, products, markets, processes, materials, or even staffing.

Critics of impact studies argue that precise measurement of EI programs is flawed for three reasons. First, the benefits of greater employee involvement will show up in individual as well as group activity and few of these studies measure group outcomes such as the launch of a new product or effective implementation of a new system. Further, some impact of EI may be observable only when organizations go through sudden and unexpected change such as technological change (e.g., EI may make employees more amenable to technological change), downsizing (e.g., employees may identify more strongly with the strategic goals of the business), or the introduction of new markets or products (e.g., EI may aid in the development of a more flexible and agile organization). Most studies in the past have not measured such effects because of the problems inherent in such measurement.

Second, critics charge that measuring EI outcomes in a narrow, short-term frame will hurt the very process the study is designed to measure. The EI process would change once the fact of measurement became known to the participants who would be likely to experience some anxiety as a result of being monitored. Consequently, in many firms managers have decided not to measure the outcomes of EI at least in the short run.[7]

Third, in field studies, it is difficult to measure the factors separate and independent of EI that are often introduced along with other workplace changes and innovations.

In practice, the decision to introduce greater employee involvement is not always made contingent upon a quick demonstration through hard data of a positive impact of EI. Often, quantitative assessment of EI and its impact on performance is made only after the program has had some time to become absorbed, in whole or in part, into the organizational culture.

EI in Unionized Environments

It is in the unionized context that EI poses the deepest challenges for all actors in the industrial relations system. Implementation of EI in a union environment is problematic because EI is an ideologically loaded intervention in the employment relationship. Many unions fear that employee involvement is a potent socialization tool through which employers can co-opt employees into a managerial agenda and, thereby, weaken collective bargaining and the union. These fears have been fuelled in part by the growth of the nonunion sector in the US, where employers have successfully resisted unionization in new nonunion plants by implementing, among other policies, greater employee involvement (Verma and Kochan, 1985).

The vast majority of unionized workplaces have experienced difficulties in implementing EI and not only for the reasons stated above. The introduction of EI requires a drastic change in the traditional labour–management relationship conventionally characterized by a separation of management and labour roles and the associated mutual distrust and adversarial bargaining. On the other hand, there is some evidence that unions play a positive "watchdog" role in ensuring that the employee involvement initiatives that come to fruition are well-reasoned, implemented with care, and fair from the employees' perspective.

Impediments to EI Adoption and Implementation

Two impediments to the introduction of EI in unionized workplaces have been identified in the literature.

1. **The History of Labour–Management Relations.** Many companies that began to introduce EI in the 1980s discovered that their enthusiasm was not universally shared. Quite often unions were not nearly as excited at the prospect of introducing EI. Part of the reason lay in the history of adversarial relations, which had taught the parties to exercise caution, if not plain mistrust, in dealing with the other side. Thus, the initial call for collaboration for mutual benefit has been generally obscured by the shadow of the past.

   In cases where EI has had a more successful start, the introduction has been preceded, generally, by a series of activities whose intent and effect has been to build the relationship up from its adversarial past. In general, the following sequence may occur at a site where EI is being introduced.

   a. Teams of employees, both from management and the union, visit other organizations where EI has proved to be successful.

   b. EI experts speak at company training sessions. Some of these sessions are attended by union and management representatives.

   c. The company and union agree to attend an off-site workshop designed especially to discuss mutual interests.

   d. Union and management agree to expand the traditional bargaining agenda by removing obstacles like a large backlog of unresolved grievances.

e. Both sides agree to form a joint steering committee to oversee the design and implementation of the EI program.

Where the parties do not invest in such prior relationship building, the results are generally unfavourable. In some cases, the union refuses to discuss the EI issue, forcing management either to implement it on its own or to drop the initiative altogether. In other cases, EI has a very slow start and proves ineffective despite several years of costly investments. Eventually the effort is either formally cancelled or it dies slowly through lack of interest.

2. **The Knowledge Gap**. Another impediment to effective introduction of EI lies in unequal knowledge of and expertise in EI matters on the part of labour and management. Management, in most cases, has had a head start on learning about the nuts and bolts of EI in the 1980s, by working closely with behavioural scientists and other experts and by using organizational resources to hire experts and to train its own personnel.

Labour, on the other hand, has lagged in educating itself and its membership on these concepts. This gap was glaring in the early- and mid-1980s. Although the knowledge gap has narrowed a great deal in the 1990s, it remains an important hurdle that must be overcome if EI is to be diffused widely in the unionized sector.

The key decision for these unionized firms is the extent or scope of union involvement in EI initiation, implementation, and evaluation.

Extent of Involvement

The extent of union involvement can be described in terms of the following five levels. Under *unilateral management decision making*, management makes all the decisions and there is no role for the union. Under *managerial information sharing*, management informs the union of its plans and actions and the union may have the right to request information. This does not allow for any direct input into decision making but it does provide additional resources (i.e., information) to the union to represent its interests through traditional channels. Under *consultation*, management provides information and solicits union input with no promise of acting on the input. The power of decision making remains with management, which becomes better informed about the needs of the union as a result of the consultative process. Progressive managers would try to accommodate union needs as often as possible. Autocratic managers or militant union leaders could, however, defeat the process by making consultation irrelevant to decision making. Under *decision making by consensus*, both sides make decisions jointly but agree to rule only by consensus. Legal authority remains with management but formal authority is delegated to a joint forum. There is no dispute resolution mechanism. In the event of a dispute that cannot be resolved, authority reverts to its traditional owner, the management. Finally, under *joint governance*, decisions are made jointly by both sides; a dispute resolution procedure is used in the event that the two sides cannot agree (Verma and Cutcher-Gershenfeld, 1993).

EXHIBIT 15.4

CEP POLICY ON EMPLOYEE INVOLVEMENT AND PARTICIPATION

CEP will enter into discussions at the sectoral or workplace level with a view to conclude agreements that enhance employment and income security and enhance productivity based on investment in the labour force and strategic investment in the enterprise or industry.

CEP will work with industry and negotiate particular programs providing that CEP is a full participant in the design, implementation, and continuous development of these programs.

Sectoral or workplace agreements may address training programs, workplace restructuring, and particular investment and production plans.

Any such agreement shall be properly negotiated, and must be subject to membership debate and approval.

Source: CEP. *New Directions: CEP Policy on Workplace Reorganization.*

Some unions have developed policies with regard to their role in workplace change interventions. Exhibit 15.4 excerpts the CEP union's requirement that programs be negotiated with the union's full participation and receive union membership approval.

Scope of Involvement

Unions can be involved in various stages of EI—idea, design, and implementation. In the vast majority of cases, unions are brought into the picture only at the implementation stage. This sets up a very dysfunctional dynamic between the parties right from the start because unions feel that by the time they are involved, most of the major parameters of the EI program have been set. Unions frequently are put into the position of either agreeing to a package designed unilaterally by management experts, or rejecting it completely.

Union Concerns about EI

Unions have articulated their concerns about EI in a variety of ways ranging from the ideological to the practical. Apart from some ideologically driven hardline opinions, most union concerns have to do with the potential impact of EI on the collective bargaining process. If union leaders perceive that EI will weaken collective bargaining and the union, they are generally opposed to it. They worry that EI may co-opt workers into a managerial agenda (i.e., improve quality and productivity) to the extent that workers will begin to see the union as irrelevant to their welfare. Unions also worry that some employers will use EI meetings to promote anti-union sentiments among workers to the point that workers will be ready to decertify their union.

Case evidence is strongly suggestive of EI's potential to thwart union interests (Verma and Kochan, 1985). But there is no evidence to indicate that this potential is innate to EI or that it is inherent in EI's dynamic as an organizational process. Rather, the evidence suggests that, like any other instrument, EI can be used for a variety of purposes, both functional and dysfunctional. Research shows that if EI is supported by the union, its outcomes are generally positive towards union as well as company goals. On the other hand, lack of union involvement leads to a perception that the union's contributions are marginal, which in turn leads to outcomes less favourable to the union.

Union leaders are concerned about EI programs because they socialize workers with pro-company and, possibly, anti-union views. Not all employers use EI as a forum to reinforce anti-unionism, but almost all programs do conduct training and provide information on a firm's competitive position as well as on the need to improve productivity and upgrade technology. Some studies have found that EI has a positive effect on the extent to which workers identify with company goals (Lischeron and Wall, 1975; Verma and McKersie, 1987)—termed a *program effect* (Verma, 1989).

A second concern for unions is the possibility that EI programs attract workers with anti-union views. In other words, EI programs result in a sorting of workers by their affinity to the union—pro-union workers stay away while anti-union workers tend to volunteer for participation in the program. This has been called the *selection effect* (Verma, 1989).

Empirical studies suggest that a union's own involvement may determine whether the program and selection effects are positive or negative. Where unions support EI programs, the program effect is positive and the selection effect zero or absent (Verma, 1989; Thacker and Fields, 1987). On the other hand, when a union is not involved in EI, there is evidence of a negative selection effect (Verma and McKersie, 1987). These results suggest that by withdrawing from EI efforts, unions may be creating a self-fulfilling prophecy; i.e., lack of union involvement may create the very effects unions fear most.

The extent to which union fears may be justified also depends on management's intent. EI can be used to undermine as well as reinforce and reform the labour–management relationship. One research study that monitored EI developments in companies like Boeing, Cummins Engine, General Motors, Xerox, Western Airlines, Alcoa, Budd, Boise Cascade, and Goodyear over a number of years found that EI tended to reinforce collective bargaining in cases where its principles were used to address external shocks such as restructuring due to recessions and other crises (Cutcher-Gershenfeld, Kochan, and Verma, 1991). On the other hand, in cases where EI principles were suspended or bypassed during these critical incidents, EI tended to either disappear or undermine the collective bargaining process.

Unions often negotiate quid-pro-quo conditions for their participation. For example, before agreeing to a work redesign at NB Tel, the CEP union demanded a written agreement from management that "It is not the intent of this initiative to reduce the workforce, reduce the level of bargaining unit work, or lower any standards of living or wages" (quoted in DiGiacomo, 1997). Similarly, in Exhibit 15.2 the union won a job security provision in exchange for the removal of restrictive work rules.

The Consequences of Non-Involvement of Unions

Management faces a series of choices when it comes to its relations with the union. The question is whether to involve the union at all and to consider the implications of implementing EI without any involvement of the union.

It is not uncommon to find managers who believe that they can "go it alone" on the issue of implementing EI. This is natural given the EI expertise that management usually can marshall on its own. Moreover, many managers feel that EI is largely a bilateral matter between themselves and their employees and that the union as a third party has no role, expertise, or contribution to make. Research shows that non-involvement of unions in the EI process can lead to a number of potential problems that managers must anticipate (Verma and McKersie, 1987).

First, lack of union involvement may be viewed by some employees as an ambiguous signal. Most employees trust the union more than management to safeguard their interests. They may wonder why the union is not saying anything about EI. This potentially disruptive effect, while discernible in some surveys, is clearly not a great threat, at least in the near term (Verma, 1989). But the lack of union involvement can also be viewed as a missed opportunity for management to marshall the union's support in making EI more effective.

Second, if the union chooses to oppose the EI program, it can very effectively compromise the program's impact on the workers. Unions have threatened and carried out anti-EI campaigns with some success. At BC Tel, the union opposed quality circles and, to make its opposition effective, conducted an education campaign to render quality circles ineffective. Other unions, including the United Steelworkers and the Communications Workers of America, have stated that if they were not given some involvement, they would carry out a campaign against EI efforts. Unions can file unfair labour practice complaints against companies, arguing that management is attempting to bypass the employees' legitimate bargaining agents, thereby preventing management from making any unilateral changes in terms and conditions of employment that would bolster the EI effort.

An active opposition campaign by the union sends confusing signals to workers who are not sure who they should believe—union leaders or managers. Employee surveys at many companies, including Boeing and Xerox, have documented a schism that develops among workers when they hear these conflicting messages about EI (Verma and McKersie, 1987; Cutcher-Gershenfeld, 1988). Those who are active in the union tend to view EI in negative terms, while those who are less interested in (or opposed to) the union tend to view EI in positive terms. Clearly, these divisions do not bode well for a successful EI effort.

Should management decide to get the union involved, it would have to make choices about the extent and scope of union involvement. There is not a great deal of systematic research on the pros and cons of different choices managers make in this regard. There is, however, much case and anecdotal evidence. The rule of thumb is to get the union involved as early in the process as possible, perhaps at the idea stage. The evidence also points to an active rather than passive union role as the key to effectiveness.

Canadian Unions and Direct Participation

When Canadian firms began to introduce direct participation processes such as quality circles, work teams, and other such forums, a number of unions saw them as an employer ploy to gain the upper hand in industrial relations. Several unions warned of the dangers of direct participation forums and urged opposition to such managerial initiatives. Many other unions, as well as the Canadian Labour Congress, issued statements of caution and provided guidelines on the conditions under which a union could get involved in such efforts.

By the end of the 1980s, a number of unions had developed their expertise in such matters, and they began to join with a small number of companies in exploring and implementing worker participation in the context of workplace reorganization. Notable among these unions were the Communications Workers of Canada (later the Communications, Energy, and Paperworkers) who adopted a policy at their annual convention in 1992, and the United Steelworkers of America who held a major policy conference on restructuring in 1991. Both of these unions released statements that endorsed the idea of proactive union involvement in introducing innovations such as direct worker participation through joint efforts with management. Recent examples of the implementation of EI initiatives in unionized Canadian workplaces are available, and most report quantifiable gains as a direct result of EI.[8]

The lack of enthusiasm for EI programs on the part of some unions can be argued to have slowed down the diffusion of EI in workplaces represented by these unions. However, it would be misleading to suggest that the examples of union opposition cited above have completely blocked the adoption of EI. Given the decentralized nature of the Canadian industrial relations system in which the power to sign collective agreements rests with union locals rather than with union centrals, a number of workplaces have adopted EI programs despite union policy statements critical of them. For example, the CAMI auto-assembly plant in Ontario, a joint venture between General Motors and Suzuki, has adopted a team-based production system in agreement with its local of the CAW.

Joint Governance

At the opposite end of the spectrum from non-involvement of unions is the process of joint governance. Under joint governance, union and management leaders bear *joint* responsibility for making decisions. Joint governance is both a radical departure from the conventional decision-making process and also a gradual extension of the principle of EI. Although it is not common in North America, there is a small but growing number of such arrangements (Verma and Cutcher-Gershenfeld, 1993).

Since joint governance is the ultimate step in union involvement, it poses the deepest problems and subsumes many of the issues previously discussed. Traditionally and legally, the authority for decision making has always resided primarily with management. It seems remarkable that any manager would give up this authority willingly. It seems equally remarkable that elected union leaders would agree to join management in making day-to-day decisions. Yet, for some parties, the benefits of joint governance outweigh the costs. It creates a forum for creative co-operation, but it also formalizes power in decision making so each side can maintain independence. In these and other ways, joint governance creates unique opportunities for innovative problem solving where other methods may fail.

What factors persuade the parties to enter into joint governance? What impact does joint governance have on employers and unions? Case evidence provides some clues (Verma and Cutcher-Gershenfeld, 1993). Some parties entering into joint governance are often pushed into it by events, while others enter into it believing that joint governance is integral to an effective labour–management relationship. The internal dynamic of joint governance is driven by the simultaneous opportunity for both co-operation and conflict. The parties have equal freedom and power to raise disputes or to develop solutions. Once implemented, joint governance requires that both direct and indirect participation be used in the workplace, that substantive rules be replaced by procedural ones, and that management and the union learn each other's skills; i.e., management must learn some political skills while the union must learn some business skills.

Despite many potential advantages, joint governance remains limited in its diffusion in Canadian, US, and other industrial relations systems.

THE LEGALITIES OF EMPLOYEE INVOLVEMENT

In this section of the chapter, we turn to the legal issues that surround the high-involvement workplace. For example:

- Is it lawful for employers to create teams, groups, and worker participation plans (particularly if they behave like unions)?
- What is the difference between employee participation in union and nonunion workplaces?
- Can employers use employee participation plans to avoid unionization?
- How far can managers and nonunion employees move in the direction of formalized representation systems without incurring legal roadblocks?
- Can employers implement employee participation plans in unionized worksites? What if the union objects?

Nonunion Workers: The Canadian Approach

To this point, we have focused on EI systems based primarily on meeting the competitive challenges of firms. But EI also brings opportunities for workers to group together, increases their ability to exert some influence on decision making, and generally makes them feel more effective. In these conditions, workers might be interested in collective representation of their own agenda, i.e., improving the terms and conditions of their employment. Industrial relations as a field accepts the premise that workers have common interests that might differ from those of management. Further, it is quite rational behaviour for workers to seek to increase their power through collective action. And in larger companies—where it is difficult to meet all employees individually—savvy managers who want greater participation and commitment from employees might find it in the corporate interest to hear and respond to workers' issues.

We turn to nonunion worksites first. Although rarely examined by industrial relations scholars in Canada, nonunion worksites deserve attention for two reasons. First, the majority of employees—currently almost 70 percent—are not unionized and thus are not protected by the collective bargaining statutory regimes described in Chapter 7. The ability of nonunion employees to seek a collective voice mechanism where unions have not—for whatever reasons—proved to be a viable option is of considerable interest. This is particularly true as management philosophies have moved in the direction of greater inclusion of and participation by employees. The Canadian approach is that all nonunion forms of employee representation are lawful (Taras, 1997). There is no ban or limitation on nonunion employee representation, so long as a company is not setting up a nonunion system for the purpose of thwarting the workers' statutory right to choose to be represented by a union.[9] Using EI for union-busting is an unfair labour practice. (By contrast, the American approach greatly restricts both the form and scope of nonunion plans. See Kaufman and Taras, 1999.)

Where does EI and nonunion representation exist in the legal web of rules governing Canadian employment? The simple answer is, nowhere. Aside from some statutes that compel larger companies to set up health-and-safety committees within union and nonunion worksites, there is no overt recognition in Canadian public policy of nonunion employee representation and participation systems.

Dissatisfied workers in an EI plan cannot simply transform themselves into a union because no labour board will certify a group of employees as a union when management has participated in, interfered with, or dominated their attempts to form a collective entity. That is, labour boards will not consider a management-dominated group to be appropriate for the purposes of collective bargaining.[10] Almost all nonunion groups involve substantial management participation. Often, the nonunion plans are encouraged or even established by management. Workers meet with managers in order to exchange ideas, usually on paid time and on company premises. Management has considerable input into the agenda and guides the discussion. Workers rarely have access to independent resources or expertise, but instead rely on information provided by management. Workers rarely pay any type of dues or charge for their participation in nonunion plans, as they are usually funded entirely by management. Two of the most formal and highly evolved Canadian nonunion representation plans are managed by the Royal Canadian Mounted Police and Imperial Oil.[11] Because of the extent of management presence in these nonunion plans, they cannot be certified as unions, and thus they exist outside collective bargaining laws.

By contrast, unionized workers meet without management presence. They collect membership dues and have access to independent expertise. Through their union, they can refuse to participate in any form of work design that violates the collective agreement.

They can strenuously resist the introduction of new participation plans, and they can link their acceptance of such plans to collective bargaining objectives such as higher wages or greater job security.

Though EI is not protected by laws, neither is it banned or interfered with by any laws. The situation in Canada is that managers and workers are free to establish whatever types of plans and vehicles they desire in nonunion worksites. Thus, in Canada, the issues involving employee participation rarely touch on legality, but more often involve implementation. The success and failure of nonunion plans depend on their design, the integrity of management, whether the workers trust that management will hear them, and the company's long-term commitment to employee participation.

Employee Involvement Plans and Unions: The Legalities

Not all Canadian employers have the unfettered right to initiate new forms of work arrangements. The legal situation is more complex in worksites that involve the coexistence of EI and collective bargaining arrangements. Canadian laws grant exclusive bargaining rights to unions that achieve certification. Various types of employee involvement programs currently are in vogue in Canada, all of which require more collaborative work arrangements between managers and workers. However, an employer cannot implement an initiative "in a manner which disregards a union's statutory bargaining rights" (Gleave, 1998: 199). While nonunion employers may freely communicate with employees, the situation is more complex in unionized settings. Employers' communication with unionized workers is constrained as follows:

- There can be no promises of reward, intimidation, threats, or coercion to interfere with, undermine, or derogate the union.

- Employers may not negotiate directly with workers on matters within the purview of the collective bargaining relationship. No "side-deals" are permitted.

- The union must not be maligned or demeaned by the employer.

Canadian labour relations boards have sufficient powers, under the various labour relations statutes, to safeguard the role of unions. Employers cannot use consultative programs to "subvert, circumvent, or replace the union in its legitimate role as exclusive bargaining agent."[12] On the other hand, the Canada Labour Relations Board commented in a leading CBC case that employee involvement initiatives were commendable, and that on their own they would not violate labour laws provided that management first attempted to deal with employees through the union.[13]

Thus, to introduce and operate high-involvement systems in unionized worksites requires a great deal of communication and collaboration with the union. It often is argued that unionization is a formidable barrier to the type of flexibility needed to run sophisticated employee involvement plans. The flip side of this assertion is that if a union accepts and oversees the implementation of such a plan, the plan is more likely to be well conceived and of lasting impact.

The Role of Public Policy

Canadian public policy generally has taken a non-interventionist role, and allows the parties to handle EI on their own. Labour and management are free to devise their own responses to workplace challenges, which might include restructuring, technological change, EI, and so on. There are concerns, however, that parties are producing inconsistent results, or are spending time inefficiently by "reinventing the wheel." Government has stepped in to "help" the parties arrive at agreements that introduce innovations such as EI to preserve jobs and improve productivity (Verma and Weiler, 1994). There are three main areas where public policy responses aimed at workplace change and innovation can be seen in recent years: amending labour codes to facilitate adoption of innovations, providing institutional support for innovations, and introducing EI into the government's own employment practices.

Amending Labour Codes

Governments in both Ontario and BC amended their labour relations acts in the early 1990s to strengthen collective bargaining and to encourage workplace reform. There are two approaches that encourage the parties to consult with each other and to make decisions jointly in the workplace. Section 53 in BC and Section 44.1 in Ontario provide for a joint consultation process that can be invoked by either party. Provision for a joint consultation committee must be included in every collective agreement. Joint consultation can begin with commencement of bargaining but must also be available during the term of the agreement. The objective of consultation is to "promote the co-operative resolution of workplace issues, to respond and adapt to changes in the economy, to foster the development of work related skills, and to promote workplace productivity." Lastly, the parties can jointly request the mediation services of the government to appoint a facilitator to assist in developing a more co-operative relationship.

An alternate approach, contained in Section 54 in BC and a similar Section 41.1 in Ontario, is to facilitate joint decision making in the area of workplace change. The BC *Labour Code* provided for joint decision making in the event of any "measure, policy, practice, or change that affects the terms, conditions, or security of employment of a significant number of employees." An adjustment plan for the change must be arrived at jointly. It thus provides for a process that is similar to that found in Germany under the works council statutes.

Institutional Support for Diffusion

Policy-makers have established various institutions and initiatives since the 1980s to support workplace innovations. Examples include: the Canadian Labour Market and Productivity Centre (CLMPC) to facilitate a mutual-interest agenda at the national level; the Canadian Labour Force Development Board (CLFDB), a labour–management board that advised the government on training policy; and the Ontario Training and Adjustment Board (OTAB), to formulate policy and administer training funds. A minister of the government may convene a meeting of the leading unions and employers in an industry or may engage in trilateral negotiations with a company and its union (Verma and Meltz, 1994). This approach has produced a number of agreements in Quebec in the last few years. Human Resources Development Canada has done a number of studies of workplace innovations in the late 1990s, and it continues to promote joint labour–management initiatives through its Labour–Management Partnerships Program. The Canadian Workplace Research Network (formed in 1994) offers another forum for information dissemination. In addition, sector-specific labour–management councils have been created by the federal government. The Canadian Steel Trade and Employment Council (CSTEC) in the steel industry and the Sectoral Skills Council for the electrical and electronics industry are two good examples (Gunderson and Sharpe, 1998).

Labour–Management Partnerships Program: labour-travail.hrdc-drhc.gc.ca/doc/fmcs-sfmc/eng/lmpp.cfm

Canadian Workplace Research Network: www.cwrn-rcrmt.org/eng/

Government as "Model Employer"

As governments are the direct employers of public-sector workers, EI can be introduced into their employment practices. In Ontario, a Liberal government mandated positions for nurses on hospital fiscal advisory committees in 1990. In the BC health care sector, a "social contract" was negotiated on an industry-wide, province-wide basis by the government, management, and three unions in 1993. In the late 1990s, many provincial governments moved aggressively to reduce deficits and balance budgets. The resulting restructuring in health care and education have put tremendous pressures on labour–management relationships in those sectors, and the parties have been forced to devise new organizational structures and workflows. It is too early to assess the full impact of these innovations at the present time.

THE SUSTAINABILITY OF EMPLOYEE INVOLVEMENT PROGRAMS

The practice of employee involvement has seen many innovations and, some would say, fads over the past 15 years. In the 1970s, the quality-of-worklife (QWL) movement was very strong, and a number of significant EI programs were launched under its banner. In the 1980s, quality circles (QCs) became very popular. The 1990s saw a major growth in total quality management (TQM) programs. The shifting sands of management fads and fashions raise a fundamental question about employee involvement: What factors sustain such innovations over time?

Although there are very few empirical studies of the sustainability issue based on large random samples, the case-study literature suggests a number of generalizations. First, as discussed earlier in the section on the organizational consequences of employee involvement, sustainability is facilitated by access to information and communication within the organization, and by corresponding changes in training and work organization. Second, a number of theorists have argued that, in unionized organizations, the support and co-operation of the union would enhance the effectiveness and sustainability of the EI process (Kochan, Katz, and Mower, 1984).

Further, as discussed earlier in the section on emergent types of EI, there is a link between sustainability and the type of EI: the narrow self-contained type such as quality circles or the integrated form such as autonomous work groups. It has been proposed that the first type is easier to introduce because its implementation requires relatively minor changes in the organization, but it is harder to sustain (at least in the North American setting) given its narrow scope. The second type is harder to implement given all the changes that need to be made, but easier to sustain because of its wide scope (Lawler and Mohrman, 1985; Cutcher-Gershenfeld, Kochan, and Verma, 1991).

Running successful nonunion employee participation plans requires a change in management style and a great deal of forethought. In Exhibit 15.5, the senior manager in charge of Imperial Oil's upstream operations' joint industrial council plan for worker representation analyzes the key elements that require management commitment. This plan is noteworthy because it involves *indirect* representation (workers are represented by elected worker delegates) and has an open mandate to advise—but not bargain—on matters normally falling within the purview of a union. Very few firms are willing to "walk the talk" on formal, nonunion representation plans. In particular, autocratic management styles, found in the "command and control" structures embedded in most firms, are incompatible with the principles necessary to run nonunion plans.

EXHIBIT 15.5

OPERATION OF THE PRODUCTION DISTRICT JOINT INDUSTRIAL COUNCIL, IMPERIAL OIL

1. MANAGEMENT VALUES, PRINCIPLES, LEADERSHIP STYLE

The values and principles of senior management are critical. Delegates and employees are sensitive to such questions as:

- Does the management team believe that employees have a role to play in influencing and setting policy?
- Is open, honest communication valued?
- Is constructive criticism welcomed?
- Are different perspectives respected and valued?
- Do the leaders do what they say they will do?

The values of the company and its leaders/managers translate into behaviours and a management "style" that can make or break the success of any form of representation, but it is especially key for nonunion representation in which there is no veil behind which management can hide.

Imperial takes care to appoint leaders/managers who demonstrate the ability to work well with a diverse workforce and have a proven track record in maintaining positive employee relations. We build this expectation into our management succession planning.

2. THE COMPETITIVENESS OF EXISTING WAGES, BENEFITS, AND WORKING CONDITIONS

It is important that a process exist to ensure we remain competitive in our wages, benefits, and working conditions. Let's not be naive. If our compensation package is not competitive, then a nonunion form of representation can break down very quickly. If employees feel they are being given fair and equitable treatment and their issues in these areas are being resolved, they typically see less value in injecting a third party such as a union into the process.

3. IMPACT AND ABILITY TO INFLUENCE

A representation vehicle that has (and is perceived to have) influence over matters within its mandate is more likely to succeed...Responsiveness is valued and expected. We keep a log of issues to ensure that response time is tracked. Delays without reasonable explanation are flagged for discussion and action.

4. HAVING BOTH FORMAL AND INFORMAL ISSUE RESOLUTION PROCESSES

The presence of formal and informal issue resolution processes is valued and the perception as to whether or not they are effective is important to monitor. The existence of a grievance procedure often is cited by people as an advantage of unions and there is a message in this for nonunion forms of representation. We have provided training for our delegates into how grievances are best handled....Equally important is a working environment where issue resolution can take place and employees are free to voice their opinions without fear of reprisal....It is most important that we "walk this talk."

5. EXTERNAL LABOUR RELATIONS AND LEGAL/HUMAN RIGHTS ENVIRONMENT

Our company does not operate nonunion representation in a vacuum. In other words, union actions, whether they be contract settlements, job actions, or grievance/arbitration decisions have some residual effect in nonunion areas. In addition, legal or human rights rulings that affect the workplace require clear understanding by our delegates. Things like alcohol and drug policy implementation have been a hot topic for us. The key in all of these areas, from my perspective, is to ensure that we have frank, open discussion of these matters....

6. THE WILL TO MAKE IT HAPPEN AND THE ABILITY TO EVOLVE

[We] press for continuous improvement in the Joint Industrial Council processes. If this evolution had not occurred, there is no doubt that JIC would not have survived to see its 50th anniversary in Imperial Oil's upstream.

Source: Excerpt from Boone (2000). Reproduced with permission of ME Sharpe, Inc. Publisher, Armonk, NY 10504.

A key area for long-term success of employee involvement in any organization, but especially a unionized one, is the issue of employment security. Since job security is fundamental to employee interests, it is only natural for employees to wonder about the effect on their own jobs of EI programs that seek to improve productivity and quality. Few people would be willing to help eliminate their own jobs. Hence, EI programs must create an implicit, if not explicit, guarantee that participants in the program will not become victims of their own success. In some organizations, such as Xerox and Saturn, explicit employment guarantees have been made. In others, implicit guarantees often accompany successful implementation.

In several documented cases, the loss of employment through major layoffs has often derailed EI programs. In firms such as Budd, Cummins Engine, US West, and even in the Edmonton hospitals, large-scale layoffs have led to a pulling back of labour–management co-operation or cancellation of the program or both. This is not to say that EI programs cannot be sustained in firms that are going through external shocks such as downsizing, restructuring, or market upheavals. However, attempts to implement EI during downsizing can have counter-productive results (Lam and Reshef, 1999). In a small number of cases, when the EI process is used to inform people about important business decisions, even if they have negative outcomes for employees, the trauma reinforces the EI process. At Xerox, when key business decisions such as subcontracting and location of a new plant were made through the EI process, that process was reinforced. On the other hand, when key decisions bypass the EI process, the effect is to undermine employee involvement.

Table 15.3 summarizes the factors that help and hinder effective employee involvement at the idea, design, and implementation stages. But underlying the specific factors listed in Table 15.3 might be a general construct relating to the tone of the relationship of workers and managers within the firm. A recent study of a Vancouver-based lumber co-operative proposed that *how* employees and managers interact and discuss issues may have a significant impact on the success of employee involvement. People with co-operative goals who discuss problems openly and constructively are more likely to experience success with EI than those who have competitive goals that result in avoidance or escalations of conflict, low productivity, and low morale (Tjosvold, 1998).

In general, EI initiatives challenge the comfort zone of employees and managers, who are accustomed to a certain "wage-effort bargain." Suddenly, people are being asked to work harder, or work "smarter," or communicate with each other in ways that were never required in the past. Psychological theories of motivation suggest that, in exchange for more effort, employees anticipate additional compensation from the corporation. Firms should acknowledge employee expectations of greater wages, benefits, and job security; satisfying training opportunities; respectful treatment; more collegial management styles; and other conditions of employment. EI will have spillover effects on many aspects of the firm, and successful interventions are those that anticipate and plan for such challenges, all within a more co-operative style of interaction.

TABLE 15.3

SUCCESSFUL AND UNSUCCESSFUL EI INITIATIVES

STAGE OF EI	FACTORS THAT HELP EI	FACTORS THAT HINDER EI
Idea Stage	• Consultation with employees and their employee representatives. • Assessment of EI readiness. • Commitment from senior managers. • Analysis of the HRM and IR systems that would need modification, including the need for change in the organization's culture.	• No consultation or advanced indication of intention to introduce EI. • No commitment of senior managers, or high rate of turnover of managers such that no EI "champion" is sustained. • Thinking about EI as a practice without ripple effects throughout the employment practices and culture of the firm.
Design Stage	• Input from employees or their representatives. • Training in skills needed for EI design. • Redefinition of the new role of supervisors. • Renegotiation of terms and conditions of employment so rewards from EI are allocated appropriately	• No input from workers, unions, or supervisors. • No training in design skills. • No coordination with line managers in integrating EI with work itself.
Implementation Stage	• Organization-wide communication on EI goals and methods. • Training for all employees in "soft" skills. • Redefinition of supervisory role as coach and mentor. • Appropriate incentives for EI efforts. • Tie-in of EI efforts with organizational goals. • Incentives for line managers to adopt EI.	• Insufficient autonomy for EI efforts. • Insufficient communication about EI to all employees. • Involuntary participation in EI. • Lack of funds to start EI. • Lack of focus on outcomes of interest to workers, e.g., safe jobs, more interesting jobs, job security, enhanced compensation.

LOOKING BEYOND: THE FUTURE FOR EI

Although the idea of greater say for workers has been accepted in principle, its implementation continues to be fraught with ambiguity and uncertainty. Battles, both ideological and tactical, continue around the scope, the extent, and the form that participation is to take within the organization.

Despite the intuitive appeal of the idea of employee involvement, its diffusion and effective implementation is far from being assured. EI requires each party to the employment relationship to alter its traditional stance towards the other party. Even as managers and union leaders grapple with ways to implement EI effectively, there is no doubt that the expectations of workers themselves will continue to rise in step with changing norms within free and democratic societies. Competitive pressures from the marketplace for better quality and greater product innovation are also unlikely to ease in the future. The net result would be to force both managers and union leaders to devise better ways of implementing greater employee involvement as an integral part of work and workplace relations.

Questions

1. What advantages and disadvantages do EI systems offer over purely Tayloristic forms of work organization?

2. Debate the proposition that EI should be implemented *only* if it improves productivity and efficiency.

3. Identify key organizational and external factors that will make an organization more likely to adopt greater EI.

4. Identify individual, group, organizational, and external factors that cause many EI programs to fail.

5. Is EI more or less likely to be adopted in a unionized organization? Why?

6. Do EI programs have the potential to destabilize labour–management relations? How can managers make EI a positive intervention in labour–management relations?

7. How can labour boards tell the difference between EI initiatives that are lawful, and those that are considered unfair labour practices?

8. Discuss the role of various management levels and functions in the successful implementation of EI: top management, middle management, first-line managers, HR/IR managers, line managers.

ENDNOTES

1 From Ann Armstrong, "Pay for Knowledge and Skill System: Chamainus Sawmill Division of MacMillan Bloedel Limited." In *Action: Developing High-Performance Work Teams*, Volume 1, Jack J. Philips, series editor. Copyright 1999 by the American Society for Training & Development, Alexandria, VA. Reprinted with permission. All rights reserved.

2 Throughout this chapter, the terms employee involvement, worker participation, and employee participation will be used interchangeably.

[3] Jeffrey Pfeffer wrote scathingly of management's preoccupation with lowering labour rates rather than over-all labour costs in his 1998 article "Six Dangerous Myths about Pay," *Harvard Business Review* (May–June), pp. 109–119.

[4] Sharing can be operationalized in practice in a variety of ways. Sharing profits or gains with workers according to a pre-set formula is one way of conveying to them that they will get an equitable return on their efforts. Employee ownership is yet another method that has gained some currency in recent years.

[5] Establishment surveys of training, in general, do not ask about the extent of coverage, i.e., two establishments, one with 100 percent of its employees covered and another with only 10 percent of its employees under training, would be counted similarly. Thus, caution in interpreting such data is advised.

[6] Reviews of many of these studies can be found in Locke and Schweiger (1979); Miller and Monge (1986); Cotton, Vollrath, Froggart, Lengnick-Hall, and Jennings (1988); Cotton (1993); and Wagner (1994).

[7] Measurement of outcomes such as costs and productivity should not be confused with general assessment and evaluation of the EI program. In fact, many of the firms that do not collect data on costs and output relating to EI do conduct employee surveys and focus groups to get subjective feedback from the employees on the EI program.

[8] These include NCR, Stelco's Lake Erie works, Canada Post, BPCO, Kruger, Abitibi-Price, NB Tel, and Norsask. Human Resource Development Canada's *Collective Bargaining Review* (1997) reproduces these studies on the Web: labour-travail.hrdc-drhc.gc.ca/wip/publications.html-ssi.

[9] See, for example, a leading Ontario Labour Relations Board [1984] decision, January 13, 1984, filed as 1146-83-R; 1682-83-U *Canadian Union of United Brewery, Flour, Cereal, Soft Drink and Distillery Workers* v. *Sevenup/Pure Spring Ottawa*.

[10] For the statutory treatment of management "domination," see, for example, *Canada Labour Code* Sections 94 and 25(1), *Alberta Labour Relations Code* Sections 146(1) and 36(1), and *Quebec Labour Code* Sections 12, 149, and 29.

[11] K. MacDougall, "Nonunion Employee Representation at the Royal Canadian Mounted Police," R. Chiesa and K. Rhyason, "Production District Join Industrial Council at Imperial Oil Ltd.: The Perspective from the Employee's Side," and D. G. Taras, "Contemporary Experience with the Rockefeller Plan: Imperial Oil's Joint Industrial Council," in *Nonunion Employee Representation*, edited by B. E. Kaufman and D. G. Taras. (Armonk, NY: ME Sharpe, 2000).

[12] According to the Canada Labour Relations Board in *C.U.P.E.* v. *C.B.C.* 1994, pp. 121–2.

[13] The difficult position unions find themselves in as a result of management's employee involvement initiatives is described from the union position by B. Hargrove (1998) and M. Wright (1998). The management perspective is offered by R. L. Heenan (1998) and by S. Gleave (1998).

REFERENCES

APPELBAUM, E., T. BAILEY, P. BERG, A. L. KALLEBERG. 2000. *Manufacturing Advantage: Why High-Performance Work Systems Pay Off*. Ithaca, NY: Economic Policy Institute and Cornell University ILR Press.

ARMSTRONG, A. 1999. "Pay for Knowledge and Skill System: Chemainus Sawmill Division of MacMillan Bloedel Limited," in *Developing High Performance Work Teams*, edited by S. D. Jones and M. M. Beyerlein. American Society for Training and Development.

BERG, P. 1999. "The Effects of High Performance Work Practices on Job Satisfaction in the United States Steel Industry." *Relations industrielles/Industrial Relations*, 54, no.1, pp. 111–135.

BETCHERMAN, G. and K. McMULLEN. 1986. *Working With Technology: A Survey of Automation in Canada*. Ottawa: Ministry of Supply and Services.

BETCHERMAN, G., K. McMULLEN, N. LECKIE, and C. CARON. 1994. *The Canadian Workplace in Transition*. Kingston, ON: IRC Press.

BOONE, D. J. 2000. "Operation of the Production District Joint Industrial Council," in *Nonunion Employee Representation*, edited by B. E. Kaufman and D. G. Taras. Armonk, NY: ME Sharpe.

CANADIAN AUTO WORKERS (CAW). *CAW Statement on The Reorganization of Work*. No date.

CANADIAN LABOUR CONGRESS (CLC). *A Trade Union QWL Agenda*. No date.

CANADIAN PAPERWORKERS UNION (CPU). 1990. "The Team Concept and the Restructuring of the Workplace." *CPU Journal*, 10, no. 2 (June).

CHAMBERLAND, R. 1997. "High-Performance Work Practices at Abitibi-Price." Innovative Workplace Practices: Case Studies, in *Collective Bargaining Review*. Workplace Information Directorate, Labour Branch, Human Resources Development Canada (March), pp. 115–119.

COHEN-ROSENTHAL, E. and F. J. WAYNO, eds. 1995. *Unions, Management, and Quality: Opportunities for Innovation and Excellence*. Chicago, Ill.; Toronto: Irwin; co-published with the Association for Quality and Participation.

COMMUNICATIONS WORKERS OF CANADA (CWC). 1992. *Prosperity and Progress: CWC's Vision for Shaping the Future*, 9th Annual Convention (June 15–19).

CONGER, J. A. and R. N. KANUNGO. 1988. "Behavioral Dimensions of Charismatic Leadership," in *Charismatic Leadership*, edited by J. A. Conger and R. N . Kanungo. San Francisco: Jossey-Bass, pp. 78–97.

COTTON, J. L. 1993. *Employee Involvement*. Newbury Park, CA: SAGE.

COTTON, J. L., D. A. VOLLRATH, K. L. FROGGATT, M. L. LENGNICK-HALL, and K. R. JENNINGS. 1988. "Employee Participation: Diverse Forms and Different Outcomes." *Academy of Management Review*, 13, no.1, pp. 8–22.

CUTCHER-GERSHENFELD, J. 1988. *Tracing a Transformation in Industrial Relations: The Case of Xerox Corporation and the Amalgamated Clothing and Textile Workers Union*. Washington, DC: Bureau of Labor-Management Relations and Cooperative Programs, US Department of Labor (BLMR 123).

CUTCHER-GERSHENFELD, J., T. A. KOCHAN, and A. VERMA. 1991. "Recent Developments in U.S. Employee Involvement Initiatives: Erosion or Transformation," in *Advances in Industrial & Labor Relations*, Vol. 5, edited by D. Sockell, D. Lewin, and D. Lipsky. JAI Press, pp. 1–31.

DACHLER, P. H. and B. WILPERT. 1978. "Conceptual Dimensions and Boundaries of Participation in Organizations: A Critical Evaluation." *Administrative Science Quarterly*, 23, no. 1 (March), pp. 1–39.

DiGIACOMO, G. 1997. "High Involvement Work Reorganization at NB Tel," in Innovative Workplace Practices: Case Studies, *Collective Bargaining Review*. Workplace Information Directorate, Labour Branch, Human Resources Development Canada (January), pp. 91–99.

FREEMAN, R. B. and J. ROGERS. 1999. *What Workers Want*. Ithaca, NY: Cornell University ILR Press.

GERWIN, D. and H. KOLODNY. 1992. *Management of Advanced Manufacturing Technology*. New York: John Wiley & Sons, Inc.

GITTLEMAN, M., M. HORRIGAN, and M. JOYCE. 1998. "'Flexible' workplace practices: Evidence from a nationally representative survey." *Industrial & Labor Relations Review*, 52, no. 2, pp. 99–115.

GLEAVE, S. F. 1998. "Worker Involvement Initiatives: A Management Viewpoint." *Labour Arbitration Yearbook*. Toronto: Lancaster House.

GODARD, J. 1997. "Beliefs About Unions and What They Should Do: A Survey of Employed Canadians." *Journal of Labor Research*, 18, pp. 619–640.

GRAHAM, L. 1995. *On the Line at Subaru-Isuzu: The Japanese Model and the American Worker*. Ithaca: Cornell University ILR Press.

GUNDERSON, M. and A. SHARPE. 1998. *Forging business-labour partnerships: The emergence of sector councils in Canada.* Toronto: Published in co-operation with the Centre for the Study of Living Standards by University of Toronto Press.

HARGROVE, B. 1998. "Decision-Making in the Workplace: A Union View." *Labour Arbitration Yearbook.* Toronto: Lancaster House.

HEENAN, R. L. 1998. "Decision-Making in the Workplace: A Management Viewpoint." *Labour Arbitration Yearbook.* Toronto: Lancaster House.

ILO. International Labour Organization. 1993. *Yearbook of Labour Statistics.* Geneva: ILO.

JACKSON, E. T. and G. DiGIACOMO. 1977. "Innovative Workplace Practices: Case Studies. Introduction," *Collective Bargaining Review.* Workplace Information Directorate, Labour Branch, Human Resources Development Canada (January), pp. 85–89.

KANIGEL, R. 1997. *The One Best Way: Frederick Winslow Taylor and the Enigma of Efficiency.* New York, NY: Penguin Books.

KAUFMAN, B. E. and D. G. TARAS. 1999. "Nonunion Employee Representation: Introduction." *Journal of Labor Research*, 20, no. 1, pp. 1–8.

KLEIN, J. A. 1988. *The Changing Role of First-Line Supervisors and Middle Managers.* Washington, DC: Bureau of Labor-Management Relations and Cooperative Programs, US Department of Labor (BLMR 126).

KLEIN, J. A. and P. A. POSEY. 1986. "A Good Supervisor is a Good Supervisor Anywhere." *Harvard Business Review* (November–December).

KOCHAN, T. A., H. C. KATZ, and N. MOWER. 1984. *Worker-Participation and American Unions: Threat or Opportunity?* Kalamazoo, MI: Upjohn.

LAM, H. and Y. RESHEF. 1999. "Are Quality Improvement and Downsizing Compatible?" *Relations industrielles/Industrial Relations*, 54, no. 4, pp. 727–47.

LAWLER, E. E. and S. A. MOHRMAN. 1985. "Quality Circles after the Fad." *Harvard Business Review*, 63, no. 1 (January–February), pp. 64–71.

LAWLER, E. E., S. A. MOHRMAN, and G. E. LEDFORD. 1992. *Employee Involvement and Total Quality Management.* San Francisco: Jossey Bass.

———. 1995. *Creating High Performance Organizations: Practices and Results of Employee Involvement and Total Quality Management in Fortune 1000 Companies: A Study Commissioned by the Association for Quality Participation.* San Francisco: Jossey Bass.

LEE, C. and R. S. SCHULER. 1982. "A Constructive Replication and Extension of a Role and Expectancy Perception Model of Participation in Decision-making." *Journal of Occupational Psychology*, 55, pp. 109–118.

LEWCHUK, W. and D. ROBERTSON. 1996. "Working Conditions under Lean Production: A Worker-based Benchmarking Study." *Asia Pacific Business Review,* 2, pp. 60–81.

LISCHERON, J. A. and T. D. WALL. 1975. "Employee Participation—An Experimental Field Study." *Human Relations,* 28, pp. 863–84.

LOCKE, E. A. and D. M. SCHWEIGER. 1979. "Participation in Decision-making: One More Look," in *Research in Organizational Behavior*, Vol. 1, edited by B. M. Staw. Greenwich, CT: JAI Press.

LONG, R. J. 1989. "Patterns of Workplace Innovations in Canada." *Relations industrielles/Industrial Relations*, 44, no. 4 (Autumn), pp. 805–25.

MILLER, K. I. and P. R. MONGE. 1986. "Participation, Satisfaction, and Productivity: A Meta-Analytic Review." *Academy of Management Journal*, 29, no. 4, pp. 727–53.

OSTERMAN, P. 1994. "How Common is Workplace Transformation and Who Adopts It?" *Industrial and Labor Relations Review*, 47, no. 2, pp. 173–188.

PORTER, M. E. 1980. *Competitive Strategy*. New York: Macmillan.

———. 1990. *The Competitive Advantage of Nations*. New York: Macmillan.

RANKIN, T. 1986. "Integrating QWL and Collective Bargaining." *Worklife Review*, 5, no. 3.

SASHKIN, M. 1976. "Changing Towards Participative Management Approaches: A Model and Methods." *Academy of Management Review*, 1, no. 3, pp. 75–86.

SCHULER, R. S. 1980. "A Role and Expectancy Perception Model of Participation in Decision-making." *Academy of Management Journal*, 23, pp. 331–40.

TARAS, D. G. 1997. "Why Nonunion Representation is Legal in Canada." *Relations industrielles/Industrial Relations*, 52, no. 4, pp. 763–86.

TARAS, D. and A. PONAK. 1999. "Petro-Canada: A Model of the Union Cooperation Strategy within the Canadian Petroleum Industry," in *From Contract to Commitment: Employment Relations at the Firm-level in Canada*, edited by A. Verma and R. P. Chaykowski. Kingston, ON: IRC Press.

TAYLOR, F. W. 1911. *The Principles of Scientific Management*. New York: Harper and Brothers.

———. 1916. "The Principles of Scientific Management." *Bulletin of the Taylor Society* (December), quoted in *Classics of Organization Theory*, 4th Edition, edited by J. M. Shafritz and J. Steven Ott. Fort Worth: Harcourt Brace, 1995.

THACKER, J. W. and M. W. FIELDS. 1987. "Union Involvement in Quality-of-Worklife Efforts: A Longitudinal Investigation." *Personnel Psychology*, 40, pp. 97–111.

TJOSVOLD, D. 1991. *Team Organization: An Enduring Competitive Advantage*. Chichester: John Wiley & Sons.

———. 1998. "Making Employee Involvement Work: Cooperative Goals and Controversy to Reduce Costs." *Human Relations*, 51, no. 2, pp. 201–14.

UNITED STEEL WORKERS OF AMERICA (Canada). 1991. *Empowering Workers in the Global Economy, A Labour Agenda for the 1990s*. Papers prepared for a conference in Toronto (October 22–23).

VERMA, A. 1989. "Joint Participation Programs: Self-help or Suicide for Labor?" *Industrial Relations*, 28, no. 3 (Fall), pp. 401–10.

———. 1990. *The Prospects for Innovation in Canadian Industrial Relations in the 1990s*. Ottawa: Canadian Federation of Labour and World Trade Centres in Canada Joint Committee on Labour Market Adjustment.

VERMA, A. and J. CUTCHER-GERSHENFELD. 1993. "Joint Governance in the Workplace: Beyond Union-Management Cooperation and Worker Participation," in *Employee Representation: Alternatives and Future Directions*, edited by B. E. Kaufman and M. M. Kleiner. Madison, WI: Industrial Relations Research Association, pp. 197–234.

VERMA, A. and D. IRVINE. 1992. *Investing in People: The Key to Canada's Growth and Prosperity*. Toronto: Information Technology Association of Canada.

VERMA, A. and T. A. KOCHAN. 1985. "The Growth & Nature of the Nonunion Sector Within a Firm," in *Challenges and Choices Facing American Labor*, edited by T. A. Kochan. Cambridge, MA: M.I.T. Press, pp. 89–118.

VERMA, A. and R. B. McKERSIE. 1987. "Employee Involvement Programs: The Implications of Non-involvement by Unions." *Industrial and Labor Relations Review*, 40, no. 4, pp. 556–68.

VERMA, A. and N. M. MELTZ. 1994. "Canadian Developments in Industrial Relations and Implications for the U.S." Paper presented to *Conference on Labor Relations Institutions and Economic Performance, Work and Technology Institute*, Washington, D.C. (March 14–15).

VERMA, A. and J. P. WEILER. 1994. *Understanding Change in Canadian Industrial Relations: Firm-level Choices and Responses*. Kingston, ON: IRC Press.

WAGER, T. 1996. *Employee Involvement, Strategic Management and Human Resources: Exploring the Linkages*. Kingston, ON: Queen's University, Industrial Relations Centre.

WAGNER, J. A. 1994. "Participation's Effects on Performance and Satisfaction: A Reconsideration of Research Evidence." *Academy of Management Review*, 19, no. 2, pp. 312–30.

WRIGHT, M. D. 1998. "Worker Involvement Initiatives: A Union Viewpoint." *Labour Arbitration Yearbook*. Toronto: Lancaster House.

CHAPTER 16

Union–Management Relations in Quebec

Esther Déom and Jean Boivin

Culinar, a Quebec-based food company, is one of the province's entre-
preneurial success stories (Fraser, 1987). It was founded in 1923 as the
Vachon's family business near Quebec City. The single-plant operation
specialized in making various pastries, the most famous of which is the
"Joe Louis."

At the end of the 1960s, the Vachon family was planning to sell the
company for $13.5 million to the American multinational Beatrice
Foods. However, Quebec's premier persuaded the leader of the
Desjardins Credit Union to ensure that Vachon control would remain
within Quebec. A deal was struck for $14 million, with Desjardins hold-
ing the majority share.

Vachon became Culinar in 1970 and the company expanded its operations after the injection of capital by the General Investment
Corporation, a financial arm of the Quebec government. The GIC also
took a majority position on the board of the newly diversified company.
In 1990, Culinar entered the American market through the purchase of

> Drake Bakeries. Drake was later sold in 1998 to the American company Interstate Bakeries after it became apparent that Culinar could not solve the distribution system issues that plagued Drake. Culinar's profitability gradually diminished in the 1990s, and the logical choice of buyer was Interstate Bakeries. However, selling to Interstate was vetoed by the GIC representatives since it would have meant the loss of another of Quebec's economic jewels. The province had already been traumatized by the sale of its largest retail food store, Provigo, to the Ontario-based Loblaws. Another large Quebec food company, Saputo, in the cheese processing business, was persuaded to outbid the Interstate Bakery offer by $15 million. The control of Culinar has thus remained in Quebec and the company is operating today as a branch of Saputo. It remains to be seen if Saputo will be able to guarantee a bright future for Culinar's 2300 employees located in five different plants in Canada.

This chapter is divided into three sections. The first provides the reader with the evolution of the socio-political and economic contexts that have shaped labour–management relations in Quebec. The second deals with employer and employee associations. The third presents some particular features of Quebec's public policies on work, such as pay equity legislation.

The Social, Political, and Economic Context

Three key factors have to be kept in mind when trying to understand the functioning of labour–management relations in Quebec: nationalism, state interventionism, and the political strength of the labour movement.

The first factor stems from the fact that 80 percent of Quebec's 7 million people are French speaking and are surrounded by more than 300 million English-speaking neighbours. Nationalism has been a permanent feature of Quebec's society since the British conquest of Canada in 1759, and Quebec's political, religious, and intellectual leaders have always nurtured the instinct of survival among the population. Such strong nationalistic sentiment exists even among citizens that want to remain part of Canada.

The second factor—the very active role played by the provincial government in all aspects of Quebec's economic and social activities—is, to a certain extent, a direct consequence of the first. It is a phenomenon that gained considerable momentum in the early 1960s with what has been called Quebec's "Quiet Revolution." A good indicator of this reality is the fact that the share of Gross Domestic Product that is related to government activities was 54.6 percent in Quebec in 1995 while the Canadian figure was 47.9 percent and the US figure 33.2 percent (Treff and Perry, 1998).

The third factor—the political strength of the labour movement—is a by-product of the "Quiet Revolution." It still exists at the turn of the millennium, even in the face of a hostile economic environment that has led to a slight decrease in the percentage of employees represented by labour unions. This political strength is not the result of formal relationships between labour unions and a specific party as is the case in the rest of Canada with the NDP, nor is it caused by the ability of labour organizations to mobilize voters during elections, although this can happen sporadically. It rather comes from two sources. First, the neo-corporatist ideology that prevails in Quebec enhances the capacity of labour organizations to influence governments. For example, after the failure of the Meech Lake Accord, leaders of central labour organizations were part of the constitutional commission that was set up by the Quebec government to examine various scenarios regarding the place of Quebec within Canada. Second, the centralized nature of collective dealings between employers and unions under the Decree System (Exhibit 16.1) or in key sectors of the economy such as construction and the public sector[1] yields considerable power to labour organizations in Quebec.

Conservative Nationalism (1900–1960)

Until the early 1960s, Quebec's nationalism was based on the preservation of two fundamental values: the French language and the Catholic religion. The Catholic church had a strong hand on almost every aspect of Quebec's socio-economic life, and it played a major role in shaping the population's attitudes and behaviours toward work, business activities, and labour unions.

In the first half of the 20th century, although rural values still predominated, industrialization was progressing rapidly and the number of factory workers was rising accordingly. The Catholic church had finally accepted the idea that workers could form labour unions, although Catholic leaders did not want workers to join locals of international unions for two major reasons: "These organizations did not share the language, nor the values nor the culture of French Canadian Catholic workers" (Babcock, 1973), and "they were socialistic since they were advocating measures like free and mandatory public schools, free universal Medicare, old age pensions, employers' liability for occupational injuries" (Rouillard, 1989). For this reason, the Catholic church took it upon itself to set up independent "confessional" labour unions run by French-speaking leaders. At the same time, similar confessional unions were also being established in countries like France, Belgium, and the Netherlands. The fear of Marxism explains why the Catholic church became involved in labour relations throughout the world. But in Quebec, the attack on international unions was dictated more by the Catholic church's fear of losing its influence and control over vital institutions such as schools, hospitals, and the welfare system than by the fact that existing international unions were leaning toward Marxism.

As one might expect, confessional unions were not militant. They very seldom engaged in strikes, and when they intended to do so, their action had to receive prior authorization from the local union's chaplain. These organizations accounted for 20 percent to 40 percent of total union membership in Quebec between 1930 and 1960 (Rouillard, 1989).

Despite the conservatism that prevailed in Quebec society, the provincial government introduced two pieces of legislation that favoured the development of union activities. In 1924, the *Professional Syndicates Act* gave individuals exercising the same profession or trade the right to set up associations and register them as civil entities. The Act recognized that an important function of these associations was the enhancement of the economic interests of their members, and it gave them the right to sign legal contracts and enforce them in courts.

In 1934, the *Act Respecting Collective Agreement Decrees* gave the minister of labour the power to extend some provisions of collective agreements (namely monetary clauses) to nonunion employers of the same economic sector. The main goals of the legislation were, first, to give nonunion workers the benefits of better working conditions found in collective agreements, and second, to eliminate competition over wages and working conditions among firms operating in the same industry. The Decree System is still in force (see Exhibit 16.1), although employers are challenging its usefulness more and more in the context of free trade agreements.

Decrees are mainly found in low-wage sectors characterized by a large number of small and medium-size firms, which operate in highly competitive markets. Despite the fact that many of them have disappeared over the years, the number of employers and employees covered by decrees has remained stable over the past 20 years. This is so because, as the more traditional trades in the manufacturing sector were covered less and less by decrees, new ones were enacted in sectors such as private security, building services, solid waste removal, and installation of petroleum equipment. At the end of 1998, 11,518 employers and 112,678 salaried workers (less than 5 percent of total employment) were covered by 27 decrees in the following sectors: garages; services such as bread distributors, building services, road haulage, security guards, and solid waste; clothing, which includes handbags, leather gloves, men's clothing, millinery, shirts, and women's clothing; hairdressers; and other industries such as building materials, caskets, furniture paper boxes, petroleum equipment, non-structural metals, and corrugated paper boxes.

During its 60 years of existence, the Decree System has often been the subject of strong criticisms. Labour organizations have complained that the system prevented them from increasing their penetration in sectors covered by decrees because unorganized workers had no incentive to join a union—they were already benefiting from some of the working conditions negotiated by unions without having to pay for the cost of unionization. However, this argument is not supported by facts because union density has been higher in sectors covered by decrees compared to the Quebec economy as a whole, at least until recently. (Bernier, 1993).

More recently, criticisms have come from employers who complain that higher labour costs imposed by the decrees put them at a competitive disadvantage vis-à-vis firms located outside Quebec. Consequently, many employers' associations are presently requesting either a complete abolition of the Decree System or, at least, that decrees not apply to sectors exposed to foreign competition. Decrees in the flat glass and woodworking sectors were eliminated recently and, at the time of writing, the government was

EXHIBIT 16.1

BASIC FUNCTIONING OF THE DECREE SYSTEM

Step one: Either a very large firm or a group of small firms of the same economic sector gathered into an association bargain a collective agreement with the local union that is representing their employees. This is done under the general rules of the *Labour Code*.

Step two: If the employers and the local union are interested in having the basic terms of their collective agreement (wages, hours of work, working days, vacations with pay, social security benefits, classification of operations, and classes of employees and employers) extended to the whole economic sector, they petition the minister of labour to this effect. The parties involved must also determine the scope of the decree by defining the type of activity that will be covered as well as the geographical area, whether the whole province or just a region.

Step three: The text of the agreement is sent to the minister of labour who publishes it in the *Gazette officielle du Québec* and in one French and one English newspaper. Third parties have 30 days to file any objections.

Step four: The minister, "if he deems the provisions of the agreement have acquired a preponderant significance and importance for establishing conditions of labour, without serious inconvenience resulting from the competition of outside countries or the other provinces, may recommend the approval of the petition...with such changes as are deemed expedient, and the passing of a decree for such purpose" (Section 6 of the legislation). The minister has the discretionary power to change some provisions of the agreement.

Step five: If the minister approves the petition, a joint committee is formed with an equal number of representatives from both the employers and the unions who signed the agreement. The minister may add an equal number recommended by employers and employees who are not parties to the agreement. The committee appoints a general manager, secretary, and inspectors, and it acts on behalf of employees in the enforcement in the courts. The committee's operating costs are mainly covered by a levy of one-half of 1 percent of the employers' payroll and of the employees' salaries. The joint committee negotiates the renewal of the decree, making the extension system a type of multi-employer and sometimes, multi-union, collective bargaining.

holding public hearings on abrogating the four decrees in the clothing sector. For their part, labour unions are in favour of maintaining the Decree System.

Despite the adoption, by the Liberal party in 1943, of legislation proclaiming the right of workers to unionize and the obligation of employers to collectively bargain with the certified representative of their workers (*Labour Relations Act*), the persistence of conservative values among the population and the overt opposition of the Union Nationale government, which stayed in power between 1944 and 1960, made it very difficult for the labour movement to make any significant progress during that period.

On the business side, people who were interested in setting up their own private commercial enterprises were often discouraged from doing so because the accumulation of wealth was considered sinful by the Catholic church. The few students who attended post-secondary institutions were mainly oriented toward theology, medicine, and law. As a result, very few French-speaking Quebecers worked as supervisors or were found on companies' executive boards. Rather, the bulk of the population was working as cheap labour for businesses that were run by English-speaking Canadians and Americans.

State Interventionism and Labour's New Legitimacy and Militancy (1960–76)

The Quiet Revolution: A Modernized Form of Nationalism

The return of the provincial Liberal party to power in 1960 signalled the beginning of Quebec's Quiet Revolution. The 1960–66 period gave a strong impetus to the modernization of Quebec's institutions through the development of state-owned enterprises and the creation of a professional civil service that replaced the old spoils system. It also provided a more favourable environment for the labour movement, whose leaders were intellectually very close to some influential ministers of the party in power. One of the key pieces of legislation adopted by the Liberal government was the replacement of the *Labour Relations Act* by a modernized *Labour Code*, which included many provisions facilitating the expansion of collective bargaining rights. Among other things, civil servants and professional workers were granted the right to join a union, all public-sector employees except police and firefighters were granted the right to strike, and conciliation procedures were simplified so as to make it less cumbersome for unions to declare a legal strike. As a result, the number of unionized workers increased by 42.8 percent between 1963 and 1966, and the unionization rate went from 30.5 percent in 1960 to 35.7 percent in 1966 (Rouillard, 1989: 289).

The modernization of Quebec would not mean an abandonment of nationalism, as was demonstrated by the slogan adopted by the Liberals in the 1960 electoral campaign, "Maîtres chez nous" (Masters of our own Destiny). A new form of nationalism emerged based on social and economic development rather than on the preservation of religious and conservative values.

Because most of the economic and financial institutions were in the hands of non-francophone Quebecers, only a strong and proactive role by the government could change the situation. The nationalization of private hydro-electrical companies, which were integrated into Hydro-Quebec in 1962, was the first expression of this "economic liberation" of French-speaking Quebecers. The immediate effect of this decision was to allow many French-speaking engineers (and other professionals) to make a career in a company that would soon be identified as the leader of Quebec's economic development and recognized as a world-class organization.

Two important economic institutions were also created during that period. The General Investment Corporation (Société générale de financement) was to accelerate industrial development by promoting and financing Quebec's companies. The Quebec Deposit and Investment Fund (Caisse de dépôt et de placement du Québec) was to manage the assets of the Quebec Pension Plan, which had been established as a separate entity from the Canada Pension Plan. Over time, these institutions have become very powerful financial instruments in the hands of the Quebec government (see opening vignette).

The role of the Quebec government as a leading agent of change in socio-economic development was put on the back burner in 1966 when, surprisingly, the Union Nationale party regained power for a final four-year stint. The loss of the election led to a split within the Liberal party: The more nationalistic elements left to form the Parti Québécois. The Union Nationale government did not abolish any of the institutions that had been put in place during the Quiet Revolution. It just slowed down the rate of involvement of the state in the economy. Unions, for their part, continued to gain new members in both the private and public sectors, and the unionization rate climbed to 37.6 percent in 1971 (Rouillard, 1989: 289).

The Liberal party returned to power between 1970 and 1976 and, although it did not create new financial or economic institutions, it did actively stimulate Quebec's socio-economic development through massive public investments in education, health, road construction, hydro-electricity, and social programs. Public-sector employees' working conditions were also considerably ameliorated as a result of the militancy of workers whose jobs were taking increased importance in the day-to-day life of Quebec citizens.

Radicalization of the Labour Movement

At the end of the 1960s and throughout most of the 1970s, many labour organizations in Quebec adopted radical ideological positions. Some of them, notably the former confessional federation which had become a lay organization in 1960 (CNTU) and the Teachers' Federation, went as far as to suggest that Quebec become a truly socialistic, independent country. Such radicalization led to a schism within the CNTU in 1972 as some 35,000 members left to set up a new federation.

Even the more pragmatic Quebec Federation of Labour flirted with radicalism. At its 1973 general meeting, the QFL president exhorted its troops to "the inescapable battle against the existing economic and political regime" (Fournier, 1994: 91) However, time and events would show that the QFL was seeking the electoral defeat of the ruling Liberal party rather than the destruction of the capitalist system.

The ideological radicalization of labour organizations combined with the inflationary period that followed the oil prices shock of 1973 and the political agitation created by the Quebec Liberation Front—a small group of individuals that was seeking Quebec's political independence by violent means—helped to create a very chaotic social situation in the 1970s. That situation was exacerbated by the numerous conflicts that took place during the renewal of collective agreements in the construction and public sectors.

In the 1972 negotiations of the public sector, labour organizations representing all categories of personnel (civil servants, teachers, hospital workers, and government agency workers) formed a Common Front to back their monetary demands. They staged an 11-day general work stoppage that was finally ended by special legislative intervention. A few weeks later, the leaders of the three main labour federations were sentenced to jail for six months because they had recommended that their members not respect court injunctions. In the next round of negotiations, public-sector unions changed their strategy and opted for sector-based strikes. Once again, injunctions were issued, labour unions defied them, and special legislative intervention was used.

The Quiet Revolution Rekindled: The First PQ Mandate (1976–1985)

The 1976 election of the Parti Québécois led to a resurgence of Quebec's economic nationalism. Reaffirming the ideal of the Quiet Revolution, the PQ government put forward an economic development strategy based on self-sufficiency, i.e., the extension of ownership and control of enterprises by Quebec interests. One of the pillars of this strategy was the nationalization of the US-owned Asbestos Corporation. Also part of that strategy was the creation of a financial institution that would provide venture capital to private enterprises—the Quebec Development Corporation (Société de développement industriel).

These and other government initiatives such as the Workers' Solidarity Fund (Exhibit 16.2) provided considerable help to firms controlled by French-speaking executives (such as Bombardier, Quebecor, Cascades, Canam-Manac, and Culinar). By the mid-1980s, the expression "Quebec-Inc." became part of the financial vocabulary in Quebec (Fraser, 1987).

The government also initiated a series of socio-economic summits between 1977 and 1984, aimed at establishing a permanent dialogue among employers' organizations, unions, the co-op movement, and community groups. The 17 sector-based summits were aimed at solving industry problems such as the lack of competitiveness of exports, while the two general summits were exercises in consensus building reflecting this party's corporate ideology. One of the positive benefits of the general summits was an appeasement of the social climate at the end of the 1970s.

When in the opposition, the PQ repeatedly presented itself as a friend of labour although there was and there still is no formal or financial links between any of the major labour organizations and the party. The Quebec Federation of Labour is the only central organization to have officially demonstrated its sympathy for the PQ (via resolutions adopted at general meetings exhorting its members to vote for the PQ). It has done so in every provincial election since 1976, except in 1985 when the Liberals were returned to power. The QFL also took the side of the 'YES' camp in both the 1980 and 1995 referendums on the political future of Quebec within Canada.

The "friendliness" of the PQ toward organized labour was demonstrated a few months after it was elected in 1976. One of the very first political decisions that the new government

Exhibit 16.2

The Quebec Federation of Labour's Workers' Solidarity Fund

In 1982, the president of the QFL brought forward the idea of setting up a labour-sponsored investment fund that would help preserve and create jobs. At first received coolly by the government, business leaders, and even some trade unionists within the QFL, the idea became feasible when the Quebec government adopted enabling legislation on June 23, 1983. The Fund officially began its operations on February 3, 1984 after the government had injected $10 million.

Contributors

- Any individual, although QFL members represented 45 percent of the subscribers in 1999.
- Income tax credit of 30 percent, subscriptions eligible for RRSP tax credit, maximum $5000/year.
- Sums invested cannot be recuperated until contributor's retirement from the labour force, except under certain circumstances such as loss of employment.
- Some collective agreements provide for employer contributions to the Fund.

Key Characteristics of the Fund

- 60 percent of the Fund must be invested as venture capital in small and medium-size firms based in Quebec. The rest is invested in bonds and equities.
- The Fund participates in many local, regional, and sectorial venture capital funds with other financial institutions and community or co-operative groups.
- Value of Fund's assets—$3 billion; investments—$1.7 billion in 1100 Quebec firms. (Largest venture capital institution in Quebec.)
- Jobs maintained or created since inception: 66,000.
- Permanent staff of 200 employees plus temporary hires during the RRSP season.

Investment Policy

Before making an investment, the Fund does an analysis that includes social, economic, and financial considerations. Once a decision to invest has been made, it carries specific conditions:

- Company must reveal financial situation to employees.
- Company must allow employees to attend two- or three-day courses on subjects such as understanding financial statements and analysis of the employer's market situation.
- Courses are offered through an education and economic development foundation, largely funded by employer contributions from firms in which the Fund has invested.
- Present on a company's board of directors, but never as a majority partner except under exceptional circumstances, the Fund ensures employees keep receiving financial information.
- Fund plays key role in promoting labour training and a good climate of industrial relations.

made was to drop all the legal charges that had been laid against labour organizations by the previous government in the aftermath of the public-sector negotiations.

The government also introduced a series of amendments to the *Labour Code*, most of which were requested by the QFL and welcomed by all labour unions, even those that were ideologically opposed to the government. Among the most important amendments were: anti-strikebreaking provisions (Exhibit 16.3); automatic deduction of union dues from all employees included in the bargaining unit whether or not they are members of the union; provisions for first collective agreement arbitration; voluntary conciliation; and certain obligations imposed on labour unions such as secret ballots to be held for the election of officers, for approval of a collective agreement, and for strike authorization.

Despite ideological criticisms by two of the four major labour federations (the CNTU and the Teachers' Federation) most private-sector union activists believed that the PQ's

EXHIBIT 16.3

ANTI-STRIKEBREAKING PROVISIONS

Article 109.1 of the *Labour Code* reads in part as follows:

For the duration of a strike declared in accordance with this Code or a lockout, every employer is prohibited from:

a) Utilizing the services of a person to discharge the duties of an employee who is a member of the bargaining unit then on strike or locked out when such person was hired between the day the negotiation stage begins and the end of the strike or lockout;

b) Utilizing, in the establishment where the strike or lockout has been declared, the services of a person employed by another employer or the services of another contractor to discharge the duties of an employee who is a member of the bargaining unit on strike or lockout;

c) Utilizing, in an establishment where a strike or lockout has been declared, the services of an employee who is a member of the bargaining unit then on strike or locked out unless certain specified conditions have been met;

d) Utilizing, in another of his establishments, the services of an employee who is a member of the bargaining unit then on strike or lockout;

e) Utilizing, in an establishment where a strike or lockout has been declared, the services of an employee he employs in another establishment;

f) Utilizing, in an establishment where a strike or lockout has been declared, the services of a person other than an employee he employs in another establishment, except where the employees of the latter establishment are members of the bargaining unit on strike or locked out;

g) Utilizing, in an establishment where a strike or lockout has been declared, the services of an employee he employs in the establishment to discharge the duties of an employee who is a member of the bargaining unit on strike or lockout.

amendments would help the development of union activities in Quebec. The relationships between the PQ and public-sector unions, however, were not so friendly, and they had negative political consequences for the government.

The first encounter of the PQ with public-sector unions came in 1979–80, a few months prior to the referendum on Quebec's political future. Despite very generous offers made by the government early in negotiations in order to prevent the usual social crisis accompanying the renewal of public-sector collective agreements, public-sector unions maintained their traditional strategy and engaged in a series of militant actions. Special legislation was used and, once again, the settlements were reached in a context of social chaos. Some PQ political strategists affirmed that the loss of the referendum (by a 60 percent to 40 percent margin) was in part caused by the militant action of labour organizations in the public sector, which antagonized both the natural clientele of the PQ (public-sector employees) and the population in general.

Despite this political defeat, the PQ handily won the 1981 election. However, it returned to power in the midst of a severe economic recession that would once again put the PQ on a collision course with public-sector unions. In 1981, the president of the Treasury Board asked the unions to forfeit the wage increase that was scheduled for the last year of the collective agreement (1982). After the unions declined the government's proposal, the latter enacted special legislation that suspended the collective bargaining process and unilaterally imposed working conditions for the next three years. Worst, in the first three months of 1983, the salaries of most public-sector employees were decreased in such a way as to allow the government to recuperate the monetary increments it had given the previous year.

This very strong stance taken by the PQ government against public-sector unions certainly contributed to its electoral defeat in the 1985 election. Contrary to what it had done in 1976 and 1981, the QFL did not endorse the PQ, and its leaders widely publicized that it was because of what the PQ had done to public-sector employees. In its last year in power, the PQ introduced amendments to the *Labour Code* to modify bargaining procedures in the public sector.

Economic Nationalism, Social Contracts, and the Recession (1985–1994)

Labour–Management Collaboration in the Private Sector

The Liberal party returned to power in the midst of the economic recovery that followed the 1980–82 recession. They would be re-elected in 1989 before once again becoming the opposition in 1994. Although the Liberals had been very critical of the increased size of government as a result of too much state intervention in the economy under the PQ administration, their actual behaviour did not match their words once they were elected. They made the same political decisions that they were decrying while in the opposition.

In regard to union–management policy, the Liberals took a slightly different approach but the objective was the same: the pursuit of union–management dialogue in order to enhance the economic competitiveness of Quebec firms. The strategy of industrial clustering developed by the minister of industry, commerce, science, and technology, inspired by the works of Michael E. Porter of the Harvard Business School (1990), pursued the same objectives as the sector-based economic summits of the PQ; it even took them one step further.

The minister was an ardent believer in union involvement in the operation of firms, and he promoted the practice of "social contracts" between unions and management. These contracts took the form of memorandums of agreement, which complemented collective agreements (Exhibit 16.4). To favour the diffusion of social contracts, the government amended the *Labour Code* to allow collective agreements to last for longer than three years (except for first agreements). Although government financial participation was not a necessary condition for a social contract, it was common practice for the Quebec Development Corporation to require that most of the elements of the social contract be present before making an investment in a particular company.

The minister also established a program favouring the development of worker-shareholder co-ops, which enabled workers to collectively own up to 30 percent of the shares of a company and have representation on its board of directors. The acquisition of shares was facilitated by the Quebec Development Corporation's guaranteeing loans to workers. Some 30 such enterprises were in existence in 1997 (Grant and Lévesque, 1997: 247). Work co-ops in general are more numerous in Quebec than anywhere else in Canada (Quarter and Melnyk, 1989).

The Quebec government also used its fiscal policy to promote greater employer–employee partnership in small and medium-size firms. The *Workers Participation Scheme in a Total Quality Management Context* provided tax deductions for both employees and employers who got involved in a profit-sharing plan. Thus, in the private sector, economic nationalism was pursued by the Liberal government, which encouraged partnership and

EXHIBIT 16.4

THE SEVEN ELEMENTS OF SOCIAL CONTRACTS

1. Labour relations stability, which must be ensured by a long-term peace agreement.
2. Employment stability.
3. Human resources development and training.
4. Flexibility and mobility in work organization.
5. Total quality management.
6. Economic transparency, i.e., information provided to employees on the financial situation of the firm.
7. Joint administration of the agreement.

dialogue between management and unions at both the workplace and sector levels. This may have contributed to the decrease in strike activity that occurred between 1980 and 1995, although that decrease occurred throughout Canada (see Chapter 11).

Government policy is neither the only nor the main factor explaining this turn of events. Private-sector unions affiliated with all central labour organizations have become more aware of the necessity of committing themselves to workplace transformation in order to save and create jobs. The CNTU, for instance, concluded that unions should even propose changes in order to achieve better productivity rather than being reactive and waiting for employers' proposals to adjust to the new economic reality.

Public Sector's Financial Crisis

In its first mandate (1986–1989), the Liberal government started to tackle one of the major problems facing all governments in Canada: annual budgetary deficits. In 1986, the government struck a deal with the unions by allowing wage and salary increases for the next three years contrary to what the new legal regulations stipulated. In exchange, the unions accepted the economic package proposed by the government, but only after the government resorted to special legislative intervention to prevent a general strike in the health sector. That legislation, which is now a permanent statute, included very stiff penalties in case of violation (Exhibit 16.5). In 1989, nurses and other hospital employees illegally struck during the electoral campaign. The government used the provisions of the above mentioned legislation, which facilitated the reaching of an agreement. It also won the election.

When the most severe economic recession since the Great Depression hit Canada in 1990, it had very negative consequences on the government's financial situation. As was the case in other Canadian provinces and with the federal government, Quebec's public-sector employees would be the preferred target of the restrictive measures since their compensation represented more than 50 percent of the provincial budget.

First, the Quebec government asked all public-sector unions to postpone, until June 1993, the renewal of collective agreements that expired in December 1991. In exchange, it granted wage increases of 4 percent over that period. The unions reluctantly accepted, but not without publicly demonstrating against the government's original proposals, which were even more drastic.

Second, in January 1993, the government adopted legislation that froze public-sector salaries for two years and gave public employers the authorization to reduce their wage bill by 1 percent annually. The law also allowed municipalities to be covered by the legislation if they chose to do so. Additional legislation required all government departments and public agencies to reduce their supervisory personnel by 20 percent in the next three years (1993–96) and to reduce the rest of their workforce by 12 percent over the next five years (1993–98).

Public-sector unions felt betrayed by these measures because they had already accepted an extension of their collective agreements. The unions recognized that Quebec had serious financial problems but they claimed that the government could solve its

EXHIBIT 16.5

ACT REGARDING THE MAINTENANCE OF ESSENTIAL SERVICES IN THE HEALTH AND SOCIAL SERVICE SECTORS

For each day of illegal strike the following penalties will be imposed:

FINES
- $25 to $100 for individual employees
- $5000 to $25,000 for union officers
- $20,000 to $100,000 for the union itself

UNION DUES
- An employer shall cease to collect union's dues for a period of 12 weeks.

REDUCTION IN PAY
- An employee's salary shall be reduced by the equivalent of two days' pay.

LOSS OF SENIORITY
- An employee shall lose one year of seniority.

This last item is the most controversial one. It is unfair to some employees because many of them nevertheless remain at work during the strike, and it is an administrative nightmare for individual employers. As a result, after the 1989 round of negotiations, the government adopted legislation restoring the seniority of many employees following the recommendations of a special inquiry committee.

problem by modifying taxation so as to eliminate many tax evasion schemes and increase taxes on higher revenues and corporate profits, rather than by realizing short-term economies on the backs of public employees. They tried to mobilize their members and the population against the government adopting these two laws but to no avail. One year later, with an election looming, the austerity plan was abandoned and the Liberals ran a record-high $6 billion deficit in 1994. Nonetheless, the government was defeated in the September 1994 election.

The Carrot and Stick Approach and the PQ's Political Agenda
The First PQ Mandate, 1994–1998: The Zero Deficit Target

The electoral victory stirred up the PQ's interest in a new referendum, which the new government slated for October 30, 1995. However, a major stumbling block stood on the road to the fateful encounter with the population: the renewal of the 450,000 public employees' collective agreements, a task that had always been very difficult for any government be it Liberal or Parti Québécois. On the positive side for the new government was the fact that all but one of the central trade union organizations in Quebec had officially endorsed the objective of an independent status for Quebec. On the negative side was the financial situation of the government. The ratio of Quebec's debt to its GDP had risen from 28.3 percent in 1990 to 44.7 percent in 1995, the second highest among Canadian provinces.

One month prior to the referendum, and without any show of power on either side, the government and the various public-sector unions of the civil service, education, and health sectors reached an accord whose major features were the following: repeal of the legislation ordering the yearly reductions of 1 percent in total compensation; lump-sum payments representing 0.5 percent of employees' salary for 1996; salary increases of 1 percent to be awarded on January 1, 1997 and 1998; reduction of actuarial penalties on pension plans to encourage early retirements; no change in clauses that would give public employers additional managerial flexibility; and collective agreements to be valid until June 30, 1998. The total cost of these measures was estimated at $930 million ($770 million for salary increases and $160 million for early retirement provisions).

A few weeks after the referendum was lost by the narrowest of margins (50.4 percent to 49.6 percent), the head of the government resigned. Under a new leader, the government's utmost priority became the fight against budgetary deficits. The provincial government had to restore the province's public finances if it wanted to convince the Quebec population and key monetary institutions that an independent Quebec could be economically viable. In order to obtain a consensus on the objective of zero deficit, the government organized an economic summit in March 1996—a characteristic common to all PQ governments—which was attended by key decision makers from the ranks of business and labour. In the end, a consensus was reached that fiscal year 1999–2000 was the target date for the obtaining of the zero deficit budget. In the weeks following the summit, the government prepared a budget that drastically cut various programs and set the goal of a recurrent reduction of $800 million in unionized public employees' labour costs starting in fiscal year 1997–98. It also requested an additional reduction of $100 million in global compensation for the year 1996–97.

How was the new premier going to sell such an idea to labour organizations? The easiest way would have been to legislatively force the unions to relinquish the 2 percent salary increases that were scheduled for 1997 and 1998. However, this course of action had already been taken by a previous PQ government in 1983, and government negotiators knew very well the risks involved if they decided to follow the same strategy. Accordingly, a proposal was made to the unions, which suggested that public employees allow the government to reduce their gross salaries by 6 percent. In exchange, employees would be exempted from contributing to their pension funds for two years; the actuarial surpluses of the various pension plans would be used to finance this contribution moratorium. The government also declared that should its proposal be rejected, some 15,000 public employees would be laid off.

Even if public employees benefited from employment security, the unions knew that the Quebec government could use its legislative power to suspend this protection, like the federal government had done a year before. Nonetheless, after carrying out extensive consultation of their members, all unions rejected the proposal. Intensive bargaining thus took place and an agreement in principle was finally reached between the government and public-sector unions: The unions accepted the government's objectives regarding the reduction of labour costs, and the government accepted the unions' proposal that the savings be achieved through a program of voluntary retirements. It was expected that some 15,000 employees would be permanently removed from the public sector before July 1, 1997. The costs involved in this operation would be borne partly by the actuarial surpluses of the pension plans and partly by the government's general revenues.

There was serious misunderstanding, however, over how to reduce the personnel in the health and education sectors because of the constraints imposed by existing collective agreements. Hence, the government came forward with specific proposals to remove these constraints. The unions systematically refused to have their collective agreements altered and threatened to resort to work stoppages. The government counterattacked by introducing special legislation, which stipulated that if its proposals were not accepted, an automatic 6 percent reduction of salaries would ensue. In the end, although legislation had to be adopted in order to cover certain categories of nonunion personnel and some recalcitrant unions in colleges, an agreement was reached with most groups. During the final talks though, the government dropped most of its demands concerning modifications to the collective agreements.

This approach to labour cost reduction in the public sector has led to very important organizational problems. First, because the program was voluntary, many more individuals left their jobs than was necessary (36,000 rather than 15,000). Secondly, the voluntary nature of the early retirement program led to the loss of many experienced employees, including many in services that were vital to the population, such as nursing. As a result, these services are now experiencing shortages and public employers are trying to entice some of the retirees to return to work as contractual employees.

The Second PQ Mandate: 1998–

As part of the fight against the deficit, the Quebec government, as many other provincial governments in Canada, undertook a major overhaul of the health care system. Despite the unpopularity of the reforms that were introduced, the PQ was re-elected in November 1998. Currently, the government is having a difficult time with some of its electoral promises, like enabling the unionization of independent contractors such as truck drivers and prohibiting the use of "grandfather" clauses in collective agreements as a way of preventing discrimination against the younger generation. Expectations have been raised within these two groups, as they have been among women with the *Pay Equity Act* of 1996 (discussed later in this chapter), and it seems that the government is backing off as a result of an effective lobby put forward by employers. The latter, for their part, have been actively seeking the abolition of the Decree System and the alleviation of the provisions of the *Labour Code* dealing with subcontracting.

As regards public-sector negotiations, the government was facing the renewal of all collective agreements, which had expired in June 1998. For the first time since 1989, the collective bargaining process was unfolding according to the normal "rules of the game," i.e., there was no economic recession justifying the extension of existing agreements, no enactment of special legislation suspending the collective bargaining process, and no upcoming referendum justifying a last-minute arrangement over monetary issues with the unions. What was under way at the time of writing was just a plain "classic" round of negotiations with the usual pressure tactics on one side and delaying tactics on the other. This time the economic perspective for the government looked much better. The zero deficit budget had been obtained one year ahead of schedule (1999) and the rate of growth of Quebec's GDP was going to be greater than the 2.3 percent figure forecast by the finance minister. The expectations of public-sector unions were thus very high, as they were anticipating that their members could share in the new prosperity and recuperate some of the purchasing power that had been lost in the last decade.

The government affirmed that, since Quebec citizens were facing the highest tax burden in Canada, one of its priorities was to lower income taxes so that all citizens could benefit from recent economic growth. As a result, public employees had to accept wage increases that were in line with what was being offered in the economy in general and forget about any "catching up" effort. Moreover, using the Compensation Research and Information Institute's 1998 Annual Report, the government claimed that public-sector employees' remuneration was already at parity with that of private-sector employees and that its actual offers maintained this parity. As a matter of fact, such parity existed because public-sector employees enjoyed better fringe benefits and a shorter workweek than private-sector employees. On the basis of salary comparisons alone, public-sector employees' wages lagged behind those in the private sector by 7.2 percent (CRII, 1998).

The first test of the government's wage policy came in the summer of 1999 when nurses belonging to the Quebec Nurses Federation engaged in 23 days of illegal strikes (despite the stiff penalties described in Exhibit 16.5). The Federation was seeking three main objectives: a reduction of the nurses' workload, which had increased considerably as a result of the drastic health care reform; better job security; and better pay. They were successful on the first two counts but, despite the great show of sympathy by the population for the nurses' cause, the government did not make any concession on salaries. It offered to create a committee whose mandate is to compare the nurses' salaries with those of other public employees, and it guaranteed to pay whatever increments would be recommended by the said committee.

EMPLOYER AND EMPLOYEE ORGANIZATIONS

The next section of this chapter is devoted to describing the major labour organizations in Quebec as well as the major employer organization (the Conseil du Patronat du Québec).

Trade Union Structure and Membership
The Quebec Federation of Labour (QFL)

The Quebec Federation of Labour (QFL) (Fédération des travailleurs et travailleuses du Québec) is by far the largest central organization in Quebec (Table 16.1). In 1997 the QFL represented 37 percent of all employees covered by collective agreements falling under the jurisdiction of the provincial *Labour Code* (that is, all employees except construction workers and workers under the federal jurisdiction). The bulk of its membership comes from the private sector, where it represents almost 60 percent of all unionized employees, but it also has considerable strength in the municipal sector (53.8 percent of all unionized employees), and significant representation in the parapublic sectors. As well, its affiliates in the construction industry have always obtained the largest share in the representation elections held periodically under the *Loi sur les relations du travail dans l'industrie de la construction* (*Construction Industry Labour Relations Act*). Almost all unionized employees who come under the jurisdiction of either the Canadian *Labour Code* or the *Public Service Staff Labour Relations Act* are affiliated with the QFL.

TABLE 16.1

DISTRIBUTION OF WORKERS ACCORDING TO UNION AFFILIATION AND SECTOR, 1997 (PERCENTAGE OF WORKERS)

UNIONS	PUBLIC PROVINCIAL CIVIL SERVICE	PARAPUBLIC HEALTH AND EDUCATION	QUASI-PUBLIC UTILITIES & GOVERNMENT ENTERPRISES	PRIVATE	MUNICIPAL ADMINIS- TRATION	ALL SECTORS
CEQ	—	28.1	1.4	0.6	—	9.9
CSD	—	1.3	0.4	6.8	2.6	3.8
CSN	0.3	38.6	22.9	18.5	10.6	23.9
QFL	0.6	9.0	49.8	59.3	53.8	37.3
Independent	99.1	23.0	25.5	12.4	32.9	24.0
Others	—	—	0.1	2.4	0.1	1.1
All unions	100.0	100.0	100.0	100.0	100.0	100.0
Percentage of workers in each sector	6.8	34.0	6.7	46.8	5.7	100.0
All unions (number of workers)	63,689	316,830	62,668	435,655	53,566	932,408

Source: R. Shawl. 1998. "La présence syndicale au Québec." *Le marché du travail,* 19, no. 9 (septembre), p. 8.

The affiliation of local unions with provincial federations such as the QFL is not mandatory under the CLC constitution. Once a local union has joined a national or international union that belongs to the CLC, the local itself decides whether or not to affiliate with the provincial body. The QFL has been able to increase substantially its percentage of CLC union affiliates, from a mere 37 percent one year after the historic 1956 merger of the TLC and the CCL to between 65 percent and 70 percent in the 1970s. Today the QFL represents virtually all CLC affiliates in Quebec.

CLC: www.clc-ctc.ca

Special Status within the CLC. The Quebec situation of trade union pluralism and cultural specificity has led the QFL to behave like an independent labour body. Unlike other provincial federations, which quickly achieved a monopoly status in their respective jurisdictions after the 1956 merger, the QFL must compete with three other major labour organizations to obtain union members' allegiance. This unique situation has gradually led QFL leaders to ask for additional powers and more autonomy from their parent body, the CLC.

As early as 1967, the QFL leadership argued that CLC success in Quebec depended on a strong provincial federation. In practice, this meant that the CLC should recognize that QFL representatives were in a better position than CLC officials to understand the specific needs and problems of Quebec workers. To be successful in attracting workers to CLC unions, the organization should grant the QFL more power, autonomy, and money. The process of gaining more autonomy has recently led to an agreement that the QFL labelled a "sovereignty-association" agreement. However, the process of gaining this new status has been a long one, occurring at the 1974 CLC convention in Vancouver and at the 1994 convention in Toronto.

In 1974, delegates to the CLC national convention in Vancouver accepted the Quebec delegation's three major requests: (1) that the QFL would henceforth have full jurisdiction over labour education services in Quebec, a prerogative exercised by the CLC itself in all other provinces; (2) that the CLC would bargain with the QFL over a formula that would permit the latter to recoup funds for services that Quebec union members pay for but do not benefit from because of linguistic, cultural, or political differences (for example, a unilingual newspaper); (3) that the CLC would yield full jurisdiction over local labour councils to the QFL—an agreement implying jurisdiction over staff and hence over the corresponding sums of money. Although it took time for these resolutions to materialize, the QFL has been able to increase its presence in most regions where it was formerly weak (or non-existent) through hiring additional union staff appointed to local councils. The QFL has also extensively expanded its education services.

From "Special Status" to "Sovereignty-Association." From 1974 to 1994, many unique situations were created by the particular status of the QFL. Those situations led to informal agreements between the QFL and the CLC. In one case, it also led the QFL to take actions not allowed by the CLC constitution but that have been more or less tolerated.

In the mid-1970s, contrary to the CLC constitution, the QFL maintained among its affiliates organizations that had either severed their affiliation with, or refused to join, an international trade union. Asked to justify this irregularity, QFL leaders always publicly affirmed that the situation was temporary. The rationale for this irregularity was based on the unique situation of the QFL, namely the trade union pluralism in Quebec. For this reason, the QFL kept those organizations within its ranks, pending their final decision to return to their former organizations or to affiliate with some other CLC organization.[2] Many building-trade unions affiliated with the AFL-CIO, but threatened to leave the CLC if it did not order the QFL to end the situation of dual unions within its ranks. The CLC leadership, under the presidency of Dennis McDermott of the Automobile Workers, decided to stand behind the QFL and refused to expel the dual unions. As a result, in March 1981, the CLC executive council suspended 14 international building-trade unions, with more than 229,700 members, for nonpayment of affiliation dues. One year later, ten of these international building-trade unions participated in the establishment of a new labour federation: the Canadian Federation of Labour (CFL).

The 1994 agreement constitutes a logical result of the 1974 agreements. It became a necessity because of the deterioration in relations between the QFL and CLC after the electoral failure of the QFL candidate at the CLC national convention in June 1992. This "sovereignty-association" agreement was adopted unanimously by the CLC delegates at the national CLC convention held in Toronto, in May 1994. In addition to occupying a seat on the CLC Executive Council, the QFL president automatically becomes a full voting member of the CLC executive committee. This agreement also gives the QFL the right to observe its own protocols on such important issues as internal jurisdictional disputes and union education, together with the corresponding sums of money. It systematically includes the QFL in the CLC international representation by inviting the QFL to designate officers or representatives to participate in activities or organizations such as the International Labour Organization (ILO) Annual Conference, the International Confederation of Trade Unions Executive Board, conferences and meetings, as well as other international conferences, particularly those associated with francophone countries. With this agreement between equal partners, the QFL has evolved from having "special status" to "sovereignty-association."

The Confédération des syndicats nationaux (CSN)

The Confédération des syndicats nationaux (CSN) was originally a confederation of Catholic trade unions created in 1921. At the time, it represented approximately 26,000 workers and was known as the Confédération des travailleurs catholiques du Canada (CTCC). By 1997, it included more than 220,000 workers, representing 24 percent of all Quebec workers covered by collective agreements under the provincial labour code (excluding the construction sector). In contrast to the QFL, the majority of whose members come largely from the private sector, more than half of the membership of the CSN is in the parapublic sector, particularly in health care.

Since its creation in 1921, the CSN has undergone profound changes in the composition of its membership, its structure, and its ideology. Rapid industrial expansion drew large numbers of French Canadians to major urban centres, where they came in contact with other workers. This led the CTCC to remove the Catholics-only clause from its constitution in 1943. Vigorous organizing campaigns by the TLC and the CCL in Quebec also forced Catholic organizations such as the CTCC to be more militant than they were at the outset under the strong involvement of the Catholic church. This militancy brought the CTCC into conflict with the Union Nationale regime of Maurice Duplessis on more than one occasion. Many historians consider the violent strike at Asbestos in 1949 to be the turning point in the evolution of the Catholic confederation.

At the time of the great union mergers that brought an end to the rivalry between the American Federation of Labour (AFL) and the Congress of Industrial Organizations (CIO) in the United States as well as their counterparts—the TLC and CCL—in Canada, the CTCC was urged to join the unification movement. However, the CTCC wanted to join as a unit in order to preserve its distinct character and identity, and the CLC was structurally designed to accommodate only individual unions organized on the basis of particular trades or industries. Thus, instead of achieving structural unity, the Quebec labour movement remained divided and continued to be prone to rivalry and conflict between the two main union bodies, the CTCC and the CLC's new Fédération du travail du Québec (QFL).

At its 1960 convention, the CTCC dropped the last vestiges of its identification with the Catholic church and renamed itself the Confédération des syndicats nationaux (CSN). It subsequently reorganized and centralized its structure (for example, it established a single strike fund financed by all of its affiliates) in order to be in a better position to compete with QFL's affiliates.

 CSN: www.csn.qc.ca

The CSN grew rapidly in size and in influence during the Quiet Revolution of the 1960s. It benefited most from the organization of professional and other salaried employees in the public service, but it also won certification campaigns over CLC-QFL on many occasions. After the 1965 departure of CSN president Jean Marchand for Ottawa, where he became a very influential minister in Pierre Trudeau's Liberal cabinet, the leaders who came to power showed a much greater propensity for radical, even revolutionary, viewpoints. The CSN's political or ideological orientation became defined increasingly by a group of influential radicals within the organization. The early 1970s were propitious to union radicalism within both the CSN and the QFL. One important consequence of this growing radicalism was serious splits within the CSN: The first led to the creation of the Centrale des syndicats démocratiques (CSD) in May 1972. Then, in September 1972, 30,000 civil servants also pulled out of the CSN; they decided to remain an independent labour organization rather than join either the QFL or the CSD. One year later, some 5000 workers in the aluminum industry also left the CSN and formed another independent organization, the Fédération des syndicats du secteur aluminium.

The loss in membership suffered by the CSN during the 1970s, as well as the severe economic crisis of the early 1980s, contributed to a reduction in the influence of the radical elements within the CSN. Once strongly opposed to co-operation with management, the CSN, as well as other labour organizations such as the QFL, are now actively involved in labour–management co-operation experiments. For instance, the president of the CSN played a decisive role in the establishment of the social contract at SAMMI-Atlas. This move from a quasi-Marxist orientation in the mid-1970s to a more pragmatic one in the mid-1980s is reflected in the themes debated by the delegates at the 1991 convention (Prendre les devants dans l'organisation du travail) and by the creation of the worker solidarity fund, Fondaction, in 1996.

The organizational structure of the CSN resembles that of any other labour federation, although the structure of the CSN remains highly political because of the strong weight given to local labour councils. It is well known that the latter are functionally oriented toward broader political issues while the professional federations tend to focus on bread-and-butter issues. Unlike the typical North American model of a craft union federation, the CSN does not affiliate construction workers on a trade-by-trade basis. All its members in this sector are grouped within a single industrial-like professional federation. Although unusual, this type of union structure conforms with Quebec's special legislation regulating labour relations in the construction industry.

The Centrale des syndicats démocratiques (CSD)

Created in 1972, the CSD is structured on the same model as the CSN except that affiliation with professional federations and labour councils is not mandatory for local unions. Since its creation in 1972, the CSD has not significantly increased its membership. As a matter of philosophy, the CSD wants to remain absolutely neutral vis-à-vis political parties. It does not profess any particular social doctrine; it even has an article in its constitution whereby the adoption of a particular ideological orientation would require a referendum of the whole membership.

The Centrale de l'enseignement du Québec (CEQ)

The unionization of teachers in Quebec dates from 1936; the first provincial federation was formed ten years later. Like most other union organizations, the Corporation des instituteurs et institutrices catholiques du Canada had a rough time during the Duplessis regime. It dropped its confessional name in 1967 and became the Corporation des enseignants du Québec (CEQ). That year also saw the first confrontation between teachers and the provincial government, which led to the first special legislation to end a wave of teachers' strikes. Like the CSN at the beginning of the 1970s, the CEQ went through a substantial ideological reorientation. One aspect of this reorientation was the transformation of the organization from a "corporation"—in which membership was mandatory according to a government charter and restricted to elementary and secondary school teachers—to a genuine labour organization, the Centrale de l'enseignement du Québec (still CEQ), representing all categories of workers in the field of education, from care-takers to classroom teachers at the elementary, secondary, and post-secondary levels. As a consequence, the CEQ became involved alongside CSN, CSD, and QFL affiliates in representation elections for certain categories of employees. Nonetheless, more than 90 percent of the CEQ's membership is still made up of elementary and secondary school teachers.

 CEQ: www.ceq.qc.ca

Independent Labour Unions

Despite the presence of four major labour federations in Quebec, almost one-quarter of the province's union members are not affiliated with any of these organizations. The most important independent unions are the Syndicat de la fonction publique du Québec (the Civil Service Union) and the nurses' associations. This situation has been an area of major concern for central labour organizations because independent labour organizations grew from 15.5 percent of unionized workers in 1975 to 27 per-cent by 1987 (Delorme and Veilleux, 1980: 17), plateauing at 25 percent by 1997 (Shawl, 1998: 8).

Employer Organizations

There are many types of employer organizations in Quebec, including sectorial groups directed towards economic and social interests, economic promotion groups, business groups, professional associations, and even employer associations responsible for negoti-ating with trade unions, also called employer unions. There are approximately 90 em-ployer unions in Quebec representing approximately 25,000 employers, mainly in construction and in sectors governed by the *Collective Agreement Decrees Act* (Delorme, Fortin, and Gosselin, 1994: 169).

More importantly, Quebec is characterized by the existence of a prominent confeder-ation of employer associations, the Conseil du Patronat du Québec (CPQ). This organ-ization was created in 1969 to address three specific goals: (1) to have a single spokesperson for employers to deal with the Quebec government, which only wanted to deal with a single organization during consultation with employers; (2) to integrate English-speaking businesses; and (3) to highlight the employers' perspective on labour legislation (Boivin, 1989). The CPQ is mainly a group of associations, not individual companies. Contributions from individual firms, or corporate members, represent a con-siderable part of its revenue; however, corporate members are not part of the CPQ decision-making structure. These members form the Bureau des Gouverneurs, which acts only as a consultative body. It is estimated that employers directly or indirectly rep-resented by the CPQ employ 70 percent of the Quebec labour force (Leclerc and Quimper, 1994: 211).

Over the years, the CPQ has managed to become the spokesperson for the employers' community in Quebec. It represents management in the majority of existing tripartite structures such as the Advisory Council on Labour and Manpower and the Superior Education Council. The CPQ presents briefs on all questions that are likely to be of interest to its members, takes part in conventions and press conferences, publishes studies, states opinions, and organizes colloquiums and conferences. In fact, the CPQ performs most activities that are usually expected from a representative organization in labour relations, with the exception of collective bargaining. There is also a Quebec branch of the Canadian Manufacturers Association (Alliance des Manufacturiers et des Exportateurs du Québec). In addition, employers are represented by branches of Chambers of Commerce, as in any other province.

CPQ: www.cpq.qc.ca

PUBLIC POLICY ON WORK

Quebec has a number of important policies on work, especially in the areas of labour standards, pay and employment equity, and occupational health and safety.

Labour Standards

The regulation of minimum working conditions constitutes one of the oldest forms of government intervention in the area of paid work (Trudeau, 1990). In Quebec, the first government interventions date back to the end of the 19th century and were aimed at protecting women and child labour. In 1937, minimum wages were to be applied universally. In 1940, the *Fair Wage Act* was amended and became the *Minimum Wage Act,* with numerous modifications from 1940 to 1979. From 1979 to the present, minimum working conditions have been governed by the *Labour Standards Act*, which replaced the *Minimum Wage Act* and codified numerous rulings previously adopted. It is similar to other labour standards legislation in Canada, in that it is applied by a labour standards commission operating on a complaint procedure. The one important distinction is the protection against unjust dismissal for workers who have been with the same employer for five years or more (Trudeau, 1990). This is the equivalent of arbitration for unjust dismissal of workers covered by collective agreements. It has been criticized, however, because the costs of the arbitration, which are divided between the parties, can stem its use (Trudeau, 1990: 1114).

In 1990, the *Labour Standards Act* was changed substantially to make working conditions for people with family responsibilities more flexible (e.g., parental leave, leave for family duties) and to improve maternity leave and leave for adoption. The unfair dismissal procedures were also altered with the cost of arbitration now being paid by the state, and with the eligibility criteria being reduced from five to three years. At the time of writing, there is debate over whether to legislate against two-tiered wage structures. According to many youth organizations, some collective agreements (6.7 percent in 1997) discriminate against new, and mostly young, workers by including provisions allowing for two-tiered wage structures or working conditions through "grandfather clauses."

Pay and Employment Equity

In all spheres of social and economic activity, the last three decades of the 20th century were characterized by an organized and systematic fight against discrimination towards certain groups, especially women. Even though current laws are meant to tackle discrimination against several groups, called "target groups," it is women who are at the forefront of the anti-discrimination movement. Thus reference will most often be made to their situation.

Discrimination at Work and Policy Responses

Although women workers have made some breakthroughs in areas of training and employment previously occupied almost exclusively by men, the majority are still concentrated in a limited number of sectors of activity and employment categories, while at the same time they are largely—even totally—absent from certain fields (Gouvernement du Québec, 1993a). Although there has been some narrowing of the wage gap between men and women since the end of the 1960s, the gap between men's and women's average income was barely reduced at all during the last ten years.[3]

The two major problems are the existence of wage differentials between men and women within the salary structures of firms, and the prevalence of occupational segregation. The latter involves the *concentration* of women in a limited number of jobs in the labour market and the *feminization* of these jobs (the fact that women occupy the majority of these jobs). Although the wage gap and occupational segregation are two aspects of discrimination against women in the labour market, they are different in nature and therefore require different policy responses.

Equal access aims first to eliminate discrimination in all human resource management practices in order to guarantee equal opportunity: This is the dimension of equality of opportunity. A further objective of equal access is equal representation of members of groups that have been discriminated against in jobs offered by a firm: This is the dimension of equality of outcome. *Pay equity* is specifically aimed at obtaining equal pay for work of equal value, which would help narrow the wage gap between men and women. These two aspects of anti-discrimination policy are dealt with in the Quebec *Charter of Human Rights and Freedoms*. However, since 1996, the *Pay Equity Act* has changed the situation.[4]

Charter of Human Rights and Freedoms

In Quebec, legislators chose to address employment discrimination in a Charter, which also guarantees fundamental freedoms. The *Charter of Human Rights and Freedoms*, ratified in 1975, is intended to be the preferred tool in the fight against discrimination at work. Quebec is alone among Canadian legislators in having adopted a definition of the concept of discrimination. Thus, to say that discrimination exists, the following three elements must be found:

- a distinction, an exclusion, or a preference,
- based on prohibited grounds (there are 13 of them, pregnancy being a distinct prohibited ground for discrimination),
- which has the effect of destroying or compromising the right to full and equal recognition and exercise of human rights and freedoms.

This definition identifies two types of discrimination: direct discrimination, which is "the fact of a distinction, exclusion, or preference directly and explicitly based on a prohibited ground for discrimination" (Côté and Lemonde, 1988: 17), and systemic discrimination resulting from customs and practices rooted in systems such as the employment systems of organizations.

Thus the Charter's objective in the area of employment is to "neutralize" work environments by eliminating all manifestations of discrimination. Two distinct and complementary series of measures have been utilized: provisions prohibiting discrimination and provisions aimed at promoting the rights of groups that have been discriminated against.

Quebec's Human Rights Commission is responsible for overseeing, in the first instance, the application of the Charter. Created in 1975, the commission was for 15 years the only organization overseeing the Charter. Although it may carry out investigations on its own initiative, its limited resources and the fact that it must oversee the application of all Charter provisions essentially means that the commission functions on the basis of complaints filed by people, groups, or organizations. This has limited the Charter's impact. Until 1990, the commission restricted its role to conciliation and was empowered to make recommendations only. The commission had to go to court if it wished to have its recommendations enforced.

The establishment of a human rights tribunal in 1990 did not alter this fundamental operating characteristic. The tribunal hears appeals against the commission's recommendations; however, the commission is still the starting point for all charter-related complaints.

When compared to the proactive laws adopted by Ontario and some other provinces to require pay equity, this method of functioning can be described as passive because it relies on complaints being filed. Even if organizations are required to respect the Charter, in reality, the law of "nothing seen, nothing done" applies. This complaints-based method of functioning is based on the idea that discrimination in the labour market is an exception rather than the rule.

Equal Access

When it was adopted in 1975, the Charter recognized only the principle of *equality of opportunity* in employment between men and women; it addressed problems of access only by prohibiting discrimination in human resource management practices. At the time, it was believed that it was sufficient to give everyone equal opportunity so that the employment systems of organizations would reflect better the diversity of the labour force. In the light of experiences with these measures and the relative failure of programs that only addressed equal opportunity, the objective of equal access was reinforced in 1982 by the introduction of the concept of equality of outcome. The Charter was then amended to include a section related to equal access programs. However, it was not until 1985 that this section came into effect.

Regulations related to equal access programs hold that they must include equality of opportunity measures whose goal is to eliminate discriminatory practices permanently, as well as corrective measures aimed at correcting the under-representation of groups discriminated against. Nevertheless, for private-sector firms, equal access programs are still voluntary, and participation in such programs remains largely dependent on a favourable economic context and an awareness of the situation by the management of these firms. Equal access includes dual objectives: (1) to detect and eliminate all sexist and discriminatory aspects of employment policies and practices, and (2) to eliminate occupational segregation by increasing the representation of women (and members of other target groups) in jobs where they are under-represented.

Pay Equity

Since it came into effect in 1976, the Charter has recognized the principle of "equal pay for work of equal value" by stipulating that "Every employer *must*, without discrimination, grant equal salary or wages to the members of his personnel who perform work of equal value at the same place" (emphasis added). The term "work of equal value" refers to a reality that is quite different from that referred to by the term "equal work." The early anti-discrimination laws included the notion of equal pay for equal work in order to end *obvious* sources of wage discrimination such as different wage scales for men and women doing the same jobs (e.g., male cashier and female cashier). Given occupational segregation, this principle could affect only a small part of the wage gap since men and women generally do not have the same jobs.

According to the principle of pay equity, an employer must pay a secretary the same wage as that of a playground maintenance worker if the two jobs are of *equal value* as determined by job evaluation. The notion of equal work was similar to comparing apples with apples. Under pay equity, different jobs are compared, and thus apples can be compared with oranges. Just as apples and oranges can be compared for their calories, vitamins, weight, and appearance, jobs can be broken down into various factors and compared using the common denominators.

The Quebec Charter may have been very progressive in its early recognition of the principle of pay equity in 1976, but since its introduction the situation in Canada has changed considerably. For example, in Ontario, all public-sector employers and all private firms with ten or more employees must achieve pay equity according to implementation deadlines established in 1988. Numerous other provinces have also adopted a proactive approach. The passive approach of the Charter, the cumbersome complaint process with its burden of proof on the complainant, and the reproaches often made about the commission's weak and ineffective process for dealing with complaints (Côté and Lemonde, 1988) help explain why few real gains have been made with regard to pay equity, and why most successes have been achieved in unionized sectors.

In 1994, the Parti Québécois won the election and emphasized its willingness to adopt proactive legislation on pay equity. After two governmental commissions, many public hearings, and a strong show of disagreement by employers' organizations, the bill was finally adopted unanimously by the National Assembly on November 21, 1996 (see Exhibit 16.6). Employers' obligations came into force in November 1997. The law allows for employee (nonunion as well as unionized) participation through a pay equity committee, mandatory for employers with more than 100 employees. Employers must pay for the committee members' training.

The general principle is "one employer—one program." However, the law allows many exceptions to this principle so that it is possible, for example, to have as many sep-

EXHIBIT 16.6

BASIC FEATURES OF THE *PAY EQUITY ACT*

- It covers all public and private employers over ten employees.
- There is extensive definition of salaried employees (including part-time and contractual employees but excluding executive managers as well as police and firefighters).
- Employers with 50 employees or more must implement a pay equity program which includes these four steps:
  Step 1. Identification of predominantly male and female job categories;
  Step 2. Description of the job evaluation method and tool;
  Step 3. Evaluation of the job categories, comparison, wage-gaps estimation, and wage adjustments calculation;
  Step 4. Methods of wage adjustments payments.
- Predominantly male and female job categories are defined as those having 60 percent or more persons of one sex.
- The job evaluation tool must include the four legally required criteria: skill, effort, responsibility, and working conditions.
- The job evaluation tool must avoid gender bias.
- Employers must achieve the pay equity program (or ascertain the wage adjustments) before November 2001.
- Pay equity adjustments must take place within a four-year period between November 2001 and November 2005.
- There are special provisions of the law for programs having been completed or being in progress before the adoption of the law.

arate programs as there are bargaining units in one organization. A Pay Equity Commission, responsible for the law's *administration* was created in March 1997. The law does not required notifying the Pay Equity Commission about the process but programs must be posted in the workplace. The minister of labour is accountable for the law's enforcement and appeals from the commission's decisions are directed to the labour tribunal instead of the existing tribunal for human rights.

Ministère du travail du Québec: www.travail.gouv.qc.ca/

Commission de L'équité Salariale: www.ces.gouv.qc.ca/

A Special Process for Firms Having Already Started or Completed Pay Equity

Certain employers, among them the Quebec government through its Treasury Board, had already started or completed an exercise of pay equity or salary relativity[5] in their organizations before the adoption of the law in 1996. In some cases this had been agreed through collective bargaining. The law takes this into account by allowing these employers to submit an implementation report by November 21, 1998 to the commission, which will determine if these exercises satisfy the requirements of the law. It may also suggest modifications. Around 170 firms submitted such reports and are awaiting the decisions of the commission. They include several important employers in the province: the Treasury Board (for all the employees of the public and parapublic sector), the Confédération des Caisses Populaires Desjardins, an important chain of food stores (Provigo), and several universities. A public-sector union (Quebec's union of public employees, which includes 35,000 members), supported by other unions, is currently challenging the validity of this section of the law. Given that the obligations of the employers in this section of the law appear more flexible than those applicable to the other employers, and that very large organizations are involved, the decisions of the commission will constitute a clear signal of its commitment to monitor the application of the law.

Review of the Current Situation on Pay Equity and Equal Access

Up to 1997, Quebec experiences with pay equity have been mostly through negotiation, occasionally through the filing of complaints, and sometimes through both channels. Negotiations were mostly undertaken in the Quebec public and parapublic sectors under pressure from unions. Just before the adoption of the *Pay Equity Act* of 1996, there were no significant settlements involving pay equity, especially in nonunion environments in the private sector where the wage gap attributable to discrimination is likely to be the most pronounced.

Even since the legislation was enacted in 1996, significant change has yet to occur. This is so for a variety of reasons. The law itself keeps employee participation at a minimum level, especially for women in nonunion workplaces. Furthermore, the commission has not fully played the role that was expected. The actors have not rallied behind the commission since its formation. Indeed, the choice of the commissioners has not been unanimous; the government created the commission when the context was one of budget cuts, and the assigned budget for the first year was insufficient to launch a wide information campaign. In March 1999, two years after its creation, the commission launched a very discreet publicity campaign in the press, which did not seem to rectify the situation. As well, the material published by the commission and the diffusion channels it favours—largely the Internet—are less accessible to women workers, unionized or not. The commission's annual report highlights that the commission has not been very active on the "pay equity" stage. Given that the firms have only until November 2001 to complete the pay equity exercise, there is little time left for them to meet their obligations.

Many are eagerly awaiting the commission's first decisions on pay equity or on the relativity programs already completed or in progress. The commission itself is waiting for the decision of the court on the challenge made to these programs. The "waiting for" attitude of the commission and the lack of information for working women, especially those who are nonunion and of the population in general, raise the distinct possibility that the "non initiatives" will be ineffective in correcting inequities. Worst of all, the completion of such a limited exercise will be considered by many as "a job done," creating the myth that pay equity is truly achieved so that the page must be turned and the issue forgotten.

With respect to equal access, the Quebec Charter is the main source of impetus, as discussed previously. However, these programs are voluntary (with the exception of the civil service), which explains why they have not been adopted more widely. Since 1986, equal access programs have been introduced in government departments and organizations. In addition, pilot projects allowing for the establishment of such programs have been set up in 76 organizations in the parapublic, private, and municipal sectors. This has had an effect on nearly 900 establishments and 150,000 people (Gouvernement du Québec, 1993a: 19). Quebec's council on the status of women, however, determined that the equal access programs had a limited effect due to their short duration and the weakness of measures adopted. The council indicated that "instead of being genuine equal access programs with established numerical goals and corrective measures, projects put into place more often resemble equal opportunity programs" (CSF, 1993: 21).

In 1989, the government established a contract compliance program modelled on the Federal Contractors Program. The Quebec program requires all firms with more than 100 employees, and with a Quebec government grant or contract for goods or services in the amount of $100,000 or more, to introduce an equal access program. According to the minister responsible for the status of women, these initiatives have not produced the expected results as only a little over 5 percent of firms with more than 100 employees are establishing an equal access program. A report issued in 1998 by the Quebec Human Rights Commission indicates that even if some significant progress for women has occurred over the past few years, there still remains a significant gap between their abilities and their share of non-traditional jobs. The same problem has been diagnosed for visible minorities and natives (Commission des droits de la personne, 1998).

Quebec Commission des droits de la personne et des droits de la jeunesse: www.cdpdj.qc.ca/htmen/htm/1_0.htm

Occupational Health and Safety

There are two laws in Quebec that provide the framework for the two main aspects usually considered in an occupational health-and-safety system: prevention and compensation. The *Occupational Health and Safety Act*, which was passed in 1979, encompasses the entire area of prevention, while the *Workers' Compensation Act*, which was passed in 1985, regulates compensation. The Occupational Health and Safety Commission was created to oversee the application of these two laws. Although Quebec was one of the last provinces to adopt health-and-safety laws, in so doing it has been able to benefit from experiences elsewhere and include some innovative provisions in the law, especially in the field of prevention.

With respect to workers' compensation, the situation in Quebec is similar to that which exists in other provinces and at the federal level: the no-fault principle, collective responsibility of employers, and mandatory insurance guaranteed by a state fund. However, in the area of prevention, Quebec, along with Ontario, Manitoba, and Alberta, are at the forefront. Provisions such as the precautionary cessation of work by pregnant workers and the recognition of the right of an injured worker or victim of an occupational disease to return to work are seen as innovative. The main distinctive feature of the legislation in Quebec, however, is in the way it is applied. Three mechanisms are used to ensure parity for and participation of both parties:

1. The board of directors of the Occupational Health and Safety Commission, which has jurisdiction over all aspects of occupational health and safety (prevention, inspection, compensation, and funding), is a joint labour–management body.

2. Occupational health and safety committees in firms are also joint committees. Most provinces also provide for the establishment of such committees.

3. Joint consultation at the sectorial level is also established through sectorial occupational health and safety associations, which are *voluntary* groupings of union and management associations.

Appeals can be made through an appeals tribunal, which is external to the Occupational Health and Safety Commission and is under the authority of the minister of justice. This body can intervene in all appeals of rulings by the Occupational Health and Safety Commission (CSST). Another peculiarity of this mechanism is that the appeals tribunal can play a conciliatory role between the parties. This has led to the unblocking of the system through out-of-court settlements of outstanding compensation claims.

Currently, the main interrelated preoccupations of the occupational health-and-safety system are: controlling the costs of administering the system, reducing the length of time taken to settle cases, and reducing the emphasis on legal aspects in the processing of files by the Occupational Health and Safety Commission. Despite a decrease in the number of accidents at work in the past few years, the costs of operating the system have continued to increase, due mainly to an increase in the average period of compensation and to an increase in the duration of relapses. However, there has been a continuous decrease in the average rate of employer contributions since 1995.

In January 1999, the CSST introduced a new insurance concept—mutual insurance—for small employers paying less than $18,000/year in contributions to the CSST. In the past, these employers had to pay their sector's rate. Now, by joining the mutual insurance program, the rates paid by employers will reflect their individual performance with respect to health and safety. This should lead to an amelioration of workers' health and safety since one of the major conditions for joining the mutual insurance group is to develop a prevention program.

CONCLUSION

We have used three key concepts to describe the evolution of union–management relations in Quebec: nationalism, state interventionism, and the political strength of the labour movement. What lessons can be drawn from the previous description?

First, Quebec's specific cultural identity explains why the state (the provincial government) is intervening to a greater extent in the economic and industrial relations spheres than is any other government in North America (e.g., through the Decree System and the particular institutional arrangements prevailing in the construction and public sectors). Quebec is a type of neo-corporatist society where interest groups are regularly consulted over major economic and political issues (e.g., the numerous economic, financial, and even constitutional summits organized by the Quebec government). Such a situation explains the presence of an organization that acts as the "official voice" of all employers in Quebec (the Conseil du patronat du Québec), something that is unique in North America. It also explains why labour unions, although divided into four separate central organizations, nevertheless have tremendous lobbying power towards all provincial governments.

Second, an important division has developed over the years between private-sector and public-sector labour relations. The main factor explaining this dual evolution is the state of the economy: The two recessions of the early 1980s and early 1990s literally transformed private-sector labour unions from ideologically oriented and very militant organizations into more pragmatic ones. On the other hand, a confrontational approach to labour relations has always prevailed in the public sector (including municipalities) except during the last recession.

This confrontation mood contrasts with the more collaborative labour–management relationships that have been developing in the private sector recently, in which unions and employers are increasingly practising "mutual gains" or "interest-based" bargaining (IBB). Signs of the changes include: Conciliation officers at the department of labour have all been trained to develop the skills required to act as "facilitator" when asked for by the parties; private consultants and some university professors run training sessions and do facilitation on IBB; "Saturn-type" collective agreements have also been signed alongside the "social contracts" described above.

Perhaps the best example of the new, more collaborative labour–management relations climate in the private sector is the publication in 1997 of a document on work re-organization (*Document de réflexion sur une nouvelle organisation du travail*) by the Joint Consultative Committee on Labour. This body acts as an adviser to the minister of labour. The committee is composed of representatives of the Conseil du patronat and the major central labour organizations in Quebec. This document, which received unanimous approval of all interested parties, states that work reorganization is no longer an exclusive "management rights" domain, that unions have a legitimate stake in it, and that they will have an increasing say in the matter. Both union and employer representatives acknowledge that, to achieve profitability, a firm must be able to adapt rapidly and use its personnel efficiently. Job protection and training must also be shared goals (Gouvernement du Québec, 1997: 9). The active role played by the government in providing the parties with a forum to reach such an agreement is another illustration of the government's policy of consensus-building in the private sector. Both the Liberal and PQ governments have pursued this policy.

Third, despite these positive signs of change in labour–management relations in the private sector, the overall situation of Quebec's labour market remains precarious. Although Quebec's economy has always been weaker than Ontario's and slightly below the Canadian average, the gap has widened over the last few years, since it took Quebec longer than most provinces to recover from the recession of the early 1990s. Some argue that this may be a result of excessive labour market regulation in Quebec (e.g., the obligation to spend at least 1 percent of payroll on training, the compulsory unionization of construction workers associated with the industry-wide bargaining structure and the regulations on hiring in this sector, and the extension of wage rates negotiated by unionized firms to unionized firms in sectors where decrees exist).

Others claim that the level of taxation—the highest in North America—deprives the province of many investment opportunities, thus hurting the growth of employment. Still others argue that the climate of uncertainty surrounding the political future of Quebec is the major culprit. For our part, we think that the explanation probably lies in a blend of all these factors plus possibly others, such as the lesser mobility of Quebec's population due to the language barrier.

Questions

1. What factors must be considered in order to understand labour–management relations in Quebec?

2. What is the official platform adopted by most central labour organizations in Quebec with regard to this province's future political status?

3. Describe the functioning of the Quebec Federation of Labour's Solidarity Fund.

4. What is meant by "social contracts" in Quebec?

5. Explain the particular relationship that exists between the CLC and QFL.

6. Explain the ideological transformation that occurred within the CSN in the late 1980s.

7. Describe the anti-strikebreaking provisions of the *Labour Code*.

8. Explain the dilemma of labour organizations when faced with a government formed by the Parti Québécois.

9. What lessons can be drawn from the experience of collective bargaining in Quebec public and quasi-public sectors between 1972 and 1999?

10. Describe the functioning of the Decree System.

11. Overall, would you say that Quebec public policy on work is substantially different from that in the rest of Canada?

ENDNOTES

[1] Special issues associated with the construction sector and the various elements of the public sector in Quebec are discussed in the chapter on Quebec by the authors in the previous edition of this volume.

[2] Quebec Federation of Labour. 1977. *Constitution*, c. art. 5f.

[3] The ratio for full-year, full-time workers was at 58.4 percent in 1969, 67.7 percent in 1990, 72.2 percent in 1993, and 72.5 percent in 1997 (Statistics Canada, 1999).

[4] Except for employers with fewer than 10 employees, who still remained covered only by the Charter.

[5] Salary relativity refers to the process of job evaluation and salary comparison throughout a sector of the organization (like production employees) or for the organization as a whole. It allows the comparison of job value and salary for a range of jobs, without special concerns for the historical impact of gender discrimination.

REFERENCES

BABCOCK, R. H. 1973. "Samuel Gompers and Quebec Workers." *American Review of Canadian Studies*, 3, pp. 47–66.

BERNIER, J. 1993. "Juridical Extension in Quebec: A New Challenge Unique in North America." *Relations industrielles/Industrial Relations*, 48, pp. 745–761.

BOIVIN, J. 1989. *Les relations patronales-syndicales au Québec*, 2nd Edition. Chicoutimi, Que.: Gaétan Morin.

COMMISSION DES DROITS DE LA PERSONNE ET DES DROITS DE LA JEUNESSE. 1998. *Les programmes d'accès à l'égalité au Québec. Bilan et perspectives*. Québec (décembre).

CÔTÉ, A. and L. LEMONDE. 1988. *Discrimination et Commission des droits de la personne*. Montréal: Saint-Martin.

CRII (Compensation Research and Information Institute). 1998. *Fourteenth Annual Report*, French version (November), p. 22.

CSF (CONSEIL DU STATUT DE LA FEMME). 1993. *Même poids, même mesure. Avis sur l'équité en emploi*. Québec: Direction des Communications.

CSN. 1992. *Une démarche syndicale pour prendre les devants dans la réorganisation du travail.*

DELORME, F., R. FORTIN, and L. GOSSELIN. 1994. "L'organisation du monde patronal au Québec: un portrait diversifié," in *Les relations industrielles au Québec. 50 ans d'évolution*. Québec: Presses de l'Université Laval, pp. 167–201.

DELORME, E. and D. VEILLEUX. 1980. *Les syndicats indépendants au Québec: un aperçu de leur situation*. Québec: Ministère du Travail et de la main-d'oeuvre.

FOURNIER, L. 1994. *Histoire de la FTQ*. Montréal: Québec-Amérique.

FRASER, M. 1987. *Quebec Inc*. Montréal: Éditions de l'Homme.

GOUVERNEMENT DU QUÉBEC. 1993a. *La politique en matière de condition féminine. Femmes des années 1990—Portrait statistique*. Québec.

———. 1993b. *Un Modèle d'entente de partenariat: le contrat social en entreprise*. Québec: Ministère de l'industrie, du commerce et de la technologie.

———. 1997. *Document de réflexion sur une nouvelle organisation du travail*. Québec: Conseil consultatif du travail et de la main d'œuvre.

GRANT, M. and B. LÉVESQUE. 1997. "Aperçu des principales transformations des rapports du travail dans les entreprises: le cas québécois," in *Nouvelles formes d'organisation du travail: études de cas et analyses comparatives*. Montréal: Harmattan.

INSTITUT DE RECHERCHE ET D'INFORMATION SUR LA RÉMUNÉRATION. 1998. *Quatorzième rapport sur les constatations de l'I.R.I.R.* (novembre).

LECLERC, M. and M. QUIMPER. 1994. *Les relations du travail au Québec: une analyse de la situation dans le secteur public*. Sainte-Foy, Qué.: Presses de l'Université du Québec.

QUARTER, J. and G. MELNYK. 1989. *Partners in Enterprise: The Worker Ownership Phenomenon*. Montreal: Black Rose.

ROUILLARD, J. 1989. *Histoire du syndicalisme québécois*. Montreal: Boréal.

SHAWL, R. 1998. "La présence syndicale au Québec," in *Le marché du travail*, 19, no. 9, pp. 6–10.

STATISTICS CANADA. 1999. *Earnings of Men and Wormen, 1997*. Catalogue no. 13-217. Ottawa.

TREFF, K. and D. B. PERRY. 1998. *Finances of the Nations*. Toronto: Canadian Tax Foundation.

TRUDEAU, G. 1990. "Les normes minimales du travail: bilan et éléments de prospective," in *Vingt-cinq ans de pratique en relations industrielles au Québec*. Cowansville, Qué.: Yvon Blais.

CHAPTER 17

Trade Unions and Labour Relations Systems in Comparative Perspective

Carla Lipsig-Mummé

On a recent trip to Haiti...I had the opportunity to visit the home of a Disney worker...She worked at N.S. Mart (Plant Number 32), where she sewed Pocahontas and Mickey Mouse shirts....

She was a typical mother with four young children. They lived in a one-room, windowless shack, 8 by 11 feet wide, lit by one bare bulb and with a tin roof that leaked....The mother told us that when she left for work that morning, she was only able to leave them...30 cents US. The four children had to feed themselves for 7.2 cents per child. Her children had been sent home from school two weeks before because she had been unable to pay their tuition. Tuition for the three older children was...more than the mother earned in a full day sewing Disney shirts.

One child had malaria, another a painful dysentery, but their mother was unable to afford the medicines....

Before leaving I asked the family what they would eat that night. Nothing, they responded. There were many days when they could not afford to eat.

> The mother had years of experience as a sewer....The Pocahontas shirts that she sewed...sell at Wal-Mart for $10.97 each....She earned the minimum of 28 cents an hour.[1]

 Centre for the Study on Living Standards: www.csls.ca/

Throughout the 20th century, national labour relations systems have remained considerably different from each other, despite economic links between countries and common international pressures. However the past 20 years have witnessed a profound transformation of the world economy (as profound as the assembly line revolution of the 1920s), which has been triggered by the wave of corporate mergers of the mid-1970s and deepened by two recessions and the revolution in information technology. Globalization, as it is loosely called, has created transnational convergence in human resource management, in government regulation of the labour market, in social and economic policy, and in political attitudes towards the social safety network and a host of other areas. What impact has globalization had on national industrial relations systems? There is considerable debate as to who benefits from globalization, who loses, and how far it will go. But there is general agreement that it has made the economies of developed and underdeveloped countries newly dependent on each other, and more vulnerable to each other, than they have been in the past generation.

In this chapter we begin by looking at established patterns in labour relations in Europe, Australia, and North America, as these developed before the wave of globalization in the 1970s. We move to summarizing the big changes in the environment for labour relations that occurred after the mid-1970s, largely because of the growing importance of global economic integration, changes that include the formation of the European Union and the North American Free Trade Agreement. We ask: How did national labour relations systems adapt and survive the impact of globalization? Why do some countries' labour movements continue to do well while others do not? We conclude the chapter by comparing Canadian trade unions and labour relations to other countries, evaluating the ways Canada has changed and failed to change in the past decade, and what we can learn from other countries.

LABOUR RELATIONS IN ADVANCED INDUSTRIAL COUNTRIES: POST-WAR PATTERNS

In this section, the national labour relations systems of advanced industrial countries in the post-war period are categorized into their main types.

National Labour Relations Systems

A national labour relations system is the web of social institutions that structure the relationships among three major actors in the regulation of the world of employment and work. These actors are: workers and their unions, employers and their associations, and the state. Each actor operates at several different levels, both internally and in interaction with the others. While most labour relations systems have as their formal goal co-operation among the actors (or social partners), conflict of interest is recognized as inherent, and conflict-resolving mechanisms are usually built in. In all countries, labour relations systems take shape slowly and continue to reflect the particular national or regional culture and class relations that have developed over time. All labour relations systems make a formal place for trade unions, and most consider them to be the workforce's most important spokesgroup. Some also make space for other workplace organizations that represent workers. Only a few labour relations systems make a place for input by citizens, consumers, and other members of civil society who are not involved in the regulation of work relations but may be affected by its outcomes.

The end of World War II—1945—usually marks the beginning of the era of modern welfare states and modern labour relations. This is true for Canada and Australia. But some countries (Sweden, the US, and the UK) began to develop their welfare states earlier, in response to the Great Depression. Still others (Germany and New Zealand, for example) date the origins of their welfare states from the last decade of the 19th century. And countries defeated in World War II (Germany, Japan, Austria, and Italy) began the reconstruction of their economies, their governing systems, and their industrial relations under the aegis of US authorities. So, although modern labour relations systems are shaped by modern welfare states, their unions and employers' associations sometimes draw on older traditions, stretching back to the 19th century.

Four Patterns

Earlier we said that labour relations systems are nationally specific and have been so for decades, if not for centuries. Does this mean that every one is so different from the rest that we cannot identify patterns and types? Jacoby (1995) proposes a categorization of labour relations systems in the developed countries on the basis of two questions: Is collective bargaining centralized or decentralized, and does the state play an interventionist or minimalist role in regulating the economy and labour relations?

Four 'types' of national labour relations system can then be identified: (1) corporatism of the macro- or meso-corporatist varieties, (2) decentralized marketism, (3) statist micro-corporatism, and (4) regional concertation.[2]

Corporatism describes a system of labour relations in which the state creates bipartite (the government with corporations *or* with unions) or tripartite (the government, employer associations, and trade unions) institutions for consulting employers and unions and formally integrates them into the process of labour market regulation and economic and social policy making. (Two examples: bipartite corporatism characterized Australia from 1983 to 1996; tripartite corporatism has characterized Scandinavia for three-quarters of a century.) These corporatist institutions may be at the national level *(macro-corporatism)*, in which case they often entail centralized wage bargaining. When macro-corporatist labour relations exist for a considerable period of time, they provoke the centralization of both unions and employers' associations, in terms of internal structure, level of negotiation, and location of power within each institution. Sweden and Austria are examples of macro-corporatism (Kjelberg, 1992). Macro-corporatist systems link centralized bargaining and government intervention to set wage patterns. They are associated with strong economies, low unemployment, and rapid recovery from international dislocations such as the 1970s oil crisis. They typically have high union density; strong unions; and comprehensive welfare, training, and education systems. Wage dispersion is less likely in macro-corporatist systems, and citizens in general, not just union members, benefit directly and indirectly from the results of macro-corporatist labour relations.

Meso-corporatism refers to the integration of employers and unions at the level of sectoral bargaining, with the state facilitating and setting parameters. Sectoral, or meso-corporatist, relationships are completed by state-level macro-corporatism in economic planning. Germany's "dual system" of industrial-sector bargaining is an example of meso-corporatism. Like the macro-corporatist labour relations systems, meso-corporatism encourages centralization of power (at the industry-wide level) and consultative relationships, while discouraging union militancy and industrial conflict. Like macro-corporatism, meso-corporatism is associated with high wages, generous welfare provisions, the sectoral ability to take wages out of competition, and national economic prosperity.

The German model, however, has several additional components (Jacobi, Keller, and Muller-Jentsch, 1992). First, the "dual structure" of representation, or co-determination, separates worker organizations in the workplace from collective bargaining at the sectoral level. Collective bargaining is the precinct of unions and employers' associations at the sectoral level: This effectively takes wages out of competition. At the workplace, works councils and local management deal with the daily issues that arise. Union members, and sometimes union officials, sit on the works councils. Second, labour relations in Germany are the subject of extensive and comprehensive regulation by law (i.e., juridification). Labour law sets the terms for collective bargaining and regulates industrial conflict and workplace labour relations. While strikes may result from collective bargaining at the sectoral level, they are illegal in the exercise of co-determination at the workplace. This "means that structural conflicts between labour and capital can be broken down and dealt with in two arenas" (Jacobi, Keller, and Muller-Jentsch, 1992: 218). Third, unions and employers' associations are designated by law to represent their entire constituencies, whether these are members or not. Fourth, as in other meso-corporatist systems, collective bargaining in Germany is highly centralized at the sectoral level. The tradition of industrial rather than craft unions goes back to before World War II, and the union commitment to centralized decision making rather than local autonomy dates from the 19th century. Although unions in the inter-war period were ideologically divided and competitive, after the war and during reconstruction the labour movement made a decision for unitary rather than pluralist and competitive union structures, and this has greatly contributed to the effectiveness both of the unions and of the collective bargaining system.

In recent years, however, employer pressure to decentralize and deregulate have put real pressure on meso-corporatist systems, opening gaps between the healthy vs. threatened industrial sectors and between large and small industry.

Decentralized marketism describes a labour relations system in which the state plays only a minimal role in labour market regulation and economic policy-making, leaving the market to make decisions and individual firms and unions to battle it out within a minimalist legislative framework. Unions have little or no formal (institutional) role in economic and labour market policy-making. Consultation is sporadic and at the will of particular governments; links (for labour) to a political party capable of gaining office are weak. The US and Canada are examples of decentralized marketism (Drache and Glasbeek, 1992).

Labor Link (American): www.laborlink.org/

In the US, the labour movement has long maintained a recognized (but often ineffectual) relationship with the Democratic Party, although this is not a formal affiliation such as the Canadian unions have with the New Democratic Party, or the Australian Council of Trade Unions (ACTU) maintains with the Australian Labour Party. In the United Kingdom, where the trade union movement has been affiliated to the Labour Party since the beginning of the 20th century, the state has been a moderate economic planner, there has traditionally been little labour relations regulation by law, and collective bargaining has been decentralized. The exceptions—important ones—have occurred when Labour was in office, particularly during the 1945–79 period when bipartite corporatism took shape, and the state intervened in economic and social planning more vigorously (Edwards, Hall, et. al, 1992). More recently, the 18 years of Conservative rule beginning in 1979 undid the Labour years. The Thatcher governments introduced extensive juridification of union–employer relations, interposed the state between the union and its members, privatized many public services, made strikes and union recognition more difficult, re-established the market as the nation's economic planner, and solidified the government's credentials as the leading force in the weakening of the oldest trade union movement in the developed world.

In decentralized market systems of labour relations, collective bargaining typically takes place in the firm or the workplace, and industrial conflict levels are often very high. There is considerable variation in wages between strong and weak sectors as well as between unionized and nonunion workers, and the flow-on of collective bargaining gains to the socially excluded is less likely to happen than in the corporatist regimes. Although the Canadian government (at national and provincial levels) is more of a regulator of the labour market than the US governments at all levels, it remains minimalist by world standards. Typically, decentralized market systems are characterized by low union density with considerable geographic and sectoral variation.

Statist micro-corporatism is Jacoby's (1995) memorable characterization of Japanese labour relations. At the macro level, the state works closely with industry to obtain markets, reduce competition among Japanese companies abroad, and regulate the currency. This might be called statist entrepreneurism. Companies are organized sectorally into industry associations and work with the government through these. Labour, however, is absent at the level of state policy-making. This model of statist industrial entrepreneurism has been reproduced elsewhere in East Asia.

In Japan, ongoing, or core, workers are organized into company unions whose real life is at the level of the workplace. Unlike German unions, Japanese unions are ineffective in negotiating sectoral agreements. Unlike Swedish and Austrian unions, they are absent at the level of national economic policy-making and wage bargaining. At the workplace, however, Japanese workers and their unions are incorporated into an elaborate web of consultative and participative structures, tying the worker to the company through socialization into corporate culture and reducing the union's ability to articulate and defend workers' interests autonomously. This has been called "private welfare corporatism" (Jacoby, 1995). Between "corporatism without labour" at the national policy-making level, and corporatist workplace relations, Japanese unions have rightly been considered weak, docile, and ineffective.

In the past few years, however, the Asian economic crisis and Japan's lingering recession have placed profound strain on this two-level system of bipartite corporate–government macro-economic policy-making, and micro-corporatism in the workplace. Although large Japanese companies had long employed a core of permanent workers and a cushion of precarious employees—the former could assume employment security until late in their working life, and the latter would be laid off or hired according to the ebbs and flows of the market—the current economic strains have led to layoffs in unprecedented numbers. This in turn has provoked internal questioning about the effectiveness of the unions and the fairness of the core/precarious tradition of employment. It has also contributed to a real decline in union density in Japan.

Twenty years ago, it was possible to classify the post–World War II labour relations systems as macro-corporatist or meso-corporatist (Scandinavia, Germany, Austria), statist and micro-corporatist (Japan), or market-driven and decentralized (the US, Canada, and sometimes the UK). Australia combined centralized wage setting through an arbitration system with little economic planning by government, but a historic structure of tariff barriers, thereby making it difficult to classify (Peetz, 1998).

Regional concertation would not come into importance in Italy and France until the later 1980s, when it emerged as an innovative way for communities to take their own economic development in hand outside the firm and outside national governments.[3] In regional concertation, municipal or regional governments attract and encourage the growth of small and medium-size businesses, often in new manufacturing sectors (Ferner and Hyman, 1992). Collaborative efforts by local unions, local government, and local employers' associations develop training facilities, research and development services for small businesses, and the social services of the region, such as co-ops and credit unions. Of particular note is the fact that regional concertation in Italy has attracted the involvement of socialist and communist unions and municipal governments.

Taking the long view, the half-century since World War II divides into two distinct periods: from 1945 to the late 1970s, and from the early 1980s to the present. The earlier period, described here, was characterized by widespread economic growth and prosperity in the developed countries, the pre-eminence of the welfare state and Keynesian economic strategies, low unemployment, and nationally autonomous labour relations systems (Trubek and Rothstein, 1998).

EXHIBIT 17.1

FOUR TYPES OF NATIONAL LABOUR RELATIONS SYSTEMS

- Corporatism (macro-corporatism or meso-corporatism)
- Decentralized Marketism
- Statist Micro-corporatism
- Regional Concertation

THE EMERGENCE OF A NEW ENVIRONMENT

The past 20 years, however, have seen a veritable revolution in world economic organization, the role of national states in economic decision making, and the profile of the labour force. A central force in triggering this "revolution" was the wave of corporate mergers that began in the mid-1970s and its impact on the national labour market policies that developed from it. In the next section, we look at the "structural" transformations that occurred in all developed countries.

These structural changes form a common context—a backdrop against which different countries have grappled with the challenges international economic integration has posed to national labour relations systems. Chief among these are six developments: the long-term shift from manufacturing to private-sector services as the basis for advanced economies, with the attendant shrinkage of the public sector; the breakdown of secure employment, the rise of precarious employment, and the formation of a precarious labour force; recession and 15 years of high unemployment; a chilly political climate in which governments of all political colours stepped back from regulating the labour market and embraced some form of trade liberalization; the increasing concentration of corporate ownership worldwide; and the emergence of new patterns of regional internationalism.

From Manufacturing to Services

Throughout the 20th century, agriculture has been declining so that today it represents less than one in ten jobs in all the high-wage countries, and in some, such as Canada, only one in fifty (Lipsig-Mummé, 1997). In the meantime, manufacturing emerged as the motor of these economies. It continued to grow as a proportion of employment in most high-wage countries in Europe and in the US, Canada, and Australia to the end of the 1960s. Since the 1970s however, manufacturing has been declining as a source of employment, but within manufacturing, this has been a two-pronged movement. The traditional "heavy" or basic industries have waned in importance, while the newer, high-tech and consumer-related goods sectors have grown. Today, manufacturing rarely accounts for more than one in three jobs in Europe or North America (Ferner and Hyman, 1992). Many manufacturing jobs have been eliminated by technological advances, but many have also migrated to the lower-wage countries of Asia, Latin America, Africa, and eastern and southern Europe. But manufacturing, and its typical full-time, lifelong job, remains the basis on which contemporary labour relations and labour law are based.

In contrast, the service sector continues to grow, so that today all high-wage countries may be defined as service economies. In Canada, 72.2 percent of all jobs are in services, the highest of any developed economy in the world (Lipsig-Mummé, 1997). Labelling an economy "service-based" means several things: The majority of jobs are in the service sector; more new jobs are being created in services than in manufacturing or agriculture; white-collar work is growing and manual labour declining; and women are being drawn rapidly into the labour force while employment patterns are feminizing. But in all the high-wage countries, the service sector has two faces: public services that are often regulated, highly unionized, with large workplaces; and private services that are weakly unionized and characterized by worker vulnerability as well as extremes of employer and workplace size and compliance with labour standards. Throughout Europe and North America, it is the private services that are growing, accounting for more than 50 percent of jobs in many high-wage countries, and the public services that are shrinking or remaining stable. Becoming a service economy places great pressure on national trade union movements, because labour relations systems and the structure of trade movements were created to regulate manufacturing-based economies and then adapted to include the public sector. Few countries have modernized their labour relations system to take into account the passage from a manufacturing to a private service economy.

Precarious Employment and the Feminization of Employment

Since the mid-1970s, male labour force participation has been declining, while female labour force participation has been growing. Yet male manufacturing workers have been the historic backbone of trade unionism.

The rise in women's labour force participation has in some measure been stimulated by the expansion of services. While the public service was a first and important port of entry for women into the post-war labour market, since the reduction in public-service employment in the 1980s, new jobs for women are largely in the least regulated parts of the economy, the private services. The spread of precarious employment in the private service sector leads to what is sometimes called "the feminization of employment patterns."

There are four dimensions to this idea: (1) Women represent a growing percentage of those employed; (2) A convergence between men's and women's labour market participation rates is occurring; (3) Women's patterns for entry to the labour market, historically characterized by non-standard, part-time, and vulnerable jobs, are now spreading to men, to young workers, and to older workers; and (4) The growth of precarious employment contributes to a polarization of wages and of working time (Lipsig-Mummé and Laxer, 1998). This poses a real challenge to unions. Women are less unionized than are men, perhaps because of the weakly unionized sectors, occupations, and employment categories in which they cluster. In Canada, however, the more rapid growth of women's than men's trade union membership since 1976 has bolstered trade union density. For unions throughout Europe and North America, the challenge to unionize women is no less than the challenge to reverse the decline in union membership rates.

Unemployment

The years from the end of the 1970s to the middle of the 1990s were marked by high and tenacious unemployment, even in countries with traditionally low levels. As unemployment rose above 10 percent in Australia, France, Germany, Canada, and the UK, governments of all political persuasions proved unable to contain or reduce it. The two recessions that bracketed the 1980s weakened trade unionism in the traditional bastions of union strength: heavy industry, mining, and the public sector. At the same time, the tenacity of high unemployment revealed the inadequacy of national governments in coping with what was a new phenomenon in the post-war years. By the time unemployment rates began dropping in the last years of the 1990s, increasing numbers of workers and former workers had fallen out of the safety net of labour standards and union membership. Young people were coming to assume that precariousness was the natural form of employment. Social exclusion resulted from the weakening of labour regulation and revealed the existing national labour relations systems as relevant only to a shrinking number of citizens in a deregulating labour market.

In sum, over the past 20 years the high-wage economies have shared a shift from manufacturing to private services, a rise and spread of precarious employment, an increase in women's labour force participation and a decrease in men's, and the deregulation of employment in ways that pose a threat both to conventional trade unionism and the contemporary structure of labour market regulation.

The Political Climate

The past two decades have provided a chilly climate for trade unions, and for government protection of unorganized workers, compared to the 30 years after World War II. Indeed, the widespread turn against the welfare state, its policies of social expenditure, and its philosophy of social responsibility for all citizens has combined with the embracing of both trade liberalization and intensified international competitiveness. These have contributed not only to the deregulation of the labour market in the quest for flexibility, but to increasing difficulties for trade unions in attracting and organizing members of the next working class.

While the political climate has been less friendly to trade unions, countries have varied considerably in the degree of changes they have made to their welfare-state-era labour relations systems. Why, in the face of common changes to the structure of their national economies, have some countries turned radically away from their post-war systems, while others have not? The growing but uneven impact of international economic interdependence may be one reason.

The Impact of Economic Transnationalism on National Labour Relations Systems

The expansion of international economic interdependence is often called globalization, but it is more complex and uneven than that. We will, instead, call it *economic transnationalism*.

Economic transnationalism is, first, the increasing integration of national economies into supra-national economic structures. These may be geographic: regional trading zones like the European Union or NAFTA. Or they may be global, such as the World Trade Organization. Second, economic transnationalism refers to the growing role that large transnational corporations play throughout the world in national and regional economies, as evidenced by their growing share of economic output, the growing number of workers who are directly or indirectly employed by them, and their growing influence on national and regional governments and on the regulation of labour relations (Ferner and Hyman, 1992). In other words, economic transnationalism refers to the growing regional integration of national economies *and* to the increased importance of transnational corporations in those economies and on those national labour relations systems.

But prior to 1970, national labour relations systems in developed countries had operated relatively autonomously. These labour relations systems were protected in their *national* autonomy by an *international* consensus. As stated by Trubek and Rothstein (1998: 6) "Firms tended to operate within national borders [as opposed to internationally], tariffs were still a significant barrier to trade, industry was largely located within the richer countries of the north, trade was heavily weighted to intra-industry exchanges, and capital markets were weak and not well integrated across national boundaries."

International support for national autonomy in labour relations came in the form of the Bretton Woods monetary system and the International Labour Organization (Trubek and Rothstein, 1998). But Bretton Woods, with its system of fixed exchange rates, ended in 1973, the oil crises began, inflation and unemployment rose simultaneously, and the whole cocktail contributed to the first wave of corporate mergers and the internationalization of production and distribution.

Three Patterns of Regional Internationalism

Out of the breakdown of the post-war system of "national autonomy internationally reinforced," three different patterns of regional internationalism emerged.

EXHIBIT 17.2

SIX CHANGES IN THE ENVIRONMENT FOR LABOUR RELATIONS SINCE 1980

1. From a manufacturing to a service economy.
2. From secure employment to precarious employment.
3. The feminization of employment patterns.
4. From low unemployment to high unemployment.
5. The transformation of national economies in developed and underdeveloped countries by transnational corporations.
6. The emergence of new patterns of regional internationalism.

The European Union (EU)

The European Union (EU) is both the oldest and the most ambitious system of regional integration. Beginning in 1950 with the United Europe project, it has moved slowly to reduce the barriers to the free movement of people, products, and services. While the EU is the most developed and successful of the three forms of regional integration, it has favoured economic integration over harmonizing social issues. Social issues have been relatively neglected. In the domain of labour relations, there have been important steps to set Europe-wide protections for workers and the free movement of labour, but "transnational markets [have been created] in the context of national industrial relations systems" (Ross and Martin, 1998). Can a regional labour movement, and a regional labour relations system, come into being?

Ross and Martin see more progress than they expected. The "market-building" emphasis in European integration pressed for trade liberalization and deregulation, rather than the creation of Europe-wide social and labour standards. Unions needed, then, to "transnationalize" their strategies and organizational structures. But the national nature of their structures, organizational patterns, and cultures created considerable obstacles. Yet against the odds, the "Europeanization" of labour relations and trade union action is occurring. The Maastricht Agreement includes the possibility of Europe-wide collective bargaining and has put into place protection for the most vulnerable workers. The European Trades Union Congress (ETUC) is coming to play a respected role in labour and economic policy formation, as well as securing the buy-in of national labour movements. But Ross and Martin conclude that Europe has a long way to go before a regional industrial relations system can be said to exist. In other words, the development of transnational markets does "hollow out" national labour relations systems and does weaken unions, but it does not necessarily lead to the transnationalization of labour relations.

The North American Free Trade Agreement (NAFTA)

The North American Free Trade Agreement (NAFTA) was signed by Canada, the US, and Mexico in 1992, following the Free Trade Agreement between the US and Canada in 1989, and in the face of opposition from the Canadian and American labour movements.[4] While it liberalizes trade among the three countries, it contains no provisions for monetary integration or for the harmonization of economic and social policies as the EU is beginning to do.

In the face of labour opposition to NAFTA, labour and environmental "side accords" to the core agreement were negotiated. Although the side agreement for labour—the North American Agreement for Labour Cooperation (NAALC)— includes formal protection for the right to bargain collectively, occupational health and safety, freedom of association and freedom from discrimination, minimum wages, and a ban on child labour, each country has considerable leeway to observe the regulation as it sees fit. Says one observer, "The NAALC provides for no regional level norms or law making, and

specifically renounces the idea of harmonizing labour standards in North America...
There are no sanctions for failure to do so except in certain very limited areas"
(Trubek and Rothstein, 1998: 34). NAFTA is, in other words, a narrow form of regional
economic integration, lacking a social dimension or effective transnational political
regulatory bodies.

While each of the three NAFTA countries is holding tenaciously to its national labour
laws and institutions, it would not be correct to suppose that NAFTA has not modified
the three national labour relations systems. NAFTA's impact has first been felt in the redistribution of manufacturing jobs from Canada and the US to Mexico, a transfer that
has impacted on the organizing ability and the collective bargaining strategies of manufacturing unions in both Canada and the US. Since many of these manufacturing unions
have reinvented themselves as general unions, organizing in the service sector to offset
membership decline in their traditional sectors, there is a flow-on of impact beyond
manufacturing as well.

Second, NAFTA has intensified the upheaval within the Mexican labour movement,
where forces inside and outside the official unions are struggling to reinstate democratic
processes in union practices (LaBotz, 1992). In addition, the *maquiladora* regions have
become contested terrain between TNCs, several levels of Mexican government, and
sometimes the official unions on one side, and workers seeking to unionize, working
with the independent unions and some Canadian and US unions, on the other (LaBotz,
1992). Within the Canadian labour movement, NAFTA has divided Quebec unions
from their English Canadian counterparts, since Quebec labour is cautiously enthusiastic about globalization. NAFTA has also stimulated the highly competitive Canadian
unions in heavy industry and mining to seek partners in Mexico and elsewhere in Latin
America, as they square off against each other. Within the US, opposition to NAFTA has
pitted the AFL-CIO against the Clinton administration, underscoring the weakness of
the union movement in influencing policies of the Democratic Party.

NAFTA, like the EU, highlights the fact that trade liberalization and the regionaliza-
tion of markets do not lead easily or quickly to the creation of a regional labour relations
system or regionally co-ordinated unions. As in the European Union, the creation of
transnational markets may well weaken the national labour relations system and national
unions, but it does not create a regionalized, international alternative.

Trade and Bilateral Accords

But what of the rest of the world? Trade and bilateral accords in the absence of formal
institutional integration is the third pattern of economic transnationalism. This is the
pattern developing in Asia, where the possibility of a multilateral trading bloc remains
on the books, and in Latin America, which hopes to join NAFTA. In southern Africa,
however, the relatively powerful South African economy is leading the way in discussion
of the construction of a southern African economic bloc.

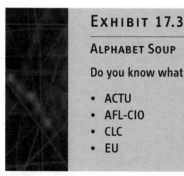

EXHIBIT 17.3

ALPHABET SOUP

Do you know what these acronyms stand for?

- ACTU
- AFL-CIO
- CLC
- EU
- ETUC
- NAFTA
- NAALC
- ILO

ECONOMIC TRANSNATIONALISM AND LABOUR

How well have trade unions faced down the turn away from the welfare state and Keynesian economic strategies that began in the 1980s? There is a great deal of variation even among developed countries.

The post-war pattern for union membership divides into two periods, as does the development of national labour relations systems. From 1950 to the mid-1970s, most advanced countries experienced growth in the proportion of workers who joined unions. From the mid-1970s onward, however, national union movements began to decline in the proportion of workers they represent, although the date of the beginning of the decline, its speed, and the magnitude of loss varies greatly. Certainly the United States, Japan, Australia, and France have been the hardest hit. All have more than halved their union density rates (i.e., union members as a percentage of the non-agricultural paid workforce). In 1950, the French labour movement represented almost one in three workers. Today union density is less than 10 percent. In 1950, Japanese unions represented 46 percent of the working class. Today they represent less than 20 percent. In 1953, the US labour movement represented 35 percent of the working class. Today its density is 12 percent, and declining. In Australia, union membership has been dropping steadily since the mid-1980s when it stood at 50 percent. Today it is 28 percent, but stable.

Some union movements withstood globalization better. The Danish and Swedish movements have sustained their high density rates at around 80 percent, and Norway has sustained its rate of around 55 percent. Union density rates have fallen slightly between 1980 and 1995 in Austria from 59.6 percent to 51.6 percent, and in Germany from 38.3 percent to 32.3 percent (see Table 17.1).

Canada is a special case. Union membership had stood steady between 31 and 33 percent for almost 30 years. Decline in density began late—after 1992. In fact, it had been the strong growth of the public sector and women's trade union membership that had supported the Canadian labour movement during the years of decline in other countries. When the growth in the public sector and women's union membership faltered (the former in the 1980s and the latter after 1992), density began to decline. It now stands at 31 percent, the same level as in 1982 (as shown in the table), but down slightly from the 1970s.

TABLE 17.1

UNION DENSITY IN VARIOUS DEVELOPED COUNTRIES, 1980 AND 1995

COUNTRY	1980	1995
Australia[5]	50.0	28.0
Austria[6]	59.6	51.6
Canada[7]	31.0[a]	31.0[b]
Denmark[8]	77.8	81.9
France[9]	19.0	9.0
Germany[10]	38.3	32.3
Great Britain[11]	55.8	32.1
Italy[12]	49.0	38.5[c]
Japan[13]	35.0	20.0
Norway[14]	55.0	56.0[d]
Sweden[15]	82.0	83.0
United States[16]	23.0	12.0

Notes:
a. Figures for 1982.
b. Figures for 1997.
c. Figures for 1993.
d. Figures for 1994.

Source: See various endnotes.

What does this tell us about the ability of unions in advanced countries to withstand the dislocations of globalization in the 1980s and 1990s? We can divide the question in two. What accounts for a strong union presence in the first place? Jacoby (1995) suggests that the small countries with concentrated economies, in which labour has control of social resources such as the unemployment system and employers seek to co-opt socialist unions rather than confront them, have historically developed a strong union presence.

Second, what allows national union movements to withstand adverse political and economic developments? Jacoby (1995) identifies the factors. Surprisingly, these seem to be located in the *structure* of national labour relations, rather than in the ideology or strategies of the unions themselves. And these structures have long histories.

Countries with centralized wage bargaining, national or sectoral level negotiating, long-standing corporatist arrangements, and a centralized labour movement suffered the fewest losses during the 1980s and 1990s. Scandinavia, Germany, and Austria fall into this category, even when their social democratic governments were replaced by conservatives. On the other hand, countries with decentralized bargaining, little state intervention in wage setting, the exclusion of labour from politics, and multiple or weak central labour bodies fared badly. The US, France, and Japan fall into this category (Jacoby, 1995).

Australia is a special case. It began the 1980s with protectionism and its highly centralized arbitration system for wage setting intact. After the election of the Australian Labour Party (ALP) in 1983, efforts were made to create a macro-corporatist social and economic framework—to "Swedify" Australia. This included the arbitration system, the Accord (a bipartite wages agreement between the government and the ACTU), and the creation of a network of consultative institutions around economic development, skills training, and macroeconomic policy. But the ALP had come to office at a time when international pressures to replace protectionism with trade liberalization were particularly strong. By the end of the 1980s, the ALP itself was dismantling the tariff barriers, weakening the arbitration system, and decentralizing wages bargaining to the workplace. By the time the ALP was voted out of office in 1996, the Australian labour movement had declined from 56 percent of the labour force to less than 30 percent.

HR Global Village (HRM site from Australia, requires membership for most information): www.hr-global-village.org./

The British experience has something in common with the Australian. After strong union growth in the public sector in the 1970s under a succession of Labour governments, the UK elected a strongly anti-union Conservative government, which held office from 1979 to 1997. While the 1960s and 1970s had been a period of moderate corporatism, the 1980s and 1990s were dominated by a strongly free-market, anti-welfare-state orientation and saw the radical weakening of trade union rights and the rapid decline of union membership. In both the Australian and the British cases, the transition from a social democratic to a free-market government led to a paradigm shift: from a large role for the state in economic planning and centralized wages bargaining, to neo-liberal free-market ideology and radically decentralized collective bargaining. In both cases, the national union movements flourished under social democratic governments, but found themselves in strategic paralysis when successor governments transformed the national labour relations systems.

In sum, the story of union decline in the 1980s and 1990s tells us that the structure of national labour relations systems—not only in the present but in their historical construction—plays a pivotal role in the national labour movement's ability to either adapt and survive, or move into strategic paralysis and decline. And the story of the impact of economic transnationalism on national labour relations systems in Europe and North America tells us that globalization has weakened national states and the laws that regulate the labour market, but has not replaced these with transnational legislation or institutions.

CANADIAN LABOUR RELATIONS AND INTERNATIONAL PATTERNS

Does Canada have anything to learn from the experience of other high-wage countries in this period of profound systemic change? We can identify four "lessons."

First, the decentralized structure of Canadian collective bargaining (typically one employer, one union), the minimalist involvement of the federal state with economic planning, and the increasing competition among unions is also characteristic of those industrial relations systems in Europe that have been most gravely weakened by globalization since the 1980s. European experience indicates that centralization of collective bargaining and rationalization of union structure buttress the shocks of internationalization better than decentralization and internal competition.

Second, the structure of Canadian unions has been changing rapidly since the 1980s, but in a direction that is likely to weaken them in a period of regional economic integration. The Canadian labour movement has historically had too many small unions. Instead of working towards mergers to build a few, strong, sectorally specific unions, the Canadian labour movement is using mergers and new organizing to create a number of large, general unions each of which organizes workers in any industry. This creates a mosaic of large, competitive unions with no clear identity. No centralized coordination is possible where unions are in competition. The picture is completed by a weak central labour body, the Canadian Labour Congress, which has little voice in social and macroeconomic policy-making.

Third, while regional economic integration and the increased clout of the TNCs can certainly weaken the autonomy of national industrial relations systems, international or regional industrial relations systems are proving very hard to create and anchor, while trade union internationalism is proceeding even more slowly. This leaves the Canadian labour relations system facing a gap between the weakening of the national system and the failure to create an international system.

Finally, comparative study of labour relations in other countries under the impact of globalization indicates that whether national systems and labour movements survive intact or emerge weakened seems to be determined by the structure of the institutions and actors. But the Canadian experience seems to tell a different story. Canada's ability to hold off the decline in union density until the 1990s is a product of conscious organizing strategy and strategizing about organization renewal, rather than of receiving protection from robust institutions of labour relation's regulation. This may be a uniquely Canadian form of voluntarism.

CONCLUSION

Setting Canada in an international context, five conclusions emerge. First, the growth of economic transnationalism has weakened national governments and the "national" definition of labour relations systems, but has failed to create an international or regional system in its place. Second, transnationalism has also generated considerable pressure towards convergence among national labour relations systems, at least in the advanced capitalist countries. Third, despite these pressures, national diversity of labour relations systems remains and is particularly sharp between the first world and the third world. Fourth, the decline of labour unions has been widespread in high-wage countries during the 1980s and the 1990s, but unions and labour relations systems have differing capacities for adaptation. Fifth, the response of countries to the economic transformations of the past 20 years underlines the continuing importance of law and politics in directing national choices in labour relations and the continued importance of trade unions as key actors.

Questions

1. Define, compare, and contrast macro-corporatism and meso-corporatism.

2. What is economic transnationalism?

3. How does Canadian trade union density compare to density in the US, the UK, Australia, and Sweden, over the past 20 years? Explain differences and similarities.

4. What are the principal differences between the European Union and the North American Free Trade Agreement in labour relations?

5. How do these differences affect trade unions?

6. Define "the Europeanization of labour relations."

7. What would have to change for a "North Americanization" of labour relations to occur?

8. Define "the feminization of employment patterns."

9. What factors contribute to the future stability of the Canadian labour relations system? To its future instability?

10. TNCs are increasingly investing in manufacturing in low-wage countries. How can this investment be made into a win-win situation?

ENDNOTES

[1] Ross, 1997, pp. 97–98.

[2] Jacoby (1995: 23–24) proposes a typology of industrial relations systems as: macro-corporatism, voluntarism, regionalism, statist micro-corporatism.

[3] Jacoby, 1995, pp. 19, 23–24; Ferner and Hyman, 1992; and Goetschy and Rozenblatt, 1992.

[4] The Quebec labour movement initially opposed the Free Trade Agreement in 1987 and 1988, but by the time NAFTA came to the table, it offered its qualified support.

[5] Evatt Foundation, 1995, p. 107, Table 6.1.

[6] Traxler in Ferner and Hyman, 1998, p. 244, Table 8.1.

[7] Lipsig-Mummé and Laxer, 1998, Table 2.

[8] Scheuer in Ferner and Hyman, 1998, p. 155, Table 5.1.

[9] Evatt Foundation, 1995, p. 107. Union membership figures in France an approximation only.

[10] Jacobi, Keller, and Muller-Jentsch in Ferner and Hyman, 1998, p. 202, Table 7.5.

[11] Edwards, Hall, et. al. in Ferner and Hyman, 1998, p. 26, Table 1.3.

[12] Regalia and Regini in Ferner and Hyman, 1998, p. 472, Table 16.2.

[13] Evatt Foundation, 1995, p. 107, Table 6.1.

[14] Dolvik and Stokke in Ferner and Hyman, 1998, p. 125, Table 4.1.

[15] Kjelberg in Ferner and Hyman, 1998, p. 99, Table 13.6.

[16] Evatt Foundation, 1995, p. 107, Table 6.1.

REFERENCES

DRACHE, D. and H. GLASBEEK. 1992. *The Changing Canadian Workplace*. Toronto: Lorimer.

EDWARDS, P., M. HALL, R. HYMAN, P. MARGINSON, K. SISSON, J. WADDINGTON, and D. WINCHESTER. 1992. "Great Britain: Still Muddling Through," in *Industrial Relations in the New Europe,* edited by A. Ferner and R. Hyman. Oxford: Blackwell.

EVATT FOUNDATION, UNIONS 2001. 1995. *A Blueprint for Union Activism*. Sydney: Evatt.

FERNER, A. and R. HYMAN. 1992. "Italy," in *Industrial Relations in the New Europe,* edited by A. Ferner and R. Hyman. Oxford: Blackwell.

——— eds. 1998. *Changing Industrial Relations in Europe*. Oxford: Blackwell.

GOETSCHY, J. and P. ROSENBLATT. 1992. "France: The Industrial Relations System at a Turning Point?" in *Industrial Relations in the New Europe,* edited by A. Ferner and R. Hyman. Oxford: Blackwell.

JACOBI, O., B. KELLER, and W. MULLER-JENTSCH. 1992. "Germany," in *Industrial Relations in the New Europe*, edited by A. Ferner and R. Hyman. Oxford: Blackwell.

JACOBY, S., ed. 1995. *The Workers of Nations: Industrial Relations in a Global Economy*. New York: Oxford University Press.

KJELBERG, A. 1992. "Sweden: Can the Model Survive?" in *Industrial Relations in the New Europe*, edited by A. Ferner and R. Hyman. Oxford: Blackwell.

LaBOTZ, D. 1992. *The Mask of Democracy*. Montreal: Black Rose Books.

LIPSIG-MUMMÉ, C. 1997. "The Politics of the New Service Economy," in *Work of the Future: Global Options,* edited by J. Paul, W. Veit, and S. Wright. Sydney: Allen and Unwin.

LIPSIG-MUMMÉ, C. and K. LAXER. 1998. *Organising and Union Membership: A Canadian Profile in 1997*. Canadian Labour Congress and Centre for Research on Work and Society.

PEETZ, D. 1998. *Unions in a Contrary World*. MacMillan.

ROSS, A. 1997. "An Appeal to Walt Disney," in *No Sweat*. London: Verso.

ROSS, G. and A. MARTIN. 1998. "Europeanization and the Integration of European Labor." mimeo.

TRUBECK, D. and J. ROTHSTEIN. 1998. "Transnational Regimes and Advocacy in Industrial Relations: A Cure for Globalization?" Labor and Global Economy Research Circle, University of Wisconsin-Madison.

INDEX